Cisco Voice Gateways and Gatekeepers

Denise Donohue, David Mallory, Ken Salhoff

Cisco Press

Cisco Press
201 West 103rd Street
Indianapolis, IN 46290 USA

Cisco Voice Gateways and Gatekeepers

Denise Donohue, David Mallory, Ken Salhoff

Copyright© 2007 Cisco Systems, Inc.

Published by:
Cisco Press
800 East 96th Street
Indianapolis, IN 46240 USA

Printed in the United States of America 4 5 6 7 8 9 0

Fourth Printing February 2008

Library of Congress Cataloging-in-Publication Number: 2005935269

ISBN: 1-58705-258-X

Warning and Disclaimer

This book is designed to provide information about configuring Cisco routers to act as Voice over IP gateways and gatekeepers. Every effort has been made to make this book as complete and as accurate as possible, but no warranty or fitness is implied.

The information is provided on an "as is" basis. The authors, Cisco Press, and Cisco Systems, Inc. shall have neither liability nor responsibility to any person or entity with respect to any loss or damages arising from the information contained in this book or from the use of the discs or programs that may accompany it.

The opinions expressed in this book belong to the author and are not necessarily those of Cisco Systems, Inc.

Trademark Acknowledgments

All terms mentioned in this book that are known to be trademarks or service marks have been appropriately capitalized. Cisco Press or Cisco Systems, Inc. cannot attest to the accuracy of this information. Use of a term in this book should not be regarded as affecting the validity of any trademark or service mark.

Feedback Information

At Cisco Press, our goal is to create in-depth technical books of the highest quality and value. Each book is crafted with care and precision, undergoing rigorous development that involves the unique expertise of members from the professional technical community.

Readers' feedback is a natural continuation of this process. If you have any comments regarding how we could improve the quality of this book, or otherwise alter it to better suit your needs, you can contact us through e-mail at feedback@ciscopress.com. Please make sure to include the book title and ISBN in your message.

We greatly appreciate your assistance.

Corporate and Government Sales

Cisco Press offers excellent discounts on this book when ordered in quantity for bulk purchases or special sales.

For more information please contact: U.S. Corporate and Government Sales 1-800-382-3419 corpsales@pearsontechgroup.com

For sales outside the U.S. please contact: International Sales international@pearsoned.com

Editor-in-Chief	Paul Boger
Cisco Representative	Anthony Wolfenden
Cisco Press Program Manager	Jeff Brady
Executive Editor	Brett Bartow
Managing Editor	Patrick Kanouse
Development Editor	Dan Young
Project Editor	Tonya Simpson
Copy Editor	Karen A. Gill
Technical Editors	Danelle Au
	Christina Hattingh
	Sibrina Shafiq
	Lingling Zhang
	Brandon Ta
Editorial Assistant	Vanessa Evans
Book and Cover Designer	Louisa Adair
Composition	Mark Shirar
Indexer	Julie Bess

Americas Headquarters
Cisco Systems, Inc.
170 West Tasman Drive
San Jose, CA 95134-1706
USA
www.cisco.com
Tel: 408 526-4000
800 553-NETS (6387)
Fax: 408 527-0883

Asia Pacific Headquarters
Cisco Systems, Inc.
168 Robinson Road
#28-01 Capital Tower
Singapore 068912
www.cisco.com
Tel: +65 6317 7777
Fax: +65 6317 7799

Europe Headquarters
Cisco Systems International BV
Haarlerbergpark
Haarlerbergweg 13-19
1101 CH Amsterdam
The Netherlands
www-europe.cisco.com
Tel: +31 0 800 020 0791
Fax: +31 0 20 357 1100

Cisco has more than 200 offices worldwide. Addresses, phone numbers, and fax numbers are listed on the Cisco Website at **www.cisco.com/go/offices.**

About the Authors

Denise Donohue, CCIE No. 9566, is a design engineer with AT&T. She is responsible for designing and implementing data and VoIP networks for SBC and AT&T customers. Prior to that, she was a Cisco instructor and course director for Global Knowledge. Her CCIE is in Routing and Switching.

David L. Mallory, CCIE No. 1933, is a technical education consultant with Cisco Systems, Inc. supporting Cisco voice certifications. Prior to this role, David was a systems engineer supporting several global enterprise customers. David has presented on voice gateways and gatekeepers at Networkers and has achieved four CCIE certifications: Routing and Switching, WAN Switching, Security, and Voice.

Ken Salhoff, CCIE No. 4915, is a systems engineer with Cisco Systems, Inc. Ken has been specializing in voice technologies with Cisco for the past six years. In the systems engineering role, Ken has supported several global enterprise customers using Cisco voice technologies. Ken has achieved two CCIE certifications: Routing and Switching, and Voice.

Contributing Author

Jayesh Chokshi has worked in the field of networking for about 10 years and has been with Cisco Systems, Inc. for the last 6 years. He has worked in the field of Voice over IP as part of the Solutions Engineering and Technical Marketing Team and helped design and deploy multiple customer voice networks. Currently, he works as a Technical Marketing Engineer and focuses on Cisco Multiservice IP-to-IP Gateway product development and customer deployments.

About the Technical Reviewers

Danelle Au is a product manager in the Access Technology Group at Cisco Systems. She defines the strategy and roadmap and drives product requirements in the areas of IP communications. She was involved in the product management and marketing activities for the introduction of the Cisco CallManager Express (CME) and Survivable Remote Site Telephony products. She is currently responsible for IP Communications security, the voice gateway module portfolio, and DSP technologies on the Cisco Integrated Services Routers. Danelle is a co-author of the *Cisco IP Communications Express* book (ISBN 158705180X) and holds an M.S. in Electrical Engineering from University of California, Berkeley.

Christina Hattingh is a member of the technical staff in the branch office IP Communications group at Cisco Systems. The products in this group, including the Cisco 2600, 2800, 3600, 3700, and 3800 series platforms, were some of the first Cisco platforms to converge voice and data by offering PSTN and PBX voice gateway interfaces and critical QoS features on WAN interfaces, while more recently integrating numerous IP network voice services, call control, and application elements such as conferencing/transcoding services, RSVP Agent, IP-IP gateway, Cisco CME, and Cisco UE into the router-based platform. In this role, she helps guide development projects, trains Cisco sales staff and Cisco resale partners on new router-based voice technologies, and advises customers on voice network deployment and design.

Sibrina Shafique, CCIE No. 10871, is a member of the technical marketing team that works on the Cisco voice gateways. She works closely with engineering teams to guide voice-related projects and sales staff to provide training and technical assistance. In her previous role as a technical support engineer her task was to analyze, configure, and troubleshoot complex product and network problems on customer networks on all Cisco Voice gateways and their interaction with PSTN, third-party PBX systems. She has end-to-end understanding of voice networks and has assisted with large voice deployments.

Lingling Zhang has been working in Cisco Systems as Product Manager for five years. The primary focus of her role is to lead definition and development of Voice over IP products and services in the portfolio of Cisco access routers and develop Cisco competitive strategy and positioning in the low-end access market. Before joining Cisco, Lingling Zhang worked in *China Network World* as a reporter and editor for two years.

Brandon Ta, CCIE No. 2494, is a Consulting Systems Engineer for the Enterprise East Voice Group at Cisco Systems, Inc. Brandon worked for Cisco Systems, Inc. for nine years and has been focusing on unified communication for the last six years. He has worked on some of larger IP Telephony designs and networks that span from 16,000 to more than 100,000 Cisco IP phones. Beside the CISSP certification and a handful of other technical certifications, Brandon has four CCIEs and was the first in the world to receive three CCIEs back in 2000, where he was featured in *Cisco Packet* magazine. Brandon has presented at the Cisco IP Telecommunication User Group (CIPTUG) conference as well as the Cisco Networkers Conference on Unified Communication Technology.

Dedications

Denise Donohue: This book is dedicated to my incredibly patient family, especially my husband, Kevin, who has done a good, if not enthusiastic, job of cooking dinners the past few months. I'd also like to dedicate this book to all the people who have been so generous in sharing their knowledge with me over the years.

David Mallory: This book is dedicated to my wife, Tammy, and my children, Melissa and Laura, who sacrifice much for my endeavors.

Ken Salhoff: This book is dedicated to my wife, Jan, and my children, Jeff and Dani, who have been encouraging and supportive through this entire process. During the many hours I've spent locked in the lab, Jan has handled the added family workload without complaint, and for that I will be forever grateful.

Acknowledgments

This book is the product of a few authors and many behind-the-scenes workers who deserve recognition. Our thanks go to our editor, Brett Bartow, who did his best to keep us on track and on time, in spite of ourselves. Thanks also to Christopher Cleveland and Dan Young, our development editors, for ensuring that our words made sense. The editing and production staff had the unenviable job of making sure all spelling, grammar, punctuation, and illustrations were correct, and we are grateful for their work.

Our technical editors on this book did a great job of making sure the book was technically correct and suggesting ways to improve the content. The book would not have been as good without them. A big thank you to Danelle Au, Christina Hattingh, Sibrina Shafique, Brandon Ta, and Lingling Zhang!

Denise would like to thank the AES Engineering and Callisma groups within AT&T for the loan of lab equipment. Thanks also to Tom Petzold for helping keep this relevant.

David would like to thank the voice TEC team for their reviews and suggestions and for their insights on instruction and certification. He also wants to thank his manager, Drew Rosen, for supporting him in this and all his other efforts.

Ken would like to thank his manager, Michael Aaron, for his support during this process.

This Book Is Safari Enabled

The Safari® Enabled icon on the cover of your favorite technology book means the book is available through Safari Bookshelf. When you buy this book, you get free access to the online edition for 45 days.

Safari Bookshelf is an electronic reference library that lets you easily search thousands of technical books, find code samples, download chapters, and access technical information whenever and wherever you need it.

To gain 45-day Safari Enabled access to this book:

- Go to http://www.ciscopress.com/safarienabled
- Complete the brief registration form
- Enter the coupon code 3AI6-Q3TG-CZHW-LFGI-3VX4

If you have difficulty registering on Safari Bookshelf or accessing the online edition, please e-mail customer-service@safaribooksonline.com.

Contents at a Glance

Contents

Icons Used in This Book

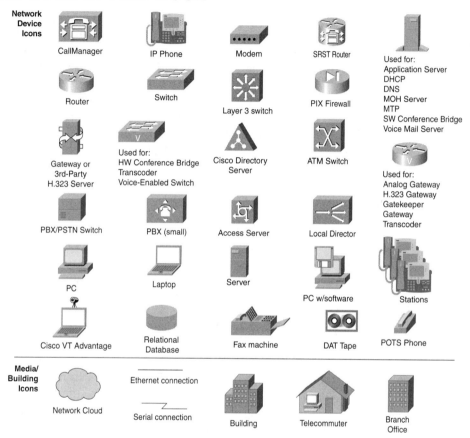

Command Syntax Conventions

The conventions used to present command syntax in this book are the same conventions used in the Cisco IOS Command Reference. The Command Reference describes these conventions as follows:

- **Boldface** indicates commands and keywords that you enter literally as shown. In actual configuration examples and output (not general command syntax), boldface indicates commands that you input manually (such as a **show** command).

- *Italic* indicates arguments for which you supply actual values.

- Vertical bars | separate alternative, mutually exclusive elements.

- Square brackets [ ] indicate optional elements.

- Braces { } indicate a required choice.

- Braces within brackets [{ }] indicate a required choice within an optional element.

Foreword

Cisco IOS routers have shipped with voice interface cards since 1997, and after this capability was available the term *voice gateway* became part of the VoIP vernacular, seemingly overnight. The voice interfaces allowed routers to provide a critical interconnectivity link between the traditional data IP networks and the traditional voice (PSTN, PBXs, and key systems) networks. With this technology, the industry widely built toll bypass networks during the late 1990s: Enterprises connected their PBXs at different sites with VoIP "trunks" instead of with TIE lines or the PSTN, and service providers leveraged IP backbone networks to offer calling-card services and cut-rate long-distance and international calling.

VoIP did not fascinate the popular imagination of the likes of Jeff Pulver of Voice-on-the Net (VON) and other industry observers until end-user–visible devices, such as IP phones, and IP-based applications brought the technology to the forefront. Voice gateway technology is still the pale sibling of the IP telephony world that creates no buzz, and yet it is also the workhorse of every single VoIP network. Even as VoIP endpoints become ever more prevalent in businesses and residences, voice gateways still provide critical interconnectivity with billions of traditional PSTN and PBX voice endpoints, without which companies cannot operate their communications networks.

Although the idea of a voice gateway is conceptually simple enough—it's a demarcation between two networks and translates the protocols from one (the TDM world) to the other (the IP world)—the technology has become increasingly sophisticated and the features more intertwined over the years. Choosing the "right" voice gateway and configuring the "right" set of features for a particular network is no longer the task for the uninitiated. The question I hear most frequently is whether to deploy MGCP, H.323, or SIP gateways. Cisco gateways are protocol agnostic and support all of these protocols and several variations thereof, and the answer to the question posed is not a simple one: The optimal network design depends on a large number of considerations. Some protocols and designs are better suited to particular types of networks, partly owing to the architecture of the protocols themselves and partly due to the features that have been chosen for implementation over the years.

A Cisco Press book with comprehensive coverage focused entirely on voice gateway technology and features was a long time coming, and at last with this book, the authors provide an in-depth look at the breadth of voice gateway features and capabilities, as well as providing voice gateway configuration guidance. The book explains the major VoIP protocols, MGCP, H.323, and SIP, their structure and operation, and the considerations to choose among them. It discusses in detail the PSTN and PBX circuit connection technologies and choices. There are often multiple connection choices on the central office or PBX switch as well as on the voice gateway side of the circuit, and which of these would provide the features, cost points, and manageability that are optimal for your network might not be obvious at first glance.

The book goes on to provide insights into many other areas of gateway selection and deployment, including the myriad choices in carrying fax and modem traffic over IP, dial plan features and digit manipulation tools, call admission control capabilities to keep voice traffic off the IP network when it does not have the quality levels to carry it, a review of DSP technology and operation, and an examination of IP connectivity implications and QoS features required to carry voice traffic with decent quality. Later chapters in the book also include discussions on pure IP-oriented topics such as TCL and VXML applications capabilities, conference mixing, transcoding, gatekeeper functions and connectivity, and IP-to-IP gateway (session border controller) services and features. All of these pure VoIP services are offered by the same platforms that are also voice gateways, even though TDM connectivity is not a necessary component for the IP-only services.

The book also covers key areas of interest in any network, including security measures and high availability. VoIP network security is a wide topic fully deserving of its own book-length treatment, but this book provides enough basic information to get your network deployed. It covers how voice gateway traffic passes through firewalls and NAT devices, how to encrypt voice signaling and media traffic to or from a voice gateway, as well as configuring class of service restrictions such that certain call patterns are allowed while others are blocked per the policy of your network. High availability is essential in all networks—a chapter in this book is dedicated to the discussion of how gateways fail over when other network components are out of contact, as well as how gateway features interoperate with IP Phone failover features such as SRST to maintain dial tone and PSTN network access for your end users at all times.

Throughout the book is a case study that solidifies the chapter discussions by providing practical, hands-on examples of how the configuration of the system implements the features. This, together with the detailed chapter-by-chapter coverage of crucial gateway topics, make this an invaluable book essential to the tool chest of anyone contemplating the implementation of a new network, actively designing a network, or evolving or optimizing the features in an existing network.

Christina Hattingh
Access Technology Group
Cisco Systems, Inc.

Introduction

The use of Voice over IP (VoIP) is rapidly expanding. You can find all sorts of glowing statistics about the adoption of VoIP by businesses and consumers. Traditional telecommunications companies are phasing in IP voice in parts of their backbone. Service providers are lowering the cost to businesses of implementing VoIP by offering hosted and managed solutions. Organizations both large and small are embracing VoIP.

Voice gateways are an essential part of VoIP networks. Gatekeepers and IP-to-IP gateways help these networks scale. Yet no definitive reference is available on these subjects. A network engineer who needs to design a VoIP network or configure these devices has to search to find the necessary information. This book strives to fill that need as much as humanly possible. It builds on the foundation laid by the Cisco CVoice course, focusing on advanced deployment options and features of Cisco IOS-based voice gateways and gatekeepers.

In a field that is constantly changing and developing, great care has been taken to make this book relevant and accurate. The authors hope that you will find it a good learning tool and a good resource for implementing and troubleshooting your voice gateways and gatekeepers.

Goals and Methods

The goal of this book is to produce a practical guide to help people both understand Cisco gateways and gatekeepers and configure them properly. This book seeks to describe the Cisco voice gateway and gatekeeper theories and protocols in a way that readers can apply to their networks. It provides examples, screen shots, configuration snips, and case studies to make this a useful guide and a reference book. The book includes the typical tasks and issues in deploying voice gateways and gatekeepers, in addition to advanced features and capabilities. Emphasis is placed on the accepted best practices and common issues encountered. It is not written specifically as a preparation for the Cisco Gateway Gatekeeper exam, but the topics that are covered on the exam are included in this book.

Who Should Read This Book?

Primary target audiences for this book are network engineers, IP Telephony engineers, and Telco engineers who are tasked with the installation, configuration, and maintenance of VoIP and IP Telephony networks. Secondary audiences include network managers and certification candidates who would like to augment their Cisco Gateway Gatekeeper exam preparatory material with more in-depth information. This book also serves as a resource to CCVP and CCIE voice candidates who are preparing for the written or lab exams.

It is assumed that the reader understands IP networking and is familiar with the topics covered in the following Cisco courses: CVoice, CIPT, QoS, and IPTT. This includes a basic understanding of VoIP and time-division multiplexing (TDM) voice fundamentals, the concepts and configuration of basic IP voice routers, and Cisco CallManager basics.

How This Book Is Organized

This book is designed to be flexible and allow you to easily move between chapters to focus on topics of interest to you. However, if you do intend to read every chapter, the order in the book is an excellent sequence to use because it progresses from basic to more advanced subjects. Chapter 1 provides an overview of the components of an IP voice network. The remainder of the book is divided into three parts: "Gateways." "Gatekeepers," and "IP-to-IP Gateways."

Part I, "Voice Gateways and Gatekeepers"

Chapter 1, "Gateways and Gatekeepers"—This chapter provides an overview of components of an IP voice network, including different types of gateways, such as routers, standalone devices, and switch modules, H.323 gatekeepers, and IP-to-IP gateways (IPIPGW). It contains a review of the Multiple Gateway Control Protocol (MGCP), H.323, Session Initiation Protocol (SIP), Skinny Client Control Protocol (SCCP), and Real-Time Transport Protocol (RTP) protocols. It also describes different types of call agents that are used in IP voice networks. In addition, it introduces the network used throughout the book in examples and case studies.

Part II, "Gateways"

Chapter 2, "Media Gateway Control Protocol"—This chapter covers how MGCP implements call signaling, describes call flow using MGCP, and discusses the pros and cons of the protocol and when to use it. It then covers implementing MGCP gateways—configuration of the router, addition of an MGCP gateway to CallManager, configuration of dual tone multifrequency (DTMF) relay, some security features, and troubleshooting of MGCP gateways.

Chapter 3, "H.323"—This chapter discusses the implemention of call signaling with the H.323 protocol, some of the protocols that are part of the H.323 suite, call flow using H.323, and the pros and cons of the protocol and when to use it. It then covers implementing H.323 gateways—configuring the router, using toll bypass, adding a gateway to CallManager, configuring DTMF relay, allowing H.323-to-H.323 connections, configuring both H.323 and MGCP on a gateway, using H.323 security features, and troubleshooting.

Chapter 4, "Session Initiation Protocol"—This chapter describes how SIP implements call signaling, describes the various SIP functions and how they participate in the call flow, and lists the pros and cons of the protocol and when to use it. It covers implementing SIP gateways—configuring the router, using SIP toll bypass, adding the gateway to CallManager, using SIP security features, allowing SIP-to-H.323 connections, and troubleshooting SIP gateways.

Chapter 5, "Circuit Options"—This chapter examines the various analog and digital circuits that gateways use to connect a VoIP network to the public switched telephone network (PSTN). It looks at the different signaling types, features, and uses of each type of circuit; issues such as echo cancellation; and selection and sizing of the circuit.

Chapter 6, "Connecting to the PSTN"—PSTN connections are examined in more depth in this chapter. The analog coverage includes a discussion on configuring and troubleshooting Foreign Exchange Office (FXO), direct inward dial (DID), and Centralized Automated Message Accounting (CAMA). The digital coverage includes explanations on configuring and troubleshooting T1 and E1 PRI, BRI, and channel-associated signaling (CAS) connections. The chapter also discusses caller ID and name delivery considerations.

Chapter 7, "Connecting to PBXs"—This chapter covers the configuration of analog PBX trunks using Ear and Mouth (E&M) and FXO interfaces, and digital PBX trunks using CAS, PRI, and BRI interfaces. It discusses Transparent Common Channel Signaling (T-CCS) and Q Signaling (QSIG).

Chapter 8, "Connecting to an IP WAN"—This chapter covers reasons for connecting a VoIP network to an IP WAN, QoS considerations, use of the modular quality of service command-line interface (MQC) to provide the needed quality of service, and QoS over an MPLS network. Handling faxes and modems in a VoIP network are discussed. This chapter also describes the need for securing voice traffic over a WAN by using SRTP and V3PN, the implications of NAT on voice traffic, and the use of firewalls with VoIP.

Chapter 9, "Dial Plans"—This chapter covers dial plan design and implementation. It discusses building a scalable dial plan, handling overlapping number ranges, and implementing a dial plan on gateways and call agents. It helps you understand the different types of dial peers and how they affect call routing by examining the way that the gateway selects dial peer matches.

Chapter 10, "Digit Manipulation"—This chapter discusses various ways for a gateway to control called and calling phone numbers, including digit stripping, forwarding only a specified number of digits, prefixing digits, and expanding numbers. It also covers voice translation rules, use of regular expressions, voice translation profiles, control of the calling-line identification information, and verification and troubleshooting of digit manipulation.

Chapter 11, "Influencing Path Selection"—This chapter covers several different ways of influencing route selection, including hunt groups, trunk groups, and tail end hop-off. The chapter examines call admission control (CAC) techniques—local CAC using maximum connections and local voice busyout; measurement-based CAC using IP SLA, PSTN fallback, and advanced local voice busyout; and resource-based CAC using Resource Reservation Protocol (RSVP) and RSVP agent, and using CAC with gatekeepers. It also discusses considerations when using POTS-to-POTS call routing.

Chapter 12, "Configuring Class of Restrictions"—This chapter explains what COR is and how it operates. It covers using COR with CallManager Express (CME) implementations, and on a gateway with Survivable Remote Site Telephony (SRST), restricting both inbound and outbound calls.

Chapter 13, "SRST and MGCP Gateway Fallback"—This chapter gives an overview of SRST with ways to adjust the failover and fallback times, and shows how to configure SRST on both the gateway and CallManager. It describes MGCP fallback and how to configure it. SRST dial plan considerations are discussed, along with configuring SRST call features, configuring SIP SRST, preserving calls, and troubleshooting SRST and MGCP fallback.

Chapter 14, "DSP Resources"—This chapter examines codec considerations and configuration, digital signal processor (DSP) considerations, determination of DSP resources needed, the DSP modes, and configuration of conferencing and transcoding resources on both the gateway and CallManager.

Chapter 15, "Using TCL Scripts and VoiceXML"—This chapter explains how to support interactive voice response (IVR) and advanced call-handling applications using Toolkit Command Language (Tcl) and VoiceXML. It gives examples, tells how to download Tcl scripts, and shows how to configure gateways to use them. This chapter also examines the auto attendant (AA) script and creation of audio files in more detail and discusses some caveats and restrictions.

Part III, "Gatekeepers"

Chapter 16, "Deploying Gatekeepers"—This chapter provides the conceptual information that you need to integrate gatekeepers into your VoIP network. It describes gatekeeper functionality in networks with and without a CallManager, gatekeeper CAC and address resolution, redundancy and load balancing, gatekeeper security, and use of hierarchical gatekeepers. A discussion of planning a gatekeeper implementation includes placement, bandwidth, and dial plan issues. Scalabilty and multizone enhancements are also addressed.

Chapter 17, "Gatekeeper Configuration"—This chapter is a practical guide to gatekeeper configuration. It covers router configuration for basic and advanced gatekeeper functions such as directory gatekeepers, gatekeeper redundancy, Resource Availability Indication (RAI), and security. CallManager configuration for gatekeeper use and gatekeeper redundancy is also discussed, along with ways to troubleshoot your gatekeeper implementation.

Part IV, "IP-to-IP Gateways"

Chapter 18, "Cisco Multiservice IP-to-IP Gateway"—This chapter explains the functions of an IP-to-IP gateway; its use in service provider and enterprise environments and in CallManager networks; its use of the Open Settlement Protocol; and the way it functions with RSVP. This chapter also covers using these gateways with both H.323 and SIP, configuring IP-to-IP gateways, configuring a via-zone gatekeeper, and troubleshooting the configuration.

Voice Gateways and Gatekeepers

CHAPTER 1

Gateways and Gatekeepers

This book will help you understand the roles of IP voice gateways and gatekeepers and how to integrate them into your voice network.

Gateways can be configured with many different features and functions and can become quite complex. It is important for network engineers to understand gateway functions, be able to choose when to use which, and be able to configure their gateways. Engineers need a thorough understanding of gatekeeper function and configuration to ensure proper call flow. In addition, they must address issues of security and redundancy.

This chapter provides an overview of the basic building blocks of a voice-over-IP (VoIP) network. It includes information on the following:

- Voice gateways, H.323 gatekeepers, and IP-to-IP gateways
- IP voice signaling and media protocols
- Call control devices

It also includes an overview of the network used in case studies throughout the book.

The Role of Voice Gateways

The basic function of a gateway is to translate between different types of networks. In the data environment, a gateway might translate between a Frame Relay network and an Ethernet network, for example. In a VoIP environment, voice gateways are the interface between a VoIP network and the public switched telephone network (PSTN), a private branch exchange (PBX), or analog devices such as fax machines. In its simplest form, a voice gateway has an IP interface and a legacy telephone interface, and it handles the many tasks involved in translating between transmission formats and protocols. At least one gateway is an essential part of any IP telephony network that interacts with the PSTN or with analog devices. In addition, when gateways are properly configured, many can take over for a Cisco CallManager when it is unreachable.

Figure 1-1 shows a simple VoIP network with a voice gateway connected to both the VoIP network and the PSTN.

Figure 1-1 *Voice Gateway Example*

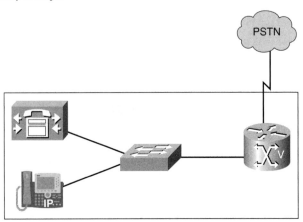

The gateway allows communication between the two networks by performing tasks such as these:

- Interfacing with the IP network and the PSTN or PBX.
- Supporting IP call control protocols, in addition to time-division multiplexing (TDM) call control protocols.
- Performing call setup and teardown for calls between the VoIP and PSTN networks by terminating and reoriginating the call media and signaling.
- Providing supplementary services, such as call hold and transfer.
- Relaying dual tone multifrequency (DTMF) tones.
- Supporting analog fax and modems over the IP network.
- In a Cisco CallManager network, a gateway also needs to do the following:
    - Support CallManager redundancy by rehoming to alternate CallManagers.
    - Support call survivability when no CallManager is available.

Gateways communicate with other gateways, gatekeepers, their endpoints, or their call control agents, such as Cisco CallManager or a PBX. The following are the protocols that Cisco gateways use for voice signaling and media:

- Media Gateway Control Protocol (MGCP)
- H.323
- Session Initiation Protocol (SIP)
- Skinny Client Control Protocol (SCCP)
- Real-Time Transport Protocol (RTP)

This chapter introduces these protocols. MGCP, H.323, and SIP are described in depth in other chapters of this book.

Types of Voice Gateways

This book deals primarily with using Cisco routers as voice gateways, but an assortment of different types and models of Cisco voice gateways is available. Gateways contain analog or digital telephony ports, in addition to IP interfaces. Analog options include Foreign Exchange Office (FXO) ports, Foreign Exchange Station (FXS) ports, and Ear and Mouth (E&M) ports. Digital options include T1/E1 PRI ports, ISDN BRI ports, and T1 channel associated signaling (CAS) ports. You can divide Cisco gateways into several categories, each with its own capabilities. For more information on the current models, visit www.Cisco.com.

Routers

You can use many Cisco routers, such as 1700, 2600, 2800, 3600, 3700, 3800, 7200, and 7500 models, as voice gateways. Voice gateway routers can contain analog ports such as FXO and FXS, and digital ports such as E1 and T1. Most can use the MGCP, SCCP, SIP, and H.323 protocols. The remainder of this book focuses mainly on router-based voice gateways.

Standalone Voice Gateways

Unlike routers, standalone voice gateways are used only as voice gateways. They come in two types: digital and analog.

Digital trunk gateways, such as the AS5000 series interface, connect an IP telephony network and the PSTN or a PBX via their trunk ports.

Analog trunk gateways, such as AT-2 or AT-4, connect to the PSTN or a PBX via analog trunks. Analog station gateways, such as an ATA186, VG224, or VG248, connect to analog devices such as telephones, fax machines, or voice-mail systems. The signaling protocols that are available vary by gateway model. The ATA186, an analog-to-IP adapter, can support two analog devices each with its own telephone number. It has one Ethernet port that connects to the VoIP network, and two voice ports for connecting analog devices. It can be controlled by Cisco CallManager and CallManager Express, and it supports SIP and SCCP protocols. However, CallManager 5.0 does not have native SIP support for the ATA186.

VG224 and VG248 are Cisco voice gateways with 24 and 48 analog FXS ports, respectively. These are line-side gateways—they do not interface with the PSTN, but with end-user analog devices. Both models allow a CallManager, CallManager Express (CME), or an SRST router multiple to control analog ports. They connect to a LAN via an Ethernet port, and they communicate with CallManager or CME using the SCCP telephony control (STC) application. The VG224 can also act as an MGCP, H.323, or SIP gateway.

The analog telephones, faxes, or modems that are attached to the gateway appear as individual endpoints to the CallManager. You must configure the gateway on the CallManager, and you must configure each port on CallManager with a directory number and any call features it needs. In CME, you must set up an e-phone for each port in use.

The VG248 gateway uses only SCCP. The VG224 gateway can use SCCP, H.323, MGCP, and SIP. CME interaction is supported only with the VG224 gateway, not VG248. The VG224 gateway is Cisco-IOS based, whereas configuration of the VG248 gateway is menu driven.

Switch Modules

Modules containing analog and digital ports are available for Cisco 6500 switches, allowing them to act as voice gateways. For example, the Communication Media Module (which you can also use in the 7600 series router) can contain a combination of T1, E1, and FXS ports. It uses MGCP, H.323, and SIP protocols, and it can provide Survivable Remote Site Telephony (SRST) functionality. The Voice T1/E1 and Services Module, or 6608 blade, can contain T1 or E1 interfaces, and it can perform as an MGCP gateway.

Role of Voice Gatekeepers

Gatekeepers help VoIP networks scale to large sizes. Companies that have geographically dispersed voice networks, or networks that have become so large that they are unwieldy, might opt to segment their network. In a CallManager network, you can create multiple clusters. In that case, you would need to configure a full mesh of connections over the IP WAN to link all the segments or clusters. You would need to configure dial information for every remote location on every gateway and CallManager cluster. A better alternative is to use gatekeepers. In a network that has gatekeepers, trunks are needed only to the gatekeeper, and the gatekeeper maintains remote endpoint information.

When you use gatekeepers, gateways and CallManagers register with their gatekeeper. Gatekeepers divide the network into "zones," or groups of devices that register with a particular gatekeeper. When an H.323 gateway receives a call that is destined to a remote phone, it queries the gatekeeper for the location of the endpoint. If the call is destined for a different zone, you can configure the gatekeeper to allow it only if sufficient bandwidth is available. In more complex networks, you can use a Directory gatekeeper to maintain information about all the zones. You can configure Cisco routers with the appropriate Cisco IOS as H.323 gatekeepers.

Figure 1-2 shows an example of a company that has three CallManager clusters and a gatekeeper. Each cluster has an intercluster trunk over the IP WAN to the gatekeeper. Each cluster is its own zone.

Figure 1-2   *H.323 Gatekeeper Example*

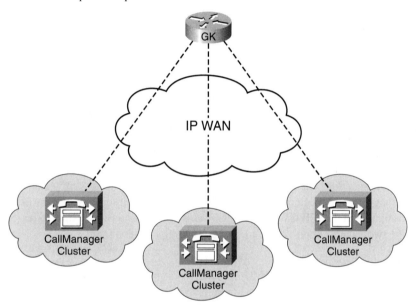

Gatekeeper functionality is part of the H.323 standard. A voice gatekeeper provides the following services:

- **Address resolution**—A gatekeeper resolves E.164 telephone numbers and H.323 IDs to endpoint IP addresses.
- **Call admission control**—A gatekeeper permits or denies a call between clusters.
- **Bandwidth control**—A gatekeeper can refuse to admit calls that exceed the allocated bandwidth.
- **Zone management**—A gatekeeper can register and manage endpoints within its zone.
- **Optional Security**—A gatekeeper can authenticate and authorize calls on an endpoint-by-endpoint basis.
- **Optional call management**—A gatekeeper can maintain information about the endpoint call state.
- **Optional routing of call control signaling**—A gatekeeper can reroute signaling to allow endpoints to communicate directly.

Role of IP-to-IP Gateways

A voice gateway joins a VoIP network and the PSTN. A gatekeeper joins separate segments of the same VoIP network. An IP-to-IP gateway (IPIPGW), often called a Session Border Controller, joins independent VoIP or Video over IP networks. It acts as a border device, allowing users in different administrative domains to exchange voice and video using IP, rather than through the PSTN. The call media can either flow through the gateway, or directly between endpoints.

For example, an Internet Telephony Service Provider (ITSP) can use IPIPGWs to route IP voice traffic through another ITSP network. An IPIPGW can provide billing information to the ITSP. IPIPGWs can allow an ITSP to offer its customers end-to-end VoIP service between each other, or between remote offices of the same company. This would allow the exchange of IP calls between CallManager, H.323, and SIP networks.

Figure 1-3 shows an example of two companies that frequently conduct videoconferences between them. They use an IPIPGW to hide the details of each network, while still allowing communication. The H.323 video systems at each location communicate with the IPIPGW, rather than with each other directly. To each network, it looks as if the call signaling originates at the IPIPGW. The IPIPGW acts as a Session Border Controller (SBC) between the two islands, controlling video conferencing between them.

Figure 1-3 *IP-to-IP Gateway Example*

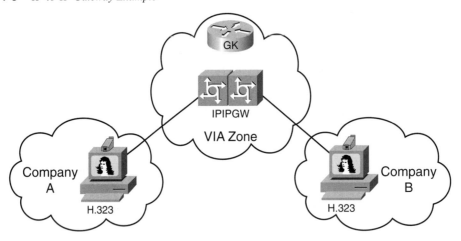

In Figure 1-3, a Voice Infrastructure and Applications (VIA) zone is used, along with a gatekeeper. This zone acts as a transit zone between the two networks. The gatekeeper is especially configured to route calls appropriately to the IPIPGW.

You can install the IP-to-IP gateway Cisco IOS feature set on many Cisco multiservice routers. The following are some features of an IP-to-IP gateway:

- Interconnecting segments of the same or different VoIP networks using different signaling types, such as H.323 and SIP
- Interconnecting segments of the same or different VoIP networks using different media types
- Billing abilities
- Coder/decoder (codec) control
- Call admission control
- Security

Introduction to Voice Protocols

VoIP has several call signaling and control protocols available for use. The protocol that you should use depends on the type of gateway, endpoint host, and call agent, and the capabilities you need in the network. Multiple protocols might be used in different portions of the network. After you set up the call, you transmit IP voice and video traffic using a different protocol, RTP. This section gives an overview of IP signaling and media protocols used in a VoIP network.

Media Gateway Control Protocol

MGCP is a client-server call control protocol, built on centralized control architecture. All the dial plan information resides on a separate call agent. The call agent, which controls the ports on the gateway, performs call control. The gateway does media translation between the PSTN and the VoIP networks for external calls. In a Cisco-based network, CallManagers function as the call agents. This book deals with CallManager-controlled MGCP gateways only; other call agents are beyond the scope of this book.

MGCP is an Internet Engineering Task Force (IETF) standard that is defined in several RFCs, including 2705 and 3435. Its capabilities can be extended by the use of "packages" that include, for example, the handling of DTMF tones, secure RTP, call hold, and call transfer.

An MGCP gateway is relatively easy to configure. Because the call agent has all the call-routing intelligence, you do not need to configure the gateway with all the dial peers it would otherwise need. A downside, however, is that a call agent must always be available. Cisco MGCP gateways can use SRST and MGCP fallback to allow the gateway to take over and provide local call routing in the absence of a CallManager. In that case, you must configure dial peers on the gateway.

NOTE	See Chapter 2, "Media Gateway Control Protocol," for more information on this protocol.

H.323

H.323 is an International Telecommunications Union Telecommunication Standardization Sector (ITU-T) standard protocol. It has its roots in legacy telecommunications protocols, so it communicates well with hosts on the PSTN. H.323 is actually a suite of protocols that specify the functions involved in sending real-time voice, video, and data over packet-switched networks. Unlike MGCP, an H.323 gateway does not require a call agent; it is built on a distributed architecture model. Gateways can independently locate a remote host and establish a media stream; thus, you must configure them with call routing information.

Although an H.323 gateway does not require a call agent, you can use it in a CallManager network. The CallManager directs calls that are bound for the PSTN to the gateway, which uses plain old telephone service (POTS) dial peers to route them. The gateway has a VoIP dial peer pointing to CallManager for calls that are bound inside the VoIP network. You can configure IP phones to register directly with an H.323 gateway using SRST when their CallManager is unavailable.

The H.323 standard defines four components of an H.323 system: terminals, gateways, gatekeepers, and multipoint control units (MCU).

- **Terminals**—These are the user endpoints, such as a video conferencing units, that communicate with each other.
- **Gateways**—Used to communicate with terminals on other networks (primarily across the PSTN).
- **Gatekeepers**—Translate phone numbers to IP addresses, and control and route calls.
- **Multipoint control units (MCU)**—Enable multiple parties to join a videoconference.

NOTE	See Chapter 3, "H.323," for more information on this protocol.

Session Initiation Protocol

SIP, like MGCP, is an IETF standard, which is defined in a number of RFCs. Its control extends to audio, video, data, and instant messaging communications, allowing them to interoperate. SIP uses a distributed architecture based somewhat on the Internet model, using clear text request and response messages and URLs for host addressing. The protocol addresses only session initiation and teardown. It relies on other protocols, such as HTTP for message format, Session Description Protocol (SDP) for negotiating capabilities, and the Domain Name System (DNS) for locating servers by name. The driving force behind SIP is enabling next-generation multimedia networks that use the Internet and Internet applications.

SIP uses several functional components in its call setup and teardown. Because these are logical functions, one device could serve several functions. SIP entities can act as a client or server, and some can act as both. Clients initiate requests for a service or information, and servers respond. One call might involve several requests and responses from several devices. Some SIP functions are as follows:

- **User agent**—The SIP endpoint, such as a SIP phone, which generates requests when it places a call and answers requests when it receives a call.
- **Proxy server**—The server that handles requests to and from a user agent, either responding to them or forwarding them as appropriate.
- **Redirect server**—The server that maintains routing information for remote locations and responds to requests from proxy servers for the location of remote servers.
- **Registrar server**—The server that keeps a database of user agents in its domain and responds to requests for this information.
- **Presence server**—The server that supports SIP for Instant Messaging and Presence Leveraging Extensions (SIMPLE) applications. It collects and communicates user and device status, communications capabilities, and other attributes.

SIP is a developing standard; therefore, interoperability between vendors and with other VoIP protocols can be a challenge. Much work is being done in this area, as SIP becomes more widely adopted.

NOTE   See Chapter 4, "Session Initiation Protocol," for more information on this protocol.

Skinny Client Control Protocol

Cisco IP phones use the Cisco proprietary Skinny Client Control Protocol (SCCP), or "Skinny," to communicate with their call agent. As the "skinny" portion of the name implies, SCCP is a lightweight protocol that is built on a client-server model. Call control messages are sent over TCP. End stations use SCCP to register with their call agent, and then to send and receive call setup and teardown instructions.

Routers in SRST mode can use SCCP to communicate with the Cisco IP phones they control. Some analog gateway devices, such as a VG224 and Analog Telephone Adapter (ATA), can also use Skinny to communicate with a call agent.

Real-Time Transport Protocol

MGCP, H.323, SIP, and SCCP are protocols that handle call signaling and control. RTP is an IETF standard protocol that uses User Datagram Protocol (UDP) to carry voice and video media after the call is set up. Its header includes a sequence number so that the receiver knows if packets are arriving in the correct order, and a timestamp field to calculate jitter. The RTP, UDP, and IP headers together equal 40 bytes, which can be much larger than the voice data carried in the packet. RTP header compression (cRTP) compresses these three headers as small as 2 to 4 bytes to save bandwidth on low-speed links. The Real-Time Transport Control Protocol (RTCP) allows monitoring of the call data, including counts of the number of packets and bytes transmitted. Secure versions of RTP (SRTP) and RTCP (SRTCP) encrypt the media streams between hosts. Chapter 8, "Connecting to an IP WAN," has more information on using cRTP and SRTP with gateways.

Call Control Agents

You can deploy gateways with many different kinds of call control agents, and they might perform different roles with different ones. The following sections examine some types of call control agents and some gateway considerations for each type.

Cisco CallManager

Cisco CallManager is a call processing application that runs on a server. It is a part of the Cisco Unified Communications solution. You can install CallManager software on multiple clustered servers to achieve high availability and scalability. CallManager can manage both local and remote phones and gateways. For increased scalability, you can deploy multiple clusters and achieve end-to-end IP voice and video communication. CallManagers handle address resolution and call admission control for their registered phones, but they can also interact with H.323 gatekeepers for those functions. Cisco CallManagers can interact with gateways using MGCP, SCCP, SIP, and H.323.

Cisco CallManager Express

CME is an application on a Cisco IOS router that provides standalone call control for small to medium sites. The number of phones supported varies with the type of router, up to a maximum of 240. With CME, the same router can perform typical gateway functions, such as PSTN connectivity, and also call processing functions. Although CME does not provide all the features of a full CallManager installation, it meets the needs of smaller sites. In addition, you can use extensible markup language (XML) applications to provide users with enhanced features. CME can interoperate with gateways using SCCP, H.323, and SIP.

CME can also integrate with a CallManager network. You can use H.323 trunks between CallManager and a CME router to carry calls over an IP WAN. If the site grows, you can expand call capacity by adding the site to a CallManager cluster and using the router solely as a gateway.

SIP Proxy Server

The Cisco SIP proxy server application runs on a server, providing call routing and control services to SIP endpoints, such as phones or PC applications. It combines the functions of a standard SIP proxy server and a SIP registrar. Endpoints register with the proxy server, which builds a database. When the server receives a SIP call setup message, it attempts to resolve the address with its local information, before forwarding a request to remote servers. It can also authenticate and encrypt SIP messages. You can use redundant servers to provide high availability and load balancing.

Cisco Enterprise Gateway

The Enterprise Gateway (EGW) is an application that runs on the same type of server as CallManager. It acts as a transition point for VoIP and legacy TDM networks, providing call control, signaling, and routing for calls between the two networks. It eases the migration to a CallManager VoIP network by allowing legacy PBXs to communicate with CallManager-controlled phones and Unity voice-mail servers. It also facilitates deploying toll bypass with legacy PBXs. When using an EGW, voice-enabled routers connect to the PBX or the PSTN, acting as media gateways. The router backhauls call control information to the EGW and does the actual media conversion between the TDM and packet networks. The EGW uses MGCP to control the media gateway, SIP, to communicate with a Unity server, and H.323 to communicate to devices in the CallManager network.

PBX with Toll Bypass

A call agent does not have to reside on the VOIP network—a PBX can perform that function for a gateway. A company that wants to retain its existing legacy telephone structure can leverage its IP WAN for intrasite calls. You would need to connect a voice gateway to the PBX using a telephony interface, such as an E&M or PRI. You also need to provide access to the WAN. When an analog phone calls another company site, the PBX can route it to the voice gateway rather than across the PSTN. The PBX can also perform call admission control, rerouting calls to the PSTN when the link between it and the gateway is busy. This is called *toll bypass*. The voice gateway translates between the legacy voice and the IP voice signaling and media.

Deployment Scenarios

Three typical CallManager deployment scenarios exist:

- Single site
- Multisite with centralized call control
- Multisite with distributed call control

Each scenario has different ways of using gateways and gatekeepers.

Single Site Deployment

In the single site model, a central call agent serves one location, such as a building or campus. In small sites, this might be a Cisco CME. Larger sites might use a CallManager cluster. All telephones calls outside the site are sent through the PSTN. Telephone calls within the site traverse the LAN or perhaps metropolitan-area network (MAN). Figure 1-4 shows a typical single site deployment.

Figure 1-4 *Single Site Deployment*

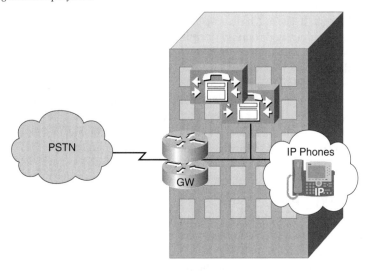

The example shows a small CallManager cluster used as the call agent. In this deployment, gatekeepers are not needed. Gateways connect the LAN to the PSTN, and sometimes to a PBX. For added redundancy, two gateway routers are used. The G.711 codec is used, because bandwidth is not an issue. The gateway Digital Signal Processor (DSP) resources provide conferencing and media termination point (MTP) resources. To simplify gateway configuration, MGCP is used as the call control protocol. If some specific H.323 or SIP functionality is needed, you could use those protocols instead.

Multisite with Centralized Call Control

A company uses this type of deployment when it wants to include multiple sites in its VoIP network, but centralize the call agents. Typically, a CallManager cluster is located at the headquarters or data center site, with perhaps redundant servers at a backup site. The IP phones in remote locations register to the centralized CallManagers, in a hub-and-spoke type arrangement. Remote sites are connected in a full mesh across an IP WAN. Both call signaling and IP voice are sent over the WAN. PSTN access is usually still provided locally. Figure 1-5 illustrates this type of scenario.

Figure 1-5 *Multisite Deployment with Centralized Call Control*

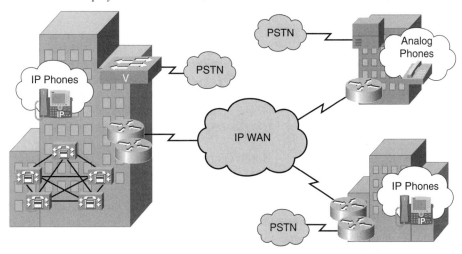

The gateways at each location interface with the PSTN, the LAN, and the IP WAN. They might also interface with a PBX at some sites. They provide backup call processing by using SRST if the CallManagers are not available because of WAN failure. You can use the G.729 codec across the WAN; use quality of service (QoS) for best results. A gatekeeper is not required for call admission control, but you can use it for dial plan resolution if many remote sites exist.

Multisite Deployment with Distributed Call Control

If the number of remotes sites grows unwieldy, or sites are widely distributed, you can use a multisite scenario with distributed call control. Each "site" in this scenario might be one of three types:

- A single location or campus using CallManager, CME, or another IP PBX
- A multisite CallManager cluster with centralized call control
- A site with a legacy PBX and a VoIP gateway

Figure 1-6 shows an example of this type of network.

Figure 1-6 *Multisite Deployment with Distributed Call Control*

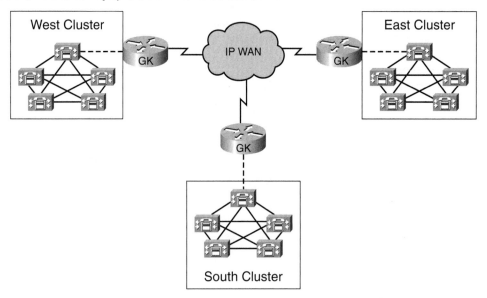

Multiple CallManager clusters are used, and gatekeepers are used for at least call admission control and address resolution. You can add a directory gatekeeper to scale the gatekeeper implementation. If gatekeepers are used, H.323 gateways are used also. Sites are connected across an IP WAN, with PSTN backup in case of WAN failure or insufficient bandwidth. You typically use the G.729 codec across the IP WAN. Use QoS for best results.

Case Study: Introduction

The case studies for this book use a fictional international company with offices in six locations, as shown in Figure 1-7. Each office has a different set of equipment and network connections to demonstrate the various technologies mentioned in this book. Every location communicates with the others over a Multiprotocol Label Switching (MPLS) network that the ISP manages. A centralized CallManager in the New York office controls phones in Miami, Boise, Shanghai, and Leeds. The Lima voice gateway router is running CME for its phones. Boise has analog phones, Shanghai has a combination of IP and analog, and the other sites have IP phones.

Figure 1-7   *Complete Case Study Network*

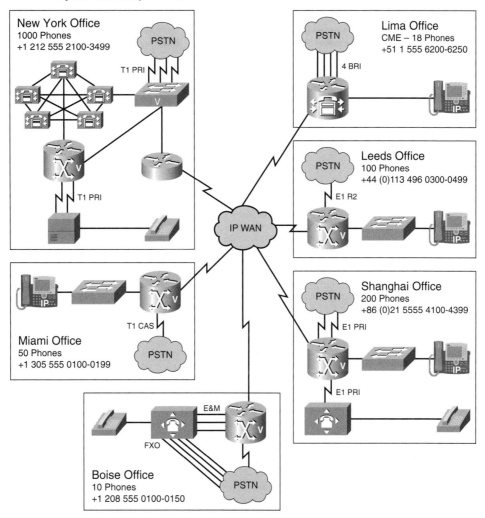

Table 1-1 lists each site and the composition of its voice network. It shows the number of IP and analog phones, the phone number range, the type of hardware, and the IP addressing scheme. You might find it helpful to refer back to this table as you read through the remaining case studies in this book.

Table 1-1 *Description of Case Study Sites*

Site	Number and Type of Phones	Telephone Number Range	Hardware/ Connections	Cisco CallManager IP Range	Data IP Subnet	Voice IP Subnet
New York City, New York, USA	1000 IP phones	1-212-555-2100 through 3499	CallManager cluster 6500 switch with a Communication Media Module (CMM) connected to three T1 PRIs A voice gateway router connected to a PBX via two T1 PRIs	10.1.10.10-20/24	10.1.25-49.0/24	10.1.50-75.0/24
Miami, Florida, USA	50 IP phones	1-305-555-0100 through 0199	Voice gateway router with SRST and one T1 CAS connection to the PSTN	N/A	10.10.25.0/24	10.10.50.0/24
Boise, Idaho, USA	10 analog phones	1-208-555-0100 through 0199	Voice gateway router with three E&M connections to a PBX and one T1 PRI connection to the PSTN	N/A	10.20.25.0/24	10.20.50.0/24
Shanghai, China	200 phones in a combination of IP and analog	86-21-5555-4100 through 4399	Voice gateway router with SRST, two E1 PRI links to the PSTN, and one E1 PRI connection to a PBX	N/A	10.30.25.0/24	10.30.50.0/24
Leeds, England	100 IP phones	44-0113-496-0300 through 0499	Voice gateway router with SRST and one E1 R2 connection to the PSTN	N/A	10.40.25.0/24	10.40.50.0/24
Lima, Peru	18 IP phones	51-1-555-6200 through 6299	Voice gateway router with CME and four BRI connections to the PSTN	N/A	10.50.25.0/24	10.50.50.0/24

Chapter Review Questions

1   What are three tasks that a voice gateway performs?

2   What are two benefits of adding an IPIPGW between networks?

3   What are four tasks that an H.323 gatekeeper performs?

4   Which call control protocol is an IETF standard that requires a call agent to function?

5   Which call control protocol is an IETF standard, uses a distributed call-control model, and is able to control multiple types of media connections?

6   Which call control protocol is an ITU-T standard and uses a distributed call-control model?

7   What are three typical CallManager deployment scenarios?

Gateways

CHAPTER 2

Media Gateway Control Protocol

The Media Gateway Control Protocol (MGCP) is described in a series of Internet Engineering Task Force (IETF) drafts and informational RFCs and was standardized by the ITU-T. MGCP grew out of two other protocols—the Internet Protocol Device Control (IPDC) and the Simple Gateway Control Protocol (SGCP). MGCP separates the functions of call control and media translation into two separate devices:

- The voice gateway handles media translation.
- A call agent handles call control.

This chapter describes how MGCP functions and how you implement it using Cisco CallManager as the call agent.

MGCP is a master/slave protocol that allows a call-control device (such as Cisco CallManager) to control and track the state of each voice port on the gateway. CallManager is able to exercise per-port control of connections to the public switched telephone network (PSTN), legacy private branch exchanges (PBX), voice-mail systems, and plain old telephone service (POTS) phones. This allows complete control of the dial plan from Cisco CallManager, which centralizes gateway management and provides scalable IP Telephony deployments.

Two versions of MGCP are in use:

- **Version 0.1**—This is the original version of MGCP that you are probably familiar with because it has been used for years on Cisco gateways and CallManagers. 0.1 is the default version in Cisco gateways and CallManagers as of the writing of this book.
- **MGCP version 1.0**—This was first defined in informational RFC 2705, which was obsoleted by RFC 3435. RFC 2705 outlined some changes based on experience implementing version 0.1 of the protocol. RFC 3435 is an enhancement of MGCP that contains some new events and features, allows IPv6 addresses in endpoint names, corrects some known issues, and provides more options for existing operations.

Cisco CallManager supports only version 0.1 as of this writing, but Cisco gateways can use version 1.0 with other call agents.

Many people choose to use MGCP gateways because the configuration is much simpler than other gateway protocols. MGCP has other capabilities that can make it a good choice, such as centralized administration and QSIG facility decoding.

This chapter covers the following topics:

- Introduction to MGCP
- MGCP Operation
- Call Flow with MGCP
- Pros and Cons of MGCP
- Dial Plan Considerations
- Implementing MGCP Gateways
- Securing MGCP Gateways
- Troubleshooting Tools

Introduction to MGCP

MGCP was created for a centralized architecture, where most of the configuration and call-control intelligence resides on a call agent, such as Cisco CallManager. The traditional role of an MGCP gateway is media translation. PSTN connections, such as Foreign Exchange Office (FXO), Foreign Exchange Station (FXS), and PRI lines, typically terminate in the gateway. The gateway then translates between the PSTN and the IP network. MGCP gateways are sometimes divided into two categories:

- **Residential gateways**—Interfaces between analog (RJ11) ports and the Voice over IP (VoIP) network
- **Trunking gateways**—Interfaces between PSTN trunks such as DS0s or PRIs and the VoIP network

This is somewhat of an artificial distinction, because MGCP gateways can contain both analog and trunk interfaces—thus functioning as both types of gateways, in addition to IP WAN interfaces.

An MGCP gateway routes calls in response to instructions from the call agent (in this case the Cisco CallManager). These calls could be to or from a telephone on the PSTN, or across a WAN to an IP or analog phone at a remote site. The gateway does not make call routing decisions. It needs to be able to reach a CallManager before it can handle calls. You can specify multiple CallManagers for the gateway to use. CallManager also controls other aspects of the call, such as the use of Resource Reservation Protocol (RSVP). Caller ID is available on digital lines but not on analog lines.

MGCP is an extensible protocol. Added functionalities are described as packages. In Chapter 8, "Connecting to an IP WAN," the section on WAN security describes the Secure Real-Time Protocol (SRTP) package that you can use to encrypt voice traffic. Other packages include capabilities for Real-Time Protocol (RTP), trunks, dual tone multifrequency (DTMF) tones, and announcement servers. You can see the full list in the output of the global configuration command **mgcp package-capability ?**.

When you are using an MGCP gateway, all the dial plan knowledge resides on the CallManager. You do not need to configure dial peers, unlike H.323 and SIP. However, this leaves the gateway unable to route calls if it cannot reach a CallManager. To remedy this, the MGCP Fallback feature was developed to allow gateways to fall back to using H.323 when a CallManager is unavailable. Fallback configuration enables the voice ports that were registered to the Cisco CallManager using MGCP to be available for routing calls to the PSTN. This is frequently used in conjunction with Survivable Remote Site Telephony (SRST) on the MGCP gateway. When IP phones register with the SRST router, they can use these voice ports.

MGCP is the protocol of choice when you need any of the following features:

- Centralized dial-plan control and management
- Simplified gateway configuration
- MGCP backhaul for Q Signaling (QSIG) connections, and PRI QSIG facility IE decoding

As with any protocol, MGCP has its pros and cons.

Pros

MGCP pros are as follows:

- **Ease of configuration**—The gateway can download much of its configuration from the CallManager. You need to configure dial peers for any voice ports that you will use for H.323 fallback, such as during SRST operation.
- **Ease of administration**—Because the call intelligence resides in the call agent, the management of multiple gateways is centralized. You can create customized, granular dial plans centrally at the Cisco CallManager, allowing the network to scale to large IP Telephony deployments.
- **Call survivability for analog and T1 channel-associated signaling (CAS) calls**— MGCP gateways preserve active calls using analog these voice ports and T1 CAS ports during failover to a backup CallManager and during transition to SRST. (However, any backhauled PRI and BRI ports are dropped when a connection to the CallManager is lost. These calls are also dropped when the CallManager connection is restored.)
- **Encryption of voice traffic**—MGCP was the first gateway protocol to support the encryption of voice traffic using SRTP in a Cisco-based network.
- **QSIG functionality**—When connecting to a PBX using QSIG, MGCP BRI/PRI Backhaul enables the decoding of facility IE messages by the CallManager. Calling name and redirect number, which are carried in the facility IE, are therefore available only when using MGCP trunks. You might need this function for voice-mail access. (See Chapter 5, "Circuit Options," for an explanation of IE messages, and Chapter 7, "Connecting to PBXs," for an explanation of QSIG.)

Cons

MGCP cons are as follows:

- **Dependence on call agent**—The lack of call intelligence on the gateway means that it must depend on a call agent, and network administrators must make backup plans in case the call agent becomes unavailable. Otherwise, you cannot place new calls. Thus, you need SRST and H.323 fallback.

- **Lack of call survivability for PRI and BRI calls**—Any active calls using a PRI and BRI port that is being backhauled to the CallManager are dropped when a connection to the CallManager is lost.

- **Fax calls**—Although MGCP supports various methods for fax calls, CallManager does not support the signaling and negotiation of any of the fax methods for MGCP gateways. H.323 now supports SRTP.

- **No caller ID with FXO ports**—The current implementation of MGCP does not pass along caller ID information when a call comes from an FXO port.

MGCP Operation

To understand MGCP, you must understand the concepts of endpoints and connections, and events and signals.

An *endpoint* can be either the source or the destination for a media stream. Some examples are an analog or digital line, or a virtual endpoint such as DSP resources used by a conference bridge. One gateway can support multiple endpoints. Endpoint names have two components—a local identifier, and a gateway identifier. The entire name consists of the local identifier, followed by the @ symbol, and then the gateway identifier. For example:

local_identifier@gateway_identifier.domain_name

The gateway identifier is its configured hostname, such as "BoiseRTR01." If the gateway is configured with a domain name, it is appended to the end of the hostname, such as "BoiseRTR01.company.com."

The format of a local identifier varies depending on the type of interface. The local identifier for *analog ports* uses the following syntax:

Endpoint type/Slot #/Subunit #/Port #

For example, an endpoint name for an FXO port might look something like this:

AALN/S0/SU0/1@VoiceGW

where

- **AALN** (Analog Access Line Endpoint) means that it is either an FXS or FXO interface.
- **S0** is the slot number that contains the voice module.
- **SU0** (for Subunit 0) is the slot within the network module that holds the voice interface card (VIC) or voice/WAN interface card (VWIC).
- **1** is the number of the voice port on the VIC or VWIC.
- **VoiceGW** is the hostname of the gateway.

The local identifier for *digital interfaces* uses the following syntax:

Slot #/Trunk type-Port #/B channel #

For example, the endpoint name for a T1 PRI interface might look something like this:

S0/ds1-0/1@VoiceGW.cisco.com

where

- **S0** is the slot number that contains the voice module.
- **ds1** means that the trunk type is a DS-1. Other trunk type values include ds3, e1, and e3.
- **-0** is the port number within the slot.
- **1** identifies ISDN B-channel number 1.
- **VoiceGW.cisco.com** is the hostname of the gateway, with its domain name appended.

Connections are created on endpoints when you need to make a call. Connections have properties, such as codec, IP address, port number, bandwidth, and encryption. MGCP uses the Session Description Protocol (or SDP, defined in RFC 2327) to inform CallManager about these details of the connection.

Endpoints generate *events*, such as when a phone on an FXS port goes off-hook or dials digits. Cisco CallManager can ask to be notified when it receives specific events on its gateways.

The CallManager can then instruct the gateway to send *signals*, such as dial tone or ringing.

MGCP Messages

MGCP uses nine types of messages between the gateway and CallManager to control the endpoints and connections. The receiver must acknowledge each message. Messages between the CallManager and the gateway are sent by default to port 2427.

Understanding these messages helps in troubleshooting issues with your MGCP gateway. The following is a description of the MGCP messages. Figures 2-1 through 2-3 illustrate their use.

When the CallManager needs to make a call to an endpoint that is connected to a gateway, it sends a **CreateConnection (CRCX)** command. Included in this message are the parameters to be used for the connection. These might include such things as the following:

- Bandwidth to be used for the call
- Codec to be used
- QoS settings
- Encryption
- Voice activity detection (VAD)
- Echo cancellation
- RSVP

The gateway responds to the CRCX message with one of the return codes. If the gateway accepts the request to create the connection, it responds with 200 OK, which includes information about the session such as IP address and media type (RTP audio, for example.) This session information is carried using SDP (RFC 2327).

If the CallManager wants the gateway to watch for certain events on an endpoint, it sends a **NotificationRequest (RQNT)** listing the type of event to watch for. Typically, the gateway is instructed to look for a phone going off or on hook, or digits being dialed.

The gateway answers with a **Notify (NTFY)** message. When the CallManager detects one of these events, it uses a NotificationRequest message to instruct the gateway to respond appropriately (for instance, to provide a dial tone.)

Based on the events received, the connection might be changed. For instance, if the gateway sets up the connection for a voice call and then notices fax tones, CallManager changes the encoding. The CallManager changes these parameters with a **ModifyConnection (MDCX)** command containing the new connection settings.

To terminate a connection, the CallManager sends the gateway a **DeleteConnection (DLCX)** command.

The gateway then sends a return code in response to the request to delete connection. If the gateway accepts the request, it sends a **200 OK** message with the following statistics about the connection to the CallManager:

- Number of packets sent
- Number of bytes sent
- Number of packets received
- Number of bytes received
- Number of packets lost
- Average jitter
- Average transmission delay

The CallManager uses an **AuditEndpoint (AUEP)** message to find information and status on the endpoint. It sends one AUEP message per endpoint.

The CallManager can learn the parameters that are associated with a connection by using the **AuditConnection (AUCX)** command.

The **EndpointConfiguration (EPCF)** command instructs the gateway about configuration to be applied to the endpoint.

The gateway initiates a **RestartInProgress (RSIP)** message to the CallManager when an endpoint or group of endpoints are going out of or coming into service, or when the gateway will restart. Three types of restarts exist:

- **Graceful**—The restart is delayed to allow any existing connections to finish their calls.
- **Forced**—This restart occurs immediately, and all connections are lost.
- **Restart**—The gateway itself is going to reboot.

Registering with CallManager

An MGCP gateway must register with its CallManager before accepting calls. Figure 2-1 illustrates the process that an MGCP gateway follows when registering with a Cisco CallManager.

Figure 2-1 *Registering an MGCP Gateway with CallManager*

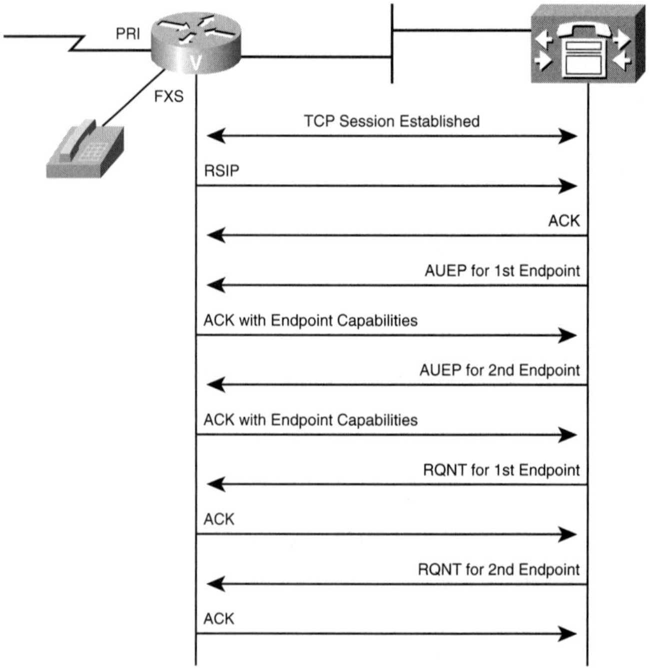

The transactions in Figure 2-1 are as follows:

1 A TCP connection is opened between the gateway and CallManager.

2 The gateway sends an RSIP message to the CallManager to inform it that it is coming into service.

3 The CallManager sends the gateway one AUEP message per endpoint. This message requests information on the attributes and capabilities of the endpoint. Figure 2-1 shows just two AUEP messages for the sake of simplicity—CallManager actually sends an AUEP message for each DS0 in the PRI.

4 The gateway acknowledges with an ACK that contains the endpoint information.

5 The CallManager responds with an RQNT message per endpoint, listing the events it wants to be notified of.

6 The gateway acknowledges those messages. The gateway, along with its endpoints, is then registered with the CallManager.

Call Flow with MGCP

MGCP uses the messages described in the previous section during call setup and teardown. The exact procedure varies depending on the type of endpoint, but completing an MGCP phone call involves four basic steps:

1 When CallManager is notified of a phone going off-hook, it asks the calling gateway to create a connection on that endpoint. The calling gateway does so and sends an SDP message describing the connection parameters.

2 CallManager asks the receiving gateway to create a connection on one of its endpoints. The message includes the SDP information from the calling gateway. The receiving gateway creates a connection and responds with its own SDP message.

3 CallManager sends the session description information for the receiving gateway to the calling gateway with a modify connection message. Communication is now bidirectional, and the call can proceed.

4 When one endpoint hangs up, CallManager sends a DLCX to both gateways, and the call ends.

Call Flow Between Analog Phones

When an MGCP gateway has an analog device connected to it, it collects the call information and sends it to CallManager. Figure 2-2 shows the process for setting up a call between two analog phones connected to FXS ports on different gateways but controlled by the same CallManager.

Figure 2-2 *Call Flow Between Analog Phones*

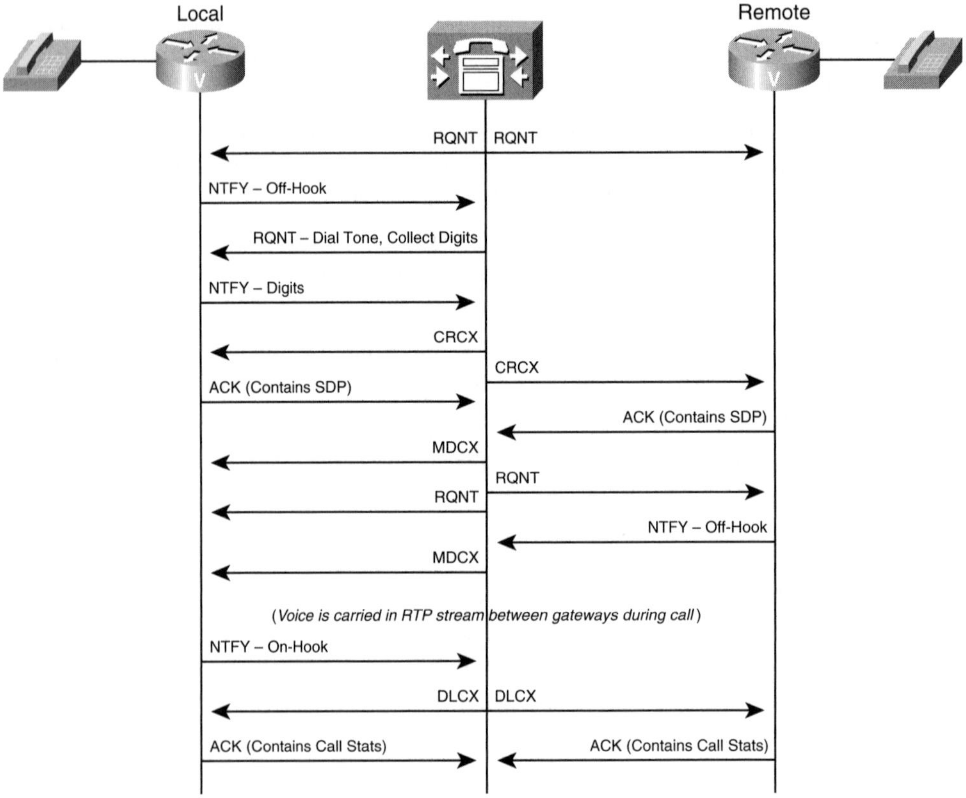

The transactions illustrated in Figure 2-2 are as follows:

1 The CallManager instructs both gateways to watch for events in a NotificationRequest message. One event that the gateway is instructed to watch for is the connected phone going off-hook.

2 The local gateway notices the phone going off-hook and sends an NTFY message with that information.

3 CallManager responds with an RQNT message to provide dial tone, collect digits, and tell it if the phone goes back on-hook. The gateway can group all the digits into one message, but it needs to know how to recognize when enough digits have been gathered. To solve this, CallManager provides the gateway with the dial plan information.

4 When the gateway finishes collecting the digits, it sends them to CallManager in a Notify message.

5 CallManager responds with a CRCX message. Included in that are the parameters that the gateway needs to create the connection to the phone. The gateway sends an ACK that contains the SDP information about its local connection.

6 CallManager also sends a CRCX message to the remote gateway, asking it to open a connection to its appropriate endpoint and passing along the SDP information from the local gateway.

7 The remote gateway responds with an ACK containing its SDP information. CallManager then sends the gateway an RQNT asking to be notified when the remote phone goes off-hook.

8 CallManager issues an MDCX message to the local gateway containing the connection information from the remote gateway. It also sends an RQNT to both gateways, telling the local gateway to provide ringback and the remote gateway to send ringing.

9 When the remote gateway sees its phone go off-hook, it sends an NTFY message to CallManager. CallManager then sends an MDCX to the local gateway telling it to go to two-way communication, and RTP takes over to carry the voice traffic.

10 In Figure 2-2, when the local user hangs up, the gateway sends an NTFY message to CallManager.

11 CallManager sends a DLCX message to both gateways, and the gateways respond with an ACK that contains all the call statistics. The call is terminated, and both gateways go back to watching for changes in the status of their endpoints.

ISDN Connections with Backhaul

Flow for an ISDN call is different from an analog one. PRI and BRI circuits carry Q.921 and Q.931 signaling messages in the D channel. An MGCP gateway responds to Layer 2 Q.921 signals but does not try to interpret Q.931 call control signals. Instead, when a call needs to be set up, gateways send the Q.931 Layer 3 messages to their CallManager. The gateway uses MGCP Backhaul to send these signals to CallManager over TCP port 2428. (You might also see this called PRI or BRI Backhaul.) The messages are marked with a quality of service (QoS) Differentiated Services Code Point (DSCP) value of 0, or best effort, by default.

The gateway needs a connection to a CallManager to process ISDN calls. If a CallManager is not available, the gateway does not bring up the D channel. If connection to CallManager is lost while an IDSN call is active, the gateway maintains the call if a backup CallManager is available. If no CallManager is reachable, the gateway drops the D channel and the call. In SRST mode, the gateway can re-establish the call if the user initiates it.

Figure 2-3 shows the call flow using a PRI circuit.

Figure 2-3 *Call Flow with a PRI Circuit*

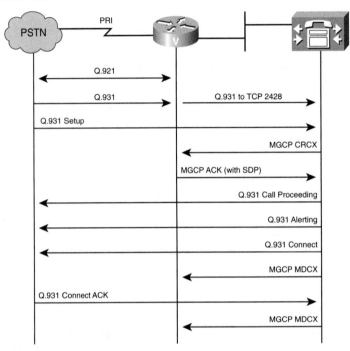

The transactions for the call flow in Figure 2-3 are as follows:

1 The gateway and the PSTN switch exchange ISDN Q.921 Layer 2 information. This registers the gateway with the ISDN switch and ensures that the ISDN connection remains active. Q.921 information stops at the gateway.

2 An ISDN Q.931 Setup call-control message arrives. The gateway puts it in a packet addressed to TCP port 2428 and sends it to the CallManager using PRI Backhaul. The CallManager responds by instructing the gateway to create a connection. The gateway sends an acknowledgement that contains SDP information about the connection.

3 The CallManager then sends three Q.931 messages: Call Proceeding, Alerting, and Connect through the gateway to the PSTN. These messages let the other side of the connection know that CallManager is placing the call, and then that the call has been answered.

4 After the call is brought up, the CallManager sends the gateway an MGCP MDCX message to tell it parameters for the connection.

5 The CallManager gets an acknowledgement of the connection from the other side of the call and then sends a message to the gateway telling it to go to two-way communication on the connection. Voice traffic can then go through the link.

MGCP Fallback

An MGCP gateway sends keepalive messages to its primary CallManager every 15 seconds. If CallManager does not respond in 30 seconds, the gateway switches over to the next configured CallManager. If no Cisco CallManagers are reachable, the gateway can fall back to using the default session application, if it is so configured. Voice ports are controlled by a Tcl scripts, and H.323 controls any VoIP dial peers. All active MGCP analog and T1 CAS calls are maintained during the fallback transition. Callers are unaware of the fallback transition, and these active MGCP calls are cleared only when the communicating callers hang up. Active MGCP PRI and BRI backhauled calls are released during fallback, however. Any transient MGCP calls (that is, calls that are not in the connected state) are cleared when the fallback transition is triggered and must be attempted again.

Enabling fallback requires the configuration of fallback commands, specifying the fallback application and defining dial peers to be used while in fallback mode. This is shown in the "Implementing MGCP Gateways" section of this chapter.

While in fallback mode, the gateway continues its attempts to contact the CallManagers that are listed in its configuration. When one of the CallManagers responds, the gateway registers with it and switches back to MGCP operation. As before, all active calls are maintained except ISDN calls, which have their signaling backhauled to CallManager.

Dial Plan Considerations

Configuring a dial plan for MGCP is fairly simple, because the call agent handles all the call control information in normal circumstances. Dial plans are configured on the call agent. Dial peers must still be configured for analog or PSTN digital ports, such as FXO, FXS, or PRI. However, these dial peers are associated with—and controlled by—the CallManager.

If the gateway falls back to H.323 when its connection to the CallManager is lost, you must plan the routing of calls during fallback. Typically, all calls are forwarded to the PSTN in this circumstance, but occasionally they are forwarded to a different gateway instead. If you want this operation to be transparent to your users, you might need to add digits such as area or long-distance access codes. If you will use the router in SRST mode, you might need other configurations to emulate CallManager capabilities. Chapter 13, "SRST and MGCP Gateway Fallback," details these.

Implementing MGCP Gateways

Basic implementation of an MGCP gateway involves enabling MGCP on the gateway, telling the gateway how to find the CallManagers, and then adding the gateway and its endpoints to the CallManager configuration. You have a choice of doing all of configuration manually or downloading a good part of it from CallManager. The following sections describe some common configuration tasks.

Basic MGCP Gateway Configuration

Before you enable MGCP, configure the router with a hostname, IP addressing, and routing information. Then the basic tasks to configure MGCP on the router are enabling MGCP, telling it how to reach its call agent, and telling it that the call agent is a Cisco CallManager. The commands to do this at global configuration mode are as follows:

```
VoiceGW(config)#mgcp
VoiceGW(config)#mgcp call-agent [ip-address | hostname] [port] service-type mgcp
[version 0.1 | 1.0 | rfc3435-1.0]
VoiceGW(config)#ccm-manager mgcp
```

If you would like the gateway to download much of its MGCP configuration from CallManager, you must code that and give it the IP address or DNS name for the TFTP server (usually CallManager). This downloads XML files with configuration such as MGCP packages, RTP settings, and fax settings. The commands to enable this are as follows:

```
VoiceGW(config)#ccm-manager config server {ip-address | dns-name}
VoiceGW(config)#ccm-manager config
```

This file is downloaded when the gateway first communicates with CallManager, before it sends the RSIP message. The file is refreshed if changes are made to CallManager that require the gateway to be reset. Be sure to save any manual configuration to NVRAM, or it might be overwritten if the router downloads a new XML file. If you manually configure both MGCP and H.323 dial peers, be sure to configure the MGCP ones first if you are using this auto-config feature.

If the download is successful, you see a message on the gateway similar to what follows:

```
VoiceGW#
Loading VoiceGW.cnf.xml from 10.6.2.10 (via FastEthernet0/0): !
[OK - 4445 bytes]
```

Next, you need to bind MGCP to the voice ports. You do this by configuring a dial peer for each voice port and binding MGCP to it using the **application MGCPAPP** command. This command is case sensitive in some IOS releases. To be safe, code MGCPAPP (all capital letters) unless you know that your release is not case sensitive.

```
VoiceGW(config)#dial-peer voice 100 pots
VoiceGW(config-dial-peer)#application MGCPAPP
VoiceGW(config-dial-peer)#port 1/0/0
```

NOTE   In IOS version 12.4 this command changed to **service MGCPAPP**. Do not use this command on a dial peer that supports PRI or BRI backhaul.

When you make a change to the MGCP configuration, such as adding or changing endpoints, it is a good idea to reinitialize MGCP by issuing **no mgcp** and then **mgcp global configuration** commands.

Configuring MGCP Fallback

To use MGCP fallback, you must tell the router to use its default call-routing application, when it loses contact with the CallManager. The command for this varies depending on IOS versions. For IOS releases 12.3(13)T or earlier, use the global command **call application alternate default**. For IOS releases 12.3(14)T or later, the command is a bit more complicated:

```
VoiceGW(config)#application
VoiceGW(config-app)#global
VoiceGW(config-app-global)#service alternate Default
```

When using MGCP fallback, you must also configure at least one dial peer with a destination pattern so that it can route outbound calls when CallManager is not available. That dial pattern is typically a wildcard that matches all outbound calls, such as "9T." Use the **incoming called-number .** wildcard if you want to enable the gateway to answer incoming calls on that port.

```
VoiceGW(config)#dial-peer voice 200 pots
VoiceGW(config-dial-peer)#destination-pattern 9T
VoiceGW(config-dial-peer)#incoming called-number .
VoiceGW(config-dial-peer)#port voice-port
```

Assigning an MGCP Source IP Address

By default, MGCP sources its messages from the IP address of Loopback 0 if it is present. If not, they are sourced from the outgoing interface. You can designate a specific interface to be used as the source IP address for either MGCP signaling, RTP media, or both. First configure the loopback interface, and then use the global configuration command **mgcp bind {control | media} source-interface** *interface-number*. After configuring this, reinitialize MGCP.

Configuring MGCP PRI and BRI Backhaul

MGCP passes the ISDN Q.931 call setup and teardown information to its CallManager. You configure this under the BRI or PRI interface, with the command **isdn bind-l3 ccm-manager**. When you are setting up the PRI-group timeslots on the controller for the PRI interface, add **service mgcp** to the end of the **pri-group timeslots** command. In addition, you must add that interface to CallManager as an MGCP endpoint and link it to a route pattern. You might need to include the **application mgcpapp** command under the dial peer for that interface, depending on your IOS version. For Cisco IOS Software Release 12.3(7)T and later, do not include this command under dial peers for ISDN interfaces that will use backhaul.

Verify MGCP Backhaul with the command **show ccm-manager backhaul**. You should see the ports being backhauled, in addition to information about the connection. The **show isdn status** command should show Layer 3 bound to CCM Manager.

Enabling Multicast Music on Hold

You might want to enable music on hold so that an off-net caller can receive streaming music as a multicast, rather than as a unicast. The command to enable multicast music on hold is given under global configuration mode: **ccm-manager music-on-hold.** You also must configure the CallManager to support music on hold.

Configuring Cisco CallManager

You need to configure the CallManager to recognize and control the gateway and its endpoints. The screen shots that follow were taken from CallManager 4.1. If you have a different version, your menus might differ.

Step 1 To add a new gateway, select **Device** from the CallManager Administration menu, and then click on **Gateway**, as shown in Figure 2-4.

Figure 2-4 *CallManager Administration Menu*

Step 2 At the next screen, shown in Figure 2-5, select the **Add a New Gateway** link.

Figure 2-5   *Adding a New Gateway to CallManager*

Step 3   This link takes you to the screen in Figure 2-6, where you select the type of
gateway you are adding. For an MGCP gateway, choose the device type, such as
router model or VG type. In this example, a Cisco 2821 router was selected. After
you select the gateway type, the only option available under Device Protocol is
"MGCP." Notice that you cannot configure CallManager to recognize the same
device as both an MGCP and an H.323 gateway.

Figure 2-6 *Selecting the Type of Gateway*

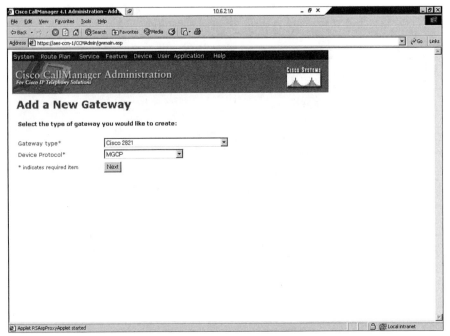

Step 4 Selecting **Next** brings you to the Gateway Configuration screen, illustrated in Figure 2-7. In the domain name field, enter the hostname of the router. (MGCP gateways are identified by hostname, not IP address.) If the router is also configured with a domain name, append that to the hostname, such as VGateway.myco.com. This name is case sensitive. Enter a description if desired. You must choose a CallManager group to use, even if it is just the default one.

Step 5 On the same screen, begin configuring the endpoints. The available router slots are listed, as is a drop-down menu to select the type of voice module they contain, if any. ISR routers contain four WIC/VWIC slots that are not part of a separate module. These are listed in the drop-down menu as "NM-4VWIC-MBRD." Be sure to choose this option, as shown in the example, if you intend to use these slots.

You can choose the type of Switchback, if desired. When a CallManager becomes unreachable and the gateway fails over to a backup CallManager, that is called *Switchover*. If the primary CallManager returns to service, the gateway reregisters with it. That is called *Switchback*. Active calls are preserved by default during both events. The Switchback Timing determines how a gateway will switch back to its primary CallManager.

When you have finished this configuration, click **Insert**.

Figure 2-7 *CallManager Gateway Configuration*

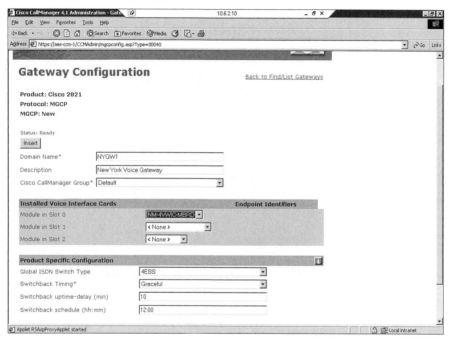

Step 6   You then specify the endpoints that CallManager controls, by selecting subunits within the modules and configuring each port. Figure 2-8 shows an example with one PRI, four FXO, and four FXS interfaces. CallManager controls all six endpoints in this one MGCP gateway. To configure a specific port, click on the link for it. The necessary configuration depends on the type of endpoint. Configure the directory number for FXS ports here, rather than on the router.

Figure 2-8 *Configuring MGCP Endpoints*

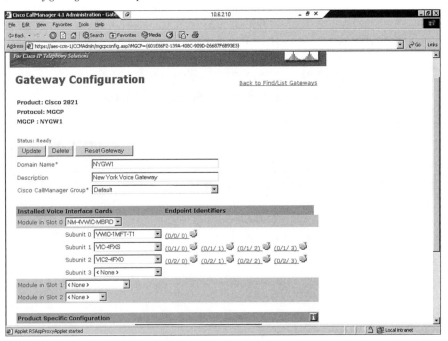

Figure 2-9 *Resetting the Gateway*

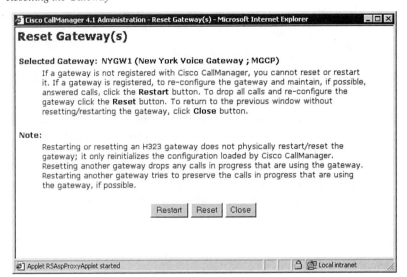

Step 7 The next step is to reset the gateway, as shown in Figure 2-9. Note that resetting an MGCP gateway drops any calls that are using that gateway.

Step 8 To verify that the gateway is registered, go back to the Find and List Gateways screen. Click on **Find**, and the gateway should be listed, as shown in Figure 2-10. Any registered endpoints are also listed.

Figure 2-10 *Verifying Gateway Registration with CallManager*

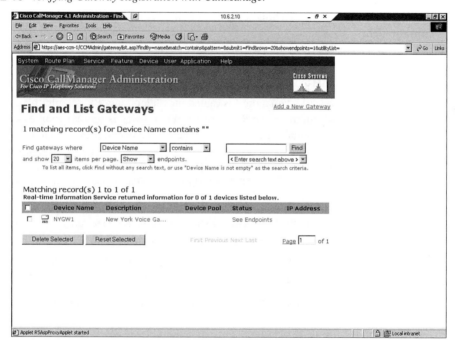

In addition, you must configure the CallManager with the appropriate route patterns, route groups, and route lists. After you do that, add the endpoints on the MGCP gateway to a route group or route list so that you can route calls to it. For dialing out to the PSTN, add the appropriate endpoints to a route pattern.

Configuring CallManager Redundancy

Because MGCP needs to communicate with a call agent for the gateway to have full functionality, the protocol allows you to specify up to three CallManagers. You configure the primary one using the global **mgcp call-agent** *ip-address\hostname* command. You can identify additional CallManagers with a global **ccm-manager redundant-host** *ip-address1\hostname1* [*ip-address2\hostname2*] command.

The gateway sends normal MGCP keepalives (an empty NTFY message) to the primary CallManager. It also establishes a TCP session with the first redundant CallManager, using port 2428, and exchanges keepalives. If the primary CallManager becomes unreachable, the gateway quickly fails over to the secondary. It then starts sending TCP keepalives to the next CallManager that is listed.

If the primary CallManager returns, the gateway switches back to using it. It does this when all the established calls have ended, by default. However, you can configure it with the **callmanager redundancy switchback** {**graceful** | **immediate** | **never** | **schedule-time** | **uptime-delay**} command.

Configuring DTMF Relay

DTMF tones are created when a digit is dialed on a telephone. By default, the gateway sends these tones within the voice RTP stream. When voice is sent uncompressed, these tones arrive in their original state. However, when voice is compressed, such as with the G.729 codec, the tones might be distorted or part of the signal lost. DTMF Relay addresses this by separating these tones from the rest of the voice and sending them in a different way. You have a choice of four types of DTMF Relay in an MGCP gateway—Cisco proprietary, Named Service Event (NSE), Named Telephony Event (NTE), and out-of-band.

The Cisco proprietary method sends the tones in the same RTP stream as voice, but it codes them differently to enable the receiver to identify them as DTMF signals.

NSE is specified in RFC 2833. It also sends the tones within the RTP stream, in a special NTE packet. This is similar to Cisco implementation, but it is based on standards.

The MGCP implementation of NTE has two flavors: gateway controlled (NTE-GW) and call agent controlled (NTE-CA). In NTE-GW, the two gateways negotiate the use of DTMF relay in SDP messages. In NTE-CA, the call agent tells its gateways the type of DTMF relay they are using.

Out-of-band DTMF relay sends the tones as signals to the CallManager, out-of-band over the control channel. CallManager interprets the signals and passes them on.

The DTMF package is loaded by default on Cisco gateways. To enable a specific type of DTMF relay, use the global command **mgcp dtmf-relay voip codec** {**all** | **low-bit-rate**} **mode** {**cisco** | **nse** | **nte-ca** | **nte-gw** | **out-of-band**}. This can be verified with the **show mgcp** command. The following line shows out-of-band DTMF relay:

```
mgcp dtmf-relay voip codec all mode out-of-band
```

You must also configure the CallManager to support the type of DTMF relay you choose.

Securing MGCP Gateways

An MGCP gateway is part of your IP network and should conform to your company security policy with user control and authentication, access control lists, and physical security applied to it. A voice gateway functioning as a WAN gateway can provide additional network protection with features such as IOS firewall or IPS, depending on your company policy.

In addition, MGCP gateways support authentication, encryption, and replay protection of voice traffic. Voice media is secured using Secure RTP (SRTP), and control traffic is handled using Secure RTCP (SRTCP). You must have a version of CallManager that supports this, and either an Advanced IP Services or Advanced Enterprise Services IOS image on the gateway. You can set up an IPsec connection to secure MGCP messages between the gateway and CallManager, going across a WAN. Recommended practice dictates that this tunnel terminates on the gateway rather than CallManager. This assumes that traffic within the LAN is trusted. Messages between CallManager and its IP phones can be encrypted by Transport Layer Security (TLS).

You must load the SRTP package onto the gateway. The ability to use SRTP and SRTP key information is contained in SDP messages. If one device along the path cannot support SRTP, the call reverts to using RTP. Chapter 8 describes the use of SRTP on an MGCP gateway.

Troubleshooting Tools

One of the first steps in troubleshooting an MGCP configuration is to verify that the gateway is registered with the correct CallManager with the command **show ccm-manager**. The result, as shown in Example 2-1, lists primary and backup CallManagers, in addition to statistics about the connection. Check that the CallManager IP addresses are configured correctly.

Example 2-1 **show ccm-manager** *Command*

```
VGateway#show ccm-manager
MGCP Domain Name: VGateway
Priority        Status                    Host
===========================================================
Primary         Registered                10.6.2.10
First Backup    Down                      10.6.2.11
Second Backup   None

Current active CallManager:     10.6.2.10
Backhaul/Redundant link port:   2428
Failover Interval:              30 seconds
Keepalive Interval:             15 seconds
Last keepalive sent:            03:46:22 EST Oct 23 2005 (elapsed time: 00:00:03)
Last MGCP traffic time:         03:46:22 EST Oct 23 2005 (elapsed time: 00:00:03)
Last failover time:             None
```

continues

Example 2-1 **show ccm-manager** *Command (Continued)*

```
Last switchback time:        None
Switchback mode:             Graceful
MGCP Fallback mode:          Not Selected
Last MGCP Fallback start time: None
Last MGCP Fallback end time:  None


Configuration Error History:
FAX mode: cisco
```

The **show mgcp** command gives a long, detailed breakdown of your MGCP configuration. The lines to check in here depend on the type of problem you are having. Some common lines to examine are highlighted in the output of Example 2-2.

Example 2-2 **show mgcp** *Command*

```
VGateway#show mgcp
MGCP Admin State ACTIVE, Oper State ACTIVE - Cause Code NONE
MGCP call-agent: 10.6.2.10 Initial protocol service is MGCP 0.1
MGCP block-newcalls DISABLED
MGCP send SGCP RSIP: forced/restart/graceful/disconnected DISABLED
MGCP quarantine mode discard/step
MGCP quarantine of persistent events is ENABLED
MGCP dtmf-relay voip codec all mode out-of-band
MGCP dtmf-relay for VoAAL2 disabled for all codec types
MGCP voip modem passthrough disabled
MGCP voaal2 modem passthrough disabled
MGCP voip modem relay: Disabled.
MGCP TSE payload: 100
MGCP T.38 Named Signaling Event (NSE) response timer: 200
MGCP Network (IP/AAL2) Continuity Test timer: 200
MGCP 'RTP stream loss' timer: 5
MGCP request timeout 500
MGCP maximum exponential request timeout 4000
MGCP gateway port: 2427, MGCP maximum waiting delay 3000
MGCP restart delay 0, MGCP vad DISABLED
MGCP rtrcac DISABLED
MGCP system resource check DISABLED
MGCP xpc-codec: DISABLED, MGCP persistent hookflash: DISABLED
MGCP persistent offhook: ENABLED, MGCP persistent onhook: DISABLED
MGCP piggyback msg ENABLED, MGCP endpoint offset DISABLED
MGCP simple-sdp DISABLED
MGCP undotted-notation DISABLED
MGCP codec type g711ulaw, MGCP packetization period 20
MGCP JB threshold lwm 30, MGCP JB threshold hwm 150
MGCP LAT threshold lwm 150, MGCP LAT threshold hwm 300
MGCP PL threshold lwm 1000, MGCP PL threshold hwm 10000
MGCP CL threshold lwm 1000, MGCP CL threshold hwm 10000
MGCP playout mode is adaptive 60, 40, 200 in msec
MGCP Fax Playout Buffer is 300 in msec
MGCP media (RTP) dscp: ef, MGCP signaling dscp: af31
MGCP default package: line-package
```

Example 2-2   **show mgcp** *Command (Continued)*

```
MGCP supported packages: gm-package dtmf-package trunk-package line-package
                         hs-package rtp-package atm-package ms-package dt-package
                         res-package mt-package fxr-package
MGCP Digit Map matching order: shortest match
SGCP Digit Map matching order: always left-to-right
MGCP VoAAL2 ignore-lco-codec DISABLED
MGCP T.38 Fax is ENABLED
MGCP T.38 Fax ECM is ENABLED
MGCP T.38 Fax NSF Override is DISABLED
MGCP T.38 Fax Low Speed Redundancy: 0MGCP T.38 Fax High Speed Redundancy: 0
MGCP control bind :INACTIVE
MGCP media bind :DISABLED
MGCP Upspeed payload type for G711ulaw: 0,  G711alaw: 8
MGCP Dynamic payload type for G.726-16K codec
MGCP Dynamic payload type for G.726-24K codec
MGCP Dynamic payload type for G.Clear codec
MGCP Guaranteed scheduler time is disabled
```

If you have made recent changes to the MGCP configuration or its endpoints, stop and start the MGCP process (**no mgcp** and then **mgcp**), and then give the **show** commands again.

The **show mgcp endpoint** command lists the active endpoints on the gateway. You can also look in CallManager under **Device > Gateways > Find and List Gateways** to see which endpoints have registered with CallManager. If a voice port is not registered, make sure you have the **application mgcpapp** command under its dial peer, and that it is configured in CallManager.

Related to this, **show voice port** gives the status of each port to verify that it is up. If a port is down but the physical connection is good, try disabling and re-enabling the port, using the **shutdown** and **no shutdown** interface commands. This is especially useful with FXS and FXO ports.

You can monitor active calls with the **show mgcp connection** command. Look for the M (for Mode) field. You should see M=3 if the connection is able to both send and receive traffic.

In addition, you can use the CallManager Performance Monitor and the Cisco Real Time Monitoring Tool (RTMT) to troubleshoot problems with MGCP gateways and endpoints.

Case Study: Configuring an MGCP Gateway

In this case study, a router is added to the New York office to act as an MGCP voice gateway. It terminates one of the PRI links, uses the CallManager at 10.1.10.10 as primary, and uses the CallManager at 10.1.10.11 as secondary. Both media and control traffic are sourced from interface Loopback99. Multicast music on hold is enabled. Out-of-band signaling for DTMF tones is enabled. The default switchback mode of Graceful is used, so no configuration is necessary for it.

Only the relevant gateway configuration is shown in Example 2-3. The CallManager configuration is not shown.

Example 2-3 *Case Study Configuration*

```
hostname NYCGateway2
!
ccm-manager redundant-host 10.1.10.11
!specifies back-up CCM ip address or DNS
!
!Starts the TCP socket 2428 and MGCP Link Monitor, which are specific to CCM
deployment
ccm-manager mgcp
!These two commands tell the gateway to download its MGCP configuration from CCM
ccm-manager config
ccm-manager config server 10.1.10.10
!
ccm-manager music-on-hold
!
!Enables the MGCP gateway to use fallback mode
ccm-manager fallback-mgcp
!DEFAULT is the H323 application
call application alternate DEFAULT
interface Loopback99
 ip address 10.1.49.99 255.255.255.0
!
interface Ethernet0/0
 ip address 10.1.25.4 255.255.255.0
!
controller T1 1/0
 framing esf
 linecode b8zs
 pri-group timeslots 1-24 service mgcp
!
interface Serial1/0:23
 no ip address
 isdn switch-type primary-ni
 isdn incoming-voice voice
 isdn bind-l3 ccm-manager
!
voice-port 1/0:23
!
!Start the MGCP process
mgcp
!Identify the primary CCM DNS or IP address
mgcp call-agent 10.1.10.10  service-type mgcp version  0.1
!Enable DTMF Relay
mgcp dtmf-relay voip codec all mode out-of-band
!Identifies the IP address used for communications to CallManager
!This command is essential when multiple IP interfaces have access to the CCM
mgcp bind control source-interface Loopback99
!
mgcp profile default
!
```

Example 2-3 *Case Study Configuration (Continued)*

```
!
dial-peer voice 1023 pots
 application mgcpapp
 port 1/0:23
!
gateway
 !
```

Review Questions

1 What role does the call agent play when using an MGCP gateway?

2 List the control messages that MGCP uses.

3 How does MGCP Backhaul function?

4 What three commands do you need to enable MGCP on a router and identify Cisco CallManager as its call agent?

5 Why is there a need for DTMF relay in a VoIP network, regardless of the gateway protocol used?

CHAPTER 3

H.323

H.323 is a standard for communication protocols from the International Telecommunications Union Telecommunication Standardization Sector (ITU-T); Version 4 is the current version. H.323 was created to provide multimedia communication across a packet network. The protocol can handle video and data, in addition to audio. H.323 interoperates well with the public switched telephone network (PSTN) in translating between call setup and control signals used in an IP network and those used in a switched-circuit network. H.323 is widely used in video conferencing deployments.

Gateways that use H.323 do not depend on a call agent, as with Media Gateway Control Protocol (MGCP). H.323 is the default gateway protocol on Cisco routers. This chapter focuses on Cisco IOS H.323 gateways, although the concepts apply to all H.323 gateways.

In this chapter you will learn

- H.323 specifications
- H.323 network components
- Call flow with H.323 gateways
- H.323 protocol pros and cons
- Dial plan considerations
- Implementing H.323 gateways
- Securing H.323 gateways
- Troubleshooting tools

H.323 Specifications

The H.323 standard is actually a suite of specifications that controls voice and video transmission over IP networks. The following are some commonly used specifications:

- **H.225**—Handles call setup and teardown between H.323 devices on a packet-based network, terminal to gatekeeper signaling using Registration, Admission, and Status Protocol (RAS), and call signaling. H.323 can use ISDN Q.931 signals, formatted as H.225 messages, to interoperate with legacy voice networks.

- **H.235**—Specifies security for messages between the gateway and gatekeeper.
- **H.245**—Controls the traffic flow, performs DTMF Relay, limits media transmission rates, negotiates capability, and controls opening and closing channels for media streams. Uses TCP.
- **H.261 and H.263**—Specify video conferencing standards.
- **H.450**—Controls supplementary services between H.323 entities. Examples of supplementary services include call waiting, hold, transfer, park, and pickup.
- **T.120**—Used for real-time multipoint data transfer during videoconferences. Allows application sharing, whiteboarding, and file transfer. Uses TCP.
- **H.320**—Defines the standard for video conferencing over ISDN networks. H.320 uses H.221 frames for media. It requires a gateway to interwork with H.323 conferencing over IP because H.221 frames must be translated into RTP packets, and vice versa.

H.323 Network Components

H.323 has several functional components, which you can implement separately on different devices, or as multiple functions on the same device. The basic components include gateways, gatekeepers, terminals, and multipoint control units (MCU). You can also use proxy servers. Figure 3-1 illustrates these components. A Cisco CallManager is also shown. It is not part of the H.323 specification, but it can interact with H.323 devices.

Figure 3-1 *H.323 Network Components*

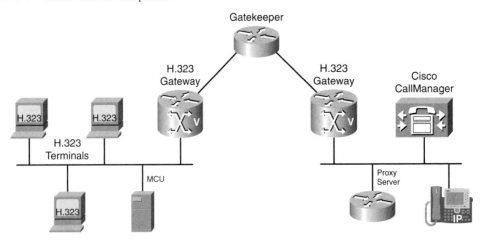

H.323 Gateways

H.323 gateways translate between different types of networks, just as any gateway does. In Figure 3-1, the gateways use H.323 to communicate with each other, the gatekeeper, CallManager, and the other H.323 devices in the network. H.323 gateways can register with a gatekeeper. They can also register analog phones in their network with the gatekeeper. H.323 gateways have the intelligence to place and receive calls, although CallManager can also control calls. Dial peers are configured on the gateway, with destination patterns. A Voice over IP (VoIP) dial peer points to the CallManager for each range of internal phone numbers it controls. CallManager sends outgoing PSTN calls to the gateway, which uses plain old telephone service (POTS) dial peers with the appropriate destination patterns to route them.

H.323 Gatekeepers

Gatekeepers provide a centralized point to resolve E.164 phone numbers to IP addresses and do call admission control. They can provide call routing and control, security, and bandwidth management, and they can simplify dial peer configuration. In Figure 3-1, when a call needs to go to an IP phone in the other network, the gateway must contact the gatekeeper before the call can proceed.

When people make calls between IP phones that the same CallManager cluster controls, the CallManager maps the called phone number to a destination IP address. When they make calls between clusters, they can optionally use an H.323 gatekeeper to route the call to the appropriate gateway or CallManager. Both CallManager and H.323 gateways can use the services of a gatekeeper. The originating gateway (or CallManager) sends a request to the gatekeeper to admit the call, and the gatekeeper responds with the IP address of the terminating gateway or CallManager. Call setup and voice media can then be sent directly between the originating and terminating peers.

H.323 Terminals

Like MGCP, H.323 uses the concept of endpoints. IP phones and video conferencing stations, in addition to gateways and CallManagers, can be H.323 endpoints. An H.323 terminal is an endpoint that is able to do real-time two-way communication. All H.323 terminals must support H.225 for call setup, H.245 for channel and capability control, RAS for communicating with a gatekeeper, and Real-Time Transport Protocol (RTP)/Real-Time Transport Control Protocol (RTCP) for media streams. They can optionally support the other H.323 specifications. The most common type of H.323 terminal is a video conferencing system.

Multipoint Control Units

An MCU allows multiple participants in a conference. In Figure 3-1, if the three H.323 video systems want to participate in a conference, the MCU controls that. An MCU is composed of a multipoint controller (MC) and a multipoint processor (MP). The MC handles the H.245 capabilities negotiation and controls the conference resources. The MP does the actual mixing and splitting of the audio and video streams, and translation between different codecs or bandwidth.

H.323 Proxy Servers

H.323 proxy servers do the call setup and teardown in place of the endpoint. They can provide security, quality of service (QoS), and application-specific routing (ASR). In Figure 3-1, a Cisco router is configured as an H.323 proxy server. It can communicate with the gatekeeper and endpoints in the other network, thus hiding their real IP address of endpoints in its network. Two proxy servers can implement Resource Reservation Protocol (RSVP) for calls between them, in proxy for their non-RSVP aware endpoints. With ASR, a proxy server routes traffic based on the application used, rather than the IP address. For instance, voice traffic could be directed to a special QoS-enabled path, instead of taking the same path as data.

Call Flow

Each protocol that is used in the call flow creates a logical channel for its traffic. Each channel is one-way, so you must open two channels in each direction for each protocol. If the call includes a T.120 data transfer, such as application sharing, T.120 creates and controls its own data channels. Basic H.323 call flow involves the following steps:

Step 1   The H.323 gateways exchange H.225 call setup messages, using TCP port 1720. One of those, the Connect message, contains the control channel address to use for H.245 signals.

Step 2   The gateways exchange several H.245 capabilities negotiation messages. When the negotiation is successful, the gateways exchange the calling endpoint IP address and RTP port numbers, and the called endpoint IP address with RTP port numbers, in OpenLogicalChannel messages.

Step 3   The call is successful, and RTP media streams are sent.

H.323 Fast Start

Recent versions of H.323 implement *H.323 Fast Start*. You might also see this called *Fast Connect*. In a sense, this tunnels H.245 traffic inside H.225 messages. When you are using H.323 Fast Start, one of the setup messages includes a FastStart element, which contains a list of capabilities and supported coder/decoder (codec) options for both sending and receiving. The other gateway responds by including a FastStart element in one of its messages, listing the capabilities and codec it has selected. After the first gateway receives this, it can begin media transmission right away, without having to open separate H.245 channels. If it needs to send other H.245 messages after the media stream has begun, it can tunnel those messages over the H.225 channel.

Figure 3-2 gives you an overview of the various protocols and signals used in an H.323 call using Fast Start. Some information has been simplified for the sake of space.

Figure 3-2   *H.323 Call Flow with Fast Start*

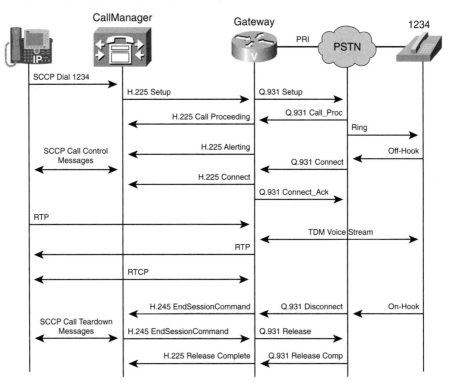

In Figure 3-2, an IP phone is making a call to a non-IP phone. The IP phone communicates with its CallManager using Skinny Client Control Protocol (SCCP). The CallManager exchanges H.323 messages with the H.323 voice gateway using Fast Start. The gateway is connected to the PSTN by a PRI line, and it uses ISDN signaling over that connection. Notice that the H.323 gateway terminates both the Q.921 and the Q.931 signaling, which is different from MGCP operation. The infrastructure on the other end (not shown) communicates with the analog phone.

The first four H.323 messages are H.225 call signaling—setup, call proceeding, alerting, and connect. Contained within these messages is the H.245 information. If all these signals succeed, the call is active. A separate unidirectional RTP channel between the IP phone and the gateway is then opened in each direction. A bidirectional RTCP channel is also opened. The gateway translates between the RTP and time-division multiplexing (TDM) networks, and it establishes a TDM media stream between it and the analog phone. When the analog phone hangs up, the gateway receives a Q.931 disconnect and translates that to an H.245 EndSession message. You do not have to configure Fast Start—it is used by default unless any of the following conditions is present:

- One of the gateways either does not support or rejects the use of Fast Start. The gateway signals this by the absence of a FastStart element in any of the setup signals, up to and including the Connect message.

- The called gateway selects different codecs for sending and receiving.

- Recent versions of the Cisco IOS use Fast Start for calls that RSVP initiates. You might have to enable slow start for backward compatibility with older versions.

When any of these occur, separate H.245 channels are opened, and the sending and receiving capabilities are negotiated the slow way.

H.323 Protocol Pros and Cons

The H.323 protocol has some benefits and some drawbacks.

Pros

The following are some H.323 protocol benefits:

- **Caller ID**—H.323 provides caller ID from Foreign Exchange Office (FXO) and T1 channel-associated signaling (CAS) ports, whereas MGCP does not.

- **Fractional PRI**—H.323 supports the use of a fractional PRI.

- **Interoperability**—H.323 is widely used and interoperates well with applications and devices from multiple vendors. Because all H.323 devices must support the core protocols, a gateway and CallManager have no version dependence.

- **Granular call control**—H.323 allows a great amount of control over the treatment of calls to and from the gateway, such as for digit manipulation, load balancing, and call rerouting. You can use Toolkit Command Language (Tcl) and voice extensible markup language (VXML) applications.

- **Legacy systems support**—You can integrate legacy systems based on POTS or ISDN lines into your H.323 network. H.323 supports more types of TDM interfaces and signaling than MGCP.

- **Multimedia support**—You can use H.323 for both voice calls and video conferencing. H.323 also allows data transfer.

- **Non-Facility Associated Signaling (NFAS) support**—H.323 supports NFAS, which allows you to control multiple ISDN PRI lines with just one D channel, thus giving you more usable channels.

- **H.323 gatekeepers**—Gateways can point to a gatekeeper for call control and address resolution.

- **PRI call preservation**—Because the gateway terminates both Q.921 and Q.931 signaling, the loss of its CallManager does not require dropping calls using the PRI line.

Cons

The H.323 protocol drawbacks include the following:

- **Configuration**—Gateway configuration is more involved than with MGCP because of the need for dial plan information for the dial peers. H.323 gateways would need a complex configuration to achieve the same functionality as CallManager partitions and Calling Search Spaces. The use of gatekeepers can eliminate some of this complexity.

- **Lack of centralized dial plan**—When you make changes to the dial plan, you must reconfigure all the gateways to reflect that change. With MGCP, however, only the CallManager needs the dial plan information. Using a Gatekeeper alleviates this somewhat.

- **Security**—H.323 does not support the use of secure RTP in Cisco IOS versions before the later releases of 12.4T.

- **Call survivability**—The default configuration of H.323 does not support call survivability. By default, if the connection to the CallManager is lost, all active calls are dropped. However, H.323 timers can be adjusted to prevent this from happening. When using Survivable Remote Site Telephony (SRST), CallManager terminates active calls when it comes back online.

- **Q Signaling (QSIG) facility IE support**—H.323 has no support for QSIG facility IE; therefore, information (such as calling name and redirect number) that is carried in the facility IE is lost. The integration of a QSIG PBX with Cisco IP Telephony requires the use of MGCP.

When to Use H.323

People sometimes avoid using H.323 gateways because they seem more complex to configure than MGCP. Because CallManager does not control H.323 endpoints, you must create dial peers on the gateway to reflect your call routing plan. This has some benefits, however. You have more flexibility and control over calls. For example, if you need to block incoming calls from a specific number, configuring that on an incoming H.323 dial peer stops the call at the gateway. No resources are wasted between the gateway and CallManager to deny the call. You can configure settings, such as QoS value, preference, and codecs, directly on the dial peers. Also, an MGCP gateway router uses H.323 dial peers when operating in SRST mode, so you need to configure those peers anyway.

H.323 is ideal for remote sites and branch offices so that the call control signaling does not have to traverse the WAN. Sites that have a PRI link should consider H.323 because they would not lose existing calls over that link during transition to SRST. H.323 is also preferred when using a fractional PRI, because it is more complicated to configure fractional PRI support on the CallManager than on an H.323 gateway. Caller ID for incoming calls on an FXO port is supported only with H.323. Sites that have Toolkit Control Language (Tcl) or VXML applications would need to use H.323.

You must use H.323 gateways in a network with H.323 gatekeepers. Use H.323 when you need to interoperate with other H.323 devices, such as videoconferencing systems, and when performing multimedia communication. If you are not using a CallManager, H.323 is the default voice gateway protocol on Cisco routers.

Dial Plan Considerations

In a voice network that has CallManagers and H.323 gateways, you need to understand the interaction between the two so that you can properly configure call flow. On the CallManager, you configure a dial plan to send calls to the H.323 gateways when needed. On the H.323 gateways, you configure dial peers to forward calls out of the gateway. You can forward calls to a CallManager using a VoIP dial peer, to the PSTN as a POTS dial peer, to another gateway using a VoIP dial peer, or to directly connected voice ports as POTS dial peers.

You can control the treatment of incoming and outgoing calls with dial peers. In your dial planning, consider the need for such things as number translations or other digit manipulations, or call restrictions. If you are using SRST, be sure the dial plan will work both with and without CallManager.

You need at least one dial peer with a destination pattern to route outgoing calls. Default incoming POTS and VoIP dial peers exist, but you should specifically configure dial peers for incoming calls if you need nondefault services. The default VoIP dial peer includes the following configuration:

- It uses G729r8 codec.
- Voice activity detection (VAD) is enabled.
- Dual tone multifrequency (DTMF) relay is disabled.
- Preference is 0.

- Voice media has differentiated services code point (DSCP) of expedited forwarding (EF); signaling is AF31.
- Huntstop is disabled.
- Both Req-qos and Acc-qos are best-effort.
- No Tcl applications are applied.
- Fax relay is disabled.
- Playout-delay is 40 ms.

The default POTS dial peer includes the following settings:

- Direct inward dial is disabled.
- Preference is 0.
- Digit strip is enabled.
- Register the E.164 phone number with a gatekeeper.
- Huntstop is disabled.
- No Interactive Voice Response (IVR) applications are applied.

Because you must configure an H.323 gateway with the information you need to route calls, the configuration can get complex in a large network. You can simplify the configuration by creating a hierarchical structure using gatekeepers and perhaps a directory gatekeeper.

When you use a gatekeeper, the gateway routes all inbound calls to its local network, but it communicates with the gatekeeper for outbound calls to unknown phone numbers. This simplifies the configuration because the gateway does not need to know how to reach every phone number in your network.

Implementing H.323 Gateways

Before you enable H.323, configure the router with a hostname, IP addressing, and routing information. Give careful thought and planning to the dial peer configurations and settings you will use. The following are some common settings to specify:

- Codec
- DTMF Relay method
- Dial peer preference
- VAD
- QoS DSCP values
- Call progress indicators
- Fax relay information
- Direct-inward-dial

Voice Class Configuration

You can create a voice class to apply configurations to specific dial peers or voice ports. Several types of configurations are possible. This section looks at two: codec and H.323 parameters.

A codec voice class allows you to control the codec negotiation by specifying which codecs will be offered, and a preference value for each codec. Use the **voice class codec** *tag#* command to create the voice class. Then list codecs and preferences with the **codec preference** *priority codec-type* command. The priority value range is 1 to 14, with 1 being the highest priority. Apply the voice class to a dial peer with the **voice-class codec** *tag#* command.

The **voice class h323** *tag#* command creates a voice class that allows you to configure the items shown in Table 3-1. The exact commands available depend on your Cisco IOS version and feature set.

Table 3-1   *Voice Class H323 Options*

Command	Use
call	Specifies H.323 fast or slow start for a particular dial peer
ccm-compatible	For CallManager connections, allows CallManager-specific behavior
encoding	Configures H.323 ASN.1 encoding options
H225	Includes H225 timeout values. Timeout has three options: • **connect**—H225 CONNECT timeout • **setup**—H225 SETUP timeout • **tcp**—TCP transport protocol
H245	Configures H245 capabilities settings
telephony-service	Used for CallManager Express (CME) H.323 connections

Example 3-1 shows a basic H.323 dial peer configuration. A voice class has been created to control the codecs that are negotiated and their preferred order.

Example 3-1   *Configuring H.323 Dial Peers*

```
NYCgateway(config)#voice class codec 1
NYCgateway(config-class)#codec preference 1 g729r8
NYCgateway(config-class)#codec preference 2 g729br8
NYCgateway(config-class)#codec preference 3 g711ulaw
!
NYCgateway(config)#dial-peer voice 100 voip
NYCgateway(config-dial-peer)#incoming called-number .
NYCgateway(config-dial-peer)#no vad
!
NYCgateway(config-dial-peer)#dial-peer voice 10 voip
```

Example 3-1 *Configuring H.323 Dial Peers (Continued)*

```
NYCgateway(config-dial-peer)#destination-pattern 1...
NYCgateway(config-dial-peer)#session target ipv4:10.1.10.10
NYCgateway(config-dial-peer)#no vad
NYCgateway(config-dial-peer)#voice-class codec 1
!
NYCgateway(config-dial-peer)#dial-peer voice 900 pots
NYCgateway(config-dial-peer)#incoming called-number .
NYCgateway(config-dial-peer)#direct-inward-dial
!
NYCgateway(config)#dial-peer voice 9 pots
NYCgateway(config-dial-peer)#destination-pattern 9T
NYCgateway(config-dial-peer)#direct-inward-dial
NYCgateway(config-dial-peer)#preference 1
NYCgateway(config-dial-peer)#port 3/0:23
!
NYCgateway(config-dial-peer)#dial-peer voice 99 pots
NYCgateway(config-dial-peer)#destination-pattern 9T
NYCgateway(config-dial-peer)#direct-inward-dial
NYCgateway(config-dial-peer)#preference 2
NYCgateway(config-dial-peer)#port 1/0/0
```

In this example, a voice class and several dial peers are configured.

1 A voice class was configured to list the preferred order for codecs to be negotiated.

2 Dial peer 100 is a default dial peer for incoming VoIP traffic. The **incoming called-number** command tells the router to look for a match to the dialed number identification service (DNIS) number of the incoming call. In this example, the command uses the . (period) wildcard, which matches all called numbers. VAD is turned off for these calls.

3 Dial peer 10 forwards calls for IP phones to the CallManager (IP address 10.1.10.10). The IP phone number range is 1000 through 1999, matched by the destination pattern 1... using wildcards for the last three digits. VAD is turned off for these calls, DTMF Relay is specified, and the codec voice class is associated with this dial peer.

4 Dial peer 900 is a default dial peer for calls that come in from the PSTN. It matches all called numbers with the . (period) wildcard and enables direct inward dial. This tells the router not to send a secondary dial tone to the caller, but to collect all the incoming digits.

5 Dial peer 9 is the preferred peer for all calls to the PSTN. The destination pattern is 9T. This assumes that users dial a 9 for outside calls. The "T" tells the router to expect a variable length dial string and to wait for the interdigit timeout to expire before matching this dial peer. 9T matches emergency calls in addition to regular ones, but you might want to explicitly configure matches for emergency numbers to avoid waiting for the interdigit timeout. This dial peer has a preference value of 1, and it is associated with the PRI port.

6 Dial peer 99 is also a POTS dial peer, and it, too, has a destination pattern of 9T and direct inward dial configured. It has a preference value of 2, so it will be used only if dial peer 9 is unavailable (lower preference wins). This dial peer is associated with FXO port 1/0/0.

NOTE   Dial peers are discussed in more detail in Chapter 9, "Dial Plans," and in the CVoice course.

Voice Service VoIP Configuration

The voice service commands cover some of the same parameters as voice classes, but these commands apply to the gateway as a whole. An individual gateway could have both voice service configuration and voice class configuration. In that case, configuration that is applied to an individual dial peer takes precedence over global configuration.

Four configuration submodes exist: POTS, Voice over ATM (VoATM), Voice over Frame Relay (VoFR), and VoIP. This section covers some of the VoIP options. The command to enter voice service configuration mode is given at the global configuration prompt: **voice service** {**pots** | **voatm** | **vofr** | **voip**}.

One use of the voice service configuration is call redirection. Consider the network shown in Figure 3-3. GW1 has a PRI line and is in a CallManager route group. GW2 has a couple of POTS lines.

Figure 3-3   *Allowing H.323 Call Redirection*

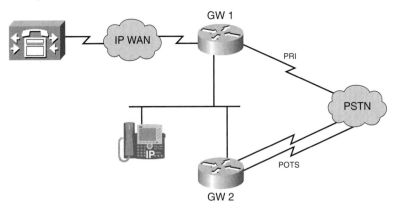

When the IP phone needs to send a call to the PSTN, the CallManager directs it to GW1. But suppose that the PRI line is full. The call could go out over one of the POTS lines on GW2, but the CallManager will not redirect it. You can configure the router to do so, however. On GW1, create a VoIP dial peer for PSTN numbers, with a higher preference value so that it is less preferred, and a session target of GW2. On Cisco IOS Software versions later than Release 12.3(7)T, you must enable this capability with the **allow-connections h323 to h323** command:

```
GW1(config)#voice service voip
GW1(conf-voi-serv)#allow-connections h323 to h323
```

The **allow-connections** command allows a Cisco router or CME to route between VoIP dial peers. You might use it when hairpinning or redirecting calls, as shown. Other options include the **allow-connections h323 to sip** command and the **allow-connections sip to h323** command.

Call survivability can be an issue with H.323. By default, an H.323 gateway exchanges H.225 keepalives with CallManager. When those keepalives fail, active calls are torn down. H.323 gateways can use SRST for backup when the CallManager is unreachable. The CallManager resets all active calls when it resumes the connection to the H.323 gateway. To prevent active calls from being terminated when the CallManager becomes unreachable, turn off H.225 keepalives between the gateway and CallManager. You do this in the **h323 submode of the voice service voip** command, as the following code shows:

```
GW1(config)#voice service voip
GW1(conf-voi-serv)#h323
GW1(conf-serv-h323)#no h225 timeout keepalive
```

You can stop the H.323 service in this submode by giving the following commands. You can then restart it in the same mode with the **no call service stop** command:

```
GW1(config)#voice service voip
GW1(conf-voi-serv)#h323
GW1(conf-serv-h323)#call service stop
```

Finally, you can control Fast Start globally. (Use a Voice Class to configure it for specific dial peers.)

```
GW1(config)#voice service voip
GW1(conf-voi-serv)#h323
GW1(conf-serv-h323)#call start slow
```

Toll Bypass

Companies that have their business in different areas might find that they spend a significant amount of money on long-distance calls between those locations. One way to minimize that cost is to use VoIP for intracompany calls. With toll bypass, calls between company locations are sent over the IP network as VoIP when bandwidth is available, and they are routed over the PSTN when no bandwidth is available. Calls can be sent over the WAN using Frame Relay or ATM, or over direct connections, such as T1 links. Voice typically shares bandwidth with data in this situation. Therefore, you must give careful consideration to QoS.

If you are using a multisite CallManager network, you are already doing something similar, with CallManager controlling the routing of intracompany calls over the WAN. However, even companies that have a PBX and analog phones can use toll bypass. They can connect the PBX to a router using standard analog or digital interfaces. The router then packetizes the voice traffic and routes it over the WAN to its peer gateway. The terminating gateway receives the IP voice traffic and, if it is also connected to a PBX, sends the call through the PBX to analog phones.

NOTE   Call Admission Control (CAC) and QoS become critical in this type of network. For more information, see Chapter 7, "Connecting to PBXs," Chapter 8, "Connecting to an IP WAN," and Chapter 11, "Influencing Path Selection."

Example 3-2 shows a voice gateway router that is configured to enable toll bypass. The Shanghai gateway router has one PRI to the PSTN (port 1/0) and another PRI to the PBX (port 2/0). It is configured to use toll bypass for its traffic to the New York office. New York also has a router that is connected to a PBX—the two routers do toll bypass between each other. Only the Shanghai configuration is shown in this example. Of course, the company needs to configure the router at the New York office similarly. This network is diagramed in Figure 3-3.

Example 3-2   *Configuring Dial Peers for Toll Bypass*

```
ShanghaiGW(config)#dial-peer voice 212 voip
ShanghaiGW(config-dial-peer)#destination-pattern 121255521..
ShanghaiGW(config-dial-peer)#session target ipv4:10.1.25.1
!
ShanghaiGW(config)#dial-peer voice 213 pots
ShanghaiGW(config-dial-peer)#destination-pattern 121255521..
ShanghaiGW(config-dial-peer)#preference 1
ShanghaiGW(config-dial-peer)#direct-inward-dial
ShanghaiGW(config-dial-peer)#forward-digits all
ShanghaiGW(config-dial-peer)#port 1/0:23
!
ShanghaiGW(config-dial-peer)#dial-peer voice 21 pots
ShanghaiGW(config-dial-peer)#destination-pattern 2155541..
ShanghaiGW(config-dial-peer)#direct-inward-dial
ShanghaiGW(config-dial-peer)#forward-digits 4
ShanghaiGW(config-dial-peer)#port 2/0:23
```

Dial peers 212 and 213 have the same destination pattern for a range of phone numbers at the New York office. Dial peer 212 will be preferred, because it has the default preference value of 0, and dial peer 213 has been given a preference of 1. Calls to the New York office will be routed over the WAN if possible, as a toll-free call. Those calls will go over the PSTN only if the WAN is down or if bandwidth is insufficient for the call.

The IP address in the dial peer 212 session target is the New York office router. The port that is specified in dial peer 213 is the PRI to the PSTN. Dial peer 21 forwards all traffic that is bound to the analog phones out the PRI to the PBX. The **forward-digits 4** command instructs the router to send only the last four digits of the called number to the PBX.

Figure 3-4 shows the network between the New York and the Shanghai offices. Toll bypass is configured on the two routers that are connected to PBXs at each location, to enable them to send interoffice calls over the IP WAN.

Figure 3-4   *Toll Bypass*

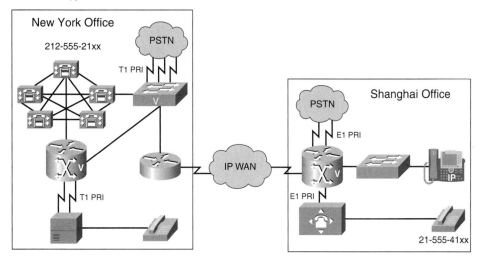

Defining H.323 Gateways on CallManager

If the gateway will be part of a Cisco Unified Communications system, you need to configure it to peer with CallManager. You must still configure the dial peers and any dial peer options you need. Configure an additional VoIP dial peer for routing calls that are bound to other phones in the cluster. List the IP address of the CallManager as its session target. The destination pattern will depend on your dial plan, but you should specify intracluster calls. If your dial plan is complex, you might need several VoIP dial peers to cover it.

After you configure the gateway, configure CallManager to recognize and use it.

Step 1   The CallManager configuration for an H.323 gateway is fairly simple. In CallManager Administration, go to the **Device** menu and select **Gateway** from the drop-down list. When the Find and List Gateways page opens, select the **Add a New Gateway link**.

Step 2   Figure 3-5 shows the next page. Select **H.323 Gateway** from the drop-down list next to Gateway Type. Notice that the server automatically fills in the Device Protocol box with H.225. Click the **Next** button.

Figure 3-5 *Adding an H.323 Gateway to CallManager*

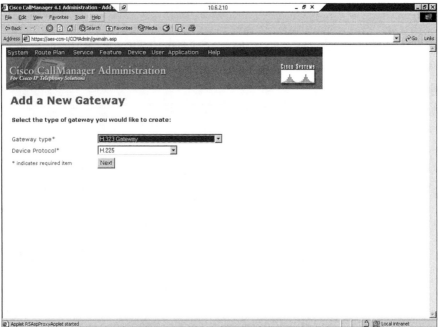

Step 3 On the next screen, shown in Figure 3-6, you enter information about the gateway.

For **Device Name**, enter the IP address of the router. Notice that only one IP address is allowed. If the router might use multiple interfaces to communicate with its CallManager, you need to tell the router which one to use as the source of its messages (possibly a loopback interface). Use the **h323-gateway voip bind srcaddr** *ip-address* command, under interface configuration mode.

Add a description and select the CallManager device pool to which the gateway will belong. The **Location** field is used to control the number of calls allowed to a site, to ensure that each call has enough bandwidth. This is typically used with a remote gateway. This page has many other options. Check your CallManager documentation for further explanation. When you are finished, click the **Insert** button. After the screen refreshes, reset the gateway.

Figure 3-6 *Configuring the Gateway on CallManager*

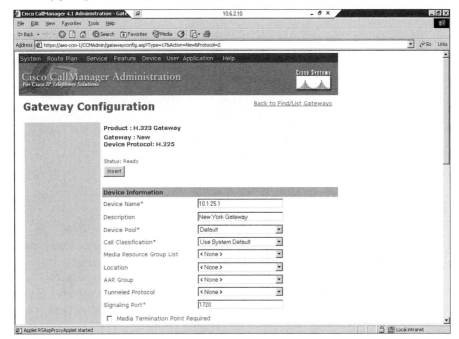

Step 4   Verify that the gateway has been defined on the CallManager by doing a search on the Find and List Gateways page of CallManager Administration. You should see the gateway listed. The gateway will show "Not Registered," which is normal because the H.323 gateway treats the CallManager as its peer.

Redundancy

In a cluster with multiple CallManagers, the gateway needs to be able to use alternates if the primary one is unavailable. You can set this up by creating VoIP dial peers pointing to each CallManager. Use a preference value under each dial peer to determine the order in which the CallManagers are used. The default preference is 0; the lowest preference wins:

```
NYCgateway(config)#dial-peer voice 11 voip
NYCgateway(config-dial-peer)#session target ipv4:10.1.10.11
NYCgateway(config-dial-peer)#preference 2
```

You might need to adjust the default timers when using multiple CallManagers, especially if the gateway has a PRI connection for inbound calls. When a call comes in that should be forwarded to a CallManager, the router attempts to set up an H.225 TCP session to its preferred VoIP dial peer. The TCP session must time out before it will try another dial peer. This takes 15 seconds by default. ISDN Q.931 has a Call Proceeding timeout of 10 seconds. A call that comes in over a PRI line will time out before the router can fail over to an alternate CallManager. Even without a PRI connection, 15 seconds might be longer than you want to wait.

To remedy this, change the H.225 TCP session establishment timer. The **voice class h323 10** command creates a voice class in global configuration mode that reduces the timer to three seconds:

```
NYCgateway(config)#voice class h323 10
NYCgateway(configs-class)#h225 timeout tcp establish 3
```

Apply that voice class under the dial peers pointing to redundant CallManagers:

```
NYCgateway(config)#dial-peer voice 1 voip
NYCgateway(config-dial-peer)#session target ipv4:10.1.10.10
NYCgateway(config-dial-peer)#voice-class h323 10
```

DTMF Relay

DTMF tones are created when a digit is dialed on a telephone. By default, the gateway sends these tones within the voice RTP stream. When voice is sent uncompressed, these tones arrive in their original state. However, when voice is compressed, such as with the G.729 codec, the tones might be distorted, or part of the signal might be lost. DTMF Relay addresses this by separating these tones from the rest of the voice and then sending them in a different way.

H.323 gateways have four different ways of sending these tones: the Cisco proprietary method, RTP-NTE, H.245 Alphanumeric, and H.245 Signal.

- **Cisco proprietary method**—Sends the tones in the same RTP stream as voice, but they are coded as payload type 121 to enable the receiver to identify them as DTMF signals. To use this method, both the originating and terminating gateways must be Cisco devices.

- **RTP-NTE**—Uses a method specified in RFC 2833 to send DTMF tones within the RTP stream, in a special Named Telephony Event (NTE) packet. The use of this method and the payload type value is negotiated on a call-by-call basis.

- **H.245 Alphanumeric**—Is specified by the ITU-T H.245 standard. Tones are sent over the H.245 signaling channel, rather than in-band with voice traffic. H.245 transmits DMTF tones to the receiving gateway as the ASCII character it represents (1, 2, 3, and so on). It does not send tone-length information. Each tone is assumed to last 500 milliseconds (ms). All H.323 gateways must support this type of DTMF Relay.

- **H.245 Signal**—Addresses a potential problem with H.245 Alphanumeric. It does not pass along the length of a tone. Sometimes it is important to know how long a particular tone lasted—that is, how long a keypad button was held down. You might notice this when placing multiple calls using a calling card. With the company-provided calling card of the author, you can avoid having to re-enter the card number by holding down the # key for two seconds. H.245 Signal DTMF Relay sends information about the tone duration along with its alphanumeric representation. Support for H.245 Signal is optional in H.323 gateways.

The Cisco method and RTP-NTE send the tones in-band, and both H.245 methods send them out-of-band. Gateways negotiate the type of DTMF Relay to be used during call establishment.

You configure DTMF Relay under the dial peer on H.323 gateways. If no method is configured, the tones are sent in-band with the voice stream. To configure a specific type of DTMF Relay, use the **dtmf-relay** [**cisco-rtp**] [**rtp-nte**] [**h245-alphanumeric**] [**h245-signal**] command.

Example 3-3 shows an H.323 gateway that is configured for H.245 alphanumeric DTMF Relay. It also shows that you can list multiple types of DTMF Relay in the command, to support the capabilities of different terminating gateways.

Example 3-3 *Configuring DTMF Relay*

```
NYCgateway(config)#dial-peer voice 10 voip
NYCgateway(config-dial-peer)#dtmf-relay h245-alphanumeric ?
  cisco-rtp    Cisco Proprietary RTP
  h245-signal  DTMF Relay via H245 Signal IE
  rtp-nte      RTP Named Telephone Event RFC 2833
  <cr>
NYCgateway(config-dial-peer)#dtmf-relay h245-alphanumeric h245-signal rtp-nte
  cisco-rtp
NYCgateway(config-dial-peer)#^Z
NYCgateway#show run
![output omitted]
dial-peer voice 10 voip
 session target ipv4:10.1.10.10
 dtmf-relay cisco-rtp rtp-nte h245-signal h245-alphanumeric
```

In Example 3-3, the DTMF Relay methods were entered in one order, but the output of the **show run** commands shows them in a different order. If you specify multiple methods, the Relay method is negotiated in the order of priority shown in the **show run** output:

1 Cisco-RTP

2 RTP-NTE

3 H.245 Signal

4 H.245 Alphanumeric

Securing H.323 Gateways

Any voice gateway is part of your IP network and should conform to your company security policy with user control and authentication, access-control lists, physical security, and so on applied to it. A voice gateway that is functioning as a WAN gateway can provide additional network protection with features, such as Cisco IOS firewall or Intrusion Detection System (IDS), depending on your company policy. The firewall must be able to examine the traffic in the control channel to learn what port numbers are being used and allow traffic only while the control channel is active. Cisco firewalls and Cisco IOS firewall feature sets are able to do this.

When you are using a gatekeeper, you can authenticate the Registration, Admission, and Status Protocol (RAS) messages between the gateway and the gatekeeper by using procedures that are specified in H.235. A password that you configure on the gateway is sent in as a Message Digest 5 (MD5) hash. Timing information is also sent; therefore, you must synchronize the gateway and gatekeeper clocks to within 30 seconds of each other. Enable this on the gateway with the **security password** *password* **level [endpoint | per-call | all]** command. Selecting **endpoint** authenticates RAS messages, selecting **per-call** authenticates call admission messages, and selecting **all** authenticates both types of messages. Also, configure the gatekeeper with the **security token required-for registration** command. In addition, you can use an authentication, authorization, and accounting (AAA) server to control the authentication.

You can also provide authentication for each call by requiring users to enter an account number and personal identification number (PIN). Configure dial peers on the gateway for IVR. In addition, download an IVR Tcl script from Cisco.com, and use the dial peer **call application voice** *application-name location* command to tell the router to use it for traffic matching that dial peer.

Secure RTP (SRTP) is supported in Cisco IOS gateways using Cisco IOS version 12.4(6)T or higher. This allows you to authenticate and encrypt RTP traffic between the IP phones and the gateways and between H.323 gateways. Only the G711 and G729 codecs are supported with SRTP. Not all modules and digital signal processors (DSP) support encryption of calls coming in from the PSTN. Check Cisco.com for a current list of supported modules. To encrypt traffic between a gateway and a gatekeeper, use IPsec for the RAS messages.

Troubleshooting Tools

Misconfigured dial peers are common problems with H.323 gateways. You can see a list of all the dial peers with the **show dial-peer voice summary** command. This gives you a summary of the configuration for each dial peer. If you have SRST configured, some dial peers will have high numbers and odd-looking ports. These are the SRST dial peers that the router created. When you are using the nondefault codec, make sure it is defined in the incoming dial peer.

The **show dialplan number** *phone-number* command tells which dial peers are matched by a specific phone number.

Several useful debug commands exist. **debug cch323 h225** and **debug cch323 h245** are good commands to troubleshoot call setup and teardown. You can also use **debug h225** and **debug h245** commands to troubleshoot call setup and teardown. The **debug voip ccapi inout** command debugs the call control application programming interface. It shows details about the call setup from both the telephony and network sides. Use the **debug ip tcp transaction** command to make sure that the TCP session for H.225 and H.245 is being established.

Debugs can be verbose, so log them to the buffer and disable terminal monitoring when you are troubleshooting a gateway that has more than one active call.

You can simulate a phone call from the router with the **csim start** *phone-number* command.

View statistics on the H.323 messages sent and received with the **show h323 gateway** command. You can reset these statistics with the **clear h323 gateway** command.

Case Study: Configuring an H.323 Gateway

In this case study, the router at the Leeds office is configured as an H.323 gateway. It will use three of the CallManagers in the New York office for internal company traffic. Users dial an 8 plus the complete number (minus international code) to call another office, and 9 to dial an outside number. All PSTN traffic, including emergency calls, will be routed out the E1 interface of the gateway. The emergency number for Leeds, England is 999. Dial peers will be created for the emergency number so that users will not have to wait for the interdigit timeout to expire. When the gateway is operating in SRST mode, only calls to the U.S. offices are allowed. Router configuration that does not directly pertain to the gateway configuration is beyond the scope of this example.

Figure 3-7 shows the networks at the New York and Leeds offices. Example 3-4 shows the Leeds gateway configuration.

In addition, you will need to configure the CallManager publisher in New York to use this router as a gateway.

Figure 3-7 *New York and Leeds Networks*

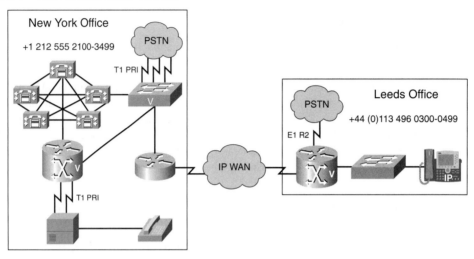

Example 3-4 *Configuring an H.323 Gateway*

```
!Create a voice class for the H.225 timeout
voice class h323 1
 h225 timeout tcp establish 3
!
!Create a voice class for codec negotiation
voice class codec 2
 codec preference 1 g729r8
 codec preference 2 g729br8
 codec preference 3 g711ulaw
!
!Create VoIP dial peers for the CallManagers
!"8" is the interoffice code
dial-peer voice 81 voip
 destination-pattern 8T
 preference 1
 no vad
 voice-class h323 1
 voice-class codec 2
 dtmf-relay h245-alphanumeric
 session target ipv4:10.1.10.10
!
dial-peer voice 82 voip
 destination-pattern 8T
 preference 2
 no vad
 voice-class h323 1
 voice-class codec 2
 dtmf-relay h245-alphanumeric
 session target ipv4:10.1.10.11
```

Example 3-4 *Configuring an H.323 Gateway (Continued)*

```
!
dial-peer voice 83 voip
 destination-pattern 8T
 preference 3
 no vad
 voice-class h323 1
 voice-class codec 2
 dtmf-relay h245-alphanumeric
 session target ipv4:10.1.10.13
!
!Create a default incoming VoIP dial peer
dial-peer voice 1 voip
 incoming called-number .
 codec g711ulaw
 no vad
 ip qos dscp ef media
 ip qos dscp cs3 signaling
!
!Create a POTS dial peer for general external numbers
dial-peer voice 9 pots
 destination-pattern 9T
 port 0/0:15
!
!Create POTS dial peers for emergency numbers
!This dial peer is for outside code of "9" plus emergency number "999"
dial-peer voice 9999 pots
 destination-pattern 9999
 port 0/0:15
!
!This dial peer is for emergency number "999" without the outside code
dial-peer voice 999 pots
 destination-pattern 999
 port 0/0:15
!
!Create a default incoming POTS dial peer
dial-peer voice 2 pots
 incoming called-number .
 direct-inward-dial
 port 0/0:23
!
!Create a POTS dial peer for intracompany traffic to the U.S. in case the WAN link
fails
!The prefix of "001" is for international access to U.S. sites
dial-peer voice 800 pots
 destination-pattern 8T
 preference 2
 prefix 001
 port 0/0:15
!
!Enable SRST on the gateway
call-manager-fallback
 ip source-address 10.40.25.1 port 2000
 max-ephones 100
 max-dn 200
```

Review Questions

1 List at least four benefits of using H.323 as a gateway protocol.

2 When you are configuring an H.323 gateway on a CallManager, what information do you enter for Device Name?

3 Name four types of DTMF Relay that H.323 uses.

4 What commands must you enter for a Cisco gateway to use H.323 Fast Start?

5 Briefly describe toll bypass.

6 If you configure conflicting commands globally under the **voice service voip** configuration mode, and under the dial peer using **voice class**, which commands will the router use?

7 How do you prevent active calls from being terminated when the CallManager becomes unreachable?

CHAPTER 4

Session Initiation Protocol

The Session Initiation Protocol (SIP) is an Internet Engineering Task Force (IETF) standard call control protocol, based on research at Columbia University by Henning Schulzrinne and his team. The first SIP RFC, number 2543, was published in 1999. Since then, much work has been done, and numerous RFCs have been published to solidify and extend SIP capabilities.

SIP is designed to provide signaling and session management for voice and multimedia connections over packet-based networks. It is a peer-to-peer protocol with intelligent endpoints and distributed call control, such as H.323. Gateways that use SIP do not depend on a call agent, although the protocol does define several functional entities that help SIP endpoints locate each other and establish a session.

In this chapter you will learn

- How SIP works
- SIP call flow
- SIP pros and cons
- Dial plan considerations
- How to implement SIP gateways
- Some ways to secure SIP gateways
- Allowing H.323 to SIP connections
- Troubleshooting tools

Description of SIP

SIP was designed as one module in an IP communications solution. This modular design allows it to integrate with and use the services of other existing protocols, such as Session Description Protocol (SDP), Real-Time Transport Protocol (RTP), Resource Reservation Protocol (RSVP), RADIUS, and Lightweight Directory Access Protocol (LDAP). SIP usually uses User Datagram Protocol (UDP) as its transport protocol, but it can also use TCP. The default SIP port for either TCP or UDP is 5060. To provide additional security, Transport Layer Security (TLS) support is included beginning with Cisco IOS Software

Release 12.3(14)T. SIP specifications do not cover all the possible aspects of a call, as does H.323. Instead, its job is to create, modify, and terminate sessions between applications, regardless of the media type or application function. The session can range from just a two-party phone call to a multiuser, multimedia conference or an interactive gaming session. SIP does not define the *type* of session, only its management. To do this, SIP performs four basic tasks:

- Locating users, resolving their SIP address to an IP address
- Negotiating capabilities and features among all the session participants
- Changing the session parameters during the call
- Managing the setup and teardown of calls for all users in the session

SIP is built on a client-server model, using requests and responses that are similar to Internet applications. It uses the same address format as e-mail, with a unique user identifier (such as telephone number) and a domain identifier. A typical SIP address looks like one of the following:

sip:1112223344@mycompany.com
sip:1112223344@10.1.1.1

This allows Domain Name System (DNS) to be used to locate users, and it also allows SIP to integrate easily with e-mail. SIP uses Multipurpose Internet Mail Extension (MIME) to describe the contents of its messages. Thus, SIP messages can contain information other than audio, such as graphics, billing data, authentication tokens, or video. Session Description Protocol (SDP) is used to exchange session capabilities and features.

One of the most unique parts of SIP is the concept of *presence*. The public switched telephone network (PSTN) can provide basic presence information—whether a phone is on- or off- hook—when a call is initiated. However, SIP takes that further. It can provide information on the *willingness* of the other party to receive calls, not just the ability, before the call is attempted. This is similar in concept to instant messaging applications—you can choose which users appear on your list, and they can choose to display different status types, such as offline, busy, and so on. Users who subscribe to that instant messaging service know the availability of those on their list before they try to contact them. With SIP, you can gather presence information from many devices, such as cell phones, SIP phones, personal digital assistants (PDA), and applications. A SIP *Watcher* subscribes to receive presence information about a SIP *Presentity*. SIP presence information is available only to subscribers.

SIP is already influencing the marketplace. A growing number of IP Telephony Service Providers (ITSP), such as Vonage, are already using it. Traditional telephony providers, such as AT&T, have created SIP-aware networks for both internal and customer use. Cellular phone providers use SIP to offer additional services in their 3G networks. The Microsoft real-time communications platform—including instant messaging, voice, video, and application-sharing—is based on SIP. Cisco applications such as MeetingPlace,

CallManager, and CallManager Express (CME) support SIP. Some hospitals are implementing SIP to allow heart monitors and other devices to send an instant message to nurses. You can expect to see its use increase as more applications and extensions are created for SIP.

SIP Functional Components

SIP endpoints are called user agents (UA) and can be various devices, including IP phones, cell phones, PDAs, Cisco routers, or computers running a SIP-based application. UAs can act as either clients or servers. The user agent client (UAC) is the device that is initiating a call, and the user agent server (UAS) is the device that is receiving the call. The SIP protocol defines several other functional components. These functional entities can be implemented as separate devices, or the same device can perform multiple functions.

- **Proxy server**—This server can perform call routing, authentication, authorization, address resolution, and loop detection. A UA sends its call setup messages through a proxy server. The proxy server can forward the messages if it knows where the called party is located, or it can query other servers to find that information. It then forwards the request to the next hop. When it receives a response to the request, it forwards that to the client UA. After the call is set up, the proxy server can elect to stay in the signaling path so that it also sees call change or termination messages, or it can withdraw from the path and let the UAs communicate directly. Cisco has a SIP proxy server product.

- **Redirect server**—UAs and proxy servers can contact a redirect server to find the location of an endpoint. This is particularly useful in a network that has mobile users whose location changes. The redirect server can let its clients know that a user has moved either temporarily or permanently. It can also return multiple possible addresses for the user, if necessary. When a UA has multiple addresses, the proxy server can *fork* the call, sending it to each address either simultaneously or sequentially. This allows "Find Me/Follow Me" type services. Cisco routers can act as SIP redirect servers.

- **Registrar server**—UAs register their location with a registrar server, which places that information into a location database. A registrar server responds to location requests from other servers. The server can maintain the location database locally, or it can employ a separate location server. Cisco routers and CallManager 5.x can act as SIP registrar servers.

- **Location server**—This server maintains the location database for registered UAs.

- **Back-to-back user agent (B2BUA)**—This server acts as a UA server and client at the same time. It terminates the signaling from the calling UA and then initiates signaling to the called UA. B2BUAs are allowed to change the content of requests, giving them more control over the call parameters. Cisco CallManager 5.x can function as a SIP B2BUA.

- **Presence server**—This server gathers presence information from Presentities and subscription information from Watchers, and sends status notifications.

All these functions work together to accomplish the goal of establishing and managing a session between two UAs. SIP servers can also interact with other application servers to provide services, such as authentication or billing.

You can configure Cisco routers as SIP gateways. As such, they can act as a SIP UAC or UAS, they can register E.164 numbers with a SIP registrar, and they can act as SIP registrar and redirect servers. In addition, they can set up SIP trunks to another SIP gateway or to CallManager.

A Cisco SIP gateway that is using Survivable Remote Site Telephony (SRST) can provide registration and redirection services to SIP phones when CallManager and proxy servers are unavailable. SRST is not on by default; you must configure it. Both SIP and SCCP phones can fail over to a router that is running SIP SRST. Cisco CME and SRST also support B2BUA functionality beginning in Cisco IOS 12.(4)T. SIP SRST is described in Chapter 13, "SRST and MGCP Gateway Fallback."

SIP Messages

SIP uses plain-text messages, following the format of standard Internet text messages. This helps in troubleshooting, because it is easy to read SIP messages. However, you must understand the types of messages and their formats to successfully troubleshoot them. This section helps you with that understanding.

SIP messages are either requests or responses to a request; the function that the request invokes on a server is called a *method*. Several types of SIP methods exist. The original SIP specification included the following six methods. Cisco gateways can both send and receive these methods, except where noted.

- **REGISTER**—A UA client sends this message to inform a SIP server of its location.
- **INVITE**—A caller sends this message to request that another endpoint join a SIP session, such as a conference or a call. This message can also be sent during a call to change session parameters.
- **ACK**—A SIP UA can receive several responses to an INVITE. This method acknowledges the final response to the INVITE.
- **CANCEL**—This message ends a call that has not yet been fully established.
- **OPTIONS**—This message queries the capabilities of a server. Cisco gateways receive these methods only.
- **BYE**—This message ends a session or declines to take a call.

Cisco gateways also support the following additional methods, but they only respond to them. They do not generate them.

- **INFO**—This message is used when data is carried within the message body.
- **PRACK**—This message acknowledges receipt of a provisional, or informational, response to a request.

- **REFER**—This message points to another address to initiate a transfer.
- **SUBSCRIBE**—This message lets the server know that you want to be notified if a specific event happens.
- **NOTIFY**—This message lets the subscriber know that a specified event has occurred. It can also transmit dual tone multifrequency (DTMF) tones.
- **UPDATE**—A UAC uses this to change the session parameters, such as codec used or quality of service (QoS) settings, before answering the initial INVITE.

SIP entities can send additional messages in response to a method; these responses are listed in Table 4-1. Responses to SIP methods fall into six categories. The **100 Series** designates informational or provisional responses, such as 100 for Trying, and 180 for Alerting. A **200 Series** response means that the request was successful; it includes 200 for OK, and 202 for Accepted. The **300 Series** redirects the user to a different location for the called endpoint. Examples include 301 for Moved Permanently and 302 for Moved Temporarily. The **400 Series** of responses indicate a request failure, such as 404 User Not Found and 480 Temporarily Unavailable. A **500 Series** response is received due to a server failure, such as 500 for Server Internal Error or 503 for Service Unavailable. The **600 Series** is used for a global failure, including 603 when the call is declined.

Table 4-1   *SIP Response Table*

Class of Response	Status Code	Explanation
Informational/provisional	100	Trying
	180	Ringing
	181	Call Is Being Forwarded
	182	Queued
	183	Session Progress
Success	200	OK
Redirection	300	Multiple Choices
	301	Moved Permanently
	302	Moved Temporarily
	305	Use Proxy
	380	Alternative Service
Client-error	400	Bad Request
	401	Unauthorized
	402	Payment Required

continues

Table 4-1   *SIP Response Table (Continued)*

Class of Response	Status Code	Explanation
	403	Forbidden
	404	Not Found
	405	Method Not Allowed
	406	Not Acceptable
	407	Proxy Authentication Required
	408	Request Timeout
	410	Gone
	413	Request Entity Too Large
	414	Requested URL Too Large
	415	Unsupported Media Type
	416	Unsupported URI* Scheme
	420	Bad Extension
	421	Extension Required
	423	Interval Too Brief
	480	Temporarily Not Available
	481	Call Leg or Transaction Does Not Exist
	482	Loop Detected
	483	Too Many Hops
	484	Address Incomplete
	485	Ambiguous
	486	Busy Here
	487	Request Terminated
	488	Not Acceptable Here
	491	Request Pending
	493	Undecipherable
Server-error	500	Internal Server Error
	501	Not Implemented
	502	Bad Gateway
	503	Service Unavailable
	504	Server Timeout
	505	SIP Version Not Supported
	513	Message Too Large

Table 4-1   *SIP Response Table (Continued)*

Class of Response	Status Code	Explanation
Global failure	600	Busy Everywhere
	603	Decline
	604	Does Not Exist Anywhere
	606	Not Acceptable

*URI = uniform resource identifier

Example 4-1 shows a SIP INVITE message and explains the different fields. This call is from an IP phone in a CME network to an IP phone in a CallManager network. Neither phone is a SIP endpoint—the IP addresses listed are for the gateway and CallManager. A SIP trunk exists between CallManager and the gateway/CME.

Example 4-1   *SIP INVITE Message*

```
SIP-GW#debug ccsip messages
Sent:
!Request-URI (Uniform Resource Identifier) field
!This is the SIP address, or SIP URL, that the INVITE is sent to
INVITE sip:3401@10.6.2.10:5060 SIP/2.0
!Each device that handles the packet adds its IP address to the VIA field
Via: SIP/2.0/UDP  10.6.3.1:5060;branch=z9hG4bKA1798
!The calling party. A tag identifies this series of messages
From: <sip:4105553501@10.6.3.1>;tag=105741C-1D5E
!The called party
To: <sip:3401@10.6.2.10>
Date: Fri, 06 Jan 2006 05:35:01 GMT
!Unique identifier for this call
Call-ID: E937365B-2C0C11D6-802FA93D-4772A3BB@10.6.3.1
!Extensions supported include reliable provisional responses and timer refreshes
Supported: 100rel,timer
!Minimum value for session interval
Min-SE:  1800
Cisco-Guid: 3892269682-738988502-2150410557-1198695355
!Identifies the device that originated the INVITE
User-Agent: Cisco-SIPGateway/IOS-12.x
!List of methods that are supported
Allow: INVITE, OPTIONS, BYE, CANCEL, ACK, PRACK, COMET, REFER, SUBSCRIBE, NOTIFY,
INFO, UPDATE, REGISTER
!Identifies call sequence number and method for this call
CSeq: 101 INVITE
!Max number of proxies or gateways that can forward this message
Max-Forwards: 70
Remote-Party-ID: <sip:4105553501@10.6.3.1>;party=calling;screen=no;privacy=off
Timestamp: 1014960901
!Identifies the user agent client, for return messages
Contact: <sip:4105553501@10.6.3.1:5060>
Expires: 180
Allow-Events: telephone-event
```

continues

Example 4-1 *SIP INVITE Message (Continued)*

```
!This INVITE carries an SDP message
Content-Type: application/sdp
Content-Length: 202
```

SIP uses SDP to exchange information about endpoint capabilities and negotiate call features. This sample INVITE contains SDP information. The SDP part of a SIP message has standard fields, as shown in Example 4-2. This is the continuation of the INVITE message in Example 4-1. The SDP fields have the following meanings:

- **v**—Tells the SDP version
- **o**—Lists the organization of the calling party
- **s**—Describes the SDP message
- **c**—Lists the IP address of the originator
- **t**—Tells the timer value
- **m**—Describes the media that the originator expects
- **a**—Gives the media attributes

Example 4-2 *SIP SDP Message Contents*

```
v=0
o=CiscoSystemsSIP-GW-UserAgent 7181 811 IN IP4 10.6.3.1
s=SIP Call
c=IN IP4 10.6.3.1
t=0 0
m=audio 18990 RT
SIP-CME#P/AVP 0 19
c=IN IP4 10.6.3.1
a=rtpmap:0 PCMU/8000
a=rtpmap:19 CN/8000
a=ptime:20
```

Continuing the call, the called side (the UAS) returns a provisional response 100 Trying, shown in Example 4-3. Note that the call sequence number, 101, and the method type it is responding to, INVITE, are sent in each message.

Example 4-3 *SIP "Trying" Response*

```
Received:
!"Trying" indicates that the gateway has received the INVITE
SIP/2.0 100 Trying
Via: SIP/2.0/UDP  10.6.3.1:5060;branch=z9hG4bKA1798
From: <sip:4105553501@10.6.3.1>;tag=105741C-1D5E
!A tag is added by the UAS to identify this series of messages
To: <sip:3401@10.6.2.10>;tag=16777231
Date: Fri, 06 Jan 2006 5:35:10 GMT
Call-ID: E937365B-2C0C11D6-802FA93D-4772A3BB@10.6.3.1
```

Example 4-3   *SIP "Trying" Response (Continued)*

```
Timestamp: 1014960901
CSeq: 101 INVITE
Allow-Events: telephone-event
Content-Length: 0
```

In Example 4-4, the UAS sends a 180 Ringing response to indicate that the remote phone is ringing.

Example 4-4   *SIP Ringing Response*

```
Received:
! Ringing indicates that the called phone is being alerted
SIP/2.0 180 Ringing
Via: SIP/2.0/UDP  10.6.3.1:5060;branch=z9hG4bKA1798
From: <sip:4105553501@10.6.3.1>;tag=105741C-1D5E
To: <sip:3401@10.6.2.10>;tag=16777231
Date: Fri, 06 Jan 2006 5:35:10 GMT
Call-ID: E937365B-2C0C11D6-802FA93D-4772A3BB@10.6.3.1
Timestamp: 1014960901
CSeq: 101 INVITE
Allow: INVITE, OPTIONS, BYE, CANCEL, ACK, PRACK
Allow-Events: telephone-event
Remote-Party-ID: <sip:3401@10.6.2.10>;party=called;screen=no;privacy=off
Contact: <sip:3401@10.6.2.10:5060>
Content-Length: 0
```

The remote phone has picked up the call, so a 200 OK response is sent, as shown in Example 4-5.

Example 4-5   *SIP OK Response*

```
Received:
! OK indicates that the called phone has answered
SIP/2.0 200 OK
Via: SIP/2.0/UDP  10.6.3.1:5060;branch=z9hG4bKA1798
From: <sip:4105553501@10.6.3.1>;tag=105741C-1D5E
To: <sip:3401@10.6.2.10>;tag=16777231
Date: Fri, 06 Jan 2006 5:35:12 GMT
Call-ID: E937365B-2C0C11D6-802FA93D-4772A3BB@10.6.3.1
0Timestamp: 1014960901
CSeq: 101 INVITE
Allow: INVITE, OPTIONS, BYE, CANCEL, ACK, PRACK
Allow-Events: telephone-event
Remote-Party-ID: <sip:3401@10.6.2.10>;party=called;screen=yes;privacy=off
Contact: <sip:3401@10.6.2.10:5060>
Content-Type: application/sdp
Content-Length: 221

v=0
o=CiscoSystemsCCM-SIP 2000 1000 IN IP4 10.6.2.10
s=SIP Call
```

continues

Example 4-5 *SIP OK Response (Continued)*

```
c=IN IP4 10.6.2.10
t=0 0
m=audio 24580 RTP/AVP 0 101
a=sendrecv
a=rtpmap:0 PCMU/8000
a=ptime:20
a=rtpmap:101 telephone-event/8000
a=fmtp:101 0-15
```

The UAC responds to the OK message with an ACK method, shown in Example 4-6. Now the call is established.

Example 4-6 *SIP ACK Message*

```
Sent:
ACK sip:3401@10.6.2.10:5060 SIP/2.0
Via: SIP/2.0/UDP  10.6.3.1:5060;branch=z9hG4bKB1C57
From: <sip:4105553501@10.6.3.1>;tag=105741C-1D5E
T0o: <sip:3401@10.6.2.10>;tag=16777231
Date: Fri, 06 Jan 2006 5:35:13 GMT
Call-ID: E937365B-2C0C11D6-802FA93D-4772A3BB@10.6.3.1
Max-Forwards: 70
CSeq: 101 ACK
Content-Length: 0
```

SIP Call Flow

Basic SIP session setup involves a SIP UA client sending a request to the SIP URL of the called endpoint (UAS), inviting it to a session. If the UAC knows the IP address of the UAS, it can send the request. Otherwise, the UAC sends the request to a proxy or redirect server to locate the user. That server might forward the request to other servers until the user is located. After the SIP address is resolved to an IP address, the request is sent to the UAS. If the user takes the call, capabilities are negotiated and the call commences. If the user does not take the call, it can be forwarded to voice mail or another number. The following sections outline various scenarios in more detail.

Call Flow Between Two SIP Gateways

Cisco routers, including CME routers, can act as SIP gateways for calls that originate from non-SIP phones. The gateways function as SIP UAs and set up a SIP session between them for each call. Figure 4-1 shows two routers handling analog phones, using SIP between them. In this example, SIP GW-A originates the calls and acts as a UAC, and SIP GW-B acts as a UAS. The signaling from the PBX to the gateway is just normal analog call signaling. Only the two gateways exchange SIP messages.

In Figure 4-1, the analog phone on the left initiates a call to the analog phone on the right.

Figure 4-1   *Call Flow Between Two SIP Gateways*

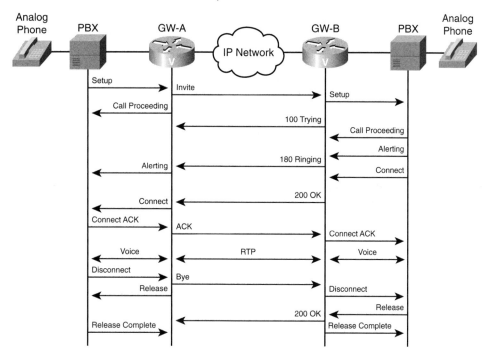

After the first phone initiates the call, the call flow proceeds as follows:

1 The PBX sends a call setup signal to GW-A, which then sends a SIP INVITE message to GW-B. This INVITE contains SDP information for capabilities negotiation. GW-A also sends a Call Proceeding message to the PBX.

2 GW-B exchanges call setup message with its PBX and sends SIP responses 100 (Trying) and 180 (Ringing) to GW-A.

3 GW-A translates these messages into analog signaling messages for its PBX.

4 When the user on the right picks up the call, his PBX sends a Connect message to GW-B, which then forwards a SIP 200 (OK) response to GW-A. This OK response contains SDP information with the capabilities that both devices support.

5 GW-A delivers a Connect message to its PBX. When the PBX acknowledges that with a Connect ACK, it sends a SIP ACK message to GW-B.

6 GW-B sends a Connect acknowledgement to its PBX, and the call is active. At this point, normal voice steams exist between the two phones and the gateways, and RTP voice streams exist between the two gateways.

7 The user on the left hangs up the phone. His PBX sends a Call Disconnect message to GW-A. GW-A then sends a SIP BYE message to GW-B and a Release message to the PBX. The PBX responds with a Release Complete message.

8 GW-B sends a Call Disconnect message to its PBX, which responds with a Release message.

9 GW-B forwards a SIP 200 (OK) response to GW-A and a Release Complete message to its PBX. The call is now completely terminated.

Call Flow Using a Proxy Server

SIP UAs register with a proxy server or a registrar. Proxy servers then act as an intermediary for SIP calls. Cisco routers that are acting as SIP gateways can use the services of a SIP proxy server, either contacting the server or receiving requests from it. They can additionally register E.164 numbers with a proxy server or a registrar.

Proxy servers can either leave the signaling path when the call is connected or can enable "Record-route" to stay in the signaling path. If Record-route is disabled, the proxy server does not know of any changes to the call or when the call is disconnected. Figure 4-2 shows call flow when Record-route is disabled.

In Figure 4-2, a SIP endpoint places a call using a proxy server. The figure shows several types of endpoints:

- A PC and a PDA running a SIP application
- A SIP phone
- A cell phone that uses SIP

Figure 4-2   *SIP Call Flow Using a Proxy Server*

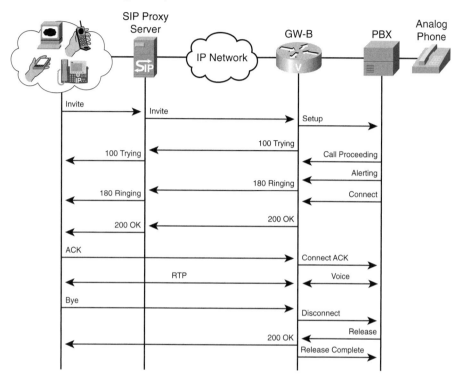

In Figure 4-2, one of these endpoints places a call to an analog phone behind SIP gateway GW-B. The call flow proceeds as follows:

1 The UAC sends an INVITE to its proxy server. In this INVITE, the Request-URI field contains the address of the called phone number as part of the SIP address. SDP information is included with this INVITE.

2 The proxy server creates a new INVITE, copying the information from the old INVITE, but replacing the Request-URI with the address of GW-B—the UAS.

3 When GW-B receives the INVITE, it initiates a call setup with the PBX. It sends a SIP response 100 (Trying) to the proxy server which, in this example, sends a 100 response to the SIP UAC. The proxy server is not required to send this response.

4 The PBX sets up an analog call with the end user and sends call progress messages to GW-B. When GW-B receives the Alerting message, it sends a SIP 180 (Ringing) message to the proxy server. The proxy server sends the same message to the UAC.

5 When the end user picks up the phone, the PBX sends a Connect message to GW-B. GW-B then sends a SIP 200 (OK) response to the proxy server, which sends it to the UAC. SDP information for the remote end is included in this OK response. The proxy server is not configured to be stateful—that is, Record Route is disabled. Therefore, the proxy server leaves the signaling path, and all further SIP signaling is directly between the UAC and GW-B.

6 The SIP UAC acknowledges the OK response, and a two-way RTP stream is established between the UAC and GW-B, the UAS. A two-way voice stream is established between GW-B and the PBX.

7 When the UAC hangs up, it exchanges SIP BYE and OK signals with GW-B. GW-B terminates the call with the PBX.

Call Flow Using Multiple Servers

SIP UAs and SIP proxy servers can contact a redirect server to determine where to send an INVITE. They typically do this when the called number is outside the local domain. The redirect server returns the most detailed information it has—either endpoint location(s) or the location of the next-hop server. Then it relies on the proxy server or UAC to route its INVITE appropriately.

Figure 4-3 shows the call flow in a more complex network with registrar, redirect, and proxy servers. (Recall that these are functional units and can all reside in the same device.) The figure shows the messages that are necessary to route the initial INVITE method to the UAS. After GW-B, the UAS, receives the INVITE, call flow is similar to the previous examples.

Figure 4-3 *SIP Call Flow with Multiple Servers*

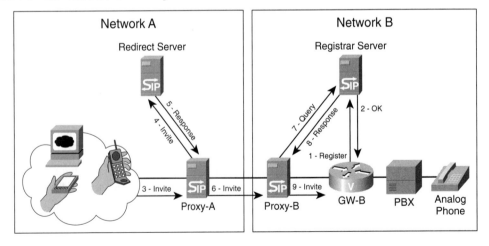

In Figure 4-3, one of the SIP endpoints in Network A calls an analog phone behind gateway GW-B in Network B. The following steps take place:

1 The gateway, GW-B, registers the E.164 phone numbers of its analog phones with the registrar server.

2 The registrar server replies with a 200 (OK) response.

3 The UAC sends an INVITE method to its proxy server, Proxy-A.

4 The proxy server recognizes that the destination number is outside its domain. It sends the INVITE to the redirect server.

5 The redirect server replies with a 300-series message listing the SIP address of the next-hop proxy server, Proxy-B.

6 Proxy-A sends an INVITE message to Proxy-B.

7 Proxy-B requests the location of the called number from its registrar server.

8 The registrar server responds with the SIP address of GW-B.

9 Proxy-B sends an INVITE to GW-B.

Following these steps, GW-B sets up the call with the PBX. It sends responses to Proxy-B, which forwards them through Proxy-A to the calling endpoint. If Record-route is enabled, all further signaling goes through the proxies. If not, call signaling proceeds as shown in Figure 4-2.

Call Flow Using Cisco CallManager 5.x

CallManager 5.x supports SIP phones and is an integral part of a SIP network. It can play different roles, such as registrar server and B2BUA.

Figure 4-4 illustrates a call flow scenario with CallManager acting as a B2BUA.

Figure 4-4 *Call Flow with CallManager 5.x*

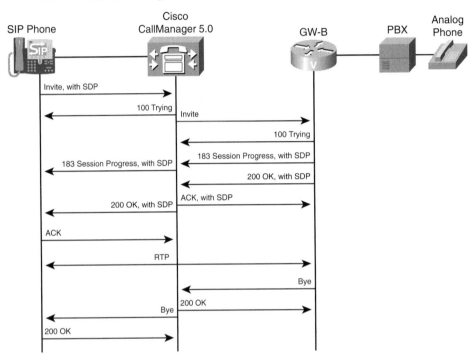

In Figure 4-4, a SIP phone is registered to a CallManager. The SIP phone places a call to an analog phone off a PBX behind the router/gateway GW-B. A SIP trunk exists between CallManager and the gateway. CallManager acts as a B2BUA—it terminates each leg of the call during the signaling phases, yet it allows the RTP stream to go directly between the two endpoints. This is accomplished by the way SDP information is sent.

1. A SIP phone that is registered to CallManager calls the analog phone. It sends an INVITE containing standard SDP information to CallManager. CallManager responds with a 100 Trying message. In this step, CallManager is acting as a UAS.

2. CallManager sends an INVITE over its SIP trunk to the remote SIP gateway, GW-B. This INVITE has a different Call-ID number than the one from the phone. In addition, this INVITE does not contain SDP fields. CallManager acts as a UAC in this step.

3. GW-B answers with a 100 Trying message and initiates a call to the PBX. (That signaling is not shown.) GW-B sends its SDP parameters in a 183 Session Progress message to CallManager. Included in this are the session parameters that the gateway supports.

4 CallManager sends a 183 Session Progress message to the SIP phone. This message contains an SDP portion with the capabilities that both endpoints support. For instance, suppose that the original SDP message of the phone indicated that it supported G.711 and G.729 codecs, but the gateway SDP message said that it supported only G.729. In that case, the 183 message from CallManager to the phone would list only G.729. It would also list the IP address of GW-B as the originator address in SDP field 'c.'

5 When the analog phone picks up, GW-B sends a 200 OK message containing its SDP information. CallManager acknowledges it with an ACK that contains the SDP information that both endpoints support. The IP address of the SIP phone is also included as the originator address in the SDP field 'c.'

6 CallManager sends a 200 OK message with SDP information to the phone. The phone acknowledges that message. Now that each endpoint has the IP address of the other, the two can establish an RTP stream between them for the duration of the call.

7 In Figure 4-4, the analog phone hangs up, so GW-B sends a SIP BYE method to CallManager.

8 CallManager replies with a 200 OK response and then sends a BYE to the SIP phone. The phone responds with a 200 OK message.

SIP Pros and Cons

People have high expectations for SIP. They hope it will enable advanced, anywhere, anytime multimedia communication. However, SIP is basically just another call control protocol, with its pros and cons. The following sections list a few of each.

Pros

- SIP works independently of the type of session, or the media used, giving it flexibility.

- It is an open standard, allowing multivendor support and integration. Applications can be written to customize SIP uses.

- SIP messages are clear text, making troubleshooting easier.

- SIP can accommodate multiple users with differing capabilities. For instance, in a conference that has some users with video capability and some only with audio capability, the video users can see each other. They do not have to drop down to audio only, as with other protocols.

Cons

- Processing text messages puts a higher load on gateways. The router must translate that text into a language that the router can understand. Code for this must be in the Cisco IOS.

- SIP is a fairly new protocol, so fewer people understand it than the older protocols. Be sure you have trained support personnel if you intend to implement SIP within your network.

- When you are using both SIP and SCCP phones on the same network, you must convert between in-band and out-of-band DTMF tones.

- SIP features are still being developed, and many vendors have proprietary implementations of the protocol.

When to Use SIP

SIP is the protocol of choice when you want to integrate multiple types of media. For example, perhaps you get an instant message on your phone screen that you want to respond to verbally. You start to press the button to call the IM sender, but you see that the sender has set his status to "Don't call me," so you refrain. Later, you would like to have a videoconference with three other people, but you notice that one of them has his phone off-hook. The other two join you, one as video and the other as audio only. You send a text message to the IP phone of the third person, asking him to join when he can. This might sound like the office of the future, but it is becoming reality.

You can use SIP trunks even without native SIP phones. You might choose them because of the simple session setup mechanism for SIP. For instance, you can use a SIP trunk between gateways with toll bypass. When you use SIP with CallManager or CME, you are not limited to Cisco-brand IP phones. You can also use other commercially available, and perhaps lower-priced, SIP phones. Be aware that CallManager might not be able to provide all the features for these phones that it can for a Cisco-brand SIP phone.

Before you implement a SIP network, plan its integration into your existing network. Determine exactly what you want to accomplish and how you will accomplish it. Remember also that you need to either find people who are knowledgeable about SIP or train your staff.

Dial Plan Considerations

SIP dial plan considerations are similar to those for an H.323 gateway, because dial peers control gateway call routing. You must configure dial peers to forward calls out of the gateway. You can forward calls to CallManager using a Voice over Internet Protocol (VoIP) dial peer, to the PSTN as a plain old telephone service (POTS) dial peer, to another gateway using a VoIP dial peer, or to directly connected voice ports as POTS dial peers.

In a voice network that has CallManagers and SIP gateways, it is important to understand the interaction between the two, because different versions of CallManager have different SIP capabilities. CallManager versions before 5.x can only have a SIP trunk to a gateway or other servers. CallManager 5.x and above also acts as a SIP B2BUA and allows SIP phones to register to it. It also can do domain routing for SIP calls. A new menu, SIP Route Pattern, allows you to configure SIP URI dialing. Therefore, your dial plan must take into account the CallManager version. No matter which version of CallManager you use, you configure a dial plan to send calls to the SIP trunk when needed. CallManager appears to the SIP gateway as a SIP-enabled VoIP dial peer.

Another consideration in SIP networks is where the dial plan will reside. The default behavior of SIP is to push down the dial plan to each endpoint. When a user dials digits on the phone, the phone compares those numbers against its internal dial plan. If the phone finds a match, it sends an INVITE. Otherwise, it must wait for the interdigit timer to expire before playing a reorder tone. The alternative is to use the Key Press Markup Language (KPML). When you use KPML, the SIP phone sends each digit to CallManager, similar to the way SCCP phones behave. CallManager can instruct the phone to play a reorder tone immediately if an incorrect number is dialed, or it can route the call as soon as enough digits are dialed. If you do not use KPML, you must configure SIP dial rules.

In your dial planning, consider the need to configure the gateway for such options as number translations or other digit manipulations, or call restrictions. If you are using SRST, be sure that the dial plan will work both with and without CallManager and, if possible, any SIP servers in the network. You need at least one dial peer with a destination pattern for routing outgoing calls. Default incoming POTS and VoIP dial peers are available, but you should specifically configure dial peers for incoming calls if you need a nondefault configuration.

As with H.323, SIP gateway configuration can become complex in a large network. You must configure each gateway with the information you need to route calls. Proxy, registrar, redirect, and DNS servers can help the network scale by providing dial plan resolution. This simplifies the gateway configuration.

Implementing SIP Gateways

Configuring a SIP gateway can be as simple as configuring SIP VoIP dial peers or as complex as tweaking SIP settings and timers. Gateway SIP configuration is done in three basic places: on dial peers, under SIP UA configuration mode, and under voice service VoIP configuration mode. The following sections discuss the types of configuration you can accomplish in each mode.

SIP Dial Peer Configuration

A basic SIP gateway configuration consists of simply adding one line under a VoIP dial peer configuration: **session protocol sipv2**. You can use additional dial peer settings; the exact options and commands vary by Cisco IOS version. For instance, to allow SIP calls to be hairpinned from one VoIP dial peer to the other, use the **redirect ip2ip** command. SIP supports both consultative and blind call transfers from Cisco gateways. It also supports call forwarding from IP phones that are registered with the gateway as e-phones. This capability is enabled per dial peer with the **application session** command in dial-peer configuration mode.

To change the transport protocol (UDP is the default), use the **session transport [udp | tcp]** command. SIP can switch from using UDP to TCP when a voice packet gets within 200 bytes of the maximum transmission unit (MTU) to avoid UDP fragmentation. To configure this for a specific dial peer, use the **voice-class sip transport switch udp tcp** command. You can also configure this globally under voice service configuration mode.

Example 4-7 shows the configuration of two SIP dial peers. On the first dial peer, the transport protocol is changed from the default UDP to TCP (an optional step). On the second dial peer, the configuration shows enabling switching from UDP to TCP for large packets.

Example 4-7 *Configuring a SIP Dial Peer*

```
SIP-GW(config)#dial-peer voice 3401 voip
SIP-GW(config-dial-peer)#session target ipv4:10.6.2.1
SIP-GW(config-dial-peer)#session protocol sipv2
SIP-GW(config-dial-peer)#session transport tcp
!
SIP-GW(config)#dial-peer voice 4404 voip
SIP-GW(config-dial-peer)#session target ipv4:10.7.1.1
SIP-GW(config-dial-peer)#session protocol sipv2
SIP-GW(config-dial-peer)#voice-class sip transport switch udp tcp
SIP-GW(config-dial-peer)#destination-pattern 4404...
```

SIP UA Configuration

The SIP UA does not require configuration to function, but you might want to make some adjustments. Enter UA configuration mode by issuing the **sip-ua** command. As with dial peers, the options vary by Cisco IOS and device. Table 4-2 shows some common UA commands.

Table 4-2 *SIP UA Commands*

Command	Description
calling-info	Controls the calling ID treatment for calls to and from the PSTN.
max-forwards *number*	Configures the maximum hops for SIP methods. Values are 1–70; default is 70.

Table 4-2   *SIP UA Commands (Continued)*

Command	Description
nat	Configures NAT traversal settings.
retry	Controls the number of times that a SIP message will be sent. Options include the following: • **bye**—Default is 10. • **cancel**—Default is 10. • **comet**—Default is 10. • **invite**—Default is 6. • **notify**—Default is 10. • **prack**—Default is 10. • **refer**—Default is 10. • **register**—Default is 10. • **rel1xx**—Default is 6. • **response**—Default is 6. • **subscribe**—Default is 10.
registrar {**dns:***address* | **ipv4:***destination-address*} [**expires** *seconds*][**tcp**] [**secondary**]	Allows a gateway to register the E.164 numbers of non-SIP phones with a registrar or proxy server.
sip-server {**dns:**[*host-name*] | **ipv4:***ip-addr* [**:***port-num*]}	Specifies the name or IP address of a SIP server, usually a proxy server. When you use this, you can configure the dial-peer session target as **session target sip-server**.
timers	Changes SIP signaling timers. Options include the following: • **connect**—Time to wait for a 200 response to an ACK. Default is 500 ms. • **disconnect**—Time to wait for a 200 response to a BYE. Default is 500 ms. • **expires**—Valid time for an INVITE. Default is 180,000 ms. • **register**—Time that UA waits before sending REGISTER message. Default is 500 ms. • **trying**—Time to wait for a 100 response to an INVITE. Default is 500 ms.
[**no**] **transport** {**udp** | **tcp**}	Configures the SIP UA to listen for messages on port 5060 of either UDP or TCP. Both are enabled by default.

Example 4-8 shows a SIP UA configuration. The gateway is configured to register its analog phones with redundant servers, the IP address of the proxy server is specified, the maximum number of hops for SIP methods is reduced to 10, and the gateway is limited to listening for TCP SIP messages. The configuration is partially verified by using the **show sip-ua status** command. The configured E.164 phone number registration is verified with the **show sip-ua register status** command.

Example 4-8 *SIP UA Configuration*

```
SIP-GW(config)#sip-ua
SIP-GW(config-sip-ua)#registrar ipv4:10.30.25.250 tcp
SIP-GW(config-sip-ua)#registrar ipv4:10.30.25.251 tcp secondary
SIP-GW(config-sip-ua)#sip-server ipv4:10.30.25.252
SIP-GW(config-sip-ua)#max-forwards 10
SIP-GW(config-sip-ua)#no transport udp
!
SIP-GW#show sip-ua status
SIP User Agent Status
SIP User Agent for UDP : DISABLED
SIP User Agent for TCP : ENABLED
SIP User Agent bind status(signaling): DISABLED
SIP User Agent bind status(media): DISABLED
SIP early-media for 180 responses with SDP: ENABLED
SIP max-forwards : 10
SIP DNS SRV version: 2 (rfc 2782)
NAT Settings for the SIP-UA
Role in SDP: NONE
Check media source packets: DISABLED
Maximum duration for a telephone-event in NOTIFYs: 1000 ms
SIP support for ISDN SUSPEND/RESUME: ENABLED
Redirection (3xx) message handling: ENABLED
Reason Header will override Response/Request Codes: DISABLED

SDP application configuration:
 Version line (v=) required
 Owner line (o=) required
 Timespec line (t=) required
 Media supported: audio image
 Network types supported: IN
 Address types supported: IP4
 Transport types supported: RTP/AVP udptl
!
SIP-GW#show sip-ua register status
Line         peer          expires(sec)  registered
============ ============  ============  ===========
4101         20001              118      yes
4102         20003              118      yes
4103         20005              118      yes
4104         20007              118      yes
```

SIP Voice Service Configuration

The voice service configuration mode is used for voice-related commands that affect the entire gateway. Enter this mode by issuing the **voice service voip** command. In this mode, you can allow hairpinned calls for all dial peers with the **redirect ip2ip** command. (You can also issue this command under dial-peer configuration mode. Then it affects only those dial peers.)

You can enter the SIP submode with the **sip** command from voice service mode. You can do several SIP-specific configurations from this mode. Table 4-3 lists some of these; specific options vary by Cisco IOS version and device.

Table 4-3   *SIP Voice Service Configuration Commands*

Command	Description
**bind {all	control	media} source-interface** *interface-id*	Sets the source IP address for control signaling or media, or both.
call service stop [forced]	Stops the SIP service. Active calls are not affected unless the **forced** option is used.
min-se *seconds*	Changes the SIP session expiration timer. Default (and recommended) value is 1800 sec. In the event of a timer mismatch, the higher value is used.
**redirect contact order [best-match	longest-match]**	Sends a SIP 300 Redirect message listing all the routes in the Contact header when the gateway knows of multiple routes to a destination. This command controls the order in which the routes are listed. **Longest-match** is default; it puts routes in order of number of digits matched in its destination patterns. **Best-match** uses the current system configuration.
registrar server [expires [max *seconds*] [**min** *seconds*]]	Configures the gateway to act as a registrar server; used when SRST is active.
**session transport {tcp	udp}**	Globally configures either TCP or UDP as the transport protocol.
**subscription maximum {accept	originate}** *number*	Controls the maximum number of subscriptions accepted or originated by the gateway. Default is twice the number of dial peers configured on the gateway.
transport switch udp tcp	Enables the router to use TCP instead of UDP when a SIP message exceeds the MTU size.

Example 4-9 shows a gateway that has been configured to hair-pin calls for all dial peers. The source IP address for all SIP signaling traffic has been set to Loopback 0, and this gateway has been configured to act as a registrar server. You can verify the interface binding with the **show sip-ua status** command.

Example 4-9   *SIP Voice Service Configuration*

```
SIP-GW(config)#voice service voip
SIP-GW(conf-voi-serv)#redirect ip2ip
SIP-GW(conf-voi-serv)#sip
SIP-GW(conf-serv-sip)#bind control source-interface lo0
SIP-GW(conf-serv-sip)#registrar server expires max 1500 min 500
```

Toll Bypass

You use toll bypass to send calls between different sites over a packet network rather than over the PSTN. Because this bypasses the PSTN, it also bypasses any long-distance toll charges. Cisco routers, functioning as edge gateways, can use SIP to pass voice traffic between them. This traffic is typically from analog phones, such as those connected to a PBX, but it can be from IP or SIP phones. Figure 4-1 shows this type of setup.

Configuring the routers for toll bypass involves two components. First, you must configure connection(s) to the internal voice network. This might be a PRI to a PBX, for instance. You must configure both the physical links and the appropriate dial peers. Second, you must configure the connection to the other router. This involves configuring the physical link and at least one SIP VoIP dial peer pointing to the remote SIP router. You configure the dial peers and gateways as detailed in the previous sections of this chapter.

Registering with CallManager

CallManager versions 4.x can register a SIP trunk connecting to a remote gateway, a proxy server, or CallManager Express. The trunk is referred to as a *signaling interface*. CallManager 5.x can register SIP phones, in addition to SIP trunks. Trunks can point to other Cisco CallManager clusters, also.

Configuring a SIP Trunk with CallManager 4.x

The following steps show how to create a SIP trunk on CallManager 4.x. The menus on other versions of CallManager might vary slightly, but the process is similar.

Step 1   To add a new trunk, select the Device menu, and then select the **Trunk** link. At the Find and List Trunks screen, shown in Figure 4-5, click the link for **Add a New Trunk**.

Step 2   On the next screen, shown in Figure 4-6, select **SIP Trunk** as the Trunk type. Notice that Device Protocol is automatically set to SIP. Click the **Next** button.

Figure 4-5   *CallManager Find and List Trunks Screen*

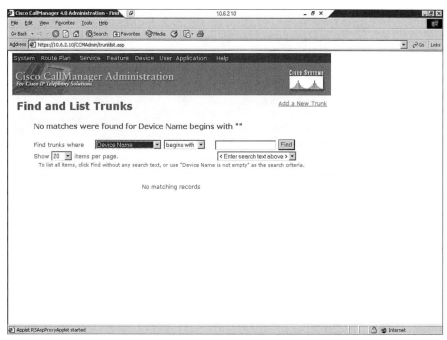

Figure 4-6   *CallManager SIP Trunk Creation*

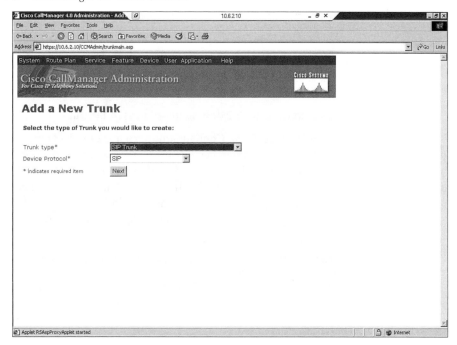

Step 3 The Trunk Configuration screen, shown in Figure 4-7, appears next. Enter the name of the device at the other end of the trunk, and optionally a description. You must select a Device Pool. Then designate whether calls to this trunk are OnNet or OffNet, or let the system decide. Note that a media termination point (MTP) is required. This is to translate DTMF signals between SIP and SCCP phones. For more information, see the later section, "DTMF Relay."

Figure 4-7 *SIP Trunk Configuration in CallManager*

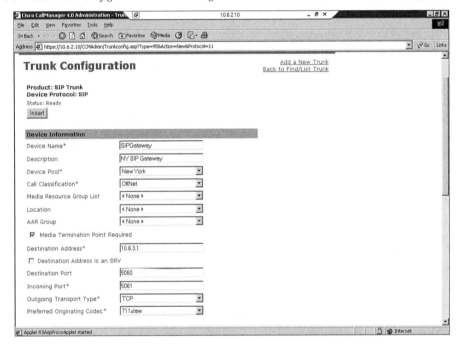

Step 4 On this same screen, enter the destination address of the trunk.

Step 5 The next options in the Trunk Configuration screen are for the Destination Port number, the Incoming Port number, and the Outgoing Transport Type (Layer 4 protocol). The default destination port for SIP is 5060, and it is typically left at that. CallManager can have multiple SIP signaling interfaces. You must use a unique incoming port for each signaling interface in CCM 4.x. Not shown in Figure 4-7 are settings for incoming and outgoing calls, further down on the screen.

Step 6 When you are finished with the configuration, click **Insert**. You are then prompted to reset the trunk.

Step 7   You can verify your trunk configuration by going back to the Find and List Trunks page. Click the **Find** button, and verify that your new trunk is there, as shown in Figure 4-8. After you have created the trunk, you can assign route patterns, list, or groups to it as normal.

Figure 4-8   *Verifying a SIP Trunk in CallManager*

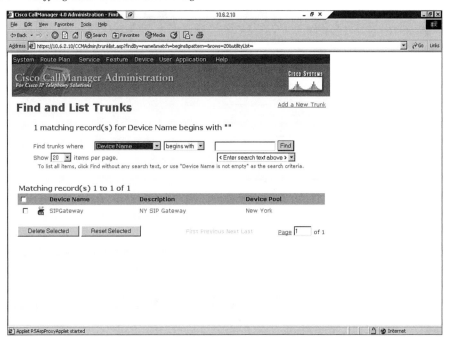

Configuring a SIP Trunk with CallManager 5.x

The process that you use to register a SIP trunk with CallManager 5.x is slightly different from the CallManager 4.x process. For instance, an MTP is not required with CallManager 5.x if the endpoints can negotiate using out-of-band DTMF relay. Multiple trunks can have the same incoming port number.

To begin adding a SIP trunk in CCM 5, follow Steps 1 and 2 in the CallManager 4.x process. The next screen, the Trunk Configuration screen, has some different fields, and some fields are in different positions in CallManager 5.x. Figures 4-9, 4-10, and 4-11 show this Trunk Configuration screen. Some items to note are that the MTP might not be required and is not checked automatically. Some SIP-specific fields have been added, such as Presence Group, SIP Trunk Security Profile, SIP Profile, and SUBSCRIBE Calling Search Space.

Figure 4-9 *Configuring a SIP Trunk in CCM 5*

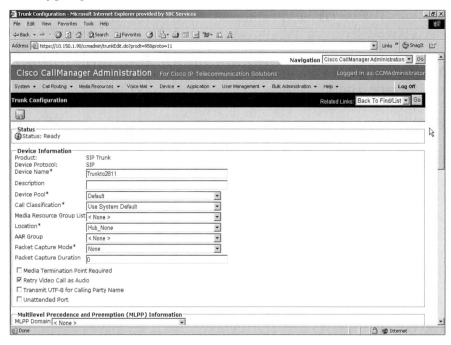

Figure 4-10 *Configuring a SIP Trunk in CCM 5*

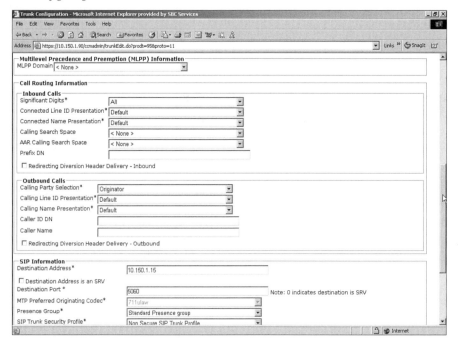

Figure 4-11 *Configuring a SIP Trunk in CCM 5*

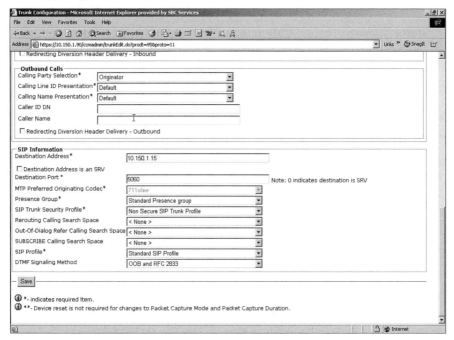

When you are finished configuring the trunk, you must save it by clicking the Save button on the bottom of the screen or the disk icon at the top of the screen. You can verify SIP trunk configuration for CallManager 5.x by using the same method that you used for CallManager 4.x—by using the Find button at the Find and List Trunks page.

Configuring the Gateway for a CallManager Trunk

Regardless of the CallManager version you use, the gateway sees it as a SIP dial peer. For redundancy, you can configure a dial peer for each CCM in the cluster, using preference to determine their order of use. Example 4-7 (shown previously) demonstrates the configuration for a basic SIP dial peer.

DTMF Relay

DTMF tones are the tones that are generated when a telephone key is pressed on a touchtone phone. Sometimes the called endpoint needs to hear those tones, such as when you enter digits during the call in response to a menu. Low-bandwidth codecs can distort the sound, however. *DTMF relay* allows that tone information to be reliably passed from one endpoint to the other. By default, SIP uses in-band signaling, sending the DTMF information in the voice stream. However, you can configure it to use RTP-NTE, SIP INFO messages, SIP NOTIFY messages, or KPML for transmitting DTMF tone information.

RTP-NTE is an in-band DTMF relay method, which uses RTP Named Telephony Event (NTE) packets to carry DTMF information instead of voice. If RTP-NTE is configured, SDP is used to negotiate the payload type value for NTE packets and the events that will be sent using NTE.

RTP-NTE can cause problems communicating with SCCP phones, which use only out-of-band DTMF relay. In a CallManager 4.x network with SCCP phones, you must provision an MTP for calls that traverse the SIP trunk. This MTP translates between in-band and out-of-band DTMF signals. You must configure a separate MTP for each side of the SIP trunk. You can do this MTP in hardware, or in software on CallManager.

Cisco has two out-of-band procedures for DTMF relay. One uses SIP INFO methods, and the other uses SIP NOTIFY methods. The SIP INFO method sends DTMF digits in INFO messages. It is always enabled. When a gateway receives an INFO message containing DTMF relay information, it sends the corresponding tone.

NOTIFY-based out-of-band DTMF relay is negotiated by including a Call-Info field in the SIP INVITE and response messages. This field indicates an ability to use NOTIFY for DTMF tones and the duration of each tone in milliseconds. Using this method can help SIP gateways interoperate with Skinny phones. You can also use it for analog phones that are connected to Foreign Exchange Station (FXS) ports on the gateway.

When a DTMF tone is generated, the gateway sends a NOTIFY message to the terminating gateway. When that gateways receives the NOTIFY, it responds with SIP 200 OK and plays the DTMF tone. To configure the DTMF relay type, use the **dtmf-relay** command in dial-peer configuration mode. To optionally configure the interval between NOTIFY messages for a single DTMF event, use the **notify telephone-event max-duration** *millisecond*s command in SIP UA configuration mode. The default is 2000 msec; the lowest value between two SIP peers is the one chosen.

Example 4-10 shows these commands. Notice that two types of DTMF relay are configured. The router prefers SIP-NOTIFY but uses RTP-NTE if the other side does not support SIP-NOTIFY. If no DTMF relay method is configured, the tones are sent in-band.

Example 4-10 *Configuring NOTIFY-Based DTMF Relay*

```
!Setting the NOTIFY interval
SIP-GW(config)#sip-ua
SIP-GW(config-sip-ua)#notify telephone-event max-duration 1000
SIP-GW(config-sip-ua)#exit
!
!Setting NOTIFY-based out-of-band DTMF relay
SIP-GW(config)#dial-peer voice 3400 voip
SIP-GW(config-dial-peer)#dtmf-relay ?
  cisco-rtp          Cisco Proprietary RTP
  h245-alphanumeric  DTMF Relay via H245 Alphanumeric IE
```

Example 4-10   *Configuring NOTIFY-Based DTMF Relay (Continued)*

```
 h245-signal        DTMF Relay via H245 Signal IE
 rtp-nte            RTP Named Telephone Event RFC 2833
 sip-notify         DTMF Relay via SIP NOTIFY messages

SIP-GW(config-dial-peer)#dtmf-relay sip-notify rtp-nte
```

KPML is another way for SIP phones to send dialed-digit information, as described previously in the "Dial Plan Considerations" section. Like SIP-NOTIFY, KPML uses a NOTIFY message to transmit each digit.

Securing SIP Gateways

Your SIP gateway, as part of your IP network, should conform to your company security policy. Deployment of basic items, such as user control and authentication, access-control lists, and physical security, should be standard. The SIP network, like most of your user devices, should be on a LAN using private IP addresses, with strong perimeter security.

Because SIP messages contain IP addresses in several different locations, it is important to use a firewall that supports SIP. Cisco IOS firewalls, PIX firewalls, and Adaptive Security Appliance (ASA) devices are all able to inspect the SIP application data and maintain call flow information.

SIP supports some authentication, authorization, and accounting (AAA) mechanisms to help authenticate communications between UAs, servers, and gateways. You can use RADIUS to preauthenticate calls. The gateway forwards incoming call information to a RADIUS server, which must authenticate it before connecting the call. To enable AAA for SIP calls, you must use the normal AAA configuration on the gateway and the RADIUS server. In addition, at global configuration mode, issue the **aaa preauth** command to enter AAA preauthentication configuration mode. Specify the RADIUS server with the command **group** {**radius** | *groupname*}.

You can also use HTTP Authentication Digest. UAs, proxy servers, and redirect servers can request authentication before they process a SIP message. Gateways can respond to authentication challenges and can respond on behalf of non-SIP phones that they have registered to a SIP server. SIP defines authentication and authorization fields that can be present in the message header. A server that receives a message—such as an INVITE— without authentication credentials issues a challenge. The response includes an authorization field with an MD5 hash and other credentials. To configure a gateway to use HTTP Authentication Digest, give the following command in each dial peer or SIP-UA configuration mode: **authentication username** *username* **password** *password* [**realm** *realm*]. *Username* is the name of the user that will be authenticating, *password* is the shared password, and *realm* is an optional entry that lets you configure multiple username/password combinations. The realm is included in the challenge, so the response will include credentials for that specific realm.

To provide a more secure, encrypted transport mechanism for SIP messages, Cisco IPT devices have added support for the TLS protocol.

Allowing H.323 to SIP Connections

SIP and H.323 dial peers can be configured on the same gateway, but call routing between the two types of dial peers is disabled by default. To enable this routing, enter voice service configuration mode and issue the command **allow-connections** *from-type* **to** *to-type*. Options for both the *from-type* and the *to-type* are **h323** and **sip**. Example 4-11 shows a router that is configured to allow multiple types of VoIP connections.

Example 4-11 *Configuring H.323 to SIP Connections*

```
H323-SIP-GW(config)#voice service voip
H323-SIP-GW (conf-voi-serv)# allow-connections h323 to h323
H323-SIP-GW (conf-voi-serv)# allow-connections h323 to sip
H323-SIP-GW (conf-voi-serv)# allow-connections sip to h323
H323-SIP-GW (conf-voi-serv)# allow-connections sip to sip
```

Troubleshooting Tools

If calls cannot be made between SIP gateways or over SIP trunks, dial peer configuration is one of the first places to check. Make sure that the dial peer is configured to use SIP and that both devices are using the same transport protocol and DTMF relay method. Make sure that destination patterns and session targets are correct, also.

Several **show** commands can troubleshoot and monitor the SIP UA function of the gateway. Example 4-12 lists them; options can vary by Cisco IOS and device.

Example 4-12 **show sip-ua** *Command Options*

```
SIP-GW#show sip-ua ?
  calls         Display Active SIP Calls
  connections   Display SIP Connections
  map           Display SIP status code to PSTN cause mapping table & vice versa
  min-se        Display Min-SE value
  mwi           Display SIP MWI server info
  register      Display SIP Register status
  retry         Display SIP Protocol Retry Counts
  service       Display SIP submode Shutdown status
  statistics    Display SIP UA Statistics
  status        Display SIP UA Listener Status
  timers        Display SIP Protocol Timers
```

The **show sip-ua connections** {**udp|tcp**} command gives you information on active connections, including those with errors. To stop a problem connection, use the **clear sip-ua** {**udp | tcp**} [**connection id** *number*] [**target ipv4:***ip-address*] command.

To ensure that the SIP is enabled on the gateway, use the **show sip-ua service** command. You should get the following result:

```
SIP-GW#show sip-ua service
SIP Service is up
```

The **show sip-ua statistics** command provides statistics on each type of method and response, errors, and total SIP traffic information. You can reset these counters with the **clear sip-ua statistics** command.

The **show sip-ua status** command can be useful in troubleshooting, also. Output from this command was shown previously in Example 4-13.

To debug SIP messages, use the **debug ccsip** command. This command has several options, as Example 4-13 shows. Use **messages** to see the SIP method and response messages, as shown previously in Example 4-1. The **media** option shows RTP information. Your options might vary by Cisco IOS and device.

Example 4-13   **debug ccsip** *Command Options*

```
SIP-GW#debug ccsip ?
  all        Enable all SIP debugging traces
  calls      Enable CCSIP SPI calls debugging trace
  error      Enable SIP error debugging trace
  events     Enable SIP events debugging trace
  info       Enable SIP info debugging trace
  media      Enable SIP media debugging trace
  messages   Enable CCSIP SPI messages debugging trace
  preauth    Enable SIP preauth debugging traces
  states     Enable CCSIP SPI states debugging trace
  transport  Enable SIP transport debugging traces
```

Case Study: Configuring SIP Between a Gateway and CallManager 5.x

In this case study, SIP is being introduced into the New York and Shanghai networks. The locations will use both SIP and SCCP phones, and a SIP trunk will be configured between the New York CallManager cluster and the Shanghai gateway, shown in Figure 4-12. CallManager 5.x is used to register the SIP phones. The preferred DTMF relay method will be SIP-NOTIFY, but RTP-NTE will be accepted as a second choice.

For redundancy, the Shanghai gateway has dial peers to two of the CallManager servers. One CallManager IP address is configured under the UA, to demonstrate that command. The gateway will register its network analog phones with registrar servers at 10.10.10.19 and 10.10.10.20. HTTP digest authentication is configured.

All SIP traffic will use interface Fa0/0 as its source IP address. Large packets will switch from UDP to TCP as their transport protocol to avoid UDP fragmentation.

Figure 4-12 *SIP Case Study Network Diagram*

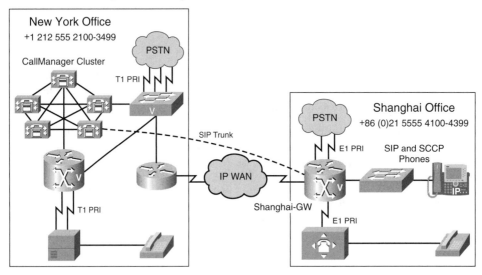

Example 4-14 shows the configuration of SIP and the SIP trunk on the Shanghai gateway. POTS dial peers to connect to the PBX are not shown in this example. CallManager configuration is outside the scope of this case study.

Example 4-14 *SIP Case Study*

```
Shanghai-GW(config)#sip-ua
Shanghai-GW(config-sip-ua)#sip-server ipv4:10.10.10.11
Shanghai-GW(config-sip-ua)#registrar ipv4:10.10.10.19
Shanghai-GW(config-sip-ua)#registrar ipv4:10.10.10.20 secondary
Shanghai-GW(config-sip-ua)#authentication username NYCServ1 password C1sc0 realm
  NYC-SIP
!
Shanghai-GW(config)#voice service voip
Shanghai-GW(conf-voi-serv)#sip
Shanghai-GW(conf-serv-sip)#bind all source-interface fa0/0
Shanghai-GW(conf-serv-sip)#transport switch udp tcp
!
Shanghai-GW(config)#dial-peer voice 2121 voip
Shanghai-GW(config-dial-peer)#destination-pattern 21255521..
Shanghai-GW(config-dial-peer)#session target sip-server
Shanghai-GW(config-dial-peer)#session protocol sipv2
Shanghai-GW(config-dial-peer)#dtmf-relay sip-notify rtp-nte
Shanghai-GW(config-dial-peer)#preference 1
```

Example 4-14 *SIP Case Study (Continued)*

```
!
Shanghai-GW(config)#dial-peer voice 2122 voip
Shanghai-GW(config-dial-peer)#destination-pattern 21255521..
Shanghai-GW(config-dial-peer)#session target 10.10.10.12
Shanghai-GW(config-dial-peer)#session protocol sipv2
Shanghai-GW(config-dial-peer)#dtmf-relay sip-notify rtp-nte
Shanghai-GW(config-dial-peer)#preference 2
```

Review Questions

1 What do the acronyms UAC and UAS stand for? Define the difference between the two entities.

2 Name five types of SIP servers, and describe what they do.

3 Name the five types of SIP methods that Cisco routers can both generate and respond to. What is the purpose of each one?

4 What command configures a dial peer to use SIP in its communication with its VoIP peer?

5 How does CallManager 4.x interact with a SIP gateway?

6 What additional SIP capabilities does CallManager 5.x add?

7 Which Layer 4 protocol does SIP use by default, and what is the default port?

8 What is the function of the SDP in SIP call setup?

CHAPTER 5

Circuit Options

In this chapter, you will learn about the various circuit types that Cisco voice gateways support, in addition to signaling methods and available features of circuits.

NOTE   For more information on the implementation details, see Chapter 6, "Connecting to the PSTN," and Chapter 7, "Connecting to PBXs."

This chapter helps you to understand the following:

- Analog circuit options and signaling methods
- Digital circuit options and signaling methods
- ISDN technology
- Voice tuning on different types of circuits

Circuit Signaling

All voice circuits use signaling methods to communicate. These signaling methods vary based on the type of circuit, but all circuits must communicate the same types of information. This information is grouped by the type of information and signaling method:

- **Supervisory signaling**—Supervisory signaling is used to indicate the state or current status of a circuit. A circuit, or circuit channel, can be either on-hook, which indicates that the circuit is available, or off-hook, which indicates that the circuit is in use.

- **Address signaling**—Address information consists of the digits that are assigned to an end station. Address signaling methods are required to transmit this information from the call originator.

  Multifrequency (MF) tones are commonly used for address signaling. MF signaling uses numerous reference frequencies sent two at a time to represent each digit. Each protocol defines the reference frequencies and how each pair of frequencies, or tone-pair, maps to a digit.

- **Informational signaling**—Informational signaling is used to provide feedback to the calling or called party. Common informational signaling includes dial tone, ring indication, and busy signal.

Various terms describe the address information. People often use these terms interchangeably, although they actually refer to specific standards or signaling methods.

- **Dialed number identification service (DNIS)**—The telephone number of the called party. Specifically, DNIS refers to the number that the service provider sends to the destination. DNIS might or might not be the digits that the calling party dials to reach the destination.

- **Automatic number identification (ANI)**—The telephone number of the calling party.

- **Calling number identification or calling name identification (CNID)**—CNID is used as a synonym to ANI.

- **Calling line identification (CLID)**—Similar to ANI. Refers to the number of the calling party.

- **Caller ID**—Generic term that describes the delivery of calling number or name. Also used as a marketing term by many service providers to refer to a chargeable feature offered on analog phone service.

Analog Circuits

Cisco voice gateways support three types of analog circuits:

- Foreign Exchange Station (FXS)
- Foreign Exchange Office (FXO)
- Ear and Mouth (E&M)

FXS/FXO

An FXO is a port type that connects subscribers to central office (CO) equipment or PBXs. You can use FXS to connect to regular analog phones or PBXs.

In general, an FXS port is a port that comes from the service offering equipment, whether it is a CO class five switch, a PBX, or a voice gateway. An FXO port is a port from an end device, such as a telephone, fax, or modem, that is connected to an FXS port to obtain telephony services.

FXS

FXS ports are the ports that you plug a telephone, fax, or modem into that provide telephony service. For example, an analog telephone that is connecting over twisted copper pairs to the port in a home or a port on a PBX is connecting to the FXS port of the telephone carrier or the private telephone exchange. FXS ports provide dial tone, battery current, and ring voltage to the subscriber device.

Dial tone is the current that the FXS port places on the analog circuit to inform the subscriber device that the line is ready to collect dual tone multifrequency (DTMF) tones for call routing.

Idle voltages range from 24V to 48V and are configurable. *Ring voltage* is the voltage that is placed on the analog circuit to inform subscriber devices of an incoming call.

Cisco routers provide 40Vrms 5 ring equivalence number (REN), which is sufficient to support on-premise equipment.

FXO

FXO ports are the ports on subscriber devices that connect to the CO or PBX to receive subscriber services. Examples are the port on a telephone, modem, or fax that connects to the FXS port in the wall, PBX, or voice gateway. PBX systems and voice gateways can also contain FXO ports that are connected to the CO. For example, you can connect an analog telephone FXO port to the FXS port from a PBX for voice service. This FXS port allows the analog phone to call other phones that are connected to the PBX. The PBX might also contain an FXO port that is connected to a CO FXS port. This FXO port allows the PBX to route calls from its FXS ports to the public switched telephone network (PSTN). On-hook/off-hook indication is delivered to the FXS port by a change in voltage on the analog line.

FXO Power Failover

If the power to the router fails, a metallic path is established between certain FXO and FXS ports. You can mark the analog phones that are connected to these FXS ports as emergency phones for calling out to the PSTN even when the router is down.

FXS/FXO Supervisory Signaling

A subscriber device that is connected to an FXS port initiates communications by delivering off-hook indication. An FXS port detects the off-hook state and prepares to gather DTMF tones used to determine how to route the call. The remote FXS port applies ring voltage to the remote subscriber FXO, and the remote FXO detects ring voltage and goes off-hook, indicating reception of the call and closing of the call circuit. The call is ended by each local segment entering the on-hook state and the FXS port sending on-hook indication. You can accomplish supervisory signaling between FXS and FXO ports in two ways: loop-start and ground-start signaling.

Loop-Start Signaling

Loop-start signaling involves the breaking and connecting of the 48V circuit loop originating from the CO equipment. During the on-hook state, the subscriber equipment has a break on the loop, so no voltage is passing. When the subscriber equipment goes off-hook, it closes the loop, and current flows. At this point, the CO detects the closing of the loop and provides a dial tone. To seize the far-end subscriber, the CO provides an analog current across the line called ring voltage. This current causes the subscriber device to "ring," indicating an incoming call. When the subscriber answers the call, or goes off-hook, the 48V circuit loop is closed and the CO turns off the ringing voltage. The call is now connected.

The loop-start method has the advantage of not requiring a common ground between the CO and subscriber equipment. However, it does not provide far-end disconnect monitoring. There is no mechanism in place to determine when the remote party has returned to the on-hook state. There is also poor glare resolution with loop-start signaling. Glare occurs when both the CO and subscriber equipment attempt to seize the line at the same time.

Ground-Start Signaling

Ground-start signaling calls for the 48V circuit loop to be grounded on both sides of the connection. In the idle state, the subscriber has a break in the ring, and the CO has a break in the tip. When the subscriber seizes the line, it grounds the ring, allowing current to flow along the path. When the CO senses the ring ground, it grounds the tip. Upon detection of the tip ground, the subscriber closes the loop and removes the ring ground. This action connects the circuit. When the CO seizes the line, it grounds the tip, causing the subscriber to detect the current, close the loop, and remove the ring ground. Ground-start signaling provides far-end disconnect information because the CO can ground the tip when the remote subscriber has entered the on-hook state. It also minimizes instances of glare. However, it requires that both CO and subscriber equipment have a common ground.

Address Signaling

The FXO port sends address signaling to the FXS port to indicate the final destination of the call. Analog address signaling can use either pulsed digits or DTMF tones. DTMF is a common implementation of MF tones that defines eight reference frequencies and tone-pair to digit mapping.

Pulsed tones are rarely used today. Pulse tones were originally sent by spinning a dial wheel on a telephone. As this mechanical device spun, it opened and closed the circuit. The pulses, or duration of open and closed, vary by country but must be consistent within a specified tolerance.

Today, most analog circuits use DTMF tones to indicate the destination address. As you push the buttons on a touch-tone phone, two different frequencies are sent on the circuit. This combination of frequencies notifies the receiving side of the digits. Table 5-1 lists the frequencies that are associated with each button on a telephone keypad.

Table 5-1   *DTMF Frequencies*

	1209	1336	1477	1633
697	1	2	3	A
770	4	5	6	B
852	7	8	9	C
941	*	0	#	D

FXS-DID

Because address signaling is transmitted only from the FXO port to the FXS port, calls from the PSTN on a typical analog circuit do not indicate the end destination of a call. For a typical residential application, this is not an issue, because all phones on the associated line will ring. When the analog service is connected to a gateway or PBX, it would be beneficial to receive addressing signaling to allow calls to be routed to individual phones on the system. Some service providers offer this service by providing an FXO port as the demarcation. You can then connect an FXS port that is configured for direct inward dial (DID) service and receive address signaling from the PSTN. You cannot configure all FXS ports to support DID service.

NOTE   You cannot use FXS ports that are configured for DID service to place outbound calls.

Informational Signaling

The FXS port provides informational signaling using call progress tones. Call progress (CP) tones are audible tones that the FXS device sends to indicate the status of calls. Functions are determined by the frequency of tone sent and the cadence of the tone. For example, in the United States, a dial tone is a continuous generation of 350 Hz and 440 Hz, whereas a busy signal is 480 Hz and 620 Hz with a .5 second on/.5 second off cadence. A sample list of call progress tones is as follows:

- Busy signal
- Call waiting
- Dial tone
- Ring tone
- Congestion tone
- Audible ringback tone

CP Tones are country specific. Cisco voice gateways default to U.S. CP tones. You can select country-specific tones using the voice port command **cptone**, as shown in Example 5-1.

Example 5-1   *Configuring CP Tones*

```
Gateway#config t
Gateway(config)#voice-port 2/0/0
Gateway(config-voiceport)#cptone ?
  locale   2 letter ISO-3166 country code

  AR Argentina          IS Iceland         PE Peru
  AU Australia          IN India           PH Philippines
  AT Austria            ID Indonesia       PL Poland
  BE Belgium            IE Ireland         PT Portugal
  BR Brazil             IL Israel          RU Russian Federation
  CA Canada             IT Italy           SA Saudi Arabia
  CN China              JP Japan           SG Singapore
  CO Colombia           JO Jordan          SK Slovakia
  C1 Custom1            KE Kenya           SI Slovenia
  C2 Custom2            KR Korea Republic  ZA South Africa
  CY Cyprus             LB Lebanon         ES Spain
  CZ Czech Republic     LU Luxembourg      SE Sweden
  DK Denmark            MY Malaysia        CH Switzerland
  EG Egypt              MX Mexico          TW Taiwan
  FI Finland            NP Nepal           TH Thailand
  FR France             NL Netherlands     TR Turkey
  DE Germany            NZ New Zealand     GB United Kingdom
  GH Ghana              NG Nigeria         US United States
  GR Greece             NO Norway          VE Venezuela
  HK Hong Kong          PK Pakistan        ZW Zimbabwe
  HU Hungary            PA Panama
```

Caller ID

Caller ID is a service provider feature that allows the receiving party to be notified of the directory number of the calling party. Caller ID is based on Telcordia Publications TR-TSY-000030 and TR-TSY-000031 and is officially known as Calling Number Delivery (CND).

CND sends the calling party information between the first and second ring of a call. The information is sent as ASCII-encoded text in a 1200 bps stream of data bytes and includes the date, time, and calling party number and name.

FXO ports support inbound Caller ID. You can also configure a name and number for FXS ports by using the **station-id** command. This information is used for calls within a system only. Calls to the PSTN present the official directory information stored in the service provider database.

NOTE   CallManager-controlled Media Gateway Control Protocol (MGCP) gateways do not support inbound caller ID on FXO ports.

Supervisory Disconnect

Traditionally, there was no need for the FXS port to inform the FXO port of disconnect because the end user was a person. During a phone conversation, people indicate the end of the discussion or assume the end of a discussion by a prolonged silence. Even if the end user is a modem or fax, disconnect indication is not required because this type of device can detect when it loses the carrier from the far end. However, complications arise when the FXO port is part of another switching system, such as a PBX or voice gateway. During loop-start signaling, the status, or battery state, of the FXS device never changes. If the FXO port is on another switching device, the remote end might become disconnected, but the PBX or Voice over IP (VoIP) gateway has no indication of the disconnect. In this case, the FXO port can be left in a hung state.

The FXS port can signal call disconnect to the FXO port using several methods:

- If you use ground-start signaling, the FXO receives a disconnect indication when the voltage level changes.

- If you use loop-start signaling, you can configure the FXS port to temporarily deny power when the call disconnects. The FXO port can sense this short loss of power and disconnect the call. Power denial support is enabled by default on Cisco FXO ports.

- You can configure the FXS for battery reversal using the **battery-reversal** command under voice port configuration. FXS ports normally reverse battery polarity at the point of far-end answer. You can set the FXS to reverse the polarity again during far-end hang-up to indicate disconnect to the FXO.

- The FXS can send a tone-based supervisory disconnect to the FXO. After receiving this tone, the FXO port knows that the call has disconnected. The tone that is sent varies by country. Example 5-2 shows how to configure Supervisory Tone Disconnect on an FXO port.

Example 5-2 *Configuring Supervisory Tone Disconnect*

```
Gateway#config t
Gateway(config)#voice-port 2/0/0
Gateway(config-voiceport)#supervisory disconnect dualtone mid-call
Gateway(config-voiceport)#cptone us
Gateway(config-voiceport)#timeouts wait-release 5
Gateway(config-voiceport)#timeouts call-disconnect 5
Gateway(config-voiceport)#exit
```

If the default disconnect tone for a country does not work, you can specifically define the tone. You can modify settings for frequencies, power, delay, and cadence. You must obtain from the service provider the information that is required to configure the tone, or you must determine it using a frequency analyzer. Example 5-3 shows how to customize the disconnect tone.

Example 5-3 *Customizing the Supervisory Disconnect Tone*

```
Gateway #configure terminal
Gateway(config)#voice-port 3/1/1
Gateway(config-voiceport)#supervisory disconnect dualtone pre-connect voice-class
10
Gateway(config-voiceport)#end

 Gateway(config)#voice class dualtone 10
    Gateway(config-voice-class)#freq-pair 1 350 440
    Gateway(config-voice-class)#freq-max-deviation 5
    Gateway(config-voice-class)#freq-max-power 6
    Gateway(config-voice-class)#freq-min-power 25
    Gateway(config-voice-class)#freq-power-twist 15
    Gateway(config-voice-class)#freq-max-delay 16
    Gateway(config-voice-class)#cadence-min-on-time 100
    Gateway(config-voice-class)#cadence-max-off-time 250
    Gateway(config-voice-class)#cadence-list 1 100 100 300 300 100 200 200 200
    Gateway(config-voice-class)#cadence-variation 8
    Gateway(config-voice-class)#exit
```

CAMA

Centralized Automated Message Accounting (CAMA) is an old telephony protocol that was developed for long-distance billing but is widely used today in the United States for enhanced 911 (E911) services. The protocol allows for both the calling and called number to be carried using in-band signaling. This is needed in 911 calling because 911 calls are routed to the appropriate service center based on the calling number. CAMA allows the telephone company to transmit the calling number to the public safety answering point (PSAP) dispatcher prior to establishing the audio connection. This is crucial information because it tells the dispatcher the exact location that the call is coming from and provides callback information if the call is disconnected.

Most E911 networks are standalone entities within their own region. Many states have laws requiring that businesses connect directly to the local E911 network, and this legislation is expected to be passed throughout the United States in the near term. More than 80 percent of the E911 networks in the United States consist of CAMA trunks, whereas some E911 regions allow alternative connections, such as ISDN. A CAMA trunk can either be an analog telephone line carrying MF signaling or a voice T1 with MF signaling. The enterprise device, whether it is a voice gateway or PBX, connects directly to the E911 device. This device routes the call to the appropriate PSAP based on the calling number of the incoming call.

You can configure VIC2 FXO ports to support CAMA signaling.

E&M

E&M signaling was developed to interconnect PBXs using dedicated circuits from the PSTN. Unlike the 2-wire FXS/FXO circuits, E&M circuits are 8-wire. The voice path uses either 2-wire or 4-wire. The remaining four wires are used for signaling. Table 5-2 lists the wires, or leads, that are used in E&M circuits.

Table 5-2   *E&M Leads*

Lead	Description	Pin
SB	-48V signaling battery	1
M	Signaling input	2
R	Ring, audio input	3
R1	Ring, audio input/output	4
T1	Tip, audio input/output	5
T	Tip, audio input	6
E	Signaling output	7
SG	Signaling ground	8

E&M comes in six common variants: E&M Types I through V and E&M SSDC5. This section discusses E&M Types I through V. The Type indicates how the various signaling leads are used to indicate an off-hook or trunk seizure condition.

Type I Signaling

Type I signaling is the most common version seen in North America. Battery is provided on both the E and the M lead. During on-hook, both of the leads are open. The trunk circuit side indicates off-hook by connecting the M lead to the battery, while the signaling unit indicates off-hook by grounding the E lead, as shown in Figure 5-1.

Figure 5-1 *E&M Type I Signaling*

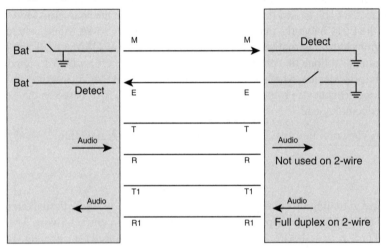

Condition	M Lead	E Lead
On-Hook	Ground	Open
Off-Hook	Battery	Ground

Type II Signaling

Type II signaling interfaces cause little interference and are typically used for sensitive environments. These interfaces use four leads for signaling: E, M, SB, and SG. During on-hook, both the E and M lead are open. The trunk side indicates off-hook by connecting the M lead to the SB lead connected to the battery of the signaling side. The signaling side indicates off-hook by connecting the E lead to the SG lead that is connected to the trunk circuit ground.

Type III Signaling

Type III signaling is not commonly used. It also uses four leads, but during on-hook, the E lead is open and the M lead is set to the ground that is connected to the SG lead of the signaling side. The trunk side indicates off-hook by moving the M lead connection from the

SG lead to the SB lead of the signaling side. The signaling unit indicates off-hook by grounding the E lead.

Type IV Signaling

Type IV signaling is similar to Type II. It also uses four leads, and during on-hook, both the E and the M leads are open. The trunk side indicates off-hook by connecting the M lead to the SB lead that is connected to the ground of the signaling side. The signaling side indicates off-hook by connecting the E lead to the SG lead that is connected to the ground of the trunk side.

NOTE	Cisco E&M voice interface cards (VIC) do not support E&M Type IV signaling.

Type V Signaling

Type V signaling is the most common mechanism used outside of North America. It is similar to Type I, and it only uses the E and M leads. During on-hook, both leads are open. The trunk side indicates off-hook by grounding the M lead, while the signaling side indicates off-hook by grounding the E lead, as shown in Figure 5-2.

Figure 5-2   *E&M Type V Signaling*

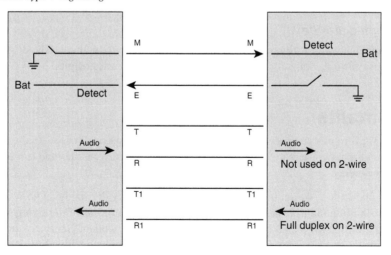

Condition	M Lead	E Lead
On-Hook	Open	Open
Off-Hook	Ground	Ground

Address Signaling

E&M supports three mechanisms of start dial signaling used between off-hook and digit collection: wink-start, delay-start, and immediate-start. Like FXS/FXO, both pulse dialing and DTMF can be used for address transmission.

Wink-Start

In wink-start operation, the originating device goes off-hook using the signaling leads as determined by the Type configuration. When the remote switch detects that the originating switch is off-hook, it transmits an off-hook pulse of approximately 140 to 290 ms in duration and then returns to the on-hook state. This is the "wink." The originating switch detects the wink, waits for at least 100 ms, and then outputs digits to the remote switch. The remote switch extends the call based on the received digits. After the called party answers the call, the remote switch indicates call answer by transmitting off-hook.

Delay-Start

During delay-start, the originating switch waits a configurable time before inspecting the incoming signal from the remote switch. If the signal indicates on-hook, the originating switch outputs digits to the remote switch. If the signal is off-hook, the originating office waits until the signal returns to on-hook before forwarding digits. The remote switch indicates call answer by transmitting off-hook.

Immediate-Start

Immediate-start is the most basic of the trunk-signaling methods. The originating switch goes off-hook, waits for at least 150 ms, and then forwards digits.

Digital Circuits

Digital circuits provide significant advantages over analog circuits. Analog circuits require one port per conversation, which can result in port density issues and can be susceptible to interference.

Digital circuits overcome some of these limitations by digitizing audio waveforms and transmitting multiple calls over a single circuit. The process of digitizing an analog signal requires that the signal be sampled, quantified, and encoded. Henry Nyquist, who was an engineer at AT&T, developed a method for digitizing analog signals in 1924. What is known as Nyquist's theorem states that to digitize an analog signal, the signal must be sampled at a rate twice that of the highest frequency. Although human speech has a wide range, analog telephone channels typically carry frequencies in ranges between 200 and 3300 Hz. Because of variations in the frequency ranges supported at the time, Nyquist set the maximum frequency at 4000 Hz, resulting in a sampling rate of 8000 times per second. Each of these 8000 samples is quantified, or assigned a numerical value, based on a reference scale. The scale uses 255 values, which can be encoded using 8 bits.

T1

T1 circuits evolved in early voice networks as a mechanism to transfer multiple calls across one copper transmission medium. The copper loop can carry significantly more bandwidth than the 4000 Hz required for voice transmission. By electronically changing the voice frequency of incoming calls, frequency division multiplexing (FDM) was used to carry 24 calls across one copper loop using 96000 Hz of spectrum. Today, digital transmission has changed the T1 into a TDM circuit transmitting 1s and 0s instead of analog signals.

One voice channel in digital form requires 64 kbps of bandwidth. This is calculated by multiplying the 8000 samples per second × 8 bits per sample = 64 kbps. This 64-kbps package is known as the *digital signal level zero*, or DS-0. At 64 kbps, the 24 voice channels represent 1.536 Mbps of data. An additional 8000 bps were added for framing, bringing the speed of the T1 circuit to 1.544 Mbps.

Framing is the mechanism used by transmitting devices to ensure the synchronization and organization of user data. A T1 time slot is an 8-bit segment for each DS-0. A frame consists of 24 time slots and one framing bit, for a total of 193 bits. The transmitting and receiving equipment use the framing bit; the bit does not contain user data. It must be recognizable in the transmission, so the receiver looks for a pattern that repeats every 12 frames: 100011011100. This 12-frame unit is called a *Super Frame* (SF), or D4. In some cases, the voice signaling is transmitted by using the least significant bit of the sixth and twelfth frame of the SF. The A-bit is robbed from the sixth frame, and the B-bit is robbed from the twelfth frame. Table 5-3 illustrates an SF. The bolded rows show the position of the signaling bits if robbed-bit signaling is used.

Table 5-3   *SF (D4)*

Frame Number	Framing Bit	Channel 1	Channel 2	Channel 3-23	Channel 24
1	1	12345678	12345678	12345678	12345678
2	0	12345678	12345678	12345678	12345678
3	0	12345678	12345678	12345678	12345678
4	0	12345678	12345678	12345678	12345678
5	1	12345678	12345678	12345678	12345678
6	**1**	**1234567A**	**1234567A**	**1234567A**	**1234567A**
7	0	12345678	12345678	12345678	12345678
8	1	12345678	12345678	12345678	12345678
9	1	12345678	12345678	12345678	12345678

continues

Table 5-3 *SF (D4) (Continued)*

Frame Number	Framing Bit	Channel 1	Channel 2	Channel 3-23	Channel 24
10	1	12345678	12345678	12345678	12345678
11	0	12345678	12345678	12345678	12345678
12	**0**	**1234567B**	**1234567B**	**1234567B**	**1234567B**

As digital technology arose, the need for more signaling states led to the development of the Extended Superframe (ESF). ESF doubled the number of frames in the SF from 12 to 24. This allowed for two more signaling bits, C and D, to be robbed from frames 18 and 24, respectively. As technology advanced, only 2 kbps were required for synchronization in a 6-bit framing pattern 001011. The other framing bits are used to carry 2 kbps of CRC error checking and 4 kbps of data link information, such as performance information or alarms. Table 5-4 illustrates an ESF frame. In the table, FPS indicates a synchronization bit, DL indicates a data link bit, and CRC indicates a CRC bit.

Table 5-4 *ESF Frame*

Frame Number	Framing Bit	Channel 1	Channel 2	Channel 3-23	Channel 24
1	1/0 DL	12345678	12345678	12345678	12345678
2	1/0 CRC1	12345678	12345678	12345678	12345678
3	1/0 DL	12345678	12345678	12345678	12345678
4	0 FPS	12345678	12345678	12345678	12345678
5	1/0 DL	12345678	12345678	12345678	12345678
6	**1/0 CRC2**	**1234567A**	**1234567A**	**1234567A**	**1234567A**
7	1/0 DL	12345678	12345678	12345678	12345678
8	0 FPS	12345678	12345678	12345678	12345678
9	1/0 DL	12345678	12345678	12345678	12345678
10	1/0 CRC3	12345678	12345678	12345678	12345678
11	1/0 DL	12345678	12345678	12345678	12345678
12	**1 FPS**	**1234567B**	**1234567B**	**1234567B**	**1234567B**
13	1/0 DL	12345678	12345678	12345678	12345678
14	1/0 CRC4	12345678	12345678	12345678	12345678
15	1/0 DL	12345678	12345678	12345678	12345678
16	0 FPS	12345678	12345678	12345678	12345678
17	1/0 DL	12345678	12345678	12345678	12345678
18	**1/0 CRC5**	**1234567C**	**1234567C**	**1234567C**	**1234567C**

Table 5-4   *ESF Frame (Continued)*

Frame Number	Framing Bit	Channel 1	Channel 2	Channel 3-23	Channel 24
19	1/0 DL	12345678	12345678	12345678	12345678
20	1 FPS	12345678	12345678	12345678	12345678
21	1/0 DL	12345678	12345678	12345678	12345678
22	1/0 CRC6	12345678	12345678	12345678	12345678
23	1/0 DL	12345678	12345678	12345678	12345678
24	**1 FPS**	**1234567D**	**1234567D**	**1234567D**	**1234567D**

Channel-Associated Signaling

As described earlier, bit robbing allows using the least significant bit in some timeslots to transmit signaling information—the sixth and twelfth frame for SF; and the sixth, twelfth, eighteenth, and twenty-fourth frame for ESF. This method of voice signaling on a T1 is known as *channel-associated signaling* (CAS) or *in-band signaling*. The common forms of signaling on CAS circuits are the same as analog circuits: loop-start, ground-start, and E&M.

In loop-start operation, the FXO uses the B bit, and the FXS uses the A bit. In the on-hook state, the FXS transmits an A bit value of 0, and the FXO transmits a B bit value of 0. To indicate an incoming call, the FXO rings the FXS by toggling the B bit between 0 and 1. The FXS responds by going into the on-hook state and setting the A bit to 1. During a disconnect, the FXO does not change signaling state, and the FXS must detect the end of the call and toggle the A bit back to 0.

Ground-start operation requires the FXO to use both the A and the B bit, whereas in most applications, the FXS still only uses the A bit. In the on-hook state, both the A and B bits of the FXO are set to 1, and the A bit of the FXS is set to 0. During a call from the FXO to the FXS, the FXO sets the A bit to 0 and toggles the B bit to indicate ringing. FXS detects the ringing and sets the A bit to 1 to indicate off-hook. The network goes off-hook by keeping the A bit at 0 and setting the B bit to 1. When the call disconnects, the FXO sets the A bit to 1; upon detection, the FXS sets the A bit to 0 to indicate on-hook.

E&M Signaling

E&M signaling is the preferred method when using T1 CAS circuits. Both network and user transmit all 0s for on-hook and all 1s for off-hook or line seizure. The different methods of E&M signaling described in the "Analog Circuits" section of this chapter are applicable for digital CAS circuits. Cisco voice gateways support the following E&M signaling types:

- **e&m-wink-start (Feature Group B [FGB])**—The receiving side acknowledges that the originator is off-hook by toggling the A and B bit from 0 to 1 for approximately 200 ms. After the wink, the originator sends the address information.

- **e&m-delay-dial**—The originator goes off-hook and waits 200 ms. Then it verifies that the receiver is on-hook before sending address information.

- **e&m-immediate-start**—The originator goes off-hook and sends the address information. The receiver goes off-hook after receiving the digits.

- **e&m-fgd (Feature Group D [FGD])**—The receiving side acknowledges that the originator is off-hook with a wink. After the wink, the originator sends the address information. The receiver acknowledges the digits with a second wink. FGD allows receipt of additional address information such as ANI.

- **fgd-eana**—FGD Exchange Access North America uses the same double-wink mechanism as FGD. FGD-EANA allows sending additional address information to support call services such as ANI or emergency calls.

- **fgd-os**—FGD Operator Services is used for calls from a Bell Operating Company sent toward the carrier switch. It is not typically used in enterprise environments.

NOTE   Only the AS5x00 family fully supports FGB. If your service provider is not sending ANI, e&m-wink-start can be used to connect an FGB circuit to other Cisco voice gateways.

Feature Group D

FGD defines the rules that are used for connection between local carriers and interexchange carriers. A trunk that is running the FGD protocol ensures equal access of services for the different carriers. This allows options for end customers and fair access to all services available from all carriers. The protocol passes information, such as the ANI, or calling number, across the FGD trunk.

Both e&m-fgd and fgd-eana support the delivery of DNIS, or called number. e&m-fgd can receive but not send ANI. Fgd-eana can send but not receive ANI. If you require both incoming and outgoing ANI information, you need to have two circuits or circuit groups, as shown in Example 5-4.

Example 5-4   *Sending and Receiving ANI Using FGD*

```
Gateway#config t
Gateway(config)#controller t1 1/0
Gateway(config)#framing esf
Gateway(config)#linecode b8zs
Gateway(config-controller)#ds0-group 1 timeslots 1-12 type e&m-fgd
Gateway(config-controller)#ds0-group 2 timeslots 13-24 type fgd-eana
Gateway(config-controller)#end
Gateway#
```

DS-0 group 1 is used for inbound calls and can receive ANI. DS-0 group 2 is used for outbound calls and can send ANI.

E1

An E1 circuit is similar to a T1 in that it is a TDM circuit that carries DS-0s in a bundled connection. The E1 is widely used in countries in Europe, Asia, and South/Central America. The framing format for E1 circuits is defined in Consultative Committee for International Telegraph and Telephone (CCITT) recommendation G.704 and is supplemented by G.732. It consists of 32 timeslots and a transmission rate of 2.048 Mbps. Of the 32 timeslots, 1 is used for framing, 1 is used for telephony signaling, and 30 are available for user data. Timeslot 0 is used for framing, alarm transport, and international bits. The standard also allows for optional CRC-4 error checking. Timeslot 16 is used to carry signaling information, whether it is CAS, ISDN, SS7, or proprietary signaling.

Cisco supports the same CAS methods on E1 circuits as T1 circuits. Cisco also supports Mercury Exchange Limited (MEL) CAS versions of E&M and FXO/FXS signaling. MEL CAS is primarily used in the United Kingdom.

E1 R2

R2 signaling is defined in ITU Recommendations Q.400 through Q.490 and uses two types of signaling: line signaling and inter-register signaling. R2 signaling is either an international version known as CCITT-R2 or a country-specific variant. Cisco supports both the International Telephony Union (ITU) standard and many country and regional variants.

Line Signaling

Line signaling is used for supervisory signals for call setup and teardown. R2 supports three methods of line signaling:

- **R2-Digital**—R2-Digital is defined in ITU-U Q.421. It is typically used for pulse code modulation (PCM) systems and is described in more detail in this section.

- **R2-Analog**—R2-Analog is defined in ITU-U Q.411 and is typically used in carrier systems. Signaling uses a Tone/A bit.

- **R2-Pulse**—R2-Pulse is defined in ITU-U Supplement 7. It is a variant of R2-Analog in which the Tone/A bit is pulsed rather than continuous, and is typically used for satellite links.

R2-Digital signaling uses CAS carried in timeslot 0 of the E1 frame. Of the four bits that are available, only the A and B bits are used by R2 line signaling. In the on-hook state, the A bit is set to 1 and the B bit is set to 0. These bits have different meanings depending on which side is initiating the call. For the purpose of this discussion, *forward* is defined as bits coming from the calling party, and *backward* is defined as bits coming from the called party. Table 5-5 lists the bit settings for CCITT-R2 signaling.

Table 5-5   *R2 Signaling Bits*

Direction	Signal Type	A Bit	B Bit
Forward	Seizure (off-hook)	1 -> 0	0
Forward	Clear (on-hook)	0 -> 1	0
Backward	Seizure-ack	1	0 -> 1
Backward	Answer	1 -> 0	1
Backward	Clear-back	0 -> 1	1
Backward	Release-guard	0 -> 1	1 -> 0

NOTE   0 -> 1 indicates a bit state transition from 0 to 1. A single digit indicates that the bit state does not change.

Inter-Register Signaling

Register is the term used to describe the switches at each end of the E1 circuit. Therefore, inter-register signaling is used between the switches, or registers, for both address and informational messaging. Informational messaging between registers includes information on priority levels, congestion notification, or charges. Inter-register signaling uses multifrequency tones in the timeslot used for the call so that it is in-band signaling. This signaling is a form of *multifrequency compelled* (MFC) signaling, meaning that a signal from one end is acknowledged by a tone from the opposite end. Most country variants of R2 involve inter-register signaling.

Forward signals are signals from the calling party toward the called party and are classified as Group-I or Group-II signals. Group-I signals convey address information, including DNIS and ANI. Group-II signals identify additional information about the calling party, such as priority level. Backward signals are signals from the called party to the calling party and are classified as Group-A or Group-B. Group-A signals acknowledge Group-I signals and convey additional information, such as congestion. Group-B signals acknowledge Group-II signals and provide called party information. Table 5-6 lists the R2 inter-register signal types.

Table 5-6   *Inter-Register Signals*

Group	Signal	Function
Group-I	I-1 to I-10	Digits 1 to 10
	I-15	Indicates end of address
Group-II	II-1	Subscriber without priority
	II-2 to II-9	Subscriber priority levels
	II-11 to II-15	For national use
Group-A	A-1	Send next digit
	A-3	Address complete
	A-4	Congestion
	A-5	Send calling party category
	A-6	Address complete, charge, setup, speech conditions
Group-B	B-3	Subscriber busy
	B-4	Congestion
	B-5	Unallocated number
	B-6	Subscriber line free charge

Cisco voice gateways support four types of inter-register signaling:

- **R2-Compelled**—Forward tones stay on until the remote end responds. The tones are compelled to stay on until you turn them off.

- **R2-Noncompelled**—Forward tones are sent as pulses. Group-B responses are also sent as pulses. Noncompelled inter-register signaling has no Group-A signals.

NOTE   Most installations use the noncompelled type of inter-register signaling.

- **R2-Semi-Compelled**—Forward tones are sent as compelled. Responses are sent as pulses. Semi-compelled is the same as compelled, except that the backward signals are pulsed instead of continuous.

- **DTMF**—In-band DTMF tones are used for address signaling.

ISDN

ISDN is a digitized service offering of telephone carriers to allow users to transmit voice, data, video, and other applications over existing telephone wiring. With ISDN, one channel, called a D-channel, is designated as the signaling channel. It is either 16 kbps or 64 kbps. User data is carried in 64-kbps channels, which are called B–channels, or bearer channels. Because all signaling occurs on the D-channel, ISDN is also called common channel signaling (CCS).

ISDN circuits come in two types: BRI and PRI. A BRI consists of two B-channels and one 16-kbps D-channel, for a total bandwidth of 144 kbps. A T1 PRI consists of 23 B-channels and 1 64-kbps D-channel. An E1 PRI consists of 30 B-channels and 1 64-kbps D-channel.

In its early history, ISDN was the high-speed connection of choice for end users. Quick connection time, the ability to have more bandwidth, and the option to connect several services to one line made ISDN much more attractive than dial services. With the advent of broadband residential services, such as cable and digital subscriber line (DSL), the popularity of ISDN in the home has diminished. The BRI is still used in many data applications, typically as a backup to a WAN connection or for voice connections in Europe, and the PRI is used widely in voice applications.

Covering all aspects of ISDN would take an entire book. This section focuses on the aspects required to connect an ISDN PRI circuit to a Cisco voice gateway.

ISDN Switch Configuration

For PRIs, a Cisco voice gateway acts as an ISDN switch. Various switch types are defined. ISDN switches use a master/slave designation to control signaling. One switch is designated as the network side, or master, and one switch is designated as the user side, or slave. The ISDN Layer 2 protocol Link Access Procedure, D-channel (LAPD) establishes and maintains the D-channel. To establish the D-channel, the network/user configuration must be correct. When connecting to the PSTN, the gateway should be the user side. When connecting to a PBX, either the gateway or the PBX must be configured for the network side. Table 5-7 lists the switch types that Cisco voice gateways support.

Table 5-7   *ISDN Switch Types for PRI*

Switch Type	Description	User Side	Network Side
4ESS	Lucent 4ESS—United States	Y	Y
5ESS	Lucent 5ESS—United States	Y	Y
DMS100	Northern Telecom DMS100—United States	Y	Y
DPNSS	DPNSS—Europe	Y	Y

Table 5-7   *ISDN Switch Types for PRI (Continued)*

Net5	United Kingdom, Europe, Asia and Australia	Y	Y
NI-2	National ISDN—United States	Y	Y
NTT	Japan	Y	Y
QSIG	QSIG	Y	Y
TS014	Australia (Obsolete)	Y	N

The following steps are required to configure a PRI on a Cisco voice gateway:

Step 1   Set the ISDN switch type in global configuration mode using the **isdn switch-type** command:

```
Gateway(config)#isdn switch-type primary-ni
```

Step 2   Configure the controller using the **pri-group** command:

```
Gateway(config)#controller T1 1/0
Gateway(config-controller)pri-group timeslots 1-24
```

Only one PRI group is supported on a T1 or E1. Fractional PRIs are supported. For example, you can configure 12 B-channels. The D-channel is always required. If you do not include the D-channel in the timeslot range, it is added for you.

When you configure a PRI group on a controller, the gateway creates a serial interface. For controller 1/0 shown in the example, this interface is referenced as Serial 1/0:23 for T1s and Serial 1/0:15 for E1s.

Step 3   If necessary, configure the serial interface for network-side support using the **isdn protocol-emulate** command:

```
Gateway(config)#interface serial1/0:23
Gateway(config-if)#isdn protocol-emulate network
```

You can also modify the switch type for each PRI if required using the **isdn switch-type** command under the serial interface.

Step 4   Verify the ISDN status using the **show isdn status** command:

```
Gateway#show isdn status
Global ISDN Switchtype = primary-ni
ISDN Serial1/0:23 interface
        dsl 0, interface ISDN Switchtype = primary-ni
    Layer 1 Status:
        ACTIVE
    Layer 2 Status:
        TEI = 0, Ces = 1, SAPI = 0, State = MULTIPLE_FRAME_ESTABLISHED
```

```
Layer 3 Status:
    0 Active Layer 3 Call(s)
Active dsl 0 CCBs = 0
The Free Channel Mask:  0x80000FFF
Number of L2 Discards = 0, L2 Session ID = 16
Total Allocated ISDN CCBs = 0
```

ISDN Call Signaling

ISDN performs supervisory, address, and informational signaling using Layer 3 messages that are sent on the D-channel. Figure 5-3 shows the ISDN Layer 3 message format.

Figure 5-3 *ISDN Layer 3 Message Format*

8	7	6	5	4	3	2	1
Protocol Discriminator							
0	0	0	0	Call Ref Value Length			
Flag	Call Reference Value						
Call Reference Value (if 2 octets)							
0	Message Type						
Information Elements (one or more octets)							

- **Protocol Discriminator**—Identifies the protocol type used.
- **Call Ref Value Length**—Indicates the length of the Call Reference Value.
- **Flag**—Set to 0 if the message sender assigned the Call Reference Value. Set to 1 if the message sender did not assign the Call Reference Value.
- **Call Reference Value**—Arbitrary number assigned to identify a call.
- **Message Type**—Defines the function of the message. Message types are described later in this section.
- **Information Elements**—Additional information as required. Information Elements are described in more detail later in this section.

The message type is typically one octet. The first bit is always 0. The next two bits are used to group message types. The last five bits define the message. Table 5-8 lists common message types. The capitalized portion of the message is what appears in a debug of ISDN messages.

Table 5-8   *Common ISDN Message Types*

Call Establishment (000)		Call Clearing (010)	
000 00001	ALERTing	010 00101	DISConnect
000 00010	CALL PROCeeding	010 00110	Restart
000 00011	PROGress	010 01110	Restart ACK
000 00101	SETUP	010 01101	RELease
000 01101	SETUP ACK	010 11010	RELease COMplete
000 00111	CONNect	–	–
000 01111	CONN ACK	–	–
Call Information (001)		Miscellaneous (011)	
001 00000	USER INFO	011 00000	SEGment
001 00101	SUSPend	011 00010	FACility
001 00001	SUSP REJ	011 01110	NOTIFY
001 01101	SUSP ACK	011 10101	STATUS ENQuiry
001 00110	RESume	011 11001	Congestion
001 00010	RES REJ	011 11011	INFO
001 01110	RES ACK	011 11101	STATUS

Call setup and call clearing message types provide the supervisory signaling. Figure 5-4 illustrates a typical message flow in an ISDN call.

Figure 5-4   *ISDN Message Flow*

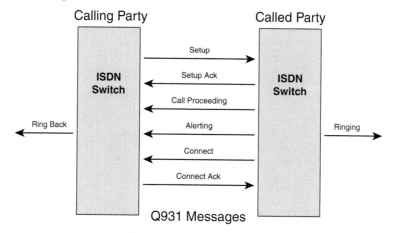

Information Elements

The Information Element (IE) field in the message type is used to convey specific information regarding the call. For example, a DISConnect or RELease message includes a CAUSE IE that indicates why the call was terminated.

The common IEs are as follows:

- **Channel ID**—Indicates the channel that is being used. Included in Call Establishment and Call Clearing messages.

- **Cause**—Indicates the reason that a call was terminated or that call setup failed.

- **Display**—Sends information to be displayed, such as calling name or number. Some switch types use Facility IEs for calling name information.

- **Facility**—Invokes supplemental services.

- **Progress**—Used for informational feedback, such as ring or network announcements. For example, "The number you have dialed is not in service."

You can view the ISDN Layer 3 messages by issuing the **debug isdn q931** command. Example 5-5 shows the debug output for a call that is placed from 4085550123 to 12012012002.

Example 5-5   *ISDN Q931 Debug*

```
Gateway#debug isdn q931
debug isdn q931 is              ON.
Gateway#
*May  2 04:07:10.727: ISDN Se1/0:23 Q931: Applying typeplan for sw-type 0xD is 0
x0 0x0, Calling num 4085550123
*May  2 04:07:10.731: ISDN Se1/0:23 Q931: Applying typeplan for sw-type 0xD is 0
x0 0x0, Called num 12012012002
*May  2 04:07:10.731: ISDN Se1/0:23 Q931: TX -> SETUP pd = 8  callref = 0x0022
        Bearer Capability i = 0x9090A2
                Standard = CCITT
                Transer Capability = 3.1kHz Audio
                Transfer Mode = Circuit
                Transfer Rate = 64 kbit/s
        Channel ID i = 0xA98381
                Exclusive, Channel 1
        Progress Ind i = 0x8183 - Origination address is non-ISDN
        Calling Party Number i = 0x80, '408550123'
                Plan:Unknown, Type:Unknown
        Called Party Number i = 0x80, '12012012002'
                Plan:Unknown, Type:Unknown
*May  2 04:07:10.779: ISDN Se1/0:23 Q931: RX <- CALL_PROC pd = 8  callref = 0x80
22
        Channel ID i = 0xA98381
                Exclusive, Channel 1
*May  2 04:07:10.923: ISDN Se1/0:23 Q931: RX <- ALERTING pd = 8  callref = 0x802
2
        Progress Ind i = 0x8088 - In-band info or appropriate now available
*May  2 04:07:19.859: ISDN Se1/0:23 Q931: RX <- CONNECT pd = 8  callref = 0x8022
```

Example 5-5   *ISDN Q931 Debug (Continued)*

```
*May  2 04:07:19.859: ISDN Se1/0:23 Q931: TX -> CONNECT_ACK pd = 8  callref = 0x
0022
*May  2 04:07:25.859: %ISDN-6-CONNECT: Interface Serial1/0:0 is now connected to
 12012012002 unknown
*May  2 04:07:42.855: %ISDN-6-DISCONNECT: Interface Serial1/0:0  disconnected fr
om 12012012002 , call lasted 22 seconds
*May  2 04:07:42.855: ISDN Se1/0:23 Q931: TX -> DISCONNECT pd = 8  callref = 0x0
022
        Cause i = 0x8090 - Normal call clearing
*May  2 04:07:42.871: ISDN Se1/0:23 Q931: RX <- RELEASE pd = 8  callref = 0x8022
*May  2 04:07:42.875: ISDN Se1/0:23 Q931: TX -> RELEASE_COMP pd = 8  callref = 0
x0022
```

Address Types

ISDN includes two identifiers that are used to classify the calling and called numbers. These are the number plan identification (NPI) and the type of number (TON). These identifiers are highlighted in the setup message in Example 5-4. The NPI and TON sometimes determine how a call is routed or how the number is displayed. They can also be used for accounting purposes. Many newer switch types ignore the NPI and TON. The NPI and TON are specified in the third octet of the Calling and Called part IEs. The NPI is specified in bits 1 through 4, and the TON is specified in bits 5 through 7. Table 5-9 lists the defined NPIs, and Table 5-10 lists the defined TONs.

Table 5-9   *NPIs*

NPI Bits	NPI	Related Standard
0 0 0 0	Unknown	–
0 0 0 1	ISDN Telephony	E.164 (described below)
0 0 1 1	Data	X.121
0 1 0 0	Telex	F.69
0 1 0 1	Maritime Mobile	E.210 and E.211
0 1 0 1	Land Mobile	E.212
0 1 1 1	ISDN/Mobile	E214
1 0 0 0	National Standard	–
1 0 0 1	Private	–
1 1 1 1	Reserved for Extension	–

Table 5-10 *TONs*

TON Bits	TON
0 0 0	Unknown
0 0 1	International
0 1 0	National
0 1 1	Network Specific
1 0 0	Subscriber
1 1 0	Abbreviated
1 1 1	Reserved for extension

ITU Recommendation E.164, "Numbering Plan for the ISDN Era," defines specifics on how to build a numbering plan to allow interoperability between the numerous public networks. E.164 specifies a format for an international ISDN number, which is variable length arranged in specific fields, as follows:

- **Country Code (CC)**—The country code is a one, two, or three-digit code representing a specific country or region.

- **National (Significant) Number (N(S)N)**—The N(S)N is the number used to select the destination subscriber. The N(S)N is further defined as containing the following fields:

  - **National Destination Code (NDC)**—The NDC is variable in length and contains Destination Network (DN) or Trunk Codes (TC) to indicate how to route a call. This is commonly called an area code.

  - **Subscriber Number (SN)**—SN is variable in length and is assigned to end subscribers.

NFAS

Non-Facility Associated Signaling (NFAS) is an ISDN feature that allows you to share one D-channel for multiple PRI lines. This allows you to use all of the DS-0s on some PRIs as B-channels and increase the amount of user data available. For example, if you have five PRI lines configured for NFAS with only the first PRI providing a D-channel, you will gain four additional B-channels across the bundle. NFAS also allows for a backup D-channel if the primary channel fails. The bundle of T1s configured in an NFAS group and signaled by a common D-channel is typically referred to as a *trunk group*.

QSIG

Q Signaling (QSIG) is an alternative to Q.931 that is used for interconnection in private integrated services network exchange (PINX), consisting of PBXs, key systems, and CallManager. It is an ISDN variant based on Q.931 that is used worldwide for the interconnection of private telephony devices. QSIG consists of three sublayers: Basic Call, Generic Function, and Supplementary Services. Basic Call is an extension of Q.931 that is used to provide call setup, maintenance, and clearing support. Generic Function enables transparent transmission of QSIG facility messages to allow supplementary services and network features. Supplementary Services provide additional functions.

One of the most important qualities of QSIG is its flexibility as a signaling agent. Feature transparency allows for features to be carried between two different QSIG endpoints even if intermediate switching devices do not support the feature set. This allows feature support across multiple vendors and the development of new proprietary features without concerns of interoperability. Flexibility in the number plan, network topology, networking transport, and application allows QSIG to be widely deployed in many environments. QSIG has also been adopted by all the major PBX manufacturers to ensure consistent development.

Echo Cancellation

Echo is an intrusive condition that has existed on telephone networks since their inception. The human ear is sensitive to fluctuations in voice, and the inherent delay that is involved in telecommunications can cause echo on the line to disrupt the user experience. The primary source of echo in traditional telephone networks is line-side echo caused by 2-wire to 4-wire hybrids. These hybrids convert the 2-wire circuit coming from the subscriber loop to the 4-wire trunk circuit. A mismatch in impedance in these devices causes a portion of the "talk" energy to be reflected back onto the receive side. If the delay in this return voice energy is sufficient, the speaker hears his own voice disruptively echoing on the line. Acoustic echo occurs when the microphone of the user picks up the voice of the user multiple times: once when the user speaks, and then again as the voice energy is reflected back from the environment and transmitted by the microphone. Acoustic echo is caused by a faulty device with poor acoustic isolation between the speaker and microphone. Some headsets and speaker phones cause acoustic echo. In modern telecommunications, the analog to digital conversion and the use of bandwidth-saving compression techniques can increase the problems that are associated with echo.

You can control echo by using several mechanisms: balancing impedance on hybrids, inserting loss into the path of the return signal, using echo cancellers, and minimizing the delay. Efforts are made to balance the impedance in a voice network, but imbalance, and the resulting echo, is inevitable. Because of the need to maintain levels and the inevitable delay inserted due to digital processing, the most practical method of controlling echo in networks is the use of an echo cancellation device. Echo cancellers work by using digital signal processors (DSP) and application-specific integrated circuits (ASIC) to sample the signal and model the signal characteristics and echo in the path. The canceller then compares the returning voice path with the model and dynamically removes the echo.

You can also effectively use cancellers to mitigate the amount of intrusive background noise by adding attenuation and effectively lowering the dB levels of the background noise. This is done by the nonlinear processor (NLP) of the echo canceller. It samples the background noise to learn the frequencies and then uses this information to drop the dB levels. Another important function of the NLP is to generate comfort noise in periods of the conversation when neither party is speaking. This white noise on the line is necessary, because if the line is entirely clean, the speakers believe that the call has been disconnected.

Review Questions

1 Which port type should you use to connect to a 2-wire analog service connecting to the PSTN for both inbound and outbound calling?

2 What types of signaling are required on a voice circuit?

3 What is the difference between CAS and CCS on an E1 circuit?

4 What is the difference between SF and ESF?

5 What two types of echo are possible on a voice circuit?

6 Which signaling type supports ANI on T1 CAS circuits?

7 Which line signaling method should you use on an E1 r2 satellite link?

8 What component of an ISDN message is used to carry information about the call?

CHAPTER 6

Connecting to the PSTN

One of the most important functions of the Cisco voice gateway is to provide an interface from a packet voice network to a time-division multiplexing (TDM) network, such as the public switched telephone network (PSTN) or a PBX. This connection enables you to place calls to, or receive calls from, the outside world, and it can also assist in migration from a TDM PBX to a Voice over IP (VoIP) solution. In this chapter, you will learn about the connection methods used between the Cisco voice gateway and the PSTN.

This chapter helps you to do the following:

- Understand the factors that affect circuit selection when connecting to the PSTN

- Understand the benefits and limitations of each of the different types of circuits available

- Understand the information needed from the PSTN to properly configure a PSTN trunk circuit

- Understand how to configure Cisco voice gateways for each circuit type when connecting to the PSTN

- Verify and troubleshoot circuit connections to the PSTN

PSTN Circuit Selection Overview

A Cisco voice gateway can connect with the PSTN using several different types of trunk circuits. Many factors determine the number and type of trunk circuits needed. These factors include the following:

- Call volume that you expect this gateway to handle. In addition to total call volume, you should take redundancy requirements into account when sizing gateways. You might want to split PSTN traffic between two or more gateways to achieve a higher level of reliability.

- The features that you need from the PSTN, such as caller ID, direct inward dial (DID), dialed number identification service (DNIS), and so on.

- Trunk types and services that are available from the carrier at the particular location. For example, in some locations, ISDN service might not be available.

- Cost, which plays an important role in design. Cost is especially a factor in PSTN trunk circuits, because these represent a recurring cost to the business. Not surprisingly, service pricing varies widely by geography and carrier. What is more of a surprise is that in some cases, trunk circuits that provide more features, such as ISDN, are less expensive than services such as analog business lines.

Connections from the PSTN to the gateway can be broken down into two basic types: analog and digital.

Supported Analog Connection Types

Analog connections are either two-wire or four-wire configuration. Cisco voice gateways support analog connections using five basic signaling formats:

- **Foreign Exchange Office (FXO)**—The FXO interface is an RJ11 two-wire connection that is typically used for single channel plain old telephone service (POTS) trunks to the PSTN central office (CO).

- **DID**—DID is a special form of POTS connection in which the PSTN provides the last three to five digits of the called number across the trunk. Using this information, the call can be directly routed to the destination.

- **Centralized Automated Message Accounting (CAMA)**—CAMA is a signaling protocol originally developed for toll call billing. It has been adapted to support the North American Enhanced 911 (E911) service. CAMA transmits both the calling and called number in-band prior to connecting the voice channel.

- **Foreign Exchange Station (FXS)**—The FXS interface is also a single-channel RJ11 two-wire connection. It is useful for connecting end station equipment (phones, fax machines, and so on). FXS interfaces provide ring voltage and dial tone, which FXO interfaces do not provide.

- **"Ear and Mouth" (E&M)**—E&M is also sometimes referred to as "rEceive and transMit" or "Earth and Magneto." The E&M interface uses an RJ48 connector and is described as either a two- or four-wire service. Although some PSTN providers still offer E&M as a tariffed service, E&M trunks are almost exclusively used as PBX tie-lines.

Of these analog types, only FXO, DID, and CAMA are commonly used for PSTN connections. POTS trunks are typically used in small sites, where only a few simultaneous calls need to be supported. The main advantage of using POTS for small installations is lower cost. The disadvantages include additional hardware interface requirements on the voice gateways, less reliable signaling mechanisms, slow call connect times, and voice quality issues, such as echo.

Supported Digital Connection Types

Digital connections to the Cisco voice gateways are supported using the following signaling methods:

- **ISDN PRI**—ISDN PRI provides 23 voice-bearer channels (B-channels) when delivered as a T1 or 30 voice-bearer channels (B-channels) when delivered as an E1. ISDN PRI also provides a dedicated 64-kbps data channel (D-channel) for signaling traffic. This service is also referred to as 23B+D for T1 or 30B+D for E1.

- **ISDN BRI**—ISDN BRI provides two voice-bearer channels and a single 16-kbps data channel (2B+D) for signaling traffic.

- **E1 R2**—R2 signaling is a channel-associated signaling (CAS) system developed in the 1960s that is still in use today in Europe, Latin America, Australia, and Asia. Unlike ISDN, a CAS circuit has no dedicated signaling channel.

- **T1 CAS**—Also known as robbed-bit signaling, in T1 CAS, the signaling is done in-band on the voice channels by "robbing" the least significant bit of the information in that channel. Common forms of CAS signaling are loop-start, ground-start, Equal Access North American (EANA), and E&M.

When connecting to the PSTN, digital trunks are always preferred if possible. Digital trunks provide higher capacity, better voice quality, and more reliable signaling methods.

Analog Trunks

POTS trunks are almost always delivered from the PSTN as a two-wire service that connects to analog interface ports on the Cisco voice gateway. Each POTS trunk supports a single call. This section covers how to configure, verify, and troubleshoot the most common types of analog ports used to connect to the PSTN. These include FXO, DID, and CAMA interfaces.

Although some PSTN service providers still offer two- and four-wire E&M, this service is almost never used to connect to the PSTN. Other available services offer similar functionality at a much lower cost. E&M is used primarily to connect to a PBX and will be discussed in Chapter 7, "Connecting to PBXs."

Configuring FXO Connections

To properly configure an FXO port, you need to gather information about the circuit that is being installed:

- Locale code (usually the country). This is used so that call progress tones (ringback, busy, reorder, and so on) are reproduced appropriately for the location where the gateway is installed.

- Whether dual tone multifrequency (DTMF) or pulse dialing is necessary.

- Whether the trunk requires loop-start or ground-start signaling.

- Supervision type: call answer/disconnect supervision indication method.

Setting up basic operation of an FXO port for a POTS trunk is simple. You configure the specifics for a given FXO port in voice port configuration mode, which you enter using the **voice-port** *slot/port* command or **voice-port** *slot/subunit/port* command, as shown in Example 6-1.

Example 6-1 *FXO Basic Configuration*

```
Boise#config t
!
!  Enter voice port configuration mode
Boise(config)#voice-port 0/3/0
!
!  Configure signal type
Boise(config-voiceport)#signal loopStart
!
!  Set the locale
Boise(config-voiceport)#cptone US
%Impedance also changed to 600Real
!
!  Set the dial type
Boise(config-voiceport)#dial-type dtmf
```

When the circuit is delivered, the telco should provide the information that you need to configure the voice port. The gateway configuration must match the telco configuration.

After these basic steps are completed, calls that are directed outbound via a dial peer or other call control agent should work properly. Remember that the call control agent needs to pass the proper digits to the PSTN to complete the call.

Incoming calls are a different matter. Remember that this is basic analog service—the PSTN is not providing in-band information to the gateway about the call destination.

By default, the call is answered after one ring, and the caller hears a secondary dial tone generated by the voice gateway. The number of rings to wait is customizable between one and ten using the **ring number** command in voice port configuration. When the secondary dial tone is presented, the caller can enter an extension number. The gateway will do normal digit analysis, attempting to match that number to a dial peer and route the call. If the gateway cannot route the call, the caller hears a reorder tone. Although this configuration works, it is not typically used. Callers will not expect the second dial tone and might not know that they are expected to dial an extension.

Another more common approach is to automatically route the call to a predetermined destination. Private line automatic ringdown (PLAR) is a feature used to automatically connect an endpoint to a predetermined destination number as soon as the line goes off-hook. This destination number can be the pilot number of an auto attendant, a hunt group, or a receptionist. Configuring the destination number is done using the **connection plar** command in voice port configuration mode, as shown in Example 6-2.

Example 6-2 *Setting a Destination for Inbound Calls*

```
Boise#config t
!
!  Go to voice port configuration
Boise(config)#voice-port 0/3/0
!
!  All inbound calls will route to extension 3000
Boise(config-voiceport)#connection plar opx 3000
```

Example 6-2 also included the **opx** keyword. This indicates to the gateway that the destination is an off-premise exchange (OPX). When **opx** is coded, the FXO port does not answer the call until the remote side is available. If the **opx** keyword is not configured, the call is answered after the specified number of rings, even if the destination number is unavailable.

Often, the PSTN offers caller ID name and number information, which is passed in-band on the POTS trunk. To receive the caller information, you need to configure the FXO port to look for it. This information is normally delivered between the first and second rings. The voice port configuration **caller-id enable** command is used to enable this feature, as shown in Example 6-3.

Example 6-3 *Enabling Caller ID*

```
Boise#config t
!
!  Go to voice port configuration
Boise(config)#voice-port 0/3/0
!
!  Enable caller ID
Boise(config-voiceport)#caller-id enable
```

Verifying and Troubleshooting

To check that the FXO ports are configured properly, you can use the **show voice port** or **show voice port summary** commands.

In Example 6-4, the two FXO ports have been configured to use loop-start signaling.

Example 6-4 *Verify FXO Port Status*

```
Boise#show voice port summary
                                IN       OUT
PORT       CH   SIG-TYPE   ADMIN OPER STATUS   STATUS   EC
========= == ============ ===== ==== ======== ======== ==
0/3/0      --   fxo-ls     up   down idle     on-hook  y
0/3/1      --   fxo-ls     up   dorm idle     on-hook  y
```

The most common problems with FXO ports are incorrect call signaling type and line polarity. The PSTN equipment is polarity sensitive, so if you are having polarity problems, you might need to reverse the tip and ring connection.

To help with troubleshooting, you can see the signaling progress of an inbound call with the **debug vpm all** command. This will show you the line seizure and the caller ID information, if available.

The supervisory disconnect detection method on FXO ports defaults to battery reversal. A port that continues to ring or remains off-hook after the caller has hung up is a symptom of a supervisory disconnect problem. If a disconnect problem occurs, you might need to change the detection method using the **supervisory disconnect** *method* command under voice port configuration. It is important to configure the port to match the method that the PSTN uses so that you can prevent this type of problem.

Caveats and Restrictions

When you are using FXO connections to the PSTN, remember to take into account the following limitations:

- No DNIS information is available on incoming calls. You must permanently route these calls to a fixed extension, hunt group pilot, or automated attendant for subsequent routing.

- Ground start connections are polarity sensitive. Failed calls or dropped calls can occur if the connection is wired incorrectly.

- Disconnect supervision problems can occur with FXO ports. For a complete discussion of FXO disconnect issues, go to http://www.cisco.com/en/US/customer/tech/tk652/tk653/technologies_tech_note09186a00800ae2d1.shtml.

Media Gateway Control Protocol

If you are using a call control agent, such as Cisco CallManager, to control the gateway using Media Gateway Control Protocol (MGCP), the situation is quite different from the FXO configuration discussed previously. With MGCP, the call control agent does all the configuration tasks for setting up the FXO port operation.

When you are configuring CallManager for an MGCP gateway, you must identify the gateway type and the voice interface modules that are included in the gateway. For FXO ports, the signaling type is set when the hardware definition is initially added. Figure 6-1 shows an example of this. The **LS** shown on FXO port 0/3/0 and 0/3/1 indicates loop-start signaling. If the ports showed **GS**, it would indicate ground-start signaling.

Figure 6-1   *Analog Port Configuration Using MGCP*

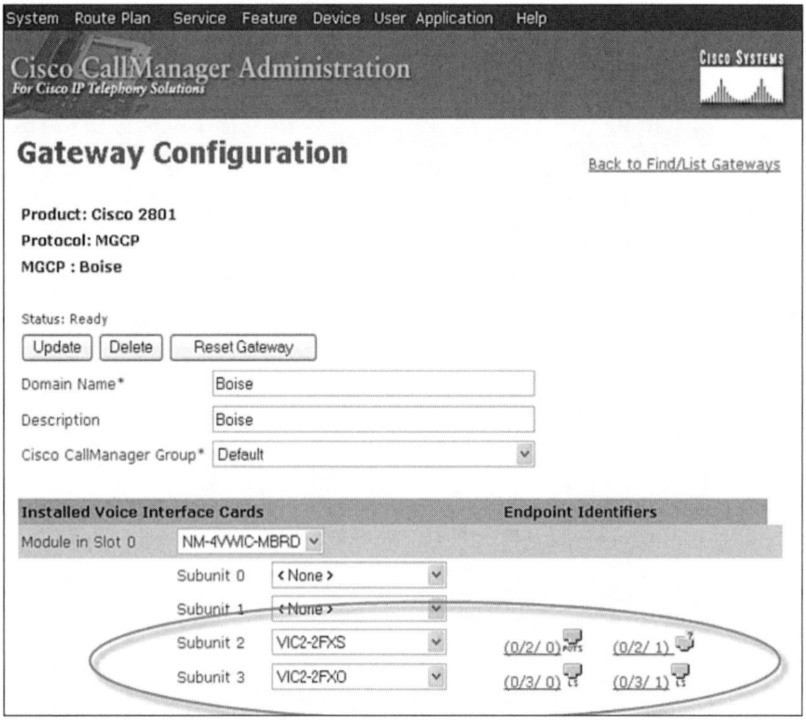

NOTE   The **?** shown on port 0/2/1 indicates that this port has not yet been configured.

Figure 6-2 shows an example of the remaining parameters that you can configure using MGCP for an FXO port. The **Attendant DN** field sets the destination for inbound calls, similar to the **connection plar** command.

NOTE   You cannot enable caller ID in the CallManager MGCP configuration. Caller ID is not supported on MGCP-controlled analog ports.

Figure 6-2 *FXO Port Configuration Options Using MGCP*

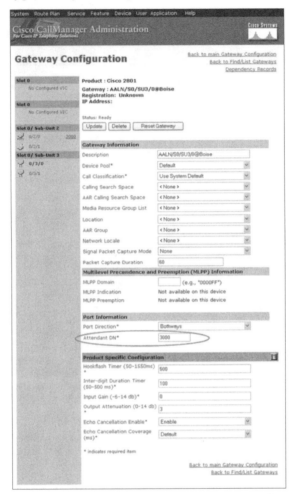

Configuring DID Connections

The PSTN might offer DID service on analog trunks. This service allows callers to be routed directly to an extension without needing to be routed to an auto-attendant or an operator as is the case with the FXO connection discussed previously. The PSTN does this by passing the dialed number information in-band across the trunk as the call is delivered to the gateway port.

For example, if a caller dials 555-1234, the PSTN might deliver 1234 across the trunk. If the trunk is connected to a port that is configured as a DID port, the gateway can collect these digits and forward them to call control (CallManager, H.323 dial peers, and so on) so that the call can be directly routed to extension 1234. Caller ID information can be sent in-band on the same trunk.

On the surface, this function looks useful because it allows calls to be directly routed to extensions. In practice, however, this function is less useful than you would think. Businesses that use analog trunks are usually small and do not require DID service. Further, PSTN service providers rarely offer the service, because most customers have switched to digital service. Finally, you can use ports that are configured to use DID signaling for inbound calls only; you need separate trunks for outbound calls.

Analog DID connections are currently supported on only three interface models available for Cisco voice gateways, including these:

- **VIC-4FXS/DID**—A four-port voice interface card (VIC)
- **VIC-2DID**—A two-port VIC
- **EVM-HD-8FXS/DID**—An eight-port enhanced voice module

To properly configure a port for a DID connection, you need the following information from the PSTN:

- **Signaling type**—The signaling types available are as follows:
  - **Immediate-start**—This is the simplest of all protocols. The PSTN seizes the line by going off-hook and starts out-pulsing the digits without waiting.
  - **Wink-start**—With wink-start, the PSTN seizes the line by going off-hook and waits for an acknowledgment from the other end before out-pulsing the digits.
  - **Delay-dial**—In the delay-dial mode, the PSTN goes off-hook, waits for about 200 ms, and then checks to see if the far end is on-hook. If it is on-hook, the PSTN outputs the dialed digits. If the far end is off-hook, the PSTN waits until it goes on-hook, and then it outputs the dialed digits.
- **Number of DID digits passed**—You need this to properly configure the call control agent to match the dialed number and route the calls.

You configure the actual port by using the **signal did** command in voice port configuration mode. Also include the signaling type on this command, as shown in Example 6-5.

Example 6-5 *Configuring DID Port*

```
Boise#config t
!
!  Go to voice port configuration
Boise(config)#voice-port 0/2/0
!
!  Set signaling for DID
Boise(config-voiceport)#signal did immediate
```

Verifying and Troubleshooting

To check that the DID ports are configured properly, you can use the **show voice port** or **show voice port summary** commands.

In Example 6-6, the first three ports have been configured to use DID signaling. Each of the three DID signaling types is shown. The last port 2/0/3 is configured as a loop-start FXS port, not DID.

Example 6-6 *Voice Port Summary*

```
Boise#show voice port summary
                                  IN       OUT
  PORT      CH  SIG-TYPE   ADMIN OPER STATUS  STATUS   EC
  ========= == ============ ===== ==== ======== ======== ==
  2/0/0     -- did-in-imd  up    dorm idle    idle     y
  2/0/1     -- did-in-dly  up    dorm idle    idle     y
  2/0/2     -- did-in-wnk  up    dorm idle    idle     y
  2/0/3     -- fxs-ls      up    dorm on-hook idle     y
```

The most common problems with DID ports are the incorrect configuration of the dial plan (how many digits are being delivered by the PSTN), incorrect call signaling type, and line polarity. The PSTN equipment is polarity sensitive, so if you are having polarity problems, you might need to reverse the tip and ring connection.

To help with troubleshooting, use the **debug vpm all** command to see the signaling progress of an inbound call. This command shows you the line seizure and the actual inbound digits that the gateway has collected.

Caveats and Restrictions

You need to keep several considerations in mind when you are setting up DID ports:

- After you have configured a port for DID signaling, you can use it only for inbound calls. You cannot place outbound calls on that port.

- DID operation is not supported when CallManager MGCP controls the voice gateway.

- The port can be damaged if it is connected to a standard PSTN line while it operates in DID mode. Ensure that lines to the PSTN are provisioned for DID.

Configuring Centralized Automated Message Accounting Connections

CAMA is an old telephony protocol that was originally developed and used for long-distance billing applications. This protocol is now used as a mechanism for handling Enhanced 911 (E911) traffic in the United States. It is necessary to handle E911 calls differently because calls to emergency services are routed based on the calling number, rather than the called number, as is normally the case. CAMA checks the calling number against a database to determine which Public Service Answering Point (PSAP) handles calls from that number. It then routes the call to the appropriate PSAP to dispatch the correct emergency services.

During setup of a call to E911, before the audio channel is connected, the calling number is transmitted to each switching point (also known as a selective router [SR]) via the CAMA protocol. Today, 80 percent of the E911 trunks in service use CAMA.

CAMA trunk connections are currently supported on a limited number of Cisco voice gateway interface modules, including these:

- **VIC-2CAMA**—This interface was specifically sold to support CAMA trunks. It is no longer available for purchase; however, you might still run in to one occasionally.

- **VIC2-2FXO or VIC2-4FXO**—These are two- or four-port FXO interface cards, respectively. You can individually configure the FXO ports to support CAMA trunk connections.

Four signaling types are supported to transmit automatic number identification (ANI) information to the SR. The PSTN determines which one is appropriate to use when the trunk is delivered. The four supported types are as follows:

- **Type 1 (KP-0-NXX-XXXX-ST)**—In Type 1, the last seven digits of the calling phone number are transmitted. The area code information (also known as Numbering Plan Area [NPA]) is implied by the trunk that the call is using and is not sent.

- **Type 2 (KP-0-NPA-NXX-XXXX-ST)**—The full ten-digit E.164 number is transmitted.

- **Type 3 (KP-2-ST)**—This mode is used if the gateway is unable to out-pulse the ANI information. For example, if the PSTN requires ten-digit ANI information and the gateway receives only a seven-digit calling number, KP-2-ST is sent. It is important to note that 911 calls are never rejected because of an ANI information mismatch. The voice call goes through even without the ANI.

- **Type 4 (KP-NPD-NXX-XXXX-ST)**—Type 4 transmits eight digits of information. Area codes are mapped to a single digit between 0 and 3. This single digit is sent first, followed by the last seven digits of the calling number. If you use Type 4, you must also configure the area code mapping in the gateway. You need to obtain proper Number Planning Digit (NPD) to area code mapping information from the PSTN. Only NPD values between 0 and 3 are valid. Values above 3 are reserved for error conditions.

After you have obtained the signaling information from the PSTN, you do the configuration in voice port configuration mode using the **signal cama** *signal type* command.

In Example 6-7, the CAMA port is configured for Type 4 (KP-NPD-NXX-XXXX-ST) signaling. Type 4 requires mapping the NPA to a single-digit NPD code using the **ani mapping** command, as shown. Also, notice the message indicating the need to shut down the port and bring it back up before the change can take effect.

Example 6-7 *Configuring a CAMA Port*

```
Boise#config t
!
! Go to voice port configuration
Boise(config)#voice-port 0/3/1
!
! Configure for CAMA signaling
Boise(config-voiceport)#signal cama KP-NPD-NXX-XXXX-ST
Note: need to shut/no shut to complete the CAMA signal type configuration.
!
Boise(config-voiceport)#shutdown
*Jan  7 02:14:19.560: %LINK-3-UPDOWN: Interface Foreign Exchange Office 0/3/1,
changed state to Administrative Shutdown
!
Boise(config-voiceport)#no shutdown
*Jan  7 02:14:24.376: %LINK-3-UPDOWN: Interface Foreign Exchange Office 0/3/1,
changed state to up
!
! Configure NPD to NPA mapping
Boise(config-voiceport)#ani mapping 0 919
Boise(config-voiceport)#ani mapping 1 843
```

Verifying and Troubleshooting

To check that the CAMA ports are configured properly, you can use the **show voice port** or **show voice port summary** commands.

In Example 6-8, you can see that the **show voice port** command lists the CAMA signaling type and ANI mapping, if present.

Example 6-8 **show voice port** *for a CAMA Type 4 Trunk*

```
Boise#show voice port 0/3/1
 ! Unnecessary output omitted
 Voice card specific Info Follows:
 Signal Type is cama
 Cama Type is KP-NPD-NXX-XXXX-ST
 NPD to NPA mapping is :
 NPD     NPA
 0       919
 1       843
 2       0
 3       0
 Battery-Reversal is enabled
 Number Of Rings is set to 1
 Supervisory Disconnect is signal
 Answer Supervision is inactive
```

The most common problem that occurs when installing a CAMA trunk is reversal of the tip and ring wiring connections. When this occurs, the voice call still goes through, but no ANI information is present, and the call disconnects within a minute or so. To identify this issue, use the **debug vpm all** command and review the debug output from a call that has failed.

Example 6-9 shows what to look for when the tip and ring wiring has been reversed. After the gateway out-pulses the dialed number, it waits for an acknowledgement from the PSTN in the form of a battery voltage reversal. Because the wires are reversed, the signal is incorrect, resulting in the error message that you see in the trace output. The gateway waits for another signal from the PSTN to begin sending the ANI information. Because the leads are reversed, the correct signal is never recognized. In this example, after about 15 seconds, the gateway times out waiting for the ANI signal from the PSTN, and the call is disconnected.

Example 6-9 *Sample Debug Output*

```
! Unnecessary output omitted

*Jan 6 02:30:40.647: htsp_process_event: [0/3/1, FGD_OS_WAIT_DIAL_DNIS_DONE,
E_DSP_SIG_0110]
*Jan 6 02:30:40.647: [0/3/1, FGD_OS_WAIT_DIAL_DNIS_DONE, E_DSP_SIG_0110] -> ERROR:
INVALID INPUT
### ERROR MESSAGE - GETTING INVALID SEIZURE FROM PSTN
*Jan 6 02:30:41.056: htsp_process_event: [0/3/1, FGD_OS_WAIT_DIAL_DNIS_DONE,
E_DSP_DIALING_DONE]fgd_os_dnis_dial_donefgd_os_start_timer: 16000 ms
*Jan 6 02:30:41.060: htsp_timer - 16000 msechtsp_alert
### WAITING FOR PSTN TO SEND SEIZURE TO REQUEST ANI
*Jan 6 02:30:41.184: htsp_process_event: [0/3/1, FGD_OS_WAIT_ANI_REQST,
E_HTSP_VOICE_CUT_THROUGH]
*Jan 6 02:30:41.420: htsp_dsp_message: SEND/RESP_SIG_STATUS: state=0x4
timestamp=43143 systime=904142
*Jan 6 02:30:41.420: htsp_process_event: [0/3/1, FGD_OS_WAIT_ANI_REQST,
E_DSP_SIG_0100]
*Jan 6 02:30:41.420: [0/3/1, FGD_OS_WAIT_ANI_REQST, E_DSP_SIG_0100] -> ERROR:
INVALID INPUT
*Jan 6 02:30:57.062: htsp_process_event: [0/3/1, FGD_OS_WAIT_ANI_REQST,
E_HTSP_EVENT_TIMER]fgd_os_wait_ani_req_timeoutfgd_os_onhook
### TIMEOUT WAITING FOR ANI REQUEST / DISCONNECT THE CALL
```

Caveats and Restrictions

CAMA trunks allow fast and reliable communication with the correct emergency service providers for a given area. Their proper operation is vital in an emergency. You need to keep several things in mind when installing CAMA trunks:

- CAMA trunks are not supported on CallManager MGCP-controlled voice gateways.

- By their nature, IP phones can be easily moved from one location to another. When you are using IP phones, put some mechanism in place to ensure that 911 calls are always routed to the proper gateway for the current location of the phone. In a larger campus or a distributed environment, consider the Cisco Emergency Responder application to control this issue.

- Always test your installation after it is complete to make certain that the proper ANI information is being transmitted and the calls are completing successfully.

Digital Trunks

Digital trunks typically offer much greater capacity, quality, and reliability than analog trunks. As such, most midsize and larger businesses use digital service connections to the PSTN. This rise in popularity has also caused the cost of this service to decline over time in most geographies, making its use even more attractive.

In this section, you will learn how to configure, verify, and troubleshoot the four types of digital service that Cisco voice gateways support. These include ISDN PRI, ISDN BRI, E1 R2, and T1 CAS trunk types.

Configuring E1/T1 Physical Layer Connections

All these trunk types—with the exception of ISDN BRI—are delivered on either an E1 or T1 digital circuit. Before you configure voice signaling methods, be sure that the interface is configured so that the circuit is operating properly on the physical signaling level (Layer 1).

E1 or T1 voice circuits are channelized, meaning they transmit information in timeslots or channels. E1 circuits have 30 timeslots available, and T1 circuits have 24 timeslots. The timeslots are carried in frames. The beginning of the frame is marked by a specific bit sequence. A more complete description of the circuit characteristics is described in Chapter 5, "Circuit Options."

At a physical level, the interface must be able to identify the beginning of each frame in the bit stream and understand the frame format that is being used so that it can read the information in the timeslots correctly. This means several things:

- The interface must be accurately clocked to prevent bit "slips." A slip occurs when there is a difference between when the interface expects a data bit and when it actually arrives. When connecting to the PSTN, you should always use line clocking—that is, obtain the clock from the PSTN circuit. PSTN equipment uses extremely accurate clock sources and provides an excellent source for precisely clocking the voice gateway interface.

- T1 or E1 framing is necessary to provide a common data format and to provide a means for synchronization on a network. For T1, two common framing standards are currently in use: Super Frame (D4) and Extended Superframe (ESF). An E1 circuit uses timeslot 0 for framing and synchronization. Timeslot 0 has two framing formats: double-frame and CRC-4. Double-frame provides synchronization but no error checking. CRC-4 adds a checksum to provide error checking of timeslots within the frame.

- Line coding identifies the way the bit stream is sent on the transmission line. T1 circuits can use either alternate mark inversion (AMI) or binary 8-zero substitution (B8ZS) line coding. E1 circuits can also use AMI, or they can use high-density Bipolar 3 (HDB3) line coding.

For T1, D4 framing is usually associated with AMI line coding, and ESF framing is usually associated with B8ZS line coding. The PSTN service provider can furnish details regarding which framing and line coding mechanism is being used on the circuit that you are installing.

Now you can begin setting up the physical characteristics of the circuit at the T1/E1 controller level. From global configuration mode, enter the **controller T1** *port/slot* or **controller E1** *port/slot* command to enter controller configuration mode.

Configure the framing using the **framing** *type* command. For T1, the valid options for *type* are **sf** or **esf**. The default for T1 is SF. For E1, the valid options for *type* are **crc4** and **no-crc4**. The default for E1 is CRC4.

Configure the line coding using the **linecode** *type* command. For T1, the valid options for *type* are **ami** and **b8zs**. The default for T1 is AMI. For E1, the valid options for *type* are **ami** and **hdb3**. The default for E1 is HDB3.

It is not normally necessary to configure the clock source for PSTN connections. The default setting is **line** clock, which allows the interface to obtain clocking from the circuit. This is typically the correct setting for a PSTN circuit.

Example 6-10 demonstrates configuring the physical interface for an E1 circuit.

Example 6-10 *E1 Physical Circuit Configuration*

```
Shanghai#config t
!
! Enter controller configuration mode
Shanghai(config)#controller E1 1/0
!
! Configure framing
Shanghai(config-controller)#framing crc4
!
! Configure line coding
Shanghai(config-controller)#linecode hdb3
*May 12 15:48:28.527: %CONTROLLER-5-UPDOWN: Controller E1 1/0, changed state to up
```

After you have configured the proper framing and line coding, the controller comes up.

Verifying and Troubleshooting

You can verify that no physical alarms exist on this circuit by using the **show controller T1** *slot/port* or **show controller E1** *slot/port* command. Both commands show you the current state of the controller, configuration information, and whether any alarms are detected. Both commands also provide error counters for the previous 24 hours in 15-minute intervals.

Example 6-11 demonstrates sample output from the **show controller e1** command. You can see in this example that this interface has had errors. Slip seconds have been recorded in the current interval, indicating a possible clocking issue.

Example 6-11   **show controller e1** *Command Output*

```
Shanghai#show controller e1 1/0
E1 1/0 is up.
  Applique type is Channelized E1 - balanced
  No alarms detected.
  alarm-trigger is not set
  Version info Firmware: 20050620, FPGA: 16, spm_count = 0
  Framing is CRC4, Line Code is HDB3, Clock Source is Internal.
  CRC Threshold is 320. Reported from firmware  is 320.
  Data in current interval (864 seconds elapsed):
     0 Line Code Violations, 0 Path Code Violations
     24 Slip Secs, 0 Fr Loss Secs, 0 Line Err Secs, 0 Degraded Mins
     24 Errored Secs, 0 Bursty Err Secs, 0 Severely Err Secs, 0 Unavail Secs
  Data in Interval 1:
     3 Line Code Violations, 29 Path Code Violations
     21 Slip Secs, 0 Fr Loss Secs, 3 Line Err Secs, 0 Degraded Mins
     22 Errored Secs, 0 Bursty Err Secs, 4 Severely Err Secs, 0 Unavail Secs
  !  Additional output omitted
```

Table 6-1 describes all the fields shown.

Table 6-1   **show controller e1** *Field Descriptions*

Field	Description
E1 1/0 Is Up	The E1 controller 0 in slot 1 is operating. The controller state can be up, down, or administratively down. Loopback conditions are shown by (Locally Looped) or (Remotely Looped).
No Alarms Detected	Any alarms that the controller detects are displayed here. Possible alarms are as follows: • Transmitter is sending remote alarm. • Transmitter is sending alarm indication signal (AIS). • Receiver has loss of signal. • Receiver is getting AIS. • Receiver has loss of frame. • Receiver has remote alarm. • Receiver has no alarms.
Data in Current Interval (864 Seconds Elapsed)	This field shows the current accumulation period, which rolls into the 24-hour accumulation every 15 minutes. The accumulation period is from 1 to 900 seconds. The oldest 15-minute period falls off the back of the 24-hour accumulation buffer.

Table 6-1   **show controller e1** *Field Descriptions (Continued)*

Field	Description
Line Code Violations	This field indicates the occurrence of either a bipolar violation (BPV) or Excessive Zeros (EXZ) error event.
Path Code Violations	This field indicates a frame synchronization bit error in the D4 and E1-noCRC formats, or a cyclic redundancy check (CRC) error in the ESF and E1-CRC formats.
Slip Secs	This field indicates the replication or deletion of the payload bits of a DS1 frame. A slip can occur if there is a difference between the timing of a synchronous receiving terminal and the received signal.
Fr Loss Secs	This field indicates the number of seconds an "out-of-frame" error is detected.
Line Err Secs	A line errored second (LES) is one in which one or more "line code violation" errors are detected.
Degraded Mins	A degraded minute is one in which the estimated error rate exceeds 1E-6 but does not exceed 1E-3.
Errored Secs	In ESF and E1-CRC links, an errored second is a second in which one of the following is detected: one or more path code violations; one or more "out-of-frame" defects; one or more Controlled Slip events; a detected AIS defect. For D4 and E1-noCRC links, the presence of bipolar violations (BPV) also triggers an errored second.
Bursty Err Secs	Count of the number of seconds with fewer than 320 and more than 1 "path coding violation" error, no "severely errored frame" defects, and no detected incoming AIS defects. Controlled slips are not included in this parameter.
Severely Err Secs	For ESF signals, count of the number of seconds with one of the following errors: 320 or more "path code violation" errors; one or more "out-of-frame" defects; a detected AIS defect. For E1-CRC signals, a second with one of the following errors: 832 or more "path code violation" errors; one or more "out-of-frame" defects. For E1-noCRC signals, a second with 2048 or more line code violations. For D4 signals, a count of 1-second intervals with "framing" errors, or an "out-of-frame" defect, or 1544 line code violations.
Unavail Secs	Count of the total number of seconds where interface has been unavailable to pass traffic.

Configuring ISDN PRI Trunks

To configure a PRI trunk, you need to gather the following information from the PSTN service provider:

- **Number of channels**—This is the number of channels provisioned for voice service.

- **ISDN channel selection order**—Determine if the PSTN service provider expects B-channel selection to be ascending (B-channel 1 first) or descending (B-channel 30 first for E1 or B-channel 23 first for T1). The default selection order on the Cisco voice gateways is descending.

- **ISDN switch type**—Specifying an ISDN switch type identifies the Layer 2 and Layer 3 signaling that the voice gateway and the PSTN are using. The ISDN switch types that Cisco voice gateways support vary depending on the Cisco IOS software release. Table 6-2 lists the switch types that Cisco IOS Software Release 12.3 supports.

Table 6-2 *ISDN PRI Switch Types Supported by Cisco IOS 12.3*

ISDN PRI Switch Type	Description
primary-4ess	Lucent 4ESS switch type for the United States
primary-5ess	Lucent 5ESS switch type for the United States
primary-dms100	Northern Telecom DMS-100 switch type for the United States
primary-dpnss	Digital Private Networking Signaling System (DPNSS) switch type for Europe
primary-net5	NET5 switch type for the United Kingdom, Europe, Asia, and Australia
primary-ni	National ISDN switch type 2 for the United States
primary-ntt	NTT switch type for Japan
primary-qsig	Q.SIG switch type
primary-ts014	TS014 switch type for Australia (now obsolete)

Basic configuration of the interface for a PRI voice trunk begins by configuring the gateway for an ISDN switch type. You do this in global configuration mode by using the **isdn switch-type** *switch type* command, where *switch type* matches the device that the PSTN service provider is using; see Table 6-2. Defining a switch type globally for the gateway is required.

NOTE   You can override the ISDN switch type at the individual interface level. This is useful when you have interfaces in the gateway that are connected to different switches.

The second step is to configure the PRI voice timeslots on the controller. Enter controller configuration and use the command **pri-group** *timeslots (1-23)* for T1 or **pri-group** *timeslots (1-31)* for E1. This command associates the specified timeslots as ISDN channels. If you do not specify timeslots, all B-channels are associated to the PRI group. It is important to understand that the D-channel is always added to the pri-group, even if it is not explicitly specified, because it is required for signaling. Further, you can specify only one PRI group on the controller because each circuit has a single D-channel available.

After you specify the PRI group, the gateway automatically creates an associated voice port and serial interface. You configure the voice port in a similar way to the FXO voice port, as shown earlier.

The serial interface actually controls the D-channel (signaling channel). You do all configuration that affects processing of the signaling on the D-channel. It is on the D-channel that you can set the B-channel selection order if necessary. You do this by entering interface configuration mode on the D-channel serial interface and using the **isdn bchan-number-order** {**ascending** | **descending**} command.

After you have completed these steps, your service should be operational. Remember that during call setup, both the calling and called numbers are signaled on the D-channel. This allows call control to match on either field to route the call. See Chapter 9, "Dial Plans," and Chapter 10, "Digit Manipulation," for more details. Example 6-12 shows a typical E1 ISDN PRI configuration. In this example, the first four B-channels are used for voice traffic.

Timeslot 16 is the E1 D-channel that was added to the PRI group automatically. The B-channel selection order was also changed to begin with B-channel 1. Interface Serial1/0:15 and voice port 1/0:15 were automatically created when the PRI group was added to the E1 controller.

Example 6-12   *Sample E1 ISDN PRI Configuration*

```
Shanghai#show running-config
Building configuration...
!
!   Unnecessary output removed
!
!   ISDN switch type set globally
!
isdn switch-type primary-net5
!
!   First 4 B-channels included in the pri-group, D-channel 16 added automatically
!
controller E1 1/0
 pri-group timeslots 1-4,16
!
!   D-channel interface
!
interface Serial1/0:15
 no ip address
 isdn switch-type primary-net5
```

continues

Example 6-12 *Sample E1 ISDN PRI Configuration (Continued)*

```
 isdn incoming-voice voice
 isdn bchan-number-order ascending
 no cdp enable
 !
 ! Voice port created for pri-group
 !
 voice-port 1/0:15
 !
 end
```

MGCP

If MGCP is going to control the ISDN PRI, a few configuration changes are required. With MGCP, the Layer 3 Q.931 messages are backhauled to the CallManager and not processed by the gateway.

When setting up the PRI group on the controller, you need to specify that MGCP will control the signaling. You do this from controller configuration mode by using the **pri-group timeslots** *number* **service mgcp** command.

Under the serial interface created for the D-channel, you also must code the **isdn bind-l3 ccm-manager** command. This attaches the D-channel Q.931 protocol to the CallManager backhaul. Example 6-13 shows the differences in configuration for an ISDN PRI under MGCP control.

Example 6-13 *MGCP E1 ISDN PRI Configuration*

```
Shanghai#show running-config
Building configuration...
 !
 !   Unnecessary output removed
 !
 !   ISDN switch type set globally
 !
isdn switch-type primary-net5
 !
 !   Added 'service mgcp' for MGCP-controlled interface
 !
controller E1 1/0
 pri-group timeslots 1-4,16 service mgcp
 !
 !   D-channel interface
 !
interface Serial1/0:15
 no ip address
 isdn switch-type primary-net5
 isdn incoming-voice voice
 isdn bind-l3 ccm-manager
 no cdp enable
 !
```

Example 6-13 *MGCP E1 ISDN PRI Configuration (Continued)*

```
! Voice port created for pri-group
!
voice-port 1/0:15
!
end
```

The **isdn bind-l3 ccm-manager** command shown under interface Serial1/0:15 is available only after you add the service mgcp keywords to the PRI group definition. If the command is unknown when you try to configure it, look at the controller to ensure that the PRI group is defined correctly.

Verifying and Troubleshooting

To verify that the circuit is operating properly, you can use the **show isdn status** command. Example 6-14 shows the output of this command.

Example 6-14 **show isdn status** *Command Output for PRI*

```
Shanghai#show isdn status
Global ISDN Switchtype = primary-net5
ISDN Serial1/0:15 interface
        dsl 0, interface ISDN Switchtype = primary-net5
    Layer 1 Status:
        ACTIVE
    Layer 2 Status:
        TEI = 0, Ces = 1, SAPI = 0, State = MULTIPLE_FRAME_ESTABLISHED
    Layer 3 Status:
        0 Active Layer 3 Call(s)
    Active dsl 0 CCBs = 0
    The Free Channel Mask:  0x8000000F
    Number of L2 Discards = 0, L2 Session ID = 2
    Total Allocated ISDN CCBs = 0
```

The example shows the status of the circuit at Layers 1, 2, and 3. Layer 1 should show ACTIVE, with the Layer 2 state as MULTIPLE FRAME ESTABLISHED. If that is not the case, check the physical interface for errors, as shown in the previous section. Also verify that the switch type is correct and that it matches the PSTN specification.

If Layer 2 is showing an incorrect state, you can use the **debug isdn q921** trace to help determine the cause. Example 6-15 shows a problem with Layer 2, where both sides of the connection are configured as network, and the Layer 2 connection cannot be established.

Example 6-15 **debug isdn 921 Trace Output** *Command Output for PRI*

```
Miami#show isdn status
Global ISDN Switchtype = primary-ni
ISDN Serial1/0:23 interface
        ******* Network side configuration *******
```

continues

Example 6-15 **debug isdn 921 Trace Output** *Command Output for PRI (Continued)*

```
              dsl 0, interface ISDN Switchtype = primary-ni
       Layer 1 Status:
              ACTIVE
       Layer 2 Status:
              TEI = 0, Ces = 1, SAPI = 0, State = AWAITING_ESTABLISHMENT
       Layer 3 Status:
              0 Active Layer 3 Call(s)
       Active dsl 0 CCBs = 0
       The Free Channel Mask:  0x80000000
       Number of L2 Discards = 0, L2 Session ID = 11
       Total Allocated ISDN CCBs = 0
Miami#debug isdn q921
debug isdn q921 is            ON.
Miami#
*Jul  5 19:31:01.477: ISDN Se1/0:23 Q921: Net TX -> SABMEp sapi=0 tei=0
*Jul  5 19:31:01.933: ISDN Se1/0:23 Q921: Net RX <- BAD FRAME(0x02017F)
*Jul  5 19:31:02.477: ISDN Se1/0:23 Q921: Net TX -> SABMEp sapi=0 tei=0
*Jul  5 19:31:02.933: ISDN Se1/0:23 Q921: Net RX <- BAD FRAME(0x02017F)
*Jul  5 19:31:03.477: ISDN Se1/0:23 Q921: L2_EstablishDataLink: sending SABME
```

If the status of Layer 1 and 2 are good and you are still having trouble placing calls, make a test call with **debug isdn q931** active. This debug shows activity on the PRI D-channel and is useful in troubleshooting. First, if your test call produces trace output, it confirms that the request is actually being sent out the PRI interface. Second, as you can see in Example 6-16, it shows a great deal of information about the call. You can see the calling and called numbers, which B-channel is requested, and failure cause codes with reasonably clear descriptive text.

Example 6-16 **debug isdn q931** *Command Output*

```
Shanghai#debug isdn q931
debug isdn q931 is            ON.
Shanghai#
*May 13 13:46:32.662: ISDN Se1/0:15 Q931: Applying typeplan for sw-type 0x12 is
0x0 0x0, Calling num 2001
*May 13 13:46:32.662: ISDN Se1/0:15 Q931: Applying typeplan for sw-type 0x12 is
0x0 0x0, Called num 19192099832
*May 13 13:46:32.662: ISDN Se1/0:15 Q931: TX -> SETUP pd = 8  callref = 0x0011
       Bearer Capability i = 0x8090A3
               Standard = CCITT
               Transfer Capability = Speech
               Transfer Mode = Circuit
               Transfer Rate = 64 kbit/s
       Channel ID i = 0xA98381
               Exclusive, Channel 1
       Calling Party Number i = 0x0081, '2001'
               Plan:Unknown, Type:Unknown
       Called Party Number i = 0x80, '1212'
               Plan:Unknown, Type:Unknown
*May 13 13:46:32.694: ISDN Se1/0:15 Q931: RX <- CALL_PROC pd = 8  callref = 0x80
```

Example 6-16   **debug isdn q931** *Command Output (Continued)*

```
11
        Channel ID i = 0xA98381
                Exclusive, Channel 1
*May 13 13:46:32.710: ISDN Se1/0:15 Q931: RX <- DISCONNECT pd = 8  callref = 0x8
011
            Cause i = 0x8281 - Unallocated/unassigned number
*May 13 13:46:32.710: ISDN Se1/0:15 Q931: TX -> RELEASE pd = 8  callref = 0x0011
*May 13 13:46:32.726: ISDN Se1/0:15 Q931: RX <- RELEASE_COMP pd = 8  callref = 0
x8011
```

This example shows that extension 2001 called 1212 on B-channel 1. The call failed because 1212 is an unassigned number—the number does not exist. The PSTN expects numbers in E.164 format. You can quickly see that the gateway is not passing numbers in the correct format to the PSTN, which is a dial plan configuration issue. You can also tell from this example that the B-channels are being selected in ascending order as was configured.

An additional command can provide assistance when you are troubleshooting CallManager MGCP-controlled trunks. It is the **show ccm-manager** command that, among other things, shows the status of the Q.931 backhaul. You can see this information at the end of Example 6-17. Other useful information provided by this command includes the destination IP address for the backhaul link, packet and error counts, and the slot and port information for the interfaces that are being backhauled.

Example 6-17   **show ccm-manager** *Command Output*

```
Shanghai#show ccm-manager
MGCP Domain Name: Shanghai
Priority        Status                      Host
=========================================================
Primary         Registered                  10.1.5.2
First Backup    None
Second Backup   None
Current active Call Manager:     10.1.5.2
Backhaul/Redundant link port:    2428
Failover Interval:               30 seconds
Keepalive Interval:              15 seconds
Last keepalive sent:             21:50:32 UTC May 13 2005 (elapsed time: 00:00:04)
Last MGCP traffic time:          21:50:35 UTC May 13 2005 (elapsed time: 00:00:020
Last failover time:              None
Last switchback time:            None
Switchback mode:                 Graceful
MGCP Fallback mode:              Not Selected
Last MGCP Fallback start time:   None
Last MGCP Fallback end time:     None
MGCP Download Tones:             Disabled
Backhaul Link info:
    Link Protocol:        TCP
    Remote Port Number: 2428
```

continues

Example 6-17 *show ccm-manager Command Output (Continued)*

```
      Remote IP Address:  10.1.5.2
      Current Link State: OPEN
      Statistics:
          Packets recvd:   1
          Recv failures:   0
          Packets xmitted: 1
          Xmit failures:   0
      PRI Ports being backhauled:
          Slot 1, port 0
  Configuration Error History:
  FAX mode: cisco
```

Q.931 information is also written to the CallManager trace files and can be viewed with the Q.931 Translator utility provided with CallManager. This helps in troubleshooting by allowing you to look at historical call data. You can also use the Voice Log Translator (VLT) tool to parse and translate CallManager trace file data. It is available for download at Cisco.com.

Configuring E1 R2 Trunks

R2 signaling is a CAS method that is defined in International Telecommunications Union Telecommunication Standardization Sector (ITU-T) recommendations Q.400 through Q.490. This signaling method is widely used in Europe, Latin America, Australia, and Asia. You need to beware of many country-specific variants before you configure R2. These variants are described in the Consultative Committee for International Telegraph and Telephone (CCITT) R2 specification.

R2 signaling has two components: line signaling, which provides supervisory control signals, and interregister signaling, which provides call setup control.

Line signaling uses the ABCD bits in timeslot 16 for supervisory purposes, such as indicating line seizure or line clearing. Only the A and B bits are used in the CCITT-R2 format. Line signaling is supported in Cisco Voice Gateways in the following formats:

- **R2-Digital**—Typically used for pulse code modulation (PCM) systems, this type is defined in ITU-U Q.421.

- **R2-Analog**—Typically used in carrier systems, this type is defined in ITU-U Q.411.

- **R2-Pulse**—This type is usually reserved for systems that employ satellite links.

Interregister signaling uses in-band multifrequency signals in each timeslot to send the calling number, called number, and call category. Three types of interregister signaling are supported:

- **R2-Compelled**—In compelled, a tone-pair is sent from the switch and stays on until the remote end responds with a pair of tones that signals the switch to turn off the tones.

- **R2-Noncompelled**—In noncompelled, the tone-pairs are sent as pulses so that they stay on for a short duration. Responses to the switch are sent as pulses.

- **R2-Semicompelled**—In semicompelled, forward tone-pairs are sent as compelled. Responses are sent as pulses.

To configure an R2 signaling on an E1 trunk, you need to gather the following information from the PSTN service provider:

- Line signaling type.

- Interregister signaling type. Most implementations use R2-Noncompelled.

- Whether or not ANI information will be sent on the trunk.

- Number of channels, and which specific channels will be used to carry voice on the E1.

- Any CCITT-R2 country-specific variations that the PSTN uses.

To begin, you need to configure the physical port, as shown previously in the section "Configuring E1/T1 Physical Layer Connections."

The next step is to set up the DS0 groups. A DS0 group is a logical grouping of individual 64-Kbps voice channels on the E1. You can configure the entire E1 as a single DS0 group, or you can set up several DS0 groups, depending on requirements. For a PSTN connection, the DS0 logical configuration must match what the PSTN provides.

You configure the DS0 groups by using the following command:

```
ds0-group group number timeslots 1-31 type line-signaling-type interregister-
signaling-type ani
```

The *group number* assigns a logical grouping to the channels defined in this DS0 group. You can specify up to 31 separate groups on an E1 trunk. Each logical DS0 group will have a separate voice port.

The **timeslots** keyword identifies the channels on the E1 that are being grouped under this DS0 group.

The *line-signaling-type* and *interregister-signaling-type* must match those that the PSTN service provider requires.

The **ani** optional keyword is added if the PSTN is providing ANI (calling number) information. The DNIS (called number) information is always provided.

Example 6-18 shows a typical E1 R2 configuration for a voice trunk in the United Kingdom. In this example, the first four channels of the E1 are used for voice. ANI information is being provided. Voice port 1/0:0 was created for the logical DS0 group 0. The **cptone GB** command under the voice port sets the locale to the United Kingdom.

Example 6-18 *E1 R2 Example Configuration for the United Kingdom*

```
Leeds#show running-config
Building configuration...
!
!  Unnecessary output deleted
!
version 12.3
!
controller E1 1/0
 ds0-group 0 timeslots 1-4 type r2-digital r2-compelled ani
!
!   Voice port 1/0:0 created for logical ds0-group 0
!
voice-port 1/0:0
 cptone GB
!
end
```

Many country-specific variations of R2 signaling exist. To customize the voice gateway for the country where it is deployed, use the **cas-custom** *channel number* subcommand in controller configuration mode. The channel number parameter must match the group number of the DS0 group that you are customizing. Whenever you are setting up customized R2, Cisco recommends that you begin by using the **country** *country* **use-defaults** subcommand of the **cas-custom** command. This subcommand automatically sets up typical parameters for the chosen country. You can customize further from that starting point. Example 6-19 shows how you can use the **cas-custom** command.

Example 6-19 *E1 R2* **cas-custom** *Example Configuration*

```
Leeds#show running-config
Building configuration...
!
!  Unnecessary output deleted
!
version 12.3
!
controller E1 1/0
 ds0-group 0 timeslots 1-4 type r2-digital r2-compelled ani
cas-custom 0
  unused-abcd 0 1 1 1
  country hongkong-china
  answer-signal group-b 1
!
!   Voice-port 1/0:0 created for logical ds0-group 0
!
voice-port 1/0:0
 cptone HK
!
end
```

In Example 6-19, the router generated the three subcommands following **cas-custom 0**. The actual command entered under **cas-custom 0** was **country hongkong-china use-defaults**.

NOTE   You can find further information on country-specific R2 protocol customization on Cisco.com:

E1 R2 customization with the **cas-custom** command—www.cisco.com/en/US/tech/tk652/tk653/technologies_tech_note09186a00800942f2.shtml

E1 R2 signaling configuration and troubleshooting—www.cisco.com/en/US/tech/tk652/tk653/technologies_configuration_example09186a00800ad389.shtml

---

MGCP

CallManager MGCP does not support E1 CAS (E1 R2) trunks.

Verifying and Troubleshooting

You can view the status and signaling of the voice ports by individual timeslot (channel) using the **show voice port summary** command, as shown in Example 6-20. This example reflects the configuration shown previously in Example 6-18. Voice port 1/0:0 is controlling associated timeslots 1 through 4 with r2-digital signaling. You can also see that channel 1 is active (seized).

Example 6-20   **show voice port summary** *Command Output with E1 R2*

```
Leeds#show voice port summary
                                    IN      OUT
PORT       CH  SIG-TYPE     ADMIN OPER STATUS  STATUS   EC
========= == ============ ===== ==== ======== ======== ==
1/0:0      01  r2-digital  up    dorm idle     seized   y
1/0:0      02  r2-digital  up    dorm idle     idle     y
1/0:0      03  r2-digital  up    dorm idle     idle     y
1/0:0      04  r2-digital  up    dorm idle     idle     y
```

You can find information about the progress of a call on the voice port with the **show voice call summary** command. In Example 6-21, you can see that a call is in progress on voice port 1/0:0 channel 4.

Example 6-21   **show voice call summary** *Example with E1 R2*

```
Leeds#show voice call summary
PORT             CODEC     VAD VTSP STATE          VPM STATE
=============== ======== === =================== =======================
1/0:0.1          -         -   -                   R2_Q421_IDLE
```

continues

Example 6-21 show voice call summary *Example with E1 R2 (Continued)*

```
1/0:0.2        -        - -           R2_Q421_IDLE
1/0:0.3        -        - -           R2_Q421_IDLE
1/0:0.4        None     y  S_R2_DIALING    R2_Q421_OG_SEIZE_ACK
```

If you are having problems completing calls on the E1 trunk, the **debug vpm signal** and **debug vtsp all** commands can provide useful information to assist in troubleshooting.

Configuring T1 CAS Trunks

T1 CAS circuits use in-band signaling, "robbing" the least significant bits from channels that carry voice to handle framing and to pass state information. The framing and state information is carried along with the voice information in each channel. This is in contrast to ISDN, which has one channel dedicated to carrying signaling for all the other voice channels.

To configure a T1 CAS trunk, you need to gather the following information from the PSTN service provider:

- **Signaling interface**—FXO, FXS, or E&M. You also need to know the specific method that the PSTN uses to signal state of the line:

  — **For FXO or FXS**—Loop-start or ground-start.

  — **For E&M**—Immediate-start, delay-dial, wink-start (also known as Feature Group B (FGB)), double-wink-start (also known as Feature Group D [FGD]), or Feature Group D Exchange Access North American (FGD-EANA).

- **Number of channels used for voice traffic**—If you are not using the full T1 for voice, you need to know which specific channels carry voice traffic.

Signaling information is passed over T1 circuits by emulating the methods used for analog trunks: FXO, FXS, and E&M. This information is passed using the A and B bits in SF circuits or the ABCD bits in ESF circuits. For more details on these signaling methods, see Chapter 5.

Loop-start signaling is the simplest CAS signaling method. Unfortunately, it has several disadvantages that make it an undesirable choice. It has no far-end answer or disconnect supervision. That is, you cannot relay when the remote side of the call answers or hangs up. Loop-start also provides no seizure of the channel on incoming calls. This can lead to a condition known as *glare* when both sides of the connection try to place a call at the same time.

Ground-start signaling has some advantages over loop-start. Ground-start can recognize far-end disconnect. It also can seize the channel on an inbound call, preventing the occurrence of glare. For this reason, ground-start is often used between PBXs or from a PBX to a voice gateway.

E&M signaling has many advantages over the other types shown so far and is the preferred choice for CAS trunks. E&M provides both answer and disconnect supervision and glare avoidance, can receive ANI information (FGD only), and can send ANI information (FGD-EANA only).

To begin, it is necessary to configure the physical port, as shown previously in the section, "Configuring E1/T1 Physical Layer Connections."

The next step is to configure DS0 groups. You configure DS0 groups in controller configuration mode using the **ds0-group** keyword. The syntax is **ds0-group** *group-number* **timeslots** *0-23* **type** *signaling-type*. The *group-number* parameter identifies the DS0 group and is a number in the range of 0–23. You can configure up to 24 DS0 groups, and you must assign each a different number. The **timeslots** *0-23* parameter establishes which channels in the T1 belong to this logical voice port. Table 6-3 lists the signaling types supported in current Cisco IOS versions that you might need for a PSTN connection.

Table 6-3   *T1 CAS Signaling Types That IOS 12.3 Supports*

T1 CAS Signaling Type	Description
e&m-delay-dial	E&M delay-dial signaling.
e&m-fgd	E&M Type II Feature Group D.
e&m-immediate-start	E&M immediate start.
e&m-wink-start	E&M wink-start signaling. Also known as Feature Group B (FGB) signaling.
fgd-eana	FGD Exchange Access North American.
fxo-ground-start	FXO ground-start signaling.
fxo-loop-start	FXO loop-start signaling.
fxs-ground-start	FXS ground-start signaling.
fxs-loop-start	FXS loop-start signaling.
none	External call control.

It is important to note that if CallManager MGCP call control is used with the T1 CAS port, only E&M wink-start and E&M delay-dial are supported.

After you define the DS0 group, the gateway creates a voice port in the form of **voice-port** *slot/port:ds0-group-number,* as shown in Example 6-22. In this example, two DS0 groups were created. The first is associated with voice port 1/0:0, which controls timeslots 1 through 4 on the T1 and uses E&M wink-start signaling. The second is associated with voice port 1/0:1, which controls timeslots 5 through 8 on the T1 using E&M FGD signaling. Call control references the voice ports individually to route calls in and out of the associated timeslots on the T1.

Example 6-22 *T1 CAS Sample Configuration*

```
Miami#show running-config
Building configuration...
!
!  Unnecessary output removed
!
version 12.3
!
controller T1 1/0
 framing esf
 linecode b8zs
 ds0-group 0 timeslots 1-4 type e&m-wink-start
 ds0-group 1 timeslots 5-8 type e&m-fgd
!
!  Voice ports created by DS0 groups defined above
voice-port 1/0:0
 !
voice-port 1/0:1
 !
end
```

MGCP

When you configure a T1 CAS connection that CallManager MGCP will control, you set all the call control parameters on the CallManager, rather than on the gateway. On the gateway, you associate the voice port created to the MGCP application with a dial peer.

CallManager MGCP supports only E&M wink-start and E&M delay dial signaling types for T1 CAS circuits.

You can control whether a port is used for inbound calls, outbound calls, or both.

You can also set the number of significant digits that CallManager should collect for an inbound call. You might need to do this if you are using DID and the last digits of the dialed number represent the extension where the call is to be routed. By setting the number of significant digits to the extension length, you can remove the need to further manipulate the incoming dialed number to deliver the call.

You can individually apply parameters to voice timeslots that are defined on the T1 controller.

Verifying and Troubleshooting

You can view the status and signaling of the voice ports by individual timeslot (channel) using the **show voice port summary** command, as demonstrated in Example 6-23. This example reflects the configuration shown previously in Example 6-22. Voice port 1/0:0 is controlling associated timeslots 1 through 4 with E&M wink-start signaling. You can also see that channel 1 is active (seized). Voice port 1/0:1 is controlling associated timeslots 5 through 8 with E&M FGD signaling.

Example 6-23 **show voice port summary** *Example with T1 CAS*

```
Miami#show voice port summary
                             IN       OUT
PORT       CH   SIG-TYPE     ADMIN OPER STATUS   STATUS   EC
========= == ============ ===== ==== ======== ======== ==
1/0:0      01   e&m-wnk      up    up   seized   idle     y
1/0:0      02   e&m-wnk      up    dorm idle     idle     y
1/0:0      03   e&m-wnk      up    dorm idle     idle     y
1/0:0      04   e&m-wnk      up    dorm idle     idle     y
1/0:1      05   e&m-fgd      up    dorm none     none     y
1/0:1      06   e&m-fgd      up    dorm none     none     y
1/0:1      07   e&m-fgd      up    dorm none     none     y
1/0:1      08   e&m-fgd      up    dorm none     none     y
```

You can also find information about the progress of a call on the voice port with the **show voice call summary** command. In Example 6-24, you can see that a call is in progress on voice port 1/0:0 channel 3.

Example 6-24 **show voice call summary** *Example with Active Call*

```
Miami#show voice call summary
PORT             CODEC      VAD VTSP STATE           VPM STATE
=============== ======== === ==================== =====================
1/0:0.1          -          -  -                    EM_ONHOOK
1/0:0.2          -          -  -                    EM_ONHOOK
1/0:0.3          None       y  S_DS_DIALING         EM_WAIT_DIAL_DONE
1/0:0.4          -          -  -                    EM_ONHOOK
1/0:1.5          -          -  -                    FGD_ONHOOK
1/0:1.6          -          -  -                    FGD_ONHOOK
1/0:1.7          -          -  -                    FGD_ONHOOK
1/0:1.8          -          -  -                    FGD_ONHOOK
```

If you are having a problem with calls on the port, you can use the **debug voip vtsp all** command, which shows the progress of the call control signaling for the call in progress on the port.

Configuring ISDN BRI Trunks

ISDN BRI the only service described that is not delivered on a T1 or E1 circuit. The information and tasks described in the section "Configuring E1/T1 Physical Layer Connections" do not apply to a BRI. BRI voice trunks are not used often in the United States; however, they are popular in other areas of the world.

An ISDN BRI is similar to a PRI in that the signaling information is carried separately from the voice-bearer traffic in a dedicated data channel. A BRI circuit has just two voice-bearer channels and one data channel (2B+D). Only two voice calls can occur simultaneously on a BRI.

BRI trunks operate in a master-slave mode. The master side is called the network termination (NT) side and is responsible for providing clocking and power. The slave side is called the terminal equipment (TE) side. This master-slave relationship extends to Layer 2 and Layer 3 protocols, as defined by ITU-T specifications Q.921 and Q.931, respectively. The master side initiates the Layer 2 and Layer 3 communications. When connecting to the PSTN, the voice gateway is always configured as the slave side (TE). An NT1 device is typically required to connect the voice gateway TE interface to the PSTN.

To configure an ISDN BRI voice trunk, you need to gather the following information:

- **ISDN switch type**—Just as in PRI service, you must specify the switch type in use for signaling to operate properly between the voice gateway and the PSTN. You must globally configure an ISDN switch type on the gateway. You can override this global definition on a port-by-port basis if necessary.

- **ISDN service profile identifiers (SPID) if required**—The PSTN assigns ISDN SPIDs and local directory numbers (LDNs). These are only used for national and DMS-100 switch types.

Begin configuration by defining the ISDN switch type in global configuration mode using the **isdn switch-type** *switch-type* command. Table 6-4 lists ISDN switch types supported by current versions of Cisco IOS that you might encounter when setting up a PSTN BRI trunk. You can override this setting at the port level if necessary to support multiple connections to different switch types.

Table 6-4   *ISDN BRI Switch Types for PSTN Trunks*

Locale	ISDN BRI Switch Type	Description
Australia, Europe, United Kingdom	**basic-1tr6**	German 1TR6 ISDN switch
	basic-net3	NET3 ISDN BRI for Norway NET3, Australia NET3, and New Zealand NET3 switch types; ETSI-compliant switch types for Euro-ISDN E-DSS1 signaling system
	vn3	French ISDN BRI switch
Japan	**ntt**	Japanese NTT ISDN switch
North America	**basic-5ess**	Lucent basic rate 5ESS switch
	basic-dms100	Northern Telecom DMS-100 BRI switch
	basic-ni	National ISDN switch

Continue the configuration in interface configuration mode using the **interface bri** *slot/port* command. If necessary, configure the first SPID using the **isdn spid1** *spid* [*ldn*] command, as well as using the PSTN-assigned SPID and LDN numbers. You can configure the second SPID in the same manner using the **isdn spid2** *spid* [*ldn*] command.

For voice calls to be properly routed to digital signal processor (DSP) resources for voice processing, you must also code the **isdn incoming-voice voice** command on the interface.

Example 6-25 shows the configuration of a typical ISDN BRI voice trunk.

Example 6-25   *ISDN BRI Voice Interface Configuration*

```
Lima#show running-config
Building configuration...
!
!   Unnecessary output removed
!
version 12.3
!
isdn switch-type basic-5ess
!
interface BRI1/0
 no ip address
 no ip directed-broadcast
 isdn switch-type basic-5ess
 isdn twait-disable
 isdn incoming-voice voice
!
voice-port 1/0
!
end
```

MGCP

CallManager versions 4.1.3SR1 and later allow you to control BRI voice ports with MGCP. With MGCP, the Layer 3 Q.931 messages are backhauled to the CallManager and are not processed by the gateway.

Under the BRI interface, you must code **isdn bind-l3 ccm-manager service mgcp**. This attaches the D-channel Q.931 protocol to the CallManager backhaul. Example 6-26 shows the configuration for an ISDN BRI under MGCP control.

Example 6-26   *MGCP ISDN BRI Configuration*

```
Lima#show running-config
Building configuration...
!
!   Unnecessary output removed
!
version 12.3
!
isdn switch-type basic-net3
!
interface BRI1/0/0
```

continues

Example 6-26 *MGCP ISDN BRI Configuration (Continued)*

```
 no ip address
 no ip directed-broadcast
 isdn switch-type basic-net3
 isdn bind-l3 ccm-manager service mgcp
 isdn incoming-voice voice
 !
voice-port 1/0/0
 !
end
```

In Example 6-26, the ISDN switch type is basic-net3. This is the only switch type supported by CallManager for MGCP control of a BRI.

Verifying and Troubleshooting

To verify that the circuit is operating properly, you can use the **show isdn status** command. Example 6-27 shows the output of this command. The example shows that Layers 1 and 2 are active and that no Layer 3 calls are currently in progress. You can also see the ISDN switch type configured globally and for the specific port.

Example 6-27 **show isdn status** *Command Output for BRI*

```
Lima#show isdn status
Global ISDN Switchtype = basic-5ess
ISDN BRI1/0 interface
        dsl 0, interface ISDN Switchtype = basic-5ess
    Layer 1 Status:
        ACTIVE
    Layer 2 Status:
        TEI = 64, Ces = 1, SAPI = 0, State = MULTIPLE_FRAME_ESTABLISHED
    Layer 3 Status:
        0 Active Layer 3 Call(s)
    Activated dsl 0 CCBs = 0
```

If you have not properly established the Layer 2 connection, use the **debug isdn q921** trace to help identify the problem. If the Layer 1 and Layer 2 output looks correct and you are still having trouble placing or receiving calls on the port, use the **debug isdn q931 trace** command. Both of these are described in the troubleshooting portion of the "Configuring ISDN PRI Trunks" section.

Case Study: Add an E1 R2 Connection to the Leeds Gateway

The Leeds office is migrating from its PBX to a VoIP solution using a Cisco voice gateway. The first task that the Leeds office needs to complete is getting a PSTN connection to the gateway and verifying that it can place and receive calls to the PSTN.

Leeds has a requirement for DID to the employee four-digit extensions. The customer also has a requirement to receive ANI information to identify callers. Because call volume is low at Leeds, it is planning to use only ten DS0s for voice calls. It has ordered an E1 R2 CAS circuit from the PSTN with HDB3 line coding and CRC4 framing. The PSTN has told you that it will be using the first ten timeslots as voice channels on this circuit and that the interregister signaling will be noncompelled.

A Cisco 2811 voice gateway has been installed with a VWIC2-2MFT-T1/E1 two-port module in slot 0 and two PVDM2-16 DSP modules on the main board. The first E1 port connects to the PSTN. The second will help Leeds with the migration by providing temporary connectivity to the PBX. The installed DSPs will provide support for the ten voice channels and two conferencing sessions after the migration is complete.

Call control will use H.323 for this gateway because CallManager MGCP does not support E1 R2 CAS trunks.

Example 6-28 illustrates the configuration of the Leeds gateway to support this PSTN trunk. The first ten timeslots are defined in the DS0 group as specified by the PSTN. You have also included the **ani** keyword to indicate that you will be expecting ANI information.

Under **cas-custom 0**, you have further specified that you are only going to accept four digits of DNIS and seven to ten digits of ANI. You can map the DNIS directly to the four-digit phone extensions at Leeds.

You have also configured **cptone GB** on the voice port to specify the Leeds location in the United Kingdom.

Example 6-28 *Leeds Gateway E1 R2 PSTN Trunk Configuration*

```
Leeds#show running-config
Building configuration...
!
!  Unnecessary output deleted
version 12.4
!
!
!
controller E1 0/1/0
 ds0-group 0 timeslots 1-10 type r2-digital r2-non-compelled ani
 cas-custom 0
  dnis-digits min 4 max 4
  ani-digits min 7 max 10
!
```

continues

Example 6-28   *Leeds Gateway E1 R2 PSTN Trunk Configuration (Continued)*

```
!
voice-port 0/1/0:0
 cptone GB
!
end
```

Example 6-29 shows that the line coding and framing are correct, that the line is up, and
that no errors are occurring. Line code HDB3 and framing CRC4 are the defaults on an E1
port, so they do not show in the configuration in Example 6-28.

Example 6-29   **show controller e1** *Command Output for Leeds E1 R2 PSTN Trunk*

```
Leeds#show controller e1 0/1/0
E1 0/1/0 is up.
  Applique type is Channelized E1 - balanced
  No alarms detected.
  alarm-trigger is not set
  Version info Firmware: 20040713, FPGA: 15, spm_count = 0
  Framing is CRC4, Line Code is HDB3, Clock Source is Line.
  CRC Threshold is 320. Reported from firmware  is 320.
  Data in current interval (340 seconds elapsed):
     0 Line Code Violations, 0 Path Code Violations
     0 Slip Secs, 0 Fr Loss Secs, 0 Line Err Secs, 0 Degraded Mins
     0 Errored Secs, 0 Bursty Err Secs, 0 Severely Err Secs, 0 Unavail Secs
```

The **show voice call summary**, shown in Example 6-30, indicates the status of the
individual DS0s in the DS0 group. An outgoing call has been answered on DS0 four. DS0
nine has an incoming call that has been answered and is using a G.729r8 codec.

Example 6-30   **show voice call summary** *Output with Calls in Progress*

```
Leeds#show voice call summary
PORT           CODEC    VAD VTSP STATE          VPM STATE
============== ======== === ==================== ======================
0/1/0:0.1      -        -   -                    R2_Q421_IDLE
0/1/0:0.2      -        -   -                    R2_Q421_IDLE
0/1/0:0.3      -        -   -                    R2_Q421_IDLE
0/1/0:0.4      None     y   S_CONNECT            R2_Q421_OG_ANSWER
0/1/0:0.5      -        -   -                    R2_Q421_IDLE
0/1/0:0.6      -        -   -                    R2_Q421_IDLE
0/1/0:0.7      -        -   -                    R2_Q421_IDLE
0/1/0:0.8      -        -   -                    R2_Q421_IDLE
0/1/0:0.9      g729r8   y   S_CONNECT            R2_Q421_IC_ANSWER
0/1/0:0.10     -        -   -                    R2_Q421_IDLE
```

With this configuration, the PSTN trunk operates correctly using H.323 call control. Leeds
can now continue with the next step of its migration.

Review Questions

1 What is a major drawback of using analog FXO trunks for inbound calls?

2 Which command must you include when configuring a CAMA type 4 (KP-NPD-NXX-XXXX-ST) trunk?

3 You issue a **show controller** command on a digital trunk and see accumulated slip seconds in every interval. What could be the cause?

4 When you are trying to set up Q.931 backhaul on an ISDN PRI using CallManager MGCP, the **isdn bind-l3 ccm-manager** command is not recognized. What could cause this?

5 What must you do prior to configuring a PRI group on an ISDN PRI circuit?

6 Which signaling type is necessary if you want to receive ANI information on a T1 CAS trunk?

7 What are the two components of R2 signaling?

8 If it is necessary to use the **cas custom** command to modify the signaling on an E1 R2 trunk, what is the recommended first step?

CHAPTER 7

Connecting to PBXs

Another useful application of a Cisco voice gateway is to connect to a company PBX. One reason to do this is to eliminate dedicated tie trunks that connect PBX systems in different locations, thus reducing costs by eliminating the monthly charge for those circuits. You can connect a PBX to a voice gateway, and you can route calls across a WAN network to another voice gateway that is connected to the remote PBX. This extends the usefulness of the data bandwidth between sites, and it allows companies to bypass any long-distance tolls that might be charged.

Most companies are either actively investigating or currently involved in replacing their PBX systems with an IP telephony system, such as the Cisco CallManager or Cisco CallManager Express (CME). This rapid change is being driven by the many benefits that IP telephony provides, including applications and XML services which enhance business productivity, simplified upgrades to add or change services to quickly adapt as business needs change, and so on.

You can connect a voice gateway to a PBX to help facilitate this migration. The PBX connection allows you to route calls between the two networks during the migration period. In this case, it is not unusual to have both public switched telephone network (PSTN) connections and PBX connections on the voice gateway.

This chapter will help you to do the following:

- Understand, properly configure, and troubleshoot the various analog connections available, including Foreign Exchange Office (FXO)/Foreign Exchange Station (FXS) and ear and mouth (E&M) connection types

- Understand how clocking works on digital circuits and be able to properly configure it for various circuit options

- Understand how ISDN works as a PBX tie trunk and be able to successfully configure and troubleshoot an ISDN PRI trunk

- Recognize the interoperability benefits of Q Signaling (QSIG) and understand how to configure a Cisco CallManager-controlled QSIG trunk

- Understand the application of Transparent Common Channel Signaling (T-CCS) and be able to configure and troubleshoot a T-CCS trunk between locations

Analog Trunks

Plain old telephone service (POTS) trunks are two- or four-wire analog service types that you can use to connect a voice gateway to a PBX. They are typically used where the call volume is low, because each trunk is capable of carrying only a single call at a time.

The analog trunk types that you can use for PBX integration include FXS, FXO, and E&M trunks.

Configuring FXO/FXS Connections

FXO and FXS ports are complementary interfaces. That is, they are meant to be connected to each other. When the PSTN supplies a POTS line to a location, it is supplying an FXS interface. To operate properly, the FXS interface must be connected to an FXO interface, such as that on analog station equipment (telephone, fax machine, modem, and so on) or to an FXO port on a voice gateway, as discussed in Chapter 6, "Connecting to the PSTN."

PBX analog trunk connections are typically FXO interfaces. They normally connect to a PSTN POTS trunk, which is an FXS interface. A PBX analog FXO trunk must be connected to an FXS interface on a Cisco voice gateway to work properly.

PBX systems usually also have FXS ports to connect to analog station equipment. This is called a *station-side* connection to the PBX. In some cases, you might want to connect a voice gateway to a PBX on the station side. Station-side PBX connections use FXO interfaces on Cisco voice gateways. You can configure these FXO ports exactly as described in Chapter 6. Station-side connections to the PBX can be useful when you are using the PBX as a pass-through device to get to the PSTN.

An example of where this might occur is during a migration from a PBX to an IP telephony solution. In the early stages of a migration, the PSTN trunks might still be connected to the PBX. The voice gateway can route calls between the PBX or PSTN and the IP voice network using station-side PBX connections if ports are available and the call volume is low enough.

FXS ports support two methods of supervisory signaling to detect on-hook or off-hook conditions and line seizure: loop-start or ground-start.

Loop-start is the most common signaling method used on PSTN trunks. It has two significant disadvantages: No mechanism exists to prevent glare from occurring, and no switch-side disconnect supervision exists to indicate the end of a call. These limitations make ground-start the preferred signaling method for tie trunks between a PBX and a voice gateway.

For ground-start signaling to function properly, the physical wiring must be correct. The connection is polarity sensitive, so you need to wire it with tip connected to tip and ring connected to ring.

After you have determined the proper connection port type and signaling, configuration is straightforward. Start by entering voice port configuration mode using the **voice-port** *slot/subunit/port* command. After you are there, you can configure signaling using the **signal** *type* subcommand, where *type* is either **groundstart** or **loopstart**. Loop-start signaling is the default. For installations outside of the United States, you can set up the locale using the **cptone** *locale* command.

To use caller ID, you must use the **caller-id enable** command on the voice port. When you are using FXO and FXS ports to set up connections to a PBX, it is important to remember that FXS ports *send* caller ID and FXO ports *receive* caller ID. Because of this relationship, caller ID is sent only one way when used on this type of connection—from FXS to FXO.

Example 7-1 shows the configuration of both an FXS and an FXO port. A station name and number is assigned to the FXS port using the **station-id name | number** *word* command. When station ID is coded, the interface sends that static information as the caller name and number.

You can verify the configured signaling and status of an FXO or FXS port using the **show voice port summary** command, as shown in Example 7-1. Output from the **show voice port summary** command shows that ground-start signaling is configured for these two ports.

Example 7-1 *FXO and FXS Port Configuration*

```
Boise#show running-config
!
!  Unnecessary output deleted
!
!  FXS Port 0/2/0
voice-port 0/2/0
 signal groundStart
 station-id name Tie Line
 station-id number 9195553456
 caller-id enable
!
!  FXO port 0/3/0
voice-port 0/3/0
 signal groundStart
 caller-id enable
!
end
Boise#show voice port summary
                                  IN       OUT
PORT       CH   SIG-TYPE   ADMIN OPER STATUS   STATUS   EC
========= == ============ ===== ==== ======== ======== ==
0/2/0      --   fxs-gs     up    dorm on-hook  idle     y
0/2/1      --   fxs-ls     up    dorm on-hook  idle     y
0/3/0      --   fxo-gs     up    dorm idle     on-hook  y
0/3/1      --   fxo-ls     up    dorm idle     on-hook  y
```

You can display more specific information by using the **show voice port** *slot/subunit/port* command. Example 7-2 shows the caller ID-specific information displayed by this command. Note that the FXS port clearly shows that it will *send* the caller ID, whereas the FXO port will *receive* the caller ID.

Example 7-2 *Verifying FXO/FXS Caller ID Using the* **show voice port** *Command*

```
Boise#show voice port 0/2/0
Foreign Exchange Station 0/2/0 Slot is 0, Sub-unit is 2, Port is 0
 Type of VoicePort is FXS  VIC2-2FXS
 Operation State is DORMANT
 Administrative State is UP
 !
 ! Unnecessary output deleted
 !
 Caller ID Info Follows:
 Standard BELLCORE
 Output attenuation is set to 14 dB
 Caller ID is transmitted after 1 ring(s)

 Voice card specific Info Follows:
 Signal Type is groundStart
 Ring Frequency is 25 Hz
 Hook Status is On Hook

Boise#show voice port 0/3/0
Foreign Exchange Office 0/3/0 Slot is 0, Sub-unit is 3, Port is 0
 Type of VoicePort is FXO
 Operation State is DORMANT
 Administrative State is UP
 !
 ! Unnecessary output deleted
 !
 Caller ID Info Follows:
 Standard BELLCORE
 Caller ID is received after 1 ring(s)

 Voice card specific Info Follows:
 Signal Type is groundStart
 Battery-Reversal is enabled
 Number Of Rings is set to 1
 Supervisory Disconnect is signal
```

MGCP

You can place both FXO and FXS ports under Media Gateway Control Protocol (MGCP) control. When defining FXO ports to CallManager for MGCP control, you must configure the signaling type. You can also control whether the port is used for inbound calls, outbound calls, or both. No signaling type is defined for FXS ports. However, when using an FXS port as a trunk, you must define the number of digits expected on an inbound call for proper call routing to occur.

Configuring E&M Trunks

The enhanced mechanisms for signaling answer and disconnect supervision available make E&M trunks a good choice for connections between a Cisco voice gateway and a PBX. Five discrete interface types are defined for E&M connections. Cisco voice gateways support Types I, II, III, and V. Cisco platforms do not support E&M Type IV.

E&M signaling defines a *trunk side,* which is usually the PBX, and a *signaling side,* which is usually the voice gateway. Cisco E&M interfaces are fixed as the signaling unit side of the interface. This might make it necessary to change the E&M trunk settings on the PBX to operate as the trunk circuit side depending on the interface type in use.

NOTE   For more information about E&M circuit wiring, operation, and troubleshooting, see Chapter 5, "Circuit Options."

Before beginning to configure an E&M trunk, you need to do the following:

- **Determine whether the trunk will be using two-wire or four-wire operation**— Clearly understand the wiring arrangement in use by the PBX and verify that the wiring to the E&M port on the voice gateway is correct. Even though these connections are described as "two-wire" or "four-wire," it is common to have six or eight wires in actual use. Incorrect wiring is one of the most common problems encountered when installing an E&M trunk.

- **Determine which interface type to use**—Cisco voice gateways support Types I, II, III, and V. Note that Type I is the most common in North America, whereas Type V is the most common throughout the rest of the world.

- **Identify the correct start dial supervision signaling to use**—Immediate start, wink-start, and delay dial are the different options that can be selected. This setting defines the signaling format to expect prior to delivering addressing information, such as dialed number identification service (DNIS).

After you have obtained the necessary information, have verified the wiring requirements, and have the port physically connected, you can begin configuration.

Enter voice port configuration mode using the **voice-port** *slot/subunit/port* command. If necessary, configure the country-specific locale parameters using the **cptone** *locale.* The default locale is **us**.

Specify how many wires are used for voice transmission using the **operation** {**2-wire** | **4-wire**} command. Note that this defines the wires used for the audio path only, not for signaling. The default is two-wire operation.

Specify the E&M interface type to which this port is connected using the **type {1 | 2 | 3 | 5}** command. On the VIC-2E/M or VIC2-2E/M interface module, you must set both ports to the same interface type.

Example 7-3 shows an E&M trunk configured for interface Type I, four-wire operation, and wink-start dial signaling.

Example 7-3 *E&M Port Basic Configuration*

```
Boise#config t
!
! Go to voice port configuration
Boise(config)#voice-port 0/1/0
!
!  Specify four-wire audio path
Boise(config-voiceport)#operation 4-wire
!
!  Configure interface type
Boise(config-voiceport)#type 1
!
!  Configure start dial signaling method
Boise(config-voiceport)#signaling wink-start
```

NOTE   The current version of CallManager MGCP does not support analog E&M trunks.

Verifying and Troubleshooting

To verify that the port is configured correctly, use the **show voice port** *slot/subunit/port* command. This command shows you the current configuration of the parameters that were already discussed in addition to many others. Example 7-4 reflects the port that was configured in the preceding example. Notice that the port was configured for four-wire operation, interface Type I, and wink-start signaling.

Example 7-4 **show voice port** *Output for E&M Interfaces*

```
Boise#show voice port 0/1/0

recEive And transMit 0/1/0 Slot is 0, Sub-unit is 1, Port is 0
 Type of VoicePort is E&M
 Operation State is DORMANT
 Administrative State is UP
 The Last Interface Down Failure Cause is Administrative Shutdown
 Description is not set
 Noise Regeneration is enabled
 Non Linear Processing is enabled
 Music On Hold Threshold is Set to -38 dBm
 In Gain is Set to 0 dB
 Out Attenuation is Set to 0 dB
 Echo Cancellation is enabled
```

Example 7-4   **show voice port** *Output for E&M Interfaces (Continued)*

```
Echo Cancel Coverage is set to 8 ms
Connection Mode is normal
Connection Number is not set
Initial Time Out is set to 10 s
Interdigit Time Out is set to 10 s
Call-Disconnect Time Out is set to 60 s
Region Tone is set for US

Analog Info Follows:
Currently processing none
Maintenance Mode Set to None (not in mtc mode)
Number of signaling protocol errors are 0
Impedance is set to 600r Ohm

Voice card specific Info Follows:
Signal Type is wink
Operation Type is 4-wire
E&M Type is 1
Dial Type is dtmf
In Seizure is inactive
Out Seizure is inactive
Digit Duration Timing is set to 100 ms
InterDigit Duration Timing is set to 100 ms
Pulse Rate Timing is set to 10 pulses/second
InterDigit Pulse Duration Timing is set to 500 ms
Clear Wait Duration Timing is set to 400 ms
Wink Wait Duration Timing is set to 200 ms
Wink Duration Timing is set to 200 ms
Delay Start Timing is set to 300 ms
Delay Duration Timing is set to 2000 ms
Dial Pulse Min. Delay is set to 140 ms
```

If the port configuration is correct and you are still having problems placing or receiving calls on the trunk, the first place to look is at the wiring between the PBX and the voice gateway. As mentioned, the most common problem encountered with E&M trunk is incorrect wiring.

NOTE   You can find detailed information about E&M interface types and wiring arrangements on Cisco.com at www.cisco.com/en/US/products/hw/gatecont/ps2250/ products_tech_note09186a008009452e.shtml.

- **E&M Type I and Type V**—Uses two leads for supervisory signaling (on-hook/off-hook signaling). Cisco voice gateways expect to see off-hook conditions on the M-lead and signal off-hook to the remote device on the E-lead.

- **E&M Type II and Type III**— Uses four leads (E, M, Signal Battery [SB], and Signal Ground [SG]) for supervisory signaling. The PBX connects the M-lead to the SB-lead to indicate the off-hook condition. The voice gateway connects the E-lead to the SG-lead to indicate the off-hook condition.

- **Voice path operation**—The two-wire or four-wire operation for the audio path is independent of the signaling type. For example, a four-wire voice operation E&M circuit has six physical wires if it is configured for Type I or Type V. It has eight physical wires if it is configured for Type II or Type III.

- **Voice path wiring**—In the four-wire mode, some PBX and key system products reverse the normal usage of the tip and ring (T&R) and Tip1 and Ring1 (T1&R1) pairs. In that case, to match up the PBX voice pairs with the voice gateway E&M voice pairs, you might need to connect T&R on the PBX side to T1&R1 on the voice gateway side, and T1&R1 on the PBX side to T&R on the voice gateway side.

The next step in troubleshooting is to look for problems with supervision signaling. You can do this by using the **debug vpm signal** command. Enable this debug mode and place a call from the PBX to the voice gateway. Verify that the gateway can see the on-hook/off-hook signaling. If you do not see the supervisory signaling in the debug output, a mismatch might exist between the interface type on the PBX and that of the Cisco voice gateway.

Finally, validate that the gateway sends and receives the correct digits to and from the PBX. You can do this by using the **debug vpm signaling** and **debug voip vtsp session** debugging commands. The **debug voip vtsp session** command displays the digits received or sent. If digits are passing but are not the *expected* digits, double-check the call control (dial peers, CallManager route patterns, and so on).

Digital Trunks

Connecting the voice gateway to the PBX using digital trunks has many advantages. Among these advantages are higher capacity, more reliable signaling methods, and advanced features, such as caller number and name display.

Configuring E1/T1 Physical Layer Connections

Successful implementation of digital tie trunks between a PBX and a voice gateway begins with establishing correct physical connections. You must properly set line coding, framing, and clocking on each end of the link. When the PSTN service provider connects to a PSTN trunk, it establishes the parameters to use for the link. When you connect to a PBX, you typically have control over both ends of the link and can optimize the configuration for your particular application.

Line coding and framing configuration are discussed in detail in Chapter 6. Be sure that you configure these parameters in the voice gateway to match what is configured on the PBX.

Clocking

It is important that you understand how clocking will be set up on a digital trunk. Improper clocking configuration shows up as clock slips on the controller interface. Slips can cause a wide variety of voice problems, including poor voice quality, static, echo, and one-way audio. Understanding how to set up a stable clocking domain prevents these problems.

In addition to the trunks, Cisco voice gateways that have a built-in TDM bus must be clocked correctly for voice traffic to flow properly and to avoid problems. By default, the time-division multiplexing (TDM) bus uses the internal oscillator as a clock source. However, this causes problems with connected circuits that use a different clock source. You can use the **show network-clocks** command to see which of the available clock sources is currently being used to time the TDM bus. In Example 7-5, a primary and a secondary clock source are configured. The secondary source link is not active at the moment, and the primary is in use. The internal oscillator (called the Backplane in this output) is also listed as a "last ditch" clock source to be used if no better clock is available.

In Cisco Integrated Services Routers (ISR), you must synchronize the clock for the digital signal processor (DSP) resources on the motherboard with the circuit to be used. The DSP resources are clocked from the TDM bus.

Example 7-5   *Output from* **show network-clocks** *Command*

```
Miami#show network-clocks
  Network Clock Configuration
  Priority        Clock Source      Clock State       Clock Type
     1            T1 1/0            GOOD              T1
     2            T1 1/1            LINK DOWN         T1
    10            Backplane         GOOD              PLL


  Current Primary Clock Source
  Priority        Clock Source      Clock State       Clock Type
     1            T1 1/0            GOOD              T1
```

When selecting a clock source to use, choose the best available one. PSTN circuits are generally the best clock sources available. Most PBX systems can pass the clock from a "master" source, such as a PSTN circuit, to other trunk ports. If the PBX has a PSTN circuit attached and can use that circuit as a master clock source, use the PBX timing on the tie trunk and set the voice gateway for loop timing, as shown in Figure 7-1.

Figure 7-1 *Using PSTN Trunk to the PBX as Master Clock Source*

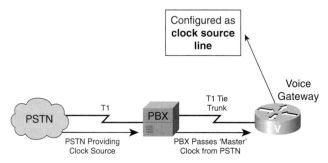

With this configuration, you can also use the clock that you recovered from the PSTN (using the PBX) for the TDM bus within the gateway. Example 7-6 shows the configuration necessary. The **network-clock-participate** command enables the module on slot 1 to be a clock source for the TDM bus. The **network-clock-select** command sets clocking recovered on T1 1/0 to be used as the priority 1 clock for the TDM bus. If additional clock sources are available, you can add them as candidates using the **network-clock-select** command and different priorities. Only one clock is in use at any given time. In controller configuration mode, the **clock source line** command instructs the voice gateway to use the clock recovered from the bit stream received on that interface as a clock source, rather than the internal clock.

Example 7-6 *Using the PBX Trunk as a Master Clock Source*

```
Miami#show running-config
!
!   Unnecessary output deleted
!
network-clock-participate slot 1
network-clock-select 1 T1 1/0
!
!
controller T1 1/0
 framing esf
 clock source line
 linecode b8zs
 ds0-group 1 timeslots 1-24 type e&m-wink-start
!
end
```

You can also reverse this configuration. If the PSTN trunk goes to the Cisco voice gateway instead of the PBX, the voice gateway can recover the clock from the PSTN circuit and use it to clock both the internal TDM bus and the tie trunk to the PBX, thus providing clocking for the PBX. Figure 7-2 shows an example of this scenario.

Figure 7-2   *Using the PSTN Trunk to the Voice Gateway as the Master Clock Source*

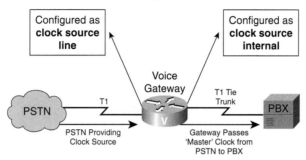

Example 7-7 shows the voice gateway configuration necessary. Notice that T1 1/1 goes to the PBX and uses the **clock source internal** command. That command gets clocking from the TDM bus, which is in turn being clocked by PSTN T1 1/0.

Example 7-7   *Using the PSTN Trunk to Clock a PBX Tie Trunk*

```
Miami#show running-config
!
!  Unnecessary output deleted
!
network-clock-participate slot 1
network-clock-select 1 T1 1/0
!
!
controller T1 1/0
 description PSTN Trunk
 framing esf
 clock source line
 linecode b8zs
 ds0-group 1 timeslots 1-24 type e&m-wink-start
!
controller T1 1/1
 description Tie Trunk to PBX
 framing esf
 clock source internal
 linecode b8zs
 ds0-group 1 timeslots 1-24 type e&m-wink-start
!
end
```

Another possibility is that two connections to the voice gateway exist and both are good clock sources. As an example, suppose that there is a PSTN trunk to the voice gateway, a PSTN trunk to the PBX, and a tie trunk from the PBX to the voice gateway. In this case, a viable clock source for the voice gateway exists on both ports. Figure 7-3 shows this scenario.

Figure 7-3 *Multiple Usable Clock Sources*

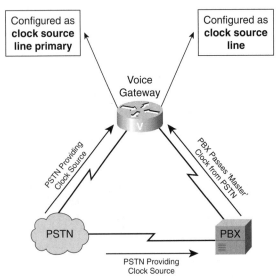

Example 7-8 shows the configuration of the voice gateway that is necessary to support this clocking scenario. The PSTN trunk uses the **clock source line primary** command, and the PBX trunk uses the **clock source line** command. The **primary** keyword indicates that, whenever possible, you should use the clock from the PSTN trunk to time the Phase-Locked Loop (PLL) on this controller.

Example 7-8 *Configuring for Multiple Usable Clock Sources*

```
Miami#show running-config
!
!  Unnecessary output deleted
!
network-clock-participate slot 1
network-clock-select 1 T1 1/0
network-clock-select 2 T1 1/1
!
!
controller T1 1/0
 description PSTN Trunk
 framing esf
 clock source line primary
 linecode b8zs
 ds0-group 1 timeslots 1-24 type e&m-wink-start
!
controller T1 1/1
 description Tie Trunk to PBX
 framing esf
 clock source line
 linecode b8zs
```

Example 7-8 *Configuring for Multiple Usable Clock Sources (Continued)*

```
 ds0-group 1 timeslots 1-24 type e&m-wink-start
!
end
```

When using a two-port network module, such as a VWIC2-2MFT-T1/E1 for two voice circuits, both ports must use the same clock source. The same DSP resources used for both ports and differences in clocking can cause sips and interface flaps. If multiple *different* clocks sources are present (such as circuits from different carriers), divide them across modules using different DSP resources. For example, one could use motherboard DSPs and another could use DSPs on a network module (NM), such as the NM-HDV2. In this case, you should not include the NM-HDV2 in the **network-clock-participate** list. Because the NM has a different clock than the other circuits in this example, it should not be a fallback candidate to clock the TDM bus.

For voice circuits, all interfaces that share a common pool of DSP resources must have synchronized clocks.

Verifying and Troubleshooting

You can verify the correct operation of the digital trunk at a physical level by using the **show controller t1 | e1** *slot/subunit/port* command. The output shows a great deal of information about the current state of the link, in addition to historical information. This information can help you isolate problems with line coding, framing, and clocking of the link. In Example 7-9, you can see that numerous slips have been recorded, which indicates a clocking issue with the circuit. Notice in this example that the clock source is set to internal. This information can immediately lead you to investigate the clocking configuration as a starting point in troubleshooting.

Example 7-9 **show controller** *Command Output*

```
Miami#show controller t1 1/1
T1 1/1 is up.
  Applique type is Channelized T1
  Cablelength is long gain36 0db
  Receiver has loss of signal.
  alarm-trigger is not set
  Version info Firmware: 20040713, FPGA: 15, spm_count = 0
  Framing is ESF, Line Code is B8ZS, Clock Source is Internal.
  CRC Threshold is 320. Reported from firmware  is 320.
  Data in current interval (890 seconds elapsed):
     2 Line Code Violations, 798 Path Code Violations
     114 Slip Secs, 0 Fr Loss Secs, 0 Line Err Secs, 0 Degraded Mins
      114 Errored Secs, 0 Bursty Err Secs, 0 Severely Err Secs, 757 Unavail Secs
```

Additional troubleshooting information, as well as a description of all the fields in the output of the **show controller** command, is covered in detail in Chapter 6.

Configuring ISDN PRI Trunks

Configuring a PRI trunk to a PBX and configuring one to the PSTN has two main differences:

- **The need to determine the network versus user role**—Layer 2 communications are established on an ISDN link using a master-slave relationship. The master side is called the network side, and the slave side is called the user side. When connecting to the PSTN, the voice gateway is always the user side and the PSTN is always the network side. This is not necessarily the case when connecting a voice gateway to a PBX.

  PBX manufacturers typically assume that the PRI trunk ports will be connecting to the PSTN, so they default to user side. The Cisco voice gateway also defaults to user side. If a connection is made from user side to user side or network side to network side, Layer 2 communications are not established. You must decide which device will be the network side of the connection and configure it correctly. Many older or smaller PBX systems do not have the option of running the PRI trunk port as the network side.

  If this is the case, you need to configure the voice gateway to be the network side. You accomplish this by using the **isdn protocol-emulate network** command. You apply this command to the serial interface that is created when you define the **pri-group**.

- **The need to determine the ISDN switch type to be used**—The ISDN switch type determines the format of the Layer 3 messages to be used on the ISDN D-channel. When you connect to the PSTN, the service provider specifies the ISDN switch type to use. When you connect to a PBX, it is important to select a switch type that is supported and provides the highest level of interoperability for supplementary services and information exchange.

  Many PBX vendors support "native" switch types that provide the highest level of capabilities for their systems. These include 5ESS for AT&T or Lucent, DMS-100 for Nortel PBX systems, and so on. Most PBX systems also support standard switch types such as NI2 for North America and NET5 for the UK, Europe, Asia, and Australia.

  The QSIG protocol was developed specifically to provide interoperability between PBXs and can be used if your PBX system supports it. Many PBX vendors have chosen to support QSIG only as an added cost upgrade. You can find more information about QSIG later in this chapter.

After you have the physical connection running and verified, have determined which side will be network and user, and have selected a switch type, you can begin to configure the PRI trunk.

Configuration begins by setting a global ISDN switch type for the voice gateway. You do this by using the **isdn switch-type** *type* command in global configuration mode. You can override this setting on a port-by-port basis later on if necessary. After you have defined the global switch type, enter controller configuration mode using the **controller T1 | E1** *slot/subunit/port* command. Add the PRI group to the interface using the **pri-group timeslots** *num* command. The *num* parameter is 1-24 for T1 or 1-31 for E1. You can only create one PRI group on an interface. The Cisco IOS includes the D-channel automatically.

After you have defined the PRI group, IOS automatically creates a corresponding voice port and serial interface. You can manipulate parameters, such as locale, station name and number, and so on, on the voice port.

The serial interface is for controlling Layer 3 (and some Layer 2) functions. This is where you can override the switch type for an individual port, change the B-channel selection order, and configure network-side protocol emulation.

Example 7-10 shows a voice gateway connected to both the PSTN and a PBX. The PSTN is connected to T1 1/0, and the PBX is connected to T1 1/1. Twelve B-channels are available on the PSTN link, which is using the NI2 protocol. The PBX has all 23 B-channels available, and it is using the 5ESS protocol. The voice gateway is the network side of the PBX connection and the user side of the PSTN connection. It is deriving clock from the PSTN trunk and supplying clock to the PBX.

Example 7-10   *Dual PRI Configuration Example*

```
Miami#show running-config
!
!    Unnecessary output deleted
!
network-clock-participate slot 1
network-clock-select 1 T1 1/0
!
!    Global ISDN Switch Type
!
isdn switch-type primary-ni
!
!
controller T1 1/0
 description PSTN Trunk
 framing esf
 clock source line
 linecode b8zs
 pri-group timeslots 1-12,24
!
controller T1 1/1
 description PBX Tie Trunk
 framing esf
```

continues

Example 7-10 *Dual PRI Configuration Example (Continued)*

```
 linecode b8zs
 clock source internal
 pri-group timeslots 1-24
 !
 !
 !
interface Serial1/0:23
 description PSTN Trunk
 no ip address
 isdn switch-type primary-ni
 isdn incoming-voice voice
 isdn bchan-number-order ascending
 no cdp enable
 !
interface Serial1/1:23
 description PBX Tie Trunk
 no ip address
 isdn switch-type primary-5ess
 isdn protocol-emulate network
 isdn incoming-voice voice
 no cdp enable
 !
 !
voice-port 1/0:23
 !
voice-port 1/1:23
 !
end
```

Verifying and Troubleshooting

For the PRI to be operating properly, the Layer 1, Layer 2, and Layer 3 protocols must be functioning correctly. Layer 1 is discussed in the earlier section "Configuring E1/T1 Physical Layer Connections." To verify Layer 2, use the **show isdn status** command. If Layer 2 is up and operating, you should see the status **Multiple Frame Established**, as shown in Example 7-11.

Example 7-11 *Verifying PRI Layer 2 Using the* **show isdn status** *Command*

```
Miami#show isdn status
Global ISDN Switchtype = primary-ni
ISDN Serial1/0:23 interface
        ******* Network side configuration *******
        dsl 0, interface ISDN Switchtype = primary-5ess
    Layer 1 Status:
        ACTIVE
    Layer 2 Status:
        TEI = 0, Ces = 1, SAPI = 0, State = MULTIPLE_FRAME_ESTABLISHED
    Layer 3 Status:
        0 Active Layer 3 Call(s)
```

Example 7-11 *Verifying PRI Layer 2 Using the* **show isdn status** *Command (Continued)*

```
Active dsl 0 CCBs = 0
The Free Channel Mask:  0x80000FFF
Number of L2 Discards = 0, L2 Session ID = 3
```

In Example 7-11, the ISDN switch type that is defined globally is **primary-ni**, whereas the switch type for this interface is **primary-5ess**. This interface is defined as network side, and Layer 2 is up. If Layer 2 was not up, the status would show **TEI Assigned** instead of **Multiple Frame Established**. If Layer 1 is active, indicating that the physical circuit is available, the Layer 2 failure might be caused by having both sides of the connection defined as either user or network. You can diagnose this using the **debug isdn q921** command.

Example 7-12 shows the output from a **debug isdn q921** trace in which Layer 2 has failed to come up properly. Notice that the Layer 2 status is shown as **TEI Assigned**. This output shows that this router is the user side and is receiving bad frames. That likely means that the remote end of the connection is set up as user side, too. To correct this error, configure one side of the trunk as the network side and the opposite side of the trunk as the user side.

Example 7-12 *Troubleshooting Layer 2 with* **debug isdn q921** *Trace*

```
Miami#show isdn status
Global ISDN Switchtype = primary-ni
ISDN Serial1/0:23 interface
        dsl 0, interface ISDN Switchtype = primary-5ess
    Layer 1 Status:
        ACTIVE
    Layer 2 Status:
        TEI = 0, Ces = 1, SAPI = 0, State = TEI_ASSIGNED
    Layer 3 Status:
        0 Active Layer 3 Call(s)
    Active dsl 0 CCBs = 0
    The Free Channel Mask:  0x80000FFF
    Number of L2 Discards = 0, L2 Session ID = 4

Miami#debug isdn q921
*Nov  9 07:44:49.543: ISDN Se1/0:23 Q921: User RX <- BAD FRAME(0x00017F)
*Nov  9 07:44:55.547: ISDN Se1/0:23 Q921: User RX <- BAD FRAME(0x00017F)
*Nov  9 07:44:56.543: ISDN Se1/0:23 Q921: User RX <- BAD FRAME(0x00017F)
```

Example 7-13 shows the same interface after you have configured **isdn protocol-emulate network**.

Example 7-13 *Layer 2 Startup with* **debug isdn q921** *Trace*

```
Miami#config t
Miami(config)#interface s1/0:23
Miami(config-if)#isdn protocol-emulate network
Miami(config-if)#end
```

continues

Example 7-13 *Layer 2 Startup with* **debug isdn q921** *Trace (Continued)*

```
Miami#debug isdn q921
*Nov  9 07:48:40.555: ISDN Se1/0:23 Q921: Net RX <- SABMEp sapi=0 tei=0
*Nov  9 07:48:40.555: ISDN Se1/0:23 Q921: S4_SABME: Sending UA
*Nov  9 07:48:40.559: %ISDN-6-LAYER2UP: Layer 2 for Interface Se1/0:23, TEI 0 changed
to up
*Nov  9 07:48:40.559: ISDN Se1/0:23 Q921: Net TX -> UAf sapi=0 tei=0
```

Troubleshooting Layer 3 problems on a PRI that is connected to a PBX can be more difficult. If you are having problems with call completion, you can trace the Layer 3 messages with the **debug isdn q931** command. Example 7-14 shows the output of a **debug isdn q931** trace. The lobby phone at 919-555-3456 called 911 on B-channel 1, and the call ended normally. This trace validates that both the calling and called numbers are being passed correctly, the calling name is being provided correctly, and the calls can complete normally.

Example 7-14 *Layer 3 Call Information with* **debug isdn q931** *Trace*

```
*Nov  9 08:02:55.955: ISDN Se1/0:23 Q931: TX -> SETUP pd = 8  callref = 0x000E
            Bearer Capability i = 0x9090A2
                    Standard = CCITT
                    Transfer Capability = 3.1kHz Audio
                    Transfer Mode = Circuit
                    Transfer Rate = 64 kbit/s
            Channel ID i = 0xA98381
                    Exclusive, Channel 1
            Progress Ind i = 0x8583 - Origination address is non-ISDN
            Display i = 'Lobby Phone'
            Calling Party Number i = 0xA1, '9195553456'
                    Plan:ISDN, Type:National
            Called Party Number i = 0x80, '911'
                    Plan:Unknown, Type:Unknown
*Nov  9 08:02:55.999: ISDN Se1/0:23 Q931: RX <- CALL_PROC pd = 8  callref = 0x80
0E
            Channel ID i = 0xA98381
                    Exclusive, Channel 1
*Nov  9 08:02:56.003: ISDN Se1/0:23 Q931: RX <- CONNECT pd = 8  callref = 0x800E
*Nov  9 08:02:56.003: ISDN Se1/0:23 Q931: TX -> CONNECT_ACK pd = 8  callref = 0x
000E
*Nov  9 08:02:58.879: ISDN Se1/0:23 Q931: RX <- DISCONNECT pd = 8  callref = 0x8
00E
            Cause i = 0x8090 - Normal call clearing
```

Occasionally, slight differences in the implementation of the Layer 3 protocol can cause problems, even though calls complete properly. These problems can manifest themselves as missing or improperly displayed caller name or number display, call transfer failures, and so on. Use the **debug isdn q931** trace information in conjunction with placing test calls to verify that everything is working correctly. If you encounter problems that are related to variations in protocol implementation, the **debug isdn q931** information can help you determine whether the problem is with the PBX or the voice gateway. You might also be able to find a case study on Cisco.com that can help. Cisco has tested interoperability with many brands of PBX systems and published case studies that can provide insight into the correct configuration parameters to use on both the voice gateway and the PBX.

MGCP

The configuration process changes when you use MGCP to control the T1 or E1 PRI trunk. The configuration on the voice gateway sets up MGCP control. This begins when you specify on the controller configuration that you will use the MGCP protocol. You do this by using the **pri-group timeslots** *num* **service mgcp** configuration command. When you are configuring CallManager MGCP, all the parameters that control the trunk are defined on the CallManager, rather than on the gateway. Further, the Layer 3 Q.931 traffic is backhauled to CallManager for processing. The Layer 3 backhaul is configured using the **isdn bind-l3 ccm-manager** command on the serial interface configuration.

Example 7-15 shows the full configuration parameters that are necessary to set up a CallManager MGCP-controlled T1 PRI tie trunk on controller 1/0. The IP address of the CallManager is specified on the **mgcp call-agent** command. The configured dial peer associates call control for port 1/0:23 to the MGCP application.

Example 7-15 *CallManager MGCP Controlled Voice Gateway Configuration*

```
Miami#show running-config
!
!      Unnecessary output deleted
!
ccm-manager mgcp
!
controller T1 1/0
 description Tie Trunk to PBX - MGCP Controlled
 framing esf
 linecode b8zs
 pri-group timeslots 1-24 service mgcp
!
!
interface Serial1/0:23
 no ip address
 isdn switch-type primary-ni
 isdn incoming-voice voice
 isdn bind-l3 ccm-manager
 no cdp enable
!
!
voice-port 1/0:23
!
mgcp
mgcp call-agent 10.1.5.2 service-type mgcp version 0.1
!
```

continues

Example 7-15 *CallManager MGCP Controlled Voice Gateway Configuration (Continued)*

```
mgcp profile default
!
dial-peer voice 1 pots
application mgcpapp
port 1/0:23
!
end
```

Figure 7-4 is an excerpt of the CallManager configuration showing how both the physical line and ISDN signaling information are configured for an MGCP-controlled PRI trunk. In CallManager configuration, the Protocol Side drop-down box controls whether the ISDN trunk operates as network or user side. You also configure line coding, framing, and clocking here.

Figure 7-4 *CallManager Configuration of MGCP PRI*

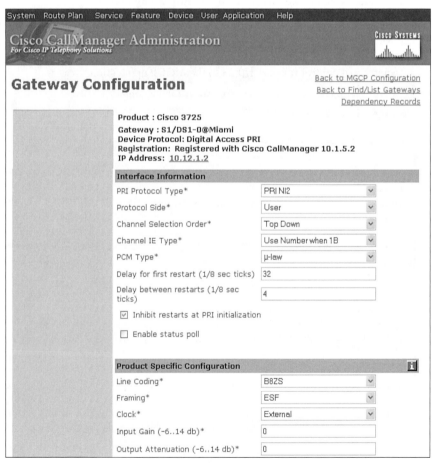

Verifying and Troubleshooting

You can verify the operational status of an MGCP-controlled PRI trunk by using the **show isdn status** command. In Example 7-16, you can see that Layer 1 is active, and Layer 2 shows **Multiple Frame Established** and is operational. The display also indicates that Layer 3 is backhauled to CallManager.

Example 7-16 *Sample **show isdn status** for an MGCP-Controlled PRI Trunk*

```
Miami#show isdn status
Global ISDN Switchtype = primary-ni
%Q.931 is backhauled to CCM MANAGER 0x0003 on DSL 0. Layer 3 output may not apply
ISDN Serial1/0:23 interface
        dsl 0, interface ISDN Switchtype = primary-ni
        L2 Protocol = Q.921 0x0000  L3 Protocol(s) = CCM MANAGER 0x0003
    Layer 1 Status:
        ACTIVE
    Layer 2 Status:
        TEI = 0, Ces = 1, SAPI = 0, State = MULTIPLE_FRAME_ESTABLISHED
    Layer 3 Status:
        0 Active Layer 3 Call(s)
    Active dsl 0 CCBs = 0
    The Free Channel Mask:  0x80000FFF
    Number of L2 Discards = 0, L2 Session ID = 4
    Total Allocated ISDN CCBs = 0
```

For information about the ISDN Layer 3 backhaul, use the **show ccm-manager** command, as shown in Example 7-17. Example 7-17 shows that the voice gateway is registered to a CallManager at IP address 10.1.5.2, and the backhaul link is open. The PRI at slot 1, port 0 is being backhauled, and you can see that messages have flowed across the backhaul link with no receive or transmit failures.

Example 7-17 *Sample **show ccm-manager** for an MGCP-Controlled PRI Trunk*

```
Miami#show ccm-manager
MGCP Domain Name: Miami
Priority        Status                  Host
=============================================================
Primary         Registered              10.1.5.2
First Backup    None
Second Backup   None
Current active Call Manager:    10.1.5.2
Backhaul/Redundant link port:   2428

!   Unnecessary output deleted
!
Backhaul Link info:
    Link Protocol:      TCP
    Remote Port Number: 2428
    Remote IP Address:  10.1.5.2
    Current Link State: OPEN
    Statistics:
```

continues

Example 7-17 *Sample* **show ccm-manager** *for an MGCP-Controlled PRI Trunk (Continued)*

```
        Packets recvd:    10
        Recv failures:   0
        Packets xmitted: 13
        Xmit failures:   0
PRI Ports being backhauled:
        Slot 1, port 0
```

To view the traffic on the backhaul link, you can use the **debug ccm-manager packets** trace command. Although this command does show the actual traffic on the backhaul link, it is typically not as useful in troubleshooting as the **debug isdn q931** trace command discussed in the previous section.

Q Signaling

The QSIG protocol is a set of international standards that define services and signaling protocols for private integrated services networks (PISN). QSIG is based on ISDN Q.921 and Q.931 and is a worldwide standard for PBX interconnection. QSIG allows you to route calls from one private integrated services network exchange (PINX) to another PINX using Cisco voice gateways. A PINX can be a PBX, key system, or CallManager node that supports the QSIG protocol. Using the QSIG protocol, all of the features that are available as a PBX user operate transparently across the network.

It is important to note that although many PBX manufacturers provide support for QSIG, the support is frequently not included as a standard feature; instead, it is offered as an extra-cost option. If the connection to the PBX is being made as an interim measure during a conversion to an IP telephony system, it might not make financial sense to pay for the QSIG option. Verify the status of QSIG support on the PBX prior to planning a QSIG implementation.

The Cisco QSIG implementation supports basic calls, identification and message waiting indication services, call forwarding, and call transfer. QSIG can transparently route call services from a PBX to a voice gateway, across a WAN or virtual private network (VPN) connection to another voice gateway, and back to a PBX. A far more common topology is a T1 or E1 PRI connection to a CallManager-controlled voice gateway.

Cisco has tested CallManager QSIG feature interoperability with the following PBX vendors: Lucent/Avaya Definity G3R, Avaya MultiVantage and Communication Manager all using T1 or E1, Alcatel 4400 using E1 or T1, Ericsson MD110 using E1, Nortel Meridian using E1 or T1, Siemens Hicom 300 E CS using T1, Siemens Hicom 300 E and Siemens HiPath 4000 both using E1.

CallManager supports many call features with QSIG, including the following:

- **Retry on busy**—When the number you are calling is busy, you can request that the call complete when the busy destination hangs up the phone and becomes available.

- **Retry on no answer**—When your call is not answered, you can request that the call be retried after activity occurs on the phone of the called party.

- **Identification service**—The ability to present or restrict the display of caller or called party number and name is configurable in CallManager.

- **Message waiting services**—Turn on or turn off voice mail message waiting indicator (MWI) indications based on QSIG directives. When a call that has been forwarded is redirected to voice mail, the called number can be determined through supplementary services, and the message is placed in the correct voice mailbox.

- **Call forwarding and call transfer**—Forwarding and transferring calls.

QSIG offers a high level of functionality and provides interoperability between equipment from different manufacturers, making its use desirable on an interconnect tie trunk between a PBX system and a voice gateway in an IP telephony environment.

Configuration of a CallManager-controlled QSIG trunk is done in the same way as an MGCP-controlled ISDN PRI trunk. The QSIG protocol is selected with the **isdn switch-type primary-qsig** command on the voice gateway or by selecting **PRI QSIG T1** or **PRI QSIG E1** on the PRI Protocol Type drop-down box in CallManager. An excerpt of the CallManager configuration page with QSIG selected is shown in Figure 7-5. Note that this also enables the Connected Line ID Presentation field, which allows you to control the display of the connected line number.

Figure 7-5 *CallManager Configuration for a QSIG Trunk*

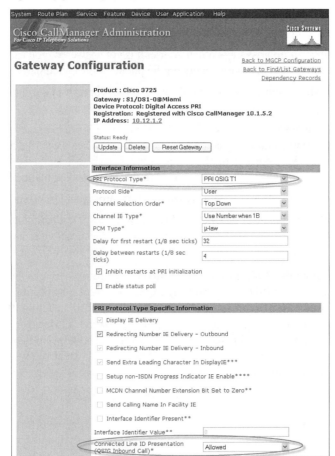

Configuring E1 R2 or T1 CAS Trunks

When setting up tie trunks to a PBX, it is always preferable to use a PRI or QSIG trunk if you can. Some PBX systems do not have PRI capability, which might force you to use a channel-associated signaling (CAS) trunk. If you must use an E1 R2 or T1 CAS connection, be sure to select a supported signaling method that provides the highest level of reliability and functionality.

Configuration of the interface on the voice gateway is done in the same way that it is for a PSTN connection. For more information, see Chapter 6.

Configuring Transparent Common Channel Signaling

When multiple PBXs exist in a private network, they are often connected using leased-line circuits from the PSTN as tie trunks between the PBXs. Many vendors have implemented proprietary protocols to carry features such as number display, name display, and networked voice mail across these tie trunks. This method makes the multiple PBXs appear to end users as a single, virtual PBX with a common dial plan and common features across all locations.

A disadvantage of this design is that dedicated point–to-point circuits are required between the PBX locations. If several locations exist, it might be necessary to implement a mesh design for the tie trunks. This can be a costly design, because there is a monthly recurring cost to each of these circuits. Further, you cannot use these circuits for any other purpose, even when call volume is low. Standard PRI or CAS circuit implementations on voice gateways do not work because of the proprietary protocols in use.

T-CCS allows the connection of two PBXs that use a proprietary or unsupported common channel signaling (CCS) protocol without the need for interpretation of CCS for call processing. The signaling is passed through transparently to the other side.

Using a T-CCS implementation, the PBX voice channels are nailed up (made permanent) and compressed between sites. You can transmit the accompanying signaling channel or channels transparently across the data network between the locations. Thus, the voice gateway does not route the calls from the PBXs on a call-by-call basis; instead, it follows a preconfigured, permanent route to the destination.

You can implement T-CCS in two primary ways:

- **Frame forwarding mode**—You can only use frame forwarding T-CCS to support PBX proprietary protocols where the signaling channel or channels are HDLC-framed and the desired VoX technology is Voice over Frame Relay (VoFR) or Voice over ATM (VoATM). In this solution, the high-level data link control (HDLC) signaling frames are encapsulated and forwarded through a channel group that is configured for the signaling on the controller. The HDLC framing is interpreted and understood, although the signaling messages are not looked at or acted upon. Idle frames are suppressed, and only real data is propagated across the signaling channel.

- **Clear-channel mode**—Clear-channel T-CCS is used to support PBX proprietary protocols in which the signaling channel(s) are ABCD-bit based or HDLC, or where the voice transport technology is Voice over IP (VoIP). In this solution, the signaling channel and voice channels are configured as DS0 groups, and all are treated as voice calls.

The voice-bearer channels are permanent trunk connections and can be compressed if desired using the voice coder/decoder (codec) of your choice. The signaling channel is also permanently connected using the clear-channel codec. The clear-channel codec passes the signaling transparently to the other side.

Use of frame forwarding mode has declined in recent years as networks have moved to an IP infrastructure and VoIP has gained popularity. When T-CCS is implemented today, it is almost always done using clear-channel mode. With clear-channel T-CCS, there is no intelligence in the software to know which channels are voice channels and which are signaling channels. You must configure the timeslots that you know carry signaling traffic to match a dial peer that assigns the clear-channel codec. The voice channels must match a dial peer that can encode voice using a compression codec scheme, such as G.729.

Figure 7-6 shows the flow of the traffic between Site A and Site B. Note that the signaling channel passes through transparently, whereas the voice channels are compressed before being sent over the network. This optimizes the use of the data network bandwidth while keeping the signaling intact.

The channels on the proprietary digital trunk from the PBX at Site A are disassembled in the voice gateway. The signaling channel is passed through transparently. The voice gateway does not see or act on any of the signaling information on the channel. The voice-bearer channels are sent individually on permanent connections between the voice gateways. You can compress voice channels by using a compression algorithm, such as G.729. At Site B, you can reassemble the channels and pass them across the digital trunk in their original form to the PBX.

Figure 7-6 *T-CCS Clear Channel Signaling Flow*

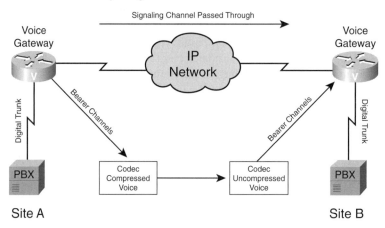

To configure T-CCS, you need to begin by creating a DS0 group for each channel on the controller that you want to transport. Each DS0 group contains a single timeslot. The type is defined as external signaling using the **ext-sig** parameter of the **ds0-group** command, as shown in Example 7-18.

Example 7-18   *Setting Up DS0 Groups for T-CCS*

```
Miami#show running-config
!
!  Unnecessary output deleted
!
controller T1 1/0
 framing esf
 clock source line primary
 linecode b8zs
 ds0-group 0 timeslots 1 type ext-sig
 ds0-group 1 timeslots 2 type ext-sig
 ds0-group 2 timeslots 3 type ext-sig
 ds0-group 3 timeslots 4 type ext-sig
 .
 .
 .
 ds0-group 23 timeslots 24 type ext-sig

!
voice-port 1/0:0
 timeouts call-disconnect 3
!
voice-port 1/0:1
 timeouts call-disconnect 3
!
voice-port 1/0:2
 timeouts call-disconnect 3
!
voice-port 1/0:3
 timeouts call-disconnect 3
 .
 .
 .
voice-port 1/0:23
 timeouts call-disconnect 3
!
end
```

Each DS0 group that is defined creates an associated voice port. After the voice ports are created, you must set them up as trunk connections using the **connection trunk** *word* command. In this case, *word* is the telephone number of the corresponding trunk on the far end of the connection. You can assign these numbers arbitrarily as long as they do not conflict with any other number used in the system. When you are configuring the trunk connections, configure one side to answer the call. You can do this by using the **connection trunk** *word* **answer-mode** command. Only use the **answer-mode** subcommand on one side of the trunk connection.

After you have configured the trunk information, you need to add a POTS dial peer for each voice port. The number on the destination pattern must match the telephone number of the trunk on the far end of the connection and is defined using the **destination-pattern** *number* command. The port must be the local voice port that connects to the far-end trunk.

You also need to set up VoIP dial peers to make the connection to the remote side. Be sure you create a separate dial peer for the bearer and signaling channels. The bearer channels can use whatever codec is appropriate, but G.729 is the default. The signaling channel must use the clear channel codec to function properly. You configure this by using the **codec clear-channel** command.

A complete sample configuration for Site A and Site B is shown in Example 7-19.

Example 7-19 *T-CCS Sample Configuration*

```
SiteA#show running-config
!
!  Unnecessary output deleted
!
network-clock-participate slot 1
network-clock-select 1 T1 1/0
!
interface Loopback0
  ip address 10.10.10.1
!
controller T1 1/0
 framing esf
 clock source line primary
 linecode b8zs
 ds0-group 0 timeslots 1 type ext-sig
 ds0-group 1 timeslots 2 type ext-sig
 ds0-group 2 timeslots 3 type ext-sig
 .
 .
 .
 ds0-group 23 timeslots 24 type ext-sig
!
voice-port 1/0:0
 timeouts call-disconnect 3
 connection trunk 6000
!
voice-port 1/0:1
 timeouts call-disconnect 3
 connection trunk 6001
!
voice-port 1/0:2
 timeouts call-disconnect 3
 connection trunk 6002
 .
 .
 .
voice-port 1/0:23
 timeouts call-disconnect 3
```

Example 7-19   *T-CCS Sample Configuration (Continued)*

```
  connection trunk 4000
 !
 !
dial-peer voice 5000 pots
 destination-pattern 5000
 port 1/0:0
 !
dial-peer voice 5001 pots
 destination-pattern 5001
 port 1/0:1
 !
dial-peer voice 5002 pots
 destination-pattern 5002
 port 1/0:2
 !
dial-peer voice 3000 pots
 destination-pattern 3000
 port 1/0:23
 !
dial-peer voice 6000 voip
 destination-pattern 6...
 session target ipv4: 10.20.20.1
 codec g729r8
 !
dial-peer voice 4000 voip
 destination-pattern 4000
 session target ipv4: 10.20.20.1
 codec clear-channel
 !
end
SiteB#show running-config
 !
 !  Unnecessary output deleted
 !
network-clock-participate slot 2
network-clock-select 1 T1 2/0
 !
interface Loopback0
  ip address 10.20.20.1
 !
controller T1 2/0
 framing esf
 clock source line primary
 linecode b8zs
 ds0-group 0 timeslots 1 type ext-sig
 ds0-group 1 timeslots 2 type ext-sig
 ds0-group 2 timeslots 3 type ext-sig
 .
 .
 .
 ds0-group 23 timeslots 24 type ext-sig
 !
```

continues

Example 7-19 *T-CCS Sample Configuration (Continued)*

```
voice-port 2/0:0
 timeouts call-disconnect 3
 connection trunk 5000
!
voice-port 2/0:1
 timeouts call-disconnect 3
 connection trunk 5001
!
voice-port 2/0:2
 timeouts call-disconnect 3
 connection trunk 5002
.
.
.
voice-port 2/0:23
 timeouts call-disconnect 3
 connection trunk 3000
!
!
dial-peer voice 6000 pots
 destination-pattern 6000
 port 2/0:0
!
dial-peer voice 6001 pots
 destination-pattern 6001
 port 2/0:1
!
dial-peer voice 6002 pots
 destination-pattern 6002
 port 2/0:2
!
dial-peer voice 4000 pots
 destination-pattern 4000
 port 2/0:23
!
dial-peer voice 5000 voip
 destination-pattern 5...
 session target ipv4: 10.10.10.1
 codec g729r8
!
dial-peer voice 3000 voip
 destination-pattern 3000
 session target ipv4: 10.10.10.1
 codec clear-channel
!
end
```

When the configuration is complete on both ends, the trunks should become active. These trunks are permanently connected between the two voice gateways.

You can use the **show voice port summary** command to verify that the trunks are connected correctly, as shown in Example 7-20.

Example 7-20 **show voice port summary** *for T-CCS*

```
SiteA#show voice port summary
                                    IN       OUT
PORT      CH  SIG-TYPE   ADMIN OPER STATUS   STATUS   EC
========= == ============ ===== ==== ======== ======== ==
1/0:0     01  ext         up   up   trunked  trunked  y
1/0:1     02  ext         up   up   trunked  trunked  y
1/0:2     03  ext         up   up   trunked  trunked  y
.
.
.
1/0:23    24  ext         up   up   trunked  trunked  y
```

You can also use the **show voice call summary** command. This command shows you the codec in use for each connected trunk, as demonstrated in Example 7-21. Note that in this example, timeslot 24 is the signaling channel and is using the clear channel codec.

Example 7-21 **show voice call summary** *for T-CCS*

```
SiteA#show voice call summary
PORT            CODEC     VAD VTSP STATE            VPM STATE
=============== ========= === ==================== ====================
1/0:0.1         g729r8    y   S_CONNECT            S_TRUNKED
1/0:1.2         g729r8    y   S_CONNECT            S_TRUNKED
1/0:2.3         g729r8    y   S_CONNECT            S_TRUNKED
.
.
.
1/0:23.24       clear-ch  y   S_CONNECT            S_TRUNKED
```

Case Study: Implementing a Cisco Voice Gateway at the Shanghai Office

The overseas office in Shanghai has nearly completed conversion from a PBX to an IP telephony solution using CallManager and Cisco voice gateways. Now it is time to move the PSTN connections from the PBX to the voice gateway. More than 200 phones have been converted to IP telephony. Only ten phones remain on the PBX, and they support a small help desk that has not yet been converted.

Help desk calls coming from the PSTN need to be routed from the voice gateway to the PBX until the migration is fully completed, which is expected to be within two months. Because this is a short-term requirement, the office does not want to spend additional money on the PBX to handle this connection. It also needs to minimize the number of configuration changes required on the PBX. The in-house staff is limited in their expertise on the PBX. Up until now, an outside company has done most of the PBX changes. This company has been reluctant to help with this migration, because it will lose this business when the migration is complete.

The PSTN has two ISDN E1 PRI circuits connecting to the PBX. The framing for both of these lines is **CRC4**, and the line coding is **HDB3**. Both circuits are using the NET5 switch type and handle incoming and outgoing calls.

Extension numbers used in the Shanghai office are in the range of 4100 to 4399. The only number that needs to be routed to the PBX is extension 4200.

The voice gateway is a Cisco 3745 with two NM-HDV-2E1-60 modules supporting four voice ports. Two ports will be used for the existing PSTN connections. The other two are spare and were included for future growth.

To begin the cutover, you will move the two PSTN E1 PRI circuits to the voice gateway router. In your design, you will put one PSTN E1 on port 1/0 and one PSTN E1 on port 2/0, so you will have one circuit on each of the two NM-HDV-2E1-60 modules. This will provide a reliable source of clocking to each module for the internal PLL. It will also provide a primary and backup clock source for the internal TDM bus. Lastly, it will provide redundancy in case one of the network modules fails.

You will also connect an E1 PRI from port 1/1 on the voice gateway to one of the PBX trunk ports that was freed up when the PSTN circuits were removed. Figure 7-7 shows the connections that reflect the design you are implementing.

Figure 7-7 *Shanghai Voice Network Design*

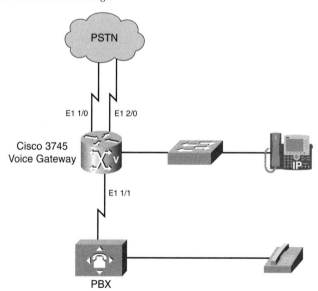

To configure this connection, you need to set up the line coding, framing, and clocking on each interface. You do this from controller configuration mode, which you enter using the **controller e1** *slot/port* command. After you are there, enter **framing crc4** and **linecode hdb3** commands to set up the physical characteristics of the line.

To set up the correct clocking for the PSTN circuits, enter the **clock source line primary** command. This tells the gateway to use the timing recovered from the line for the line itself and the internal PLL on the network module. Because the PSTN circuits will be removed from the PBX, it will no longer have a reliable clock source. You must provide clocking of the PBX tie trunk from the voice gateway. You do this using the **clock source internal** command. At this point, you can verify that each of the circuits is up and operating properly at the physical level using the **show controller e1** *slot/port* command.

The next step is to set up the clocking for the TDM bus in the gateway. Begin in global configuration mode by entering the **network-clock-participate slot 1** and **network-clock-participate slot 2** commands. Set up one E1 as priority 1 clock source using the **network-clock-select 1 e1 1/0** command. The 1 indicates that this is the clock that will be selected first for use if it is available. Use the **network-clock-select 2 e1 2/0** command to set up the other PSTN connection as a backup clock. You can verify proper clocking configuration by using the **show network-clocks** command.

Now that the physical circuit configuration is complete, you can begin configuring the ISDN portion. Begin by setting up the ISDN switch type in global configuration mode using the **isdn switch-type primary-net5** command. Next, enter **pri-group timeslots 1-31** on each of the controllers to define the three PRI groups. This creates the associate voice ports and serial interfaces where you can do further configuration if necessary.

To complete the ISDN configuration, go to the serial1/1:15 interface and enter the **isdn protocol-emulate network** command. This makes the voice gateway the network side of the PBX connection just as the PSTN was, helping to meet the requirement of minimizing changes to the PBX.

Check to be sure that the ISDN Layer 1 and Layer 2 connections on all the circuits have come up properly using the **show isdn status** command. You can verify Layer 3 either by successfully placing calls or by using the **debug isdn q931** trace command.

This should complete the basic configuration necessary to meet the requirements outlined for the Shanghai office. At this point, you need to configure call control to properly route the calls to either an IP phone destination or the PBX. The configuration done in this study reflects using H.323 call control. You could use MGCP just as easily with some minor modifications to set up the D-channel backhaul.

Example 7-22 shows the configuration statements to support this design.

Example 7-22 *Configuration for Shanghai Case Study*

```
Shanghai#show running-config
!
!  Unnecessary output deleted
isdn switch-type primary-net5
!
network-clock-participate slot 1
network-clock-participate slot 2
network-clock-select 1 E1 1/0
network-clock-select 2 E1 2/0
!
!
controller E1 1/0
 description PSTN Trunk 1
 framing crc4
 clock source line primary
 linecode hdb3
 pri-group timeslots 1-31
!
controller E1 1/1
 description PBX Tie Trunk
 framing crc4
 clock source internal
 linecode hdb3
 pri-group timeslots 1-31
!
controller E1 2/0
 description PSTN Trunk 2
 framing crc4
 clock source line primary
 linecode hdb3
 pri-group timeslots 1-31
!
controller E1 2/1
 description spare
 shutdown
!
interface Serial1/0:15
 no ip address
 isdn switch-type primary-net5
 isdn incoming-voice voice
 no cdp enable
!
interface Serial1/1:15
 no ip address
 isdn switch-type primary-net5
 isdn protocol-emulate network
 isdn incoming-voice voice
```

Example 7-22 *Configuration for Shanghai Case Study (Continued)*

```
 no cdp enable
 !
interface Serial2/0:15
 no ip address
 isdn switch-type primary-net5
 isdn incoming-voice voice
 no cdp enable
 !
voice-port 1/0:15
 !
voice-port 1/1:15
 !
voice-port 2/0:15
 !
end
```

Review Questions

1 How will caller ID work on an FXO to FXS connection between a PBX and a Cisco voice gateway?

2 Which E&M trunk type is most commonly in use?

3 A four-wire E&M Type V trunk uses how many physical wires?

4 Which command confirms the status of clocking for the TDM bus of a voice gateway?

5 How can you control the master/slave Layer 2 function of an ISDN PRI trunk?

6 What type of signaling is configured on DS0s that are used for T-CCS?

7 How do you configure the D-channel for an MGCP-controlled ISDN PRI trunk?

8 When you are using an MGCP-controlled PRI trunk, how can you verify the status of the ISDN Q.931 backhaul?

CHAPTER 8

Connecting to an IP WAN

The previous chapters have focused on voice-over IP (VoIP) within the IP network at a single site. The gateway in such a setup would interconnect public switched telephone network (PSTN), PBX, and other plain old telephone service (POTS) endpoints with voice-enabled IP endpoints, such as IP phones. VoIP over the WAN has several applications, such as connecting multiple sites, allowing service providers to terminate long-distance and local voice calls, providing voice services to telecommuters, and so on.

In this chapter you will learn

- Applications for connecting to an IP WAN
- Design considerations when using VoIP over an IP WAN
- Quality of Service issues and solutions
- Configuring Quality of Service to fit a provider's MPLS standards
- Providing fax and modem services within a VoIP network
- Ways to secure your VoIP traffic

Applications for Connecting to an IP WAN

Connecting voice gateways over an IP WAN allows you to send voice and video to other locations as IP packets. For businesses that have geographically distributed offices, using IP telephony to call between offices can be more cost effective than making long-distance calls. IP telephony is increasingly becoming a need for businesses that spread their offices globally. It lets you leverage your investment in WAN bandwidth between offices. The WAN connection can be a direct circuit between sites, such as a T1; a virtual circuit, including Frame Relay; ATM permanent virtual circuit (PVC); or a shared connection, as with a Synchronous Optical Network (SONET) ring. Communication between the voice gateways could rely on your service provider, such as with Multiprotocol Label Switching (MPLS), or on the Internet, as when using a virtual private network (VPN) between sites. Satellite links are also an option, provided their speed and reliability are acceptable.

The following are some situations in which IP WAN connections might be appropriate:

- Your company is using VoIP at multiple sites. Sending voice over the WAN connections between them is a way to make intracompany phone calls without using the PSTN. Voice performance is better with a full-mesh topology. In a hub-and-spoke design, spoke-to-spoke phone calls have to go through the hub, adding extra delay to the call. Careful attention to quality of service (QoS) is essential when sending Voice over Frame Relay (VoFR) or Voice over ATM (VoATM). PPP has no built-in QoS mechanisms; therefore, it needs multilevel precedence and preemption (MLPP) to be deployed to ensure that latency and delay requirements for voice are met.

- You want to do "tail end hop-off," which turns a long-distance call into a local one. (In tail end hop-off, you route voice traffic that is bound for a phone in a particular area to your voice gateway in that area. The voice gateway then routes the traffic out to the PSTN as a local call.)

- A company that wants to preserve its PBX investment yet avoid the cost of POTS lines and trunks can take advantage of existing WAN links for voice between sites. In this case, the voice gateway translates between the internal analog voice and the external VoIP. You need to create dial peers that point to the PBX and to the other voice gateways.

- Companies might want to centralize their PSTN connections and require remote sites to route all voice traffic bound to the PSTN through a central site. The central site needs enough PRI connections to handle the calls, and each remote site needs only minimal POTS lines in case the WAN connection is lost or for emergency calls. This centralization is normally done when all the sites are located in the same area.

- Centralizing Cisco CallManagers reduces the financial investment in IP telephony. In a centralized design, Cisco CallManagers communicate with the other voice devices over an IP WAN. Signaling between phones and CallManagers, and between gateways and CallManagers, is sent over the WAN. Voice media traffic flows directly between the IP phones and the gateway at the remote site and might not traverse the WAN.

Design Considerations

In most scenarios, voice and data are sent together on the same WAN connection. Sending voice along with data over a WAN network requires additional planning and configuration. This book focuses on gateways, but you must plan for voice flow throughout your network and configure every network device appropriately.

Be sure to consider the following areas when designing a voice-enabled WAN:

- **Bandwidth**—Estimate the number of calls you anticipate over the WAN, plus the amount of data traffic, and ensure that you have enough bandwidth. For more information on bandwidth planning, see Chapter 16, "Deploying Gatekeepers."

- **Call admission control (CAC)**—If the gateway sends out more calls than the WAN can handle, the quality of all calls suffers. Chapter 11, "Influencing Path Selection," covers CAC.

- **QoS**—If voice will share the WAN link with data, you should protect voice (and video) from data. The next section of this chapter covers QoS.

- **Security**—Consider how secure your network must be and what devices the voice traffic will traverse. For more information on security, see the "Security" section later in this chapter.

Quality of Service

Typically, data and voice traffic travel across the same WAN link. This can be a problem, because data tends to be transmitted in bursts and could use up all the bandwidth, leaving none for voice. QoS techniques help protect voice (and video) from data.

Planning is the most important part of QoS. In most networks, it is not enough to classify traffic as "voice" and "nonvoice" and give preference to voice. Most networks have various types of traffic, each with its own network needs and importance to the company. Although this book concentrates on voice, an effective QoS policy examines all the network applications and involves policy makers in deciding how to handle that data through the network. Your goal should be a consistent, end-to-end QoS strategy throughout your company.

One of your first tasks is to determine the needs of each network application. Voice is sensitive to delay, jitter, and drops. High-quality voice and interactive video have the following recommendations:

- A maximum of 150 ms of one-way delay
- A maximum of 30 ms of jitter
- A maximum of 1 percent packet loss

One cause of delay is small voice packets having to wait behind larger data packets to be sent out an interface. Jitter, which is variable delay, can result when some voice packets are sent out quickly and some have to wait. Drops happen when an interface queue is completely full—something much more likely to occur if voice has to share a queue with data. Thus, when you are sending voice and data across a WAN it is especially important to plan and implement QoS measures to increase the chances of voice always having the bandwidth it needs.

QoS involves three tasks:

* Classifying traffic
* Marking the classified traffic
* Configuring network devices to treat traffic differently based on the markings

    The modular quality of service command-line interface (MQC) is the recommended method of implementing QoS. It involves using class maps to classify traffic, using policy maps to mark traffic or specify how it will be treated, and applying the policy using the **service-policy** command. In the following sections, you will look at using MQC with voice gateways.

NOTE   A full explanation of QoS is beyond the scope of this book. You can find detailed information in the Cisco QoS Solution Reference Network Design document at www.cisco.com/go/srnd, or in these books:

* *Cisco Catalyst QOS: Quality of Service in Campus Networks* by Michael Flannagan, Richard Froom, and Kevin Turek

* *End-to-End QoS Network Design: Quality of Service in LANs, WANs, and VPNs* by Christina Hattinghand and Tim Szigeti

---

Using Class Maps to Classify Traffic

Classifying traffic requires looking at it and identifying it according to some characteristic, such as port number or source address. After you classify traffic, you can configure routers and switches to treat it differently from other traffic. The MQC uses class maps to classify traffic. Classification can be based on many different things, but voice is typically identified by looking in the OSI Layer 4, Layer 3, or Layer 2 packet headers.

Classifying at Layer 4

You can classify traffic based on the port number in the TCP or User Datagram Protocol (UDP) packet header. Each voice application uses specific port numbers. Table 8-1 lists the default port numbers that common voice-related protocols use.

Table 8-1   *Voice Protocols and Port Numbers*

Protocol	Port(s) Used
SCCP[1]	TCP ports 2000–2002
MGCP[2]	UDP 2427 and 2727; TCP 2428
H.323	UDP 1718 and 1719; TCP 1720 and 1721
RTP[3]	UDP ports 16,384–32,767
SIP[4]	TCP and UDP port 5060 (Cisco implementation)

1 SCCP = Skinny Client Control Protocol

2 MGCP = Media Gateway Control Protocol

3 RTP = Real-Time Transport Protocol

4 SIP = Session Initiation Protocol

You can use either an access list or a class map to identify this traffic based on the port number. Example 8-1 shows how to do this with an access list. The access list is created and then referenced in a class map. This example classifies the SCCP signaling traffic separately from the voice RTP traffic.

Example 8-1   *Configuring Access Lists and Class Maps*

```
VGateway#conf t
VGateway(config)#ip access-list extended RTP
VGateway(config-ext-nacl)#permit udp any any range 16383 32767
!
VGateway(config-ext-nacl)#ip access-list extended SCCP
VGateway(config-ext-nacl)#permit tcp any any range 2000 2002
VGateway(config-ext-nacl)#exit
!
VGateway(config)#class-map match-all VOICE
VGateway(configs-cmap)#match access-group name RTP
!
VGateway(configs-cmap)#class-map match-all SIGNALING
VGateway(configs-cmap)#match access-group name SCCP
```

This configuration gives you two class maps that break out two types of traffic, as verified in Example 8-2. The class map VOICE identifies the RTP traffic that is permitted in access list RTP, and the class map SIGNALING identifies the SCCP traffic that is permitted in access list SCCP. What about the rest of the data traveling around the network? A default class exists, and anything that is not explicitly identified falls into that, as shown in Example 8-2.

Example 8-2 *Verifying Class Map Configuration*

```
VGateway#show class-map
Class Map match-any class-default (id 0)
   Match any

 Class Map match-all VOICE (id 2)
   Match access-group name RTP

 Class Map match-all SIGNALING (id 3)
   Match access-group name SCCP
```

Example 8-3 shows a class map that matches RTP traffic directly. Using a class map in this way lets you bypass configuring an access list for RTP. However, you need to beware of two pitfalls in this technique.

First, using a class map this way matches only the even ports in the range you specify. RTP bearer traffic uses the even ports, and control traffic uses the odd ports. Therefore, matching against RTP in a class map breaks out only the voice-bearer traffic, not the control traffic.

Second, the way you specify the range of ports is not intuitive. In the access list shown in Example 8-1, the starting and ending port numbers are listed. In a class map, the starting port is specified, but the second number is not the ending port number. The second number is what you would add to the first number to get the ending port. For instance, suppose that you wanted to start at port 16383 and match the next 2000 ports. In that case, you would give the **match ip rtp 16383 2000** command. That would match ports 16383 through 18383 (16383 plus 2000). In Example 8-3, class map Voice-Bearer matches the even ports in the range 16383 through 32766 (16383 plus 16383.) Notice that no option is available to match SCCP, MGCP, H.323, or SIP.

Example 8-3 *Using a Class Map to Identify RTP Traffic*

```
VGateway(config)#class-map Voice-Bearer
VGateway(config-cmap)#match ?
  access-group        Access group
  any                 Any packets
  class-map           Class map
  cos                 IEEE 802.1Q/ISL class of service/user priority values
  destination-address Destination address
  fr-de               Match on Frame-relay DE bit
  input-interface     Select an input interface to match
  ip                  IP specific values
  mpls                Multi Protocol Label Switching specific values
  not                 Negate this match result
  protocol            Protocol
  qos-group           Qos-group
  source-address      Source address

VGateway(config-cmap)#match ip ?
  dscp       Match IP DSCP (DiffServ CodePoints)
  precedence Match IP precedence
```

Example 8-3 *Using a Class Map to Identify RTP Traffic (Continued)*

```
  rtp          Match RTP port nos
VGateway(config-cmap)#match ip rtp 16383 16383
!
VGateway(config-cmap)#do show class-map
Class Map match-any class-default (id 0)
   Match any

 Class Map match-all Voice-Bearer (id 2)
   Match ip  rtp 16383 16383
```

Classifying at Layer 3

A second way to identify traffic is to look at the Type of Service (ToS) field in the Layer 3
IP header. The first six bits of this field are called the differentiated services code point
(DSCP) bits. They are typically set to a decimal value of 46 for voice-bearer traffic. In the
past, Cisco recommended setting voice signaling traffic to DSCP 31. However, the current
recommendation is to set it to Class Selector (CS)3. You can use an access list to identify
traffic with a certain DSCP value, or match against it in a class map. Example 8-4 shows an
access list that looks at the DSCP value in packets. As you can see from the example, you
can list the DSCP either as a decimal value or its DiffServ per-hop behavior (PHB) value.
The second access list, VOICE-SIG, permits both CS3 and Assured Forwarding (AF)31 to
allow for devices that might not yet be transitioned to using only CS3 for signaling. After
you create the access lists, you associate them with class maps.

Example 8-4 *Using an Access List to Match DSCP*

```
VGateway(config)#ip access-list extended VOICE-BRR
VGateway(config-ext-nacl)#permit ip any any dscp ?
  <0-63>   Differentiated services codepoint value
  af11     Match packets with AF11 dscp (001010)
  af12     Match packets with AF12 dscp (001100)
  af13     Match packets with AF13 dscp (001110)
  af21     Match packets with AF21 dscp (010010)
  af22     Match packets with AF22 dscp (010100)
  af23     Match packets with AF23 dscp (010110)
  af31     Match packets with AF31 dscp (011010)
  af32     Match packets with AF32 dscp (011100)
  af33     Match packets with AF33 dscp (011110)
  af41     Match packets with AF41 dscp (100010)
  af42     Match packets with AF42 dscp (100100)
  af43     Match packets with AF43 dscp (100110)
  cs1      Match packets with CS1(precedence 1) dscp (001000)
  cs2      Match packets with CS2(precedence 2) dscp (010000)
  cs3      Match packets with CS3(precedence 3) dscp (011000)
  cs4      Match packets with CS4(precedence 4) dscp (100000)
  cs5      Match packets with CS5(precedence 5) dscp (101000)
  cs6      Match packets with CS6(precedence 6) dscp (110000)
  cs7      Match packets with CS7(precedence 7) dscp (111000)
  default  Match packets with default dscp (000000)
```

Example 8-4 *Using an Access List to Match DSCP (Continued)*

```
   ef        Match packets with EF dscp (101110)
VGateway(config-ext-nacl)#permit ip any any dscp ef
!
VGateway(config-ext-nacl)#ip access-list extended VOICE-SIG
VGateway(config-ext-nacl)#permit ip any any dscp cs3
VGateway(config-ext-nacl)#permit ip any any dscp af31
```

Using a class map to identify traffic based on a DSCP value is shown in Example 8-5. Notice in the output of the **show class-map** command that, although you specified the decimal DSCP value when configuring the class map, the router has translated that to its Diffserv value of expedited forwarding (EF). The number in parenthesis in Example 8-5 is the decimal value.

Example 8-5 *Using a Class Map to Match DSCP*

```
VGateway(config)#class-map DSCP_46
VGateway(config-cmap)#match dscp 46
!
VGateway(config-cmap)#class-map CS3
VGateway(config-cmap)#match ip dscp cs3
!
VGateway#show class-map
Class Map match-all CS3 (id 6)
   Match ip  dscp cs1 (8)

 Class Map match-all DSCP_46 (id 5)
   Match   dscp ef (46)
```

Classifying at Layer 2

A third way to identify traffic is by looking at the 802.1Q trunking tag or ISL trunking header. There are three bits called the class of service (COS), which are bits that you can set to identify different types of traffic. These bits are usually set to a decimal value of 5 for voice. You can match these bits in a class map. Of course, this only works if the router has an interface that is performing Ethernet trunking. Example 8-6 shows a class map that identifies traffic at Layer 2 by the CoS value.

Example 8-6 *Using a Class Map to Match CoS*

```
VGateway(config)#class-map COS-Voice
VGateway(config-cmap)#match cos ?
  <0-7>  Enter up to 4 class-of-service values separated by white-spaces

VGateway(config-cmap)#match cos 5
!
VGateway#show class-map

 Class Map match-all COS-Voice (id 4)
   Match cos   5
```

Cisco IP phones place an 802.1 tag on the voice traffic they send. The CoS is set to 5 for voice-bearer traffic and 3 for voice-signaling traffic. Any traffic from a PC that is connected to the phone is sent untagged. QoS should be enabled on the directly connected switch, and the switch interface should be set to trust the Cisco phone. When this happens, the switch looks at the CoS value before it removes the Layer 2 header, and it translates it into a DSCP value as the packet moves through the switch. Untagged PC traffic gets a DSCP value of 0 by default. When the packet is sent out a switch interface, it is marked at Layer 3 with that DSCP value. (It might also have a CoS value if the outgoing interface is a trunk interface.) Configure the switch to put the desired DSCP value on any packets that you want marked. Their Layer 2 header changes as they move through the network, but you can match against that unchanging Layer 3 DSCP value.

Using Policy Maps

After you have identified the interesting traffic, you can mark it or set policies for it. Marking traffic involves setting the DSCP bits or the CoS bits. You should classify and mark traffic as close to the end devices as possible, because classifying traffic uses router and switch resources. This is most important for routers, which perform QoS in software. Imagine if every router and switch in the network had to look into every packet to examine its port number. It is much more efficient if the first switch that a packet touches does the classifying and then sets a DSCP value based on the type of traffic it is. Then every other switch and router in the network can trust that the marking is correct and treat the traffic accordingly. This creates a trust boundary at the access switch.

The MQC applies policies to the traffic that has been classified by using a policy map. A policy map references the previously created class maps and then specifies what is to be done with traffic in each class. The traffic could, for example, be marked, allocated a minimum bandwidth, limited to a maximum bandwidth, prioritized, or even dropped altogether. You apply policy maps to interfaces. A separate queue is created at the interface for each class map, and the traffic that is identified by each class map is placed in its queue. This allows you to treat each of the classes of traffic differently.

Example 8-7 shows an example of marking traffic in a policy map. The class map CoS-Voice was created in Example 8-6. It identifies traffic with a CoS value of 5 in the 802.1Q trunking tag. This example creates a policy map that marks all the traffic classified by CoS-Voice with a DSCP value of 46 (or EF).

Example 8-7   *Marking Traffic Using a Policy Map*

```
VGateway(config)#policy-map COS-TO-DSCP
VGateway(config-pmap)#class COS-Voice
VGateway(config-pmap-c)#set dscp 46
!
VGateway(config-pmap-c)#class class-default
VGateway(config-pmap-c)#set dscp 0
!
VGateway#show policy-map
```

Example 8-7 *Marking Traffic Using a Policy Map (Continued)*

```
Policy Map COS-TO-DSCP
   Class COS-Voice
      set dscp ef
   Class class-default
      set dscp default
```

Notice that in Example 8-7, all traffic other than that marked with a CoS of 5 is set to a DSCP of 0 under the default class. If you have routing traffic, it is a good idea to break that out separately before classifying everything else as DSCP 0. Notice also that even though the policy map was configured using decimal values, when you display it, those are translated to the PHB values.

You most commonly use a policy map to specify different treatment for the traffic in each queue created by a class map. Setting policy and marking traffic are not mutually exclusive—you can do both of them to the same class. Voice is typically placed in a priority queue, called a low-latency queue (LLQ). It is important to understand that this is a strict priority queue. If any traffic is in the queue, it is sent out before other traffic. You can limit the amount of bandwidth used by the priority queue, however, so that other traffic is not starved.

How much bandwidth should you allow in the priority queue? In planning your bandwidth requirements, take into account the anticipated data load plus the voice load. The amount of bandwidth allocated per call varies depending on the coding/decoding (codec) used. Codec describes methods of compressing voice. The most typically used are G.711, which is uncompressed voice, and G.729, which is a type of compressed voice. G.711 is usually used in the LAN where bandwidth is plentiful. G.729 is typically used in the WAN, where you have lower bandwidth links. A G.711 call, sent at 64 kbps, has a payload size of 160 bytes. A G.729 call, sent at 8 kbps, uses a payload size of 20 bytes.

IP, UDP, and RTP headers are put onto each packet. The IP header is 20 bytes, UDP is 8 bytes, and RTP is 12 bytes, totaling an additional 40 bytes for each VoIP packet. You have the option of compressing the IP, UDP, and RTP headers, which reduces the header overhead to 2 to 4 bytes, thus reducing the entire packet size and using less bandwidth. For more information on compression, see the "Compression" section later in this chapter.

When you are planning bandwidth allocation, also take into consideration the Layer 2 headers to be used. For instance, Ethernet adds an 18-byte header, whereas Frame Relay adds only 6 bytes. Multilink PPP also has a 6-byte header. The ATM header is 5 bytes. If you use MPLS in your WAN network, the MPLS edge router adds a 4-byte header. If you are sending voice over the Internet, you might want to encrypt it in an IPsec tunnel for added security. IPsec adds 50 to 57 bytes of overhead. Secure Real-Time Transport Protocol (SRTP) encrypts the payload of IP voice packets and adds 4 bytes to the packet.

As a general rule, 21 to 320 kbps of bandwidth is required per call, depending on the codec and overhead. A good recommendation when running voice and data through the same interface is to limit the LLQ to about one-third of the bandwidth. This usually allows enough remaining bandwidth to divide between the data classes.

IP video conferencing (IP/VC) adds additional considerations to your QoS design. Interactive video has the same network needs as voice—150 ms maximum delay, jitter of 30 ms or less, and loss of 1 percent or less—so it is frequently put in a LLQ. However, video traffic varies widely in packet sizes and transmission rates. A typical video conferencing stream averages 384 kpbs of bandwidth. Cisco recommends overprovisioning the bandwidth by 20 percent, bringing it to 460 kbps per IP/VC stream. LLQ allows bursts of up to 200 ms, which is usually enough for one video stream. If you will be sending multiple streams through an interface, you might need to adjust the burst size. You can specify the burst parameter when you create the LLQ in the policy map, as part of the **priority** command, as shown in Example 8-8. No hard and fast rule is available about how much to increase the burst parameter. You need to test as multiple IP/VC streams are added.

NOTE	See Chapter 16 for more detailed information on bandwidth planning.

In Example 8-8, classes are created for voice, video conferencing, and call signaling. These classes are allotted bandwidth in the policy map. Voice and video are put into the LLQ, and the burst value for video is changed. Keep in mind that this is a simplistic example. In your network, you will most likely have other traffic that should be classified and included in the policy map.

Example 8-8   *Policy Map for Voice and Video Traffic*

```
VGateway(config)#class-map Voice
VGateway(config-cmap)#match dscp ef
!
VGateway(config-cmap)#class-map Video
VGateway(config-cmap)#match dscp 41
!
VGateway(config)#class-map match-any Call_Signaling
VGateway(config-cmap)#match dscp cs3
VGateway(config-cmap)#match dscp af31
!
VGateway(config-cmap)#policy-map VOICE-VIDEO
VGateway(config-pmap)#class Voice
VGateway(config-pmap-c)#priority percent 15
!
VGateway(config-pmap-c)#class Video
VGateway(config-pmap-c)#priority percent 18 ?
  <32-2000000>  Burst in bytes
  <cr>
VGateway(config-pmap-c)#priority percent 18 30000
!
VGateway(config-pmap-c)#class Call_Signaling
```

Example 8-8 *Policy Map for Voice and Video Traffic (Continued)*

```
VGateway(config-pmap-c)#bandwidth percent 5
!
VGateway(config-pmap-c)#class class-default
VGateway(config-pmap-c)#fair-queue
VGateway(config-pmap-c)#random-detect dscp-based
!
VGateway(config-pmap-c)#int s0/0
VGateway(config-if)#service-policy output VOICE-VIDEO
```

Notice the **fair-queue** and **random-detect dscp-based** commands under the class-default. The **fair-queue** command tells the router to create a separate queue for each conversation, or traffic flow, that falls into the default class. The **random-detect** command enables weighted random early detection (WRED) within that class. It tells the router to drop random packets from flows as the queue begins to fill up. This is done in an attempt to prevent the queue from filling completely and dropping all new packets. When the **dscp-based** command is added, the router drops packets based on their DSCP value. Packets with higher DSCP values are dropped later than lower valued ones.

The policy is applied to interface serial 0/0 and affects outbound traffic. An extremely useful command to verify and monitor your QoS configuration is **show policy interface** *interface_number*. Example 8-9 shows the output from this command. Although the router currently has no traffic, you can see that the command gives a detailed picture of the policy and its effect on traffic through that interface.

Example 8-9 **show policy interface** *Command Output*

```
VGateway#show policy interface s0/0
 Serial0/0

  Service-policy output: VOICE-VIDEO

    Class-map: Voice (match-all)
      0 packets, 0 bytes
      5 minute offered rate 0 bps, drop rate 0 bps
      Match: dscp ef (46)
      Queueing
        Strict Priority
        Output Queue: Conversation 264
        Bandwidth 15 (%)
        Bandwidth 450 (kbps) Burst 11250 (Bytes)
        (pkts matched/bytes matched) 0/0
        (total drops/bytes drops) 0/0

    Class-map: Video (match-all)
      0 packets, 0 bytes
      5 minute offered rate 0 bps, drop rate 0 bps
      Match: dscp 41
      Queueing
        Strict Priority
```

Example 8-9 **show policy interface** *Command Output (Continued)*

```
              Output Queue: Conversation 264
              Bandwidth 18 (%)
              Bandwidth 540 (kbps) Burst 30000 (Bytes)
              (pkts matched/bytes matched) 0/0
              (total drops/bytes drops) 0/0

          Class-map: Call_Signaling (match-any)
            0 packets, 0 bytes
            5 minute offered rate 0 bps, drop rate 0 bps
            Match:  dscp cs3 (24)
              0 packets, 0 bytes
              5 minute rate 0 bps
            Match:  dscp af31 (26)
              0 packets, 0 bytes
              5 minute rate 0 bps
            Queueing
              Output Queue: Conversation 265
              Bandwidth 5 (%)
              Bandwidth 150 (kbps) Max Threshold 64 (packets)
              (pkts matched/bytes matched) 0/0
              (depth/total drops/no-buffer drops) 0/0/0

          Class-map: class-default (match-any)
            0 packets, 0 bytes
            5 minute offered rate 0 bps, drop rate 0 bps
            Match: any
            Queueing
              Flow Based Fair Queueing
              Maximum Number of Hashed Queues 256
              (total queued/total drops/no-buffer drops) 0/0/0
              exponential weight: 9

          dscp    Transmitted     Random drop     Tail drop     Minimum Maximum  Mark
                  pkts/bytes      pkts/bytes      pkts/bytes    thresh  thresh   prob
          af11      0/0             0/0             0/0             32      40   1/10
          af12      0/0             0/0             0/0             28      40   1/10
          af13      0/0             0/0             0/0             24      40   1/10
          af21      0/0             0/0             0/0             32      40   1/10
          af22      0/0             0/0             0/0             28      40   1/10
          af23      0/0             0/0             0/0             24      40   1/10
          af31      0/0             0/0             0/0             32      40   1/10
          af32      0/0             0/0             0/0             28      40   1/10
          af33      0/0             0/0             0/0             24      40   1/10
          af41      0/0             0/0             0/0             32      40   1/10
          af42      0/0             0/0             0/0             28      40   1/10
          af43      0/0             0/0             0/0             24      40   1/10
          cs1       0/0             0/0             0/0             22      40   1/10
          cs2       0/0             0/0             0/0             24      40   1/10
          cs3       0/0             0/0             0/0             26      40   1/10
          cs4       0/0             0/0             0/0             28      40   1/10
          cs5       0/0             0/0             0/0             30      40   1/10
          cs6       0/0             0/0             0/0             32      40   1/10
```

continues

Example 8-9 **show policy interface** *Command Output (Continued)*

```
    cs7     0/0        0/0         0/0         34      40   1/10
     ef     0/0        0/0         0/0         36      40   1/10
   rsvp     0/0        0/0         0/0         36      40   1/10
default     0/0        0/0         0/0         20      40   1/10
```

Based on the output from the **show policy interface** command, you can tell the name of the policy map that is applied to the interface, the names of all the class maps in that policy map, and which type of traffic they match against. You can determine the policy applied to each class. Notice that both Voice and Video are shown as a strict priority queue, whereas Class-default shows flow-based fair queuing. If no queuing method is listed, the queue is using FIFO. The amount of bandwidth allocated and actually used is shown. Because the Class-default is using DSCP-based WRED, drop statistics are shown for each PHB value. This is an excellent command to remember when configuring class-based QoS because it shows both the policy and the effect of the policy. To verify specific components of a policy, use the **show policy-map**, **show class-map**, and **show queueing** commands.

Mapping to MPLS Classes

In a well-designed network, traffic generally arrives at the voice gateway already marked appropriately. You might need to change those markings, however, when sending voice over an MPLS VPN network. MPLS networks change the typical WAN paradigm. Instead of having a link between two sites, or a hub-and-spoke topology, MPLS provides connectivity to all your sites through a single WAN link. It is similar to an Ethernet network or a full-mesh Frame Relay network in that you have any-to-any connectivity through one physical link. Traffic switching between sites is done in the cloud, by the service provider.

The popularity of MPLS is growing due not only to its ability to provide full-mesh connectivity, but also for its ability to provide differing levels of service for user traffic. This makes it ideal for intraoffice voice and video, in addition to data. However, cooperation is needed between the company and the service provider to ensure consistent treatment of traffic throughout the MPLS network. It is not enough for each site to regulate the way it sends traffic out its own WAN interface, because the service provider routers are also involved in the equation. Consider a simple MPLS network such as the one shown in Figure 8-1.

Figure 8-1   *A Simple MPLS Network*

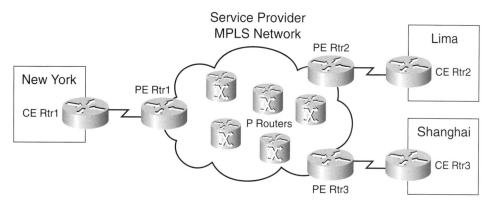

In this situation, the company has three sites. Each site has a DS3 WAN link to the MPLS network. Notice the different routers involved. Each company site has an edge router—the customer edge (CE) router. Each CE router has a DS3 link to a provider edge (PE) router. Within the provider network are multiple provider (P) routers, in addition to other devices. Suppose that a videoconference is held between users in New York and Lima. QoS on the WAN interface of each CE router ensures that the video traffic has the right amount of bandwidth as it leaves the site. However, what if a user at Shanghai starts a large data file download from New York? QoS on the CE3 router, which does not have the video traffic, would not hinder the download. If the PE router to New York does not have QoS controls configured on it, that data traffic could monopolize the bandwidth on the PE1 to CE1 link. At the very least, it would cause jitter and a high drop rate for the videoconference. A better solution is for the MPLS provider to honor the customer DSCP markings and guarantee bandwidth to the video traffic. You must do this at the egress from the PE router to the CE router, and between the P routers within the MPLS network.

MPLS providers typically have a limited number of service levels, and their equipment is programmed to respond to specific DSCP values. Many companies find it easiest to just adopt the service provider marking throughout their own network. But that is not always the best design for every network. Companies that administer their own MPLS network must also plan how to provide the needed levels of service.

Proper planning can make this a lot easier. Keep the MPLS service classes in mind when you plan your internal QoS classes. Consider the company in the example with three large sites connected with an MPLS network. When the IT staff analyzes their traffic, they find IP voice and video conferencing—each with its own signaling, stock market data, SQL database data, e-mail, web browsing, network management, and other miscellaneous traffic. They decide to use the following classes and DSCP values within their network:

- **Voice bearer**—EF
- **Video**—AF41

- **Call signaling**—CS3
- **Market data**—AF32
- **Network management**—AF33 (they also put routing updates, which are marked at CS6, in this class)
- **SQL database**—AF21
- **Email**—AF23
- **Best effort (for all other traffic)**—0

This company has selected a service provider that has four CoS levels available:

- **Real-time**—EF or CS5
- **Mission Critical**—AF31
- **Business Critical**—AF21
- **Other**—0

This creates a problem because the company has eight types of traffic that must be provided different QoS levels within its internal network. Clearly, the service provider is not going to change its setup, so the company must map its traffic to the service provider classes before sending it into the MPLS cloud. At each site, it also needs to reclassify the traffic back into its original seven groups and remark it accordingly.

The company decides to place voice, video, and call signaling in the real-time, prioritized class. It would not be a good idea to mix voice and video over a slow link (less than 768 kbps), because video packets tend to be large and thus take longer to serialize onto the link than small voice packets. It might introduce delay and jitter into voice calls if they share a queue. In this example, each site has a DS3 to the MPLS network, so serialization problems are not an issue. Voice retains its EF marking; video and call signaling are marked as CS5.

Market data, network management, and routing traffic go into the second class, Mission Critical. SQL and e-mail traffic go together into the Business Critical class. Both applications use TCP, so WRED is also enabled on the CE routers for this class. All other traffic goes into the Default class. WRED is also enabled on this class at the CE routers.

Voice can retain its current EF marking, but video and call signaling need to be remarked as CS5. Market data, network management, and routing traffic need to be remarked as AF31, and SQL and e-mail traffic need to be remarked as AF21. All other traffic already has a DSCP value of 0, so it does not need to be changed.

Consolidating the classes is fairly easy to do. Example 8-10 shows how to do this. Recall that class maps have two options: **match all** and **match any**. This example takes advantage of the **match any** option to match multiple DSCP values in one class map.

Example 8-10 *Mapping Internal Classes to MPLS Classes*

```
VGateway(config)#class-map match-all TO-MPLS-EF
VGateway(config-cmap)#match dscp ef
!
VGateway(config)#class-map match-any TO-MPLS-CS5
VGateway(config-cmap)#match dscp af41
VGateway(config-cmap)#match dscp cs3
!
VGateway(config-cmap)#class-map match-any TO-MPLS-AF31
VGateway(config-cmap)#match dscp af32
VGateway(config-cmap)#match dscp af33
VGateway(config-cmap)#match dscp cs6
!
VGateway(config-cmap)#class-map match-any TO-MPLS-AF21
VGateway(config-cmap)#match dscp af21
VGateway(config-cmap)#match dscp af23
```

The basic purpose behind identifying traffic is to configure the router to treat that traffic a certain way. You can manipulate data based on its markings in many ways, such as prioritizing it, guaranteeing bandwidth, policing to a specific bandwidth, dropping it, dropping random packets, or remarking it, as Example 8-11 shows. In the MQC, you do this using a policy map. After you have created the class maps that group the traffic, you use a policy map to change the DSCP values and allocated bandwidth.

Example 8-11 *Marking the MPLS DSCP Values with a Policy Map*

```
VGateway(config)#policy-map TO-MPLS
VGateway(config-pmap)#class TO-MPLS-EF
VGateway(config-pmap-c)#priority percent 18
VGateway(config-pmap-c)#set dscp ef
!
VGateway(config-pmap)#class TO-MPLS-CS5
VGateway(config-pmap-c)#priority percent 15
VGateway(config-pmap-c)#set dscp cs5
!
VGateway(config-pmap-c)#class TO-MPLS-AF31
VGateway(config-pmap-c)#bandwidth percent 12
VGateway(config-pmap-c)#set dscp af31
!
VGateway(config-pmap-c)#class TO-MPLS-AF21
VGateway(config-pmap-c)#bandwidth percent 10
VGateway(config-pmap-c)#set dscp af21
VGateway(config-pmap-c)#random-detect
!
VGateway(config-pmap-c)#class class-default
VGateway(config-pmap-c)#set dscp 0
VGateway(config-pmap-c)#fair-queue
VGateway(config-cmap)#random-detect
```

Then you apply this policy map to the WAN interface, outbound, with the following commands:

```
VGateway(config)#int atm 1/0.110 point-to-point
VGateway(config-subif)#pvc 10/110
VGateway(config-if-atm-vc)#service-policy output TO-MPLS
```

As a result, traffic from the eight internal QoS classes is mapped to the four classes of the MPLS provider. These same commands are needed on every CE router, applied outbound on the WAN interface. This is fairly easy. However, you must break the traffic back out into the original eight classes when it arrives at its destination CE router. That is a little more involved.

Recall that several types of traffic are sharing the same DSCP value. You must find a way to distinguish between them so that you can group them into the correct class inside the network. In the first group, identifying voice is no problem because it retained its previous marking of EF. Video and call signaling were given the same DSCP value, CS5, and placed into the same class as voice. An access list is used to break out call signaling traffic. Video uses RTP, so you can identify it in that way.

Three types of traffic are in the second group: routing, market data, and network management. The routing protocol used is Border Gateway Protocol (BGP), which you can identify by an access list. The market data uses several different ports, but all traffic is bound either to or from a specific subnet of servers. An access list can also be used to identify them. After those two are broken out, any other traffic with DSCP AF31 must be network management traffic.

The third group consists of SQL and e-mail traffic. The SQL servers share a subnet with the e-mail servers, so a simple access list specifying address is not enough. Fortunately, the Structured Query Language (SQL) and Simple Mail Transfer Protocol (SMTP) ports are both known, so you can use them to identify their respective traffic.

Example 8-12 shows how this might look when you put it all together. In this example, the policy is applied to the CE router at New York, where the servers are located. The access lists at the other sites need to flip the source and destination addresses and ports.

Example 8-12 *Mapping MPLS Classes Back to Internal Classes*

```
! This is the first group:
VGateway(config)#ip access-list extended SCCP
VGateway(config-ext-nacl)#permit tcp any any range 2000 2002
!
VGateway(config-ext-nacl)#ip access-list extended RTP
VGateway(config-ext-nacl)#permit udp any any range 16383 32767
!
VGateway(config-ext-nacl)#class-map VOICE
VGat VGateway(config-cmap)#match dscp ef
!
VGateway(config-cmap)#class-map match-all MPLS_CALL_SIG
VGateway(config-cmap)#match dscp cs5
VGateway(config-cmap)#match access-group name SCCP
```

Example 8-12 *Mapping MPLS Classes Back to Internal Classes (Continued)*

```
!
VGateway(configs-cmap)#class-map match-all MPLS_VIDEO
VGateway(config-cmap)#match dscp cs5
VGateway(config-cmap)#match access-group name RTP
!
! This is the second group:
VGateway(config)#ip access-list extended BGP
VGateway(config-ext-nacl)#permit tcp any any eq bgp
VGateway(config-ext-nacl)#permit tcp any eq bgp any
!
VGateway(config-ext-nacl)#ip access-list extended Market-Data
! The following is the Market Data server subnet
VGateway(config-ext-nacl)#permit ip any 10.1.17.0 0.0.0.255
!
VGateway(config-cmap)#class-map match-all Routing
VGateway(config-cmap)#match dscp af31
VGateway(config-cmap)#match access-group name BGP
!
VGateway(config-cmap)#class-map match-all Mkt-Data
VGateway(config-cmap)#match dscp af31
VGateway(config-cmap)#match access-group name Market-Data
!
VGateway(config-cmap)#class-map Network-Mgmt
VGateway(config-cmap)#match dscp af31
!
! This is the third group:
VGateway(config)#ip access-list extended SQL
VGateway(config-ext-nacl)#permit tcp any any eq 1433
!
VGateway(config-ext-nacl)#ip access-list extended SMTP
VGateway(config-ext-nacl)#permit tcp any any eq 25
!
VGateway(config-cmap)#class-map match-all SQL
VGateway(config-cmap)#match dscp 21
VGateway(config-cmap)#match access-group name SQL
!
VGateway(config-cmap)#class-map match-all EMAIL
VGateway(config-cmap)#match dscp 21
VGateway(config-cmap)#match access-group name SMTP
```

With the access lists and class maps, you now can classify the traffic incoming from the MPLS cloud into groups that correspond to your company policy. You do this using a policy map, as shown in Example 8-13.

Example 8-13 *Converting MPLS Markings to Internal Markings*

```
VGateway(config)#policy-map FROM-MPLS
VGateway(config-pmap)#class VOICE
VGateway(config-pmap-c)#set dscp ef
!
VGateway(config-pmap-c)#class MPLS_CALL_SIG
```

continues

Example 8-13 *Converting MPLS Markings to Internal Markings (Continued)*

```
VGateway(config-pmap-c)#set dscp cs3
!
VGateway(config-pmap-c)#class MPLS_VIDEO
VGateway(config-pmap-c)#set dscp af41
!
VGateway(config-pmap-c)#class Routing
VGateway(config-pmap-c)#set dscp cs6
!
VGateway(config-pmap-c)#class Mkt-Data
VGateway(config-pmap-c)#set dscp af32
!
VGateway(config-pmap-c)#class Network-Mgmt
VGateway(config-pmap-c)#set dscp af33
!
VGateway(config-pmap-c)#class SQL
VGateway(config-pmap-c)#set dscp 21
!
VGateway(config-pmap-c)#class EMAIL
VGateway(config-pmap-c)#set dscp 23
!
VGateway(config-pmap-c)#class class-default
VGateway(config-pmap-c)#set dscp 0
!
VGateway(config-pmap-c)#interface ATM1/0.110
VGateway(config-subif)#pvc 10/110
VGateway(config-if-atm-vc)#service-policy input FROM-MPLS
```

You apply the policy map inbound on the interface so that it affects traffic coming in from the MPLS cloud. Notice that policy map FROM-MPLS just sets DSCP values; it does not allocate bandwidth or prioritize traffic. Those tasks must be done at the outbound interfaces.

After the entire configuration is done, each CE router has two service policies on its WAN interface, as shown in Figure 8-2. The outbound policy aggregates the internally used classes of the company into ones that map to the standards of the MPLS provider. It remarks DSCP values where necessary. The inbound policy looks at the traffic coming from the MPLS cloud and then reclassifies and remarks it to comply with the internal QoS policy of the company.

Figure 8-2   *Mapping QoS to MPLS Standards*

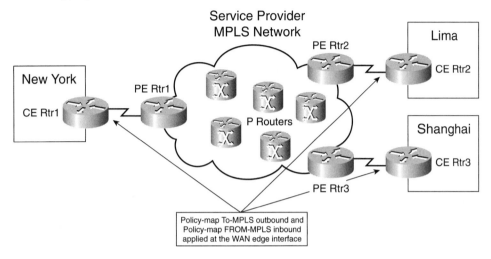

As stated earlier, it is important to thoughtfully plan your QoS strategy. You need to decide how to group traffic and what DSCP value to give to each of those groups. This is not a trivial task.

Link Fragmentation and Interleave

Voice and video traffic are sensitive to delay and jitter. You might recall that the delay target for voice is 150 ms, and for jitter it is 30 ms. LLQ, as described in the previous section, is one way to cut down on delay and jitter. When voice traffic is placed into an LLQ, it is sent out before other traffic. However, suppose that a small voice packet arrives at an interface just after a large data packet has begun being placed on the wire (or *serialized*). Even though the voice packet is placed in the priority LLQ, transmission of the data packet is not going to stop. The voice packet has to wait. This can be another cause of delay and jitter.

The time it takes for a packet to be placed onto the wire is known as *serialization delay*. This value varies by speed of the link and size of the packet. Naturally, any size packet takes longer to transmit out a slower interface than a faster one. And the more bits that must be transmitted out an interface, the longer it takes. To meet the requirements for voice, each interface along the path has a target serialization delay of no more than 10 ms. In the LAN, links are fast enough that serialization delay is not a factor. But on WAN links, it can be an issue.

One way to solve this is to break up large data packets into smaller pieces that take no more than 10 ms to serialize, which is known as *fragmentation*. Then voice packets can be transmitted between each piece of the data packet, which is known as *interleaving*. When combined, the technique is known as *Link Fragmentation and Interleave*.

You can calculate an approximate value for serialization delay using the following formula:

([packet-size * 8]/link-speed)

Packet size is in bytes, so you multiply by 8 to convert it to bits. Then you divide that product by the link speed in kbps. For example, the formula for a 1500-byte packet being sent out a T1 interface (1544 kbps) would look like this:

([1500 * 8]/1544 kbps) = 7.8 ms delay

As you can see, 1500 bytes takes less than 10 ms to serialize on a T1 interface. The same number of bytes takes 15.6 ms on a 768-kbps interface, however. As a general rule, fragmentation is not recommended on interfaces of T1 speed or greater. It can be helpful on lower-speed interfaces, if they tend to carry large data packets along with voice.

This leads to the question of what size the fragments should be. Tables are available in QoS texts detailing this, but you can also estimate the correct fragment size. At 64 kbps, it takes about 10 ms to serialize 80 bytes. You can use this fact to calculate fragment size—for instance, a 256-kbps link is four times a 64 kbps one. So the packet size can be four times 80 bytes, or 320 bytes.

Fragmentation is configured in different ways depending on the type of interface. You can do it on a leased line by using Multilink PPP (MLP), on a Frame Relay circuit by using FRF.12, on a Frame Relay circuit by using Multilink PPP over Frame Relay (MLPoFR), and with ATM by using Multilink PPP over ATM (MLPoATM). (An alternative for both Frame Relay and ATM is to use separate PVCs for voice.)

Multilink PPP

Multilink PPP was created to allow multiple PPP links to be treated as one, for load balancing and ease of administration. You can also use it with a single PPP link, as the example that follows shows. One good thing about using MLP is that you do not have to figure out the desired fragment size—PPP does that for you. You only have to specify the desired serialization delay value. Configuration is done with both a logical and a physical interface. Configuring MLP involves the following steps:

Step 1 Create a logical Multilink interface. Notice that logical configurations, such as the IP address, service policy, and bandwidth, are all configured on the Multilink interface.

```
VGateway(config-if)#interface multilink1
VGateway(config-if)#ip address 172.18.1.1 255.255.255.252
VGateway(config-if)#service-policy output VOICE-VIDEO
VGateway(config-if)#bandwidth 768
```

Step 2   Enable Multilink PPP, and associate the interface with a Multilink group. Configure the desired delay on the Multilink interface.

```
VGateway(config-if)#ppp multilink
VGateway(config-if)#ppp multilink group 1
VGateway(config-if)#ppp multilink fragment-delay 10
```

Step 3   Configure interleaving on the Multilink interface.

```
VGateway(config-if)#ppp multilink interleave
```

Step 4   At the physical PPP interface, configure PPP encapsulation, and enable PPP Multilink.

```
VGateway(config-if)#int s 0/0
VGateway(config-if)#encapsulation ppp
VGateway(config-if)#ppp multilink
```

Step 5   Place the physical interface into the Multilink group that is associated with the Multilink interface created earlier.

```
VGateway(config-if)#ppp multilink group 1
```

A useful verification command for MLP is **show interface multilink** *interface-number*. Example 8-14 shows the output from this command. Link control protocol (LCP) and multilink must both be open for the interface to be active. Under the Output queue line, which is highlighted, you can see the number of interleaves performed.

Example 8-14   **show interface multilink 1** *Command Output*

```
VGateway#show interface multilink 1
Multilink1 is up, line protocol is up
  Hardware is multilink group interface
  Internet address is 172.18.1.1/30
  MTU 1500 bytes, BW 768 Kbit, DLY 100000 usec,
    reliability 255/255, txload 9/255, rxload 9/255
  Encapsulation PPP, LCP Open, multilink Open
  Open: CDPCP, IPCP, loopback not set
  Keepalive set (10 sec)
  DTR is pulsed for 2 seconds on reset
  Last input 00:00:04, output never, output hang never
  Last clearing of "show interface" counters 01:21:31
  Input queue: 0/75/0/0 (size/max/drops/flushes); Total output drops: 0
  Queueing strategy: Class-based queueing
  Output queue: 0/1000/64/0/138 (size/max total/threshold/drops/interleaves)
      Conversations  0/2/256 (active/max active/max total)
      Reserved Conversations 0/0 (allocated/max allocated)
. . .
```

You must do this configuration on both sides of the link for fragmentation and interleave to work properly. One caveat is that any traffic in an LLQ will not be fragmented. Because video packets can go up to 1500 bytes in size, do not place video in the LLQ on slow links.

If you must run video through an interface with less than T1 bandwidth, put it in a class-based queue and assign bandwidth to it.

Frame Relay FRF.12 Fragmentation

FRF.12 is a standards-based way to do fragmentation on Frame Relay links. This standard allows you to fragment and interleave long frames with smaller frames at Layer 2. Frame Relay does not look into the packets to see whether traffic is voice or data. It fragments all packets larger than the specified size, regardless of what payload they carry. Therefore, be sure to configure a fragment size larger than the biggest voice traffic, with headers included.

Fragmentation is configured at the PVC level and applied to all traffic within that PVC. If multiple PVCs share the same physical interface, configure fragmentation on all of them because they share the same transmit ring at the interface. If any PVCs send large unfragmented frames, it could delay the voice traffic. Configure fragmentation on routers at both ends of the PVC, because it is end to end. Frames are fragmented at one router, and reassembled by the router on the other end of the virtual circuit. A special FRF.12 header is put on traffic from the PVC when fragmentation is configured.

When you are sending VoFR, shape the traffic from each PVC to avoid drops or delays from buffering within the provider cloud. Frame Relay traffic shaping (FRTS) causes the router to control the amount of traffic sent out the interface so that it conforms to the committed information rate (CIR) of each PVC. The traditional way to configure shaping is to place the commands under a Frame Relay map class. However, current versions of the Cisco IOS can do class-based FRTS. Configuring class-based Frame Relay fragmentation and shaping involves the following steps:

Step 1 Configure a policy map that puts voice in an LLQ and sets policies for other traffic as desired. Be sure that the total bandwidth allocated does not exceed the circuit CIR.

```
VGateway(config)#policy-map LLQ
VGateway(config-pmap)#class VOICE
VGateway(config-pmap-c)#priority 128
```

Step 2 Configure a second policy map. Configure traffic shaping parameters under the default class. In the following output, the first number is the configured CIR, in bits per second. Cisco recommends configuring the CIR to be 95 percent of the actual CIR to allow for overhead. The second number is the number of bits allowed per interval. Set this to the CIR/100, which forces that interval to be 10 ms. The last number is the excess burst (Be) allowed. Set this to 0 when sending VoIP over Frame Relay.

```
Gateway(config-pmap-c)#policy-map SHAPE
VGateway(config-pmap)#class class-default
VGateway(config-pmap-c)#shape average 729600 7296 0
```

Step 3   Associate the first policy map with the second under the default class.

```
VGateway(config-pmap-c)#service-policy LLQ
```

Step 4   Configure a Frame Relay map class. Configure the fragmentation parameter under this map class and associate the service policy with it. Set the fragment size to 960 by using the method given in the "Link Fragmentation and Interleave" section earlier in this chapter. Take advantage of the fact that at 64 kbps, it takes about 10 ms to serialize 80 bytes. The link speed in this example is 768 kbps. Thus, 768 divided by 64 equals 12. Multiplying 80 bytes times 12 gives you a fragment size of 960 bytes.

```
VGateway(config)#map-class frame-relay LFI-SHAPE
VGateway(config-map-class)#frame-relay fragment 960
VGateway(config-map-class)#service-policy output SHAPE
```

Step 5   Associate the map class with a PVC:

```
VGateway(config)#interface s0/0.112 point-to-point
VGateway(config-subif)#frame-relay interface-dlci 112
VGateway(config-fr-dlci)#class LFI-SHAPE
```

You can verify the configuration by the output of the **show policy interface** command, as follows in Example 8-15.

Example 8-15   **show policy interface** *Command Output*

```
VGateway#show policy interface s0/0.112
 Serial0/0.112: DLCI 112 -

  Service-policy output: SHAPE

    Class-map: class-default (match-any)
      0 packets, 0 bytes
      5 minute offered rate 0 bps, drop rate 0 bps
      Match: any
      Traffic Shaping
            Target/Average   Byte    Sustain   Excess    Interval  Increment
                  Rate       Limit   bits/int  bits/int  (ms)      (bytes)
            729600/729600    1825    7296      7296      10        912

        Adapt  Queue    Packets   Bytes    Packets   Bytes    Shaping
        Active Depth                       Delayed   Delayed  Active
         -       0        0         0        0         0        no

      Service-policy : LLQ

        Class-map: VOICE (match-all)
          0 packets, 0 bytes
          5 minute offered rate 0 bps, drop rate 0 bps
          Match: access-group name RTP
          Queueing
            Strict Priority
```

continues

Example 8-15 *show policy interface Command Output (Continued)*

```
                        Output Queue: Conversation 72
                        Bandwidth 128 (kbps) Burst 3200 (Bytes)
                        (pkts matched/bytes matched) 0/0
                        (total drops/bytes drops) 0/0

                Class-map: class-default (match-any)
                    0 packets, 0 bytes
                    5 minute offered rate 0 bps, drop rate 0 bps
                    Match: any
```

The **show frame-relay fragment** command lets you monitor the fragmentation occurring, as shown in Example 8-16. You can obtain more detailed information by specifying an interface after the command.

Example 8-16 **show frame-relay fragment** *Command Output*

```
VGateway#show frame-relay fragment
interface            dlci frag-type  size in-frag   out-frag   dropped-frag
Se0/0.112            112  end-to-end 960  0          0          0
```

Frame Relay Fragmentation Using MLPoFR

Link fragmentation and interleave can be done over Frame Relay using MLPoFR. Instead of creating a Multilink interface, the logical interface is called a Virtual-Template. Example 8-17 shows the configuration needed. You create a Virtual-Template interface and give almost the same configuration as shown in the Multilink interface example in the preceding "Multilink PPP" section. Fragmentation delay is specified, as is interleaving. The service policy LLQ is associated with this Virtual-Template interface, not the physical interface.

Example 8-17 *Configuring MLPoFR*

```
VGateway(config)#interface virtual-template1
VGateway(config-if)#
00:10:39: %LINK-3-UPDOWN: Interface Virtual-Template1, changed state to down
VGateway(config-if)#bandwidth 768
VGateway(config-if)#ip address 172.18.1.1 255.255.255.252
VGateway(config-if)#ppp multilink
VGateway(config-if)#ppp multilink fragment delay 10
VGateway(config-if)#ppp multilink interleave
VGateway(config-if)#service-policy output LLQ
!
VGateway(config-if)#map-class frame-relay MLPoFR
VGateway(config-map-class)#frame-relay cir 729600
VGateway(config-map-class)#frame-relay bc 7296
VGateway(config-map-class)#frame-relay be 0
VGateway(config-map-class)#no frame-relay adaptive-shaping becn
!
VGateway(config-map-class)#)#interface s0/0
VGateway(config-if)#encapsulation frame-relay
```

Example 8-17 *Configuring MLPoFR (Continued)*

```
VGateway(config-if)#frame-relay traffic-shaping
!
VGateway(config-if)#interface s0/0.112 point-to-point
VGateway(config-subif)#frame-relay interface-dlci 112 ppp virtual-template1
Class Based Weighted Fair Queueing will be applied only to the Virtual-Access
interfaces associated with an MLP bundle.
VGateway(config-fr-dlci)#
00:38:48: %LINK-3-UPDOWN: Interface Virtual-Access2, changed state to up
VGateway(config-fr-dlci)#class MLPoFR
```

A Frame Relay map class, MLPoFR, is configured with shaping parameters. Under that map class, the CIR is set to 95 percent of the link speed of 768 kbps to allow for overhead. Committed burst (Bc) is set to link-speed/100 to force the burst interval to be 10 ms. No Be is allowed. Adaptive traffic shaping in response to backward explicit congestion notification (BECN) frames is disabled.

Enable Frame Relay traffic shaping on the physical interface and apply the map class to the PVC. Notice the command to associate that PVC with the Virtual-Template interface: **frame-relay interface-dlci** *dlci-number* **ppp virtual-template1**. When MLPoFR is configured, the router automatically creates two additional logical interfaces: Virtual-Access1 and Virtual-Access2. (Notice in the example the message saying that interface Virtual-Access2 is up.) Virtual-Access1 is a logical PPP interface, and Virtual-Access2 is a logical Multilink PPP Bundle interface. You can verify this by looking at the output from a **show interface** command. The router messages shown are normal.

MLPoATM

You can also use MLP with an ATM PVC. Using MLPoATM allows ATM traffic to be fragmented and interleaved, something that ATM itself cannot accomplish. The most frequently used ATM adaptation layers assume that cells will arrive in the correct order, so they do not place a sequence number on the cells. Interleaving would make the cells arrive out of order. MLP handles the fragmenting, interleaving, sequence numbering, and reordering of the cells transparently to ATM.

When using MLPoATM, a Virtual-Template interface is created with the same commands as with MLPoFR. As a reminder, Example 8-18 shows the configuration.

Example 8-18 *Configuring MLPoATM*

```
VGateway#show run interface virtual-template1
interface Virtual-Template1
 bandwidth 768
 ip address 172.18.1.1 255.255.255.252
 ppp multilink
 ppp multilink fragment delay 10
 ppp multilink interleave
```

continues

Example 8-18 *Configuring MLPoATM (Continued)*

```
  service-policy output LLQ

VGateway(config)#interface atm 1/0
VGateway(config-if)#bandwidth 768
!
VGateway(config-if)#interface atm 1/0.110 point-to-point
VGateway(config-subif)#pvc 10/110
VGateway(config-if-atm-vc)#vbr-nrt 768 768
VGateway(config-if-atm-vc)#protocol ppp virtual-template1
VGateway(config-if-atm-vc)#tx-ring-limit 3
```

There is no equivalent to a Frame-Relay map class needed to specify shaping parameters; instead, you configure shaping parameters under the virtual circuit configuration, as shown in Example 8-18. The example PVC uses variable bit rate, nonreal-time (VBR-nrt). The first number is the peak cell rate (PCR), the maximum rate at which you expect to transmit traffic. The second number is the sustainable cell rate (SCR), which is the bandwidth of the virtual circuit. Setting the PCR and SCR to the same value effectively eliminates bursts, causing traffic to be shaped to a constant rate.

If you are experiencing excessive delay when using VoIP with ATM, try lowering the size of the interface transmit ring. Generally, setting the transmit ring size to 3 or 4 particles works well for voice. You do that under the virtual circuit configuration, as shown in Example 8-18.

Commands to verify the configuration include **show atm vc** and **show policy-map interface**.

Compression

Another way to lower serialization delay values is to send smaller packets. The payload in voice packets tends to be fairly small. However, each packet has to carry an IP header, a UDP header, and an RTP header that totals 40 bytes of overhead. When voice is sent across a WAN, it is usually compressed using G729, with a payload of 20 bytes. Thus, the headers are twice the size of the payload. Most of the header information in any given conversation is the same, so it can be reliably compressed. Compressed RTP (cRTP) compresses the IP, UDP, and RTP headers; it does not change the payload. With cRTP you can usually reduce the three headers to 2 bytes when checksum data is not sent, and 4 bytes when checksums are used. As you can imagine, this is especially helpful on slow links.

You can enable RTP compression on a Frame Relay, high-level data link control (HDLC), PPP, or MLP link. It is configured either at the interface level, on a particular virtual circuit, or for a class of traffic using the MQC. You must enable RTP compression on routers at both ends of a link, because each router in the path needs to uncompress the headers to know how to route the data.

Use cRTP with slow links, small voice payloads, and a need to save bandwidth. It is typically not needed on links over 2 Mbps in speed. Compression and decompression do use router resources, with more resources used the more calls you have. The trade-off in router performance is usually not worth the gain in bandwidth with link speeds over 2 Mbps. Understand that cRTP only compresses the headers for RTP traffic, not other types of data. If fast-switching or Cisco Express Forwarding (CEF) is enabled on the interface, compression is done on these paths. If neither is enabled on the interface, traffic that needs to be compressed is process switched.

To enable CRTP on an HDLC or PPP serial interface, use the following command under the physical interface configuration:

```
ip rtp header-compression [passive]
```

If you include the optional **passive** keyword, the router does CRTP only if it receives compressed packets.

To enable CRTP on a Frame Relay interface, use the following command:

```
frame-relay ip rtp header-compression [passive]
```

You can configure the preceding command either under the physical interface configuration or under the subinterface.

If this command is given on the physical Frame Relay interface, all PVCs that are associated with that interface inherit it.

MQC class-based compression allows more granular control of RTP compression. It is configured in a policy map and applies only to RTP traffic in the specific class(es) where it is enabled. For instance, in the following commands, RTP header compression is enabled for all traffic in the Voice class. If the **rtp keyword** is not specified, both RTP and TCP header compression are done. You should also configure the gateway to place this traffic in the LLQ.

```
VGateway(config)#policy-map VOICE-VIDEO
VGateway(config-pmap)#class Voice
VGateway(config-pmap-c)#compression header ip rtp
```

Then you can apply the policy outbound to an interface, virtual circuit, Frame Relay map class, or virtual interface. You can verify your configuration with the **show policy-map** and **show policy interface** commands, as shown in Example 8-19.

NOTE   For simplicity, only relevant output is displayed in Example 8-19.

Example 8-19   *Verifying RTP Compression*

```
VGateway#show policy VOICE-VIDEO
  Policy Map VOICE-VIDEO
    Class Voice
      Strict Priority
```

continues

Example 8-19 *Verifying RTP Compression (Continued)*

```
            Bandwidth 15 (%)
            compress:
                header ip rtp
VGateway#
VGateway#show policy interface s0/0
 Serial0/0

  Service-policy output: VOICE-VIDEO

    Class-map: Voice (match-all)
      2153 packets, 137792 bytes
      5 minute offered rate 10000 bps, drop rate 0 bps
      Match:  dscp ef (46)
      Queueing
        Strict Priority
        Output Queue: Conversation 264
        Bandwidth 15 (%)
        Bandwidth 231 (kbps) Burst 5775 (Bytes)
        (pkts matched/bytes matched) 2152/36584
        (total drops/bytes drops) 0/0
      compress:
          header ip rtp
          UDP/RTP compression:
          Sent: 2152 total, 2147 compressed,
                101208 bytes saved, 36584 bytes sent
```

AutoQos

Cisco has an AutoQoS feature that you can enable. When enabled, this feature configures QoS policies for the device in accordance with Cisco best practices. It is useful for network administrators who do not have in-depth knowledge of QoS techniques, or for those who need to deploy QoS quickly.

AutoQoS has the following features when used at a WAN voice gateway router:

- It uses the MQC.
- It creates class maps to classify voice-bearer and voice-control traffic, in addition to other traffic.
- It creates policy maps that place voice traffic in an LLQ and guarantee bandwidth to voice control traffic.
- Frame Relay traffic shaping is configured for Frame Relay links.
- Link Fragmentation and Interleaving (LFI) and RTP header compression are configured for links under 768 kbps.
- When you are using LFI, any IP address that is configured under the subinterface is automatically moved to the multilink or Virtual-Template interface.

- It supports Frame Relay, ATM, Frame Relay-to-ATM Internetworking, PPP, and HDLC links.
- It can send SNMP and SYSLOG notices for such things as VoIP packet drops.

AutoQos is configured on a WAN interface, subinterface, or PVC with the following command:

```
auto qos voip [trust] [fr-atm]
```

The optional keyword **trust** tells the router to trust the DSCP markings that are already on the traffic. The default is not to trust those markings, but to remark traffic based on its type. AutoQos uses Network-Based Application Recognition (NBAR) to determine types of traffic. The optional **fr-atm** keyword is used with low-speed Frame Relay PVCs that participate in Frame Relay-to-ATM Internetworking. You must manually configure bandwidth on the interface or subinterface when you are using AutoQoS.

Using AutoQos can be helpful, but a basic understanding of good QoS practices is still important. You might need to tweak the automatic configuration to suit the exact needs of your company. In addition, it is always good to understand what is happening in your network.

Providing Fax and Modem Services

Analog faxes and modems provide an extra challenge in a VoIP network. These devices assume that they have a physical circuit between the transmitting and receiving ends, such as over the PSTN, but IP networks do not provide this. Thus, fax and modem data requires special handling when sending over an IP network. There are two basic methods for handing fax and modem calls:

- **Relay**—The analog data is demodulated by the sending gateway, which packetizes the data and sends it over the IP network. The receiving gateway remodulates it and forwards it as analog data to the fax or modem. The actions of the gateways are transparent to the end devices—they receive analog data just as if they were communicating over a PSTN link. In general, relay is not as affected by packet loss, delay, and jitter as is passthrough. It also uses less bandwidth.

- **Passthrough**—Fax and modem calls are treated as any other analog voice call, with the data carried in-band in RTP packets to the remote fax or modem. This requires the G.711 codec, no echo cancellation, and no voice activity detection (VAD). When the gateways recognize the type of call, they change to these settings for the duration of the call. Passthrough is sensitive to packet loss, delay, and jitter. You can use redundancy with passthrough to send an extra copy of each packet, to help mitigate packet loss. This does result in higher bandwidth use, however.

NOTE	A third method, Store and Forward, is used only for faxes. It uses a separate e-mail server and allows faxes to be sent as TIFF attachments to e-mails. You can use Toolkit Command Language (Tcl) scripts to provide some fax-related services, also. Tcl interactive voice response (IVR) scripts are typically used with Store and Forward faxing. Tcl scripts can also provide fax detection and fax rollover applications. Fax detection allows one phone number to be used for both voice and fax calls. Fax rollover involves switching to Store and Forward mode if fax relay fails. See Chapter 15, "Using TCL Scripts and VoiceXML," for more information on Tcl scripts for fax applications.

Providing Fax Services

Several standards govern fax transmissions. It is not necessary to know all of them to get faxes working over IP, but an understanding of the major ones helps. International Telecommunications Union Telecommunication Standardization Sector (ITU-T) standards govern such things as fax resolution, identifying tones, handshaking procedures, and transmission speeds. They have developed over time from Group 1 to Group 3 standards. The Group 3, or "G3," standard is currently the most commonly used. It allows fax transmission rates over analog lines of up to 14,400 bps. Group 4 (G4) is a standard for transmitting faxes over ISDN, and it can send at a rate of 64,000 bps. By using two B-channels, G4 faxes can send and receive at the same time. Super G3 (SG3) is a newer standard, which allows sending faxes at 33,600 bps.

Session management between two G3 fax machines is specified in the T.30 standard of the ITU-T, and T.4 describes the image transmission. Communication between gateways using fax relay is standardized by T.38.

T.30 divides fax calls into five phases:

- **Phase A: Call Setup**—In Phase A, a call is established, and the two endpoints identify themselves as fax machines. The calling device repeatedly sends a CalliNG (CNG) tone. The called device sends a Called Station Identification (CED) tone. After the devices exchange these tones, they know that they are communicating with a fax machine.

- **Phase B: Capabilities Exchang**e—The called machine sends a V.21 standard Digital Identification Signal (DIS), which lists its capabilities, such as page length, resolution, error correction, and handshake speed. When the gateway sees this DIS message, it switches the call from a voice codec to a fax codec.

  The calling machine responds with a Digital Command Signal (DCS), telling the called device which of its settings to use. The calling machine then sends a Training Check Field (TCF) signal at the agreed-upon modulation. If the called machine receives this properly, it responds with a Confirmation to Receive (CFR) message. Otherwise, it sends a Failure to Train (FTT).

- **Phase C**: **Data Transmission**—The T.4 standard specifies message transmission standards. It handles such things as encoding type and error correction. At the end of the transmission, the fax sends a Return to Control (RTC) message, which initiates Phase D.

- **Phase D**: **Confirming the Transmission**—After the sending fax has returned to control mode, it sends a message that it has finished transmitting. The receiving fax responds with a Message Confirmation (MCF).

- **Phase E**: **Releasing the Call**—Either fax machine can send a Disconnect (DCN) message. Both sides then release the call.

Phases A and B are handled differently in Super G3 faxes. In Phase A, the called device sends a Modified Answer (ANSam) tone instead of a CED tone. In Phase B, the calling device sends a Call Menu message, and the called fax responds with a Joint Menu message. If the SG3 handshake does not succeed, the fax machines fall back to G3 mode. These differences in operation might require some special configuration, as you will see in the following sections.

You can configure the type of fax treatment used in two places: under an individual dial peer, or in the **voice service voip** configuration mode. The command syntax is **fax protocol {cisco | none | pass-through {g711ulaw | g711alaw}| system | t38}**. The exact options available vary by Cisco IOS version.

Configuring Cisco Fax Relay

Cisco gateways use two versions of fax relay: the Cisco proprietary version, and one that uses the ITU-T T.38 standard. Cisco fax relay is the default way of handling faxing by Cisco gateways. It uses RTP to exchange the demodulated T.30 fax signals with its peer gateway. Cisco fax relay is supported on most Cisco gateways, with the exception of some models in the AS5000 series. It does not need to be enabled, unless you have used a different method and want to re-enable it. The command to enable Cisco fax relay is **fax protocol cisco**. You can give this command under an individual dial peer, or under **voice service voip** configuration mode to affect all dial peers.

You can tweak Cisco fax relay in a few ways. For instance, Error Correction Mode (ECM) is enabled by default. Fax machines that use ECM require any frames that have errors to be retransmitted. If the fax cannot receive an error-free page, it might terminate the call. In networks that have more than two percent packet loss, you might see a high rate of fax failure because of ECM. If you disable it, more faxes succeed, although they might contain some errors. Disable ECM with the VoIP dial peer command **fax-relay ecm disable**.

Some fax machine manufacturers use proprietary features, which are negotiated during Phase B using an optional Non-Standard Facilities (NSF) field. The Cisco fax relay handles fax calls based on T.30 standards, and thus cannot interpret these capabilities. You can cause the gateway to overwrite the NSF field with zeros using the VoIP dial peer command **fax nsf 000000**.

You might need to change the rate at which faxes are sent. By default, faxes use the same bandwidth as voice calls. In networks that use low-bandwidth codecs, such as G.729, this might cause faxes to transmit too slowly. Also, some fax machines might operate better at a different speed than the default. You can change fax bandwidth for a VoIP dial peer with the command **fax rate** {*speed* | **disable** | **voice**}, where *speed* is a value from 2400 to 14400 bps, **disable** disables all fax transfer methods, and **voice** uses the voice call bandwidth. This command is also valid for T.38 fax relay.

In Example 8-20, Cisco fax relay is enabled, ECM is disabled, use of proprietary features is disabled, and the fax rate is set at 14400 bps.

Example 8-20 *Configuring Cisco Fax Relay*

```
VoiceGW(config)#dial-peer voice 4000 voip
VoiceGW(config-dial-peer)#fax protocol cisco
VoiceGW(config-dial-peer)#fax-relay ecm disable
VoiceGW(config-dial-peer)#fax nsf 000000
VoiceGW(config-dial-peer)#fax rate 14400
```

Configuring T.38 Fax Relay for MGCP Gateways

T.38 is a standards-based type of fax relay, which treats the communication between gateways differently from Cisco fax relay. After the gateway demodulates the T.30 messages from the fax machine, it translates them into T.38 Internet Fax Protocol (IFP) packets for transmission to its peer gateway. When the other gateway receives these packets, it translates them back into T.30 signals and sends those to the fax machine.

T.38 fax relay is handled differently on MGCP gateways than on H.323 and SIP gateways. MGCP gateways can rely on the call agent to direct the T.38 traffic flow, when using call agent (CA)-controlled fax relay mode. They can also make those decisions themselves, when using gateway-controlled fax relay mode.

In gateway-controlled mode, fax relay capabilities are exchanged in the Session Description Protocol (SDP) packets during call setup. If both gateways support fax relay, they signal the switch to T.38 using Named Service Event (NSE) or Named Telephony Event (NTE) messages after they detect a DIS fax tone. NSE messages are a Cisco-proprietary form of NTE messages. They are used to send call signaling that would be sent using tones, such as fax tones, in a non-VoIP network. The content of the NSE messages has information to allow the receiving gateway to re-create the original tones. NSE and NTE messages travel in the RTP stream, but they use a different RTP payload type (usually 100) to distinguish them from voice packets. NSE and NTE differ in the values used to represent tones and events.

If neither gateway supports fax relay, the gateways fall back to fax passthrough. The CA knows only that a voice call exists; the fact that it is a fax call is transparent to it. MGCP auto-configuration using the **ccm-manager config** command disables T.38 fax relay before Cisco IOS version 12.4T. It is enabled by default on IOS versions after that, and in CallManager version 4.2(3).

You can make some adjustments to MGCP T.38 with the global command **mgcp fax t38** {**ecm** | **gateway force** | **hs_redundancy** *value* | **inhibit** | **ls_redundancy** *value* | **nsf** *hexcode*}, where

- **ecm** enables error correction mode.

- **gateway force** forces the gateway to use T.38 and NSEs even if they are not negotiated during call setup. This allows MGCP gateways to use T.38 fax relay with H.323 and SIP gateways.

- **hs-redundancy** *factor* causes the router to send redundant packets when doing high-speed faxing, to cover for any dropped packets. The default value is 0, which means no redundancy.

- **inhibit** disables T.38 fax relay on the gateway. To enable T.38 fax relay, use the command **no mgcp fax t38 inhibit.**

- **ls-redundancy** causes the router to send redundant packets when doing low-speed faxing, to cover for any dropped packets. The default value is 0, which means no redundancy.

- **nsf** *hexcode* disables the use of proprietary fax features when the hexcode used is 000000.

Use the **show mgcp** command to verify your configuration, as shown in Example 8-21. Only relevant portions of the lengthy output are displayed. Note that MGCP T.38 commands are given at the global configuration mode.

Example 8-21 *Configuring MGCP T.38 Fax Relay*

```
VoiceGW(config)#no mgcp fax t38 inhibit
VoiceGW(config)#no mgcp fax t38 ecm
VoiceGW(config)#^Z
VoiceGW#show mgcp
...
MGCP TSE payload: 100
MGCP T.38 Named Signalling Event (NSE) response timer: 200
...
MGCP T.38 Fax is ENABLED
MGCP T.38 Fax ECM is DISABLED
MGCP T.38 Fax NSF Override is DISABLED
MGCP T.38 Fax Low Speed Redundancy: 0MGCP T.38 Fax High Speed Redundancy: 0
```

Configuring T.38 Fax Relay for H.323 and SIP Gateways

H.323 and SIP gateways use the same basic configuration for T.38 fax relay. They do not use NSE messages to signal the other gateway to switch to fax mode, unless you specifically configure it. Instead, they use H.323 or SIP messages. Configure dial peers for fax destinations, enable T.38 fax relay, and set parameters under each dial peer. If several dial peers share the same T.38 settings, you might prefer to configure them globally under the **voice service voip mode** instead. Dial peer configuration takes precedence over global configuration if both exist.

The command to configure T.38 fax relay under a dial peer is **fax protocol {system | t38 [nse [force]] [ls-redundancy** *value* **[hs-redundancy** *value*]] **[fallback {cisco | none| pass-through {g711ulaw | g711alaw}}]}**, where

- **system** is the default. It causes the dial peer to use the global fax protocol that is configured.

- **t38** tells the dial peer to use T.38 fax relay. The **nse** option to this command negotiates the use of NSE messages to signal the switch to fax relay. The **force** option requires the use of NSE messages, even if the other side does not signal that capability. This allows H.323 and SIP gateways to exchange faxes with MGCP gateways.

- **ls-redundancy** *value* causes the router to send redundant packets when doing low-speed faxing, to cover for any dropped packets. The default value is 0, which means no redundancy.

- **hs-redundancy** *value* causes the router to send redundant packets when doing high-speed faxing, to cover for any dropped packets. The default value is 0, which means no redundancy.

- **fallback** configures a fallback way to handle faxing if the gateway cannot negotiate T.38 fax relay with its peer gateway. **cisco** uses Cisco fax relay, **none** disables fax handling, and **pass-through** enables fax passthrough. You must specify the codec to use—either **g711ulaw** or **g711alaw**.

The same command is available under **voice service voip** configuration mode, although the **system** option is not available. When configuring fax relay in this way, make sure that at least one dial peer matches the incoming calls. Commands that you configure under a dial peer take precedence over those you configure in **voice service voip** mode.

Example 8-22 shows a dial peer that is configured for T.38 fax relay. It forces the use of NSE messages and falls back to Cisco fax relay if the gateways cannot negotiate T.38.

Example 8-22 *Configuring T.38 Fax Relay on H.323 and SIP Gateways*

```
VoiceGW(config)#dial-peer voice 4000 voip
VoiceGW(config-dial-peer)#fax protocol t38 nse force fallback cisco
```

When you are troubleshooting T.38 fax relay, be sure that an IP path exists between the two gateways. Check that the dial peers are configured properly. The **debug fax relay t30** command gives you information about the phone numbers and T.30 messages in your fax transmissions.

NOTE	Debug commands can affect the performance of the router.

Configuring Super G3 Fax Relay

Super G3 (SG3) fax machines negotiate the use of SG3 speed during call setup, using Call Menu and Joint Menu messages. They use the V.34 standard for modulation and the V.8 standard for signaling. V.34 is a form of pulse code modulation (PCM) that allows data transmission up to 33,600 bps. The V.8 standard describes SG3 signaling such as ANSam, Call Menu, and Joint Menu.

SG3 machines can interoperate with G3 faxes. If an SG3 machine is on one end and a G3 machine is on the other, the SG3 machine receives a DIS instead of the expected Menu message, and it falls back to G3 mode. When the gateway hears the DIS, it switches the call to a fax call. Fax relay between SG3 and G3 machines is not usually a problem in Cisco VoIP networks.

Fax relay between two SG3 machines can be a problem, however. SG3 was not designed to work with T.38 fax relay. The two fax machines exchange V.8 signaling, so the gateways never hear a DIS and do not switch the call over to fax mode. The current solution for this is SG3 fax spoofing. SG3 fax spoofing is available on most voice gateways in Cisco IOS versions 12.4(4)T and later. It blocks the Call Menu message from being sent. This causes the receiving fax machine to fall back to G3 mode and send V.21 DIS and DCS messages. Both gateways then use G3 mode.

You can configure SG3 fax spoofing on one or both gateways, but you at least must configure it on the calling gateway so that it suppresses the Call Menu message. You can configure the **fax-relay sg3-to-g3** [**system**] command under a dial peer or in **voice service voip** configuration mode on H.323 or SIP gateways. Configure SG3 spoofing in global configuration mode on MGCP gateways. The "system" option is available only in dial peer configuration mode and causes the dial peer to use the protocol set in **voice service voip** configuration mode. Example 8-23 shows a router configured under the **voice service** mode to use SG3 fax spoofing.

Example 8-23 *Configuring SG3 Fax Spoofing*

```
VoiceGW(config)#voice service voip
VoiceGW(conf-voi-serv)#fax-relay sg3-to-g3
```

Configuring Fax Passthrough

In fax passthrough, the gateway does not demodulate the call—it treats fax calls similar to analog voice calls. Fax data is sent in-band, in RTP packets, to the other gateway. Fax passthrough uses the G.711 codec and requires 64 kbps per call, plus 32 kbps per call for overhead. Echo cancellation and VAD are turned off. Passthrough is sensitive to jitter, latency, and packet loss. You can use redundancy, which sends two copies of each packet, to mitigate packet loss, but it also requires extra network bandwidth.

Configuring Fax Passthrough for MGCP Gateways

As with fax relay, MGCP gateways use NSE messages to signal their peer to switch to fax mode. You configure fax passthrough for MGCP gateways globally rather than under the dial peer, using options of the **mgcp modem passthrough** command. MGCP gateways use NSE messages to signal their peer gateway to switch to fax mode. Passthrough using NSEs is called "modem passthrough"; thus, the command to configure fax passthrough on an MGCP gateway is the same command you use to configure modem passthrough. The following commands are available:

- **mgcp modem passthrough** {**cisco** | **ca**}—Configures the type of fax/modem passthrough used. The **cisco** option causes the gateway to switch to G711 codec when it detects a fax tone, and notify its peer gateway. The **ca** option, which is the default, causes the gateway to alert its call agent when a fax tone is detected. The call agent then signals a switch to the G711 codec.

- **mgcp modem passthrough** {**voip** | **voaal2**} **codec** {**g711alaw** | **g711ulaw**}— Configures the codec used in either VoIP or Voice over ATM Adaptation Layer 2 (VoAAL2) networks. If you do not specify the codec, the router uses G711ulaw. After the router detects fax or modem traffic, it switches to using the specified codec for that call.

- **mgcp modem passthrough voip redundancy**—Enables redundant fax packets to be sent, to mitigate packet loss. Redundancy is disabled by default.

- **mgcp modem passthrough mode** {**voip** | **voaal2**} **mode** {**cisco** | **nse**}—Configures the method used to signal the switch to fax speed in either VoIP or VoAAL2 networks. The **cisco** option uses whatever Cisco proprietary method is available. The **nse** option, which is the default, uses NSE messages to signal the switch. If **nse** is used, you can also configure the **mgcp tse payload** value.

- **mgcp tse payload** *value*—Enables the use of in-band Telephony Signaling Events (TSE) and specifies a payload value. Both receiving and sending gateways must use the same value; the default is 100.

Example 8-24 shows an MGCP gateway configured for fax passthrough, with redundancy, using NSE message for upspeeding. The TSE payload value is left at its default of 100. This is verified with the **show mgcp** command. Only the relevant output of the command is shown.

Example 8-24 *Configuring MGCP Fax Passthrough*

```
VoiceGW(config)#mgcp modem passthrough voip mode nse
VoiceGW(config)#mgcp modem passthrough voip redundancy
!
VoiceGW#show mgcp
MGCP voip modem passthrough mode: NSE, codec: g711ulaw, redundancy: ENABLED,
MGCP voaal2 modem passthrough disabled
MGCP voip modem relay: Disabled.
MGCP TSE payload: 100
```

Configuring Fax Passthrough for H.323 and SIP Gateways

H.323 and SIP gateways typically signal the switchover to fax mode using H.323 or SIP protocol messages. However, you can configure them to use NSE messages. Using NSEs is actually called "modem passthrough." You must use modem passthrough when you are interacting with Cisco CallManager, because it uses NSE messages.

The command to configure fax passthrough is the same whether given in dial peer or **voice service voip** configuration mode: **fax protocol pass-through** {**g711ulaw** | **g711alaw**{. To force the use of NSE messages, configure modem passthrough with the **modem passthrough nse** [**payload-type** *number*] {codec {*g711alaw* | *g711ulaw*}} [**redundancy**] [**maximum-sessions** *sessions*] command, where

- **nse** signifies that NSEs will be used to signal the peer gateway to switch to fax passthrough.

- **payload-type** *number* specifies the number to assign to the NSE payload. The default is 100.

- **codec** is a required element, and you must specify either g711alaw or g711ulaw.

- **redundancy** enables the sending of two copies of each packet to mitigate packet loss.

- **maximum-sessions** *sessions* configures the maximum number of simultaneous passthrough sessions allowed. This option applies only if redundancy is also configured, and only under voice service configuration mode.

Use the same settings on both the sending and receiving gateways. When you configure fax or modem passthrough globally, be sure that at least one dial peer matches the incoming fax or modem calls.

In Example 8-25, a dial peer is configured to match all incoming calls using the . (period) wildcard. Fax passthrough is then enabled on the dial peer, using the G711ulaw codec.

Example 8-25 *Configuring Fax Passthrough for H.323 or SIP*

```
AA03(config)#dial-peer voice 904 voip
AA03(config-dial-peer)#incoming called-number .
AA03(config-dial-peer)#fax protocol pass-through g711ulaw
```

Providing Modem Services

As with faxes, a VoIP network can carry modem traffic using either a relay method or a passthrough method.

In modem relay, the modem traffic is demodulated at one gateway, digitized, and carried to the other gateway using the Simple Packet Relay Transfer (SPRT) protocol. At the receiving gateway, the traffic is remodulated and sent to the receiving modem. Modem relay is not as affected by packet loss, delay, and jitter as is modem passthrough. It also uses less bandwidth.

When a gateway that is configured for modem relay first detects a modem tone, it switches to modem passthrough mode. Then, if it detects a Call Menu (CM) tone, and the gateways have negotiated modem relay support, it switches to modem relay mode. The gateways use NSE messages to tell the other gateway to switch modes. Call Menu tones are discussed in the earlier section "Providing Fax Services."

In modem passthrough, RTP packets are used to carry the modem traffic between the two gateways. When the gateways detect a modem signal, they exchange NSE messages. Both the originating and terminating gateway switch to using a G.711 codec, and they disable the high-pass filter, echo cancellation, and VAD for the duration of the modem call. As with fax passthrough, modem passthrough is sensitive to packet loss, delay, and jitter. You can use redundancy with modem passthrough to send an extra copy of each packet to help mitigate packet loss. This does result in higher bandwidth use, however. Modem passthrough is also referred to as Voice Band Data (VBD).

Configuring Cisco Modem Relay

To use Cisco modem relay, several requirements must be met:

- Both the originating and terminating gateways must be Cisco gateways.
- Both modems must be high-speed modems—V.34 or V.90—and must use V.42bis compression.
- Error correction must be enabled on both modems.
- Modem relay is supported on both C5510 and C549 digital signal processors (DSP), and the DSPs must be set to either high or flex codec.

If these conditions are not met, modem passthrough is used. Cisco modem relay supports a transfer rate of 33.6 Kbps, which means that faster modems need to train down to that speed.

You configure modem relay on MGCP gateways at the global configuration mode with the **mgcp modem relay voip mode [nse] [codec (g711alaw | g711ulaw}] [redundancy] gw-controlled** command, where

- **nse** tells the gateway to use NSE messages to signal the switch to modem relay.

- **codec {g711alaw | g711ulaw}** specifies the codec to be used for modem calls.

- **redundancy** enables the sending of two copies of each packet.

- **gw-controlled** specifies that modem relay configuration is done on the gateway instead of being controlled by the call agent.

If you are using several of the options for this command, give them on the same line, as shown next, or the later command will overwrite them.

```
VoiceGW(config)#mgcp modem relay voip mode nse codec g711ulaw redundancy gw-
controlled
```

You can configure modem relay on H.323 and SIP gateways either in voice service mode, to apply to all VoIP modem calls, or in dial peer mode, to apply to only that dial peer. If both modes are used, the dial peer configuration takes precedent over the global configuration. Use the **modem relay {nse [payload-type** *number*] **[codec {g711alaw | g711ulaw}] [redundancy] | system} gw-controlled** command, where

- **payload-type** *number* sets the NSE payload type. The default is 100.

- **codec {g711alaw | g711ulaw}** sets the codec type for the modem relay calls.

- **redundancy** enables the sending of two copies of each packet.

- **system** is an option available only under dial peer configuration mode. It tells the gateway to use the globally configured type of modem relay for that dial peer.

- **gw-controlled** specifies that the gateway is controlling the modem relay parameters.

Be sure to use the same codec type for both the originating and the terminating gateways. Use G.711ulaw for T1 links, and G.711alaw for E1 links.

Configuring Modem Passthrough

As with fax passthrough, modem passthrough configuration for MGCP gateways differs from H.323 and SIP configuration. Modem passthrough for MGCP gateways is configured globally rather than under the dial peer, using options of the **mgcp modem passthrough** command. See the previous section "Configuring Fax Passthrough for MGCP Gateways" for a complete description and examples of this command.

For H.323 and SIP gateways, you can configure modem passthrough either under voice service configuration mode or under individual dial peers. When you configure under voice service mode, the command is **modem passthrough nse** [**payload-type** *number*] **codec** {**g711ulaw** | **g711alaw**} [**redundancy**] [**maximum-sessions** *value*], where

- **payload-type** *number* sets the NSE payload type. The default is 100.
- **codec** {**g711alaw** | **g711ulaw**} sets the codec type for the modem passthrough calls.
- **redundancy** enables the sending of two copies of each packet.
- **maximum-sessions** *sessions* configures the maximum number of simultaneous passthrough sessions allowed. This option applies only if redundancy is also configured, and only under voice service configuration mode.

When you give the command under a dial peer configuration, the **maximum-sessions** option is not available. An additional option, **modem passthrough system**, is available only in dial peer mode; it tells the dial peer to use the globally configured modem passthrough mode.

If a gateway that is using modem passthrough connects to the PSTN, it is important to synch the gateway clock with the PSTN clock so that modem passthrough can work correctly. Configure the PSTN interface to provide clocking for the gateway.

Example 8-26 shows modem passthrough configured for a SIP dial peer. NSE messages are used, along with the G.711alaw codec, and redundant packets are sent.

Example 8-26 *Configuring Modem Passthrough for a SIP Dial Peer*

```
VoiceGW(config)#dial-peer voice 706 voip
VoiceGW (config-dial-peer)#incoming called-number .
VoiceGW (config-dial-peer)#session protocol sipv2
VoiceGW (config-dial-peer)#modem passthrough nse codec g711alaw redundancy
```

Security

Voice and video traffic that you send over a WAN has unique security issues. For one thing, the traffic might be exposed to all the inherent dangers of the Internet. This is especially true for IP telephony services offered by Internet service providers (ISPs). Managed VoIP services are available in which the service provider owns and maintains the call control equipment. Another service allows companies to have just a WAN connection to an MPLS network—no local PSTN connections. All voice traffic is sent as VoIP to the provider network, where calls that are bound for the PSTN are split out from calls that are bound to a company site across the MPLS cloud. Both service providers and companies who use these services must be aware of security issues and cooperate to mitigate them. The tools that are covered in this section help with that.

For companies that manage their own VoIP network, another consideration is the security policies and devices on the network. Will the internal IP addresses be translated by Network

Address Translation (NAT) as they exit the local network? Will voice traffic have to traverse a firewall? These are issues you do not normally face when using VoIP on a LAN.

Fortunately, because voice is carried over an IP network, you can use the same tools to protect it as you use to protect your data network. Firewalls, intrusion detection and prevention systems, encryption, authentication, replay protection, and voice-enabled VPNs all work together to provide a secure voice network. The Cisco firewall devices and Cisco IOS firewalls can look into the payload section of packets and recognize voice protocols. They can then maintain stateful information for voice connections. In addition, you should configure the firewall to allow only voice traffic into the voice portion of the network.

This section discusses four security areas that relate to voice gateways:

- Securing voice media and signaling
- V3PN
- NAT and VoIP
- Firewalls and VoIP

Securing Voice Media and Signaling

Consider the various types of voice traffic that are traversing your LAN and WAN if your network uses a centralized Cisco CallManager design.

- Real-Time Control Protocol (RTCP) voice control
- RTP voice media
- SCCP signaling between phones and CallManager
- MGCP, H.323, or SIP signaling between the gateway and CallManager, and between gateways

Cisco routers can encrypt RTP voice traffic between the gateway and IP phones, and between two gateways. They can also authenticate and encrypt their communications with Cisco CallManager. Encryption of voice media and control payload is done via SRTP. Encrypting communication with CallManager is accomplished by IPsec for MGCP and H.323 gateways, and by Transport Layer Security (TLS) for SIP gateways. Encryption of the signaling between CallManager or an SRST router and IP phones uses TLS.

Securing Voice Media with Secure RTP

Media encryption and authentication using SRTP are included for MGCP gateways in the Advanced IP Services and the Advanced Enterprise Services IOS software, beginning with version 12.3(11)T1. They are included for H.323 and IP-to-IP gateways beginning in Cisco IOS version 12.4(6)T. SRTP was designed just for IP voice (not video) packets, and it was standardized in RFC 3711. SRTP encrypts the RTP payload using Advanced Encryption

Standard (AES) encryption. It does not encrypt the RTP header. You can use IPsec along with, or instead of, SRTP if you need header encryption. RTP header and payload contents are authenticated by the sender computing a one-way HMAC-SHA1 hash and placing the results in an authentication tag at the end of the packet. The receiver runs the same computation and compares its result to the contents of the authentication tag. If they do not match, the packet is dropped. SRTP also includes a replay protection process to avoid denial of service (DoS) attacks.

Most of the recent Cisco IP phones used with at least version 4.1 of Cisco CallManager can use SRTP to encrypt their signaling and voice traffic. By configuring both the phones and the gateways for encryption, you can have end-to-end security for your voice traffic. Encryption on the gateway also allows the encryption of voice traffic from analog phones and fax machines inside the network.

You must configure both the gateway and the CallManager to enable the capability for SRTP on the gateway. Negotiation of SRTP is part of the call setup process. All devices along the path must support it; otherwise, RTP is used (called SRTP-to-RTP fallback). After you negotiate encryption for a call, the encryption keys are sent over the signaling path, for use with the SRTP stream. Keys are sent clear text unless the signaling path is secured with IPsec (described in the next section).

To enable SRTP on an MGCP gateway, give the **mgcp package-capability srtp-package** command from global configuration mode. You must also configure the CallManager to support SRTP. After you negotiate encryption for a call, the CallManager sends an encryption key to the gateway for use with the SRTP stream. Configure IPsec protection for the encryption key exchange before enabling SRTP if the communication will traverse an untrusted network.

For H.323 gateways, you must configure a trunk from the gateway to CallManager. On the gateway, add the **srtp [fallback]** command under the dial peers that point to your CallManagers. The **fallback** option allows secure calls to fall back to unsecure when SRTP is not supported on the call path. Alternatively, this same command can be given under the voice service voip configuration mode. All VoIP calls then use SRTP. When you configure the trunk on CallManager, check the SRTP Allowed check box. CallManager tries to negotiate SRTP for any calls over that trunk. The H.323 gateway generates media encryption keys, which are passed to CallManager in the signaling path.

SIP gateways did not support SRTP media encryption at the time this book was written.

To enable SRTP on the IP phones and thus have end-to-end encryption, make sure that CallManager has the Certificate Trust List (CTL) client loaded. This allows for authentication between the phones and CallManager. Also verify that all the appropriate phones are set up for encrypted mode in CallManager. When a secure call is in progress, a lock icon is displayed on the phone.

Some caveats are involved in using encryption for voice traffic. One caveat is that it makes the packets a little larger. SRTP adds from 4 to 10 bytes to each packet for an authentication tag. Encryption is not used for Music on Hold (MoH) or conferencing. It only supports G.711 and G.729 codecs. When you use G.711, the number of calls supported per c5510 DSP drops from 16 to 10. The number does not change for G.729—it is still 6 for G.729 and 8 for G.729A. When you are using modules with c549 and c5421 DSPs, such as the NM-HDV and AIM-VOICE-30 modules, SRTP supports only two calls per DSP.

By default, SRTP does not operate when the gateway is in SRST mode. However, you can configure the gateway and CallManager to support Secure SRST, which uses SRTP. Detailed instructions for configuring Secure SRST can be found in Chapter 13, "SRST and MGCP Gateway Fallback."

Securing Voice Signaling with IPsec

Encrypting the signaling traffic between CallManager and its gateways is optional but highly recommended in a secure environment. If you are encrypting the media and control traffic, it makes sense to protect signaling traffic also. Otherwise, such things as passwords, dual tone multifrequency (DTMF) tones, call setup signals, and encryption keys are sent across the network in the clear. You can protect signaling traffic by using IPsec with MGCP and H.323 gateways. TLS is used for SIP gateways.

You can configure IPsec encryption between the gateway and the CallManager server; you might do this if you need to secure signaling on a LAN, but it is not recommended if the gateway is at a remote site across the WAN. For remote sites, a more scalable solution is to configure an IPsec tunnel between the gateway and another device in the trusted network, such as a firewall or VPN concentrator. Terminating the connection on a firewall means that the tunnel will not drop if a CallManager goes out of service. It also allows the firewall to examine and perhaps manipulate the traffic. IPsec configuration varies depending on the firewall, gateway, or concentrator used, and it is beyond the scope of this book. Go to Cisco.com for information on configuring it for Cisco devices.

If you decide to use IPsec between the gateway and CallManager, you must set up an IPsec association between the two. See the *Cisco IP Telephony Platform Administration Guide* at Cisco.com for information on configuring CallManager.

Securing Voice Signaling with TLS

SIP trunks use TLS to secure the call setup and teardown signaling sent over them. TLS is a protocol that provides authentication and encryption of the SIP signaling data.

When configuring the SIP trunk in CallManager, you must configure a trunk security profile. Select TLS as both the Incoming and Outgoing Transport Type, and then select Encrypted as the Device Security Mode. Apply the profile to the trunk. The security negotiation and key exchange are done in the clear, so be sure to secure that communication using IPsec if it will go over an untrusted network.

You must configure the gateway to use TLS for its communication with CallManager (or other SIP endpoints that support TLS). First, configure the use of the public key infrastructure (PKI) certificate management. This requires generating a key pair, configuring a PKI trustpoint, and enrolling the trustpoint with a CA. This configuration is beyond the scope of this book; see the Cisco IOS Security Configuration Guide at Cisco.com for detailed instructions. After that configuration is complete, configure the gateway to use TLS. If both the gateway and CallManager share the same CA, configure the gateway to use the trustpoint when initiating or accepting TLS connections. In **sip-ua** configuration mode, use the **crypto signaling [(remote-addr (ipv4:**_address_ **| dns:**_hostname_**) default] trustpoint** _string_ **[strict-cipher]** command, where

- **remote-addr ipv4:**_address_—Lists an IP address for the trustpoint
- **remote-addr dns:**_hostname_—Lists a DNS name for the trustpoint
- **default**—Tells the router to use this trustpoint as the default one
- **trustpoint** _string_—Lists the name of the certificate generated during PKI enrollment
- **strict-cipher**—Configures the gateway to use only TLS_RSA_with_AES_128_CBC_SHA

In addition, configure the gateway to use TLS as its transport method. This is shown in Example 8-27, along with the trustpoint configuration.

Example 8-27 *Configuring SIP TLS*

```
VoiceGW(config)#sip-ua
VoiceGW(configs-sip-ua)#crypto signaling default trustpoint cert1
!
VoiceGW(config)#voice service voip
VoiceGW(configs-voi-serv)#sip
VoiceGW(configs-serv-sip)#session transport tcp tls
```

V3PN

When you use SRTP, the IP phones and CallManagers participate in encrypting voice traffic. Another option is to use a voice and video-enabled VPN, or V3PN. When you set up a V3PN, the encryption is transparent to the end devices, including CallManager. Encryption is not end to end, however. It is just over the WAN, between the two ends of the VPN tunnel.

To use V3PN, site-to-site VPN tunnels are created between the voice gateways in each site. This is typical in a hub-and-spoke design, with the hub being the location of the CallManager. After the tunnels are up, you can send voice, video, and signaling traffic over them. SRTP traffic can also traverse a V3VPN. V3PN provides security for voice where it is the most vulnerable—in the Internet.

You can use IPsec in Transport or Tunnel mode, use it to encrypt a GRE tunnel, or use it just by itself. If you plan to send only IP unicast traffic over the VPN, and no multicast video or routing protocols, a straight IPsec tunnel (with no Generic Routing Encapsulation [GRE]) is sufficient. Only IP unicast traffic is then encrypted. This implementation uses fewer router resources and a smaller header but requires static routing. If you plan to carry multicast video or routing protocols over the VPN, use IPsec in tunnel mode to encrypt a GRE tunnel. This has a larger header and more resource overhead than the first option, but it allows more flexibility in the traffic it carries.

NOTE   For further details on designing and configuring V3PNs, see the *Solution Reference Network Design Guide* at http://www.cisco.com/go/srnd.

NAT and VoIP

Typical NAT does its translation based on the IP addresses in the Layer 3 header and the port numbers in the Layer 4 header. This is usually enough to identify a stream of traffic. One problem with some of the voice protocols is that they include essential information in the packet payload; thus, NAT does not see it. For instance, H.323 RAS might include an IP address in the message body when a device is registering with a gatekeeper or seeking another registered device. You must translate that address, in addition to the Layer 3 addresses. SIP and its SDP send IP addresses embedded in the packet payload. Traditional NAT and even Port Address Translation (PAT) would never see these addresses.

To solve this limitation, Cisco has an Application Layer Gateway (ALG) feature that looks inside the packets to be translated and finds embedded IP addresses. Then it can translate them properly. ALG can handle all H.323 message types, SIP messages, SCCP, and even Real Time Streaming Protocol (RTSP). Support for these protocols in the Cisco IOS has developed over time, but all are supported as of version 12.3(7)T.

You can change the port that SCCP uses if another application in your network is already using that port. If the port is already occupied, you must tell NAT the new port number. NAT on Cisco routers assumes that traffic bound to TCP port 2000 is SCCP traffic, and it uses ALG to look for embedded information. Use the following command at global configuration mode to change the port that NAT associates with SCCP:

```
ip nat service skinny tcp port port-number
```

Configure static translations for the CallManager and Unity server addresses, because you need to specify their IP addresses in the TFTP download. Alternatively, you can use Domain Name System (DNS) to resolve the IP addresses of these servers.

Firewalls and VoIP

Cisco firewall devices and Cisco IOS firewalls can look inside the payload, or data, portion of a packet to recognize voice protocols and identify voice sessions. They can maintain stateful information even when the protocols are using dynamically negotiated ports, such as with RTP. In addition, you should configure your firewalls to allow only voice traffic onto the voice network.

Voice has various protocols that it might use. RTP and RTCP together use a range of more than 16,000 UDP ports. Other protocols, such as H.323, SCCP, SIP, and MGCP, can be used in the voice network. Table 8-1, earlier in this chapter, shows the ports that the most common voice protocols use. If these protocols must traverse the WAN, the firewall must allow the appropriate ports.

Although not every network will use every port, that is still potentially a lot of ports to have open in a firewall. Your network security administrator might prefer voice to be sent over an IPsec tunnel, as already outlined in the "V3PN" section of this chapter. When you do that, only ports that support the tunnel need to be opened. This has the added benefit of encrypting the voice traffic, preventing anyone who is capturing packets from listening to your phone calls.

Termination of the IPsec connection, when using V3PN or SRTP, affects the ability of a firewall to protect the network.

- If the IPsec tunnel terminates on one of the CallManagers, or on a VPN concentrator placed on the LAN side of the firewall, the firewall will only see IPsec traffic. It will not decrypt or look further into the packets. Thus, it will not recognize that this is voice traffic. If the firewall is also performing NAT, the embedded IP addresses will not be translated properly. If the remote voice gateway has been compromised and is sending malicious data, the firewall will not see it. This solution also does not scale well in large VoIP deployments. A benefit to terminating on the CallManager is that the traffic is protected as it travels on the LAN.

- If the IPsec connection terminates on a VPN concentrator that is placed on the WAN side of the firewall, the packet will be decrypted and the original packet will be sent to the firewall. It will be recognized as voice traffic, and any inspection or filtering rules will be applied. NAT can be done on the embedded IP addresses, and internal session information can be recognized.

- If the IPsec tunnel terminates on the firewall, the firewall will decrypt the traffic and apply any necessary rules to it. The firewall can look into the data portion of the packet and take appropriate action based on its contents.

Keeping these considerations in mind when designing your network is important, especially if you plan to secure voice traffic carried over the WAN.

Case Study: Using a T1 Link as a Tie Line

Consider the scenario shown in Figure 8-3. This is a partial diagram of the networks at two sites: New York and Boise. Both the New York and the Boise office have a PBX connected with an analog trunk line. Analog telephones are connected to the PBX at both places. The offices exchange data between them over the WAN using a T1 line. The dotted line in the diagram shows the path taken by intraoffice phone calls before the network changes were made.

Figure 8-3   *Using a T1 Link Between Offices—Before Network Changes*

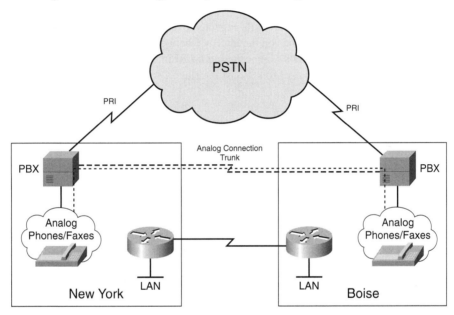

The company would like to avoid the cost of the analog trunk line. A traffic analysis found that minimal data, usually with small packet sizes, was sent over the T1 line. The Boise office primarily used the T1 to input data into a database server at New York. Also, few phone calls were made between the sites. The company decided to leverage the existing T1 line for phone calls between the two offices. The routers and PBXs will be reconfigured so that they can send phone calls between the two sites over the T1.

NOTE   If the two offices had a lot of activity between them, this type of setup would not be a good idea.

This company would like to convert the analog portion of the office to VoIP in the future, so it invested in new routers that are capable of being voice gateways. When you select the router, make sure that it has a Cisco IOS that includes voice features, and sufficient DSP resources. Another consideration is the interface between the router and the PBX. The type of interface used typically depends on two things:

- The PBX, because you will usually repurpose an existing interface (or interfaces) on the PBX to connect to the router. Thus, you might need to use Foreign Exchange Office (FXO), Ear and Mouth (E&M), or PRI ports depending on what is available on the PBX.

- The maximum number of calls expected over the tie line. The number of possible intraoffice calls depends on the interface between the PBX and router. Each FXO and E&M interface supports one call, and a PRI interface can support 23 calls. The following scenario uses four E&M interfaces, so it supports four simultaneous intraoffice calls.

NOTE   For more information on E&M interfaces, see Chapter 7, "Connecting to PBXs."

Consider the telephone numbering scheme of each office early in your planning. In this example, the users dialed 8 and then three digits to reach the other office. They did not want to change that practice. With only three digits available, the potential is great for overlapping phone numbers. If any overlapping existed, it would have required either doing some fancy digit manipulation or convincing users to change numbers. After investigating, the dial plan used by the PBX to reach the analog phones was found to be as follows.

- New York:
    - 0 for their local receptionist
    - 8-0 for the receptionist in Boise
    - 212-555-2100 to 212-555-2119 for analog telephones
- Boise:
    - 0 for their local receptionist
    - 208-555-0120 to 208-555-0199 for analog telephones

Only the last three digits for this task are significant—they are the ones that the users dial. Notice that the 100 range is split between the two sites. In addition, the users in New York need to be connected to the receptionist in Boise when they dial 8-0. You will see how the following configurations accomplished these potential issues.

Several tasks are required to enable voice traffic to flow between the PBXs over the T1 line. You need to reconfigure the PBX. It must send traffic that has a prefix of 8 to the router, rather than over the old trunk. The PBX will strip the digit 8 and send only three digits to the router. PBX configuration is beyond the scope of this book. On the voice gateway routers, you need to configure the connections to the PBX. In this case, they are E&M

interfaces, and the configuration looks like Example 8-28. Only one interface is shown, because the configuration is the same on all of them.

Example 8-28 *Configuring E&M Interfaces*

```
voice-port 0/0/0
 operation 4-wire
 type 2
 signal immediate
 description To tn 1.0 on the PBX
```

Next, you need to configure dial peers for each site. A VoIP dial peer points to the router on the other side of the T1. The New York router needs to send all traffic with a destination phone number in the 120 to 199 range across the WAN. The VoIP dial peers for New York are shown in Example 8-29. (10.100.100.33 is the IP address of the router at Boise.) Configure similar dial peers on the Boise router for each of the telephone number ranges at Building 1. These dial peers will point to the IP address of the router at New York.

Example 8-29 *Configuring VoIP Dial Peers*

```
dial-peer voice 129 voip
 destination-pattern 1[2-9].
 session target ipv4:10.100.100.33
 !
dial-peer voice 1 voip
 destination-pattern 0
 session target ipv4:10.100.100.33
```

You also must configure POTS dial peers on each router for their own internal phone numbers. These will point to the E&M interfaces. The New York POTS dial peers are used in Example 8-30. Traffic that is coming from Boise will either go to the New York analog number range or to its receptionist. Example 8-30 shows the POTS dial peers for the 100 to 119 range. Notice that four dial peers exist—one for each E&M interface. Each has a different preference value.

Example 8-30 *Configuring POTS Dial Peers*

```
dial-peer voice 100 pots
 preference 1
 destination-pattern 1[01].
 port 0/0/0
 forward-digits all
 !
dial-peer voice 101 pots
 preference 2
 destination-pattern 1[01].
 port 0/0/1
 forward-digits all
 !
dial-peer voice 102 pots
 preference 3
```

continues

Example 8-30 *Configuring POTS Dial Peers (Continued)*

```
 destination-pattern 1[01].
 port 0/1/0
 forward-digits all
!
dial-peer voice 103 pots
 preference 4
 destination-pattern 1[01].
 port 0/1/1
 forward-digits all
```

The next task is to adjust the configuration on the T1 interface of the router to accommodate the voice traffic. A QoS policy was created to prioritize voice media and guarantee bandwidth to voice signaling traffic. Voice media was given 30 percent of the bandwidth. It will not use nearly that much now with only four phone calls, but use might increase as the site expands and converts to IP telephony. The link speed of 1544 kbps is fast enough that no fragmentation or compression is needed. The policy is applied to the serial interface outbound, as shown in Example 8-31.

Example 8-31 *Configuring QoS*

```
ip access-list extended RTP
 permit udp any any range 16383 32767
 permit udp any range 16383 32767 any
ip access-list extended H323
 permit tcp any eq 1720 any
 permit tcp any any eq 1720
!
class-map match-all VOIP-Media
  match access-group name RTP
class-map match-all VOIP-Signal
  match access-group name H323
!
policy-map Tie-Line
  class VOIP-Media
   priority percent 30
  class VOIP-Signal
   bandwidth percent 5
  class class-default
   fair-queue
   random-detect
!
interface Serial0/0
 service-policy output Tie-Line
```

The QoS policy was examined after a couple of successful test calls, and it appeared to accomplish its goals, as shown in Example 8-32. The CS3 traffic that is shown in the output is Telnet traffic.

Example 8-32   *Verifying the QoS Policy*

```
Serial0/0

  Service-policy output: Tie-Line

    Class-map: VOIP (match-all)
      39 packets, 3069 bytes
      5 minute offered rate 0 bps, drop rate 0 bps
      Match: access-group name RTP-H323
      Queueing
        Strict Priority
        Output Queue: Conversation 264
        Bandwidth 30 (%)
        Bandwidth 3000 (kbps) Burst 75000 (Bytes)
        (pkts matched/bytes matched) 39/3069
        (total drops/bytes drops) 0/0

    Class-map: class-default (match-any)
      603 packets, 62083 bytes
      5 minute offered rate 0 bps, drop rate 0 bps
      Match: any
      Queueing
        Flow Based Fair Queueing
        Maximum Number of Hashed Queues 256
        (total queued/total drops/no-buffer drops) 0/0/0
        exponential weight: 9

    class     Transmitted     Random drop      Tail drop      Minimum Maximum  Mark
              pkts/bytes      pkts/bytes       pkts/bytes      thresh  thresh  prob
      0       536/52113          0/0             0/0              20      40    1/10
      1          0/0             0/0             0/0              22      40    1/10
      2          0/0             0/0             0/0              24      40    1/10
      3        36/2649           0/0             0/0              26      40    1/10
      4          0/0             0/0             0/0              28      40    1/10
      5          0/0             0/0             0/0              30      40    1/10
      6        32/7381           0/0             0/0              32      40    1/10
      7          0/0             0/0             0/0              34      40    1/10
    rsvp         0/0             0/0             0/0              36      40    1/10
```

Figure 8-4 illustrates the network topology after the changes. The dotted line shows the path taken by intraoffice calls since the network has been reconfigured. Now a telephone call between sites will go through the local PBX, to the local router, over the T1 to the router on the other side, to that PBX, and then on to the receiving telephone.

Figure 8-4 *Using a T1 Link Between Offices—After Network Changes*

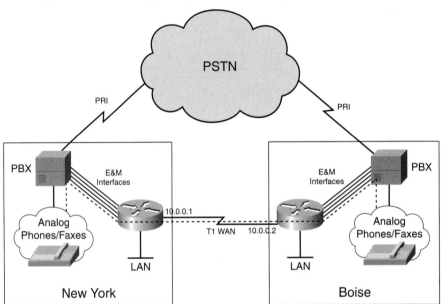

Review Questions

1   Voice is sensitive to delay, jitter, and packet drops. What are the recommended maximum values for each of these?

2   When you use the Modular QoS CLI, or MQC, what steps are involved in setting a bandwidth limit for voice traffic that is sent out an interface?

3   Data packets can be large compared to voice packets. Why is this a problem across a WAN link, and how can you remedy it?

4   What is the difference between fax/modem relay and passthrough?

5   What are the two types of fax relay that Cisco routers use, and which is the default type?

6   In which configuration mode are fax/modem commands given on MGCP gateways? How about H.323 and SIP gateways?

7 How does SRTP protect voice media traffic?

8 When using encrypted voice within a LAN, why is it a good idea to also encrypt traffic between the voice gateway and Cisco CallManager?

9 How is firewall function affected if an IPsec tunnel from a remote gateway terminates on the Cisco CallManager, rather than another device?

CHAPTER 9

Dial Plans

Designing and implementing a dial plan has always been one of the more difficult aspects of a voice system. Every decision requires balancing ease of operation for the end user with ease of administration and scalability. Because all companies have different business requirements, a simple one-size-fits-all formula is not applicable.

A dial plan is composed of five components:

- Endpoint addressing
- Path selection
- Calling privileges
- Digit manipulation
- Call coverage

This chapter provides an overview of the decisions that you must make and the guidelines for working through common dial plan issues. The focus is on endpoint addressing and the fundamentals of how a gateway selects an appropriate path for a call. Chapter 10, "Digit Manipulation," covers digit manipulation in more detail. Chapter 11, "Influencing Path Selection," covers methods for influencing the path selection, and Chapter 12, "Configuring Class of Restrictions," covers calling privileges. *Call coverage* is defined as a group of devices created to handle incoming calls according to specific rules. The call processing system provides call coverage features, such as call park, pickup groups, and automated call distribution (ACD). You can find more information on these features at Cisco.com

This chapter helps you to do the following:

- Design a numbering plan
- Interact with a public switched telephone network (PSTN) numbering plan
- Design a scalable dial plan
- Overcome the issues with overlapping dial plans
- Understand how a gateway processes dial peers

Numbering Plans

A numbering plan describes the endpoint addressing used in a voice system and is analogous to the IP addressing used in a data network. Unlike a data network, today the end user must know and enter the endpoint address to communicate with another endpoint. Because the end user must know and enter the address of the endpoint he wants to communicate with, ease of use is a major focus of numbering plans.

Numbering plans are classified as private or public. A private numbering plan is used within a single organization, and the organization defines and administers it. A public, or PSTN, numbering plan is defined for a single country or group of countries. Government agencies or service providers typically administer PSTN numbering plans, subject to governmental oversight.

Private Numbering Plans

When you are designing a private numbering plan, you must consider numerous factors. The most important factor is the number of devices requiring a number. This includes devices such as end-user phones, common area phones, fax machines, modems, and security systems. You should select an extension length that accommodates the existing number of devices and allows for growth. If you have 700 devices, you would probably want to use four-digit extensions, which allow for 10,000 numbers, even though you could assign a three-digit extension, allowing for 1000 numbers, to all existing devices. Increasing the extension length of an existing system to accommodate additional devices requires substantial planning to ensure that all devices are reachable during the changeover period. It also requires that end users are informed and possibly retrained.

Another important factor is how many locations you have. Consider the following two companies. Company A has a single location with 4000 devices. Company B has 200 locations, each with 20 devices. Both companies have to address 4000 devices, but Company B has to consider more factors than Company A. Calling patterns, PSTN connections, and alternate routing requirements impact the Company B numbering plan.

Private Numbering Plan Design Considerations

When you are designing a private numbering plan, you need to address the following considerations:

- **Number of addressable devices**—Most organizations try to use the fewest possible digits for internal calling to make it easy for users to remember and dial extensions. To allow for growth, use at least one more digit than the minimum required. For example, if you have 7,000 addressable stations, it is possible to use a four-digit numbering plan, but a five-digit numbering plan, which allows for 100,000 numbers, supports significantly more growth.

- **Number of locations**—Organizations typically use fewer digits for calls within a location, and site codes plus extensions for calls between locations. The number of digits in the site code must support the number of sites.

- **Methods for assigning site codes**—Some organizations use a mnemonic, assigning site codes based on the location. For example, New York City (NYC) would be assigned a site code of 692, and Tampa (TPA) would be assigned a site code of 872. Other organizations use existing numeric codes assigned to branch offices.

- **Inbound call routing**—The method that is used to accept calls from the PSTN determines how numbers are assigned to devices.

  Service providers offer direct inward dial (DID or DDI) services to provide a range of PSTN numbers. Organizations can pay for a sequential block of these DIDs and allow external callers to place calls directly to the intended recipients. In this case, organizations use the DID number to assign the extension.

  Many organizations opt to publish a single number for external callers. This number is routed to an auto attendant (AA) or receptionist who forwards the call to the intended recipient. This option is less expensive than DID services and allows more flexibility in assigning extensions.

  Some organizations use a combination of DID and AAs. They might assign DIDs to employees who frequently receive outside calls, such as salespeople. Calls to all other employees are routed through the AA.

- **PSTN access codes**—A PSTN access code distinguishes internal calls from external calls. This eliminates interdigit timeout when an internal numbering plan uses fewer digits than a PSTN numbering plan. It is customary to use 9 as a PSTN access code in the United States. In many other countries, 8 is used as the PSTN access code.

  One effect of using a PSTN access code is that you cannot use extensions beginning with this number. Consider a company using a four-digit numbering plan and a PSTN access code of 9. The company has purchased a 10,000 DID range from the service provider of 813 555-0000 thru 813 555-9999. If the company assigns extensions in the 9XXX range, the call processing system will not be able to distinguish internal calls from external calls. When a call is placed to extension 9500, the system will have to wait to see if additional digits will be dialed to determine if this is an internal call or an external call.

PSTN Numbering Plans

PSTN numbering plans are different for every country, but they share some common elements. Most PSTN numbering plans support the following types or classes of numbers:

- **Emergency services**—Many countries provide a single number to reach all emergency services. Others have separate numbers for police, fire, ambulance, and so on.

- **Information or directory services**—Most service providers have a number that can be used to reach directory services. In the United States, this is typically 411. Other services, such as current time or weather, might also be offered.

- **Local**—Local calls are calls within the same geographic area and typically can be dialed using fewer digits than long-distance calls. Local calls are typically free but might incur per-minute or per-call charges.

- **Mobile**—Most countries, with the exception of the United States, bill the caller for calls placed to mobile phones. This requires mobile phones to be assigned a distinct number range. In the United States, the owner of the mobile phone is billed for both incoming and outgoing calls, so mobile phones are assigned numbers from the same pool as traditional phones.

- **Toll or long distance**—Long-distance calls are directed to numbers outside the local area and commonly require an access code and area code in addition to the subscriber number. Historically, long-distance calls always incurred a per-minute toll. Many service providers now offer unlimited long-distance calls for a fixed fee.

- **Toll free**—Toll-free calls are free to the person who is making the call. The service provider bills the recipient.

- **Premium**—Premium calls are calls to businesses or services that invoke per-minute or per-call charges. Premium calls are classified distinctly from long-distance because they are frequently used for entertainment purposes, such as obtaining sports scores or using adult entertainment services. Most businesses block all outbound access to premium numbers, because these are rarely appropriate in a business environment.

- **International**—International calls are calls to other countries. They are placed using an access code followed by an International Telecommunications Union (ITU)-assigned country code and the full subscriber number, including any area or city codes.

The numbering plan for a country or region is typically complex. Over time, dramatic growth has caused most numbering plans to be revised, resulting in various exceptions or regional peculiarities. The following sections briefly introduce two common numbering plans for reference to show how various countries have implemented their numbering plans. For complete information on a particular country or regional numbering plan, please refer to the appropriate governing body.

As described in Chapter 5, "Circuit Options," the ITU Recommendation E.164 specifies how to build a numbering plan to allow interoperability between the numerous public networks. The E.164 segments a publicly assigned number into a country code (CC) and a national (significant) number, or N(S)N. The N(S)N is further segmented into a national destination code (NDC) and a subscriber number (SN). The DID numbers that a service provider assigns conform to the E.164 recommendation and are referred to as the E.164 number.

North American Numbering Plan

The North American Numbering Plan (NANP) is based on a ten-digit number assigned to each endpoint. This number is represented as XXX XXX-XXXX. The first three digits are the area code. The next three digits are the prefix and were originally used to route calls to the appropriate phone company switch. The last four digits are the subscriber number. Area codes are assigned geographically. Calls made within an area code typically use seven digits—the prefix and the subscriber number. Some densely populated areas have more than one area code assigned.

Determining whether a call is considered a local or toll call can be problematic. In sparsely populated areas, calls within a single area code might be considered long distance. In a densely populated area, calls between area codes might be considered local. To confuse matters more, some densely populated areas use ten-digit dialing for all local calls, whereas others use both seven-digit and ten-digit local dialing.

UK National Numbering Plan

The UK National Numbering Plan (NNP) also uses an area code system. The area codes are known as city codes. Unlike the NANP, the UK NNP does not have a fixed length subscriber number. The number of digits assigned to a subscriber varies based on the city. Because of the variable length of the subscriber number, the area codes are also a variable length. Larger cities have a three-digit area code, whereas smaller cities might have a four- or five-digit area code. For example, Liverpool subscribers are assigned a seven-digit subscriber number and a three-digit area code of 151, whereas subscribers in Coventry are assigned a six-digit subscriber number and a four-digit area code of 2476. This allows most calls between city codes to use 11 digits.

Table 9-1 illustrates the structuring of the UK NNP.

Table 9-1   *UK NNP*

Area Code Prefix	Service Type	Example Format
00	International	00+countrycode+number
01	Area codes	Liverpool 0151 xxx xxxx Leeds 0113 2xx xxxx
02	Area codes	London 020[378] xxx xxxx Coventry 0247 6xx xxxx
03	Area codes (expansion)	—
04	Reserved	—
05	Corporate	BT broadband voice 055 xxxx xxxx
06	Reserved	—
07	Mobile/pager/personal	Mobile 07[789]xx xxxxxx
08	Freephone (also shared cost)	0800 xxx xxx 0800 xxx xxxx 0808 xxx xxxx
09	Premium	09xx xxx xxxx

NOTE   The area code prefix is commonly depicted with a leading 0, as shown in Table 9-1. The 0 is actually an access code indicating that the call is a national call, similar to the 1 used to indicate a long-distance call in the NANP.

Table 9-2 lists the format for the various classes of numbers for the NANP and the UK NNP.

Table 9-2   *NANP and UK NNP Numbering Plans*

Call Type	NANP	UK NNP
Emergency	911	112 or 999
Services	[2–8]11	118 xxx
Local	[2–9]xx-xxxx [2–9]xx [2–9]xx-xxxx	Varies by area code
Long distance or national	1[2–9]xx [2–9]xx-xxxx	0+[1–3]xx xxx xxxx
International	011+country code+number	00+country code+number

Table 9-2 *NANP and UK NNP Numbering Plans (Continued)*

Call Type	NANP	UK NNP
Toll free	1[800,866,877,888]xxx-xxxx	0800 xxx xxx 0800 xxx xxxx 0808 xxx xxxx
Premium	1 900 xxx-xxxx 976-xxxx	09xxx xxxxxx
Mobile	N/A	07[7–9]xx xxxxxx

Overlapping Numbering Plans

Overlapping numbering plans occur when the DIDs that the service provider assigns result in the same extension ranges being used at two or more locations. In Figure 9-1, the Miami office phone numbers are 305 555 0100-0199, and the Boise office uses 208 555 0100-0150. The extensions at the Miami location will overlap with the extensions at the Boise location if less than eight digits are used for intersite dialing. For calls placed either to Miami or Boise from the New York site, the call processing system will not know to which location the calls should be routed.

Fortunately, this problem has several solutions. Selecting a solution requires balancing ease of use and provisioning complexity.

One of the easier solutions to provision is not to assign DIDs. This allows you to select nonoverlapping extension ranges without having to be concerned about aligning with the public number. A single public number is published for the location, and inbound calls are routed to an AA or a receptionist. Whether or not to assign DIDs is primarily a business decision.

An alternate solution is to use an intersite access code and a site code to call between locations. For example, you could use an intersite access code of 8 and assign a three-digit site code to each location. Using a four-digit extension, this approach would support up to 999 sites with 9,999 devices per site. Use a site code that is easily remembered to simplify calling. Many companies try to map the site code to the area code or prefix. This works for widely distributed companies, but it can be problematic for companies that have many locations in a single area. Other companies try to use a mnemonic, such as the first three characters of the location. For example, Miami would be assigned a site code of 642, corresponding to MIA. Using site codes is fairly easy from an end-user perspective but can result in complicated implementations. To provide redundancy, digit manipulation is required to route calls over the PSTN in the event of an IP WAN failure or oversubscription. For enterprises that have numerous sites, this manipulation can result in substantial configuration.

Figure 9-1 *Overlapping Numbering Plans*

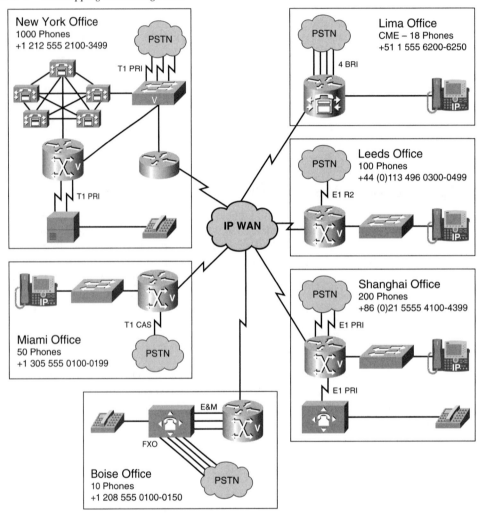

Because of the complexities associated with mapping site codes to DIDs, many large enterprises require the user to dial an access code plus the full E.164 number for intersite calls. This minimizes the complexity of the dial plan but removes the benefit of abbreviated dialing for end users.

Building a Scalable Dial Plan

Most of the dial plan decisions you make will be greatly influenced by business and political considerations. Thus, keep the following practical considerations in mind when designing and implementing your scalable dial plan:

- **Hierarchical numbering plan**—A hierarchical numbering plan is required to scale the number of devices without introducing interdigit timeout issues or call routing issues because of overlapping extension ranges. A hierarchical numbering plan also reduces the complexity of digit manipulation required to direct calls over alternate paths.

- **Dial plan distribution**—Components of the dial plan are configured in the call processing system, the voice gateways, and, if implemented, the gatekeepers. Isolating the gateway to a specific portion of the dial plan simplifies the dial plan provisioning by reducing the number of required dial peers. For H.323 gateways, consider configuring only local PSTN details and using gatekeepers for higher-level routing decisions.

- **Post dial delay**—To enhance the user experience, minimize the processing post dial delay. *Post dial delay* is the time between the last digit being dialed and the phone ringing at the remote end. Digit manipulations, multiple paths, and gateway processing affect post dial delay. To reduce post dial delay, try to minimize the amount of dial peers and voice translations. Also consider other process-intensive functions that the router might be performing, such as virtual private networking (VPN) or Network Address Translation (NAT), because these might impact the ability of the gateway to process calls.

- **Fault tolerance**—One of the advantages of VoIP is the ability to provide fault tolerance. Calls are automatically routed over redundant IP paths if available. You can configure additional dial peers to route calls over the PSTN if the IP path has failed completely. For critical sites, you can deploy redundant gateways.

    Cisco Survivable Remote Site Telephony (SRST) is a gateway feature that provides call processing redundancy, allowing an IP phone to register with the gateway if no CallManager is available. SRST is discussed in detail in Chapter 13, "SRST and MGCP Gateway Fallback."

Dial Peers

Dial peers are the primary construct used to implement a dial plan on Cisco voice gateways. Dial peers are used to determine which calls are routed and the path a call should take. Dial peers are also used to set configurable options, such as the codec or the Dual-tone Multifrequency (DTMF) relay method to be used for the call.

You can configure two types of voice dial peers in a Cisco gateway:

- **POTS dial peers**—Plain old telephone service (POTS) dial peers are used to process calls that are connected to traditional telephony equipment. The path that is associated with a POTS dial peer is a voice port on the gateway.

- **Voice-network dial peers**—Voice-network dial peers are used to process calls to or from the data network. Cisco voice gateways support Voice over Frame Relay (VoFR) and Voice over ATM (VoATM) dial peers, in addition to VoIP dial peers. VoFR and VoATM are rarely implemented and are not discussed in this book.

Inbound Versus Outbound Dial Peers

Each call that a Cisco voice gateway processes requires two dial peers, as shown in Figure 9-2. These dial peers are defined as the inbound and the outbound dial peer from the perspective of the gateway.

Figure 9-2 *Inbound Versus Outbound Dial Peers*

Call Legs

From the gateway perspective, you can view a call as two distinct call legs associated with the inbound and outbound dial peers.

When Cisco introduced voice gateways, each call matched a POTS dial peer and a VoIP dial peer. One call leg was always associated with a voice port, and one call leg was always associated with the data network. This enabled the toll bypass implementation shown in Figure 9-3. Over time, time-division multiplexing (TDM) switching capabilities were added to the gateways, allowing both incoming and outgoing call legs to be POTS. And with the addition of the IP-to-IP gateway (IPIPGW) feature, both incoming and outgoing call legs can be VoIP.

NOTE   For more information on the IPIPGW feature, see Chapter 18, "Cisco Multiservice IP-to-IP Gateway."

Figure 9-3 *Toll Bypass Topology*

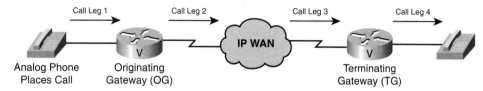

The toll bypass topology uses exactly two gateways in the call path. The gateway that is closest to the device placing the call is designated the originating gateway (OG), and the gateway closest to the device being called is designated the terminating gateway (TG). It is now much more common for an enterprise to have a single voice gateway connecting a Cisco CallManager to the PSTN or a PBX. It is also possible to have multiple gateways (as opposed to routers) in the call path using IPIPGW. In these new possible topologies, the terms OG and TG can be confusing because one, two, or many gateways can be in the call path. Many documents on Cisco.com still refer to OG and TG when describing call legs and dial peer matching. In the CallManager case, a gateway is considered a TG when CallManager originates the call, and it is considered an OG when CallManager is the destination. Although the terms OG and TG are now somewhat arbitrary, understanding the origin of these terms is important to deciphering Cisco documentation. When analyzing call flows, however, it is typically easier to consider each gateway independently and look at the incoming and outgoing legs that are specific to that gateway instead of applying arbitrary terms.

Dial Peer Matching

You can match a call to a dial peer in many ways, including called or calling number, physical port, and type of call. Because the matching process can vary for inbound and outbound dial peers, each is described separately.

Inbound Dial Peer Matching

Calls that are coming into a gateway match dial peers based on the source of the call. If a call enters using a voice port, the inbound dial peer is a POTS dial peer. If the call enters using IP, the inbound dial peer is a VoIP dial peer. The steps for matching inbound dial peers are as follows:

Step 1 Match the called number to the incoming called number that is configured on the dial peers.

For voice ports that provide call setup information, this is the more common method of matching the inbound dial peer.

Step 2   Match the calling number to the answer address that is configured on the dial peers.

In most cases, an enterprise is more concerned with where an incoming call is going than with where it originates, but sometimes you might want to route a call differently based on its source. For example, calls to a contact center might be routed to different queues based on where the call originates.

Step 3   Match the calling number to the destination pattern that is configured on the dial peers.

This configuration allows you to use a single dial peer and destination pattern to provide both inbound and outbound matching. Although this can reduce the number of required dial peers, following the call flow can become confusing.

NOTE   If an incoming POTS call has an empty calling number, it matches a dial peer that is configured with any destination pattern. The value of the destination pattern is used as the calling number on the outgoing call leg. Configure a dial peer with the **incoming called-number .** command to prevent this behavior.

Step 4   Match the voice port that is associated with the call to the port that is configured on the dial peers. This step applies only to calls that originate on voice ports.

Step 5   Match the "default" dial peer.

The "default" dial peer, or dial peer 0, is matched when no other inbound dial peer is used. It is not possible to modify parameters for these calls, such as codec or voice activity detection (VAD). Therefore, it is advisable to always configure a specific dial peer to match incoming calls.

NOTE   The AS5xxx family of gateways requires an inbound dial peer match for a call to be processed as a voice call. These gateways support both modem and voice termination. If a call does not match an incoming voice dial peer, it is processed as a modem call.

Eliminating a dial peer at one step of the process does not exclude it from consideration during subsequent steps. Example 9-1 shows a gateway with a single POTS dial peer configured with both an incoming called number and an answer address.

Example 9-1 *Inbound Dial Peer Matching*

```
Gateway#show run | begin dial-peer voice
dial-peer voice 1 pots
answer-address 408555....
incoming called-number 82..
```

Assume that port 1/0:23 receives a call setup message with a called number of 8193 and a calling number of 408 555-0123. The called number does not match the configured incoming called number on dial peer 1, so the gateway proceeds to Step 2. At this step, all dial peers are considered again. The calling number matches the answer address, so dial peer 1 is used as the inbound dial peer even though it failed Step 1.

At each step, the most specific dial peer is matched. Example 9-2 has added a dial peer to the previous example.

Example 9-2 *Multiple Potential Dial Peer Matches*

```
Gateway#show run | begin dial-peer voice
dial-peer voice 1 pots
answer-address 408555....
incoming called-number 82..
!
dial-peer voice 2 pots
answer-address 919555....
incoming called-number 820.
```

A call setup message arrives on port 1/0:23 with a called number of 8200 and a calling number of 4085550123. At this point, both dial peer 1 and dial peer 2 are potential matches for the call. Because the incoming called number for dial peer 2 is more specific, it is used as the inbound dial peer.

NOTE   Even though the calling number does not match the answer address, the dial peer is used. After a match is found for a step, no further matching analysis is performed.

Outbound Dial Peer Matching

Before discussing destination pattern matching, it is necessary to understand how digit strings are built. Wildcards are used in digit strings to allow a single digit string to match multiple numbers. Table 9-3 lists the wildcards that can be used in digit string arguments.

Table 9-3   *Digit String Wildcards*

Wildcard	Function	Examples
.	This matches any single digit.	
[ ]	This indicates a range of digits. Continuous ranges are separated by a hyphen. A comma separates individual numbers.	[2–4] matches 2, 3, or 4 [2,4] matches 2 or 4 [2–4,7] matches 2, 3, 4, or 7
+	The previous digit or pattern occurred one or more times.	4085+ matches 4085 followed by any number of 5s
?	The previous digit or pattern occurred zero or one time.	4085? matches 408 or 4085
%	The previous digit or pattern occurred zero or more times.	4085% matches 408 or 408 followed by any number of 5s
( )	This is used to designate a pattern.	408(555)? matches 408 or 408555

NOTE   Only the period (.) wildcard is allowed with the **incoming called-number** and **answer-address** commands.

For outbound dial peer matching, both POTS and VoIP dial peers are considered together, and the best match is selected. The called number is matched against the configured destination-pattern in the dial peers. The way this comparison is done depends on whether the **direct-inward-dial** command is configured on the inbound dial peer.

direct-inward-dial Is Not Configured

If the **direct-inward-dial** command is not configured on the selected inbound POTS dial peer, digit-by-digit analysis is performed. This is the case for all circuit types. After the inbound dial peer is matched, the gateway plays a second dial tone to the caller and waits for him to enter additional digits. Even with ISDN, in which the DNIS is included in the call setup message, a second dial tone is played and the original DNIS is not used to route the call. This is referred to as *two-stage dialing*. As the caller enters digits, the digits are compared to the configured destination patterns. As soon as a destination pattern is fully matched, the call is routed.

direct-inward-dial Is Configured

If the **direct-inward-dial** command is configured on the selected inbound POTS dial peer, the entire called number is used to match outbound dial peers. This is referred to as *one-stage dialing*.

The only case in which the complete called number is not used to match the destination pattern is when overlap receiving is set on an ISDN interface. With overlap receiving, digits are sent after the initial setup message. Because the entire digit string might not be received when the inbound dial peer is matched, digit-by-digit matching is used.

By default, gateways use variable-length matching when selecting outbound dial peers, as shown in Example 9-3.

Example 9-3 *Variable-Length Matching*

```
Gateway#show run | begin dial-peer voice
dial-peer voice 555 pots
destination-pattern 555
forward-digits all
port 1/0:23
!
dial-peer voice 5550123 pots
destination-pattern 555…
forward-digits all
port 1/0:23
```

If the gateway receives a call setup message with a called number of 5550123, both dial peer 555 and dial peer 5550123 match the call.

To disable variable-length matching, you can configure dial peer 555 with a destination pattern of 555$. The $ indicates that extra digits are not allowed.

Verifying Dial Peers

For a complex dial plan that results in multiple dial peers, you can use the **show dialplan** command to find the matching inbound dial peers based on calling number or voice port and matching outbound dial peers based on inbound dial peer matched and DNIS.

Example 9-4 shows which dial peer is matched for the called number 15015012001. The output shows which dial peer is matched, which port or session target is used to route the call, and which digits are sent in the outgoing setup message.

Example 9-4 *Verifying Outbound Dial Peers*

```
Gateway#sh dialplan number 15015012001
Macro Exp.: 15015012001

VoiceEncapPeer501
        peer type = voice, system default peer = FALSE, information type = voice,
```

continues

Example 9-4   *Verifying Outbound Dial Peers (Continued)*

```
          description = `',
          tag = 501, destination-pattern = `1501501....',
          answer-address = `', preference=0,
          CLID Restriction = None
          CLID Network Number = `'
          CLID Second Number sent
          CLID Override RDNIS = disabled,
          source carrier-id = `',        target carrier-id = `',
          source trunk-group-label = `',        target trunk-group-label = `',
          numbering Type = `unknown'
          group = 501, Admin state is up, Operation state is up,
          Outbound state is up,
          incoming called-number = `', connections/maximum = 0/unlimited,
          DTMF Relay = disabled,
          URI classes:
              Destination =
          huntstop = disabled,
          in bound application associated: 'DEFAULT'
          out bound application associated: ''
          dnis-map =
          permission :both
          incoming COR list:maximum capability
          outgoing COR list:minimum requirement
          Translation profile (Incoming):
          Translation profile (Outgoing):
          incoming call blocking:
          translation-profile = `'
          disconnect-cause = `no-service'
          advertise 0x40 capacity_update_timer 25 addrFamily 4 oldAddrFamily 4
          type = pots, prefix = `',
          forward-digits 10
          session-target = `', voice-port = `1/0:1',
          direct-inward-dial = disabled,
          digit_strip = enabled,
          register E.164 number with H323 GK and/or SIP Registrar = TRUE
          fax rate = system,   payload size =  20 bytes
          supported-language = ''

          Time elapsed since last clearing of voice call statistics never
          Connect Time = 0, Charged Units = 0,
          Successful Calls = 10, Failed Calls = 0, Incomplete Calls = 0
          Accepted Calls = 0, Refused Calls = 0,
          Last Disconnect Cause is "10  ",
          Last Disconnect Text is "normal call clearing (16)",
          Last Setup Time = 5526712.
          Last Disconnect Time = 5527420.
  Matched: 15015012001   Digits: 7
  Target:
```

Outbound Dial Peer Targets

You must configure outbound dial peers with a target, or path for the call. The target for outbound POTS dial peers is a voice port or trunk group. The target for outbound VoIP dial peers is an IP address.

Trunk Groups

Trunk groups are used to group multiple voice ports or ISDN channels into a single logical target for an outbound dial peer, reducing the number of peers required. Each trunk group is configured with a "hunting scheme" that determines the order in which channels are selected. The following are the hunt schemes that are available:

- **least-idle**—The interface with the timeslot that has been idle the least is selected.
- **least-used**—The interface with maximum free timeslots is selected.
- **longest-idle**—The interface with the timeslot that has been idle the longest is selected.
- **random**—The timeslot is selected randomly.
- **round-robin**—The next interface with free timeslots is selected.
- **sequential**—The interface with the highest preference is selected.

You can apply attributes, such as priority level or translations, to the trunk group. A voice port that is assigned to a trunk group can still be the target of a POTS dial peer. In this situation, the attributes of the trunk group are not applied to the call. You can also configure a dial peer with multiple trunk groups by assigning a preference to each. The dial peer attempts to extend the call over the highest priority trunk group. If this is unsuccessful, the next trunk group is attempted.

A useful feature of trunk groups is their ability to dedicate some channels of an ISDN circuit to particular dial peers. For example, you might want to reserve two channels of a PRI for emergency calls and route all other PSTN calls over the remaining channels.

NOTE   Trunk groups apply only to outbound calls. The gateway cannot control channel assignment of incoming calls.

Example 9-5 illustrates the configuration steps for each of the possible outbound dial peer targets.

Example 9-5 *Outbound Dial Peer Targets*

```
Gateway#config t
!
! VoIP dial peer
!
Gateway(config)#dial-peer voice 4 voip
Gateway(config-dial-peer)#destination-pattern 4...
Gateway(config-dial-peer)#session target ipv4:10.1.1.100
!
! POTS dial peer - single voice port
!
Gateway(config)#dial-peer voice 7 pots
Gateway(config-dial-peer)#destination-pattern 9[2-9]......
Gateway(config-dial-peer)#port 1/0:23
!
! POTS dial peer - trunk groups
! Create trunk groups
!
Gateway(config)#trunk group Emergency
Gateway(config-trunk-group)#description B Channels reserved for Emergency Calls
Gateway(config-trunk-group)#hunt-scheme round-robin
Gateway(config)#trunk group Standard
Gateway(config-trunk-group)#hunt-scheme least-used
!
! Controller config to select channels
!
Gateway(config)#controller t1 2/0
Gateway(config-controller)#framing esf
Gateway(config-controller)#linecode b8zs
Gateway(config-controller)#pri-group timeslots 1-24
Gateway(config-controller)#trunk-group Emergency timeslots 1-2
Gateway(config-controller)#trunk-group Standard timeslots 3-23
!
! Set additional voice ports into standard trunk group
!
Gateway(config)#voice-port 1/0/0
Gateway(config-voice-port)#trunk-group Standard
Gateway(config-voice-port)#interface s1/0:23
Gateway(config-if)#trunk-group standard
!
! Apply trunk groups to dial peers
!
Gateway(config)#dial-peer voice 911 pots
Gateway(config-dial-peer)#destination-pattern 911
Gateway(config-dial-peer)#trunkgroup Emergency 1
Gateway(config-dial-peer)#trunkgroup Standard 2
!
Gateway(config)#dial-peer voice 11 pots
Gateway(config-dial-peer)#destination-pattern 91[2-9]..[2-9]......
Gateway(config-dial-peer)#trunkgroup Standard
!
```

Dial Peer Hunting

If a call matches more than one outbound dial peer, the router hunts through the dial peers trying them in order. If the call setup is unsuccessful, the next matching dial peer is attempted. The following factors determine the hunt order:

- Longest match
- Preference
- Random selection

The longest match dial peer is always attempted first. If the call cannot be completed using this dial peer, the next longest match is attempted.

If you configure multiple dial peers with the same destination pattern but different voice ports, you can determine the dial peer selected using the **preference** command. You typically do this when you want a call to be extended first over the IP network and alternately over the PSTN. This scenario is discussed in more detail in Chapter 11. If you have multiple dial peers with the same destination pattern and do not specify a preference, the dial peer match is random.

You can modify the default hunt order logic using the **dial-peer hunt** command, as shown in Example 9-6.

Example 9-6   **dial-peer hunt** *Command Options*

```
BR2(config)#dial-peer hunt ?
  <0-7>  Dial-peer hunting choices, listed in hunting order within each choice:
  0 - Longest match in phone number, explicit preference, random selection.
  1 - Longest match in phone number, explicit preference, least recent use.
  2 - Explicit preference, longest match in phone number, random selection.
  3 - Explicit preference, longest match in phone number, least recent use.
  4 - Least recent use, longest match in phone number, explicit preference.
  5 - Least recent use, explicit preference, longest match in phone number.
  6 - Random selection.
  7 - Least recent use.
```

POTS Versus VoIP Outbound Dial Peers

Outbound POTS dial peers are different from outbound VoIP dial peers in one significant way: With POTS dial peers, digits that explicitly match the destination pattern are stripped from the outgoing call setup. Table 9-4 lists various destination patterns and the corresponding called numbers sent in the setup message.

Table 9-4   *POTS Digit Stripping Examples*

Destination Pattern	Dialed String	Resulting Called Number
911	911	Empty
91800.......	918005550123	5550123
91[2–9]..[2–9]....	918005550123	8005550123

To send the correct called number, you can use the **forward-digits** or **prefix** commands.

Outbound VoIP dial peers do not strip explicitly matched digits.

Dial Peer Operational Status

For a dial peer to be included in either inbound or outbound matching, it must be operationally active. It must meet one of the following conditions to be considered operationally active:

- **Destination-pattern** configured and a target (voice port, trunk group or session target) configured
- **Incoming called-number** configured
- **Answer-address** configured

If the dial peer is not operationally active, it will not be considered while doing dial peer matching.

POTS dial peers are also operationally down if the target voice port is not physically active. For most circuit types this is the preferred behavior. However, some ISDN BRI circuits are only activated when a call is placed. This can result in outbound calls failing because the dial peer is operationally down. The **no dial-peer outbound status-check pots** command will cause the gateway to ignore the oprational status and attempt to place the call on the circuit. For these BRI circuits, the call setup attempt will result in the circuit being activated.

Many people believe they can block calls to certain destinations by configuring an appropriate destination pattern and not including a target. As stated, this results in the dial peer not being included in the searching, so it does not result in call blocking if another dial peer can be matched. Example 9-7 shows how dial peer matching is performed when a dial peer is operationally inactive. Dial peer 11 is used to route NANP long-distance calls. Dial peer 900 has been added in an attempt to block calls to this premium service.

Example 9-7   *Dial Peer Operational Status*

```
Gateway#show run | begin dial-peer voice
dial-peer voice 11 pots
 destination-pattern 91[2-9]..[2-9]......
 port 2/0/0
 prefix 1
!
dial-peer voice 900 pots
 destination-pattern 91900.......
!
Gateway#debug voice dialpeer all
!
Gateway#csim start 919005550123
csim start 919005550123
csim: called number = 919005550123, loop count = 1 ping count = 0

*Aug 14 11:30:08.526: //-1/xxxxxxxxxxxx/DPM/dpMatchPeersCore:
   Calling Number=, Called Number=919005550123, Peer Info Type=DIALPEER_INFO_SPE
ECH
*Aug 14 11:30:08.526: //-1/xxxxxxxxxxxx/DPM/dpMatchPeersCore:
   Match Rule=DP_MATCH_DEST; Called Number=919005550123
*Aug 14 11:30:08.526: //-1/xxxxxxxxxxxx/DPM/dpMatchCore:
```

Example 9-7   *Dial Peer Operational Status (Continued)*

```
    Dial String=919005550123, Expanded String=919005550123, Calling Number=
    Timeout=TRUE, Is Incoming=FALSE, Peer Info Type=DIALPEER_INFO_SPEECH
*Aug 14 11:30:08.530: //-1/xxxxxxxxxxxx/DPM/MatchNextPeer:
    Result=Success(0); Outgoing Dial-peer=11 Is Matched
*Aug 14 11:30:08.530: //-1/xxxxxxxxxxxx/DPM/dpMatchPeersCore:
    Result=Success(0) after DP_MATCH_DEST
*Aug 14 11:30:08.530: //-1/xxxxxxxxxxxx/DPM/dpMatchPeers:
    Result=SUCCESS(0)
    List of Matched Outgoing Dial-peer(s):
      1: Dial-peer Tag=11
```

As you can see from the debug, this premium call will match dial peer 11, and call setup will be attempted. Because the outbound dial peer is a POTS dial peer, the gateway will strip the explicitly matched digits—91900—and will prefix in the 1. This will result in a called number of 15550123 being sent to the service provider, and the call will be rejected because of an invalid format, not because dial peer 900 was added. If dial peer 11 would have been configured with **forward-digits 11** instead of the **prefix** command, the call would have been set up successfully.

The proper method of blocking certain destination patterns depends on your topology. In most cases, the call processing system blocks calls. If the gateway is the call processing system, you can use Class of Restrictions (COR) or, for CallManager Express (CME), time of day routing to block calls. You can also use voice translation rules to block incoming calls to a gateway. Chapter 10 covers voice translation rules in greater detail.

When implementaing redundant gateways in a CallManager environment, the operational status of a dial peer can affect cal routing. If a call is sent to gateway and the appropriate dial peer is down due to a circuit issue, the gateway will return an Unallocated Number message to the CallManager. By default, CallManager stops processing the call when it receives this message. Even if there is a secondary gateway with an active circuit, CallManager will not attempt to send the call. There are two ways to correct this situation. You can set the "Stop Routing On Unallocated Number Flag" service parameter to "False" in CallManager. This will cause the CallManager to attempt all gateways in a Route Group. You can also enter the **no dial-peer outbound status-check pots** command in the gateway. This will result in the gateway returning a Temporary Failure message to the CallManager instead of an Unallocated Number message.

Dial Peers Versus Cisco CallManager

The way that gateways and CallManager perform digit-by-digit matching to determine the correct path for a call is different in one major sense. Table 9-5 illustrates how CallManager matches a dialed string of 1134. CallManager compiles a table consisting of all directory numbers (DNs), route patterns, and translation patterns. As digits are processed, the list of possible matches is narrowed down. Processing continues as long as there is a longer possible match in the table, even if a more specific match has already occurred. It is possible to change this behavior by configuring a route pattern as "Urgent Priority." Translation patterns are always considered to be Urgent Priority.

Table 9-5 *CallManager Digit Analysis*

Route Plan	Potential Matches			
	Dial 1	Dial 1	Dial 3	Dial 4
11XXX	11XXX	11XXX	11XXX	11XXX
12XXX	1134	1134	1134	1134
1134	1145	1145	—	—
1145	—	—	—	—
1250	—	—	—	—

After the caller dials a 4, the digit string still has two potential matches. CallManager waits for the caller to enter an additional digit. If the caller does not enter a digit before the interdigit timer expires, pattern 1134 is matched.

As described previously, gateways also compare digits to dial peer destination patterns, eliminating potential matches as digits are processed. The difference is that as soon as a dial peer matches, it is used even if a longer possible match exists. This is similar to configuring all your CallManager route patterns as Urgent Priority.

To understand how significant this difference is, consider the situation described previously in the NANP. Because of growth, many areas now require more than one area code to cover a "local" calling area. In some areas, both seven-digit and ten-digit dialing is used for local calls, which can lead to issues with interdigit timeout. In the Tampa, Florida area, several area codes are assigned, including 813 and 727. Most calls between these area codes do not incur per-minute charges. Table 9-6 lists some of the CallManager route patterns to support a gateway that is located in the 813 area code.

Table 9-6 *CallManager Dial Plan for Seven-Digit and Ten-Digit Local Calling*

Route Pattern	Gateway	Description
911	Local T1	Emergency—Urgent Priority
9.911	Local T1	Emergency—Urgent Priority
9.[2–9]xxxxxx	Local T1	Local seven-digit calls
9.727[2–9]xxxxxx	Local T1	Local ten-digit calls
9.1[2–9]xx[2–9]xxxxxx	LD T1	Long-distance calls

The following dialed digit strings illustrate how CallManager processes the digits and what strings result in the user experiencing interdigit timeout.

- **Dialed string**—9 555-0123

  The third pattern is the only pattern matched, so the call proceeds immediately.

- **Dialed string**—9 727 555-0123

  Both the third and fourth patterns match the first eight digits (97275550). When the caller dials a 1, the third pattern is eliminated, and the fourth pattern is used immediately after the caller dials the last digit.

- **Dialed string**—9 727-0123

  Both the third and fourth patterns match the dialed digits. CallManager must wait for additional digits to determine which pattern to use. When the interdigit timer has expired, the call is processed using the third pattern.

The only time that a user experiences interdigit timeout is when the prefix, or first three digits of a local seven-digit number, matches a "local" area code. Most service providers would avoid this situation by not assigning the 727xxxx block to a customer in the 813 area code.

Example 9-8 shows the dial peer configurations to support the same numbering plan taken from a CME gateway.

Example 9-8 *Gateway Dial Plan for Seven-Digit and Ten-Digit Local Calling*

```
Gateway#show run | begin dial-peer voice
dial-peer voice 911 pots
 destination-pattern 911
 port 1/0:23
 prefix 911
!
dial-peer voice 9911 pots
 destination-pattern 9911
 port 1/0:23
 prefix 911
!
dial-peer voice 7 pots
 destination-pattern 9[2-9]......
 port 1/0:23
!
dial-peer voice 10 pots
 destination-pattern 9727[2-9]......
 port 1/0:23
 prefix 727
!
dial-peer voice 11 pots
 destination-pattern 91[2-9]..[2-9]......
 port 2/0:23
 prefix 1
!
```

The same dialed digit strings are used to illustrate how the gateway will process the digits.

- **Dialed string**—9 555-0123

  Dial peer 7 is the only pattern matched, so the call proceeds immediately.

- **Dialed string**—9 727 555-0123

  Both dial peer 7 and dial peer 10 match the first eight digits (97275550). Dial peer 7 is used immediately after the caller presses 0, sending the incorrect digits to the service provider.

- **Dialed string**—9 727-0123

  Both dial peer 7 and dial peer 10 match the dialed digits. Dial peer 7 is used immediately after the caller presses 3, sending the correct digits to the service provider.

As you can see, the user cannot dial 10-digit local numbers using these dial peers. You must modify dial peer 7 to instruct it to wait to determine whether it should consider additional digits. Example 9-9 shows the correct configuration for dial peer 7.

Example 9-9 *Corrected Dial Peer 7*

```
dial-peer voice 7 pots
 destination-pattern 9[2-9]......T
 port 1/0:23
 !
```

The "T" added to the end of the destination pattern instructs the gateway to wait until the interdigit timer expires before matching the string. The result of this configuration change is that all seven-digit local calls must wait for the interdigit timer to expire before the call is placed, even though there are no other possible dial peer matches. You can adjust the interdigit timeout to minimize the wait of the end user, but delay will still be noticeable.

Case Study: Configuring PSTN Access

You need to configure the Miami and Leeds gateways with a dial plan to allow calls to the PSTN. Both sites should allow calls to emergency services, local, long-distance, and international numbers. You should also configure Leeds to allow calls to mobile numbers. The PSTN access code at both locations is 9.

Example 9-10 shows the dial peer configuration that is necessary to allow the Miami location to place calls to the PSTN. This example implements a portion of the NANP.

Example 9-10 *Miami PSTN Dial Peers*

```
Miami#show run | begin dial-peer voice
dial-peer voice 1 pots
description Inbound Dial Peer
incoming called-number .
direct-inward-dial
port 1/0:2
!
dial-peer voice 911 pots
description Emergency Services
destination-pattern 911
port 1/0:1
prefix 911
!
dial-peer voice 9911 pots
description Emergency Services
destination-pattern 9911
port 1/0:1
prefix 911
!
dial-peer voice 7 pots
description Local Calling
```

Example 9-10 *Miami PSTN Dial Peers (Continued)*

```
destination-pattern 9[2-9]......
port 1/0:1
!
dial-peer voice 11 pots
description Long Distance Calling
destination-pattern 91[2-9]..[2-9]......
port 1/0:1
prefix 1
!
dial-peer voice 9011 pots
description International Calling
destination-pattern 9011T
port 1/0:1
prefix 011
```

Example 9-11 shows the dial peer configuration that is necessary to allow the Leeds
location to place calls to the PSTN. This example implements a portion of the UK NNP.

Example 9-11 *Leeds PSTN Dial Peers*

```
Leeds#show run | begin dial-peer voice
dial-peer voice 1 pots
description Inbound Dial Peer
incoming called-number .
direct-inward-dial
port 1/0:1
!
dial-peer voice 999 pots
description Emergency Services
destination-pattern 999
port 1/0:1
prefix 999
!
dial-peer voice 112 pots
description Emergency Services
destination-pattern 112
port 1/0:1
prefix 112
!
dial-peer voice 9112 pots
description Emergency Services
destination-pattern 9112
port 1/0:1
prefix 112
!
dial-peer voice 10 pots
description Local Calling
destination-pattern 9[2-9].....
port 1/0:1
!
dial-peer voice 90 pots
```

continues

Example 9-11 *Leeds PSTN Dial Peers (Continued)*

```
 description National Calling
 destination-pattern 90[1-3].........
 port 1/0:1
 prefix 0
 !
 dial-peer voice 70 pots
 description Mobile Calling
 destination-pattern 907[7-9]........
 port 1/0:1
 prefix 07
 !
 dial-peer voice 900 pots
 description International Calling
 destination-pattern 900T
 port 1/0:1
 prefix 00
 !
```

The dial peers that are configured in Examples 9-10 and 9-11 enable calls to the PSTN numbering plan for each country, as described in Table 9-2. You do not need to configure two dial peers to support calls to 999 in the Leeds location. This is because of the variable-length matching. If the user dials the 9 access code, followed by three additional 9s, dial peer 999 is matched. This is not the case for the other emergency numbers, so it is recommended that you include both destination patterns.

NOTE   Consider the preceding configuration a scenario and not a complete dial plan. Additional dial peers might be required to meet local calling customs. You can also implement measures to prevent toll fraud or other misuse of the system, as discussed in Chapter 12.

Review Questions

1 What determines whether a gateway does digit-by-digit matching?

2 What is the default order of operation for matching outbound dial peers?

3 What is necessary for a dial peer to be considered operational?

4 Which factors must you balance when designing a dial plan?

5 What end-user issue can be caused by an overlapping dial plan?

6 What is the default dial peer?

7 Which number is used to match the destination pattern on a dial peer?

8 How are dial peers configured to accommodate an overlapping dial plan?

CHAPTER 10

Digit Manipulation

You might encounter situations where you need to control the actual digits contained in the telephone numbers that enter or leave the gateway. You might need to add the area code to a call that is routed out of the public switched telephone network (PSTN), or remove a site code from an intracompany call, for instance. Digit manipulation encompasses adding, subtracting, and changing telephone numbers. You can manipulate calling numbers, called numbers, and redirecting numbers, in addition to the numbering plan and ISDN number type. You can use techniques that are applied to incoming or outgoing calls, or globally to all calls. You can manipulate telephone numbers before a dial peer is matched, or afterward.

In this chapter, you will learn

- Ways that a router applies digit manipulation
- Basic digit manipulation techniques, such as digit stripping, prefixing, and forwarding
- Number expansion
- Number translation
- Control of the calling line identification (CLID) number
- Ways to troubleshoot and verify the telephone number changes that are applied

Basic Digit Manipulation

Several different digit manipulation techniques exist, each of which controls telephone numbers in a different way and can be applied at specific points in the call flow. Table 10-1 summarizes the techniques covered in this chapter, where they are applied, and where their effect is felt.

You can perform digit manipulation only on H.323 and SIP gateways; on MGCP gateways, the call agent must perform any manipulation because it controls the calls. Cisco CallManager Express and routers that are using Survivable Remote Site Telephony (SRST) offer some additional manipulation options to those discussed in this chapter, such as dial plan patterns. CallManager Express techniques are beyond the scope of this book. Chapter 13, "SRST and MGCP Gateway Fallback," discusses SRST digit manipulation in greater detail. You can also use Toolkit Command Language (Tcl) scripts to manipulate the called and calling numbers, as described in Chapter 15, "Using TCL Scripts and VoiceXML."

Table 10-1   *Digit Manipulation Techniques*

Technique	Where You Apply It	When Action Is Taken	What Can Be Manipulated
Digit stripping (default router action)	To POTS[1] dial peer	After outbound dial peer is matched, but before digits are sent out	Called number only
Forward digits	To dial peer	After outbound dial peer is matched, but before digits are sent out	Called number only
Prefix digits	To dial peer	After outbound dial peer is matched, but before digits are sent out	Called number only
Number expansion	Globally, applies to all calls	Before outbound dial peer is matched	Called number only
CLID	To dial peer	After outbound dial peer is matched, but before digits are sent out	Calling numbers, calling name
Voice translation profiles	To dial peer, voice port, trunk group, all incoming VoIP[2] calls, Source IP group, or NFAS[3] interface	Can translate before incoming dial peer is matched, before outgoing dial peer is matched, or before call is set up	Calling, called, and redirecting numbers; numbering plan; numbering type; and calls

[1] POTS = Plain old telephone service

[2] VoIP = Voice over IP

[3] NFAS = Non-Facility Associated Signaling

Digit Stripping

VoIP dial peers transmit all digits in the called number by default; however, POTS dial peers remove, or strip, any outbound digits that explicitly match their destination pattern. For instance, given a destination pattern of **55512..** the called number transmitted to the PSTN would contain just the last two digits. The first five digits, **55512**, would be stripped. Only explicitly matched digits are stripped. Given a destination pattern of **555[2-9]..** and a digit string of **555422**, only the **555** would be stripped. If all the digits in a called number are removed, the caller hears only a reorder tone.

Digit stripping is the default behavior of POTS dial peers. It can work to your advantage, as long as you understand its effect. For instance, if users dial **9** to reach an outside number, you would not want the number **9** sent to the PSTN as part of the called number. When you configure the destination pattern of a POTS dial peer as **9T**, the **9** is matched, so it is stripped. The remaining digits are transmitted. However, suppose that you have a dial peer for an emergency number, such as **911** in the United States. In that case, you would not want any of those digits removed, so you must disable the default behavior for that dial peer.

You can disable digit stripping with the command **no digit-strip** under POTS dial-peer configuration mode. Re-enable it with the command **digit-strip**. The relevant command syntax is as follows:

```
dial-peer voice 1 pots
[no] digit-strip
```

Forward Digits

You can achieve more precise control over the number of digits in the called number that are transmitted to the PSTN with the following command, which applies only to POTS dial peers:

```
forward-digits [number | all | extra]
```

where

- *number* gives the number of digits to be forwarded.

- **all** means to forward all digits.

- **extra** tells the gateway to forward any digits that are longer than the length of the destination pattern.

This command lets you specify the exact number of digits to be forwarded. If the number of digits presented exceeds the number allowed, the rightmost digits are sent. One place this can be useful is when you must dial a code (such as **9**) to reach an outside number, and there is an emergency situation. The previous section showed how to ensure that the entire emergency number (such as **911**) is sent. In an emergency, a person might be confused about whether to dial the outside code. That is why dial peers are typically set up to match both the emergency number, and that number plus the code number. If the destination pattern of a dial peer is **9911**, you should send only **911**. You can use the **forward-digits** command to transmit only the last three digits, **911**, to the PSTN.

The following examples show what digits are sent when you dial the number **111-222-3333** and use various options of the **forward-digits** command.

For this first case, the rightmost seven digits, 222-3333, are sent.

```
Miami(config)#dial-peer voice 111 pots
Miami(config-dial-peer)#destination-pattern 111222....
Miami(config-dial-peer)#forward-digits 7
```

With the configuration that follows, the entire number, **111-222-3333**, is sent. This is an alternative to using the **no digit-strip** command shown in the previous section.

```
Miami(config)#dial-peer voice 111 pots
Miami(config-dial-peer)#destination-pattern 111222....
Miami(config-dial-peer)#forward-digits all
```

Finally, with the final configuration that follows, because the destination pattern is now six digits long and the dialed number is ten digits, the "extra" digits—**3333**—are sent.

```
Miami(config)#dial-peer voice 111 pots
Miami(config-dial-peer)#destination-pattern 111222
Miami(config-dial-peer)#forward-digits extra
```

Prefix Digits

In some cases, you might need to transmit more than the dialed digits of a called number. For example, perhaps a call that would normally go across your VoIP network needs to be rerouted through the PSTN, requiring the addition of the appropriate area code and prefix. Or, a destination pattern might specify the first six digits of the number, with wildcards for the other digits. By default, those six digits are stripped. You can use the **prefix** *string* command to replace some of those digits. This command is given under dial-peer configuration mode, and it is only for POTS dial peers. The prefixed string can be any number from 0 to 9 and a comma that inserts a one-second pause. The gateway prefixes digits after the outgoing dial peer is matched and after any digits are stripped, but before it sends out the call.

In Example 10-1, long-distance calls need to go to a particular carrier and must have a separate dial peer from external local calls. The destination pattern is **91** to capture long-distance traffic; however, the PSTN needs the number **1** transmitted as part of the called number to route the call properly. Thus, the **prefix** command is added to replace that digit.

Example 10-1 *Prefixing Digits to an Outgoing Call*

```
Miami(config)#dial-peer voice 91 pots
Miami(config-dial-peer)#destination-pattern 91T
Miami(config-dial-peer)#prefix 1
Miami(config-dial-peer)#port 1/0:23
```

When a user dials the outside long-distance number **9-1-111-222-3333**, the digits are manipulated before being sent to the PSTN. The original digits **9** and **1** are stripped, and a **1** is prefixed to the remaining number. Thus, the PSTN receives the number **1-111-222-3333**.

Number Expansion

Number expansion is another way to add digits to an outgoing called number; however, number expansion is applied to the gateway as a whole, and acts on all calls, not just those matching a designated dial peer. As with the previous three techniques, this manipulates only the called number. Number expansion manipulation occurs before any outbound dial peer is matched. Thus, you must configure outbound dial peers to match the expanded numbers, not the original ones.

The command for number expansion is **num-exp** *original-number expanded-number*, configured at global configuration mode. Although it is called *number expansion*, the manipulated number can contain fewer digits than the original, or it can contain more.

Example 10-2 shows two instances of number expansion configured. The first expands any four-number extension beginning with **1** to a seven-digit number beginning with **5551**. The second changes any seven-digit number beginning with **5551** to a four-digit extension.

Example 10-2   *Number Expansion*

```
Miami(config)#num-exp 1... 5551...
Miami(config)#num-exp 5551... 1...
!
!Verifying the first number expansion
Miami#show dialplan number 1111
Macro Exp.: 5551111
!
!Verifying the second number expansion
Miami#show dialplan number 5551098
Macro Exp.: 1098
```

In the results of the **show dialplan number** command, notice that although the number entered in the command is the original number, the router looked for a match to the expanded number. The **show dialplan number** command is also useful for verifying that you have a dial peer to match the expanded number.

Voice Translation Rules and Profiles

You can accomplish more precise, granular manipulation using voice translation profiles, which contain voice translation rules. The techniques that were previously discussed can alter only the called number, or dialed number identification service (DNIS), digits. Translation profiles are much more powerful. They can change both the DNIS and the calling number, or automatic number identification (ANI), digits plus the redirecting number. With translation profiles you can adjust the numbering type and plan, reject unwanted calls based on a rule match, and remove specific digits (such as hyphens).

NOTE	A legacy technique called *translation rules* (without the *voice*) can manipulate ANI and DNIS numbers. This technique is still supported, but the recommended method is to use voice translation rules and voice translation profiles.

Using voice translation profiles for digit manipulation requires three steps:

Step 1   Create one or more voice translation rules and a prioritized list of translations associated with each rule. A maximum of 128 rules is supported, with 15 translations per rule.

Step 2   Create one or more voice translation profiles and associate the translation rules to the profile. You can define up to 1000 profiles, each with its own unique name. Within the profile, you can apply one voice translation rule to calling numbers, one to called numbers, and one to redirected called numbers.

Step 3   Apply the voice translation profile to all VoIP calls globally, a dial peer, a voice port, a trunk group, a source IP group, or an interface.

Creating Voice Translation Rules

To create a voice translation rule, use the command **voice translation-rule** *tag* in global configuration mode. Then create an ordered list of one or more rules with the following command:

```
rule precedence /match pattern/ /replace pattern/ [type {match-type replace-type}
   [plan {match-type replace-type}]]
```

You can enter rules in any order; the *precedence* value determines the order in which the rules are executed. You can configure up to 15 rules.

A basic voice translation rule replaces one group of digits with another. Each group is delineated with // (frontslash) characters. In Example 10-3, voice translation Rule 1 replaces **111** with **222,** and **333** with **444**. A test of the translations shows that they are carried out as specified.

Example 10-3   *Using a Basic Voice Translation Rule*

```
Boise(config)#voice translation-rule 1
Boise(cfg-translation-rule)#rule 1 /111/ /222/
Boise(cfg-translation-rule)#rule 2 /333/ /444/

Boise#test voice translation-rule 1 111
Matched with rule 1
Original number: 111    Translated number: 222
Original number type: none      Translated number type: none
Original number plan: none      Translated number plan: none

Boise#test voice translation-rule 1 13335
Matched with rule 2
Original number: 13335  Translated number: 14445
Original number type: none      Translated number type: none
Original number plan: none      Translated number plan: none
```

When the number **1335** is tested, notice that the number patterns are translated no matter where they appear in the string. Notice also that any digits that are not expressly matched— the numbers **1** and **5** in this example—are simply carried through. For more precise control, you can use some special characters and wildcards to build regular expressions, as shown in the next section.

Building Regular Expressions

A regular expression is a text-parsing tool that combines a string of literal characters and special characters, called *metacharacters*. Voice translation rules can use regular expressions to find matches in the digit strings, and replace a match with a different string. Table 10-2 lists some commonly used special characters and their meaning.

Table 10-2   *Regular Expression Special Characters*

Character	Meaning
.	Matches any single character
[ ]	Matches one number within the brackets; for example, the expression [234] would match either 2, 3, or 4
[^]	Matches a number except one within the bracket
-	Indicates a range of numbers when used within brackets
^	When used before a string, denotes the beginning of a string
$	Denotes the end of a string
*	Matches 0 or more occurrences of the previous expression
+	Matches 1 or more occurrences of the previous expression
?	Matches 0 or 1 occurrence of the previous expression (use **Ctrl-v ?** to enter in the IOS)
( )	Groups digits into sets
\	Changes the meaning of the following character
&	Brings all the matched digits into the replacement string

Previously in Example 10-3, the string **333** was matched even when it was in the middle of the list. If you wanted to match **333** only when it appeared at the beginning of a string, you could use the caret character:

```
rule 2 /^333/ /444/
```

To match a string containing only **333**, add the dollar sign at the end and the caret at the beginning:

```
rule 2 /^333$/ /444/
```

Using Regular Expressions When Rerouting a Call over the PSTN

The real power of regular expressions comes from using them in more complex ways. One common use is when intrasite calls that would normally traverse an IP WAN must be rerouted over the PSTN. You must remove any private numbering, such as site codes, from the called number and format it for use on the PSTN.

In Example 10-4, a company has two locations in Maryland, USA. One has a site code of 758, and the other has a site code of 759. The remainder of intrasite the number is the last seven digits of the actual phone number. In the national numbering plan, the area code for both locations is 410. To route intraoffice calls to these locations over the PSTN, you must substitute the long-distance code and area code for the site code. In this example, the first four numbers are translated to **1410,** but the rest of the number is left untouched.

Example 10-4 *Using Regular Expressions: Replacing Digits*

```
Boise(config)#voice translation-rule 2
Boise(cfg-translation-rule)#rule 1 /^75[89]\(.*\)/ /1410\1/
Boise#
Boise#test voice translation-rule 2 7591234567
Matched with rule 1
Original number: 7591234567     Translated number: 14101234567
```

To understand a regular expression, break it into its component parts and decipher each part individually. Breaking the match portion of Rule 1 into its component parts:

- **^75** are literal characters. The caret (^) designates the beginning of a string. This only matches a string that begins with a **7** and is followed by a **5**.

- **[89]** matches a literal character 8 or 9. The brackets tell the router to match just one of the numbers that the expression contains.

- In **\(.*\)**, the backslashes change the parentheses from literal characters to set-delimiters. The characters within the set are **.***, which matches any character that is repeated zero or more times.

The following list breaks down the replacement portion of the rule into its component parts:

- **1410** replaces the initial literal characters.

- In the **\1** part of the expression, the backslash changes the meaning of the digit 1. It is no longer a literal number—instead, it points to the first set in the matching part of the rule. The first set is **(.*)**. Thus, any digits matching that set are inserted after **1410**.

Instead of replacing site codes, your gateway might need to add digits when it reroutes an intrasite call to the PSTN. One way it can do this is to create multiple dial peers, each with a destination pattern of a remote site, and then prefix digits. If PSTN calls to multiple locations will go out the same PRI, the gateway can accomplish this more efficiently by using a set of voice translation rules grouped under one translation profile. For instance, suppose that your company uses seven-digit dialing between three internal sites over your

MPLS WAN. One site is local to you, but your phone company uses ten-digit dialing locally. The other two sites are long distance. You would need to add three additional digits to the called number for the local site, and the appropriate long-distance and area codes for the other sites. The original seven digits must remain unchanged.

Example 10-5 shows the voice translation rules to accomplish this for three sites in the United States. Numbers in the local site begin with 789, with an area code of 410. Numbers in one remote site begin with 123, with an area code of 212, and the other site begins with 456 with an area code of 617. The long-distance code is 1. Also shown in the example is the translation rules grouped under a voice translation profile; this could then be applied to the POTS dial peer pointing to the PRI. The section "Creating Voice Translation Profiles," later in this chapter, covers voice translation profiles in greater detail.

Example 10-5   *Using Regular Expressions: Prefixing Digits*

```
VoiceGW(config)#voice translation-rule 15
VoiceGW(cfg-translation-rule)#rule 1 /^789/ /410&/
VoiceGW(cfg-translation-rule)#rule 2 /^123/ /1212&/
VoiceGW(cfg-translation-rule)#rule 3 /^456/ /1617&/
!
VoiceGW(config)#voice translation-profile TO-PSTN
VoiceGW(cfg-translation-profile)#translate called 15
!
VoiceGW#test voice translation-rule 15 7891234
Matched with rule 1
Original number: 7891234        Translated number: 4107891234
Original number type: none      Translated number type: none
Original number plan: none      Translated number plan: none


VoiceGW#test voice translation-rule 15 1234567
Matched with rule 2
Original number: 1234567        Translated number: 12121234567
Original number type: none      Translated number type: none
Original number plan: none      Translated number plan: none


VoiceGW#test voice translation-rule 15 4561111
Matched with rule 3
Original number: 4561111        Translated number: 16174561111
Original number type: none      Translated number type: none
Original number plan: none      Translated number plan: none
```

Breaking the match portion of Rule 1 into its component parts:

- **^789** designates the literal characters **789** at the beginning of the string. This matches any string, of any number of digits, that begins with **789** so it will match the entire seven-digit called number.

Breaking the replacement portion of Rule 1 into its component parts:

- **410** tells the router to place the digits **410** at the beginning of the replacement string.
- **&** (ampersand) pulls all the matched digits into the replacement string.

The logic behind the other two rules is the same as Rule 1.

Using Regular Expressions to Delete Specific Digits

One of the company locations in Maryland, USA has a legacy PBX with a few users connected to it. Users in other company sites dial a site code of **758** to reach this location, and then a seven-digit number. The seven-digit number for PBX users begins with **4445**. The PBX was programmed to expect to receive an incoming called number consisting of the site code and the last four digits of the phone number. So you must keep the site code, remove the next three digits (**444**), and keep the last four digits.

In Example 10-6, **voice translation rule 3** accomplishes this by making the site code one set, and the last four numbers another set, but leaving the middle string of **444** out of any sets. It then tells the router to create a string consisting only of the two sets.

Example 10-6 *Using Regular Expressions: Deleting Digits*

```
Boise(config)#voice translation-rule 3
Boise(cfg-translation-rule)#rule 1 /^\(758\)444\(5...\)$/ /\1\2/
!
Boise#test voice translation-rule 1 7584445111
Matched with rule 1
Original number: 7584445111     Translated number: 7585111
```

Breaking the match portion of this rule into its component parts

- **^\(758\)** creates a set that contains the string **758** at the beginning of the digit string. The caret designates the beginning of a string, and the backslashes change the meaning of the parenthesis from literal characters to set delimiters.

- **444** designates three literal number fours

- The last four digits are grouped into a second set with **\(5...\)**. This set matches any four digits at the end of the string, if they begin with the number **5**. The end of the string is designated with the character **$**.

Breaking the replacement part of the rule into its component parts

- In the expression **\1**, the backslash changes the number **1** from a literal character. In the translated number, it is replaced with the contents of the first set—**758**.

- The expression **\2** points to the second set. In the translated number, it is replaced with the contents of the second set—in this example, the string **5111**.

Using Regular Expressions with Sets and Replacement Digits

Notice that in Example 10-6, the middle string of **444** is not included in the replacement pattern. Suppose that the rule is changed to include a replacement for that string, as shown in Example 10-7. Now the translated number matches those three fours and replaces them with three sevens.

Example 10-7 *Using Regular Expressions: Digit Replacement Using Sets*

```
Boise(config)#voice translation-rule 4
Boise(cfg-translation-rule)#rule 1 /^\(758\)444\(5...\)$/ /\1777\2/
Boise#test voice translation-rule 4 7584445111
Matched with rule 1
Original number: 7584445111      Translated number: 7587775111
```

Breaking the match portion of this rule into its component parts

- **^\(758\)** creates a set that contains the string **758** at the beginning of the digit string. The caret designates the beginning of a string, and the backslashes change the meaning of the parenthesis from literal characters to set delimiters.

- **444** designates three literal number fours.

- The last four digits are grouped into a second set with **\(5...\)**. This set matches any four digits at the end of the string, if they begin with the number **5**. The end of the string is designated with the character **$**.

The replacement part of this equation can look confusing because there is no visual break between its three components, so it is important to understand how the router interprets it. Breaking the replacement part of the rule into its component parts

- In the expression **\1**, the backslash changes the number **1** from a literal character. In the translated number, it is replaced with the contents of the first set—**758**.

- The next three digits, **777**, are a literal replacement for **444**.

- The expression **\2** points to the second set. In the translated number, it is replaced with the contents of the second set—in this example, the string **5111**.

Using Regular Expressions to Change the Call Type or Numbering Plan

You can also match and replace the type of call, such as national or international, and the numbering plan, such as ISDN or national. For instance, the commands in Example 10-8 replace the string **011** with **1** and change the call type from international to national.

Example 10-8 *Using Regular Expressions: Changing the Call Type and Numbering Plan*

```
Boise(config)#voice translation-rule 4
Boise(cfg-translation-rule)#rule 1 /^011/ /1/ type international national plan isdn
  national
!
Boise#test voice translation-rule 4 0115551212 type international plan isdn
Matched with rule 1
Original number: 0115551212      Translated number: 15551212
Original number type: international      Translated number type: national
Original number plan: isdn       Translated number plan: national
```

In this example, the match and replacement expressions follow a slightly different pattern. This expression has three components:

- In the first component, **/^011/ /1/**, the number **011** at the beginning of the string is replaced with the number **1**.

- The second component, **type international national**, replaces the numbering type **international** with **national**.

- The third component, **plan isdn national**, replaces a numbering plan of **isdn** with a **national** numbering plan.

For a call to be matched by a rule, it must fulfill all the conditions. In this case, the call must begin with **011**, have a type value of **international**, and have a plan value of **isdn**. If any of these values is not matched, this rule will not process the call.

Creating Voice Translation Profiles

Voice translation rules are associated with voice translation profiles. Using a voice translation profile gives you flexibility and scalability by allowing the use of multiple voice translation rules. You can apply voice translation rules to called numbers, calling numbers, and redirected numbers in the same profile. A voice translation profile is typically associated with a dial peer, a voice port, a trunk group, or all VoIP calls globally.

Create a translation profile and enter profile configuration mode with the command **voice translation-profile** *name*. Then specify what type of number will be translated, and the rule to apply to that number. Example 10-9 shows a sample translation profile.

Example 10-9 *Creating a Translation Profile*

```
Boise(config)#voice translation-profile TEST
Boise(cfg-translation-profile)#translate ?
  called           Translation rule for the called-number
  calling          Translation rule for the calling-number
  redirect-called  Translation rule for the redirect-number
!
Boise(cfg-translation-profile)#translate called 2
Boise(cfg-translation-profile)#translate calling 3
Boise(cfg-translation-profile)#translate redirect-called 1
```

In Example 10-9, translation Rule 2 is applied to called numbers, translation Rule 3 is applied to calling numbers, and translation Rule 1 is applied to redirecting numbers. You can apply the same translation rule to each type of number, if appropriate.

Applying Voice Translation Profiles

After you create a voice translation profile, you can assign it to a dial peer, a voice port, a trunk group, or all VoIP calls globally. Where the voice translation profile is applied affects the matching of inbound and outbound dial peers. A profile that is applied to a voice port is carried out before the inbound dial peer is matched. A profile that is applied to an inbound dial peer is carried out before the outbound dial peer is matched. A profile that is applied to an outbound dial peer is carried out before the call is transmitted. Be sure to take this into consideration when placing your voice profiles and configuring your dial peers.

- **To assign to a dial peer**—Use the command **translation-profile [incoming | outgoing]** *name* in dial-peer configuration mode. A dial peer can have one incoming and one outgoing translation profile, as the following configuration demonstrates:

```
Boise(config)#dial-peer voice 4 voip
Boise(config-dial-peer)#translation-profile incoming TEST
Boise(config-dial-peer)#translation-profile outgoing TEST
```

- **To assign to a voice port**—Use the command **translation-profile [incoming | outgoing]** *name* in voice-port configuration mode. A voice port can have one incoming and one outgoing translation profile. Inbound profiles are executed before the incoming dial peer is matched. If the port is a member of a trunk group, the profile that you apply to the port overrides any profile that you apply to the trunk group. The following configuration demonstrates assigning a voice translation profile to a voice port:

```
Boise(config)#voice-port 2/0:23
Boise(config-voiceport)#translation-profile incoming TEST
```

- **To assign to a trunk group**—You use the same command to assign a voice translation profile to a trunk group that you use to assign a dial peer or voice port: **translation-profile [incoming | outgoing]** *name*. All members of the trunk group inherit the voice translation profile, unless a different one is explicitly applied to a port or dial peer in the group. The command is given in trunk-group configuration mode, as the following configuration shows:

```
Boise(config)#trunk group 1
Boise(config-trunk-group)#translation-profile incoming TEST
```

- **To assign to all VoIP calls globally**—To associate a voice translation profile with all incoming VoIP calls, use the global command **voip-incoming translation-profile** *name*, as the following configuration demonstrates:

```
Boise(config)#voip-incoming translation-profile TEST
```

Blocking Calls Using Voice Translation Rules and Profiles

You can also use voice translation rules and profiles to block incoming calls, either for a specific number or all calls matching a specific dial peer. To do this, first create a voice translation rule with the **reject** keyword. This rule blocks any incoming calls from phone number 410-111-2222:

```
Boise(config)#voice translation-rule 410
Boise(cfg-translation-rule)#rule 1 reject /4101112222/
```

Next, create a translation profile, and assign that rule to it:

```
Boise(config)#voice translation-profile BLOCK
Boise(cfg-translation-profile)#translate calling 410
```

Finally, apply the translation profile to the appropriate dial peer(s) with the command **call-block translation-profile incoming** *name*. When the call is blocked, a reason code is sent to the caller. You can control that message with the **call-block disconnect-cause** command, as shown here:

```
Boise(config)#dial-peer voice 99 pots
Boise(config-dial-peer)#call-block translation-profile incoming BLOCK
Boise(config-dial-peer)#call-block disconnect-cause incoming call-reject
```

Testing Voice Translation Rules

Because number translations can get complex, testing your translations before putting them into production is crucial. The easiest way to test is with the **test voice translation-rule** *rule-number digit-string* command. (Output from this command is shown in Examples 10-3 through 10-8.) To see the translations in action, enter **debug voice translation** before giving this command. This command shows whether the number is matched or not, and what is replaced. Example 10-10 shows the combination of testing the voice translation rule with debugging voice translation. The **debug** output shows that there was a successful substitution, the original number, the pattern that was matched, the replacement pattern, and the translated number.

Example 10-10 *Testing and Debugging Voice Translation Rules*

```
Boise(config)#voice translation-rule 4
Boise(cfg-translation-rule)#rule 1 /^\(22\)444\(5...\)$/ /\1777\2/
Boise(cfg-translation-rule)#^Z
Boise#test voice translation-rule 4 224445678
Matched with rule 1
Original number: 224445678        Translated number: 227775678
Original number type: none        Translated number type: none
Original number plan: none        Translated number plan: none

Boise#
*Mar  1 03:42:08.636: sed_subst: Successful substitution; pattern=224445678
   matchPattern=^(22)444(5...)$ replacePattern=\1777\2 replaced pattern=227775678
*Mar  1 03:42:08.640: regxrule_subst_num_type: Match Type = none, Replace Type = none
   Input Type = none
*Mar  1 03:42:08.640: regxrule_subst_num_plan: Match Plan = none, Replace Plan = none
   Input Plan = none
```

The commands **show voice translation-rule** and **show voice translation-profile** help verify the configuration.

Manipulating Caller ID

During an outgoing call, the CLID is sent as part of the call information. CLID information includes at least one calling party number. The CLID might also include a name, a second number, and redirecting number information. You can control the information sent at the CallManager, and you can configure the gateway to control the information that shows up on caller ID. Some companies prefer that the main corporate number is displayed, rather than the actual extension of the person calling, for instance. The receiver can use CLID information in many ways, such as to route emergency services calls, so you must take this into account if you manipulate the CLID.

CLID Commands

You can manipulate caller ID information by a set of **clid** commands. These commands allow you to remove or change the calling party information transmitted with a call, or send it but prevent it from being displayed. **clid** commands apply to specific dial peers when given under dial-peer configuration mode. They apply globally when given under the voice service voip configuration mode (available in Cisco IOS Software Release 12.4(4)T and later). Not all options are available when configuring CLID in this mode. The commands include the following (those available under voice service voip are noted):

- **clid network-number** *number*—Specifies the network number to be sent in the CLID information. It sets the presentation indicator to "Y" and the screening indicator to "network provided." Available in both dial-peer and voice service voip configuration modes.

- **clid second-number strip**—Removes the original calling number from the H.225 source address field. You can also give this command on the same line as the **clid network-number** command. It is valid only if you have configured a network number.

- **clid restrict**—Transmits the calling party information but sets the presentation indicator to "N" so that it is not displayed to the called party.

- **clid strip [name | pi-restrict [all]]**—Removes the CLID number if just the **clid strip** command is given and sets the presentation indicator to "N." It removes the CLID name if the **name** option is added. To remove both the name and number, you must enter both commands separately. The **pi-restrict** option causes the CLID number to be stripped only when you set the progress indicator to "restricted." Adding the **all** keyword strips both the CLID number and name. The **pi-restrict all** option is available in both dial-peer and voice service voip configuration modes.

- **clid substitute name**—Substitutes the calling number for the display name. Available in both dial-peer and voice service voip configuration modes.

Station ID Commands

You can control the caller ID information that FXS and FXO ports send with the **station-id** [**name** | **number**] *string* command. Using either the **name** or **number** keywords also enables caller ID on that port. The **station-id** command is typically used on FXS voice ports that are attached to a phone or fax that might originate on-net calls. The information that you configure with this command shows up as the caller ID on the device connected to the remote FXS port. You might also use this command on an FXO port to supply caller ID information if that does not come from the central office, for example:

```
VoiceGW(config)#voice-port 1/0/0
VoiceGW(config-voiceport)#station-id name C.P. Ryan
VoiceGW(config-voiceport)#station-id number 1112223000
```

Order of Operation in Digit Manipulation

As you have seen, some digit manipulation techniques accomplish the same result. You can use all the various methods of digit manipulation on the same gateway, but it is not recommended and usually not needed. Choosing which technique to use is sometimes more of an art than a science. For instance, an emergency call to 911 routed out a POTS interface would have all of its digits stripped before tranmission, so the call would not go through. To remedy this, you could configure **no digit-strip**, or **forward-digits 3**, or **prefix 911** on the dial peer. You could even configure a translation profile or number expansion to change the called number so that the digits 911 would be sent, although that would be the hardest way to do it.

The point at which you must perform the manipulation is also is a factor. If the digit manipulation should apply to all calls, or be done before a dial peer is matched, you can use one of the global techniques. If the manipulation will apply only to certain calls, you can configure it under the dial peers for those calls. Some techniques are specific to POTS or VoIP dial peers, so that might aid your decision.

Consistency is a major consideration if you have many gateways needing similar digit manipulations to manage. Pick a technique (or techniques, if necessary), and standardize on it. In general, stick to the simplest way of accomplishing what you want. This consistency makes the gateways easier to configure, easier to manage, easier to troubleshoot, and probably easier on the router.

A good understanding of how the different methods interact will help your decision making, and in troubleshooting problems, also. Figure 10-1 shows how a call flows through the router, and where each technique is applied.

A POTS call first comes in a voice port, is matched to an incoming dial peer, and then is matched to an outgoing dial peer. Rules that are assigned to the voice port are applied first, next any global number expansion, then those on the incoming dial peer, and lastly those on the outgoing dial peer. If a **prefix** command is under the dial peer, the translation is done first.

Figure 10-1 *Order of Operation in Digit Manipulation*

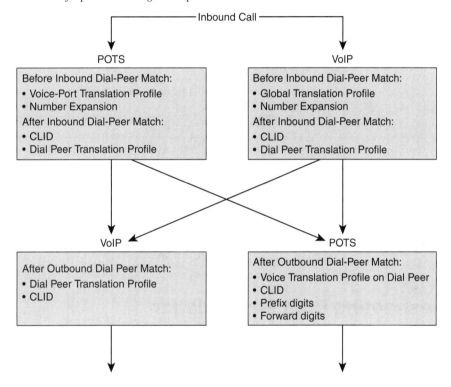

A VoIP call matches an incoming dial peer, then an outgoing dial peer, and possibly a POTS voice port. Globally assigned rules such as VoIP incoming translation profile and number expansion are executed first, then any rules on the incoming dial peer, and finally any rules on the outgoing dial peer. If a Tcl script is associated with a dial peer to manipulate the ANI or DNIS, the script runs after the dial peer is matched but before any translation profile associated with that dial peer.

Table 10-3 summarizes the order of operation for techniques discussed in this chapter.

Table 10-3 *Digit Manipulation Techniques—Order of Operation*

Type of Call	When You Apply It	Digit Manipulation Technique
POTS	Before the inbound dial peer is matched	Translation rule or profile on voice port
		Number expansion
	After the inbound dial peer is matched	CLID operations
		Translation rule or profile on POTS dial peer
	After the outbound POTS dial peer is matched	Translation rule or profile on POTS dial peer
	After the inbound dial peer is matched	CLID operations
		Prefix digits
VoIP	Before the inbound dial peer is matched	VoIP incoming translation profile
		Number expansion
	After the inbound dial peer is matched	CLID operations
		Translation rule or profile on VoIP dial peer
	After the outbound VoIP dial peer is matched	Translation rule or profile on VoIP dial peer
		CLID operations

Troubleshooting Digit Manipulation

When you are troubleshooting digit manipulation, first verify the configuration. Test the digit manipulations as much as possible before deploying them in a live network. If they do not work as expected, check to make sure that they are correctly configured and that other rules do not interfere. Remember the order in which the router processes rules.

This chapter discussed several troubleshooting and verification commands, some of the most useful of which are as follows:

- **test voice translation-rule** *rule-number phone-number*—Shows the results of a translation rule, enabling you to test it to ensure that it does what you planned
- **debug voice translation**—Shows the translations happening
- **show dialplan number** *number*—Verifies number expansion and which dial peers a phone number matches
- **debug voip ccapi inout**—Shows inbound and outbound dial peers being matched
- **show num-exp** [*number*]—Displays the number expansion rules configured

- **show dial-peer voice** [*tag*]—Displays any CLID, translation profiles, call blocking, disconnect cause, digit stripping, forwarding, or prefixing that is configured on the dial peer

- **show voice translation-rule** [*number* | **sort** [**ascending**|**descending**]]—Lists the translation rules that are configured on the router and all translation patterns configured for each one

- **show voice translation-profile** [*name* | **sort** [**ascending**|**descending**]]—Lists the translation profiles configured on the router and all translation rules associated with each one

- **debug isdn q931**—Shows the called and calling numbers sent out a PRI link for troubleshooting CLID commands

- **csim start** *phone-number*—Simulates a phone call from the router; can be used with debugs

Case Study

Figure 10-2 shows the Boise, Idaho office network. In this case study, the Boise office has the following telephone network requirements:

- The office has been experiencing spam faxes lately from one specific phone number, **410-111-2222**. That number needs to be blocked incoming on the Boise PRI.

- The office has a small help desk staff that takes calls from the Miami, Florida office and the Lima, Peru office. Both locations call the same help desk number, **3-0150**. (**3** is a site code.) You need to route calls from Miami to the English-speaking group at **3-0148**, and you need to route calls from Lima to the Spanish-speaking group at **3-0149**. Both calls will go through the local PBX. The internal company numbers for Miami are **2-0100** through **2-0199**. The internal numbers for Lima are **6-6200** through **6-6250**.

- Caller ID should show only the main office number of **208-555-0100** for outgoing calls.

- Outgoing local PSTN calls should have the initial **9** stripped and ten digits sent to the PSTN.

Figure 10-2 *Case Study Network*

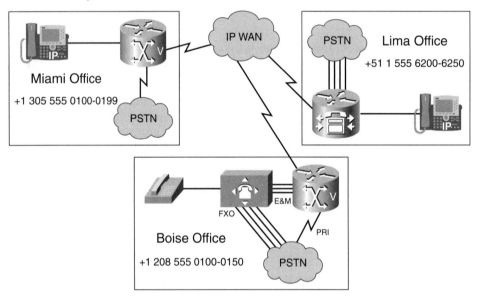

Example 10-11 shows the configuration that is necessary on the Boise router to block the spam faxes, route the help desk calls, change the caller ID, and send the appropriate called number to the PSTN.

Example 10-11 *Digit Manipulation Case Study*

```
!Configure the router to block calls from the fax spam number
!Create the rule to reject 410-111-2222
Boise(config)#voice translation-rule 410
Boise(cfg-translation-rule)#rule 1 reject /4101112222/
!
!Create a translation profile, and associate that rule with it
Boise(config)#voice translation-profile BlockFax
Boise(cfg-translation-profile)#translate calling 410
!
!Apply the translation profile to the dial peer, incoming. Specify a disconnect cause
Boise(config)#dial-peer voice 99 pots
Boise(config-dial-peer)#incoming called-number .
Boise(config-dial-peer)#call-block translation-profile incoming BlockFax
Boise(config-dial-peer)#call-block disconnect-cause incoming call-reject
Boise(config-dial-peer)#direct-inward-dial
!
!Configure the router to route help desk calls based on the ANI
!First create a rule that will be used to translate the DNIS on calls from Miami
Boise(config)#voice translation-rule 100
Boise(cfg-translation-rule)#rule 1 /\(.*\)/ /30148/
!
!Create a rule that will translate the DNIS on calls from Lima
```

Example 10-11 *Digit Manipulation Case Study (Continued)*

```
Boise(cfg-translation-rule)#voice translation-rule 200
Boise(cfg-translation-rule)#rule 1 /\(.*\)/ /30149/
!
!Create translation profiles to translate the called numbers
Boise(config)#voice translation-profile Miami
Boise(cfg-translation-profile)#translate called 100
!
Boise(cfg-translation-profile)#voice translation-profile Lima
Boise(cfg-translation-profile)#translate called 200
!
!Apply the translation profiles to dial peers that will match the incoming ANI
Boise(config)#dial-peer voice 100 voip
Boise(config-dial-peer)#answer-address 221..
Boise(config-dial-peer)#translation-profile outgoing Miami
!
Boise(config-dial-peer)#dial-peer voice 200 voip
Boise(config-dial-peer)#answer-address 662[0-5].
Boise(config-dial-peer)#translation-profile outgoing Lima
!
!Create dial peers for the help desk numbers, pointing to the PBX
Boise(config)#dial-peer voice 30148 pots
Boise(config-dial-peer)#destination-pattern 30148
Boise(config-dial-peer)#port 0/0/0
!
Boise(config-dial-peer)#dial-peer voice 30149 pots
Boise(config-dial-peer)#destination-pattern 30149
Boise(config-dial-peer)#port 0/0/1
!
!Configure CLID to send only the main office number in calls to the PSTN
Boise(config-dial-peer)#dial-peer voice 9 pots
Boise(config-dial-peer)#clid network-number 2085550100 second-number strip
Boise(config-dial-peer)#destination-pattern 9T
Boise(config-dial-peer)#port 1/0:23
!
!On the same dial peer, allow exactly ten digits to be sent as called number
Boise(config-dial-peer)#forward-digits 10
```

Review Questions

1 Define *digit manipulation*.

2 Of the digit manipulation techniques digit stripping, digit forwarding, digit prefixing, number expansion, and CLID, which are executed after the outbound dial peer is matched but before the numbers are transmitted?

3 By default, POTS dial peers strip any outbound digits that explicitly match their destination pattern. What are two simple ways to prevent the router from stripping all the digits?

4 When is a number expansion executed, and how can you test its action?

5 Given the following voice translation rule, how would a dialed string of **913012345678** be translated?

```
/^\(91\)301\(.......\)/ /1\2/
```

6 Given the following voice translation rule, how would a dialed string of **913012345678** be translated?

```
/^\(91\)301\(.......\)/ /\1700\2/
```

CHAPTER 11

Influencing Path Selection

Thus far, this book has discussed various ways to configure a gateway to ensure that your calls go through. This chapter introduces ways to control the path that calls take and to prevent calls from being placed without adequate resources to support them.

It is usually desirable to have more than one path for a call to take. Multiple paths provide redundancy in the event of a link failure or insufficient resources and sometimes are used to reduce the transport cost of a call. These paths might consist completely of voice-over IP (VoIP), or they might be a mixture of VoIP and plain old telephone service (POTS).

When you are using VoIP, keep in mind that voice is an application on the network, and voice messages are carried in IP packets. You can implement techniques to choose which VoIP dial peer is used for a call, but the IP routing structure of your network determines the path to that target IP address. This chapter talks about ways to control call routing using commands and techniques that apply to the voice application, but IP routing ultimately controls VoIP routing. VoIP traffic can be affected by router configuration such as access lists that might block a voice subnet, or policy-based routing that might send voice traffic out a different interface than the one desired. Various commands enable you to control the source IP address of voice packets; you must consider this when you are configuring policies along the entire voice path so that you avoid inadvertently blocking that traffic.

When you are planning and troubleshooting VoIP path selection, take these two levels of call routing into account. In planning, be sure that your voice calls will take the path at each hop that you want them to. When troubleshooting, test the IP path chosen through the network.

Many different ways exist to control call routing and make call admission decisions. With some methods, you make the decisions on the gateway. With others, you use a separate device. In H.323 networks, gatekeepers can control call routing; in Session Initiation Protocol (SIP) networks, proxy servers can perform that function. In Cisco Unified Communications Systems, CallManager makes call routing and admission decisions. In this chapter, you will learn about the following:

- Use of hunt groups and trunk groups
- Use of tail-end hop-off
- CAC techniques based on local gateway settings, on measurements of network performance, and on router resource availability

- Use of the IP Service Level Agreement (SLA) tool
- Use of Resource Reservation Protocol (RSVP) and the RSVP Agent
- Considerations when routing between POTS calls

Hunt Groups

One of the most straightforward ways to control call route selection on a gateway is to create hunt groups. A hunt group is a set of dial peers, all referencing the same destination pattern. You can use hunt groups to provide load balancing over multiple ports or to provide redundancy if a primary port is unusable.

You can use hunt groups with both POTS and VOIP interfaces. This section shows how to configure hunt groups for those gateway protocols that use dial peers: H.323 and SIP. You must configure hunt groups on the call agent when using MGCP gateways.

You can mix POTS and VoIP dial peers in the same hunt group. By default, a router selects which dial peer in a hunt group to use by the following criteria:

1 **Longest match**—This is the destination pattern that matches the most number of digits.

2 **Preference value**—Dial peers are chosen in order of preference.

3 **Random selection**—If all dial peers have the same preference, they are used in random order.

The **dial-peer hunt** *value* command gives you a fourth option—least recently used dial peer—and a way to alter the default order of the choice selection criteria. Example 11-1 shows the options that are available with the **dial-peer hunt** command.

Example 11-1 **dial-peer hunt** *Command*

```
Shanghai-GW(config)#dial-peer hunt ?
  <0-7>  Dial-peer hunting choices, listed in hunting order within each choice:
  0 - Longest match in phone number, explicit preference, random selection.
  1 - Longest match in phone number, explicit preference, least recent use.
  2 - Explicit preference, longest match in phone number, random selection.
  3 - Explicit preference, longest match in phone number, least recent use.
  4 - Least recent use, longest match in phone number, explicit preference.
  5 - Least recent use, explicit preference, longest match in phone number.
  6 - Random selection.
  7 - Least recent use.
```

Using the preference Command

You create a hunt group by using the **preference** command under the dial peer configuration mode, as shown in Example 11-2. Preference values can range from 0 to 10, with the lowest number being the most preferred. Thus, a dial peer with a preference value of 1 would be used before a dial peer with a preference value of 2, all other things being equal. The default preference for dial peers is 0, which is the most preferred, or highest priority, value. If the most preferred dial peer is not available, the router tries the dial peer with the next higher preference value, and so on.

If the same preference value and destination pattern are configured on a POTS and a VoIP dial peer, the POTS dial peer is used.

Example 11-2 *Configuring a Hunt Group Using Preference*

```
!The primary dial peer uses the default preference value of 0
dial-peer voice 3400 voip
 destination-pattern 34..
 session target ipv4:10.6.2.10
!
!The dial peer to use if the primary is unavailable
dial-peer voice 3401 pots
 destination-pattern 34..
 preference 1
 port 1/0:23
```

Using the huntstop Command

Dial peer hunting is enabled by default. If a call fails on one dial peer in a hunt group, the gateway continues hunting. The dial peer **huntstop** command stops the gateway from searching for other matches if the call fails on that dial peer. One use for this is a gateway with dial peers using an explicit destination pattern (such as 221.) pointing to one set of ports, and a dial peer using a less explicit destination pattern (such as 2...) pointing to another port. If you do not want the router to use the less explicit dial peer, add the **huntstop** command under the dial peer where you want the router to stop hunting, as shown in Example 11-3. Note the **huntstop** command under dial peer 2212. To re-enable hunting, use **no huntstop**.

Example 11-3 *Using the* **huntstop** *Command*

```
!The preferred dial peer for calls to 221x
dial-peer voice 2211 pots
 preference 1
 destination-pattern 221.
 forward-digits all
 port 0/0/0
!
!The secondary dial peer for calls to 221x
dial-peer voice 2212 pots
 preference 2
 huntstop
 destination-pattern 221.
 forward-digits all
 port 0/0/1
!
!A less explicit dial peer that should not be used for calls to 221x
```

continues

Example 11-3 *Using the* **huntstop** *Command (Continued)*

```
dial-peer voice 2200 pots
  destination-pattern 2...
  forward-digits all
  preference 3
  port 1/0:23
```

Using Digit Manipulation

When you are using alternate dial peers, you might have to adjust the call information that is sent. Various digit manipulation techniques are available to do this. See Chapter 10, "Digit Manipulation," for detailed information on digit manipulation techniques and commands.

Figure 11-1 illustrates some typical situations in which you might need digit manipulation. The figure shows a simple network with two sites connected over an IP network. If the IP WAN is unavailable, each gateway is configured to reroute calls over the public switched telephone network (PSTN). The remote site on each gateway has a primary VoIP and a secondary POTS dial peer.

Figure 11-1 *Using Digit Manipulation with Hunt Groups*

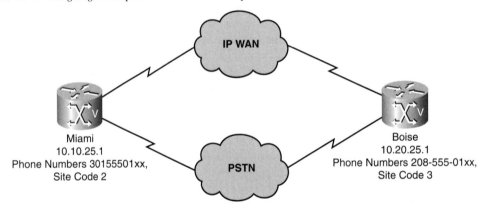

Potential problems with this voice network include the following issues. Example 11-4 shows a configuration that uses digit manipulation to solve these problems.

- A VoIP dial peer transmits all digits by default, but a POTS dial peer truncates digits that match the destination pattern. If a POTS dial peer serves as backup to a VoIP dial peer, you need to specify the number of digits to send. In networks in which the entire phone number is dialed, this can be as simple as coding **forward-digits all** under the POTS dial peer. In Figure 11-1, a site code of 3 is used for Boise. This should not be sent to the terminating gateway. In Example 11-4, the VoIP dial peer 1112 of the Miami router has a translation profile that allows just the last four digits of the dialed number to be transmitted.

- VoIP dial peers usually connect internal networks, so users usually do not dial the entire destination telephone number. If the alternate dial peer routes the call over the PSTN, you need to add information that the PSTN needs to route the call, such as long-distance code, area code, and prefix. In Figure 11-1, the POTS dial peer strips all but the last two digits, so a **prefix** command is coded on the Miami router under POTS dial peer 202 to add the long-distance access number (1), the Boise area code (208), and the next five digits of the phone number (55501). The site code of 3 is not sent. Similarly, on the POTS dial peer 202 of the Boise router, the long-distance access code (1), the Miami area code (301), and the next five digits of the phone number (55501) are prefixed. The site code of 2 is stripped.

- You might need to manipulate the called number on the terminating gateway. The Boise gateway expects to route calls to its LAN phones based on a four-digit DNIS. If the PSTN sends more digits, you need to strip some digits from the incoming called number. You might also want to manipulate the calling number to provide the caller ID that users expect to see. In Figure 11-1, the PSTN sends a ten-digit dialed number identification service (DNIS) to Boise. Example 11-4 shows that the Boise gateway translates that to just the last four digits under POTS dial peer 202.

Example 11-4 *Configuring Digit Manipulation with Hunt Groups*

```
!Miami Router Configuration

!Creates a translation rule to remove the site code
voice translation-rule 3
 rule 1 /^301/ /01/
!
!Creates the translation profile associated with Rule 3
voice translation-profile BOISE-VOIP
 translate called 3
!
!Primary dial peer, pointing to Boise router, site code is removed, four digits sent
dial-peer voice 1112 voip
 translation-profile outgoing BOISE-VOIP
 preference 1
 destination-pattern 301..
 session target ipv4:10.20.25.1
!
!Backup dial peer, sends calls to PSTN and adds necessary digits
dial-peer voice 202 pots
 preference 2
 destination-pattern 301..
 direct-inward-dial
 prefix 120855501
 port 1/0:23
```

```
!Boise Router Configuration
!
```

continues

Example 11-4 *Configuring Digit Manipulation with Hunt Groups (Continued)*

```
!Creates a translation rule to remove the site code
voice translation-rule 2
 rule 1 /^201/ /01/
 !
!Creates a translation rule to remove the extra digits sent by the PSTN
voice translation-rule 22
 rule 1 /^208555/ //
 !
!Creates a translation profile associated with Rule 2
voice translation-profile MIAMI-VOIP
 translate called 2
 !
 !
!Creates a translation profile associated with Rule 22
voice translation-profile MIAMI-POTS
 translate called 22
 !
!Primary dial peer, pointing to Miami router, site code is removed, four digits sent
dial-peer voice 1112 voip
 translation-profile outgoing MIAMI-VOIP
 preference 1
 destination-pattern 201..
 session target ipv4:10.10.25.1
 !
!Backup dial peer, sends call to PSTN, adds necessary digits to outbound calls
dial-peer voice 202 pots
!Translation profile removes all but four digits on incoming calls from Miami
 translation-profile incoming MIAMI-POTS
 preference 2
 destination-pattern 201,,
 direct-inward-dial
 prefix 130155501
 port 1/0:23
```

Using Trunk Groups

BRI, PRI, and CAS interfaces and FXO, FXO, and Ear and Mouth (E&M) voice ports can be combined into trunk groups. When you create a trunk group, you can add configuration to control path selection. Create a trunk group with the global **trunk group** *name* command. This puts you in trunk group configuration mode. You can then add commands that will apply to all the circuits in the group. The **max-call voice** *number* command limits the number of incoming and outgoing calls that the trunk group will accept. By default, the least-used trunk is selected when the gateway hunts through a trunk group. You can change this with the **hunt-scheme** command. This command has the following options:

- **least-idle** [**even** | **odd** | **both**]—Looks for the most recently released channel.

- **least-used** [**even** | **odd** | **both** [**up** | **down**]]—Is the default hunt method for a trunk group. It looks for the trunk member with the most unused channels.

- **longest-idle [even | odd | both]**—Looks for the trunk member that has been idle the longest amount of time.

- **Random**—Chooses a trunk member at random and a random channel within that trunk member.

- **round-robin [even | odd | both[up | down]]**—Looks at trunk group members in a round robin fashion, one after the other.

- **sequential [even | odd | both[up | down]]**—Always starts looking for a free channel with the highest priority trunk.

In each command, **even** selects even-numbered channels within a trunk member first, **odd** selects odd-numbered channels within a trunk member first, and **both** considers all channels for selection. The option **up** hunts through the channels in ascending order, whereas the option **down** hunts through them in descending order.

Add an interface or voice port to a hunt group with the **trunk group** *name* [*preference*] command. The *preference* value indicates the priority of the trunk within the group. A lower preference value equates to a higher priority trunk. You can then assign multiple trunk groups to dial peers, with a priority value to determine their use by the dial peer.

Tail-End Hop-Off

Tail-End Hop-Off (TEHO) allows a company to reduce its long-distance toll charges. When remotes sites are connected by an IP WAN, you can route calls that are bound to those cities—and those sites—over the WAN. The terminating gateway then routes them out to the PSTN as a local call. This sounds like a good idea in theory, but it can be complex in practice.

You need a separate dial peer for each area code/prefix combination in each remote location. Large cities have many prefixes and might have several area codes also. Small cities or regions might have some prefixes within the same area code that are local calls, and some that are long-distance calls. You might need a gatekeeper for an extensive TEHO implementation.

Regulatory issues might curtail the use of TEHO, also. TEHO results in a loss of revenue for telecommunications companies, so some countries regulate calls carried across country or regional borders. Careful planning and research on the most recent laws concerning mixed VoIP and PSTN calls is necessary before implementing TEHO in your network.

Example 11-5 shows a possible TEHO configuration for the network shown in Figure 11-1. In this example, the Miami office implements TEHO for calls to the Boise area code 208.

For purposes of the example, it is assumed that prefix 555 in area code 208 is a local call from the Boise office and that Boise uses ten-digit local dialing.

Example 11-5 *TEHO Configuration*

```
!Miami Router Configuration
!
!The primary dial peer for TEHO; calls go across the IP WAN
dial-peer voice 2081 voip
 preference 1
 destination-pattern 9208555....
 session target ipv4:10.20.25.1
!
!Backup dial peer; calls go to the PSTN
dial-peer voice 2082 pots
 preference 2
 destination-pattern 9208555....
 prefix 1208555
 port 1/0:23

!Boise Router Configuration
!
!Dial peer that sends local calls to the PSTN
dial-peer voice 208 pots
 destination-pattern 9208555....
 prefix 208555
 port 1/0:23
```

Call Admission Control

Call admission control (CAC) is used to protect the quality of your voice calls by preventing call completion if not enough resources are available to support it. CAC is needed over an IP WAN because IP does not possess the ability of the time-division multiplexing (TDM) world to meter calls. When a POTS line is in use, or a DS0 in a PRI is in use, the gateway cannot use that link for additional calls. But nothing is inherent in an IP interface that stops more packets from attempting to use it.

It is generally recognized that a voice network needs quality of service (QoS) mechanisms. However, QoS just protects voice from interference by data traffic. It does not protect voice from voice. Consider a router that is configured with a low-latency queue (LLQ) for voice, and that queue is allocated enough bandwidth for ten calls. Then suppose that an eleventh call is placed. QoS would not prevent the router from sending that call. Instead, the queue would fill up faster, and voice packets would start to be dropped. This would affect the quality of all 11 calls, not just the extra one.

CAC techniques attempt to remedy this. If CAC were implemented, the eleventh call could be rerouted to another VoIP dial peer or out to the PSTN. If the call came from a TDM switch, it could be returned to that switch for handling.

Many different types of CAC exist, and each uses different methods to decide whether to allow a call. CAC techniques can be divided into three categories:

- Local
- Measurement based
- Resource based

This section discusses each CAC type to help you decide which ones to use in your network. You can deploy multiple types of CAC mechanisms on the same gateway. If so, the gateway goes through a sequence of checks against the CAC types. If any of these tests rejects the call, the process ends at that point, and no further checking is done.

When multiple CAC mechanisms are configured, the selection process follows these steps:

Step 1   The gateway checks for the **max-conn** configuration on the outbound dial peer.

If the limit has been reached, the call is rejected. If no **max-conn** is configured, or the limit has not been reached, the router goes to Step 2.

Step 2   The router checks for CAC mechanisms based on local system resources, such as CPU use.

If these resources are not configured, or if the test succeeds, the router goes to Step 3.

Step 3   If a gatekeeper is used, and it is configured to do CAC based on bandwidth, the gatekeeper is checked.

If this test succeeds, or no gatekeeper CAC is used, the router proceeds to Step 4.

Step 4   If RSVP is configured, an RSVP reservation is attempted. When RSVP is used, this is the last test.

If the call is allowed, call setup continues. If not, the router rejects the call. *Only if RSVP is not configured does the router go to Step 5.*

Step 5   Any CAC mechanism that use probes to measure network availability is now checked.

This is the last test. If the call is allowed, setup proceeds. If not, it is rejected.

Network components other than a gateway can also make CAC decisions. In a network that uses Cisco CallManager, it is the CallManager, not the gateway, that usually makes CAC decisions. You can configure CallManagers with locations. You assign phones and other devices to a location when you add them to CallManager. Configure CallManager with a maximum bandwidth for audio and for video calls for each location. It then allows calls to or from that location across the WAN only if sufficient bandwidth is available. In addition, you can configure CallManager to use RSVP for some locations and not for others.

You can also configure gatekeepers to do CAC. Gatekeepers base their decisions either on bandwidth between zones or gateway resource availability. The section "Resource-Based CAC Mechanisms" has more information. SIP proxy servers can make CAC decisions in SIP networks.

Local CAC Mechanisms

Local CAC mechanisms are configured on the outgoing gateway, and they are aware only of local conditions. They base their call routing decisions on either the number of current calls or the state of the interface to which calls are routed. If that works for your network, you do not need to introduce the extra complexity of other techniques. Local CAC mechanisms are relatively easy to configure, and they have low overhead.

Physical DS0 Limitation

A straightforward way to limit the number of calls over the IP WAN is to limit the number of internal calls coming to the gateway. A router that is connected to a PBX with six POTS lines will never have more than six calls active over the WAN. If the router is connected to the PBX with a PRI, the number of timeslots can be configured. When all the DS0 channels are in use, the PBX is responsible for rerouting outbound calls to the PSTN.

Maximum Connections

You can configure the number of calls allowed per dial peer by using the **max-conn** *number* command under dial-peer configuration mode. The default is to allow an unlimited number of calls. In Example 11-6, five connections are allowed to phone numbers beginning with 11.

Example 11-6 *Configuring the Maximum Connections for a Dial Peer*

```
VoiceGW(config)#dial-peer voice 11 voip
VoiceGW(config-dial-peer)#destination-pattern 11T
VoiceGW(config-dial-peer)#max-conn 5
```

Keep in mind that this is just for the specific dial peer, not for the interface or the network as a whole. Limiting connections could be useful in a network with a few sites having a small number of phones and low WAN bandwidth. You must configure a separate dial peer for each remote site. The number of calls allowed on the egress interface is equal to the sum of all the connections that are allowed. The **max-conn** command helps limit the bandwidth use of the gateway WAN interface, and it prevents remote sites from being overwhelmed by calls that they will deny. However, it does not adjust to topology changes or WAN usage, and it works only in gateways that use dial peers.

Local Voice Busyout

Local voice busyout (LVBO) is used on a gateway that is connected to a PBX and an IP WAN. It tells the router to watch an interface, and if that interface goes down, the router busies out the ports or trunks to the PBX. This appears to the PBX as if the ports are off-hook. Multiple interfaces can be tracked; all must be down before the router busies out a voice port.

You should only use LVBO when the gateway is connected to a PBX, and the PBX connects to the PSTN. The PBX can then reroute internal callers to the PSTN instead of over the IP WAN. If you use it on a router that is a PSTN gateway, the PSTN interfaces are taken out of service, which stops external calls from coming into the network. That is usually not the desired result.

NOTE   LVBO tracks only the up or down status of an interface, not its usage.

LVBO can monitor LAN, WAN, and virtual interfaces and subinterfaces. You configure LVBO under the voice port configuration mode, as shown in Example 11-7.

Example 11-7 *Configuring LVBO*

```
VoiceGW(config)#voice-port 0/0/0
VoiceGW(config-voiceport)#busyout monitor interface fa 2/0
VoiceGW(config-voiceport)#busyout monitor interface atm 1/0.10
```

You can add an additional command, **busyout action graceful**, to the voice port configuration. The router then busies out the port only after active calls hang up. In H.323 networks that use gatekeepers, you can monitor the gatekeeper, and busy out ports if the gateway is unreachable, by using the **busyout monitor gatekeeper** command.

Measurement-Based CAC Mechanisms

Measurement-based CAC mechanisms look beyond the local router, into the network between the originating and terminating gateways. They attempt to measure network congestion by sending probes through the network to measure latency, delay, and jitter. The outgoing gateway uses this information to permit or deny calls. The router can reroute calls when network delay or packet loss is too high, or it can busy out voice ports so that they will not be used. The functionality to send and respond to probes is part of the Cisco IOS. In Cisco IOS releases after 12.3(14)T, the feature is called IP Service Level Agreement (IP SLA). IP SLA is an extension to the Service Assurance Agent (SAA) and Response Time Reporter (RTR) features that are present in Cisco IOS versions prior to 12.3(14)T. New commands using the **ip sla** syntax have been released beginning with Cisco IOS version 12.4.

IP SLA

IP SLA is a network monitoring and management feature that is part of the Cisco IOS. It enables you to proactively monitor and measure network performance for specific applications, not just in general. IP SLA works by sending probes to the IP address of a target device, which responds to them. When a Cisco router is the target, you can configure it as an IP SLA responder and return more accurate information. For instance, an IP SLA responder adds timestamps to the response packets so that router processing delay is not counted as part of the round-trip time. You can configure an IP SLA responder to listen only on a certain port for probe packets. You can use MD5 authentication between IP SLA sources and responders for enhanced security.

You can schedule IP SLA probes to run at a certain time, or you can run them at periodic intervals. These probes can emulate many different types of network traffic, such as FTP, Dynamic Host Configuration Protocol (DHCP), and HTTP. For VoIP and CAC, typically User Datagram Protocol (UDP) and Real-Time Transport Protocol (RTP) headers are used to emulate voice traffic, measuring jitter, gatekeeper delay, post dial delay, and RTP operations. Codec can be specified for the probes, and IP SLA will send a configurable number of packets sized appropriately for the type of codec. You can set type of service (TOS) values so that the probes receive the same QoS treatment as voice.

Measurements include jitter, round-trip time, packet loss, and one-way delay. From this information, IP SLA estimates voice quality using the Calculated Planning Impairment Factor (ICPIF) and Mean Opinion Scores (MOS) described in the next section of this chapter.

You can retrieve this information from the command line with **show** commands, but its real usefulness lies in the ability of the router to store the results in MIBs. Then you can retrieve the information via Simple Network Management Protocol (SNMP) so that applications, such as CiscoWorks and some third-party applications, can use it. A change in network performance can trigger alerts or other types of probes to troubleshoot the problem, for instance. Companies that are considering moving to VoIP need to be sure that their network will support it, and IP SLA is one way to test that.

Calculated Planning Impairment Factor and Mean Opinion Scores

IP SLA uses the information it gathers from its probes to provide estimates of probable voice quality. If network conditions are such that voice quality will be too low, calls can be rejected or rerouted, or troubleshooting measures can be triggered. Voice quality is measured in two ways:

- ICPIF
- MOS

ICPIF is an International Telecommunications Union Telecommunication Standardization Sector (ITU-T) recommendation that attempts to objectively measure voice quality by measuring network elements that impair voice call quality. In calculating an ICPIF value, Cisco uses a formula that simplifies to $icpif = idd + ie - A$, where

- idd (delay impairment factor) equals one-way delay.

- ie (equipment impairment factor) equals percent of packet loss.

- A (advantage factor, sometimes called expect factor) equals a value that is meant to reflect the fact that users accept some quality degradation under certain circumstances. Cisco assumes a value of 0 for this variable, but that is configurable.

The result of this calculation is a value representing the probable voice quality of a call sent across the circuits traversed by the probe, at the moment the probe is sent. ICPIF values range between 5 and 55, and they are assigned the meanings shown in Table 11-1.

Table 11-1   *ICPIF Scores*

ICPIF Value	Voice Quality
5	Very good
10	Good
20	Adequate
30	Limiting case
45	Exceptionally limiting case
55	Customers likely to react strongly

Voice quality is a fairly subjective thing. What might be adequate for one person might be intolerable for another. MOS is a rating of voice quality obtained by averaging the opinions of a wide range of listeners. Table 11-2 shows the MOS values, their meanings, and the equivalent ICPIF values.

Table 11-2   *Mean Opinion Score Values*

MOS Value	Description of Impairment	Corresponding ICPIF Values
5	Imperceptible	0–3
4	Just perceptible, but not annoying	4–13
3	Perceptible and slightly annoying	14–23
2	Annoying but not objectionable	24–33
1	Very annoying and objectionable	34 and up

IP SLA calculates the ICPIF and MOS values, and measurement-based CAC mechanisms can use these values to allow or disallow a call. You can also configure a maximum ICPIF value for calls that a VoIP dial peer sends.

Configuring IP SLA

Begin configuring IP SLA by choosing the routers on which it will be used. If you are using it to test a network, configure it on the routers at each end of the network. If you are using it to troubleshoot a problem, you might want to test network performance between each hop. If you plan to use IP SLA as a network monitoring tool, sending probes regularly, you should be aware that the tool has a performance cost. If you need to send a lot of probes, such as at a hub site that monitors remote sites, consider using a dedicated router as the IP SLA source router. This also gives you one central location from which to gather measurements.

Enter IP SLA configuration mode with the **ip sla** *operation-number* global command. The *operation-number* identifies a unique IP SLA instance. From there, you can configure the type of traffic to be measured. The measurements typically of concern to voice are contained under UDP jitter commands. For UDP jitter, the minimum required command is **udp-jitter** {*destination_IP-address* | *destination_hostname*} {*port-number*}. Additional options to this command include the following:

- **codec**—Configures the codec type for IP SLA packets to use. When codec is specified, you can optionally configure **codec-interval**, **codec-numpackets**, and **codec-size**. The default interval between packets is 20 ms, the default number of packets sent is 1000, and the default size is 160 bytes for G711 and 20 bytes for G729.

- **control {enable | disable}**—Enables or disables the sending of IP SLA control packets from the source to the responder. It is enabled by default; disabling it results in less accurate measurements.

- **interval** *interval*—Configures the interpacket interval in milliseconds. The default is 20 ms.

- **num-packets** *packets*—Sets the number of packets to send. The default is ten.

- **source-ip** {ip-address | hostname}—Specifies a source IP address or hostname. Without this option, the router uses the IP address of the exit interface.

- **source-port** {*port-number*}—Configures the source port for IP SLA packets. When this option is not set, the router chooses a port.

You can also set a TOS value for the IP SLA packets. IP SLA looks at the first 4 bits of the TOS byte in the IP header, but the value of these bits is calculated as if all 8 bits were used. For instance, an IP precedence of 5 and a differentiated services code point (DSCP) value of 40 both equate to an IP SLA TOS of 160. In IP SLA jitter configuration mode, give the **tos** *value* command.

After you have configured an IP SLA operation, you can schedule it. You can have it run immediately, on a regular basis, or at some point in the future. Use the **ip sla schedule** *operation-number* [**ageout** *seconds*] [**life** {**forever** | *seconds*}] [**start-time** {*hh:mm*[*:ss*] [*month day* | *day month*] | **pending** | **now** | **after** *hh:mm:ss*}] [**recurring**] global command. After you have scheduled an operation, you cannot change its configuration. If you need to make changes, you must delete and re-create that operation.

To configure a router as an IP SLA responder, code the **ip sla responder** command in global configuration mode.

To enable MD5 authentication of IP SLA packets, complete the following steps on both the source and the responder routers:

Step 1 Create a key chain and enter key chain configuration mode with the global **key chain** *name* command.

Step 2 Create a key with the **key** *number* command.

Step 3 Create the key string with the **key-string** *key-text* command.

You can create several keys for a specific key chain, but be sure to create them in the same order on both routers. If multiple keys exist, the routers will rotate key use during their communication. After the key chain is complete, configure IP SLA to use authentication with the **ip sla key-chain** *name* global command.

Example 11-8 shows the configuration of IP SLA source (Boise) and responder (Miami) routers. The routers use MD5 authentication for the IP SLA packets. UDP jitter is being measured using a destination port of 65424 and the G729 codec. A TOS value of 176 is used, which corresponds to an IP precedence of 5, and DSCP of 46 (expedited forwarding). The probe is scheduled to run every day at 9:00 am. In the output of the **show ip sla statistics** command, you can see the measured round-trip time, latency, jitter, and packet loss. The calculated ICPIF and MOS values are shown in the shaded area. PSTN fallback can use these values, which is discussed in the next section.

Example 11-8 *Configuring IP SLA Source and Responder*

```
!Configure the router that will respond to the IP SLA probes
MiamiGW#conf t
Enter configuration commands, one per line. End with CNTL/Z.
MiamiGW(config)#ip sla responder
!
!Configure MD5 authentication
MiamiGW(config)#key chain IP-SLA
MiamiGW(config-keychain)#key 1
MiamiGW(config-keychain-key)#key-string cisco
!
!MiamiGW(config)#ip sla key-chain IP-SLA

!Configure the router that will originate the IP SLA probes
BoiseGW#conf t
Enter configuration commands, one per line. End with CNTL/Z.
BoiseGW(config)#ip sla 10
```

continues

Example 11-8 *Configuring IP SLA Source and Responder (Continued)*

```
BoiseGW(config-ip-sla)#udp-jitter 10.6.2.1 65424 codec g729a
Boise GW(config-ip-sla-jitter)#tos 176
! Boise GW(config-ip-sla-jitter)#exit
Boise GW(config)# ip sla schedule 10 recurring start-time 9:00:00
!
!Configure MD5 authentication
BoiseGW(config)#key chain IP-SLA
BoiseGW(config-keychain)#key 1
BoiseGW(config-keychain-key)#key-string cisco
!
BoiseGW(config)#ip sla key-chain IP-SLA

!Observe the ICPIF and MOS results
BoiseGW#show ip sla statistics

Round Trip Time (RTT) for        Index 10
        Latest RTT: 2 milliseconds
Latest operation start time: 9:00:00.000 EDT Tue May 16 2006
Latest operation return code: OK
RTT Values:
        Number Of RTT: 10            RTT Min/Avg/Max: 2/2/3 milliseconds
Latency one-way time:
        Number of Latency one-way Samples: 0
        Source to Destination Latency one way Min/Avg/Max: 0/0/0 milliseconds
        Destination to Source Latency one way Min/Avg/Max: 0/0/0 milliseconds
Jitter Time:
        Number of Jitter Samples: 9
        Source to Destination Jitter Min/Avg/Max: 1/1/1 milliseconds
        Destination to Source Jitter Min/Avg/Max: 0/0/0 milliseconds
Packet Loss Values:
        Loss Source to Destination: 0          Loss Destination to Source: 0
        Out Of Sequence: 0      Tail Drop: 0    Packet Late Arrival: 0
Voice Score Values:
        Calculated Planning Impairment Factor (ICPIF): 10
        Mean Opinion Score (MOS): 3.3
Number of successes: 60
Number of failures: 0
Operation time to live: 0
```

IP Service Assurance Agent and Response Time Reporter

For routers with IOS version prior to 12.3(14)T, you will need to configure probes using the SAA and RTR. Begin configuring SAA with the **rtr** *number* global command. The number simply identifies an RTR instance and takes you to RTR configuration mode. From there, enable RTR measurement **type jitter**, and then add the additional configuration needed. The entire command syntax is **type jitter dest-ipaddr** {*hostname | ip-address*} **dest-port** *port-number* **codec** *codec-type* [**codec-numpackets** *number-of-packets*] [**codec-size** *number-of-bytes*][**codec-interval** *time-interval*] [**advantage-factor** *value*][**source-ipaddr**

{*hostname* I *ip-address*}] [**source-port** *port-number*] [**control** {**enable** I **disable**}].
Table 11-3 lists the meaning of each of these command options.

Table 11-3   *Configuring SAA Using the RTR Commands*

Command	Usage
type jitter	Configures the type of SAA operation.
dest-ipaddr {*hostname* I *ip-address*}	Identifies the router that responds to the SAA probes.
dest-port *port-number*	Destination port used by the probes. For voice, an even port between 16384–32767 or 49152–65535 is recommended.
codec *codec-type*	This keyword must be present for ICPIF and MOS values to be generated. Options are • **g711alaw**—Uses 64 Kbps • **g711ulaw**—Uses 64 Kbps • **g729alaw**—Uses 8 Kbps The codec specified should match the one used in the network.
codec-numpackets *number-of-packets*	Optional. The number of packets transmitted in each probe. Possible values are 1–60,000; the default is 1000.
codec-size *number-of-bytes*	Optional. The size of the packets transmitted. Possible values are 16–1500 bytes; the default varies by codec specified.
codec-interval *time-interval*	Optional. Specifies the delay between packets. Valid range is 1–60,000 ms; the default is 20 ms.
advantage-factor *value*	Optional. Sets the expectation/advantage factor used in calculating the ICPIF. Valid range is 0–20; the default is 0.
source-ipaddr {*hostname* I *ip-address*}	Optional. Specifies the source IP address or hostname used by SAA probes.
source-port *port-number*	Optional. Specifies the source port used by SAA probes.
control {**enable** I **disable**}	Optional. Sets the sending of SAA control messages to the RTR responder. If you disable it, SAA statistics will not be collected correctly. The default is enabled.

On the router that will be the RTR responder, the only command needed is **rtr responder** at global configuration mode. Once SAA is configured, you can either schedule it to run at another time or tell it to run immediately. The command is given at global configuration mode: **rtr schedule** *rtr-number* **start-time** {**after** | **pending** | *hh:mm* | *hh:mm:ss* | **now**}. Verify your SAA configuration with the **show rtr configuration** *rtr-number* command. After SAA has run, the ICPIF and MOS values can be observed with the **show rtr operational-state** *rtr-number* command or the **show rtr collection-statistics** *rtr-number* command.

PSTN Fallback

PSTN fallback, also referred to as call fallback, is a feature that uses statistics collected by probes to decide when to reroute a call to the PSTN or another IP path, or when to deny a call altogether. This call fallback feature lets you specify the thresholds to use based either on ICPIF or solely on delay and packet loss. You can use it on both H.323 and SIP gateways. PSTN fallback is typically used for toll bypass situations, where VoIP gateways connect PBX voice networks.

PSTN fallback makes call admission decisions on a call-by-call basis. The router keeps a cache of recently used destinations and the call quality values associated with them. After a destination is in the cache, the router sends probes periodically to keep the information accurate. If a destination gateway has no more calls, its entry ages out of the cache.

When an outgoing call arrives at the gateway, one of three things happens:

- The gateway checks its cache and does not find an entry for the destination gateway. It then sends a probe to that IP address and waits for a response. Call setup does not continue until the probe results are received. This causes some post call delay, but only for the first call to that remote gateway. If the ICPIF or packet loss and delay values are below the configured threshold, the call is allowed, and the probe results are added to the cache. Call setup proceeds.

- The gateway checks its cache, finds an entry for the destination gateway, and determines that the results are okay. No probe is sent, and the call is allowed. Call setup proceeds.

- The gateway checks its cache, finds an entry for the destination gateway, and determines that the results were above the configured threshold. The call is rejected. If a secondary dial peer is available, the call is sent to that dial peer. If that peer is not available, and the call came from a PBX, the call can be hairpinned back to the PBX.

You can use a series of **call fallback** commands to configure PSTN fallback on the outgoing gateway. Some of the most frequently used commands are described in Table 11-4. For a complete list of the **call fallback** commands, go to Cisco.com. Call fallback configuration is done at global configuration mode, so it applies to all calls. However, you can disable fallback for a specific dial peer so that calls denied by the primary dial peer do not fall back to it. The only configuration needed on the terminating gateway is the **ip sla responder** global command. For Cisco IOS versions prior to 12.4, use the **rtr responder** global command.

Table 11-4 **call fallback** *Commands*

Command	Usage
call fallback active	Required command to enable PSTN/call fallback.
call fallback cache size *number*	Optional. It specifies the number of entries to keep in cache. The valid range is 1–256, and the default is 128. Give this command before enabling call fallback.
call fallback cache-timeout *seconds*	Specifies the number of seconds to keep entries in cache. The default is 600 seconds.
call fallback jitter-probe	Configure the jitter probe parameters. Options include these: **dscp**—Sets the DSCP used in probe packets. No default DSCP value exists. **num-packets**—Sets the number of packets sent per probe. The default is 15. **precedence**—Sets the IP precedence used in packets. The default is 2. **priority-queue**—Tells the router to place probes in the priority queue, if configured. This is disabled by default.
call fallback instantaneous-value-weight *weight*	Tells the router to average the last two probes in making CAC decisions. That way, temporary network congestion or lulls do not affect the CAC as much. The weight factor is applied to the newest probe when calculating the average.
call fallback monitor	Lets all calls go through, but allows statistics collection about ICPIF value or packet delay and loss.
call fallback threshold delay *ms* **loss** *percent-loss*	Configures the router to make CAC decision based on delay and loss, and specifies the limit at which to reject calls.
call fallback threshold *icpif-value*	Configures an ICPIF threshold value for rejecting calls. The valid range is 0–34. 34 equals total packet loss. Cisco routers use ICPIF for call fallback by default, using a default threshold value of 5.

Verify PSTN fallback configuration with the **show call fallback config** command. If you have enabled fallback without other adjustments, this command shows you the default values. If you have changed any of the parameters, this command allows you to verify the changes. The **show call fallback cache** command reveals the current cache entries. The **show call fallback stats** command exhibits fallback statistics, such as accepted and rejected calls. You can send a test probe and view the ICPIF values with the **test call fallback probe** *ip-address* command. Two **debug** commands that can be helpful are **debug call fallback probe** and **debug call fallback details**.

Advanced Voice Busyout

Like LVBO, advanced voice busyout (AVBO) is used on routers that are connected to PBXs. It can busy out voice ports or trunks, causing the connected PBX to reroute its calls. AVBO, however, can make its decisions based on measurements of network conditions as well as interface status. Call fallback must first be enabled in order for probes to be sent. AVBO configuration is done either under the voice port or **voice class busyout** configuration modes. The command syntax to configure AVBO using probes is **busyout monitor probe ip-address** [**codec** *codec-type*] [**icpif** *number* | **loss** *percent* **delay** *milliseconds*].

Specifying the codec is optional, and the CAC decision can be made on either ICPIF results or packet loss and delay. The default codec is G711alaw. The default threshold is the one that the **call fallback** command uses. You must configure the terminating gateway as an IP SLA or RTR responder.

If you have multiple dial peers, you can use the same command in a voice class. If you are using the **voice class busyout** configuration, you can also trigger ABVO based on interface status with the **busyout monitor** *interface* command. You must then assign the voice class to a voice port with the **voice class busyout** *tag* command.

Resource-Based CAC Mechanisms

Resource-based CAC mechanisms examine the resources that are available for a call. These can be resources that are local to the router, such as CPU and memory, or they can be network resources, such as bandwidth. Two types of resource-based CAC—resource availability indication (RAI) and gatekeeper zone bandwidth—are used in H.323 networks with gatekeepers.

Local Gateway Resources

You can configure CAC based on local system resources when using H.323 and SIP gateways. The global **call threshold** command has options for global resources, such as CPU, memory, and total calls, and interface resources based on number of calls. You configure a high and low threshold. **Call threshold** is used in conjunction with the **call treatment** command, as shown in the following steps:

Step 1   Configure high and low thresholds for the appropriate router resources with the **call threshold** command.

Step 2 Enable treatment with **call treatment on**.

Step 3 Configure the type of treatment with the **call treatment** command.

Treatment can include hairpinning the call to a POTS dial peer, playing a message to the caller, busying out the voice interfaces, or rejecting the call and sending a cause code. When the high threshold is reached, the specified treatment is enabled. This continues until the low threshold is reached.

Additionally, you can limit the number of PSTN calls that the router receives within a configurable time with the **call spike** global command.

To verify your configuration, use the following commands:

- **show call threshold {config | stats | status}**
- **show call treatment {config | stats}**
- **show call spike status**

Gatekeeper Zone Bandwidth

In this chapter you have learned some ways that gateways can control the number of calls they allow outside their local network. In a CallManager network, CallManager can also control call admission. However, in a network that has multiple CallManager clusters or multiple gateways, it can help to have a central authority. One device (or group of devices) that tracks the available bandwidth for every cluster and location could make intelligent, dynamic call admission decisions. In an H.323 network, you can configure gatekeepers to perform that function. When using a gatekeeper, you divide your network into zones and then tell the gatekeeper the bandwidth allowed for calls within and between zones. Gateways are configured to contact the gatekeeper before allowing a call to be set up. The gatekeeper tracks the number of calls for each zone and does not allow calls that exceed the maximum bandwidth.

On the gateways, under the VoIP dial peer, configure the command **session target ras**. That command tells the gateway to send a Registration, Admission, and Status (RAS) message to the gatekeeper before continuing the call setup for that dial peer. You can configure a backup to the gatekeeper by using preference values with your dial peers. Set the primary dial peer with a session target of RAS so that in normal circumstances, the gatekeeper can make CAC decisions. Use preference to set a secondary dial peer pointing to the PSTN or some other local link.

For more detailed information on this topic, see Chapter 16, "Deploying Gatekeepers."

Resource Availability Indication

Resource Availability Indication (RAI) also involves RAS messages between an H.323 gateway and gatekeeper, but in this case, it is the gateway that makes the CAC decision. The gateway sends a RAS message to its gatekeeper indicating whether it is able to accept incoming calls. RAI is useful in networks in which the gateway connects to a PBX or the PSTN via PRI circuits and processes incoming called numbers that would need to be routed out that PBX or PSTN link. RAI uses a high and a low threshold value based on the digital signal processor (DSP) and DS0 use within the gateway. When resource usage reaches the high threshold, the gateway sends an "AlmostOutOfResources" message to the gatekeeper. The gatekeeper stops sending calls for those phone numbers to that gateway. When usage falls below the low threshold value, the gateway notifies its gatekeeper, and calls are routed to that gateway once again.

For more detailed information on this topic, see Chapter 16.

Resource Reservation Protocol

RSVP is also a resource-based CAC mechanism. It is an Internet Engineering Task Force (IETF) protocol that is unique among CAC mechanisms in that it can reserve end-to-end resources for the length of the call. Other mechanisms might measure network resources at the time the call is initiated, but they cannot guarantee that conditions will remain acceptable during the call. When using RSVP, each RSVP-enabled router along the call path reserves bandwidth and the requested QoS for the duration of that call. Reservations are made on a flow-by-flow basis, so each call has its own reservation. If any router along the path cannot reserve the requested resources, the originating gateway or CallManager can reroute the call or send it as unreserved traffic.

RSVP is typically used in networks that have limited bandwidth and frequent congestion. It is most appropriate for traffic that cannot tolerate much delay or packet loss, such as voice and video, although it can be used for data, too. One drawback to RSVP is that the reservation process causes some delay in call setup. To minimize this, include RSVP control messages in your QoS configuration to ensure bandwidth and prioritized handling for them.

Some applications and devices are RSVP aware, and initiate their own reservations. More typically, either the gateways or CallManager controls the reservation process, acting in proxy for the devices to create a reserved path.

Although RSVP acts independently of the call signaling protocol, the traditional way to use it for CAC requires configuration of VoIP dial peers. Thus, traditional gateway-controlled RSVP can be used only with H.323 and SIP gateways, which require dial peers. H.323 and SIP gateways must know to delay call setup until reservations have been made; extensions to those protocols have been created to allow this. Network routers should be running at least Cisco IOS 12.1(5)T to implement gateway-controlled RSVP for H.323 traffic and 12.2(8)T for SIP. RSVP operates with both IPv4 and IPv6.

In CallManager 5.0, Cisco introduced an RSVP agent that allows RSVP to be used with all gateway protocols, including Media Gateway Control Protocol (MGCP). With RSVP agent, CallManager initiates the reservations. When a call needs a reservation to be created, CallManager instructs the RSVP agent on the gateway to begin the reservation process. The gateway reports back to the CallManager on the success or failure of the reservation, and CallManager then allows or disallows the call. This process is described in the section "CallManager-Controlled RSVP with RSVP Agent." RSVP agent requires CallManager version 5.0 or above. It is supported in router Cisco IOS version 12.4(6)T or above on Cisco 2600XM, 2691, 2800, 3700, and 3800 routers.

Gateway-Controlled RSVP

Figure 11-2 shows how a reservation is created between two gateways when using traditional gateway-controlled RSVP. Keep in mind that this process happens in both directions. Reservations are made per flow; a flow is identified in RSVP by a destination IP address, protocol ID, and destination port. One reservation is made from terminating to originating gateway, and another reservation is made from originating to terminating gateway.

In Figure 11-2, both endpoints are IP phones that are not RSVP aware.

Figure 11-2 *RSVP Reservation Process*

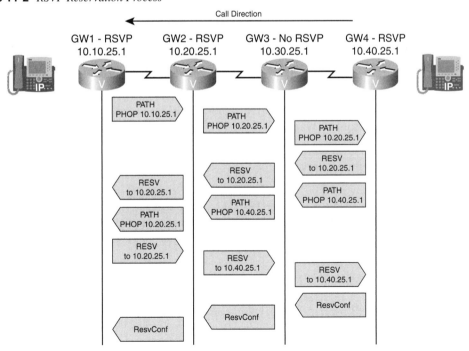

The RSVP portion of call setup proceeds as follows:

1 A phone behind GW4 initiates an H.323 call to a phone behind GW1. When the terminating gateway, GW1, receives the call setup information, it sends an RSVP PATH message toward the IP address of the originating gateway. It does this before it tells the phone to ring. PATH messages contain the IP address of the previous hop (PHOP) so that return messages can follow the same path back. They also describe the bandwidth and QoS needs of the call traffic.

2 The next hop router, GW2, is configured with RSVP. It records the previous hop information and forwards the PATH message. Notice that it inserts its IP address as the PHOP address. The destination address is still the remote gateway.

3 The third router, GW3, does not have RSVP configured. The PATH message looks just like a normal IP packet to this router, and it routes the message untouched toward the destination, just as it does any IP packet.

4 The fourth router, GW4, is the originating gateway. When it receives the PATH, it sends an RESV message to the previous hop address listed in the PATH message. This RESV message requests the needed QoS. If any router along the way does not have sufficient resources, it returns an error message and discards the RESV message. GW4 also initiates a PATH message toward GW1 to reserve resources in the other direction.

5 The RESV and PATH messages again look like normal IP packets to GW3, the non-RSVP router, so it simply routes the packets toward GW2. No resources are reserved on this gateway.

6 GW2 receives the RESV message and checks to see if it can supply the requested resources. If the check succeeds, it creates a reservation for that flow and then forwards the RESV message to the previous hop IP address listed in the PATH message it received earlier. When the other PATH message arrives, GW2 processes it and sends it to GW1.

7 When GW1 receives the RESV message, it knows that its reservation has succeeded. However, the reservation must succeed in each direction before it can continue call setup.

   GW1 responds to the second PATH message with an RESV message, which proceeds through the network as before. When GW4 receives the RESV message, resources have been reserved in both directions. GW4 responds with a ResvConf message, confirming the reservation.

8 Call setup has been delayed during the exchange of messages. When GW1 receives the ResvConf message, it knows that reservations have been made in both directions. Call setup can now proceed. RSVP then sends periodic refresh messages along the call path, enabling it to dynamically adjust to routing changes.

Configuring Gateway-Controlled RSVP

Before you configure RSVP, you need to decide how much bandwidth to allocate per flow and how much total bandwidth to allow RSVP to use, per interface. By default, you can reserve up to 75 percent of the interface bandwidth. Consider how much bandwidth is used per flow. This amount depends on the codec. By default, any flow can use up to the total reserved bandwidth, but this is configurable. Consider the expected call volume through that interface to determine the total amount of bandwidth to reserve. Remember to allow bandwidth for any other applications that use that interface.

You must configure RSVP on each router that will create reservations. It is enabled at the interface configuration mode with the **ip rsvp bandwidth** [*total-kbps*] [*single-flow-kbps*] command. If you do not specify the total bandwidth to reserve, the router reserves 75 percent of the interface bandwidth. If no flow value is specified, any flow can reserve the entire bandwidth.

To set the DSCP value for RSVP control messages, use the **ip rsvp signalling dscp** {*dscp-value*} interface command.

Synchronization between RSVP and call setup is enabled by default. If it has been disabled, the command to enable it is **call rsvp-sync**.

For RSVP to act as a CAC mechanism, also configure the requested and acceptable QoS parameters under any dial peers that RSVP will use. The **req-qos** command instructs the gateway to initiate an RSVP reservation for a call to that dial peer and specifies the type of QoS to request. The **acc-qos** command determines how strict the CAC must be. This must be done on both the originating and terminating gateways. It is recommended that both the requested and acceptable QoS be set to **guaranteed-delay**. The **guaranteed-delay** option tells RSVP to reserve bandwidth and to guarantee a minimum bit rate and priority treatment. The commands, under dial-peer configuration mode, are **req-qos guaranteed-delay** and **acc-qos guaranteed-delay**.

Example 11-9 shows a basic RSVP configuration. RSVP is enabled, and its signaling is marked with DSCP 31 under the interface configuration mode. The guaranteed delay commands are given under the outgoing dial peer.

Example 11-9 *Configuring Basic RSVP*

```
!Configure RSVP on the outgoing interface
Shanghai-GW(config)#int s2/0
Shanghai-GW(config-if)#bandwidth 1544
Shanghai-GW(config-if)#ip rsvp bandwidth 400 40
Shanghai-GW(config-if)#ip rsvp signalling dscp 31
!
!Configure QoS on the outgoing dial peer
Shanghai-GW(config-if)#dial-peer voice 3400 voip
Shanghai-GW(config-dial-peer)#req-qos guaranteed-delay
Shanghai-GW(config-dial-peer)#acc-qos guaranteed-delay
```

A useful command to verify your RSVP configuration is **show ip rsvp interface** [**detail**]. Example 11-10 shows the output from this command, based on the configuration in Example 11-9. After RSVP is working within your network, you can observe the reservations made with the **show ip rsvp installed detail** command.

Example 11-10   *Verifying RSVP Configuration*

```
Shanghai-GW#show ip rsvp interface detail
Se0/0:
   Bandwidth:
     Curr allocated: 0 bits/sec
     Max. allowed (total): 400K bits/sec
     Max. allowed (per flow): 40K bits/sec
     Max. allowed for LSP tunnels using sub-pools: 0 bits/sec
     Set aside by policy (total): 0 bits/sec
   Admission Control:
     Header Compression methods supported:
        rtp (36 bytes-saved), udp (20 bytes-saved)
   Traffic Control:
     RSVP Data Packet Classification is OFF
     RSVP resource provider is: none
   Signalling:
     DSCP value used in RSVP msgs: 0x1F
     Number of refresh intervals to enforce blockade state: 4
     Number of missed refresh messages: 4
     Refresh interval: 30
   Authentication: disabled
```

CallManager-Controlled RSVP with RSVP Agent

Cisco CallManager can use the RSVP agent feature on its gateways to provide CAC and reserve resources for calls. Resource reservation policies are configured on CallManager, and the RSVP agent on the gateway carries out these policies. The agent is a transcoding or media termination point (MTP) resource that is configured on the gateway and registered with CallManager as RSVP capable. It communicates with CallManager using Skinny Client Control Protocol (SCCP), which you must enable on the gateway.

RSVP agent provides some additional functionality over traditional gateway-controlled RSVP, including the following:

- **Multilevel precedence and preemption (MLPP)**—With MLPP, high-priority calls can preempt low-priority calls if bandwidth is unavailable.

- **Application ID**—You can create separate bandwidth pools within the total bandwidth that is allocated to RSVP. Then you can allocate traffic to those pools by application, based on an application ID. You can give video and voice traffic different application IDs and assign them to different bandwidth pools. This prevents video from using all the reservable bandwidth.

- **Multiprotocol support**—Because CallManager is controlling the reservation policies, no additional configuration of dial peers is needed. Thus, MGCP gateways are supported in addition to SIP and H.323.

- **Interoperability with location-based CAC**—You can enable RSVP use on CallManager by location, thus allowing its use for some locations but not others.

- **Site awareness**—If multiple calls are made to the same site, only one RSVP connection is made to that site.

Cisco RSVP agent is useful only for intracluster calls, because the same CallManager cluster must be able to control the RSVP agent on the gateway at each end of the call. You can use a Cisco IP-to-IP gateway to reserve bandwidth for intercluster calls. You cannot use the RSVP agent with device mobility, and it is not supported in Cisco CallManager Express (CME). See Cisco.com for a current list of RSVP agent capabilities.

The same router can be both an RSVP agent and a media gateway. Some overhead is involved with RSVP, however, and in a busy network you might want to use dedicated RSVP agent routers.

NOTE   Because RSVP reservations are made before media negotiation is done, Cisco CallManager assumes a worst-case per-flow bandwidth and asks for more bandwidth than might actually be needed. This is to prevent a post-ring failure caused by adjusting the bandwidth upward. The amount is adjusted down after media negotiation is complete. In a CallManager network, allow 96 Kbps for G.711 calls and 40 Kbps for G.729 calls when planning bandwidth.

Call flow with RSVP agents adds the SCCP communication between CallManager and the gateway. Router-to-router communication is still the same as in the traditional RSVP call flow, and reservations can be made on each router in the path. Figure 11-3 illustrates protocols that you might use in a CallManager network with RSVP agent. Both the SCCP phone and the RSVP agents on the gateways exchange SCCP messages with CallManager. The SIP phone exchanges SIP messages with CallManager. Each gateway also communicates with CallManager using its call control protocol—MGCP and SIP in Figure 11-3. The two gateways establish RSVP reservations across the IP WAN using the process shown in Figure 11-2. After the call is established, the two phones use RTP for the call media.

Figure 11-3 *Using RSVP Agent with Cisco CallManager*

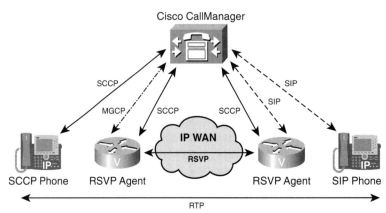

Configuring RSVP Agent

Configuration is needed both on the gateway and CallManager. This section describes the gateway configuration. Example 11-11 shows a gateway configuration for RSVP agent. Perform the following steps to configure a gateway to use RSVP agent:

Step 1 **Enable SCCP**—CallManager uses SCCP to communicate with the RSVP agent on the gateway, so you must enable it on the router and bind it to the interface used to reach CallManager. You must also specify the IP addresses or DNS names of the CallManagers. Table 11-5 shows these commands.

Table 11-5 *Enabling SCCP for RSVP Agent*

Command	Description
For routers with NM-HDV modules: **sccp ccm** {*ip-address* | *dns*} **priority** *priority* [**port** *port-number*] [**version** *version-number*]	Gives the IP address or DNS name of a CallManager and its priority if multiple CallManagers exist. It optionally specifies a port number to use and the CallManager version. For RSVP agent, use **version 5.0.1**. Repeat this command for each CallManager server.
For all other routers: **sccp ccm** {*ip-address* | *dns*} **identifier** *identifier-number* [**port** *port-number*] [**version** *version-number*]	Gives the IP address or DNS name of a CallManager and a number to identify it if multiple CallManagers exist. It optionally specifies a port number to use and the CallManager version. For RSVP agent, use **version 5.0.1**. Repeat this command for each CallManager server.

Table 11-5   *Enabling SCCP for RSVP Agent (Continued)*

Command	Description
sccp local *interface*	Identifies the interface used to communicate with CallManager. You can list only one interface.
sccp	Enables SCCP and its associated applications on the router.
show sccp	Verifies the SCCP configuration and registration with CallManager.

Step 2   **Configure DSP resource pooling**—Enable DSP farm services on any voice cards with DSP resources that you will use for transcoding or MTPs. Under voice card configuration mode, use the **dspfarm** command.

Step 3   **Configure transcoding or MTP resources**—You must configure transcoding or MTP resources on the gateway. This involves creating a DSP farm profile and associating the SCCP application with it. A transcode profile is needed when more than one codec is used. An MTP profile is configured for calls that use the same codec end to end. Table 11-6 shows these commands.

Table 11-6   *Enabling Transcoding and MTP for RSVP Agent*

Command	Description
dspfarm profile *profile-identifier* {**mtp** | **transcode**}	Creates either an MTP or transcoder DSP farm profile. You can have multiple profiles; each needs a unique identifier number.
associate application sccp	Associates SCCP with this DSP farm profile, enabling it to use SCCP to communicate with CallManager.
codec {*codec-type* | **pass-through**}	Codec passthrough is required for RSVP agent. This causes the media stream to be processed using a software MTP regardless of whether it is video or voice, even if it is a transcode profile. Other codec types can also be configured. An MTP profile supports only one codec in addition to passthrough.
In a transcode profile: **maximum sessions** *number* In an MTP profile: **maximum sessions** {**hardware** | **software**} *number*	Configures the maximum number of sessions allowed for this profile. In an MTP profile, you must specify hardware or software sessions separately. Use **hardware** when the session uses one codec but different packetization periods.
rsvp	Enables the DSP farm profile to support RSVP.

continues

Table 11-6 *Enabling Transcoding and MTP for RSVP Agent (Continued)*

Command	Description
no shut	Activates the DSP farm profile.
show dspfarm {profile *number* | **all}**	Verifies the DSP farm configuration, either for one profile or all of them.

Step 4 **Associate the DSP farm profiles with a CallManager group**—Create a CallManager group, assign CallManager servers to it, and associate DSP farm profiles with the group. Table 11-7 shows these commands.

Table 11-7 *Associating a DSP Farm Profile with a CallManager Group*

Command	Description
sccp ccm group *group-number*	Creates a CallManager group and assigns an identifying number to it.
associate ccm *identifier-number* **priority** *priority-number*	Associates one of the CallManagers configured in Step 1 with this CallManager group, and prioritizes the order in which it will be used. Repeat this command for each server in the group.
associate profile *profile-identifier* **register** *device-name*	Associates a profile configured in Step 3 with this group. This allows CallManagers in the group to control DSP resources. Use the profile number previously configured and the device name configured in CallManager for this MTP or transcoding resource. Repeat this command for each profile that is associated with the group.
bind interface *interface*	(Optional) Specifies the interface used for all calls that are associated with this profile. If no interface is listed, the router selects it.
show sccp ccm group [*group-number*]	Verifies the CallManager group configuration.

Step 5 **Enable RSVP on interfaces**—Enable RSVP on all the gateway interfaces that will participate in making reservations. Unlike gateway-controlled RSVP, the reservable bandwidth does not need to be specified, because CallManager controls it. Use the **ip rsvp bandwidth** interface command.

Step 6 **Enable call preemption if desired**—Enable this if you would like higher-priority calls to be able to preempt lower-priority calls when all the available bandwidth is reserved. Use the **ip rsvp policy preempt** global command.

The previous commands are demonstrated in Example 11-11, which shows a gateway that is configured for RSVP agent. The gateway has a primary and a backup CallManager in addition to MTP and transcode DSP farm profiles, and it is using interface Gi0/0 to communicate with CallManager.

Example 11-11   *Configuring a Gateway for RSVP Agent*

```
!Configure SCCP
VG3(config)#sccp ccm 10.6.2.1 identifier 1 version 5.0.1
VG3(config)#sccp ccm 10.6.2.2 identifier 2 version 5.0.1
VG3(config)#sccp local gi0/0
VG3(config)#sccp
!
!Configure the voice card for DSP farm
VG3(config)#voice-card 1
VG3(config-voicecard)#dspfarm
!
!Configure DSP farms
VG3(config)#dspfarm profile 1 mtp
VG3(config-dspfarm-profile)#associate application sccp
VG3(config-dspfarm-profile)#codec pass-through
VG3(config-dspfarm-profile)#maximum sessions software 10
VG3(config-dspfarm-profile)#rsvp
VG3(config-dspfarm-profile)#no shut
!
VG3(config)#dspfarm profile 2 transcode
VG3(config-dspfarm-profile)#associate application sccp
VG3(config-dspfarm-profile)#codec g711ulaw
VG3(config-dspfarm-profile)#codec g729ar8
VG3(config-dspfarm-profile)#codec pass-through
VG3(config-dspfarm-profile)#maximum sessions 5
VG3(config-dspfarm-profile)#rsvp
VG3(config-dspfarm-profile)#no shut
!
!Create a CallManager group and associate the profiles with it
VG3(config)#sccp ccm group 1
VG3(config-sccp-ccm)#bind interface gi0/0
VG3(config-sccp-ccm)#associate ccm 1 priority 1
VG3(config-sccp-ccm)#associate ccm 2 priority 2
VG3(config-sccp-ccm)#associate profile 1 register mtp_1
VG3(config-sccp-ccm)#associate profile 2 register xcoder_1
!
!Enable RSVP on each interface that will create reservations
VG3(config)#interface gi0/0
VG3(config-if)#ip rsvp bandwidth
!
!Enable call preemption
VG3(config)#ip rsvp policy preempt
```

You must also configure the CallManager Publisher to use RSVP. Configure RSVP policies for locations or for the cluster as a whole. To use RSVP, the two call endpoints must belong to different locations. Create media resource groups, and add any transcoders or MTPs that will be registered as an RSVP agent. Then configure a media resource group list (MRGL) and assign a media resource group to the list. Assign the MRGL to a device pool. See Cisco.com for complete information on configuring Cisco CallManager for RSVP agent.

RSVP and the IntServ/DiffServ Model

RSVP reserves resources, but it is up to each router to implement the appropriate QoS techniques to deliver those resources. Low-latency queuing (LLQ) is the QoS mechanism typically used for voice, putting voice in a priority queue with guaranteed but policed bandwidth. This is part of the DiffServ model of QoS. However, RSVP has its own set of queues that it puts reserved traffic into by default. These queues have a low weight, but they are not prioritized. This is part of the IntServ model of QoS. What is needed is a way to put reserved voice traffic into the LLQ—the IntServ/DiffServ model.

By default, RSVP uses weighted fair queuing (WFQ) to provide its QoS. When using LLQ with class-based weighted fair queuing (CBWFQ), disable the RSVP use of WFQ with the **ip rsvp resource-provider none** interface command. Also, by default, RSVP attempts to process every packet—not just provide CAC. Turn this off with the **ip rsvp data-packet classification none** interface command. Then you can configure the LLQ and CBWFQ as usual. RSVP reserves bandwidth for voice calls, and the QoS processes of the gateway place that voice traffic into the priority queue. In Example 11-10, note under the Traffic Control section that these two commands have been given.

When you are using LLQ, the priority queue size includes Layer 2 overhead. The RSVP bandwidth statement does not take Layer 2 overhead into consideration. Therefore, when you are using both LLQ and RSVP, set the RSVP bandwidth equal to the priority queue minus the Layer 2 overhead. You can find instructions for configuring LLQ, CBWFQ, and RSVP on Cisco.com in the "Quality of Service Solutions Configuration Guide" and in Cisco IOS Command Reference Guides. See the case study at the end of this chapter for an example of using RSVP with LLQ.

Incorporating RSVP into the Voice Network

It is not necessary to configure RSVP on every router within your enterprise. Because RSVP messages are passed through non-RSVP-enabled routers, you can use RSVP selectively. You might enable it in sections of the network that are prone to congestion, such as areas with low bandwidth. In the core of the network, where bandwidth is higher, you might rely on LLQ/CBWFQ to handle voice and video traffic. This helps in scaling RSVP, cutting down on the number of routers that must track each session and be involved in RSVP messaging.

Figure 11-4 shows a network with remote sites connecting to a core IP WAN. The core might be enterprise owned, or it might, for example, be a Multiprotocol Label Switching (MPLS) network of the service provider. All the remote site links are T1 and carry both voice and data. All WAN interfaces of the remote site routers are configured for RSVP. Bandwidth is reserved when sites place calls between each other. When these calls go across the core IP WAN, reservations are made on the WAN interfaces of the edge routers, and CAC is done based on resources that are available on the remote site routers. The core does not participate in RSVP, so you must use other means of QoS in that part of the network.

Figure 11-4 *Using RSVP in a Large Network*

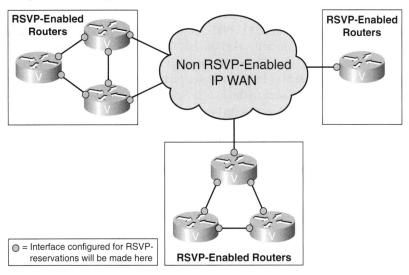

POTS-to-POTS Call Routing Considerations

Occasionally, you must route calls between POTS dial peers. CAC might cause this, such as when a call from a PBX is denied admission to the WAN and sent back to the PBX. Or a call from an analog phone might be routed over the PSTN. The ability to switch calls between POTS dial peers is enabled by default on Cisco gateways.

Many of the CAC mechanisms that are described in this chapter use *hairpinning,* or *tromboning*, in which a call both enters and exits on the same interface. Suppose that a router doing toll bypass receives an analog call from its PBX. This call is matched to an incoming POTS dial peer. Typically the analog call is terminated, regenerated as a VoIP call, and then routed out a VoIP dial peer. However, the CAC configuration of the gateway might cause the call to be rejected for sending over the IP network. When a call is rejected, you can redirect (or hairpin) it back to the PBX. Both legs of the call thus traverse the same router interface. The PBX then looks for an alternate route, such as out to the PSTN.

A hairpinned POTS call is terminated on the gateway and then routed out another POTS dial peer as a new call leg. When this happens, DSPs are assigned to the incoming leg of the POTS call and also to the outgoing (hairpinned) leg. These DSP resources stay assigned for the duration of the call; thus, each hairpinned call doubles the DSP usage.

Routing between ISDN POTS dial peers can use TDM switching, but this must be done across a bus that supports it. With TDM switching, DSP resources are assigned when the call is received, but media DSPs are dropped after the call is switched to another POTS port. No DSP is needed for the media because an internal TDM connection is made between the incoming and outgoing ports on the TDM bus. This is an advantage with nonvoice calls, such as modem, fax, and video.

Older routers, such as the 1700, 2600, 3600, and 3700 series, support TDM switching only between ports on certain network modules. Both legs of the call must stay on the same module. Cisco Integrated Services Routers (ISR) support TDM switching across the backplane; thus, POTS-to-POTS calls can be routed between different network modules. Other Cisco gateways, such as the Access Server (AS) and Integrated Access Device (IAD) lines, also support TDM switching across their backplane, and thus, can route POTS calls between interfaces. These are typically used in a service provider environment.

Modules that support intramodule TDM switching include these:

- NM-HDV
- NM-HDV2
- NM-HDV2-1T1/E1
- NM-HDV2-2T1/E1
- NM-HD-1V/2V/2VE
- EVM-HD-8FXS/DID
- AIM-VOICE-30
- VWIC

ISRs allow intermodule TDM call routing between the following modules:

- VWIC
- NM-HDV2
- NM-HD-1V/2V/2VE
- EVM-HD-8FXS/DID

You must synchronize clocking when you are switching between these ports and modules. Chapter 7, "Connecting to PBXs," describes how to do this.

Case Study: Implementing Gateway-Controlled RSVP

The link between the New York and the Leeds office tends to be fairly congested, so the decision is made to implement RSVP between the two gateways. In addition, LLQ and

CVWFQ are applied to the IP WAN interface. RSVP signaling is marked with DSCP 31 and is given a share of the interface bandwidth.

Example 11-12 shows the configuration of the New York gateway to implement RSVP and add the desired queueing. Only the New York router configuration is shown, but you must configure the Leeds router similarly. Use the same required and acceptable QoS dial peer configuration on both gateways. The LLQ and CBWFQ configuration should be the same on both routers, also.

Example 11-12   *Case Study: Configuring RSVP and LLQ for Voice*

```
!Identifies RTP traffic
NY-GW1(config)#ip access-list extended RTP
NY-GW1(config-ext-nacl)#permit udp any any range 16383 32767
NY-GW1(config-ext-nacl)#permit udp any range 16383 32767 any
!
!Identifies H.323 signaling traffic
NY-GW1(config-ext-nacl)#ip access-list extended H323
NY-GW1(config-ext-nacl)#permit tcp any eq 1720 any
NY-GW1(config-ext-nacl)#permit tcp any any eq 1720
!
!
!Creates a class for voice media matching ACL RTP
NY-GW1(config-ext-nacl)#class-map match-all VOIP-Media
NY-GW1(config-cmap)#match access-group name RTP
!
!Creates a class for voice signaling matching ACL H323
NY-GW1(config-cmap)#class-map match-all VOIP-Signal
NY-GW1(config-cmap)#match access-group name H323
!
!Creates a class for RSVP signaling matching DSCP configured on interface S0/0
NY-GW1(config)#class-map RSVP-Signal
NY-GW1(config-cmap)#match dscp 31
!
!Creates a policy for LLQ and CBWFQ
NY-GW1(config-cmap)#policy-map RSVP
NY-GW1(config-pmap)#class VOIP-Media
NY-GW1(config-pmap-c)#priority percent 30
NY-GW1(config-pmap-c)#class VOIP-Signal
NY-GW1(config-pmap-c)#bandwidth percent 5
NY-GW1(config-pmap-c)#class RSVP-Signal
NY-GW1(config-pmap-c)#bandwidth percent 5
NY-GW1(config-pmap-c)#class class-default
NY-GW1(config-pmap-c)#fair-queue
NY-GW1(config-pmap-c)#random-detect
!
!Configures the interface for RSVP and applies the policy
NY-GW1(config-pmap-c)#int s0/0
NY-GW1(config-if)#ip rsvp bandwidth 400 40
NY-GW1(config-if)#ip rsvp resource-provider none
NY-GW1(config-if)#ip rsvp data-packet classification none
NY-GW1(config-if)#ip rsvp signalling dscp 31
NY-GW1(config-if)#service-policy output RSVP
```

continues

Example 11-12 *Case Study: Configuring RSVP and LLQ for Voice (Continued)*

```
!
!Configures the dial peer to Leeds for RSVP
NY-GW1(config-if)#dial-peer voice 50300 voip
NY-GW1(config-dial-peer)#destination-pattern 50[34]..
NY-GW1(config-dial-peer)#session target ipv4:10.40.25.1
NY-GW1(config-dial-peer)#req-qos guaranteed-delay
NY-GW1(config-dial-peer)#acc-qos guaranteed-delay
NY-GW1(config-dial-peer)#forward-digits 4
```

Review Questions

1 Name three types of CAC.

2 What CAC mechanism would you use to guarantee enough bandwidth for the duration of a call?

3 How are dial peers configured to be part of the same hunt group?

4 What is the difference between LVBO and AVBO?

5 Which CAC mechanism, other than AVBO, uses probes in making its call admission decision?

6 What is TEHO used for, and what are two issues with its use?

7 What are some differences between gateway-controlled RSVP and CallManager-controlled RSVP?

8 Given the following dial peers, which would the gateway use first? Second? Third?

dial-peer voice 2200 voip

preference 1

destination-pattern 2200

session target ipv4:10.20.25.1

dial-peer voice 2201 voip

destination-pattern 2200

session target ipv4:10.20.26.2

dial-peer voice 2202 voip

preference 4

destination-pattern 2200

session target ipv4:10.20.27.3

CHAPTER 12

Configuring Class of Restrictions

Chapter 9, "Dial Plans," listed the five components of a dial plan. This chapter focuses on implementing calling privileges. The calling privileges component of building a dial plan in a voice gateway is accomplished using Class of Restrictions (COR). COR is typically used in conjunction with Survivable Remote Site Telephony (SRST) or CallManager Express, but you can apply it to any dial peer on a voice gateway to restrict access.

This chapter helps you to do the following:

- Understand how COR operates.
- Use COR to restrict outbound and inbound calls in an SRST gateway.
- Use COR to restrict outbound and inbound calls in a CallManager Express gateway.
- Describe best practices for implementing COR.

COR Overview

Calling privileges describe the types of calls that a phone, or a class of phones, is able to place. For example, you might not want your lobby phones to be able to place long-distance calls, or you might want to restrict some employees from placing international calls. The call processing system typically controls these types of restrictions. When the router is the call processing system, running either SRST or CallManager Express, you implement calling privileges using COR.

COR is required only when you want to restrict some phones from making certain types of calls while allowing other phones to place those calls. If you do not want to allow any phones to call 1-900 "premium" calls in the United States, you can build your dial peers to prevent these calls. This is much simpler than implementing COR to restrict all phones from placing 1-900 calls.

COR is often described as a *lock and key mechanism*. Locks are assigned to dial peers using an outgoing COR list. Keys are assigned to dial peers using an incoming COR list. For a call to succeed, the inbound dial peer must have the key for each of the locks that is assigned to the outbound dial peer.

Assume that you want to allow users in Dept. A to make international calls, but users in Dept. B should not be allowed to call internationally. In that case, you would assign an

International outgoing COR list containing a lock called "International" to the outgoing dial peer. You would assign an incoming COR list that contains "International" (and possibly other types of calls) to the incoming dial peers associated with Dept. A. The incoming dial peers that are associated with Dept. B would not include "International." Figure 12-1 illustrates the concept of incoming and outgoing COR lists.

Figure 12-1 *Incoming and Outgoing COR Lists*

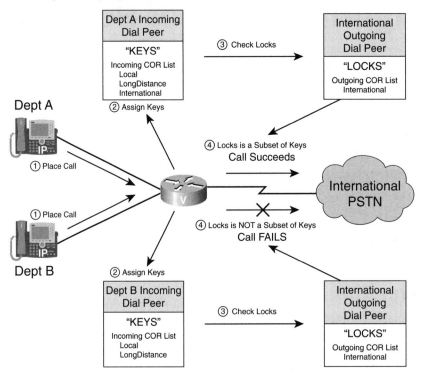

As always, some exceptions cause the lock and key analogy to break down. The most important exception is when no incoming COR list is assigned to the inbound dial peer. In this case, the call succeeds even if an outgoing COR list is assigned to the outbound dial peer.

COR Operation

Two definitions are critical to understanding COR operation. In mathematics, a *set* is a list of numbers or labels. A *subset* is a set whose members are wholly contained in another set. Applying these concepts makes understanding COR operation simple. Calls succeed as long as the outgoing COR list is a subset of the incoming COR list. Table 12-1 shows the relationship between incoming and outgoing COR lists.

Table 12-1   *COR Operation*

Incoming COR List	Outgoing COR List	Result
None	None	Call succeeds
None	Applied	Call succeeds
Applied	None	Call succeeds
Applied	Subset of incoming COR list	Call succeeds
Applied	Not a subset of incoming COR list	Call fails

NOTE   If either the incoming dial peer or the outgoing dial peer does not have a COR list applied, the call succeeds.

Implementing COR

The commands to implement COR are straightforward, but getting the logic correct takes some practice. Always remember that for the call to *fail*, both an incoming and an outgoing COR list must exist, and the outgoing COR list must be a *superset* of the incoming COR list.

Four steps are required to implement COR:

Step 1   Define COR labels using the **dial-peer cor custom name** *label* command.

This step is analogous to defining variables when writing a program. You are creating a series of placeholders to be used to create the COR logic.

The COR labels that you define here will be the members of the COR lists, or permissions groups, that you define in the next step. The labels define the types of calls that you can make. A typical set of labels includes local, long-distance, and international calls. The following example shows the creation of four labels: Local, LongDistance, Mobile, and International.

```
Leeds(config)#dial-peer cor custom
Leeds(config-dp-cor)#name Local
Leeds(config-dp-cor)#name LongDistance
Leeds(config-dp-cor)#name Mobile
Leeds(config-dp-cor)#name International
```

You need to define call types only if some phones will be restricted from making those calls. For example, if all phones should be able to call emergency services, you do not need to define a COR label for emergency calls, because you will not be restricting calls to this dial peer using an outgoing COR list.

Step 2   Build the permissions groups using the **dial-peer cor list** *list-name* **member** *label* command.

Because a call is restricted only when the outgoing COR list is not a subset of the incoming COR list, you have a great deal of flexibility in the way you build your permissions groups. However, this flexibility can make this step confusing. To keep your COR implementation simple and reproducible, you should follow these two guidelines:

— All outgoing COR lists should have a single member.

— Incoming COR lists should contain a member for each call type that the phone should be able to place.

If you follow these two rules, your COR implementation will be similar to Partitions and Calling Search Spaces in Cisco CallManager. The outgoing COR list is analogous to a partition. You place the outbound dial peer into a single permissions group just like you would assign a partition to a route pattern. The incoming COR list contains all the "partitions" that the inbound dial peer can call. This is analogous to assigning a calling search space to a device. This is especially useful in SRST mode because you can easily duplicate the calling privileges that Cisco CallManager grants. The following example shows how to build permission groups by defining outgoing and incoming COR lists. Notice that the outgoing lists have only one member, whereas the incoming ones might have several.

```
! OUTGOING COR LISTS
!
Leeds(config)#dial-peer cor list LocalCalls
Leeds(config-dp-corlist)#member Local
!
Leeds(config)#dial-peer cor list LDCalls
Leeds(config-dp-corlist)#member LongDistance
!
Leeds(config)#dial-peer cor list MobileCalls
Leeds(config-dp-corlist)#member Mobile
!
Leeds(config)#dial-peer cor list InternationalCalls
Leeds(config-dp-corlist)#member International
```

```
! INCOMING COR LISTS
!
```

```
Leeds(config)#dial-peer cor list LobbyPhones
Leeds(config-dp-corlist)#member Local
!
Leeds(config)#dial-peer cor list Employees
Leeds(config-dp-corlist)#member Local
Leeds(config-dp-corlist)#member Mobile
!
Leeds(config)#dial-peer cor list Managers
Leeds(config-dp-corlist)#member Local
Leeds(config-dp-corlist)#member Mobile
Leeds(config-dp-corlist)#member LongDistance
!
Leeds(config)#dial-peer cor list Executives
Leeds(config-dp-corlist)#member Local
Leeds(config-dp-corlist)#member Mobile
Leeds(config-dp-corlist)#member LongDistance
Leeds(config-dp-corlist)#member International
```

This configuration defines the four call types described in Step 1 (LocalCalls, LDCalls, MobileCalls, and InternationalCalls.) It also defines four COR lists that are used to group phones (LobbyPhones, Employees, Managers, and Executives) and states which type of calls each group is permitted to make.

Step 3 Apply COR lists to the outgoing dial peers using the **corlist outgoing** *list-name* command. Only one outgoing COR list is supported per dial peer.

The following example shows assignment of an outgoing COR list to each dial peer so that you can permit or deny calls appropriately. The example is based on a partial implementation of the UK National numbering plan that was described in Chapter 9.

```
Leeds(config)#dial-peer voice 7 pots
Leeds(config-dial-peer)#description Local calls within Leeds
Leeds(config-dial-peer)#destination-pattern [2-9]......
Leeds(config-dial-peer)#corlist outgoing LocalCalls
Leeds(config-dial-peer)#port 1/0/0:15
!
Leeds(config)#dial-peer voice 77 pots
Leeds(config-dial-peer)#description Calls to Mobile phones
Leeds(config-dial-peer)#destination-pattern 07[7-9]........
Leeds(config-dial-peer)#corlist outgoing MobileCalls
Leeds(config-dial-peer)#port 1/0/0:15
!
Leeds(config)#dial-peer voice 11 pots
Leeds(config-dial-peer)#description Long Distance Calls
Leeds(config-dial-peer)#destination-pattern 0[1-3]........
```

```
Leeds(config-dial-peer)#corlist outgoing LDCalls
Leeds(config-dial-peer)#port 1/0/0:15
!
Leeds(config)#dial-peer voice 100 pots
Leeds(config-dial-peer)#description International Calls
Leeds(config-dial-peer)#destination-pattern 00T
Leeds(config-dial-peer)#corlist outgoing InternationalCalls
Leeds(config-dial-peer)#port 1/0/0:15
```

Step 4 Apply COR lists to the incoming dial peers using the **corlist incoming** *list-name* command.

The method that you use to assign incoming COR lists depends on whether you are running Cisco CallManager Express, SRST or want to restrict inbound plain old telephone service (POTS) calls. Cisco CallManager Express and SRST are discussed in the next sections. You can assign an incoming COR list to any inbound POTS or Voice over IP (VoIP) dial peer. This allows you to control calling privileges for all call flows through a gateway. The following example demonstrates how to configure an analog phone that is connected to a Foreign Exchange Station (FXS) port to allow only local calling.

```
Leeds(config)#dial-peer voice 4001 pots
Leeds(config-dial-peer)#description Leeds Main Lobby Phone
Leeds(config-dial-peer)#destination-pattern 4001
Leeds(config-dial-peer)#corlist incoming LobbyPhone
Leeds(config-dial-peer)#port 2/0/0
```

Assigning COR Lists with SRST

When you are running SRST, you assign COR lists to your IP phones under the **call-manager fallback** configuration. You are limited to 20 incoming and 20 outgoing COR lists in SRST mode, but you can assign ranges of numbers to a list. If you plan your number assignments carefully, you should be able to accommodate all of your calling permissions.

You can also assign a default COR list in SRST mode. Any number that is not explicitly assigned to a COR list will be assigned to the default COR list. If the majority of your users will have the same privileges, you can assign them the same COR list even if the numbers are not consecutive.

In Example 12-1, IP phones with extensions 4005 through 4009 are assigned to the Employees COR list that is defined in Step 2 of the "Implementing COR" section, so employees will be able to make calls to local numbers and to mobile numbers. Extension 4010 is assigned to the Managers COR list created in Step 2 of the "Implementing COR" section, so managers will be able to make calls to local, mobile, and long-distance numbers. Extension 4050 is assigned to the Executives COR list, so executives will be able to make calls to local, mobile, long-distance, and international numbers. All other SRST phones will be assigned the default LobbyPhones COR list, which allows only local calls.

Example 12-1 *Assigning Incoming COR Lists in SRST*

```
Leeds(config)#call-manager-fallback
Leeds(config-cm-fallback)#ip source address 10.1.1.1 port 2000
Leeds(config-cm-fallback)#max-phones 8
Leeds(config-cm-fallback)#max-dns 16
Leeds(config-cm-fallback)#cor incoming LobbyPhones default
Leeds(config-cm-fallback)#cor incoming Employees 1 4005 - 4009
Leeds(config-cm-fallback)#cor incoming Managers 2 4010
Leeds(config-cm-fallback)#cor incoming Executives 3 4050
```

Assigning COR Lists with Cisco CallManager Express

In CallManager Express, you add an IP phone in two steps:

Step 1 You add the physical IP phone using the **ephone** configuration mode. In this step, you define the physical attributes of the phone so that it can register with CallManager Express. Each IP phone, or ephone, can have multiple lines.

Step 2 You define the lines using the **ephone-dn** configuration. In this step, you assign the extension that is associated with the line. In CallManager Express, lines, or extensions, are often referred to as *ephone-dns*.

When you are running Cisco CallManager Express, you assign incoming COR lists to your IP phones under the **ephone-dn** configuration. Because the COR lists are assigned to the ephone-dn, you can configure different calling privileges on a single IP phone. Example 12-2 illustrates how to assign incoming COR lists to ephone-dns.

Example 12-2 *Assigning Incoming COR Lists in Cisco CallManager Express*

```
Leeds(config)#ephone-dn 1
Leeds(config-ephone-dn)#description Leeds Admin
Leeds(config-ephone-dn)#number 4005
Leeds(config-ephone-dn)#cor incoming Employees
!
Leeds(config)#ephone-dn 2
Leeds(config-ephone-dn)#description Leeds Manager
Leeds(config-ephone-dn)#number 4010
Leeds(config-ephone-dn)#cor incoming Managers
!
Leeds(config)#ephone-dn 3
Leeds(config-ephone-dn)#description Leeds Executive
Leeds(config-ephone-dn)#number 4050
Leeds(config-ephone-dn)#cor incoming Executives
```

You can also assign outgoing COR lists to an ephone-dn to restrict who can call an IP phone. This requires additional labels to maintain compliance with the guidelines for configuring COR. The section "Restricting Inbound Calls" discusses this in more detail.

Assigning COR Lists to SIP Phones with CallManager Express

CallManager Express 3.4 added support for SIP phones. SIP phones are defined using the **voice register dn** *dn-tag* and the **voice register pool** *pool-tag* commands. You can assign incoming and outgoing COR lists under the **voice register pool configuration**. Assigning COR lists to SIP phones is similar to assigning COR lists to SRST phones. You can assign COR lists to a single SIP directory number or to a range of numbers using the following command:

cor {**incoming** | **outgoing**} *cor-list-name* {*cor-list-number starting-number* [- *ending-number]* | **default**}

Example 12-3 illustrates how to assign COR lists to SIP phones in CallManager Express.

Example 12-3 *Assigning COR Lists to SIP Phones in CallManager Express*

```
Leeds(config)#voice register pool 1
Leeds(config-register-pool)#id mac 000D.ED22.ED33
Leeds(config-register-pool)#type 7960-7940
Leeds(config-register-pool)#number 1 dn 1
Leeds(config-register-pool)#cor incoming Executives 1 4060
```

Restricting Inbound Calls

Restricting inbound calls adds a little complexity to your COR configuration. Reusing existing COR lists that are built to restrict outbound calls is usually possible, but your list names are not likely to be meaningful, and the logic might be difficult to follow.

In Example 12-4, calls from the PSTN to the lobby phone that is connected to port 2/0/0 are restricted. (Recall from Step 4 of the "Implementing COR" section that the lobby phone is an analog telephone.) Calls from the PSTN to IP phones are not restricted, as illustrated in Figure 12-2. To accomplish this, two new labels are added and assigned to a COR list with the same name:

- **InToLobby**—Assigned as an incoming COR list on the inbound dial peer from the PSTN

- **OutToLobby**—Assigned as an outgoing COR list on the dial peer that is associated with the lobby phone

Figure 12-2 *Restricting Inbound Calls*

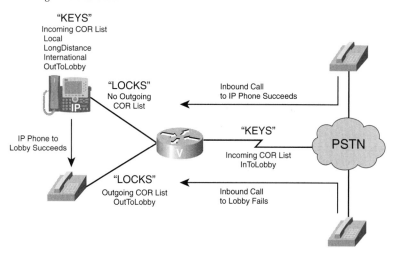

Example 12-4 *Restricting Inbound Calls*

```
Leeds(config)#dial-peer cor custom
Leeds(config-dp-cor)#name Local
Leeds(config-dp-cor)#name LongDistance
Leeds(config-dp-cor)#name Mobile
Leeds(config-dp-cor)#name International
! additional label for inbound COR list
Leeds(config-dp-cor)#name InToLobby
! additional label for outbound COR list
Leeds(config-dp-cor)#name OutToLobby
!
! INCOMING COR LISTS
Leeds(config)#dial-peer cor list LocalCalls
Leeds(config-dp-corlist)#member Local
!
Leeds(config)#dial-peer cor list LDCalls
Leeds(config-dp-corlist)#member LongDistance
!
Leeds(config)#dial-peer cor list MobileCalls
Leeds(config-dp-corlist)#member Mobile
!
Leeds(config)#dial-peer cor list InternationalCalls
Leeds(config-dp-corlist)#member International
!
Leeds(config)#dial-peer cor list LobbyPhones
Leeds(config-dp-corlist)#member Local
!
Leeds(config)#dial-peer cor list InToLobby
Leeds(config-dp-corlist)#member InToLobby
!
Leeds(config)#dial-peer cor list OutToLobby
```

continues

Example 12-4 *Restricting Inbound Calls (Continued)*

```
Leeds(config-dp-corlist)#member OutToLobby
!
! OUTGOING COR LISTS
!
Leeds(config)#dial-peer cor list Employees
Leeds(config-dp-corlist)#member Local
Leeds(config-dp-corlist)#member Mobile
Leeds(config-dp-corlist)#member OutToLobby
!
Leeds(config)#dial-peer cor list Managers
Leeds(config-dp-corlist)#member Local
Leeds(config-dp-corlist)#member Mobile
Leeds(config-dp-corlist)#member LongDistance
Leeds(config-dp-corlist)#member OutToLobby
!
Leeds(config)#dial-peer cor list Executives
Leeds(config-dp-corlist)#member Local
Leeds(config-dp-corlist)#member Mobile
Leeds(config-dp-corlist)#member International
Leeds(config-dp-corlist)#member OutToLobby
!
! ASSIGNING COR LISTS TO DIAL PEERS
!
Leeds(config)#dial-peer voice 1 pots
Leeds(config-dp-corlist)#description Inbound From PSTN
Leeds(config-dp-corlist)#incoming called-number .
Leeds(config-dp-corlist)#corlist incoming InToLobby
Leeds(config-dp-corlist)#port 1/0/0:15
!
Leeds(config)#dial-peer voice 4001 pots
Leeds(config-dp-corlist)#description Main Lobby Phone
Leeds(config-dp-corlist)#destination-pattern 4001
Leeds(config-dp-corlist)#corlist incoming LobbyPhone
Leeds(config-dp-corlist)#corlist outgoing OutToLobby
Leeds(config-dp-corlist)#port 2/0/0
```

Because the inbound COR list is not a subset of the outbound COR list, the goal of restricting PSTN calls to the lobby phone has been met. For the IP phones to call the lobby phone, you must add the OutToLobby label to the Employees, Managers, and Executives incoming COR lists. Because no outgoing COR lists are assigned to the IP phones, calls from the PSTN to IP phones will still be completed.

Case Study: Implementing COR for Miami

The gateway at the Miami location routes all toll calls to the New York gateway to take advantage of volume discounts, as shown in Figure 12-3. A recent audit has uncovered numerous calls to international numbers, and senior management has instructed you that only the Miami branch manager should be able to make international calls. The Cisco CallManager server was reconfigured to handle this restriction during normal operation. You must reconfigure the gateway with COR to maintain the restriction when its CallManager server is unavailable.

Figure 12-3 *Restricting International Calls from Miami*

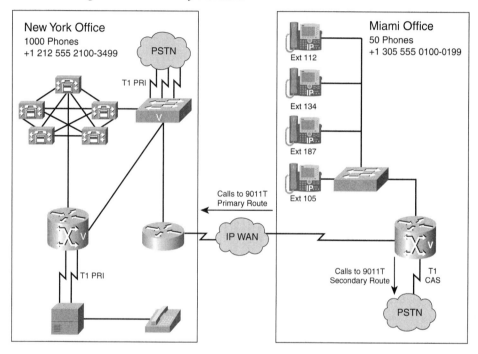

The Miami branch manager is assigned extension 150. The configuration in Example 12-5 allows only extension 150 to place international calls when the gateway is operating in SRST mode.

Example 12-5 *Configuring COR in the Miami Gateway*

```
Miami#show configuration
Building configuration...

Current configuration : 3077 bytes
!
! Unnecessary Output Omitted...
!
!
interface FastEthernet0/0
 no ip address
 duplex auto
 speed auto
```

continues

Example 12-5 *Configuring COR in the Miami Gateway (Continued)*

```
!
interface FastEthernet0/0.25
 encapsulation dot1Q 25
 ip address 10.10.25.1 255.255.255.0
!
interface FastEthernet0/0.50
 encapsulation dot1Q 50
 ip address 10.10.50.1 255.255.255.0
!
interface FastEthernet0/1
 no ip address
 shutdown
 duplex auto
 speed auto
!
controller T1 0/3/0
 framing esf
 linecode b8zs
 ds0-group 1 timeslots 1-12 type e&m-fgd
 ds0-group 2 timeslots 13-24 type fgd-eana
!
ip classless
!
!
!
voice-port 0/0/0
!
voice-port 0/0/1
!
voice-port 0/1/0
!
voice-port 0/1/1
!
voice-port 0/3/0:1
!
voice-port 0/3/0:2
!
!Define COR Labels
!
dial-peer cor custom
 name International
 name NoInternational
!
!Create Outgoing COR List
!
dial-peer cor list International
 member International
!
! Create Incoming COR List To DENY International Calls
!
dial-peer cor list Employee
 member NoInternational
```

Example 12-5 *Configuring COR in the Miami Gateway (Continued)*

```
!
! Create Incoming COR List To PERMIT International Calls
!
dial-peer cor list Manager
 member International
!
!
dial-peer voice 1 pots
 description Inbound Calls from PSTN
 incoming called-number .
 port 0/3/0:1
!
dial-peer voice 911 pots
 description Emergency Calls
 destination-pattern 911
 port 0/3/0:2
 prefix 911
!
dial-peer voice 9911 pots
 description Emergency Calls
 destination-pattern 9911
 port 0/3/0:2
 prefix 911
!
dial-peer voice 7 pots
 description Local Calls
 destination-pattern 9[2-9]......
 port 0/3/0:2
!
dial-peer voice 11 voip
 description Long Distance via NY Gateway
 destination-pattern 91[2-9]..[2-9]......
 session target ipv4:10.1.50.1
 preference 1
!
dial-peer voice 112 pots
 description Long Distance
 destination-pattern 91[2-9]..[2-9]......
 port 0/3/0:2
 prefix 1
 preferenece 2
!
dial-peer voice 9011 voip
 Description International Calls via NY Gateway
 corlist outgoing International
 destination-pattern 9011T
 session target ipv4:10.1.50.1
 preference 1

dial-peer voice 90112 pots
 description International Calls
 corlist outgoing International
```

continues

Example 12-5 *Configuring COR in the Miami Gateway (Continued)*

```
  destination-pattern 9011T
  port 0/3/0:2
  prefix 011
  preference 2
 !
dial-peer voice 900 pots
 description Block 1-900 Calls
 destination-pattern 91900.......
 !
dial-peer voice 976 pots
 description Block 1-976 Calls
 destination-pattern 91976....
 !
call-manager-fallback
 max-conferences 8
 ip source-address 10.10.50.1 port 2000
 max-ephones 64
 max-dn 192
 !
 ! Deny International Calls By Default
 !
  cor incoming Employee default
 !
 ! Permit International Calls for Ext 150
 !
  cor incoming Manager 1 150
 !
```

To restrict international calls to just the branch manager, you need to create an outgoing COR list and two incoming COR lists. The outgoing COR list is applied to the international dial peers and contains a single member, **International**. The branch manager is assigned an incoming COR list that also contains **International**. All other extensions are assigned an incoming COR list with **NoInternational**. You could also meet the requirements with a single incoming COR list assigned to all extensions except extension 150. If extension 150 is not assigned an incoming COR list, it is not restricted from outbound dial peers. To use this approach, you would have to assign the incoming COR list to each of the other extensions—you could not use the **default** keyword—which will most likely result in additional configuration and might exhaust the number of COR lists that you can assign. Explicitly defining the incoming COR lists also makes the configuration more intuitive to understand.

Review Questions

1 What conditions must exist for COR to restrict a call?

2 An outgoing COR list is analogous to which Cisco CallManager Class of Control setting?

3 An incoming COR list is analogous to which Cisco CallManager Class of Control setting?

4 How many COR lists can you assign in SRST?

CHAPTER 13

SRST and MGCP Gateway Fallback

One of the primary benefits of a centralized call processing model is the ability to provide remote sites with all the advanced calling features that were previously available only on large campuses. Survivable Remote Site Telephony (SRST) allows a Cisco voice gateway to handle call processing if the connection between the remote site and the central site is severed.

H.323 and Session Initiation Protocol (SIP) gateways are intrinsically resilient to network connectivity failures because the dial plan and call control are in the gateway, and the gateway is always in control of call-routing decisions. Media Gateway Control Protocol (MGCP) gateways are under the control of the call agent, and only the call agent can make dial-plan and call-routing decisions. Therefore, when the call agent and the MGCP gateway have a connectivity failure, you must use a fallback method to return call control to the gateway for the period of the failure. The MGCP Gateway Fallback feature allows the gateway to assume call control for MGCP-controlled voice ports. The gateway uses this feature in conjunction with SRST to allow the router to take care of IP phone and public switched telephone network (PSTN) gateway call routing during network failures.

This chapter helps you to do the following:

- Understand how SRST operates
- Understand the difference between SRST and MGCP Gateway Fallback
- Configure SRST and MGCP Gateway Fallback
- Implement your dial plan
- Configure SRST features
- Verify and troubleshoot SRST and MGCP Gateway Fallback

SRST Overview

During normal operation, Cisco IP phones exchange keepalive messages with their configured Cisco CallManagers. SRST is a licensed feature available on Cisco voice routers that allows Cisco IP phones to register with the gateway if these keepalive messages are lost. Cisco IP phones exchange the keepalive messages every 30 seconds by default. If three keepalive messages are missed, the IP phone initiates registration with the next device in its

CallManager list. If the IP phone cannot reach a Cisco CallManager, it initiates registration with the gateway.

When the gateway receives a registration request from an IP phone, it acknowledges the request and enters SRST mode. The IP phone then sends its configuration settings to the SRST gateway. The gateway uses these settings to configure virtual dial peers on the SRST gateway for each IP phone directory number (DN), as shown in Figure 13-1.

Figure 13-1 *SRST Registration Process*

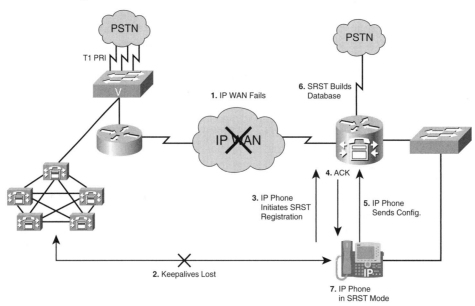

Fallback Time

The time that it takes for an IP phone to initiate registration with the SRST gateway depends on what caused the failover. Three scenarios can lead to the phone registering with the SRST gateway:

- **The CallManager process on the active CallManager is manually shut down**—This results in the TCP connection between the IP phone and the CallManager being closed. If no backup CallManager is available, the IP phone immediately attempts to register with the SRST gateway.

- **IP connectivity between the IP phone and the CallManager is broken**—When the IP phone sends its first keepalive after the TCP connection is broken, it sends TCP retries for 20 to 25 seconds. Then it initiates registration with the SRST gateway.

- **The CallManager process is locked**—In this case, the TCP connection is not closed. The IP phone waits for the keepalives to expire before initiating registration with the SRST gateway. This can take up to 90 seconds. This occurs when the server operating system (OS) is still functioning. If the entire server fails or is shut down, the TCP retries fail, as described in the previous bullet.

Other factors that can affect the fallback time include the number of CallManagers configured, the phone types used, and the number of phones registering with the SRST router.

NOTE   You can configure the keepalive timer in CallManager. This is a CallManager service parameter called StationKeepAliveInterval.

Restoral Time

By default, the IP phone waits for 120 seconds after the CallManager connection is restored before unregistering with the SRST gateway. This prevents a flapping link or other intermittent problem from causing the IP phone to repeatedly unregister and reregister with SRST.

You can adjust the time that the IP phone waits to register to CallManager. You configure this time in CallManager by using the **Device Pool>Connection Configuration Monitor** menu option.

Configuring SRST

You must configure SRST on the gateway and on CallManager. The CallManager configuration tells the IP phone that an SRST gateway is available. This is normally the tertiary device in the IP phone CallManager list.

Gateway Configuration

You enter SRST configuration mode by using the **call-manager-fallback** command. At a minimum, you must configure the source address and the number of e-phones and e-phone-dns for the SRST gateway to support. The source address is the IP address that the SRST gateway uses to communicate with the IP phones. Example 13-1 shows the initial SRST configuration.

Example 13-1 *Initial SRST Gateway Configuration*

```
Miami(config)#call-manager-fallback
Miami(config-cm-fallback)#ip source address 10.10.50.1
Miami(config-cm-fallback)#max-ephones 24
Miami(config-cm-fallback)#max-dn 48
```

The **max-ephones** command specifies how many IP phones can register with the SRST gateway. This value varies by router platform and the license you purchase. The **max-dn** command specifies how many virtual SRST voice ports are created. The number of DNs is limited by platform and memory; it is not limited to your license. This allows you to maintain multiple lines on your IP phones while in SRST mode. When you enter the **max-dn** command, the virtual voice ports are created immediately and reside in memory. These virtual voice ports are not saved in the config but are displayed when you enter a **show dial-peer voice** command, as shown in Example 13-2.

Example 13-2 *Virtual Dial Peers*

```
Miami#show dial-peer voice
VoiceEncapPeer20001
 peer type = voice, information type = voice,
 description = `',
 tag = 20001, destination-pattern = `',
 answer-address = `', preference=0,
 CLID Restriction = None
 CLID Network Number = `'
 CLID Second Number sent
 CLID Override RDNIS = disabled,
 source carrier-id = `',
 source trunk-group-label = `',
target trunk-group-label = `',
 numbering Type = `unknown'
 group = 20001, Admin state is up, Operation state is down,
 incoming called-number = `', connections/maximum = 0/unlimited,
 DTMF Relay = disabled,
 URI classes:
 Destination =
 huntstop = enabled,
 in bound application associated: 'DEFAULT'
 out bound application associated: ''
 dnis-map =
 permission :both
 incoming COR list:maximum capability
 outgoing COR list:minimum requirement
 Translation profile (Incoming):
 Translation profile (Outgoing):
 incoming call blocking:
 translation-profile = `'
 disconnect-cause = `no-service'
 advertise 0x40 capacity_update_timer 25 addrFamily 4 oldAddrFamily 4
 type = pots, prefix = `',
 forward-digits 0
```

Example 13-2 *Virtual Dial Peers (Continued)*

```
session-target = `', voice-port = `50/0/1',
direct-inward-dial = disabled,
digit_strip = enabled,
register E.164 number with H323 GK and/or SIP Registrar = TRUE
fax rate = system,   payload size =  20 bytes
supported-language = ''

Time elapsed since last clearing of voice call statistics never
Connect Time = 0, Charged Units = 0,
Successful Calls = 0, Failed Calls = 0, Incomplete Calls = 0
Accepted Calls = 0, Refused Calls = 0,
Last Disconnect Cause is "",
Last Disconnect Text is "",
Last Setup Time = 0.
```

To limit the impact on the gateway, you should determine how many lines you actually need rather than configure the maximum possible. You can also use the **limit-dn** command to limit the number of DNs that can register per IP phone type. For example, if your 7960s have four lines, you might choose just to have the primary DN register with the SRST router to conserve resources. Table 13-1 lists the maximum number of ephones and ephone-dns supported in currently available platforms. Verify these numbers on Cisco.com, because they might change with new Cisco IOS versions or increases in router CPU or memory capabilities.

Table 13-1 *Gateway SRST Support*

Router Platform	Max Ephones	Max Ephone-dns
1751-V	24	144
1760, 1760-V	24	144
2600XM	36	144
2650XM, 2651XM	48	192
2691	72	288
2801	24	256
2811	36	144
2821	48	192
2851	96	288
3725	144	960
3745	480	960
3825	336	960
3845	720	960
CMM	480	800

CallManager Configuration

You must specifically configure an IP phone with an SRST reference for it to attempt to register with a gateway. You configure the SRST reference in the device pool. In most implementations, the SRST gateway is also the default gateway for the IP phones. In this situation, you can select **Use Default Gateway** in the device pool configuration. Figure 13-2 shows the device pool configuration for the Miami phones.

Figure 13-2 *Configuring SRST Reference to Use Default Gateway*

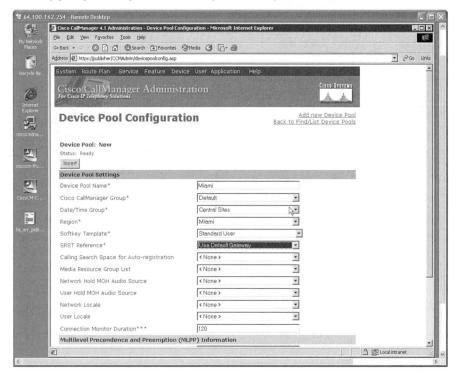

If the SRST gateway is not the default gateway for the IP phones, you must create an SRST reference that contains the IP address of the SRST gateway. You do this under the **System>SRST** menu option. Figure 13-3 illustrates an SRST reference configuration.

If the number of IP phones at a remote site exceeds the capability of the SRST gateway, you can control which IP phones register by creating two device pools for the site. Configure one device pool with an appropriate SRST reference, and assign it to the IP phones that should register with the SRST gateway. Configure a second device pool with the SRST reference set to Disable. This device pool is assigned to IP phones that are not business critical, such as break room or conference room phones.

Figure 13-3 *Creating an SRST Reference*

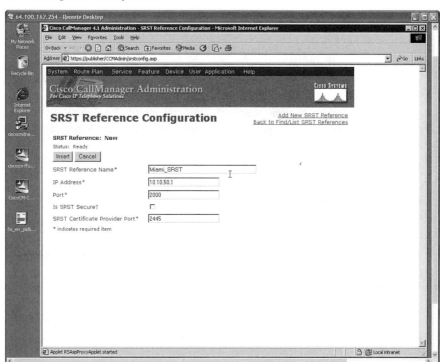

Dial Plan Considerations

When you are running in SRST mode, the gateway is responsible for processing all calls. This means you must configure appropriate dial peers, translations, and class of service (COS) to support your requirements. For H.323 and SIP gateways, the impact is minimal, because you already have dial peers to route calls to the PSTN. For MGCP gateways, the impact can be considerable, because the dial plan in the call agent is no longer available. You need to add dial peers for the voice ports that MGCP typically controls.

Planning

You need to consider several factors when implementing your dial plan in CallManager. The considerations vary by gateway type and are detailed in the sections that follow.

H.323 Gateways

One common issue with H.323 gateways and SRST is the access code. Assume that your users dial an access code of 9 to get an outside line. The service provider does not expect to receive this access code, so you must strip it before the digits are sent so that the call is routed correctly. If you strip the access code in CallManager, your dial peers in the H.323 gateway will be built without the access code. If your users dial the access code while in SRST mode, the call either will not match the appropriate dial peer or the access code will not be stripped before the digits are sent to the service provider. To prevent this, always send the access code to the H.323 gateway and build your dial peers to match the digit strings appropriately.

You might also need to duplicate digit translations in the gateway. For example, your company policy might be to send only the main number for your site instead of the individual direct inward dial (DID) numbers. You should also implement Class of Restrictions (COR) to mimic your CallManager Class of Control configuration, as described in Chapter 12, "Configuring Class of Restrictions."

An additional consideration is route patterns that you are blocking in CallManager. In many countries, blocks of numbers are reserved for "premium" calls with high per-minute charges. These numbers are typically used for things like playing sports scores or for adult-themed businesses. Many companies block access to these premium calls by building a specific route pattern in CallManager and selecting the option Block instead of Route. Because the premium call is never sent to the gateway, it is not necessary to block the route pattern using a dial peer. In SRST mode, it might be possible for your users to place these calls unless you specifically configure the gateway to deny them.

MGCP Gateways

MGCP gateways require you to build an appropriate dial plan when running in MGCP Gateway Fallback mode. In addition to all the H.323 considerations, you also have to build dial peers for basic PSTN connectivity and to properly route inbound calls from the PSTN. Example 13-3 shows an MGCP dial plan for basic connectivity to the U.S. PSTN.

Example 13-3 *MGCP Gateway Fallback Dial Plan Configuration*

```
Miami(config)#dial-peer voice 1 pots
!
! Dial peer controlled by MGCP under normal operation
!
Miami(config-dial-peer)#application mgcpapp
!
! Allows incoming calls under MGCP Fallback
!
Miami(config-dial-peer)#incoming called-number .
Miami(config-dial-peer)#direct-inward-dial
Miami(config-dial-peer)#port 1/0/0:1
!
! Outbound dial peers
```

Example 13-3   *MGCP Gateway Fallback Dial Plan Configuration (Continued)*

```
!
Miami(config)#dial-peer voice 911 pots
Miami(config-dial-peer)#destination-pattern 911
Miami(config-dial-peer)#prefix 911
Miami(config-dial-peer)#port 1/0/0:2
!
Miami(config)#dial-peer voice 9911 pots
Miami(config-dial-peer)#destination-pattern 9911
Miami(config-dial-peer)#prefix 911
Miami(config-dial-peer)#port 1/0/0:2
!
! Additional outbound dial peers omitted
```

Direct Extension Dialing

The dial plan in a centralized call processing design typically allows your remote site users to dial other locations directly using their extension or by using their site code plus their extension. For both H.323 and MGCP gateways, you should consider adding plain old telephone service (POTS) dial peers to allow direct extension dialing while in SRST mode. The destination patterns for these POTS dial peers will match your existing extension ranges or site codes and prefix the appropriate digits to route the call over the PSTN, as shown in Example 13-4.

Example 13-4   *Enabling Direct Extension Dialing in SRST*

```
!
Miami(config)#dial-peer voice 32 pots
Miami(config-dial-peer)#destination-pattern 3...
Miami(config-dial-peer)#prefix 12125553
Miami(config-dial-peer)#port 1/0/0:2
```

This configuration minimizes the impact on your remote site users. CallManager 4.2 has added a feature that minimizes the impact of SRST on your centralized phones. When a remote site is in SRST mode, those phones appear as unregistered to CallManager. CallManager has no way to know that those phones are reachable over the PSTN. In previous versions, calls to unregistered phones were forwarded to voice mail if it was configured, or callers received a reorder tone. CallManager 4.2 added a Call Forward on Unregistered field to the Line Configuration. This feature allows other users to dial the extension and be routed over the PSTN if the destination phone is in SRST mode.

Configuring SRST Dial Plan Patterns

When an IP phone registers with the SRST gateway, each extension on the phone is associated with one of the virtual dial peers created when you entered the **max-dn** command. This allows the IP phones to call each other but might result in problems with inbound calls from the PSTN. Unless the dialed number identification service (DNIS) information sent by the service provider matches the extension, inbound calls are not routed to the correct phone. You can resolve this issue by using voice translation rules to map the DNIS to the extension. You can also use the **dialplan-pattern** command if the service provider is sending the E.164 address as the DNIS:

    dialplan-pattern *tag pattern* extension-length *digits*

When you configure the **dialplan-pattern**, the gateway creates two virtual dial peers per extension: one with a destination pattern of the extension, and one matching the pattern in the **dialplan-pattern** configuration. Figure 13-4 illustrates the use of the **dialplan-pattern** command.

Figure 13-4 **dialplan-pattern** *Configuration*

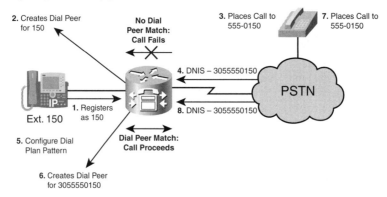

The IP phone has registered with the Miami gateway with its extension of 150. The service provider is sending the full E.164 address of 3055550105 as the DNIS. You would configure **dialplan-pattern 1 3055550... extension-length 3** to create the two virtual dial peers you need. This configuration has the added benefit of sending the E.164 address as the automatic number identification (ANI) on outbound calls from this IP phone.

SRST Features

SRST supports numerous features that are fairly intuitive. For example, you can configure the SRST gateway to play a secondary dial tone after a caller dials the access code, to mimic the behavior of CallManager, using the **secondary-dialtone** *digit* command. This section details the configuration of the less intuitive SRST features.

Auto Attendant

Auto attendant (AA) functionality in SRST is provided using a Tcl script. Existing AA scripts are available on Cisco.com for both SRST and CallManager Express (CME). Obtaining and applying Tcl scripts is described in detail in Chapter 15, "Using Tcl Scripts and VoiceXML." If the router has a Cisco Unity Express (CUE) module, you can also use that to provide AA functionality.

Maximum Line Appearances

Sometimes the number of extensions on your IP phones might exceed the number of e-phone-dns that the SRST gateway supports. For example, a 3845 supports 720 IP phones but only 960 e-phone-dns. If you have 720 IP phones with two lines each, not all of them will be able to register with the 3845. To prevent multiline IP phones from using all the available e-phone-dns, you can configure a maximum number of lines per model of phone:

```
limit-dn phone-model max-lines
```

Conferencing

SRST currently supports only ad-hoc three-party conferences. Digital signal processors (DSP) do not handle these audio streams for the conferences—the gateway mixes them. To enable conferencing, you configure the maximum number of simultaneous conferences you want to support using the **max-conferences** command.

To initiate a conference, the IP phone must have two lines. If your IP phones do not have two lines, you can use the **dual-line** keyword on the **max-dn** configuration:

```
max-dn 24 [dual-line]
```

This creates two audio channels for each virtual voice port that is providing support for call waiting and consultative transfer, in addition to conferencing.

If you have IP phones with multiple lines, using the **dual-line** option on the **max-dn** command can result in undesirable behavior. If the first line is busy and a call comes in, it hunts to the second channel of the first line instead of hunting to the second line. The **huntstop channel** command prevents calls from hunting to the second channel.

Transferring Calls

SRST supports transfers to other IP phones that are registered to the gateway. Additional configuration is required to transfer calls to external numbers.

Transfer-Pattern

If you want to allow calls to be transferred to numbers other than IP phones, you must specifically allow these numbers using the **transfer-pattern** command. A common request is to allow your users to transfer their calls to their mobile phone. To allow this, configure the transfer pattern to allow a specific number or a range of numbers using wildcards, as shown in Example 13-5. You can configure up to 32 transfer patterns.

Example 13-5 *Configuring Transfer Patterns*

```
Miami(config)#call-manager-fallback
!
! Transfer pattern to permit calls to a single long-distance number
!
Miami(config-cm-fallback)#transfer-pattern 918135550199
!
! Transfer pattern to permit calls to a range of local numbers
!
Miami(config-cm-fallback)#transfer-pattern 9555....
```

A transfer pattern allows all IP phones to initiate transfers to the specified numbers. If you want to limit who can initiate transfers to certain numbers, you can accomplish this using COR.

Consultative Transfers

In a blind transfer, the call is connected to the destination prior to the ringing tone. In a consultative transfer, the person who is initiating the transfer is connected to the destination. This allows the transfer initiator to make sure that the recipient is available and willing to accept the transfer. SRST supports four transfer methods that are configured using the **transfer-system** command. They are as follows:

- **Blind**—Blind uses a Cisco proprietary transfer method and a single line. It is recommended that you use either full-blind or consultative transfers.

- **Full-blind**—Full-blind uses H.450.2 standards to initiate the transfer.

- **Full-consult**—Full-consult uses H.450.2 standards to initiate a consultative transfer. A second line is required for a consultative transfer. If a second line is not available, the transfer is initiated as a full-blind.

- **Local-consult**—Local-consult also uses H.450.2 to initiate a consultative transfer but only for local calls—that is, calls to other IP phones. Calls to nonlocal numbers use blind.

NOTE   H.450.2 is standard for providing call transfer supplementary services in an H.323 network that is defined by the International Telecommunications Union (ITU).

Forwarding Calls

Call forwarding is restricted to local IP phones by default. To allow users to forward their phones to nonlocal numbers, you configure specific numbers or ranges of numbers by using the **call-forward** command just like you did for transfer patterns.

```
call-forward pattern number
```

You can also use the **call-forward** command to specify where a call should be forwarded if the IP phone is busy or does not answer:

```
call-forward busy digits
call-forward noan digits [timeout sec]
```

Voice-Mail Integration

Several possibilities exist for providing voice-mail services to IP phones that are registered to an SRST router. The router can be equipped with a CUE module to provide local voice-mail services, or a centralized voice-mail system, such as Unity, can be used.

Integrating with CUE

To effectively integrate with CUE, the IP phones should be configured to use CUE for voice mail whether they are registered with CallManager or the SRST router. You can use Voice Profile for Internet Mail (VPIM) to network up to 500 CUE locations. You can also use VPIM to network CUE and Cisco Unity systems.

For more information on configuring CUE and VPIM networking, refer to *Cisco IP Communications Express: CallManager Express with Cisco Unity Express* by Cisco Press.

Integrating with a Centralized Voice-Mail System

Several components are involved in configuring voice mail to integrate with a centralized voice-mail system. The first is forwarding the IP phones correctly, which was discussed in the previous section. You also configure the number that the system should dial when the Messages button is pressed:

```
voicemail digit-string
```

Depending on your PSTN connectivity, these two steps might be sufficient to support having the centralized voice-mail system answer calls.

If the connection to the PSTN is a BRI or PRI, the voice-mail system routes calls to the correct mailbox by looking at the ANI or Redirected Dialed Number Information Service (RDNIS) fields. If the call is forwarded to the voice-mail system because of no answer or a busy condition, the forwarding phone number is placed in the RDNIS field. If the RDNIS matches a mailbox address in the voice-mail system, the greeting for that mailbox is played, and the caller can leave a message. If the Messages button on the IP phone is pressed, the extension of the phone is placed in the ANI field. If this matches a mailbox, the voice-mail system plays the login prompt for that mailbox. If neither the DNIS nor the ANI matches a mailbox, the default opening greeting is played.

NOTE   You might need to select **Redirecting Number IE Delivery – Outgoing** on the Gateway
         Configuration page in CallManager for the gateway at the central location to support
         RDNIS delivery to the voice-mail system.

If the connection to the PSTN is via analog or channel-associated signaling (CAS) circuits,
additional steps are required. In this case, dual tone multifrequency (DTMF) tones are used
to route the call to the appropriate mailbox. Different voice-mail vendors expect different
formats for these DTMF tones. Because no standard format exists, you need to instruct the
SRST gateway how to send the appropriate DTMF tones using the **vm-integration**
command from global config mode. To understand how **vm-integration** works, you need
to define the participants in a call and the possible call flows. Figure 13-5 shows the
participants and the possible call flows.

Figure 13-5 *Voice-Mail Call Flows*

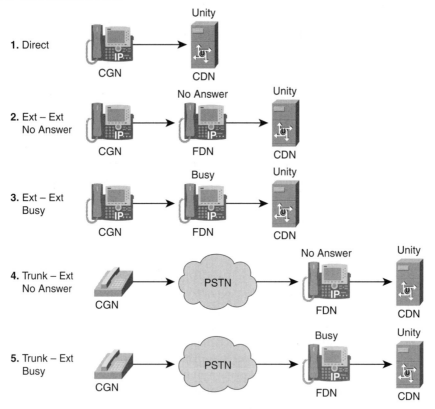

The call participants are defined from the perspective of the voice-mail system. Calling number (CGN) is the original calling party. Forwarding number (FDN) is the extension that forwarded the call to voice mail. Called number (CDN) is the called party, which in this case is the voice-mail system.

The **vm-integration** command defines how the DTMF tones are sent based on the call flow. This is done using the **pattern** command. Each of the possible call flows has a **pattern** command. Example 13-6 shows a configuration for integrating SRST with a voice-mail system over analog circuits.

Example 13-6 *Integrating SRST with a Voice Mail System over Analog Circuits*

```
Miami(config)#vm-integration
Miami(config-vm-int)#pattern direct * CGN
Miami(config-vm-int)#pattern ext-to-ext no-answer # FDN #2
Miami(config-vm-int)#pattern ext-to-ext busy # FDN #2
Miami(config-vm-int)#pattern trunk-to-ext no-answer # FDN #2
Miami(config-vm-int)#pattern trunk-to-ext busy # FDN #2
```

In this example, when a user presses the Messages button, a call is placed to the voice-mail system. When voice mail answers, a DTMF tone for * is played, followed by the CGN. For all other call flows, the DTMF tones sent are # followed by the extension of the forwarding phone followed by #2.

Some carriers do not propagate RDNIS, which results in the default opening greeting being played. If you cannot get RDNIS through your service provider network, you might be able to use the **vm-integration** commands in conjunction with the **forward-digits extra inband** command. This should be configured on the POTS dial peer that is used to forward the call to the voice-mail system. Example 13-7 shows the configuration for integrating SRST with a voice-mail system over a PRI circuit that does not support RDNIS.

Example 13-7 *Integrating SRST with a Voice-Mail System over ISDN Circuits*

```
Miami(config)#dial-peer voice 50 pots
Miami(config-dial-peer)#destination-pattern 912125553000
Miami(config-dial-peer)#prefix 12125553000
!
! Send digits after call setup inband as DTMF
!
Miami(config-dial-peer)#forward-digits extra inband
!
Miami(config-dial-peer)#port 1/0/0:23
!
Miami(config)#vm-integration
Miami(config-vm-int)#pattern direct * CGN
Miami(config-vm-int)#pattern ext-to-ext no-answer # FDN #2
Miami(config-vm-int)#pattern ext-to-ext busy # FDN #2
Miami(config-vm-int)#pattern trunk-to-ext no-answer # FDN #2
Miami(config-vm-int)#pattern trunk-to-ext busy # FDN #2
```

This solution is available in Cisco IOS Release 12.3(11)T and later.

Music on Hold

The SRST gateway can play Music on Hold (MoH) from a file on flash, but only for G.711 VoIP or PSTN calls. Internal calls between IP phones will hear tone on hold. To enable MoH from flash, use the **moh** *filename* command. Your MoH file can be a wav or au file, but it must be 8-bit, 8 KHz.

You can also use a live audio feed for MoH. The live audio feed is connected to an E&M port in the SRST gateway. Connect the standard RCA jack to pins 3 and 6 of the Ear and Mouth (E&M) port, and disable E&M signaling using the **signal-immediate** and **auto-cut-through** commands. After you have physically connected the audio feed to the E&M port, create a dial peer that you can use to "call" the audio feed. The final step is the **moh-live** command. This command creates a dummy number that initiates the MoH. Example 13-8 shows how to configure a live audio MoH feed.

Example 13-8 *Configuring a Live Audio MoH Feed*

```
Miami(config)#voice-port 0/1/0
Miami(config-voiceport)#input gain 3
Miami(config-voiceport)#auto-cut-through
Miami(config-voiceport)#operation 4-wire
Miami(config-voiceport)#signal immediate
!
Miami(config)#dial-peer voice 5555 pots
Miami(config-dial-peer)#destination-pattern 5555
Miami(config-dial-peer)#port 0/1/0
!
Miami(config)#call-manager-fallback
Miami(config-cm-fallback)#moh-live dn-number 4444 out-call 5555
!
```

NOTE The **moh-live** command uses one of the virtual voice ports that the **max-dn** command creates.

You can also use a Foreign Exchange Office (FXO) port for a live MoH feed. This requires an external adapter such as the ST-TC1 Telephone System Coupler from Radio Design Labs to provide normal telco battery voltage.

SIP SRST

SIP SRST allows a Cisco voice gateway to provide SRST support to SIP phones that are registered to a SIP proxy server. To accomplish this, the SIP SRST gateway acts as a SIP registrar. Ideally, the SIP phone should support dual registration. This allows it to be registered with the SIP proxy server and the SIP SRST gateway simultaneously. If the SIP phone does not support dual registration, the SIP SRST gateway cannot route incoming calls to the SIP phone until the SIP phone establishes registration with the SIP SRST router. You can place outbound calls, but they will experience some delay while the SIP phone is waiting for a response to INVITE messages that are sent to the SIP proxy server.

SIP SRST 3.4 added support for back-to-back user agent (B2BUA). B2BUA supports more features than a redirect server, which was used previously. SIP SRST 3.4 supports calls between SIP phones, between SIP and SCCP phones, and between SIP phones and router voice ports.

Configuring SIP Registrar Server

You can use the **voice service voip** command to configure the SIP registrar server on the SIP SRST gateway. You must also specify the call flows that you want to enable. Example 13-9 shows the steps for enabling the SIP registrar server and allowing all call combinations.

Example 13-9 *SIP Registrar Server*

```
Miami(config)#voice service voip
Miami(config-voi-serv)#allow-connections h323 to h323
Miami(config-voi-serv)#allow-connections h323 to sip
Miami(config-voi-serv)#allow-connections sip to h323
Miami(config-voi-serv)#allow-connections sip to sip
Miami(config-voi-serv)#sip
Miami(config-serv-sip)#registrar server
```

The **allow-connections** commands allow the gateway to act as a B2BUA. The **registrar server** command initiates the gateway as a SIP registrar server.

Configuring a Voice Register Pool

After you enable the SIP registrar server, you create a voice register pool that is used to determine which devices can register with the SIP SRST gateway. You can specify allowed devices by a range of IP addresses, a specific IP address, or a specific MAC address. You can configure multiple pools. Example 13-10 shows a register pool that allows all IP phones in the 10.10.50.0/24 subnet to register with the SIP SRST gateway.

Example 13-10 *Creating a Voice Register Pool*

```
!
! Set global voice register parameters
!
Miami(config)#voice register global
Miami(config-register-global)#max-dn 10
Miami(config-register-global)#max-pool 10
!
! Create voice register pool
!
Miami(config)#voice register pool 1
Miami(config-register-pool)#id network 10.10.50.0 mask 255.255.255.0
Miami(config-register-pool)#call-forward b2bua busy 5000
Miami(config-register-pool)#call-forward b2bua noan 5000 timeout 30
Miami(config-register-pool)#preference 2
Miami(config-register-pool)#proxy 10.1.10.10 preference 1 monitor-probe icmp-ping
Miami(config-register-pool)#voice-class codec 1
```

The **proxy** command in the voice register pool is the address of the SIP proxy server. This is the preferred server, so the preference is set to 1. The preference for the SIP SRST gateway is set to 2. The optional **monitor-probe icmp-ping** keyword instructs the SIP SRST gateway to monitor the availability of the proxy using pings, allowing quicker failover. Response Time Reporter (RTR) monitoring is also supported.

In addition, you can configure COR lists, dialplan-patterns, and outgoing voice translation rules to a voice register pool. Apply outgoing translation rules before the **dialplan-pattern** or the **alias** command is used in a voice register pool.

Call Preservation

One of the primary decision factors in selecting which gateway protocol to run is the preservation of calls during a failover situation. As discussed previously, MGCP gateways preserve active calls when an IP phone fails over from its primary CallManager to its secondary CallManager. Failover from CallManager to SRST is a little different.

For H.323 gateways, active calls are preserved until the H225 keepalive timer expires. You can disable the H225 keepalive timer so that active calls through an H.323 gateway are preserved indefinitely. Example 13-11 demonstrates how to disable the H225 timer.

Example 13-11 *Preserving H.323 Calls on SRST Fallback*

```
Miami(config)#voice service voip
Miami(conf-voi-serv)#h323
Miami(conf-serv-h323)#no h225 timeout keepalive
```

For MGCP gateways, call preservation depends on the type of circuit. For analog or CAS circuits, calls are preserved on failover from CallManager to SRST. For ISDN circuits, active calls are dropped on failover. Technically, the call is dropped when you initiate MGCP Gateway Fallback. This is because the D channel of the ISDN circuit is backhauled to CallManager. When MGCP Gateway Fallback is initiated, the gateway tears down and reestablishes the D channel, resulting in all active calls being dropped. Calls are also dropped when communication is reestablished with CallManager.

Two of the primary reasons for selecting MGCP are call preservation and not having to build the dial plan in each gateway. Cisco IOS 12.4(4)XC introduced a new feature that allows calls through an H.323 gateway to be preserved when an IP phone fails over its primary CallManager to its secondary CallManager. This feature requires CallManager 4.1(3)SR3. Example 13-12 illustrates the configuration for preserving H.323 calls on a CallManager failover.

Example 13-12 *Preserving H.323 Calls on CallManager Failover*

```
Miami(config)#voice service voip
Miami(conf-voi-serv)#h323
Miami(conf-serv-h323)#call preserve
```

As discussed earlier, each gateway needs appropriate dial peers to function in SRST mode. Because H.323 call preservation is more robust for SRST, and the dial plan must be configured, most people select H.323 for their remote gateways.

Secure SRST

CallManager supports secure communication with IP phones. SRST 3.3 added support for secure communication when an IP phone is registered to an SRST router. The security features include support for authentication, integrity, and media encryption. Authentication assures to one device that the other device is who it claims to be. Integrity assures that the data exchanged between two devices has not been altered. Media encryption provides a level of confidentiality by scrambling the data so that only the intended recipient can read it.

Configuring Secure SRST

Follow these steps to configure Secure SRST:

Step 1   Configure a certification authority (CA).

To support secure communications, the network must have a CA server. The CA server can be a Cisco IOS certificate server or a third-party server. Example 13-13 illustrates how to configure a Cisco IOS certificate server.

Example 13-13 *Configuring a Cisco IOS Certificate Server*

```
CA_Rtr#config t
!
! Enable the certificate server
!
CA_Rtr(config)#crypto pki server srstca
CA_Rtr(cs-server)#database level minimum
CA_Rtr(cs-server)#database url nvram
CA_Rtr(cs-server)#issuer-name CN=srstca
CA_Rtr(cs-server)#grant auto
*May  2 16:51:12.664: %PKI-6-CS_GRANT_AUTO: All enrollment requests will be
automatically granted.
CA_Rtr(cs-server)#no shutdown
%Some server settings cannot be changed after CA certificate generation.
% Please enter a passphrase to protect the private key
% or type Return to exit
Password:MiamiSRST

Re-enter password:MiamiSRST
% Generating 1024 bit RSA keys, keys will be non-exportable...[OK]
% Exporting Certificate Server signing certificate and keys...

% Certificate Server enabled.
CA_Rtr(cs-server)#
*May  2 16:53:45.800: %SSH-5-ENABLED: SSH 1.99 has been enabled
*May  2 16:53:47.288: %PKI-6-CS_ENABLED: Certificate server now enabled.
```

NOTE   The password entry, **MiamiSRST**, is shown in the example for illustration purposes. The password you type will not be visible.

The **database level** command sets what type of data is stored in the certificate database. The default is **minimal**, which stores the minimal information to continue issuing new certificates. The other options are **names**, which adds the serial number and name of each certificate, and **complete**, which writes each certificate issued. If you use the **complete** option, you should store the data on an external TFTP server. The **database url** command specifies where the database entries will be stored. The default is flash memory, but it is recommended that you store the entries in nvram.

Step 2   Autoenroll and authenticate the Secure SRST router to the CA server.

The SRST router must obtain a device certificate from the CA server. Example 13-14 illustrates the procedure for enrolling the Secure SRST router to a Cisco IOS certificate server. If you are using a third-party certificate server, you need to cut and paste in the certificate or use TFTP.

Example 13-14 *Autoenroll the Secure SRST Router*

```
Miami#config t
Miami(config)#crypto pki trustpoint srst
Miami(ca-trustpoint)#enrollment url http://10.1.10.1
Miami(ca-trustpoint)#revocation-check none
Miami(ca-trustpoint)#exit
Miami(config)#crypto pki authenticate srst
!
! Note: The crypto pki authenticate command is not necessary if the
! IOS CA server is configured on the SRST router.
!
Certificate has the following attributes:
Fingerprint MD5: 4C324B3D 71ABD56F 54532FE7 782D2C4A
Fingerprint SHA1: 5C3B6B9E EFA40927 9DF6A826 58DA618A BF39F291
% Do you accept this certificate? [yes/no]: y
Trustpoint CA certificate accepted.

Miami(config)#crypto pki enroll srst
%
% Start certificate enrollment ..
% Create a challenge password. You will need to verbally provide this
password to the CA Administrator in order to revoke your certificate.
For security reasons your password will not be saved in the configuration.
Please make a note of it.
Password: MiamiSRST
Re-enter password: MiamiSRST
% The fully-qualified domain name in the certificate will be: Miami.cisco.com
% The subject name in the certificate will be: Miami.cisco.com
% Include the router serial number in the subject name? [yes/no]: Y
% The serial number in the certificate will be: D0B9E79C

% Include an IP address in the subject name? [no]: n

Request certificate from CA? [yes/no]: y

% Certificate request sent to Certificate Authority
% Certificate request sent to file system
% The 'show crypto ca certificate srst verbose' command will show the fingerprint.
Miami(config)#Writing file to flash:srst.req
*May  2 18:54:53.843: CRYPTO_PKI:  Certificate Request Fingerprint MD5: E7DE5ADE
 1C9FE495 543783C0 85D369A4
*May  2 18:54:53.843: CRYPTO_PKI:  Certificate Request Fingerprint SHA1: C008A45
7 8FBFD73A E48E7232 AED19BD1 A857C47A
Miami(config)#end
```

After you enroll the SRST router with the CA server, enter the **no auto grant** command on the Cisco IOS certificate server. You must shut down the certificate server to turn off auto grant.

Step 3 Enable credentials service on the SRST router.

Enabling credentials service allows CallManager to retrieve the device certificate of the SRST router and place it in the IP phone configuration files. Example 13-15 illustrates how to enable credentials service.

Example 13-15 *Enabling Credentials Service*

```
Miami#conf t
Miami(config)#credentials
Miami(config-credentials)#ip source address 10.10.25.1
Miami(config-credentials)#trustpoint srst
Miami(config-credentials)#end
```

The **ip source address** is a local address on the SRST router that you will use as the source address when communicating with CallManager. You can also modify the port number for retrieving certificates by using the **port** option on the **ip source address** command. The default port is 2445.

Step 4 Import phone certificate files.

For the SRST router to authenticate the IP phones, it must retrieve the certificate of the phone. The SRST router must manually import the phone certificates. The certificates required vary by phone model and version of CallManager you are running. Example 13-16 illustrates importing a certificate for 7960 phones with CallManager 4.1.3. Prior to entering the SRST configuration, you should obtain the appropriate certificates on CallManager. The certificates are stored in C:\Program Files\Cisco\Certificates and have a .0 extension. Open the appropriate certificate with WordPad and copy the contents between "-----BEGIN CERTIFICATE-----" and "-----END CERTIFICATE-----".

Example 13-16 *Importing Phone Certificate Files*

```
Miami#config
Miami(config)#crypto pki trustpoint 7960
Miami(ca-trustpoint)#revocation-check none
Miami(ca-trustpoint)#enrollment terminal
Miami(ca-trustpoint)#exit
Miami(config)#crypto pki authenticate 7960

Enter the base 64 encoded CA certificate.
End with a blank line or the word "quit" on a line by itself

MIIDqDCCApCgAwIBAgIQNT+yS9cPFKNGwfOprHJWdTANBgkqhkiG9w0BAQUFADAu
MRYwFAYDVQQKEw1DaXNjbyBTeXN0ZW1zMRQwEgYDVQQDEwtDQVAtUlRQLTAwMjAe
Fw0wMzEwMTAyMDE4NDlaFw0yMzEwMTAyMDI3MzdaMC4xFjAUBgNVBAoTDUNpc2Nv
IFN5c3RlbXMxFDASBgNVBAMTC0NBUC1SVFAtMDAyMIIBIDANBgkqhkiG9w0BAQEF
AAOCAQ0AMIIBCAKCAQEAxCZlBK19w/2NZVVvpjCPrpW1cCY7V1q9lhzI85RZZdnQ
2M4CufgIzNa3zYxGJIAYeFfcRECnMB3f5A+x7xNiEuzE87UPvK+7S80uWCY0Uhtl
AVVf5NQgZ3YDNoNXg5MmONb8lT86F55EZyVac0XGne77TSIbIdejrTgYQXGP2MJx
```

Example 13-16 *Importing Phone Certificate Files (Continued)*

```
Qhg+ZQlGFDRzbHfM84Duv2Msez+l+Sqmq080kIckqE9Nr3/XCSj1hXZNNVg8D+mv
Hth2P6KZqAKXAAStGRLSZX3jNbS8tveJ3Gi5+sj9+F6KKK2PD0iDwHcRKkcUHb7g
1I++U/5nswjUDIAph715Ds2rn9ehkMGipGLF8kpuCwIBA60BwzCBwDALBgNVHQ8E
BAMCAYYwDwYDVR0TAQH/BAUwAwEB/zAdBgNVHQ4EFgQUUpIr4ojuLgmKTn5wLFal
mrTUm5YwbwYDVR0fBGgwZjBkoGKgYIYYtaHR0cDovL2NhcC1ydHAtMDAyL0NlcnRF
bnJvbGwvQ0FQLVJUUC0wMDIuY3Jshi9maWxlOi8vXFxjYXAtcnRwLTAwMlxDZXJ0J0
RW5yb2xsXENBUC1SVFAtMDAyLmNybDAQBgkrBgEEAYI3FQEEAwIBADANBgkqhkiG
9w0BAQUFAAOCAQEAVoOM78TaOtHqj7sVL/5u5VChlyvU168f0piJLNWip2vDRihm
E+DlXdwMS5JaqUtuaSd/m/xzxpcRJm4ZRRwPq6VeaiiQGkjFuZEe5jSKiSAK7eHg
tup4HP/ZfKSwPA40DlsGSYsKNMm30mVOCQUMH021PkS/eEQ9sIw6QS7uuHN4y4CJ
NPnRbpFRLw06hnStCZHtGpKEHnY213QOy3h/EWhbnp0MZ+hdr20FujSI6G1+L391
aRjeD708f2fYoz9wnEpZbtn2Kzse3uhU1Ygq1D1x9yuPq388C18HWdmCj40VTXux
V6Y47H1yv/GJM8FvdgvKlExbGTFnlHpPiaG9tQ==
quit
Certificate has the following attributes:
      Fingerprint MD5: F7E150EA 5E6E3AC5 615FC696 66415C9F
      Fingerprint SHA1: 1BE2B503 DC72EE28 0C0F6B18 798236D8 D3B18BE6

% Do you accept this certificate? [yes/no]: y
Trustpoint CA certificate accepted.
% Certificate successfully imported

Miami(config)#end
```

Step 5   Configure CallManager.

After the SRST router has the appropriate phone certificates, you must enable Secure SRST on CallManager. You do this by checking the **Is SRST Secure?** checkbox in the SRST Reference configuration page in CallManager. You should also modify the Certificate Provider port if you did not use the default port in Step 3. If the IP phones are already registered, you must reset them for this change to take effect.

Step 6   Configure SRST.

After you have completed and verified the certificate configuration, you configure SRST the same as if certificates were not in use.

MGCP Gateway Fallback

In an H.323 or SIP gateway, the router controls the voice ports locally, and a CallManager failure is automatically handled by rerouting calls to lower preference dial peers. In an MGCP gateway, CallManager controls the voice ports. If the IP phones cannot communicate with their configured CallManagers, it is likely that the MGCP gateway has also lost communication with the cluster. For IP phones to be able to make calls using the voice ports, MGCP must relinquish control. To accommodate this, MGCP gateways also send keepalive messages to their configured CallManagers. You can configure an MGCP gateway to "fall back" from MGCP mode to another call control application when these keepalive messages are lost. This is often referred to as falling back to H.323 mode, but this is not technically correct. SRST is typically invoked when the IP WAN fails, so any H.323 or SIP dial peers that are configured to route calls to CCM will most likely also be unavailable. Secondary, or lower preference, dial peers that point to other destinations, however, can route calls successfully. The gateway is actually falling back to an application, or Toolkit Command Language (Tcl) script, loaded in the gateway that determines the way calls are processed. All Cisco voice gateways have an application named *default* that allows the gateway to process calls using locally defined POTS dial peers. You can load other applications to provide this capability, but that topic is beyond the scope of this book.

Configuring MGCP Gateway Fallback

You configure MGCP Gateway Fallback using the **ccm-manager fallback-mgcp** command. You also specify that the default application should take over for the MGCP-controlled voice ports. The configuration for setting this application varies depending on the Cisco IOS version. Example 13-17 illustrates the methods of setting the application when in MGCP Gateway Fallback mode.

Example 13-17 *Configuring MGCP Gateway Fallback Alternate Application*

```
Miami(config)#ccm-manager fallback-mgcp
!
! PRE-12.3(14)T alternate application configuration
!
Miami(config)#call application alternate default
!
! 12.3(14)T & later alternate application configuration
!
Miami(config)#application
Miami(config-app)#global
Miami(config-app-global)#service alternate default
```

Verifying and Troubleshooting SRST

To verify your SRST configuration, you should initiate a failover condition and thoroughly test typical calls and features. To minimize the impact to operations, follow these steps to create a test bed:

Step 1 Create an SRST reference.

Step 2 Create a new device pool using the SRST reference from Step 1. All other parameters should match your existing device pool that you used at the remote site.

Step 3   Assign the new device pool to IP phones for testing. You should test with at least three IP phones. If you are implementing COR, you need at least one IP phone per incoming COR list.

Step 4   If no IP phones exist, or if you are testing an MGCP gateway, add a null route to CallManager.

```
ip route 10.1.10.0 255.255.255.0 null0
```

Step 5   If IP phones do exist, place the test phones in their own VLAN. Create an extended access control list (ACL) to block traffic from this VLAN to the CallManager addresses.

NOTE   To fully test MGCP gateways, you need to invoke MGCP Gateway Fallback. This impacts all IP phones and should be planned accordingly.

The most useful tools to troubleshoot SRST are the **show ephone** and **debug ephone** commands. These commands show any registration issues. SRST issues are commonly related to the dial plan. To troubleshoot dial plan issues, use the **debug voice dial peer** command. For ISDN circuits, use **debug isdn q931**.

The **debug voice ccapi inout** command can also be useful, but this debug generates significant output. You should use this as a last resort.

Verifying and Troubleshooting MGCP Gateway Fallback

To verify that MGCP Gateway Fallback is configured, use the **show ccm-manager** command. This shows whether MGCP Gateway Fallback is configured and whether it is active. It also shows the last time MGCP Gateway Fallback was invoked.

Case Study: Integrating SRST with an Analog Voice-Mail System

The Lima location was recently converted to IP phones. It experienced a WAN outage and failed over to SRST. While the company was running SRST, all unanswered calls were forwarded to the Cisco Unity voice-mail system in New York over the PSTN, incurring international toll rates. To eliminate these toll rates, you have decided to use the recently removed analog voice-mail system for the Lima office until you can install a Cisco Unity Express module, as shown in Figure 13-6.

Figure 13-6 *Integrating the Lima Gateway with Analog Voice Mail*

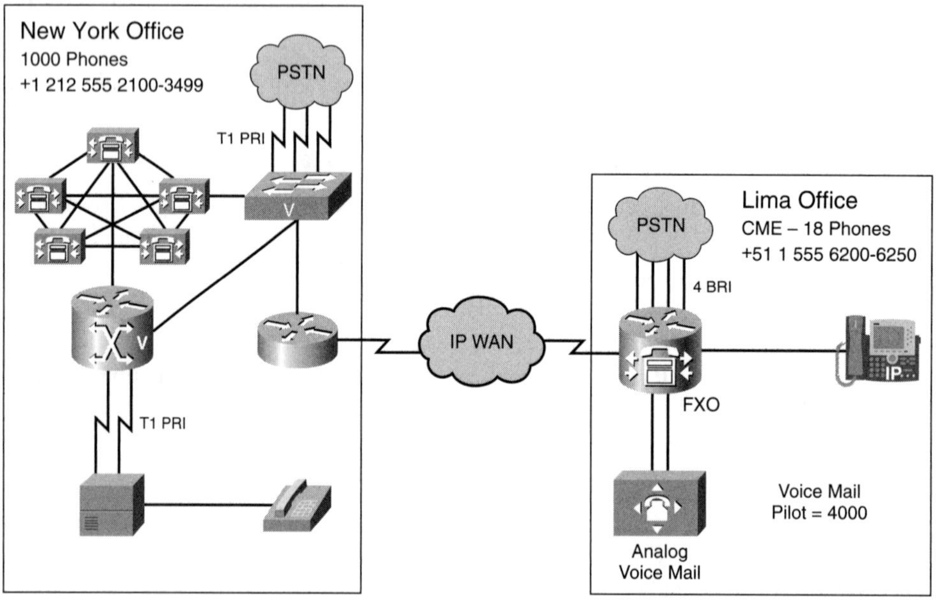

The analog voice-mail system expects the following:

- Direct calls send an *, followed by the station extension, followed by ##.

- Calls forwarded because of no answer send *2#, followed by the station extension, #, the original calling number, ##.

- Calls forwarded because of a busy signal send *3#, followed by the station's extension, #, the original calling number, ##.

- The voice-mail system does not distinguish between internal and external calls.

Example 13-18 shows the configuration necessary to integrate the Lima gateway with the analog voice-mail system when running SRST.

Example 13-18 *Integrating the Lima Gateway with Analog Voice Mail*

```
Lima#show configuration
Building configuration...

Current configuration : 3077 bytes
!
! Unnecessary output omitted...
!
!
interface FastEthernet0/0
 no ip address
 duplex auto
```

Example 13-18 *Integrating the Lima Gateway with Analog Voice Mail (Continued)*

```
 speed auto
!
interface FastEthernet0/0.25
 encapsulation dot1Q 25
 ip address 10.50.25.1 255.255.255.0
!
interface FastEthernet0/0.50
 encapsulation dot1Q 50
 ip address 10.50.50.1 255.255.255.0
!
interface FastEthernet0/1
 no ip address
 shutdown
 duplex auto
 speed auto
!
ip classless
!
!
!
voice-port 0/0/0
!
voice-port 0/0/1
!
!Dial peers to route calls to 4000 to voice mail
!
dial-peer voice 40001 pots
 description Calls to VoiceMail
 destination-pattern 4000
 preference 1
 port 0/0/0
!
dial-peer voice 40002 pots
 description Calls to VoiceMail
 destination-pattern 4000
 preference 2
 port 0/0/1
!
!Other dial peers omitted
!
 !
call-manager-fallback
 max-conferences 8
 ip source-address 10.50.50.1 port 2000
 voicemail 4000
 max-ephones 24
 max-dn 72 dual-channel
 call-forward noan 4000 timeout 10
 call-forward busy 4000
!
!VM INTEGRATION
!
```

continues

Example 13-18 *Integrating the Lima Gateway with Analog Voice Mail (Continued)*

```
vm-integration
 pattern direct * CGN ##
 pattern ext-to-ext no-answer *2# FDN # CGN ##
 pattern ext-to-ext busy *3# FDN # CGN ##
 pattern trunk-to-ext no-answer *2# FDN # CGN ##
 pattern trunk-to ext busy *3# FDN # CGN ##
 !
 ! Unnecessary output omitted
 !
```

To forward calls to the analog voice-mail system, complete the following steps:

Step 1 Create dial peers to route calls to voice mail to the correct ports. In the Lima office, the analog voice-mail system has two Foreign Exchange Station (FXS) ports connected to two FXO ports in the gateway. This requires two dial peers.

Step 2 Configure the Messages button to dial the voice-mail pilot number.

Step 3 Configure SRST to forward calls to voice mail on busy or no answer.

Step 4 Configure the vm-integration to send the appropriate DTMF tones to the voice-mail system.

Review Questions

1 Which two steps are required to enable MGCP Gateway Fallback?

2 Which device initiates SRST?

3 Which gateway protocol can provide call preservation when using ISDN to the PSTN?

4 Which command supports both extension addressing and E.164 addressing?

5 Which two SIP functions does a gateway perform to enable SIP SRST?

6 Which certificate server can a Secure SRST router autoenroll with?

7 Which gateway protocol should you use for a remote site with an E1 PRI to provide the best call preservation?

8 What is required to support integration to a centralized voice-mail system over a PRI?

CHAPTER 14

DSP Resources

This chapter covers the use of digital signal processors (DSP) in Cisco voice gateways. Voice gateways use DSPs to terminate voice calls from time-division multiplexing (TDM) systems and convert those calls to Voice over IP (VoIP). DSPs can also provide transcoding and conference bridge resources to a Cisco CallManager.

This chapter helps you to do the following:

- Understand the capabilities of DSPs
- Determine the number of DSPs required to support your requirements
- Configure a gateway to provide conferencing resources for CallManager
- Configure a gateway to provide transcoding resources for CallManager and Cisco CallManager Express (CME)
- Understand the methods available for supporting fax and modem traffic
- Configure the gateway to support fax and modem traffic

Need for DSP Resources

DSPs provide four major functions in a voice gateway:

- Voice termination
- Transcoding
- Conferencing
- Media termination point (MTP)

Voice termination is the process of digitizing and packetizing the audio stream on a TDM interface. A DSP is required to convert the traditional audio stream to VoIP. DSPs can handle multiple TDM calls. The quantity of DSPs required depends on the type of DSP and the complexity of the coder/decoder (codec) in use. While the DSP is performing voice termination, it provides echo cancellation, voice activity detection, and jitter management.

Transcoding is the process of matching two disparate VoIP streams. This is required when the codecs or sampling rate of two VoIP streams do not match. Figure 14-1 illustrates a common requirement for a transcoder.

Figure 14-1 *Transcoder Operation*

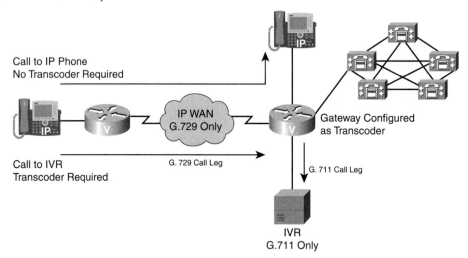

The DSPs in a Cisco voice gateway can be registered to a CallManager to provide hardware-based conferencing. The number of supported conferences and conference participants is detailed in the next section, "Determining the Resources Required."

You insert MTPs into a call to provide supplementary services if H323v2 is not supported end to end. Supplementary services include hold, conference, or other signaling instructions that are invoked during a call. MTPs might also be required with Session Initiation Protocol (SIP) gateways or endpoints. As standards evolve, supplementary services should have more interoperability, thus reducing the requirements for MTPs. Cisco voice gateways support both software-based MTPs, which do not require DSPs, and hardware-based MTPs, which do require them. A software-based MTP supports G.711 to G.711 or G.729 to G.729 calls. A hardware-based MTP supports only G.711 calls.

Determining the DSP Resources Required

Calculating the number of DSP resources required is a challenging task because of the number of variables involved. Cisco has published a DSP calculator on Cisco.com that helps simplify the calculation. Even with this excellent tool, you need to thoroughly understand all the variables involved.

NOTE   The URL for the DSP calculator is http://www.cisco.com/cgi-bin/Support/DSP/cisco_dsp_calc.pl.

DSP Types

Cisco voice gateways use various DSP models with different capabilities. Some gateway models and Network Modules (NM) use modular DSPs, or Packet Voice DSP Modules (PVDM). Some gateways and NMs, such as the NM-HD-2V, have fixed DSPs. These NMs are provisioned with the number of DSPs required to support the voice interfaces in the NM and are not usable for any other purpose. Table 14-1 lists the most common DSPs and where they are found.

Table 14-1   *DSP Types*

DSP Type	Where Found
C542	NM-1V
	NM-2v
	AS5300 VCF (single-density)
	MC3810 VCM
C544	WS-SVC-CMM-ACT
C5421	NM-HDA
	AIM-VOICE-30
	AIM-ATM-VOICE-30
C549	PVDM-12
	WS-X6608-T1/E1
	AS5800
	AS5300 VFC (double-density)
	7200/7500 HC Voice PA
	1750, 1751, 1760
	MC3810 HCM
C5510 (2505)	PVDM2-8
C5510 (2510)	PVDM2-16 (1 DSP)
	PVDM2-32 (2 DSPs)
	PVDM2-48 (3 DSPs)
	PVDM2-64 (4 DSPs)

NOTE   Cisco.com refers to the DSPs that are installed in the PVDM2 modules as both C5510s and 2505/2510s. Cisco IOS references the DSP as C5510. 2505/2510 refers to the actual part number of the DSP.

PVDM Versus PVDM2

The remainder of this section focuses on the capabilities of the PVDM and PVDM2. The PVDM utilizes the C549 DSP and is available on the NM-HDV series of network modules. Only one model of PVDM exists, and it is equipped with three C549 DSPs. The actual part number is the PVDM-12. The -12 indicates that the PVDM can terminate a maximum of 12 voice calls—four calls on each of the C549 DSPs.

The PVDM2 utilizes the C5510 DSP and is available in the NM-HDV2 series of network modules and the Integrated Services Routers (ISR) family of routers. The newer DSP that is used in the PVDM2 allows for higher-density voice termination and increased transcoding and conferencing sessions. Five models of the PVDM2 exist, as shown in Table 14-1, each equipped with a different number of DSPs. As with the PVDM-12, the –xx in the PVDM2 part number indicates the maximum number of voice channels that the PVDM2 can terminate.

The C549 DSPs are dedicated to one task. When you use PVDMs, the DSPs are statically assigned to voice termination when the router is started, or in the case of T1 and E1 ports, when the voice port is created. If additional DSPs are available, you can configure them to provide transcoding or conference bridge resources.

C5510 DSP allocation is more complex. For analog and BRI ports, C5510 DSPs are statically assigned to voice termination when the router is started. C5510 DSPs are dynamically assigned to provide voice port termination for T1 and E1 ports and for transcoding. A single C5510 DSP can provide both functions simultaneously. Conferencing is still statically defined, and a C5510 DSP that is configured as a conferencing resource cannot serve any other function.

NOTE   A PVDM-12 or PVDM2 (32 or higher) can provide voice termination, transcoding, and conferencing simultaneously. The restriction on conferencing is per DSP, not per PVDM.

Voice Termination

The number of voice calls that a DSP can terminate depends on both the model of the DSP and the codec complexity that is configured on the voice card. Example 14-1 illustrates the process of defining a ds0-group on a T1, which results in the assignment of C549 DSPs to voice port 1/0:1.

Example 14-1   *Assigning C549 DSPs to Voice Ports*

```
Gateway#show voice dsp voice

DSP  DSP              DSPWARE CURR  BOOT                         PAK     TX/RX
TYPE NUM CH CODEC     VERSION STATE STATE   RST AI VOICEPORT TS ABORT   PACK COUNT
==== === == ========  ======= ===== =======  === == ========= == =====  ============
```

Example 14-1 *Assigning C549 DSPs to Voice Ports (Continued)*

```
Gateway#config terminal
Enter configuration commands, one per line. End with CNTL/Z.
Gateway(config)#controller t1 1/0
Gateway(config-controller)#framing esf
Gateway(config-controller)#linecode b8zs
*Apr 16 19:25:37.727: %CONTROLLER-5-UPDOWN: Controller T1 1/0, changed state to up
Gateway(config-controller)#ds0-group 1 timeslots 1-4 type e&m-wink
Gateway(config-controller)#
*Apr 16 19:26:03.303: %LINK-3-UPDOWN: Interface recEive and transMit1/0:1(1),
changed state to up
*Apr 16 19:26:03.303: %LINK-3-UPDOWN: Interface recEive and transMit1/0:1(2),
changed state to up
*Apr 16 19:26:03.303: %LINK-3-UPDOWN: Interface recEive and transMit1/0:1(3),
changed state to up
*Apr 16 19:26:03.303: %LINK-3-UPDOWN: Interface recEive and transMit1/0:1(4),
changed state to up
Gateway(config-controller)#end
Gateway#
*Apr 16 19:26:07.831: %SYS-5-CONFIG_I: Configured from console by console
Gateway#
Gateway#show voice dsp voice

DSP  DSP                 DSPWARE CURR  BOOT                      PAK    TX/RX
TYPE NUM CH CODEC        VERSION STATE STATE   RST AI VOICEPORT TS ABORT PACK COUNT
==== === == ======== ======= ===== ======= === == ========= == ===== ============
C549 004 01 {medium} 4.4.702 IDLE  idle     0  0 1/0:1     01  0         0/0
         02 {medium} 4.4.702 IDLE  idle        0 1/0:1     02  0         0/0
         03 {medium} 4.4.702 IDLE  idle        0 1/0:1     03  0         0/0
         04 {medium} 4.4.702 IDLE  idle        0 1/0:1     04  0         0/0
```

The output of the **show voice dsp voice** command in the example lists the model of the DSP in use. The DSP NUM lists the number of the DSP. The DSP numbering scheme varies depending on the router platform and the NM in which the DSP is installed. The CH column indicates the DSP channel used for each physical DS0. The number of channels that a DSP can support depends on both the DSP model and the codec complexity in use, which is indicated in the fourth column of the output.

If you try to configure more voice port terminations than your DSP configuration can support, you will receive an error message similar to Example 14-2.

Example 14-2 *Insufficient DSP Resources*

```
Gateway#config terminal
Gateway(config)#controller e1 3/0
Gateway(config-controller)#pri-group timeslots 1-31

Current dsp resources can support 12 timeslots;need 5 extra dsps
to support the requested configuration

Gateway(config-controller)#
```

Examples 14-3, 14-4, and 14-5 illustrate the process of configuring a T1 port in an ISR gateway using a PVDM2 that is installed on the main board.

Example 14-3 *Assigning C5510 DSPs to Voice Ports*

```
GW_2811#show voice dsp voice
----------------------------FLEX VOICE CARD 0 ----------------------------
                             *DSP VOICE CHANNELS*
DSP   DSP            DSPWARE CURR  BOOT                      PAK   TX/RX
TYPE  NUM CH CODEC   VERSION STATE STATE  RST AI VOICEPORT TS ABRT PACK COUNT
===== === == ======== ======= ===== ======= === == ========= == ==== ============
C5510 001 01 None     5.4.1   idle  idle    0  0                    0      0/0
C5510 001 02 None     5.4.1   idle  idle    0  0                    0      0/0
C5510 001 03 None     5.4.1   idle  idle    0  0                    0      0/0
C5510 001 04 None     5.4.1   idle  idle    0  0                    0      0/0
C5510 001 05 None     5.4.1   idle  idle    0  0                    0      0/0
C5510 001 06 None     5.4.1   idle  idle    0  0                    0      0/0
C5510 001 07 None     5.4.1   idle  idle    0  0                    0      0/0
C5510 001 08 None     5.4.1   idle  idle    0  0                    0      0/0
C5510 001 09 None     5.4.1   idle  idle    0  0                    0      0/0
C5510 001 10 None     5.4.1   idle  idle    0  0                    0      0/0
C5510 001 11 None     5.4.1   idle  idle    0  0                    0      0/0
C5510 001 12 None     5.4.1   idle  idle    0  0                    0      0/0
C5510 001 13 None     5.4.1   idle  idle    0  0                    0      0/0
C5510 001 14 None     5.4.1   idle  idle    0  0                    0      0/0
C5510 001 15 None     5.4.1   idle  idle    0  0                    0      0/0
C5510 001 16 None     5.4.1   idle  idle    0  0                    0      0/0
----------------------------END OF FLEX VOICE CARD 0 ----------------------------

GW_2811#config terminal
Enter configuration commands, one per line. End with CNTL/Z.
GW_2811(config)#network-clock-participate wic 2
GW_2811(config)#controller t1 0/2/0
GW_2811(config-controller)#ds0-group 1 timeslots 1-4 type e&m-wink
GW_2811(config-controller)#
*Dec 31 15:20:59.839: %LINK-3-UPDOWN: Interface recEive and transMit0/2/0:1(1),
changed state to up
*Dec 31 15:20:59.839: %LINK-3-UPDOWN: Interface recEive and transMit0/2/0:1(2),
changed state to up
*Dec 31 15:20:59.839: %LINK-3-UPDOWN: Interface recEive and transMit0/2/0:1(3),
changed state to up
*Dec 31 15:20:59.839: %LINK-3-UPDOWN: Interface recEive and transMit0/2/0:1(4),
changed state to up
GW_2811(config-controller)#end
!
```

As shown in the initial **show voice dsp voice** output, the router has a PVDM2-16 installed on the main board. This is indicated by the 16 channels that are available on a single C5510 DSP in voice card 0. The **network-clock-participate wic 2** command is required to synchronize the clock on the voice port in HWIC slot 2 and the DSP on the main board.

In Example 14-4, the **show voice dsp voice** command shows available DSPs but does not show them assigned to a physical port. This is because C5510 DSPs are dynamically assigned to T1 and E1 ports.

Example 14-4   *Displaying C5510 DSP Assignment*

```
!
GW_2811#show voice dsp voice
--------------------------FLEX VOICE CARD 0 ----------------------------
                          *DSP VOICE CHANNELS*
DSP    DSP              DSPWARE  CURR  BOOT                      PAK   TX/RX
TYPE   NUM CH CODEC     VERSION STATE STATE   RST AI VOICEPORT TS ABRT PACK COUNT
=====  === == ======== ======= ===== ======= === == ========= == ==== ============
C5510 001 01 None       5.4.1 idle  idle      0  0                  0         0/0
C5510 001 02 None       5.4.1 idle  idle      0  0                  0         0/0
C5510 001 03 None       5.4.1 idle  idle      0  0                  0         0/0
C5510 001 04 None       5.4.1 idle  idle      0  0                  0         0/0
C5510 001 05 None       5.4.1 idle  idle      0  0                  0         0/0
C5510 001 06 None       5.4.1 idle  idle      0  0                  0         0/0
C5510 001 07 None       5.4.1 idle  idle      0  0                  0         0/0
C5510 001 08 None       5.4.1 idle  idle      0  0                  0         0/0
C5510 001 09 None       5.4.1 idle  idle      0  0                  0         0/0
C5510 001 10 None       5.4.1 idle  idle      0  0                  0         0/0
C5510 001 11 None       5.4.1 idle  idle      0  0                  0         0/0
C5510 001 12 None       5.4.1 idle  idle      0  0                  0         0/0
C5510 001 13 None       5.4.1 idle  idle      0  0                  0         0/0
C5510 001 14 None       5.4.1 idle  idle      0  0                  0         0/0
C5510 001 15 None       5.4.1 idle  idle      0  0                  0         0/0
C5510 001 16 None       5.4.1 idle  idle      0  0                  0         0/0
----------------------END OF FLEX VOICE CARD 0 ----------------------
!
```

The gateway does track the number of voice ports that are allocated to prevent oversubscription of DSPs. Even though the DSPs are not assigned to a specific voice port, the number of DSPs available for other purposes has been reduced.

Example 14-5 illustrates the eight channels that are reserved for the voice port signaling. Four of these channels are assigned to the DS0 group that is added to the T1. The other four channels support analog voice ports that are installed in HWIC slots 0/0/0 and 0/1/0.

Example 14-5   *Displaying Detailed C5510 DSP Assignment*

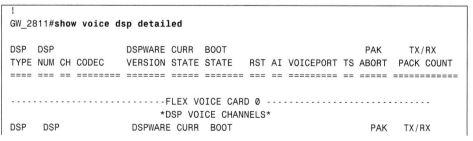

```
!
GW_2811#show voice dsp detailed

DSP   DSP              DSPWARE  CURR  BOOT                      PAK    TX/RX
TYPE  NUM CH CODEC     VERSION STATE STATE   RST AI VOICEPORT TS ABORT PACK COUNT
====  === == ======== ======= ===== ======= === == ========= == ===== ============

--------------------------FLEX VOICE CARD 0 ----------------------------
                          *DSP VOICE CHANNELS*
DSP   DSP              DSPWARE  CURR  BOOT                      PAK    TX/RX
```

continues

Example 14-5 *Displaying Detailed C5510 DSP Assignment (Continued)*

```
TYPE   NUM CH CODEC    VERSION STATE STATE   RST AI VOICEPORT TS ABRT PACK COUNT
=====  === == ======== ======= ===== ======= === == ========= == ==== ============
C5510  001 01 None      7.4.1  idle  idle     0  0                    0          0/0
C5510  001 02 None      7.4.1  idle  idle     0  0                    0          0/0
C5510  001 03 None      7.4.1  idle  idle     0  0                    0          0/0
C5510  001 04 None      7.4.1  idle  idle     0  0                    0          0/0
C5510  001 05 None      7.4.1  idle  idle     0  0                    0          0/0
C5510  001 06 None      7.4.1  idle  idle     0  0                    0          0/0
C5510  001 07 None      7.4.1  idle  idle     0  0                    0          0/0
C5510  001 08 None      7.4.1  idle  idle     0  0                    0          0/0
C5510  001 09 None      7.4.1  idle  idle     0  0                    0          0/0
C5510  001 10 None      7.4.1  idle  idle     0  0                    0          0/0
C5510  001 11 None      7.4.1  idle  idle     0  0                    0          0/0
C5510  001 12 None      7.4.1  idle  idle     0  0                    0          0/0
C5510  001 13 None      7.4.1  idle  idle     0  0                    0          0/0
C5510  001 14 None      7.4.1  idle  idle     0  0                    0          0/0
C5510  001 15 None      7.4.1  idle  idle     0  0                    0          0/0
C5510  001 16 None      7.4.1  idle  idle     0  0                    0          0/0
                    *DSP SIGNALING CHANNELS*
DSP    DSP           DSPWARE CURR  BOOT                      PAK   TX/RX
TYPE   NUM CH CODEC    VERSION STATE STATE   RST AI VOICEPORT TS ABRT PACK COUNT
=====  === == ======== ======= ===== ======= === == ========= == ==== ============
C5510  001 01 {flex}    7.4.1  alloc idle     0  0 0/0/0     02   0         36/0
C5510  001 02 {flex}    7.4.1  alloc idle     0  0 0/0/1     06   0         36/0
C5510  001 03 {flex}    7.4.1  alloc idle     0  0 0/1/0     02   0         15/0
C5510  001 04 {flex}    7.4.1  alloc idle     0  0 0/1/1     02   0         15/0
C5510  001 05 {flex}    7.4.1  alloc idle     0  0 0/2/0:1   01   0         3/12
C5510  001 06 {flex}    7.4.1  alloc idle     0  0 0/2/0:1   02   0         3/12
C5510  001 07 {flex}    7.4.1  alloc idle     0  0 0/2/0:1   03   0         3/12
C5510  001 08 {flex}    7.4.1  alloc idle     0  0 0/2/0:1   04   0         3/12
----------------------END OF FLEX VOICE CARD 0 ----------------------------
GW_2811#
```

Codec Complexity

Codec complexity groups the various codecs into three categories based on the amount of DSP processing that is required to support the particular codec. Codecs are classified as low, medium, or high complexity. Table 14-2 shows the codecs and features that each complexity level supports.

Table 14-2 *Codec Complexity*

Codec Complexity	Codec
Low	G.711 (μ-law, a-law)
	Fax passthrough
	Modem passthrough
	Clear channel

Table 14-2 *Codec Complexity (Continued)*

Codec Complexity	Codec
Medium	All low-complexity codecs plus the following: G.729A G.729AB Fax Relay G.726
High	All low- and medium-complexity codecs plus the following: G.729 G.729B Modem RelayG.728 G.723.1, G.723.1A

The gateway determines how many voice calls each DSP can terminate based on codec complexity. If the codec complexity is set to medium, the number of voice ports that can be terminated per DSP is higher than if the codec complexity is set to high.

Voice cards that do not have C5510 DSPs can be configured only for medium or high complexity. Voice cards that are equipped with C5510 DSPs have an additional complexity option called flex complexity. Setting the codec complexity to medium or high sets the number of voice terminations per DSP to a static number. Flex complexity allows a variable number of calls per DSP based on runtime calculations. Flex complexity is the default for voice cards that have C5510 DSPs. This configuration allows the DSPs to support the maximum number of voice calls but introduces the possibility of oversubscribing the DSP resources.

Configuring Codec Complexity

You configure codec complexity by using the **codec complexity** command under voice-card configuration mode, as shown in Examples 14-6 and 14-7.

Example 14-6 *Configuring Codec Complexity (C549)*

```
!
! 3725 with NM-HDV in slot 0
!
Gateway#config terminal
Gateway(config)#voice-card 0
Gateway(config-voicecard)#codec complexity ?
  high    Set codec complexity high. High complexity, lower call density.
  medium  Set codec complexity medium. Mid range complexity and call density.
  <cr>
Gateway(config-voicecard)#end
Gateway#
```

Example 14-7   *Configuring Codec Complexity (C5510)*

```
!
! 2811 with PVDM2-16 installed on main board.
!
GW_2811#config terminal
Enter configuration commands, one per line. End with CNTL/Z.
GW_2811(config)#voice-card 0
GW_2811(config-voicecard)#codec complexity ?
  flex    Set codec complexity Flex. Flex complexity, higher call density.
  high    Set codec complexity high. High complexity, lower call density.
  medium  Set codec complexity medium. Mid range complexity and call density.

GW_2811(config-voicecard)#end
GW_2811#
```

NOTE   To simplify DSP engineering, it is recommended that you set all voice cards in a gateway to the same codec complexity.

You should set codec complexity before you allocate DSPs. You cannot change codec complexity if the DSP is allocated to a voice port. If you need to change something after you have allocated the voice ports, you must remove the voice ports. This also removes the port configuration in the corresponding plain old telephone service (POTS) dial peers.

PVDMs support medium and high complexity, with medium complexity being the default. PVDM2s support medium, high, and flex complexity, with flex being the default.

Flex Complexity

Flex complexity allows a mix of low-, medium-, and high-complexity calls to be supported. This enables more calls to be supported when multiple codecs are in use. The risk is that you can oversubscribe the DSPs if more high-complexity codecs are used than the DSPs can support. If the DSPs are oversubscribed, calls will be connected, but no audio path will exist when all available DSP channels are in use.

NOTE   Low complexity is not configurable. You must configure flex complexity to enable the DSP to terminate additional low-complexity calls.

Table 14-3 lists the number of voice calls that each DSP can terminate per codec complexity.

Table 14-3   *Number of Voice Calls Supported by DSP Type*

Codec Complexity	C549	C5510 (PVDM2-8)	C5510
Low	N/A	8	16
Medium	4	4	8
High	2	4	6
Flex	N/A	4–8	6–16

DSP Sharing

The "DSP sharing" and "DSP farming" terms are sometimes used interchangeably in Cisco documentation. Because the Cisco IOS **dspfarm** command is used for both DSP sharing and DSP farming, people are confused about what these functions are. The DSP farming term was originally used to describe using DSPs as media resources for CallManager. DSP sharing allows C5510 DSPs to terminate a voice call from a voice port that is located in another hardware slot. This can reduce the possibility of oversubscription when using flex complexity. It can also make it easier to add DSPs to an existing gateway. It is physically much easier to add PVDM2s to an NM-HDV2 than it is to add them to the main board of an ISR.

DSP sharing has the following rules and definitions:

- A *local* DSP is on the same voice card as the voice port.
- A *remote* DSP is on a different voice card than the voice port.
- The DSPs on the main board of an ISR are local to the High-Performance WAN Interface Card (HWIC) and Extension Voice Module (EVM) slots and are remote to the NM slots.
- DSP sharing supports only voice termination—not transcoding.
- DSP sharing is supported on T1/E1 interfaces only.
- DSP sharing is supported on PVDM2s that are installed on the main board of 2800 and 3800 ISRs.
- DSP sharing is supported on NM-HDV2s that are installed in a 2800, 3700, or 3800 router.
- All voice cards that share DSPs must have synchronized clocks.
- You should configure all voice cards that share DSPs for the same complexity.

When you enable DSP sharing, voice cards "export" their DSPs so that another voice card can "import" the resource. When a call comes in a T1 or E1 voice port, the gateway must allocate a DSP for the call. If no local DSP is available for the call, the gateway searches for a remote DSP. The search begins with the DSPs in slot 0 and progresses through the configured voice cards. After the gateway allocates a remote DSP, the DSP remains allocated for the duration of the call, even if a local DSP becomes available.

Enabling DSP Sharing

To enable DSP sharing, you must configure at least one voice card to export its DSPs. All voice cards can import DSPs by default. DSP sharing is enabled with the **dspfarm** command in voice-card configuration. Example 14-8 illustrates the enabling of DSP sharing on a 2811 ISR with a PVDM2-16 installed on the main board and NM-HDV2 in slot 1. With this configuration, the DSPs on the main board are exported, allowing them to be allocated to voice calls arriving on a T1 or E1 port in the NM-HDV2. The DSPs in the NM-HDV2 are not being exported in this example.

NOTE   The DSPs that are installed on the main board of an ISR are configured under **voice-card 0**.

Example 14-8   *Enabling DSP Sharing*

```
GW_2811#config terminal
GW_2811(config)#network-clock-participate wic 2
GW_2811(config)#network-clock-participate slot 1
GW_2811(config)#voice-card 0
GW_2811(config-voicecard)#dspfarm
GW_2811(config-voicecard)#end
GW_2811#
```

Although DSP sharing can reduce the possibility of DSP oversubscription, it does not eliminate it. To ensure that sufficient DSP resources are always available, configure either medium or high complexity and provide sufficient local DSPs to terminate all possible voice calls.

Transcoding and MTP Resources

You can configure transcoding on the following devices:

- WS-X6608-T1/E1
- WS-SVC-CMM-ACT
- PVDM installed in NM-HDV
- PVDM2s installed in NM-HDV2
- PVDM2s installed in ISRs

- NM-HD-1V/2V/2VE (C5510)
- 1751/1760

Transcoding on the C549 DSP is not based on codec complexity. Each C549 DSP on a PVDM-12 supports four transcoding sessions. In the 1751/1760 gateways, two transcoding sessions are supported per DSP. Codec complexity does impact the C5510 DSP. The transcoding capabilities of the C5510 DSP are the same as the voice termination capabilities.

Table 14-4 lists the number of transcoding sessions that each DSP supports.

Table 14-4   *Transcoding Session Capacities*

Device	Transcoding Sessions
WS-6608-T1/E1	24 per port, 192 per module
WS-SVC-CMM-ACT	64
C549	4
C549 in 1751/1760	2
C5510 medium complexity	8
C5510 high complexity	6
c5510 flex complexity	16 (see the following Note)

NOTE   It is only possible to support 16 transcoding sessions when you are transcoding between two low-complexity codecs. Because this situation is rare, the practical maximum number of transcoding sessions per DSP is 8.

Software-based MTPs can support two voice streams with the same packetization rates. If the voice streams use different packetization rates, a DSP is required. The number of software-based MTP sessions is CPU bound and varies per router platform. You can configure only the C5510 DSP to provide hardware-based MTP services. Each DSP can support 16 MTP sessions. If a call requires MTP services and no MTP is configured, a transcoder is used if available.

Conference Bridge Resources

You need to consider only one factor when calculating conference bridge DSP requirements: the number of conferences required. Many documents on Cisco.com list only a maximum number of conference participants derived by multiplying the number of conferences by the maximum participants per conference. This leads to much confusion as to the actual capabilities of the DSPs. For example, the C5510 supports two mixed-mode conferences with up to eight participants each. Therefore, it is technically accurate to say that the C5510 supports 16 conference participants. When only the absolute maximum number of participants is listed, many people infer that you could have one conference with 16 participants or four conferences with 4 participants. When you are determining the number of DSPs required, only the number of conferences matters. The number of participants per conference is not relevant.

NOTE	Conferences cannot span a DSP. The maximum number of conferences per DSP and the maximum participants per conference are independent of each other.

Table 14-5 lists the conference capabilities of the various platforms, per DSP. The maximum number of conferences supported on a single Cisco IOS gateway is 50. This is because of CPU and I/O limitations.

Table 14-5 *Conference Bridge Capacities*

Device	Maximum Conferences	Maximum Participants per Conference
WS-6608-T1/E1	See the following Note	16
WS-SVC-CMM-ACT	42	128
C549	1	6
C5510 (G.711 only)	8	8
C5510 (G.729a/G.729)	2	8
1751/1760	1/DSP, 5/Gateway	6

NOTE	The WS-X6608 module does not follow the same rules for calculating DSP requirements as the IOS-based gateways. Each port on the 6608 can support up to 32 G.711/G.723 conference participants or 24 G.729 conference participants. The number of conferences per port is not a limitation, but there can be no more than 16 participants in a single conference.

Configuring DSP Resources

Configuring a DSP to provide transcoding or conferencing resources is often referred to as *DSP farming*. As noted earlier, this term is also sometimes applied to DSP sharing because the command-line interface (CLI) **dspfarm** command is used to configure both applications. Because the term DSP farming is somewhat ambiguous, it is preferable to explicitly state which of the features you are referring to.

The configuration is similar for transcoding and conference bridging but is significantly different for C549 DSPs versus C5510 DSPs. To distinguish between the DSP types, Cisco refers to the C5510 DSPs as "Cisco IOS Enhanced Transcoding and Conferencing" DSPs.

NOTE   A gateway might have both C549 and C5510 DSPs installed. If this is the case, you can register only one type of DSP with CallManager. You can use both DSP types for voice termination.

Configuring Transcoding and Conferencing (C549)

To configure transcoding and conferencing on an NM-HDV, follow these steps:

Step 1   Set the interface used for Skinny Client Control Protocol (SCCP).

```
Gateway(config)#sccp local interface
```
The IP address of the configured interface is used to register with CallManager. For C549 DSPs, the MAC address of the physical interface is used for the device name. Transcoders will use the device name MTPxxxxxxxxxxxx, and Conference bridges will use the device name CFBxxxxxxxxxxxx, where xxxxxxxxxxxx is the MAC address.

Step 2   Configure the CallManager address.

```
Gateway(config)#sccp ccm ipaddr [priority priority-level]
```
The default priority level is 1. You can configure up to three redundant CallManagers by using the priority option.

Step 3   Enable SCCP.

```
Gateway(config)#sccp
```
You must set the sccp local interface before you enter the **sccp** command. When you enter the **sccp** command, the gateway initiates the registration process with CallManager.

Step 4   Configure the voice card to support transcoding and conferencing.

```
Gateway(config-voicecard)#dsp services dspfarm
```

Step 5   Set the number of transcoder and conference sessions.

```
Gateway(config)#dspfarm transcoder maximum sessions number
Gateway(config)#dspfarm confbridge maximum sessions number
```

Step 6   Enable DSP farming.

```
Gateway(config)#dspfarm
```

Step 7 Configure the transcoder and conference bridge resources in CallManager.

After you complete these steps, the gateway attempts to register with the configured CallManager using a device ID of the interface MAC address preceded by "MTP" for a transcoder resource and "CFB" for a conference resource.

Example 14-9 illustrates configuration of an NM-HDV installed in a 3725 to support both transcoding and conferencing. Figures 14-2 and 14-3 show the associated CallManager configurations.

Example 14-9 *Configuring Transcoding and Conferencing on an NM-HDV*

```
Gateway#config terminal
Enter configuration commands, one per line. End with CNTL/Z.
Gateway(config)#sccp local vlan20
Gateway(config)#sccp ccm 10.1.5.2 priority 1
Gateway(config)#sccp ccm 10.1.5.3 priority 2
Gateway(config)#sccp
Gateway(config)#voice-card 1
Gateway(config-voicecard)#dsp services dspfarm
Gateway(config-voicecard)#exit
Gateway(config)#dspfarm transcoder maximum sessions ?
  <1-48>  Specify the maximum transcoding sessions value

Gateway(config)#dspfarm transcoder maximum sessions 4
Gateway(config)#dspfarm confbridge maximum sessions ?
  <1-11>  Specify the maximum conferencing sessions value

Gateway(config)#dspfarm confbridge maximum sessions 1
Gateway(config)#dspfarm
Gateway(config)#end
Gateway#
*Apr 18 16:50:00.647: %SYS-5-CONFIG_I: Configured from console by console
*Apr 18 16:50:02.039: %DSPRM-5-UPDOWN: DSP 3 in slot 1, changed state to up
*Apr 18 16:50:02.059: %DSPRM-5-UPDOWN: DSP 4 in slot 1, changed state to up
*Apr 18 16:50:02.139: DSPFARM all DSPs are UP with DSPFARM FW. Informed DSPFARM
!
Gateway#show dspfarm all
DSPFARM Configuration Information:
Admin State: UP, Oper Status: ACTIVE - Cause code: NONE
Transcoding Sessions: 4(Avail: 4), Conferencing Sessions: 1 (Avail: 1)
Trans sessions for mixed-mode conf: 0 (Avail: 0), RTP Timeout: 600
Connection check interval 600 Codec G729 VAD: ENABLED

Total number of active session(s) 0, and connection(s) 0

SLOT  DSP   CHNL  STATUS USE    TYPE   SESS-ID   CONN-ID   PKTS-RXED PKTS-TXED

1     3     1     UP     FREE   conf   -         -         -         -
1     3     2     UP     FREE   conf   -         -         -         -
1     3     3     UP     FREE   conf   -         -         -         -
1     3     4     UP     FREE   conf   -         -         -         -
1     3     5     UP     FREE   conf   -         -         -         -
```

Example 14-9 *Configuring Transcoding and Conferencing on an NM-HDV (Continued)*

```
1    3    6    UP    FREE    conf    -        -        -        -
1    4    1    UP    FREE    xcode   -        -        -        -
1    4    2    UP    FREE    xcode   -        -        -        -
1    4    3    UP    FREE    xcode   -        -        -        -
1    4    4    UP    FREE    xcode   -        -        -        -
1    4    5    UP    FREE    xcode   -        -        -        -
1    4    6    UP    FREE    xcode   -        -        -        -
1    4    7    UP    FREE    xcode   -        -        -        -
1    4    8    UP    FREE    xcode   -        -        -        -

Total number of DSPFARM DSP channel(s) 14
!
! Show interface to obtain mac address
!
Gateway#show interface vlan20
Vlan20 is up, line protocol is up
  Hardware is EtherSVI, address is 0007.b35b.d890 (bia 0007.b35b.d890)
  Internet address is 10.2.20.1/24
  MTU 1500 bytes, BW 100000 Kbit, DLY 1000000 usec,
     reliability 255/255, txload 1/255, rxload 1/255
  Encapsulation ARPA, loopback not set
  ARP type: ARPA, ARP Timeout 04:00:00
  Last input never, output never, output hang never
  Last clearing of "show interface" counters never
  Input queue: 0/75/0/0 (size/max/drops/flushes); Total output drops: 0
  Queueing strategy: fifo
  Output queue: 0/40 (size/max)
  5 minute input rate 0 bits/sec, 0 packets/sec
  5 minute output rate 0 bits/sec, 0 packets/sec
     0 packets input, 0 bytes, 0 no buffer
     Received 0 broadcasts, 0 runts, 0 giants, 0 throttles
     0 input errors, 0 CRC, 0 frame, 0 overrun, 0 ignored
     100 packets output, 7403 bytes, 0 underruns
     0 output errors, 1 interface resets
     0 output buffer failures, 0 output buffers swapped out
Gateway#
```

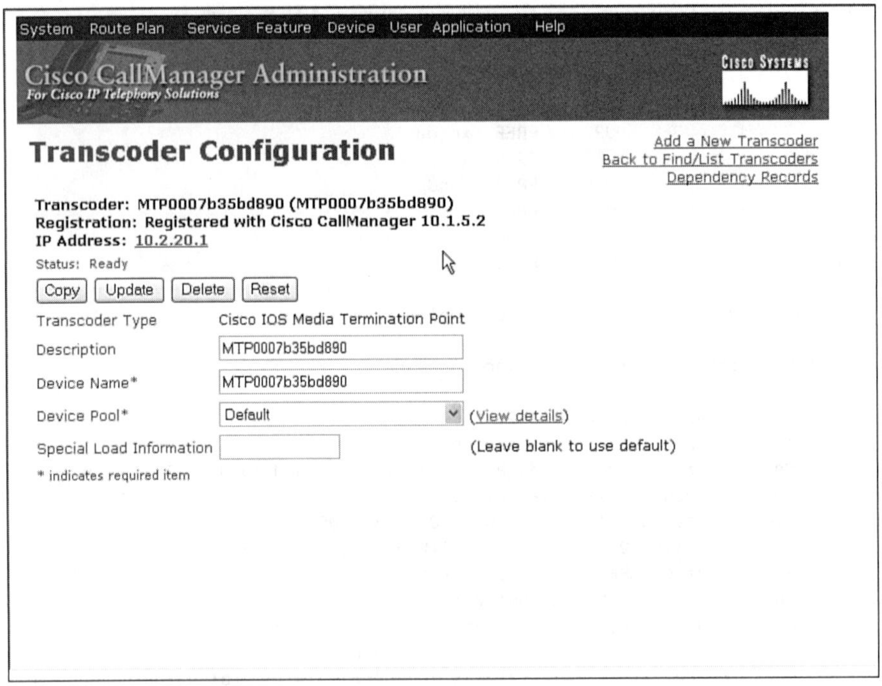

Figure 14-2 *CallManager IOS Transcoder Configuration*

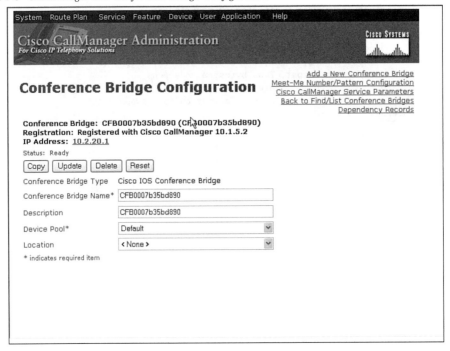

Figure 14-3 *CallManager IOS Conference Bridge Configuration*

Configuring Enhanced Transcoding and Conferencing (C5510)

One of the features of Enhanced Transcoding and Conferencing is the ability to create multiple profiles. Profiles allow more granular control of resources and enable a gateway to register resources with multiple CallManager groups. To configure an NM-HDV2 or ISR to register with a CallManager, follow these steps:

Step 1 Set the interface used for SCCP.

```
GW_2811(config)#sccp local interface
```

For Enhanced Transcoding and Conferencing, this command only determines which IP address CallManager will use to communicate with the gateway. The device name(s) are defined in a later step.

Step 2 Configure the CallManager addresses.

```
GW_2811(config)#sccp ccm ipaddr identifier identifier [version ccm version]
```

Each CallManager that the gateway will register with must be configured with a unique identifier. In a later step, one or more CallManager groups will be created. You will associate the CallManager identifiers that you create here with a CallManager group and assign them a priority for registration.

Specifying the CallManager version is optional but should be set to avoid registration issues.

Step 3 Initialize SCCP.

```
GW_2811(config)#sccp
```

Step 4 Configure the voice card to support transcoding and conferencing.

```
GW_2811(config)#voice-card 0
GW_2811(config-voicecard)#dsp services dspfarm
```

Step 5 Create a DSP farm profile for transcoding.

```
GW_2811(config)#dspfarm profile profile transcoder
GW_2811(config-dsp-profile)#associate application sccp
GW_2811(config-dsp-profile)#maximum sessions number
GW_2811(config-dsp-profile)#no shutdown
```

With Enhanced Transcoding and Conferencing, you create one or more profiles for each service type. You can associate each profile with a CallManager group. The profiles are always associated with the application *sccp*.

Step 6 Create a DSP farm profile for conferencing.

```
GW_2811(config)#dspfarm profile profile conference
GW_2811(config-dsp-profile)#associate application sccp
GW_2811(config-dsp-profile)#maximum sessions sessions
GW_2811(config-dsp-profile)#no shutdown
```

Step 7 Create a DSP farm profile for MTP.

```
GW_2811(config)#dspfarm profile profile mtp
GW_2811(config-dsp-profile)#associate application sccp
GW_2811(config-dsp-profile)#maximum sessions {hardware¦software}
sessions
GW_2811(config-dsp-profile)#no shutdown
```

You can configure software MTPs without enabling DSP services on the voice-card, even if no voice card is installed in the router.

Step 8 Associate profiles with CallManager groups.

```
GW_2811(config)#sccp ccm group number
GW_2811(config-sccp-ccm)#associate ccm identifier priority priority
GW_2811(config-sccp-ccm)#associate profile profile register device-name
GW_2811(config-sccp-ccm)#bind interface interface
```

You can associate multiple profiles with a CallManager group. Each profile is assigned a unique *device-name* between 6 and 16 characters long, which is used to register with CallManager. The device-name must be unique to the ccm group.

Step 9 Define the resources in CallManager.

Example 14-10 illustrates the configuration of a 2811 with two PVDM2-16s installed on the main board to support transcoding, conferencing, and MTP resources. Figures 14-4, 14-5, and 14-6 show the associated CallManager configurations.

Example 14-10 *Configuring Transcoding and Conferencing on a PVDM2*

```
GW_2811#config terminal

Enter configuration commands, one per line. End with CNTL/Z.
GW_2811(config)#sccp local vlan5
GW_2811(config)#sccp ccm 10.1.5.2 identifier 1 version 4.1
GW_2811(config)#sccp ccm 10.1.5.3 identifier 2 version 4.1
GW_2811(config)#sccp
GW_2811(config)#voice-card 0
GW_2811(config-voicecard)#dsp services dspfarm
GW_2811(config-voicecard)#exit
GW_2811(config)#dspfarm profile 1 transcode
GW_2811(config-dspfarm-profile)#associate application sccp
GW_2811(config-dspfarm-profile)#maximum sessions ?
  <1-15>  Number of sessions assigned to this profile
```

Example 14-10 *Configuring Transcoding and Conferencing on a PVDM2 (Continued)*

```
GW_2811(config-dspfarm-profile)#maximum sessions 4
GW_2811(config-dspfarm-profile)#no shutdown
GW_2811(config-dspfarm-profile)#exit
GW_2811(config)#dsp profile 1 conference

Profile id 1 is being used for service TRANSCODING
 please select a different profile id
GW_2811(config)#dsp profile 2 conference
GW_2811(config-dspfarm-profile)#associate application sccp
GW_2811(config-dspfarm-profile)#maximum sessions ?
  <1-2>  Number of sessions assigned to this profile

GW_2811(config-dspfarm-profile)#maximum sessions 2
GW_2811(config-dspfarm-profile)#no shutdown
GW_2811(config-dspfarm-profile)#exit
GW_2811(config)#dspfarm profile 3 mtp
GW_2811(config-dspfarm-profile)#associate application sccp
GW_2811(config-dspfarm-profile)#maximum sessions hardware ?
  <1-8>  Number of sessions assigned to this profile

GW_2811(config-dspfarm-profile)#maximum sessions hardware 4
GW_2811(config-dspfarm-profile)#maximum sessions software ?
  <1-500>  Number of sessions assigned to this profile

GW_2811(config-dspfarm-profile)#maximum sessions software 10
GW_2811(config-dspfarm-profile)#no shutdown
GW_2811(config-dspfarm-profile)#exit
GW_2811(config)#sccp ccm group 10
GW_2811(config-sccp-ccm)#associate ccm 1 priority 1
GW_2811(config-sccp-ccm)#associate ccm 2 priority 2
GW_2811(config-sccp-ccm)#associate profile 1 register XCD123456
GW_2811(config-sccp-ccm)#associate profile 2 register CFB123456
GW_2811(config-sccp-ccm)#associate profile 3 register MTP123456
GW_2811(config-sccp-ccm)#bind interface vlan5
GW_2811(config-sccp-ccm)#^Z
GW_2811#show dspfarm all
Dspfarm Profile Configuration

 Profile ID = 1, Service = TRANSCODING, Resource ID = 1
 Profile Description :
 Profile Admin State : UP
 Profile Operation State : ACTIVE
 Application : SCCP    Status : ASSOCIATED
 Resource Provider : FLEX_DSPRM    Status : UP
 Number of Resource Configured : 4
 Number of Resource Available : 4
 Codec Configuration
 Codec : g711ulaw, Maximum Packetization Period : 30
 Codec : g711alaw, Maximum Packetization Period : 30
 Codec : g729ar8, Maximum Packetization Period : 60
 Codec : g729abr8, Maximum Packetization Period : 60
 Codec : gsmfr, Maximum Packetization Period : 20
```

continues

Example 14-10 *Configuring Transcoding and Conferencing on a PVDM2 (Continued)*

```
Dspfarm Profile Configuration

 Profile ID = 2, Service = CONFERENCING, Resource ID = 2
 Profile Description :
 Profile Admin State : UP
 Profile Operation State : ACTIVE
 Application : SCCP    Status : ASSOCIATED
 Resource Provider : FLEX_DSPRM    Status : UP
 Number of Resource Configured : 2
 Number of Resource Available : 2
 Codec Configuration
 Codec : g711ulaw, Maximum Packetization Period : 30 , Transcoder: Not Required
 Codec : g711alaw, Maximum Packetization Period : 30 , Transcoder: Not Required
 Codec : g729ar8, Maximum Packetization Period : 60 , Transcoder: Not Required
 Codec : g729abr8, Maximum Packetization Period : 60 , Transcoder: Not Required
 Codec : g729r8, Maximum Packetization Period : 60 , Transcoder: Not Required
 Codec : g729br8, Maximum Packetization Period : 60 , Transcoder: Not Required
Dspfarm Profile Configuration

 Profile ID = 3, Service = MTP, Resource ID = 3
 Profile Description :
 Profile Admin State : UP
 Profile Operation State : ACTIVE
 Application : SCCP    Status : ASSOCIATED
 Resource Provider : FLEX_DSPRM    Status : UP
 Number of Resource Configured : 14
 Number of Resource Available : 14
 Hardware Configured Resources : 4
 Hardware Available Resources : 4
 Software Resources : 10
 Codec Configuration
 Codec : g711ulaw, Maximum Packetization Period : 30



 SLOT DSP VERSION  STATUS CHNL USE    TYPE   RSC_ID BRIDGE_ID PKTS_TXED PKTS_RXED

 0   1   4.4.12    UP     N/A  FREE   xcode  1      -         -         -
 0   1   4.4.12    UP     N/A  FREE   xcode  1      -         -         -
 0   1   4.4.12    UP     N/A  FREE   xcode  1      -         -         -
 0   1   4.4.12    UP     N/A  FREE   xcode  1      -         -         -
 0   1   4.4.12    UP     N/A  FREE   mtp    3      -         -         -
 0   1   4.4.12    UP     N/A  FREE   mtp    3      -         -         -
 0   1   4.4.12    UP     N/A  FREE   mtp    3      -         -         -
 0   1   4.4.12    UP     N/A  FREE   mtp    3      -         -         -
 0   5   1.0.6     UP     N/A  FREE   conf   2      -         -         -
 0   5   1.0.6     UP     N/A  FREE   conf   2      -         -         -

 Total number of DSPFARM DSP channel(s) 10
```

Figure 14-4 *CallManager Enhanced IOS Transcoder Configuration*

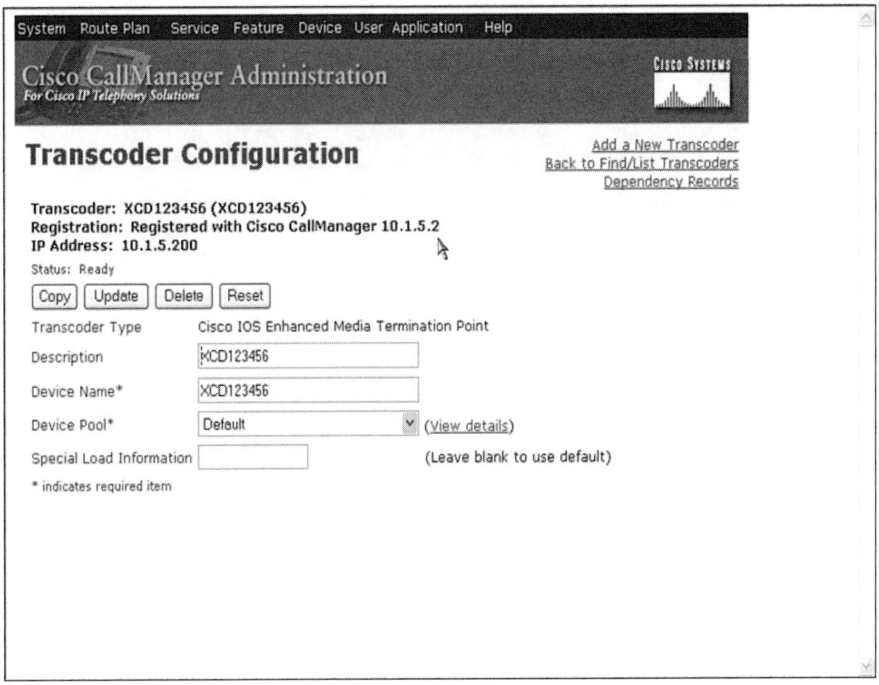

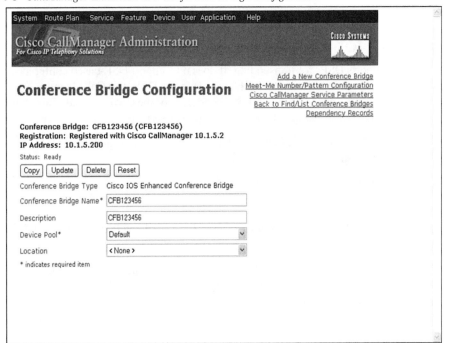

Figure 14-5 *CallManager Enhanced IOS Conference Bridge Configuration*

Figure 14-6 *CallManager Enhanced MTP Configuration*

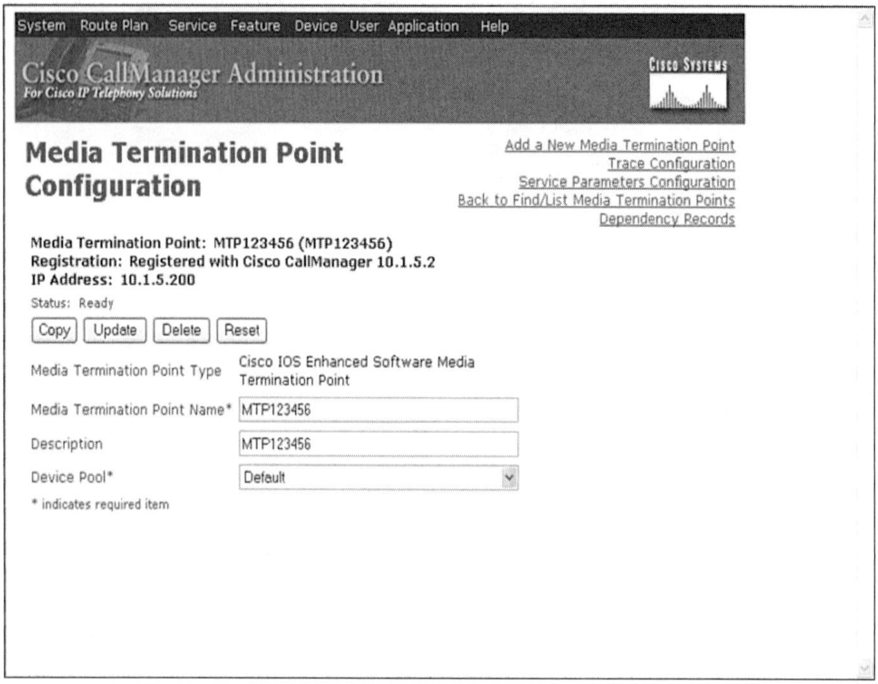

Transcoding for CallManager Express

CME supports DSPs for transcoding. It does not support DSP-based conference bridges at this time. The configuration is similar to registering DSPs to a CallManager. The IP address used in the **sccp ccm** command is the IP address of the CME service. This should match the **ip source-address** specified under telephony-service.

After you have completed Step 6 for C549 DSPs or Step 8 for C5510 DSPs, the following steps register the transcoders to CME:

Step 1 Enter telephony-service configuration mode.

```
GW_2811(config)#telephony-service
```

Step 2 Set the maximum number of DSP farms that can be registered to CME.

```
GW_2811(config-telephony)#sdspfarm units number
```

A CME can support up to five transcoder sessions. These can be locally defined transcoders on the CME gateway or DSPs that are defined on other gateways.

Step 3   Specify the maximum number of transcoding sessions supported across all
registered transcoders.

```
GW_2811(config-telephony)#sdspfarm transcode sessions number
```

This is the total number of sessions provided by all registered
transcoders. Valid entries are 1 through 128.

Step 4   Specify the name of the DSP farm.

```
GW_2811(config-telephony)#sdspfarm tag number device-name
```

The device name follows the same rules as CallManager registrations.
For C549 DSPs, the device-name is "MTP" plus the MAC address of the
SCCP local interface. For C5510 DSPs, the device-name is specified
when you associate the transcoder profile to the ccm group.

Case Study: Add DSP Resources to the Miami Gateway

Employees at the Miami location frequently conference in their supervisor when talking to
customers. You have been asked to provision local DSP resources to prevent these calls
from using DSP resources at headquarters.

The Miami location has a Cisco 2811 with two PVDM2-16s installed on the main board.
There is a channel-associated signaling (CAS) T1 to the PSTN installed in HWIC slot 3. A
VIC2-2FXO is installed in HWIC slot 0, and a VIC2-2FXS is installed in HWIC slot 1.
How many simultaneous conferences can the Miami gateway support?

At the default flex complexity, 32 channels are available to support voice termination.
Twenty-eight channels are required to support the four analog ports and 24 DS0s. This
requires the DSPs from both PVDM2-16s. Conference bridge resources require a dedicated
DSP—so the Miami gateway will not support conferences without some modification.

The best solution to this problem is to add additional PVDM2s to the gateway. The other
possible solution is to reduce the number of voice calls that the router handles. Because the
Miami call volume is light and consists mostly of inbound calls, you have decided to reduce
the number of DS0s allocated to the outbound DS0-group and remove the analog voice
ports that are not currently being used.

Example 14-11 illustrates the configuration for the Miami gateway after the voice port
modifications.

Example 14-11   *Configuring Conference Resources in Miami Gateway*

```
Miami#show configuration
Building configuration...

Current configuration : 3077 bytes
!
! Unnecessary output omitted...
```

continues

Example 14-11 *Configuring Conference Resources in Miami Gateway (Continued)*

```
!
! Enable DSP services on voice-card 0
!
voice-card 0
 dsp services dspfarm
!
!
interface FastEthernet0/0
 no ip address
 duplex auto
 speed auto
!
interface FastEthernet0/0.25
 encapsulation dot1Q 25
 ip address 10.10.25.1 255.255.255.0
!
interface FastEthernet0/0.50
 encapsulation dot1Q 50
 ip address 10.10.50.1 255.255.255.0
!
interface FastEthernet0/1
 no ip address
 shutdown
 duplex auto
 speed auto
!
controller T1 0/3/0
 framing esf
 linecode b8zs
 ds0-group 1 timeslots 1-12 type e&m-fgd
 ds0-group 2 timeslots 13-16 type fgd-eana
!
ip classless
!
!
voice-port 0/3/0:1
!
voice-port 0/3/0:2
!
! Define cmm addresses
!
sccp local FastEthernet0/0.25
sccp ccm 10.1.10.10 identifier 1 version 4.1
sccp ccm 10.1.10.11 identifier 2 version 4.1
sccp
!
!Create the CCM Group
!
sccp ccm group 10
 bind interface FastEthernet0/0.25
 associate ccm 1 priority 1
 associate profile 1 register CFB_Miami
```

Example 14-11   *Configuring Conference Resources in Miami Gateway (Continued)*

```
!
!Create the Conference Bridge Profile
!
dspfarm profile 1 conference
 codec g711ulaw
 codec g711alaw
 codec g729ar8
 codec g729abr8
 codec g729r8
 codec g729br8
 maximum sessions 2
 associate application SCCP
!
!
```

With this configuration, the Miami gateway will attempt to register its conferencing resources with CallManager, using a device-name of "CFB_Miami."

Review Questions

1 What is the purpose of a DSPFarm Profile?

2 When is a DSP needed for an MTP?

3 What is the default codec complexity for a C5510 DSP?

4 What is the major difference in the way C549 and C5510 DSPs handle voice termination?

5 You need to terminate 14 G.711 calls, provide transcoding for 6 G.729a to G.711 calls, and support 5 G.711 conference sessions with up to eight participants in each conference. What is the minimum number of DSPs required?

6 You need to support one mixed-mode conference with up to eight participants. How should you configure the maximum sessions under the conference profile?

7 Describe two benefits of DSP sharing.

8 Your ISR 2811 has an NM-HDV with five PVDM-12s and two PVDM2-48s installed on the main board. The NM-HDV is configured for medium complexity and has one E1 voice port. There are also two E1 voice ports in HWIC slots. What is the maximum number of G.711 conferences that you can support with the extra DSPs?

CHAPTER 15

Using Tcl Scripts and VoiceXML

Cisco voice gateways have the ability to support interactive voice response (IVR) and advanced call-handling applications using Toolkit Command Language (Tcl) or VoiceXML (sometimes referenced as VXML). Tcl and VoiceXML are scripting languages that allow the gateway to provide specialized call treatment, such as playing audio prompts and accepting user input using dual-tone multifrequency (DTMF) tones.

Dr. John Ousterhout developed the Tcl script language at the University of California, Berkeley. Cisco voice gateways run Tcl IVR 2.0, which is based on Tcl with a proprietary Cisco application programming interface (API). On the Cisco website, you will sometimes see Tcl referred to as "TCL," but the official name is Tcl.

VoiceXML is a standards-based markup language for voice browsers. VoiceXML can utilize existing web server and application logic, which can reduce development time and expense.

This chapter helps you to do the following:

- Understand how Tcl and VoiceXML applications operate
- Understand the difference between Tcl and VoiceXML applications
- Review sample Tcl scripts that are available from Cisco
- Implement Tcl scripts in a voice gateway
- Create audio files for use with Tcl scripts
- Verify and troubleshoot applications

Tcl IVR and VoiceXML Application Overview

Both Tcl IVR 2.0 and VoiceXML can support extremely complex applications. These complex applications are built by stringing together basic functions that fall into the following categories:

- Play audio prompts
- Collect user input in the form of DTMF tones
- Modify automatic number identification (ANI) or dialed number identification service (DNIS)

- Influence call routing
- Record call information
- Perform call admission control

NOTE   MGCP is not supported with Tcl or VoiceXML applications. To support applications, the gateway must have local control of the call.

The main difference between Tcl and VoiceXML is that the router executes a Tcl script, whereas a VoiceXML script is a client-server model. If the gateway associates a call with a VoiceXML application, the application loads the appropriate VoiceXML document that can call for the gateway to interact with various web applications. This document might play audio prompts and collect digits. You can load additional VoiceXML documents based on the caller input.

Both Tcl and VoiceXML servers can utilize external RADIUS authentication, authorization, and accounting (AAA) servers for authentication and billing and TFTP servers for storing of scripts or prompts.

Figure 15-1 shows the interaction between a caller and a typical Tcl application providing prepaid calling card service. The caller dials a toll-free access number. The Tcl script prompts the caller for his calling card number, his personal identification number (PIN), and the number he wants to reach. After the Tcl application authenticates the calling card number and PIN with the AAA server, it extends the call to the remote gateway. The remote gateway then completes the call to the destination.

Figure 15-1 *Caller Interaction with a Tcl Application*

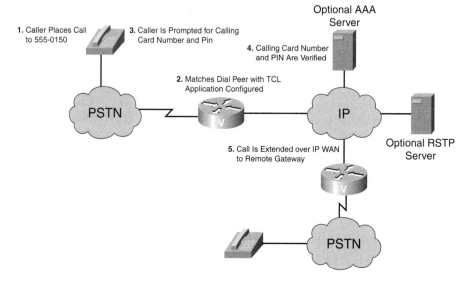

Figure 15-2 shows the interaction between a caller and a VoiceXML auto attendant (AA) application. The application prompts the user for his account number and uses this to access the customer records. The web application can then prompt the caller through checking balances, transferring funds, or other self-help activities, or it can transfer the caller to an agent for personalized service.

Figure 15-2 *Caller Interaction with a VoiceXML Application*

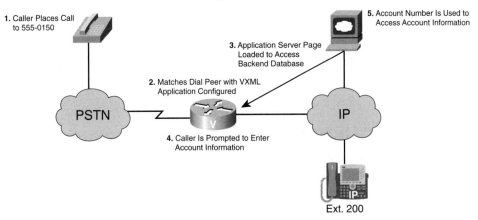

Tcl IVR 2.0 added support for Real Time Streaming Protocol (RTSP) servers. This allows you to store the audio files, or prompts, on the external server and stream them directly to the caller. This increases both the size and number of prompts that you can use in an application. Prompts that you store in the flash of the gateway or on a TFTP server are loaded into the DRAM and are played from DRAM to the caller. The applications discussed in this chapter would not typically require an RTSP server.

If a custom application requires access to servers for prompts or data retrieval, you should consider survivability if the servers are not accessible. For example, Cisco Voice Portal (CVP) includes a call survivability script that attempts to transfer callers to an alternate location in the event of CVP application errors.

Developing Tcl or VoiceXML scripts requires knowledge of programming that is beyond the scope of this book. Cisco provides numerous Tcl applications, some of which are described in the next section. This chapter focuses on implementing Tcl scripts using these Cisco-provided applications for illustration purposes. The methods for implementing VoiceXML applications are similar from the gateway perspective.

Programming Resources

Cisco provides two excellent resources for developing your own Tcl or VoiceXML applications. The *TCL IVR API Version 2.0 Programmer's Guide* and *Cisco VoiceXML*

Programmer's Guide are available from Cisco.com to registered users. Aspiring Tcl programmers should also review the wealth of information that is available at http://www.tcl.tk.

Cisco Systems also has a fee-based application development group that can develop an application to your specifications. In addition, a Cisco Technology Developer Program can provide support to third-party developers. Information on these programs is available from Cisco.com or from your Cisco account team.

NOTE	Only Tcl/VoiceXML applications that are developed through the Cisco Technology Developer Program are supported by the Cisco Technical Assistance Center (TAC).

Sample Applications

Cisco provides numerous Tcl applications for download from Cisco.com. The majority of these applications are focused on service provider needs, but several are useful to enterprise customers.

Auto Attendant

The auto attendant (AA) script is available for Survivable Remote Site Telephony (SRST) and Cisco CallManager Express (CME). This script provides basic call redirect based on caller input. When it is not possible or desirable to acquire a direct number for each phone at the location, the AA script allows you to use a single number, called the pilot number, to route calls. For example, a caller to the AA pilot number hears a customizable prompt to enter the desired extension or press 0 for the operator. When the caller enters a valid extension, the call is transferred. If the caller enters an invalid extension or does not enter any digits, the prompt is replayed. The steps for implementing the AA script are detailed in "Implementing the AA Tcl Script," later in this chapter.

NOTE	If Cisco Unity Express (CUE) is installed in an SRST/CME router, you should use it to provide AA functionality.

NOTE	Both SRST and CME have an AA script, but the scripts are not compatible. Make sure you download the correct script for your application.

Basic ACD

The Basic-ACD (B-ACD) script provides automatic call distribution (ACD) support for basic call center or help desk-type applications. The B-ACD script works in conjunction with the CME AA. It provides an IVR, which prompts callers through a menu to determine into which queue they should be placed. Each queue has an associated AA. The AA uses an e-phone hunt group to route the call to the next available agent. The B-ACD also provides statistics about calls, such as how long a caller waited before his call was answered and how many calls were routed to voice mail because the configurable max call timer expired.

Fax Detect

The Fax Detect script allows you to use a single number for both voice and fax calls. The script provides an option for prompting callers to press a particular key if they are placing a fax call. Alternatively, the script can detect that a call is a fax by listening for CalliNG (CNG) tones. When the script detects a fax call, it routes the call to the dial peer that is associated with the appropriate fax machine.

CAUTION   Fax Detect has several caveats, including a delay in call setup. Before you deploy the Fax Detect script, test it thoroughly to understand its possible side effects.

T.37 Store and Forward Fax

T.37 is a standard for converting faxes to Tagged Image File Format (TIFF) attachments that are sent via e-mail. T.37 Store and Forward Fax consists of an on-ramp and an off-ramp process. The on-ramp process converts an incoming fax to an e-mail message with a TIFF file attached. It can route an e-mail to an inbox or to an off-ramp process. The off-ramp process converts an e-mail that has a TIFF attachment back to a fax. You can load the on-ramp and off-ramp scripts on the same gateway or on different gateways.

Malicious Call ID

The Malicious Call ID (MCID) script works in conjunction with the MCID feature in Cisco CallManager 4.0. MCID allows a call recipient to press a programmable key on a Cisco IP phone if he receives a malicious call. This notifies the system administrator, flags the call in the call detail record (CDR) database, and instructs the gateway to send a message to the public switched telephone network (PSTN), allowing the service provider to take appropriate action. MCID is supported only on NET5 switches and must be enabled by the service provider.

Cisco Voice Portal

The Cisco Voice Portal (CVP) is a component of the Cisco customer contact product suite. CVP provides call treatment with self-service IVR options for both time-division multiplexing (TDM) and Voice over IP (VoIP) systems. Unlike the other sample applications listed here, CVP is not downloaded from Cisco.com.

CVP is included in this list because of the ability for a gateway to act as a remote site VoiceXML-controlled gateway for a centralized CVP server in a distributed contact center design. This is becoming a compelling network design for many Cisco customers. It allows the remote gateway to answer a call, play prompts, and collect the caller input. It keeps Real-Time Transport Protocol (RTP) streams off the network until the central ACD selects an agent to answer the call. If the caller uses the self-service features to complete his transaction and does not require an agent, the RTP call almost never uses bandwidth on the IP network.

Embedded Event Manager

The Cisco IOS Software Embedded Event Manager (EEM) is not a voice application; rather, it is a powerful tool that uses Tcl to greatly enhance network management. With EEM, you can define policies to take specific actions when Cisco IOS recognizes certain events. EEM uses event detectors to detect certain conditions in the device. EEM v2.2 has 15 event detectors; new event detectors are added with each version. The event detectors can either trigger an application policy included in EEM or can trigger custom Tcl scripts.

Downloading Tcl Scripts from Cisco.com

Tcl scripts are available in several locations on Cisco.com, depending on the application. You can find most Tcl applications by searching for "tclware." The notable exceptions are the AA and B-ACD Tcl scripts, which you can find in the CallManager Express/SRST software download section of Cisco.com.

It can be difficult to find the CME and SRST scripts because they are handled differently on Cisco.com. The CME AA and B-ACD scripts are available as individual downloads in zip and tar formats. The B-ACD script is also contained within some of the CME bundles. The SRST AA script is contained in a zip file called SRST-2.0.zip. This file is described as optional files for use with SRST 2.0. "Optional files" are also available for SRST 3.0 and SRST 3.3, but they do not include the AA Tcl script. The SRST 2.0 version of the AA script currently works with all available versions of SRST.

One of the most common problems with the AA script is using the wrong version. This is easy to do because only the CME script is labeled as an AA script, and the SRST AA script is not clearly labeled. If you use the CME version on an SRST router, the application loads and even answers the call. However, the caller does not hear prompts even though debugs indicate that the prompts are being played.

Configuring the Gateway to Use a Tcl Script

Five steps are required to implement a Tcl application on a Cisco voice gateway:

1 Load the script to flash memory or the TFTP server.

2 Load the associated audio prompts to flash memory or the RTSP server.

3 Initialize the application.

4 Specify the initial parameter values.

5 Configure the dial peers to use the script.

Cisco-developed Tcl scripts include a Readme file that describes the associated audio prompts and parameters that are associated with the script. Default audio prompts are typically included in the script, but you can rerecord them to meet your business needs.

Initializing Tcl Scripts and Specifying Parameters

The method of initializing a Tcl script and specifying initial parameter values changed in Cisco IOS Release 12.3(14)T. Prior to Cisco IOS Release 12.3(14)T, the **call application voice** command was used.

```
call application voice application-name location
```

The *application-name* is a label used within the gateway configuration, and the location is where the actual script is loaded from—either flash or a TFTP server.

After you load the application, you set parameters to their initial states:

```
call application voice application-name parameter-name value
```

This command is repeated for each parameter within the script.

Cisco IOS Release 12.3(14)T introduced an application configuration mode. This method is more hierarchical, which makes it much easier to read the configuration file and understand what is being loaded.

```
application
    service application-name location
    param parameter-name value
```

Applying Tcl Scripts

After you load the application and set the parameters to their initial values, you assign the application to a dial peer. You do this by using the **service command** under the dial-peer configuration.

```
service application-name
```

Configuring Inbound Applications

You run most applications on the inbound dial peer. For example, you run the AA script on the dial peer that is associated with calls coming from the PSTN. It is important to understand which dial peer will be matched for these inbound calls. To ensure that calls are routed as you expect, configure an explicit dial peer with an appropriate **incoming called-number** command.

You can associate applications with both plain old telephone service (POTS) and VoIP dial peers. When you associate an application with an inbound VoIP dial peer, the session target should point to a loopback interface on the local router. If you use an interface address, the application will be unavailable if that interface is down.

Configuring Outbound Applications

You can also configure applications on outbound dial peers. You use an outbound application when some preliminary processing is required before you enter the application. An inbound application must process a call before an outbound application can process it. You configure an outbound application by using the **outbound** keyword on the **service** *application-name* command.

```
service application-name outbound
```

A typical scenario would be routing calls to different VoIP dial peers based on the caller response to a prompt. The inbound application plays the prompt and collects the caller input. You can use the caller input to modify the DNIS, resulting in a specific outbound dial peer being selected. The outbound application on this dial peer can then perform additional functions.

Tcl Packages and Parameter Namespaces

Cisco IOS Release 12.3(14)T also provided a method to define packages and added the Parameter Namespace, or parameterspace. Tcl packages are Tcl or C functions or subroutines that Tcl scripts call. These packages give programmers a method of creating a "toolbox" of common functions, which can reduce the development time for new applications. Cisco gateways are preloaded with some packages. The packages vary by Cisco IOS version. The **show call application voice summary** command lists all available packages. Developers can create and load new packages using the **package** command in application configuration mode.

```
package package-name location
```

Parameter Namespaces, or parameterspaces, were added to prevent problems with two or more applications or packages that use the same parameter names. When you load an application or package, its parameterspace is defined. The parameterspace allows you to set initial values for parameters outside your local parameterspace. For example, your application might call functions that are defined in a package. Because the package has a defined parameterspace, you can set the initial values for the package parameter under your service configuration.

Tcl Parameters in Cisco IOS Release 12.3(14)T and Above

Cisco gateways support both global and local parameters. Global parameters are available to all scripts that run in the gateway. An example of a global parameter is a parameter used in a package, as just described. A single script or package uses local parameters. You set initial values for global parameters by using the **paramspace** command.

```
paramspace parameter-namespace parameter-name parameter-value
```

You set initial values for local parameters by using the **param** command:

```
param parameter-name parameter-value
```

The **param** command is used under the service or package. The "Implementing the AA Tcl Script" section in this chapter demonstrates the use of the **paramspace** and **param** commands.

NOTE   If you change a parameter value, you must reload the script for the changes to take effect.

With the introduction of parameterspaces, you can set parameter values under the service, package, or dial peer using the **paramspace** command. The ability to set parameter values in the dial peer strongly influences the way that a script functions. For example, assume that a company has two departmental receptionists—one for sales at extension 2000 and one for service at extension 3000. The company has published unique numbers for the two departments, so it has an incoming dial peer for each departmental number. You can load the same AA application on the two incoming dial peers. In one dial peer, you could set the operator number to 2000, whereas in the other, you could set the operator number to 3000. Prior to this Parameterspace feature, you would have needed to load the AA application twice, with two unique application names.

NOTE   You should register parameters in an application per the *TCL IVR 2.0 Programmer's Guide.* Some Tcl scripts available from Cisco have not been updated to register their parameters. When you set the initial value for these parameters using the **param** command, you might receive a warning message stating that the parameter has not been registered under the namespace. This should not affect the operation of the script.

Order of Parameter Precedence

If you configure the same parameter in multiple locations, the value that you assign in the dial peer takes precedence over the value that you assign in the service configuration mode. The value that you assign in the package configuration mode has the lowest precedence.

Upgrading to Cisco IOS Release 12.3(14)T and Later

The **call application voice** commands in previous versions of Cisco IOS are automatically updated to the new format. No manual reconfiguration is required. In Cisco IOS Release 12.3(14)T, the call application voice command is still available, but no help exists for the command. If you enter the **call application voice** commands, they appear in your configuration file in the new application format.

CAUTION   Downgrading from 12.3.14T to an earlier version does not automatically modify the application commands. You should always back up your configuration file before upgrading to a new Cisco IOS release.

Implementing the AA Tcl Script

Figure 15-3 shows the call flow that is associated with the AA script for CME.

Figure 15-3 *CME AA Call Flow*

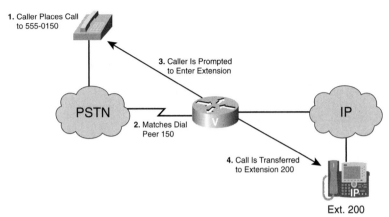

The script takes the following actions when a call matches the incoming dial peer that is configured with the AA script:

- A caller places a call to the AA pilot number.

- The script plays Prompt en_welcome.au, thanking the caller. Then it plays Prompt en_enter_dest.au, asking the caller to enter an extension.

- If the caller enters no digits or presses 0, the script transfers the call to the operator extension that is configured in the command-line interface (CLI).

- If the caller enters an invalid destination, the script plays en_reenter_dest.au prompt, asking the caller to reenter the destination. The script repeats this up to three times. After the third time, the script plays en_disconnect.au prompt and disconnects the call.

- If the caller enters a valid extension, the script transfers the call.

- If the extension is busy, the script plays the en_dest_busy.au prompt, asking the caller to enter a different extension or try the call at a later time.

- If the extension is unreachable, the script plays the en_dest_unreachable.au prompt, asking the caller to enter a different extension or try the call at a later time.

Example 15-1 illustrates the configuration required to load the Tcl AA script for CME from the flash of the router.

Example 15-1 *Loading the Tcl AA Script for SRST*

```
Miami#config t
Miami(config)#application
!
! Load the AA script from flash
!
Miami(config-app)#service aa flash:its_CISCO.2.0.1.0.tcl
```

continues

Example 15-1   *Loading the Tcl AA Script for SRST (Continued)*

```
!
! Configure the AA parameters that are associated with the English package
!
Miami(config-app-param)#paramspace english language en
Miami(config-app-param)#paramspace english location flash:
Miami(config-app-param)#paramspace english prefix en
Miami(config-app-param)#paramspace english index 1
!
!Configure the AA application local parameters
!
Miami(config-app-param)#param operator 150
Miami(config-app-param)#param aa-pilot 100
!
! Apply the AA script to the dial peer
!
Miami(config)#dial-peer voice 100 pots
Miami(config-dial-peer)#incoming called-number 100
Miami(config-dial-peer)#service aa
Miami(config-dial-peer)#direct-inward-dial
Miami(config-dial-peer)#port 1/0/0:1
```

Example 15-2 illustrates the configuration required to load the Tcl AA script for CME prior to Cisco IOS Release 12.3(14)T. The dial peer configuration is the same as in Example 15-1.

Example 15-2   *Loading the Tcl AA Script Prior to Cisco IOS Release 12.3(14)T*

```
Miami#config t
Miami(config)#call application voice aa flash:its_CISCO.2.0.1.0.tcl
Miami(config)#call application voice aa language 1 en
Miami(config)#call application voice aa operator 150
Miami(config)#call application voice aa aa-pilot 100
Miami(config)#call application voice aa set-location en 1 flash:
```

Creating Audio Files

You can rerecord audio files to meet your business needs. When you are using Cisco-provided Tcl scripts, you must save audio files using the same names. Audio files must have these properties:

- au format
- 8-bit
- μ-law
- 8-KHz encoding

Restrictions and Caveats

You need to keep several important restrictions in mind when you are applying or developing applications:

- To collect digits over an IP call leg, configure DTMF-Relay.

- RTSP multicast is not supported.

- Tcl IVR 1.0 and Tcl IVR 2.0 are not compatible.

- For VoiceXML, the web server must support HTTP 1.1.

- Load Dynamic VoiceXML documents by using HTTP. Using FTP or TFTP impacts performance.

- VoiceXML does not support ISDN Overlap signaling.

- You cannot apply applications to CallManager-controlled Multiple Gateway Control Point (MGCP) gateways.

- The SRST and CME AA scripts only work on POTS dial peers. They do not support calls from IP phones.

Case Study: Implementing ACD Application

The Leeds branch wants to implement a simple ACD for the service department, as shown in Figure 15-4. The three service technicians will answer calls to the pilot number of 496-0400. The manager wants all available phones to ring simultaneously to reduce the amount of time that callers have to wait.

Figure 15-4 *Leeds Branch ACD Call Flow*

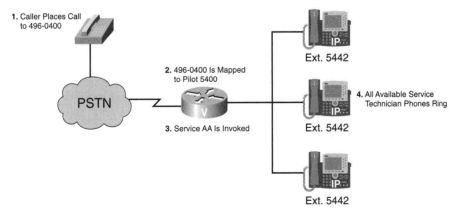

To implement this solution, download the B-ACD version 2.1.0.0 Tcl script, load it on the flash of the Leeds gateway, and rerecord the prompts. Because only one queue is available, you can implement the B-ACD script in "drop-through" mode. This mode plays an optional welcome audio prompt and then sends the call to the queue. If multiple queues exist, you can configure the AA application with multiple pilot numbers and provide the capability to dial by extension. Example 15-3 details the configuration required to enable the B-ACD application. The parameters are subject to change based on the version of the script. Always review the Readme file for any script downloaded from Cisco.com to determine how to set parameters.

Example 15-3 *Configuring the B-ACD Tcl Script*

```
Leeds#show config
!
!Unnecessary output omitted
!
ip dhcp excluded-address 10.40.25.1 10.40.25.99
ip dhcp excluded-address 10.40.50.1 10.40.50.99
!
ip dhcp pool Data
   network 10.40.25.0 255.255.255.0
   default-router 10.40.25.1
   dns-server 10.1.25.100
!
ip dhcp pool voice
   network 10.40.50.0 255.255.255.0
   default-router 10.40.50.1
   dns-server 10.1.25.100
   option 150 ip 10.40.50.1
!
application
!
! Load the acd script from flash and define the service name as queue
!
 service queue flash:app_b_acd_x.x.x.x.tcl
  param queue-len 10
  param aa-hunt1 6400
  param number-of-hunt-grps 1
  param queue-manager-debugs 1
!
! Load the acd-aa script from flash and associate it with the queue service
!
 service aa flash:app_b_acd_aa_x.x.x.x.tcl
  paramspace english location flash:
  paramspace english index 0
  paramspace english language en
  param aa-pilot 5400
  param call-retry-timer 15
  param second-greeting-time 60
  param max-time-call-retry 600
  param max-time-vm-retry 2
  param service-name queue
  param hand-off string aa
  param drop-through-option 1
  param drop-through-prompt Leeds_svc_welcome.au
```

Example 15-3   *Configuring the B-ACD Tcl Script (Continued)*

```
   param voice-mail  5350
   param number-of-hunt-grps 1
 !
voice translation-rule 1
 rule 1 /\(4960\)\(...\)/ /5\2/
 !
voice translation-profile Chg_DNIS
 translate called 1
 !
controller E1 1/0
 ds0-group 1 timeslots 1-31 type r2-digital r2-compelled ani
 !
voice-port 1/0/0:1
 translation-profile incoming Chg_DNIS
 !
dial-peer voice 5400 pots
 service aa
 incoming called-number 5400
 port 1/0/0:1
 !
telephony-service
 load 7960-7940 P00307020200
 max-ephones 120
 max-dn 240
 ip source-address 10.40.50.1 port 2000
 max-conferences 8 gain -6
 !
ephone-dn 42
 number 5442
 !
ephone-dn 43
 number 5443
 !
ephone-dn 44
 number 5444
 !
ephone 42
 mac-address 4242.4242.4242
 button 1o42,43,44
 !
ephone 43
 mac-address 4343.4343.4343
 button 1o42,43,44
 !
ephone 44
 mac-address 4444.4444.4444
 button 1o42,43,44
 !
 ! Build the hunt group with the three technician phones
 ! Selected a pilot number outside the range for Leeds
 ! since only the queue application will use this number
 !
```

continues

Example 15-3 *Configuring the B-ACD Tcl Script (Continued)*

```
ephone-hunt 1 sequential
 pilot 6400
 list 5442,5443,5444
 !
```

Review Questions

  1 Why would you choose to implement an application in Tcl instead of VoiceXML?

  2 Why would you choose to implement an application in VoiceXML instead of Tcl?

  3 What is the precedence order for setting parameter values?

  4 What is a package?

  5 What is the purpose of a parameter namespace?

  6 What application enhances the network management capabilities of Cisco routers?

  7 What protocol can you use to increase the size and number of prompts available to an application?

  8 What are the requirements for recording an application prompt?

Gatekeepers

CHAPTER 16

Deploying Gatekeepers

A gatekeeper is an H.323 device that can provide services such as address translation, admission control, bandwidth management, and centralized dial plan management to facilitate network scalability. Gatekeepers can provide these services for H.323 terminals, gateways, and multipoint control units (MCU). Cisco CallManager can also take advantage of gatekeeper services.

The Cisco IOS gatekeeper feature is supported on the Cisco 2600, 3600, 3700, 2800, 3800, and 7200 families of routers using the appropriate Cisco IOS and feature license.

Although gatekeeper usage is optional, a gatekeeper can provide many benefits to improve scalability and management. It this chapter, you will learn about the benefits that gatekeepers can provide in an IP Telephony network.

This chapter helps you to do the following:

- Comprehend the terminology used when discussing gatekeepers
- Understand gatekeeper mandatory and optional functions that you can use in an IP Telephony network
- Know the protocols and signaling methods that gatekeepers use
- Be able to select appropriate hardware and software to use for gatekeeper deployments
- Learn the various deployment models that you can use to enhance scalability of a gatekeeper-controlled network
- Discover how CallManager interacts with an H.323 gatekeeper

Gatekeeper Functionality

The concept of a *zone* is used to define the group of H.323 devices that an individual gatekeeper controls. That is, the devices that belong to the zone register with the controlling gatekeeper. Zones can cross subnets, and a gatekeeper can manage devices in one or more subnets. Up to 100 zones can be registered to an individual gatekeeper.

Prior to H.323 Version 2, only one gatekeeper could be active in a zone at a time. H.323 Version 2 introduced the concept of alternate gatekeepers. Implementing the alternate gatekeeper feature allows multiple gatekeepers to control one zone. This helps to provide redundancy and load sharing for large installations. The gateway must also support the alternate gatekeeper to use this feature.

Figure 16-1 is an example of two gatekeepers controlling devices in two separate zones. Notice that communication and signaling can cross between the zones.

Figure 16-1 *Multiple Gatekeepers and Zones*

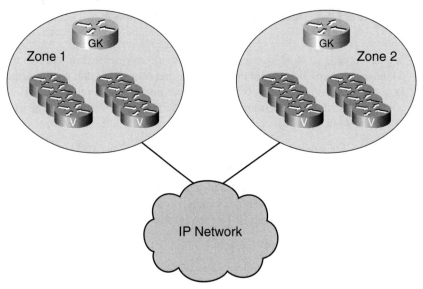

The following are services for voice calls that the gatekeeper can provide:

- **Address resolution**—H.323 IDs and E.164 telephone numbers can be resolved to an IP address for the destination gateway. This is similar to the way Domain Name Services (DNS) resolve fully qualified domain names to their associated IP addresses.

- **Admission control**—Gateways or endpoints that are initiating a call request admission into the H.323 network. For example, a gateway can request to place a phone call, and the gateway then presents the called number to the gatekeeper. If the gatekeeper can resolve the number, security requirements are met, and bandwidth is available, the gatekeeper permits the call to be placed.

  Bandwidth management—The gatekeeper can track bandwidth that active calls use both within and between zones. You can configure the maximum bandwidth available. When you place a call, the bandwidth used is subtracted from the maximum. If bandwidth is insufficient to place the call, the call is rejected. When a call terminates, the bandwidth for that call is returned to the available pool.

Bandwidth is initially managed during admission control. If the bandwidth requirements change during a call, the gateway makes a bandwidth request of the gatekeeper. If the new bandwidth is available, the request is accepted; otherwise, it is rejected.

- **Zone management**—The gatekeeper controls gateway registration within the controlled zone. Gateways make registration requests to the gatekeeper. The gatekeeper either allows the gateway to register or rejects the request.

- **Call authorization**—This option allows a gatekeeper to control access to and from certain gateways or endpoints. You can do this using authentication, authorization, and accounting (AAA) services that Cisco IOS provides in conjunction with a RADIUS server.

Gatekeeper Signaling

Cisco IOS gatekeepers use a variety of signaling methods to provide control capabilities, redundancy, and extensibility of the H.323 network. These include the H.323 Registration, Admission, and Status Protocol (RAS), the Gatekeeper Update Protocol (GUP), and the Gatekeeper Transaction Messaging Protocol (GKTMP).

RAS Signaling

Gatekeepers are H.323 devices that use the RAS protocol to communicate with Cisco voice gateways. RAS is a subset of the H.225 signaling protocol.

Call control and call setup are also done using H.225 signaling. If the call control/call setup H.225 messages go directly between gateways (not through the gatekeeper), it is known as direct endpoint signaling. Some gatekeeper implementations support gatekeeper-routed call signaling (GKRCS). With GKRCS, all H.225 signaling (RAS and call control/call setup) is passed from the gateway to the gatekeeper. No H.225 messages are sent directly between gateways.

NOTE	Cisco gatekeeper implementations do not support GKRCS. Only direct endpoint signaling is supported.

H.245 signaling is another subset of H.323 that is used for media control. H.245 flows directly between gateways to facilitate setup of the media stream.

Figure 16-2 shows the H.323 signaling and media flow for a typical voice call.

Figure 16-2 *H.323 Signaling Flow*

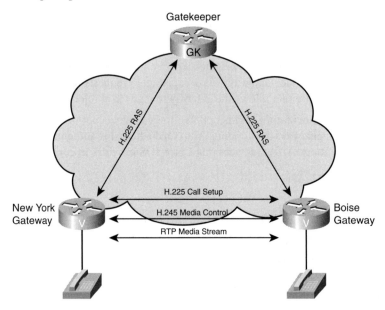

H.225 RAS uses defined message types to communicate between the gatekeeper and the gateway. Table 16-1 lists the specific RAS messages.

Table 16-1 *H.225 RAS Messages*

Message Type	Message Code	Message Code Expansion	Description
Gatekeeper discovery messages	GRQ	Gatekeeper Request	Message that a gateway sends during the gatekeeper discovery process.
	GCF	Gatekeeper Confirm	Reply from the gatekeeper to the gateway, which indicates the transport address (port) of the gatekeeper RAS channel.
	GRJ	Gatekeeper Reject	Reply from the gatekeeper to gateway that rejects the gateway request for registration. Usually due to gateway or gatekeeper configuration error.

Table 16-1   *H.225 RAS Messages (Continued)*

Message Type	Message Code	Message Code Expansion	Description
Gatekeeper registration messages	RRQ	Registration Request	Message sent from a gateway to the gatekeeper.
	RCF	Registration Confirm	Message acknowledging that the gatekeeper has allowed gateway registration.
	RRJ	Registration Reject	Message acknowledging that the gatekeeper has not allowed the gateway to register.
	URQ	Unregister Request	Message sent from a gateway or gatekeeper requesting cancellation of the registration.
	UCF	Unregister Confirm	Message sent from a gateway or the gatekeeper to confirm unregistration.
	URJ	Unregister Reject	Response to a URQ when the gateway was not registered.
Admission control messages	ARQ	Admission Request	Message that a gateway sends to initiate a call.
	ACF	Admission Confirm	Reply from the gatekeeper to the gateway admitting the call. This message also contains the IP address of the destination gateway so that the originating gateway can begin call control signaling.
	ARJ	Admission Reject	Reply from the gatekeeper denying the call request. This can be for many reasons, including a number that could not be resolved to an IP address, insufficient available bandwidth, and so on.
Location request messages	LRQ	Location Request	Message sent between gatekeepers to find a gateway in a different zone.
	LCF	Location Confirm	Message sent between gatekeepers to provide the IP address of the requested gateway.
	LRJ	Location Reject	Message sent between gatekeepers in response to an LRQ when the requested gateway is unknown or not registered.

continues

Table 16-1 *H.225 RAS Messages (Continued)*

Message Type	Message Code	Message Code Expansion	Description
Status information messages	IRQ	Information Request	Message sent from the gatekeeper to a gateway.
	IRR	Information Response	Message sent from the gateway to tell the gatekeeper about active calls.
	IACK	Information Request Acknowledgement	Response from the gatekeeper to a successfully handled IRR.
	INACK	Information Request Negative Acknowledgement	Response from the gatekeeper for an unsuccessful IRR.
	RIP	Request in Progress	Message sent from a gatekeeper to a gateway when the gatekeeper must use an LRQ to resolve an ACF in a different zone.
Bandwidth control messages	BRQ	Bandwidth Request	A request for an increase/decrease in call bandwidth that the gateway sends to the gatekeeper.
	BCF	Bandwidth Confirm	Message that the gatekeeper sends to confirm the acceptance of the bandwidth change request.
	BRJ	Bandwidth Reject	Message that the gatekeeper sends to reject the bandwidth change request.
	RAI	Resource Availability Indication	Message that gateways use to inform the gatekeeper whether resources are available in the gateway to take on additional calls.
	RAC	Resource Availability Confirm	Response from the gatekeeper to the gateway that acknowledges the reception of the RAI message.

Gatekeeper Discovery Process

A gateway will send a GRQ RAS message when trying to identify the gatekeeper for its zone. An H.323 gateway can discover its zone gatekeeper in two ways:

- **Unicast discovery**—This method requires that the IP address of the gatekeeper is configured in the gateway. The gateway immediately sends a GRQ using User Datagram Protocol (UDP) port 1718. The gatekeeper either responds with a GCF or a GRJ.

- **Multicast discovery**—This method enables a gateway to automatically discover its gatekeeper through a multicast GRQ message sent on multicast address 224.0.1.41. Using this method has less administrative overhead because the gateways do not have to be statically configured with the gatekeeper address. A gatekeeper can be configured to respond only to certain subnets.

  If multiple gatekeepers are on the network, using multicast discovery might require you to implement an IP network design such that a gateway or other endpoint can reach only the correct gatekeeper using the multicast message, or use unicast gatekeeper discovery. If multiple gatekeepers are reachable, you will not know which gatekeeper is discovered by the multicast, and unpredictable behavior can result.

If a gatekeeper is not available, the gateway attempts to rediscover one. If a gateway discovers that its gatekeeper has gone off-line, it no longer accepts new calls; however, calls in progress are not affected.

Because of the criticality of the gatekeeper in the network, most users implement redundancy to minimize the possibility of a network outage because of a failure. Methods of implementing redundancy are discussed later in this chapter.

Figure 16-3 illustrates both methods of gatekeeper discovery.

Figure 16-3   *Gatekeeper Discovery*

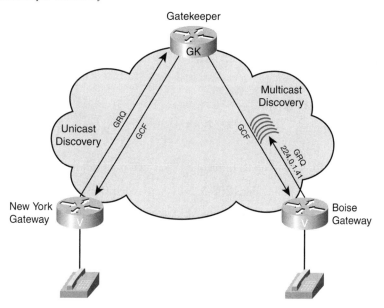

H.323 Call Flows Using Gatekeepers

Figure 16-4 shows an example of a call flow between two gateways within the same zone when a gatekeeper is used for E.164 number resolution. Both sides must successfully request admission before the call can be completed. Both gateways send IRRs to the gatekeeper after the call setup is complete and again when the call is terminated. The IRR messages are especially important if you are using the gatekeeper to collect call detail records (CDR) or for call admission control (CAC). When the IRR is received at the end of a call, the CDR is logged and the bandwidth that is used by that call is freed.

Figure 16-4 *H.323 Intrazone Call Setup*

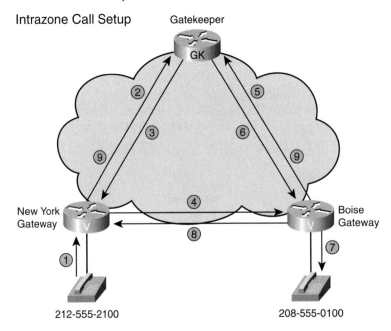

The process for setting up an intrazone H.323 call is as follows:

1   A New York phone dials 208-555-0100 to reach Boise.

2   A New York gateway sends an ARQ, asking permission to call Boise.

3   The gatekeeper does a lookup and finds that the Boise gateway is registered. The gatekeeper returns an ACF to the New York gateway with the IP address of Boise.

4   The New York gateway sends an H.225 (Q.931) call setup message to the Boise gateway, including the phone number.

5   The Boise gateway sends an ARQ to the gatekeeper requesting permission to answer the call.

6 The gatekeeper returns an ACF message, which includes the IP address of the New York gateway.

7 The Boise gateway sets up a plain old telephone service (POTS) call to the phone at 208-555-0100.

8 When the phone is answered, the Boise gateway sends an H.225 (Q.931) Connect message to the New York gateway.

9 Both gateways send an IRR to the gatekeeper after the call setup is complete.

Figure 16-5 shows an example of the signaling flow for the same call with each of the gateways belonging to a different gatekeeper zone.

Figure 16-5 *H.323 Interzone Call Setup*

Interzone Call Setup

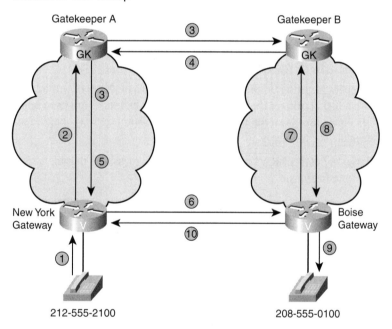

212-555-2100   208-555-0100

The process for setting up an interzone H.323 call is as follows:

1 A New York phone calls the Boise phone at 208-555-0100.

2 A New York gateway sends Gatekeeper A (the gatekeeper where the New York gateway is registered) an ARQ, requesting permission to make the call.

3 Gatekeeper A does not find a match for the requested phone number; however, it does a prefix lookup and finds Gatekeeper B. Gatekeeper A sends an LRQ to Gatekeeper B. At the same time, Gatekeeper A sends an RIP message to the New York gateway.

4 Gatekeeper B finds a match on the number with the Boise gateway. Gatekeeper B returns an LCF to Gatekeeper A with the IP address of Boise.

5 Gatekeeper A sends an ACF to the New York gateway with the IP address of Boise.

6 The New York gateway sends an H.225 (Q.931) call setup request to the Boise gateway, including the 208-555-0100 called phone number.

7 The Boise gateway sends Gatekeeper B an ARQ requesting permission to complete the call.

8 Gatekeeper B returns an ACF that includes the IP address of the New York gateway.

9 The Boise gateway sets up a POTS call to the phone at 208-555-0100.

10 When the phone is answered, the Boise gateway sends an H.225 (Q.931) Connect message to the New York gateway.

11 Both gateways send an IRR to the gatekeeper after the call setup is complete.

Gatekeeper Update Protocol

Gatekeeper clustering or alternate gatekeepers are methods of providing gatekeeper redundancy that utilizes the GUP protocol. GUP messages are used both to establish the initial connections between members of the cluster and to exchange status information between cluster members.

GUP uses versions of RAS gatekeeper discovery messages that include nonstandard fields for communications.

When the cluster is first established, the gatekeeper opens and maintains a TCP connection to the other members of the cluster (the alternate gatekeepers). The gatekeeper announces its presence by sending a GRQ message containing nonstandard data; then it flags it as an announcement. The announcement also carries information about bandwidth utilization for a zone. This allows the alternate gatekeepers to manage the bandwidth for a zone even though they are separate devices.

GUP GRQ messages can be one of the following formats: announcementIndication, announcementReject, registrationIndication, unregistrationIndication, or resourceIndication.

GUP announcements are sent every 30 seconds by default. Cluster members assume that a gatekeeper has failed if nothing is heard from that gatekeeper for six consecutive announcement periods or if the TCP connection is lost.

When a gateway registers/unregisters with a gatekeeper in a cluster, that gatekeeper uses the registrationIndication/ unregistrationIndication message to update all other gatekeepers in that cluster.

If a gateway reports a resource change using an RAI message to a gatekeeper in a cluster, that gatekeeper reports the change to all alternate gatekeepers in the cluster using the GUP resourceIndication message.

GUP messages allow all the gatekeepers in a cluster to have knowledge about the registration status, bandwidth, active calls, and resource status for every gateway in the zone.

Gatekeeper Transaction Message Protocol

Although the Cisco gatekeeper provides a rich set of functions to assist in controlling an H.323 network, additional functionality might be needed sometimes. Examples might include requirements for additional authentication, the need to implement additional specific policy controls, the desire to use Internet call waiting, or any other customized application logic used to direct call setup and control.

GKTMP was developed along with the gatekeeper application programming interface (API) to facilitate communication between the gatekeeper and an external application.

GKTMP is based on RAS and provides a set of messages that can be used to exchange information between the Cisco gatekeeper and an external application over a TCP connection.

Through the use of GKTMP and the gatekeeper API, organizations can add new functionality to the gatekeeper by using external applications. This can be done transparently to the H.323 gateways.

You can find more information about GKTMP and the gatekeeper API in the *Cisco Gatekeeper External Interface Reference* available at Cisco.com.

E.164 Number Resolution

Cisco gatekeepers group gateways into logical zones and perform call routing between them. Cisco gatekeepers handle call routing among gateways in the H.323 network and provide centralized dial plan administration. Without a Cisco gatekeeper, Voice over IP (VoIP) dial peers would need to be configured in every originating gateway for each possible termination gateway within the network. These would need to point to the specific IP address (or DNS name) for each terminating gateway. With a Cisco gatekeeper, gateways query the gatekeeper when trying to establish VoIP calls with a remote VoIP gateway.

For example, when a call request is made, the gateway determines whether to send it to a connected trunk (public switched telephone network [PSTN] or PBX) or to an IP destination based on the configured dial plan. In the case of an IP destination, the gateway queries the Cisco gatekeeper to select the best gateway.

ARQ and LRQ are the two RAS messages that initiate call routing. Gatekeepers receive ARQ messages from a gateway registered to a local zone either as a result of an outbound call initiation from the gateway or to request permission to accept an incoming call.

LRQ messages are passed between different gatekeepers and are used to route calls from a local to a remote zone (interzone routing).

Zone Prefixes

A zone prefix is the part of a called number that identifies the destination zone (local or remote) for the call. Zone prefixes can be based on area codes and local exchanges, or any characteristic of the called number prefix that makes it unique to the call routing domain. If the network is supporting extension dialing between locations, the zone prefix might be the first number of the extension or a location code used to identify a remote site. Whatever prefix is selected must be unique so that the gatekeeper can select the proper destination zone for the call.

In Example 16-1, calls beginning with 212 are routed to the NY local zone, and calls beginning with 208 are routed to the BO local zone.

Example 16-1 *Zone Prefixes*

```
gatekeeper
    zone local NY cisco.com 10.1.5.1 1719
    zone local BO cisco.com
    zone prefix NY 212.......
    zone prefix BO 208.......
```

You can configure zone prefixes manually, as shown in the example. Cisco IOS Versions 12.1T and later support an H.323 Version 2 enhancement that allows automatic creation of zone prefixes for devices with assigned E.164 addresses that are attached to the gateway, such as phones connected to Foreign Exchange Station (FXS) ports. Cisco IOS Versions 12.2.15T and later support an H.323 Version 4 feature that allows gateways to dynamically register prefixes that are assigned to POTS dial peers.

Multiple prefixes can exist for a single local zone, and a gateway belonging to multiple zone prefixes might register to the gatekeeper.

Prefixes can have overlapping number ranges. If prefixes overlap, the prefix that has the longest match is used. For example, if you have defined a prefix for the NY gateway as "212" and one for the Boise gateway as "2..", the prefixes will overlap. In this case, both prefixes begin with a "2," and numbers beginning with "212" could match either prefix. However, the longest match is to the NY prefix of "212," and it will always be selected. Conversely, a "212" number will never match the "2" prefix, even if the NY gateway is not registered to the gatekeeper. In this case, the "212" prefix will still be matched, but the address of the gateway will be unknown, so an ARJ will be sent. An exception to this is if the prefixes are dynamically learned from the gateways. In this case, if the NY gateway is unregistered, the "212" prefix will be deleted, and the "2.." prefix will be matched.

It is important to understand how prefix matching is done so that you can properly design a gatekeeper-controlled dial plan.

Technology Prefixes

A technology prefix is an optional H.323 feature that the Cisco gatekeeper uses to group gateways by type (such as voice or video) or class or to define a pool of gateways.

When you are routing a call, you use the technology prefix when no registered E.164 address matches the called number.

To use technology prefixes, you must do two things:

- **Assign the gateway a technology prefix**—You can do this on the gateway so that the prefix is registered with the gatekeeper as part of the RRQ. You can also configure it statically on the gatekeeper so that the technology prefix is associated with the gateway IP address.

  This identifies the technology (type, class, or pool) that the gatekeeper associates with this particular gateway when performing call routing.

- **Prepend a technology prefix to the called number sent in the ARQ to the gatekeeper**—You can do this on the H.323 VoIP dial-peer configuration within the gateways. The gatekeeper attempts to match the appended technology prefix with the prefix of a registered gateway to identify the destination zone for routing.

  The technology prefix is stripped from the called number when the gatekeeper attempts to match a zone prefix. However, the full number with the technology prefix is delivered to the destination gateway. Be sure that POTS dial-peers are updated to handle this properly.

You can also configure a default technology prefix in the gatekeeper. Registered gateways with the matching technology prefix are used as default for routing call addresses that are unresolved. Some H.323 endpoints do not support coding a technology prefix. The default technology that is defined on the gatekeeper is also used for those devices.

You can also configure hop-offs on the gatekeeper based on technology prefix. A hop-off is used to override the zone prefix and force the call to be routed to the specified hop-off zone regardless of the called number zone prefix.

Technology prefixes are most often used in multimedia H.323 networks to identify the type of call as either video or voice. They are also used in large networks where multiple gateways are pooled to provide greater capacity and redundancy.

Gatekeeper Call Routing Process

Figure 16-6 illustrates the overall process that the Cisco gatekeeper uses to try to route a call. The Cisco multiservice IP-to-IP gateway (IPIPGW) feature introduces gatekeeper via-zones. The sections of the diagram that are labeled "Via-Zone Processing" refer to a separate decision tree process that the via-zone-enabled gatekeepers use in an IPIPGW environment. This concept is discussed in Chapter 18, "Cisco Multiservice IP-to-IP Gateway."

Figure 16-6 *Gatekeeper Call Routing Decision Tree*

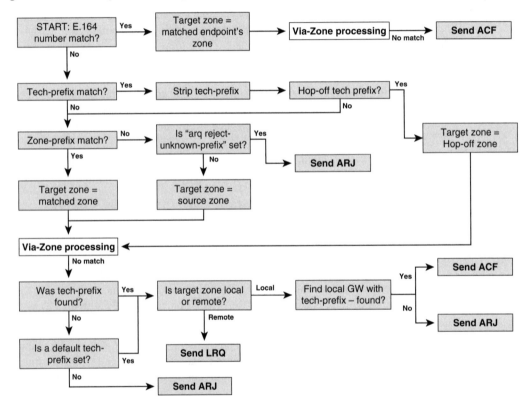

Call Admission Control

Call admission control (CAC) is important to the successful implementation of an IP voice network. If the amount of bandwidth required to support active calls exceeds that which is available on the network, voice quality suffers for all calls. Several mechanisms are available to provide CAC services. The methods selected depend heavily on the overall design of the network. Available CAC mechanisms include CallManager location-based

CAC and Resource Reservation Protocol (RSVP). You can also configure the Cisco gatekeeper to provide CAC on an H.323 network.

The gatekeeper maintains a record of all active calls so that it can manage the bandwidth in a zone. When calculating whether enough bandwidth is available to accept a call ARQ, the gatekeeper uses the following formula:

Available bandwidth = (Total allocated bandwidth) × (Bandwidth used locally) × (Bandwidth used by all alternates)

If the available bandwidth is sufficient for the call, an ACF is returned; otherwise, an ARJ is sent.

When you configure bandwidth control, you need to consider the coder/decoder (codec) in use for the call, Layer 2 encapsulation, and compression techniques (such as RTP header compression) that are in use.

You can request bandwidth changes if necessary after call setup. As of Cisco IOS Release 12.2(2)XA and later, Cisco voice gateways can request a bandwidth change if the codec in use changes. Prior to this release, calls were always reported to require a bandwidth of 64 Kb, the unidirectional bandwidth for a G.711 codec. Cisco IOS Release 12.2(2)XA and later conform to H.323 Version 3 specification, and the reported bandwidth is bidirectional. Initially, 128 Kb of bandwidth is reserved for the call using a G.711 codec, or 16 Kb for a call using the G.729 codec. If a change in bandwidth is required during the call, the gateway notifies the gatekeeper of a bandwidth change using a BRQ message.

You handle Cisco CallManager CAC for voice calls in the same way that you handle CAC for Cisco IOS voice gateways. A difference is that CallManager also can place video calls. When you are designing a CAC implementation that includes video endpoints such as those on CallManager, you must also take the video bandwidth into account. With CallManager, the bandwidth requested from the gatekeeper for a video call is two times the bit rate of the call—a 384-Kb video call counts as 768 Kb, a 512-Kb video call counts as 1024 Kb, and so on. Besides limiting the total available bandwidth, you can limit the maximum bandwidth that a single call can request. This is useful when voice and video are both present on the network. CallManager is discussed more fully later in this chapter.

You can configure the following types of zone bandwidth controls on a Cisco gatekeeper:

- The maximum bandwidth for all traffic between the local zone and a specified remote zone. You can set up this limitation individually for multiple remote zones.
- The maximum bandwidth for all traffic from a zone to all remote zones.
- Perform a check of the destination gateway bandwidth before responding to the ARQ (Cisco IOS Release 12.3(1) and later).
- The maximum bandwidth for a single session within the local zone. As mentioned, this is typically used for video traffic and not voice.

It is important to consider the network topology when planning gatekeeper-controlled CAC implementations.

Figure 16-7 shows an example of an implementation over a simple network topology. In this example, the WAN connection between New York and Boise can only support two calls because of bandwidth limitations. If you are using the G.729 codec, you could configure the gatekeeper to limit the bandwidth to 32 kbps. The first two calls would complete successfully. The third call would exceed the bandwidth limitation and be denied.

Figure 16-7   *Simple CAC Implementation*

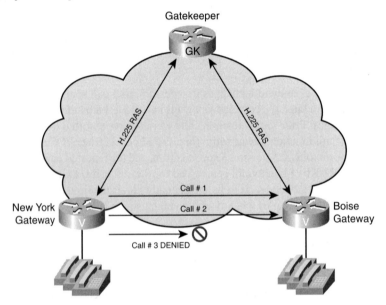

Unfortunately, most networks are not as simple as the one shown in Figure 16-7. A more complex scenario would be to have separate gateways at multiple locations with differing WAN bandwidths between locations. In our sample network, the New York location can handle 24 simultaneous calls; the Boise location can handle two calls; the Leeds location can handle four simultaneous calls.

You could set the bandwidth limits based on the site with the least capacity within the zone. In this example, you would set the gatekeeper to allow only two concurrent calls, based on the capacity at the Boise location. This would ensure good voice quality, but you would place inefficient limits on the other locations that can handle more calls.

A better approach would be to set up multiple gatekeeper zones. If you set up a single zone per site, you could have much more control over the bandwidth allocation. Figure 16-8 depicts the interzone bandwidth limits.

Figure 16-8 *Complex Multizone CAC Implementation*

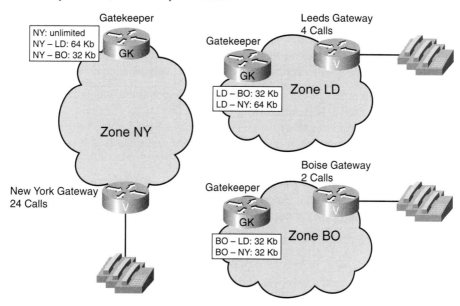

The configuration shown limits the traffic in various ways:

- Between New York and Leeds to four calls maximum
- Between New York and Boise to two calls maximum
- Between Leeds and Boise to two calls maximum

In this configuration, you are ensuring good voice quality and making the best use of the available bandwidth at each site. The gatekeepers shown are logical, not physical. You can control the zones from a single physical gatekeeper.

As you can see from this example, when you are designing gatekeeper-based CAC on an H.323 network, it is important to consider all aspects of the network topology: paths to destination; bandwidth to destination; and the number of gateways that can reach the destination. The gatekeeper is not aware of the topology of the network. Decisions about whether or not to admit a call are based solely on static configurations and calculations of available versus used bandwidth. For gatekeeper CAC to function correctly, the network must be laid out in a hub-and-spoke design. Alternate paths are not taken into account. Other CAC mechanisms such as CallManager location-based CAC have the same limitations. Although using these methods is much better than not implementing CAC, RSVP can make dynamic CAC decisions based on currently available bandwidth along the selected path to a destination. If RSVP is available on your network, it can be a better choice for implementation of CAC.

Gatekeeper Deployment Models

Without the use of a gatekeeper, as the number of gateways in an H.323 network increases, the effort to manage the dial plan grows exponentially. For each gateway, you must specifically code VoIP dial-peers pointing to the IP addresses (or DNS names) of every destination gateway that can be reached from that originating gateway.

When a gatekeeper is used, the dial plan is vastly simplified. Only the local trunk connections need to be defined in the gateways using POTS dial peers. The E.164 addresses to reach these local trunks are then registered with the gatekeeper. You can do this manually by coding *zone prefix* statements in the gatekeeper, or the gatekeeper can dynamically learn them from the gateway when it registers.

In this configuration, the gateway is only aware of local trunk connections and the gatekeeper. It has no direct knowledge of any of the other gateways in the network. When a call comes into the gateway, one of two things happens:

- A POTS dial peer is matched, and the call goes out a local trunk connection.
- The gateway issues an ARQ to the gatekeeper to find the destination for the call.

Figure 16-9 illustrates the effect of this simplification on even a small network.

Figure 16-9 *Dial Plan Simplification Using a Gatekeeper*

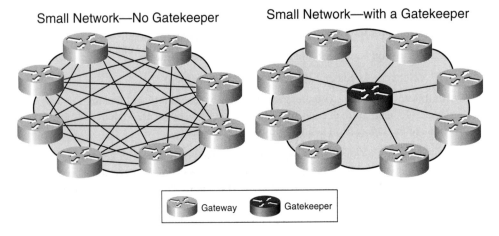

Small Network—No Gatekeeper   Small Network—with a Gatekeeper

Gateway   Gatekeeper

Redundancy

A gatekeeper is a critical network component. It is responsible for most or all of the call routing, bandwidth management, and CAC. Because the gatekeeper centrally controls the dial plan, a failure can cause disruptions across the entire network under its control. Because of this criticality, it is advisable to implement gatekeeper redundancy to reduce the possibility of service interruptions.

Several options are available to provide redundancy in a gatekeeper-controlled network:

- **Gateway dial peers**—Gateways use dial peers that are coded with RAS as the session target to communicate with the gatekeeper. You can code additional VoIP dial peers in the gateway with a lower priority than the RAS dial peer. These lower-priority dial peers have as session targets the IP addresses of the gateways to which they can send calls.

  If the gatekeeper becomes unreachable, the RAS dial peer becomes inactive. At that point, the gateway begins using the lower-priority dial peers to resolve destination addresses.

  Although this might work for smaller networks, the added administrative overhead for coding and maintaining the redundant dial peers removes much of the advantage of using a gatekeeper for centralized dial plan management.

- **Hot Standby Routing Protocol (HSRP)**—Another method of gatekeeper redundancy is the use of HSRP. HSRP has been available for some time in Cisco IOS. Guidelines and caveats for implementing HSRP on a Cisco IOS gatekeeper are as follows:

  — Only one gatekeeper is active at any given time.

  — The standby gatekeeper does not process calls unless the primary gatekeeper fails.

  — No load balancing is supported.

  — All gatekeepers must reside on the same subnet.

  — No state information is maintained between the gatekeepers, and current state information is lost in the event of a failover.

  — Outage duration during a failover might be substantial. All endpoints must reregister with the standby gatekeeper before you can place calls. Active calls are not affected.

  — Gatekeeper configurations must match exactly between the primary and standby gatekeepers. You must replicate any changes or updates manually to the standby.

- **Alternate gatekeeper**—H.323 Version 2 introduced the alternate gatekeeper concept for providing gatekeeper redundancy. The alternate gatekeeper feature allows multiple gatekeepers to control one zone. When an endpoint, such as a voice gateway, registers with a gatekeeper, it is provided with a list of alternate gatekeepers for the zone in which it registers. These alternates were specified in the gatekeeper configuration. If the gatekeeper fails, the endpoint can use the alternate gatekeepers to continue operation. As with HSRP, state information is not maintained between redundant gatekeepers. The alternate gatekeeper feature is the best alternative for networks with non-Cisco gatekeepers.

- **Gatekeeper clustering**—Gatekeeper clustering is a Cisco proprietary feature that uses GUP to maintain state information.

  A gatekeeper cluster is a group of up to five gatekeepers within a zone. The cluster shares information about the zone, including the following:

  — Current calls

  — Gateways within the zone

  — Bandwidth

  — Alternate gatekeepers available for the zone

  — Remote gatekeepers

  You can redirect gateways to other gatekeepers in the cluster either because of a gatekeeper failure or to load-balance gatekeeper traffic.

  Clustering permits rapid failover in the event of a failure, without losing call state, so CAC information is maintained. Gatekeeper clustering also enhances scalability by allowing load balancing between cluster members based on number of calls, number of endpoints, memory usage, or CPU usage.

  These advanced features make gatekeeper clustering the recommended method of implementing redundancy. Cisco recommends using HSRP only if your software feature set does not support clustering.

Resource Availability Indicator

The Resource Availability Indicator (RAI) is a mechanism by which gateways can report the status of resources to the gatekeeper. If RAI is enabled, the gateway tracks the status of DS0 channels and DSP resources.

If a low resource condition occurs, the gateway sends a RAS RAI message to the gatekeeper. The low resource condition is determined by a configurable available resource threshold within the gateway. When the resource level goes above the high resource threshold, the gateway again notifies the gatekeeper that a low resource condition no longer exists. These thresholds are configured as a percentage of total resources.

The RAI feature was introduced in H.323 Version 2 and is available in Cisco IOS Release 12.1.1T and later.

The gateway determines the utilization with the following formulas:

- Accessible channels = In-use channels + free channels
- Utilization = In-use channels ÷ accessible channels

Both DS0 channels of active trunks and DSP resources are monitored in the same manner. If the utilization for either exceeds the configured threshold, an RAI message is generated.

Note that this feature is useful only if multiple gateways are servicing the same call destinations. When more than one gateway can satisfy a request, the gatekeeper selects the gateway to use based on priority and resource threshold. If all gateways have the same priority and resources, the gatekeeper does load balancing among the gateways.

After a gateway is marked as "low on resources," the gatekeeper puts the gateway in the bottom of the priority list. (It changes the gateway priority to 1.) If no other gateway has a higher priority or if all gateways in that zone have priority 1, the gatekeeper still sends calls to the gateway that sent an RAI message declaring that it is almost out of resources.

To cause the gatekeeper to reject interzone calls if all the gateways in that zone are marked as "low on resources," use the **lrq reject-resource-low** command. If you do not use this command, the gatekeeper does not reject calls from other zones even when all gateways in that zone are marked as low on resources.

Directory Gatekeeper

As H.323 networks continue to grow, you might need additional gatekeepers to be included in the design. This might be necessary if numerous gateways exist, if the call volume is high, or perhaps for geographic or some other type of segmentation.

Each time a new gatekeeper is added, you must update all the gatekeepers in the network so that they are aware of the zones that are local to the newly installed gatekeeper. Configure zones as a full mesh to all the gatekeepers in the network. As more gatekeepers are added, the complexity involved in updating all the zone information grows exponentially.

You can solve this issue in large networks by implementing a directory gatekeeper. A directory gatekeeper contains a registry of all the different zones throughout the network and coordinates the LRQ forwarding process. This is also known as a *hierarchical gatekeeper implementation*.

Directory gatekeeper is not an industry standard but rather a feature provided on Cisco IOS gatekeepers to facilitate implementation of large H.323 networks.

You can see the impact on network simplification for a large network provided by a hierarchical gatekeeper implementation in Figure 16-10.

Figure 16-10 *Simplifying Large Network Implementations with a Directory Gatekeeper*

Large Network—Multiple Gatekeepers

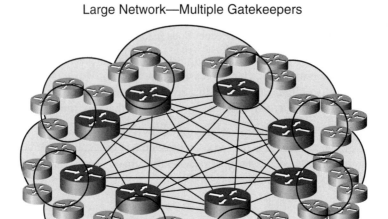

Large Network—Multiple Gatekeepers and a Directory Gatekeeper

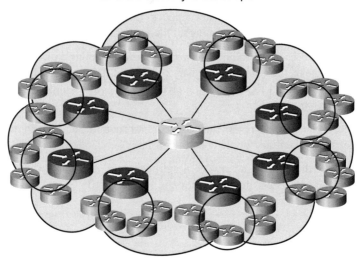

 Gateway Gatekeeper Directory Gatekeeper

Gatekeepers with CallManager

Gatekeepers can provide many of the same benefits in IP Telephony networks using CallManager. The gatekeeper can provide CAC and call routing between CallManager clusters, Cisco CallManager Express (CME), and H.323 gateways that are connected to legacy PBX systems.

As discussed, the gatekeeper is not aware of network topology, so it is limited to network hub-and-spoke topologies for CAC. When the gatekeeper is used for CAC with a CallManager-distributed call processing model, it is usually placed at the hub of the network.

When you are configuring the bandwidth available in the gatekeeper, be sure to consider the codec in use, as specified in the CallManager *Region* configuration. Include the bandwidth required for the voice codec in use and video bandwidth requirements, as shown in the *Region* configuration for CallManager 4.0 and higher systems.

In either a multicluster single campus or a distributed call processing model, you must set up connections between CallManager clusters. One type of connection is known as an intercluster trunk and is the simplest type of trunk that CallManager supports.

You must define intercluster trunks each way between clusters. You can also set them up among a maximum of three separate servers in the destination cluster for redundancy and load balancing. This means that as many as six trunks might need to be configured between two clusters.

This works for smaller deployments, but it becomes administratively difficult to manage the full mesh configuration that is required for a larger number of clusters.

It is recommended that gatekeeper-controlled intercluster trunks (or H.225 gatekeeper-controlled trunks on CallManager 3.2 and higher systems) be used to simplify the administration. Gatekeeper-controlled trunks also provide faster failover if a subscriber server in a cluster becomes unreachable. It is only necessary to configure a single gatekeeper-controlled trunk from each cluster to the gatekeeper. You can assign up to three CallManager servers to the single trunk for load balancing and redundancy. Even though you configure only a single trunk, the gatekeeper registers multiple trunks, one from each assigned CallManager server.

After you configure the trunk, you can direct route patterns to use it. The gatekeeper provides E.164 number resolution for the CallManager cluster. You can use this same mechanism to integrate CallManager clusters into a hybrid H.323 network environment containing CME or H.323 gateways that are connected to PBX systems.

It is recommended that you register each CallManager cluster to a separate zone on the gatekeeper.

For more information on using gatekeepers with CallManager, see the Solution Reference Network Design (SRND) guide available at http://www.cisco.com/go/srnd.

Security with Gatekeepers

A gatekeeper-controlled H.323 network has two primary areas of security concern:

- **Intradomain gateway-to-gatekeeper security**—Based on the H.235 specification within H.323, a gatekeeper authenticates, authorizes, and routes calls. The gatekeeper is considered a known and trusted entity in a sense that the gateway does not authenticate it when the gateway tries to register with it. You can perform authentication both on the gateway when it registers and for each call you place if desired.

  Authenticating gateways on registration helps to ensure that only known, trusted gateways on the network can register to use the gatekeeper. An example of where this might be important is if the gatekeeper is accessible from the Internet or some other untrusted network.

  Authenticating each placed call might be useful if, for example, you want to bill an end user for each call made. Usually, per-call authentication uses an interactive voice response (IVR) system to prompt the caller for a user ID, password, or pin number, which are then forwarded to the gatekeeper for authentication.

- **Interdomain gatekeeper-to-gatekeeper security**—This security covers authenticating and authorizing H.323 calls between the administrative domains of Internet Telephony Service Providers (ITSP) using InterZone Clear Token (IZCT).

This section focuses on intradomain gateway-to-gatekeeper security because it is most commonly used by enterprise customers.

Cisco uses an authentication scheme that is similar to Challenge Handshake Authentication Protocol (CHAP) as the basis for its gateway-to-gatekeeper H.235 implementation. This allows you to leverage the AAA feature within Cisco IOS to perform the actual authentication. Using AAA, the credentials used for authentication can exist locally on the gatekeeper or can be retrieved from an external RADIUS server. Using RADIUS is usually preferred because it allows for management of the security credentials without direct access to the gatekeeper. Also, AAA used with a RADIUS server provides an accounting function, which you can use to track things such as valid and invalid access attempts and call durations.

The H.235 portion of H.323 defines the use of H.225 cryptoTokens for authentication. Instead of cryptoTokens, Cisco uses H.235 clearTokens with fields populated appropriately for use with RADIUS. This token is referred to as the Cisco Access Token (CAT).

Using cryptoTokens would require that the gatekeeper have a way to acquire passwords for all the users and gateways. This is because the token field of the cryptoToken requires that the authenticating entity needs the password to generate its own token against which to compare the received one.

Cisco gatekeepers completely ignore cryptoTokens and look for a CAT for authentication. However, some third-party gatekeepers use the cryptoTokens to authenticate the gateway. Because the gateway does not know what type of gatekeeper it talks to, it sends both in the RRQ.

A timestamp is also included in the RRQ with the CAT. The timestamp must nearly match the current time; otherwise, the RRQ is rejected. This mechanism is employed to prevent use of replay attacks to gain access to the gatekeeper. The amount of variance allowed between the timestamp and the current time is determined by implementation parameters. It is important that the time is synchronized on all gateways and gatekeepers in the network, or failures can occur. You can accomplish this synchronization by configuring the gateways and gatekeepers to use the Network Time Protocol (NTP).

Tokenless Call Authentication

Some endpoints do not support the use of IZCTs or CATs for authentication. An example of this is CallManager. The tokenless call authentication feature was introduced in Cisco IOS Version 12.2.15T as an alternative to token-based authentication mechanisms.

With the tokenless call authorization feature, an access list of all known endpoints is configured on the gatekeeper. The gatekeeper is configured to use the access list when it processes calls. Rather than rejecting all calls that do not contain IZCTs or CATs, gatekeepers reject only calls that do not have tokens and are not from endpoints on the access list.

Review Questions

1 List the two primary functions of a gatekeeper in an H.323 network.

2 What is a gatekeeper zone?

3 What is a technology prefix?

4 Where is bandwidth management initially done?

5 What is another name for a *directory gatekeeper*?

6 What is GUP, and what is it used for?

CHAPTER 17

Gatekeeper Configuration

Previous chapters looked at how Cisco IOS gatekeepers function, what protocols they use, and what benefits they provide in an H.323 network. This chapter discusses how to actually implement Cisco IOS gatekeepers in the network.

This chapter will help you to do the following:

- Complete the basic configuration of a Cisco router as a gatekeeper

- Troubleshoot basic gatekeeper configurations

- Configure a Cisco CallManager system to use a gatekeeper for both H.323 and intercluster trunks

- Understand and configure gatekeeper redundancy using both HSRP and gatekeeper clusters

- Troubleshoot gatekeeper redundancy issues

Configuring Basic Gatekeeper Functionality

Successful gatekeeper implementation requires configuration of both the gatekeeper and the gateways that are going to use it. For the implementation to work properly, you should plan carefully the zone coverage, dial plan, and bandwidth limits before you begin the actual configuration.

The first step is to complete the configuration necessary to allow the gateways to successfully register to the gatekeeper.

Figure 17-1 shows the network topology used in the following examples to begin the gatekeeper configuration. As you can see, it consists of two H.323 gateways in Boise and Miami and a gateway in New York under CallManager control, which will be discussed later in this chapter. The Boise gateway has two Foreign Exchange Station (FXS) connections, and the Miami gateway has a T1 channel-associated signaling (CAS) connection to the public switched telephone network (PSTN). The gatekeeper is physically located in the Miami office. It is set up with a loopback interface having an IP address of 10.100.100.1, which you can use as the gatekeeper address.

Figure 17-1 *Basic Network Topology*

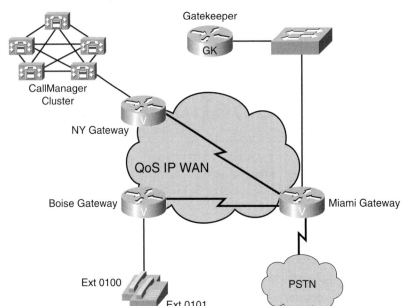

Configuring Gatekeeper Zones

Begin by configuring zones on the gatekeeper. Zones are logical groups of H.323 devices that the gatekeeper controls. Zone definitions include the zone name and domain name. The first zone definition also includes the IP address for the gateways to use when connecting to the gatekeeper.

Because the gatekeepers will be used for both call routing and call admission control (CAC), each of the gateways will be placed in a separate zone.

The gatekeeper stores its configuration in a separate section of the Cisco IOS configuration. To begin, enter the **gatekeeper** command from global configuration mode. After that, you can add the zone definitions by using the **zone local** *zonename domain ip-address* command. You enter subsequent zone commands the same way, but without the *ip-address,* which you enter only once.

After you define the zones, start the gatekeeper service by entering the **no shutdown** command. The gatekeeper is now ready to accept gateway registrations.

Example 17-1 shows the configuration done to this point.

Example 17-1   *Basic Gatekeeper Zone Definitions*

```
GK_A#show running-config
Building configuration...
!
!  Unnecessary output deleted
!
interface Loopback0
 description Gatekeeper Interface
 ip address 10.100.100.1 255.255.255.255
!
!
gatekeeper
 zone local miami cisco.com 10.100.100.1
 zone local boise cisco.com
 no shutdown
!
end
```

Configuring Gateways to Use H.323 Gatekeepers

After you have defined the zones on the gatekeeper, you must configure each of the gateways. To configure a Cisco device as an H.323 gateway, configure at least one of its interfaces as a gateway interface. Use of a reliable interface, such as a loopback interface or a LAN interface, is recommended.

Begin the configuration in interface configuration mode for the selected interface. Define this interface to be a gateway interface using the **h323-gateway voip interface** command.

Define the name and location of the gatekeeper for this gateway using the following command:

> **h323-gateway voip id** *gatekeeper-id* {**ipaddr** *ip-address* | **multicast**} [**priority** *priority*]

The *gatekeeper-id* must match the zone name that is defined to the gatekeeper for the zone that will control this gateway. The *ip-address* is the address of the gatekeeper. You can alternatively use the **multicast** keyword to let the gateway automatically discover the gatekeeper.

Optionally, you can define the H.323 name of the gateway, to help identify this gateway to the gatekeeper. The H.323 name is usually the gateway hostname and the gateway domain name. The **h323-gateway voip h323-id** *interface-id* command is used to configure the name.

After you define a gateway interface, you can activate the gateway service by entering the **gateway** command in global configuration mode. The gateway immediately tries to register with its gatekeeper.

You can verify that the gateways have registered properly by using the **show gatekeeper endpoints** command.

Example 17-2 shows the necessary configuration for both of the gateways in this sample network. The **show gatekeeper endpoints** command indicates that both gateways have registered properly.

Example 17-2 *Basic Gatekeeper and Gateway Configurations*

```
BOISE GATEWAY

Boise#show running-config
Building configuration...
!
!  Unnecessary output deleted
!
!
interface Serial1/0.100 point-to-point
 ip address 10.1.5.200 255.255.255.0
 frame-relay interface-dlci 100
 h323-gateway voip interface
 h323-gateway voip id boise multicast
 h323-gateway voip h323-id boise@cisco.com
 !
gateway
 !
end
MIAMI GATEWAY

Miami#show running-config
Building configuration...
!
!  Unnecessary output deleted
!
!
interface FastEthernet1/0
 ip address 10.12.1.2 255.255.255.0
 h323-gateway voip interface
 h323-gateway voip id miami multicast
 h323-gateway voip h323-id miami@cisco.com
 !
gateway
 !
end
GATEKEEPER A

GK_A#show gatekeeper endpoints
                  GATEKEEPER ENDPOINT REGISTRATION
                  ================================
CallSignalAddr  Port  RASSignalAddr  Port  Zone Name       Type      Flags
--------------- ----- --------------- ----- ---------       ----      -----
10.12.1.2       1720  10.12.1.2       55765 miami           VOIP-GW
    H323-ID: miami@cisco.com
```

Example 17-2 *Basic Gatekeeper and Gateway Configurations (Continued)*

```
      Voice Capacity Max.=  Avail.=  Current.= 0
 10.1.5.200      1720  10.1.5.200      53857 boise              VOIP-GW
    H323-ID: boise@cisco.com
      Voice Capacity Max.=  Avail.=  Current.= 0
 Total number of active registrations = 2
```

Although both gateways are registered to the gatekeeper, they still cannot use it to route calls. To do that, you must properly set up the dial plan within the gateways and configure technology prefixes and zone prefixes in the gatekeeper.

Technology Prefixes

A technology prefix identifies H.323 endpoints by type or class or identifies a resource pool to the gatekeeper. It is important to configure a default technology prefix on the gatekeeper and a technology prefix on the gateway for everything to work correctly. Select a technology prefix to identify the type of gateway—in this case, a *voice* gateway—to the gatekeeper.

NOTE	Defining a technology prefix is important for proper operation because in most cases, calls do not route properly if this step is not done. Typically, the called number matches a zone prefix, not a registered E.164 address. In this case, if a technology prefix is not also matched, the call is rejected. To understand why, review Figure 16-6 in Chapter 16, "Deploying Gatekeepers."

For the sample network, **1#** is selected as the technology prefix associated with a *voice gateway*. Because this is a voice network, 1# is also the default technology prefix for the network.

To configure the default technology prefix on the gatekeeper, use the **gw-type-prefix** *prefix* **default-technology** command in gatekeeper configuration mode. For this network, configure **gw-type-prefix 1#* default-technology** on the gatekeeper. The wildcard symbol * indicates that any number of digits can follow the prefix.

The next step is to set up the technology prefix on the voice gateways. You do this by using the **h323-gateway voip tech-prefix** *prefix* command, which is applied to the gateway interface defined earlier. For this sample network, configure **h323-gateway voip tech-prefix 1#** on each gateway.

Configuring Zone Prefixes and Dial Peers

The last task you need to do before routing calls is to set up the dial plan. You define the dial plan to the gateways in a gatekeeper-controlled network by using dial peers in much the same way as you do without a gatekeeper. POTS dial peers are defined for all phone numbers that are reachable through connected trunks or devices. The difference is in configuration of the Voice over IP (VoIP) dial peers for remote locations.

Without a gatekeeper, you need to set up a VoIP dial peer for each remote site, directly referencing the remote gateway IP address (or Domain Name Services [DNS] name). When a gatekeeper is installed in the network, it resolves phone numbers to the appropriate IP address of the destination gateway. This makes configuring the VoIP dial peer simple. All you need to set up is one or more dial peers that send all unknown numbers to the gatekeeper. You can construct these in different ways. Although some examples are included here, for more specific details on building dial peers, please refer to Chapter 9, "Dial Plans."

The complete dial plan is centrally managed on the gatekeeper. You configure *prefixes* on the gatekeeper, which identify the numbers that are reachable using each voice gateway within the network. A prefix can be equated to a destination pattern on a dial peer. In fact, the prefixes that are defined on the gatekeeper are typically the same as those that are defined on the POTS dial peers on the gateways throughout the network.

In the sample network, extensions 0100 and 0101 need to go to the phones in Boise, and all PSTN access is through Miami. The number 9 is the access code for all calls that are going to the PSTN. Plain old telephone service (POTS) dial peers are set up in both gateways for the connected devices and trunks. The VoIP dial peers are configured to use a wildcard match so that any other number matches the VoIP peer. In place of the IP address that is normally coded as the session target, use the **session target ras** command. This tells the gateway to issue a RAS Admission Request (ARQ) message for any call that matches this dial peer, using the gatekeeper to resolve the IP address of the destination.

You can configure a prefix in the gatekeeper by using the **zone prefix** *zonename prefix* command. In the sample network, the command is **zone prefix miami 9***. This command tells the gatekeeper that any call beginning with a 9 belongs to the Miami zone. You can look at the zone prefixes that have been defined using the **show gatekeeper zone prefix** command.

Because the Boise gateway is running a current version of Cisco IOS, you do not need to configure a zone prefix for the phones that are attached to the FXS ports on the gateway. When the gateway creates the dial peers for those phones, it automatically registers their E.164 addresses. This is an H.323 Version 2 feature and is available in Cisco IOS version 12.1T and later. You can verify that the addresses have registered using the **show gatekeeper endpoints** command. You can override this behavior on the dial peer if desired using the **no register e164** command.

Example 17-3 shows the configuration of the devices in the sample network after you make these changes. At this point, you should be able to route calls properly.

Example 17-3   *Basic Call Routing Configuration*

```
BOISE GATEWAY

Boise#show running-config
Building configuration...
!
!  Unnecessary output deleted
!
interface Serial1/0.100 point-to-point
 ip address 10.1.5.200 255.255.255.0
 frame-relay interface-dlci 100
 h323-gateway voip interface
 h323-gateway voip id boise multicast
 h323-gateway voip h323-id boise@cisco.com
 h323-gateway voip tech-prefix 1#
!
voice-port 0/2/0
!
voice-port 0/2/1
!
voice-port 0/3/0
!
voice-port 0/3/1
!
dial-peer voice 20 pots
 destination-pattern 0100
 port 0/2/0
!
dial-peer voice 21 pots
 destination-pattern 0101
 port 0/2/1
!
dial-peer voice 911 pots
 destination-pattern 911
 port 0/3/0
 no digit-strip
!
dial-peer voice 91 voip
 destination-pattern 9T
 session target ras
!

gateway
!
end
```
```
MIAMI GATEWAY

Miami#show running-config
Building configuration...
!
```

continues

Example 17-3 *Basic Call Routing Configuration (Continued)*

```
! Unnecessary output deleted
!
interface FastEthernet 1/0
 ip address 10.12.1.2 255.255.255.0
 h323-gateway voip interface
 h323-gateway voip id miami multicast
 h323-gateway voip h323-id miami@cisco.com
 h323-gateway voip tech-prefix 1#
!
dial-peer voice 999 voip
 destination-pattern .T
 session target ras
!
dial-peer voice 1 pots
 destination-pattern 91[2-9]..[2-9]......
 port 1/0:23
 prefix 1
!
dial-peer voice 2 pots
 destination-pattern 9011T
 port 1/0:23
 prefix 011
!
dial-peer voice 3 pots
 destination-pattern 911
 port 1/0:23
 prefix 911
!
dial-peer voice 4 pots
 destination-pattern 9[2-9]......
 port 1/0:23
!
gateway
!
end
GATEKEEPER A

GK_A#show running-config
Building configuration...
!
! Unnecessary output deleted
!
interface Loopback0
 ip address 10.100.100.1 255.255.255.255
!
!
gatekeeper
 zone local miami cisco.com 10.100.100.1
 zone local boise cisco.com
 zone prefix miami 9*
 gw-type-prefix 1#* default-technology
 no shutdown
```

Example 17-3 *Basic Call Routing Configuration (Continued)*

```
!
end

GK_A#show gatekeeper endpoints
                GATEKEEPER ENDPOINT REGISTRATION
                ================================
CallSignalAddr  Port  RASSignalAddr   Port  Zone Name    Type     Flags
--------------  ----  --------------  ----- ---------    ----     -----
10.12.1.2       1720  10.12.1.2       51335 miami        VOIP-GW
    H323-ID: miami@cisco.com
    Voice Capacity Max.=  Avail.=  Current.= 0
10.1.5.200      1720  10.1.5.200      55132 boise        VOIP-GW
    E164-ID: 0100
    E164-ID: 0101
    H323-ID: boise@cisco.com
    Voice Capacity Max.=  Avail.=  Current.= 0
Total number of active registrations = 2

GK_A#show gatekeeper zone prefix
    ZONE PREFIX TABLE
    =================
GK-NAME                E164-PREFIX
-------                -----------
miami                  9*
```

When this configuration is complete, you can verify that calls will route successfully. The **show gatekeeper calls** command provides information about any calls that are currently in progress.

A PSTN call from the phone at extension 0100 to phone number 12012012002 is shown in Example 17-4. Notice that the source and destination are identified, as is the bandwidth that this call is using. The bidirectional bandwidth used by the call is reported as 16Kb in the example, indicating that the G.729 codec is being used. You can also tell how long the call has been active—342 seconds in this example.

Example 17-4 *Viewing Calls in Progress on the Gatekeeper*

```
GK_A#show gatekeeper calls
Total number of active calls = 1.
                GATEKEEPER CALL INFO
                ====================
LocalCallID                     Age(secs)  BW
13-34686                        342        16(Kbps)
 Endpt(s): Alias                E.164Addr
   src EP: boise@cisco.com      0100
           CallSignalAddr  Port  RASSignalAddr   Port
           10.1.5.200      1720  10.1.5.200      55132
 Endpt(s): Alias                E.164Addr
   dst EP: miami                912012012002
           CallSignalAddr  Port  RASSignalAddr   Port
           10.12.1.2       1720  10.12.1.2       51335
```

Dynamic Prefix Registration

H.323 Version 4 added a feature that makes it even easier to set up prefixes on the gatekeeper—dynamic prefix registration. This feature allows the gateways to automatically register prefixes with the gatekeeper that are configured as destination patterns on the gateway POTS dial peers. Not only does this mean that you no longer have to manually configure zone prefixes on the gatekeeper, but it also automatically tracks any new, changed, or deleted destination patterns on voice gateways that are registered to the gatekeeper zone. This lowers the administrative effort of implementing the dial plan and reduces the chance of errors caused by the configurations being out of sync.

NOTE   Complex destination patterns do not dynamically register. For example, if you code **destination-pattern 91[2-9]..[2-9]......**, which is common in North America, it does not dynamically register with the gatekeeper. In this example, you can simplify the entry to **destination-pattern 91...........** The latter does register properly. This may result in inter-digit timeout issues, however, for short patterns such as 911. If so, adjust the default inter-digit timeout.

To enable this feature, you need to configure the gateway H.323 service to send the prefixes in the gatekeeper Registration Request (RRQ). You do this by coding the **ras rrq dynamic prefixes** command under the H.323 service configuration. You can get to H.323 service configuration mode by entering **voice service voip** from global command mode and then **h323** to configure H.323-specific parameters.

Configure the gatekeeper to accept dynamic prefixes by coding the **rrq dynamic-prefixes-accept** command. By default, this feature is disabled. The gatekeeper must be in a shutdown state before you can apply this command.

When the preceding configuration is added to both the gateway and gatekeeper, all the destination patterns that are coded on the POTS dial peers for the gateway automatically register as zone prefixes on the gatekeeper.

To verify that the gateway is sending the prefix information, use the **show h323 gateway prefixes** command. This command lists the prefixes that the gateway is requesting be added to the gatekeeper as well as the status of those add requests.

The **show gatekeeper zone prefix** command does not show you the dynamically registered prefixes. To see them, you need to use the **show gatekeeper zone prefix all** command. Without the **all** parameter, only the statically defined prefixes are displayed. You can use both static and dynamic zone prefixes within the same gatekeeper zone.

Example 17-5 demonstrates the use of the dynamic prefix registration feature.

Example 17-5 *Dynamic Prefix Registration*

```
MIAMI GATEWAY

Miami#show running-config
Building configuration...
!
!  Unnecessary output deleted
!
voice service voip
 h323
  ras rrq dynamic prefixes
!
interface FastEthernet 1/0
 ip address 10.12.1.2 255.255.255.0
 h323-gateway voip interface
 h323-gateway voip id miami multicast
 h323-gateway voip h323-id miami@cisco.com
 h323-gateway voip tech-prefix 1#
!
dial-peer voice 999 voip
 destination-pattern .T
 session target ras
!
dial-peer voice 1 pots
 destination-pattern 91.........
 port 1/0:23
 prefix 1
!
dial-peer voice 2 pots
 destination-pattern 9011T
 port 1/0:23
 prefix 011
!
dial-peer voice 3 pots
 destination-pattern 911
 port 1/0:23
 no digit-strip
!
dial-peer voice 4 pots
 destination-pattern 9[2-9].........
 port 1/0:23
!
gateway
!
end
GATEKEEPER A

GK_A#show running-config
Building configuration...
!
!  Unnecessary output deleted
```

continues

Example 17-5 *Dynamic Prefix Registration (Continued)*

```
!
interface Loopback0
 ip address 10.100.100.1 255.255.255.255
 !
 !
gatekeeper
 zone local miami cisco.com 10.100.100.1
 zone local boise cisco.com
 rrq dynamic-prefixes-accept
 gw-type-prefix 1#* default-technology
 no shutdown
 !
end
```

```
Miami#show h323 gateway prefixes

GK Supports Additive RRQ        : True
GW Additive RRQ Support Enabled : True
Pattern Database Status         : Active


Destination                                    Active
Pattern                         Status         Dial-Peers
============================================================
9011*                           ADD ACKNOWLEDGED    1
911*                            ADD ACKNOWLEDGED    1
91.........                     ADD ACKNOWLEDGED    1


VERIFY THE PREFIXES ARE REGISTERED
```

```
GK_A#show gatekeeper zone prefix all
                ZONE PREFIX TABLE
        ================================================
GK-NAME             E164-PREFIX              Dynamic GW-priority
-------             -----------              -------------------
miami               9011*                    miami /5
miami               911*                     miami /5
miami               91.........              miami /5
```

Configuring Call Admission Control

You can also configure the gatekeeper to limit the calls that are traversing the WAN based on available bandwidth. The gatekeeper is not aware of the topology of the network, so proper design is essential if bandwidth management is to work properly. For more details, see Chapter 16.

You have five options for configuring bandwidth limits on a Cisco IOS gatekeeper:

- **Interzone**—Configure max bandwidth from a zone to all other zones.
- **Remote**—Configure max bandwidth allowed to all remote zones.
- **Total**—Configure max bandwidth allowed for all calls in a zone.

- **Check destination**—The destination zone bandwidth is checked before responding.

- **Session**—Configure the max bandwidth that is allowed for a session in a zone. You use this primarily for video.

It is easier to implement gatekeeper bandwidth management if each site is in a different zone. This allows you to use the **bandwidth interzone** command to assign a maximum to each remote site separately. This level of granularity helps to make the most efficient use of the available bandwidth, while protecting call quality.

In the sample network, the number of calls using the WAN bandwidth is limited by the number of phones at the Boise site. Using the G.729 codec, the two calls from Boise have no problem on the 128-kbps Frame Relay WAN link. If more phones were in Boise, the low-speed Frame Relay link would be a concern.

You can easily configure the gatekeeper to limit the bandwidth that is used for voice calls to Boise. Because calls over the WAN use a G.729 codec, the gatekeeper counts 16 Kb of interzone bandwidth for each active call.

Because each site is in a separate local zone, use the **bandwidth interzone zone** *zonename bw-in-Kb* command to implement the restriction. For example, if you want to allow only a single call to Boise from any other site, you can configure **bandwidth interzone zone boise 16** on the gatekeeper.

You can view the current traffic and maximum limits using the **show gatekeeper zone status** command on the gatekeeper. The configuration to set up this restriction in the sample network is shown in Example 17-6.

Example 17-6 *CAC Using Bandwidth Limits with Gatekeepers*

```
GATEKEEPER A

GK_A#show running-config
Building configuration...
!
!  Unnecessary output deleted
!
interface Loopback0
 ip address 10.100.100.1 255.255.255.255
!
!
gatekeeper
 zone local miami cisco.com 10.100.100.1
 zone local boise cisco.com
 rrq dynamic-prefixes-accept
 gw-type-prefix 1#* default-technology
 bandwidth interzone zone boise 16
 no shutdown
!
end

VERIFY THE LIMITS
```

continues

Example 17-6 *CAC Using Bandwidth Limits with Gatekeepers (Continued)*

```
GK_A#show gatekeeper zone status | begin boise
boise        cisco.com     10.100.100.1    1719  LS
  BANDWIDTH INFORMATION (kbps) :
    Maximum total bandwidth : unlimited
    Current total bandwidth : 16
    Maximum interzone bandwidth : 16
    Current interzone bandwidth : 16
    Maximum session bandwidth : unlimited
    Total number of concurrent calls : 1
  SUBNET ATTRIBUTES :
    All Other Subnets : (Enabled)
```

In Example 17-6, a call is already in progress. The maximum interzone bandwidth is set to 16, so no other calls can proceed until the first call ends and releases the bandwidth. Because the maximum assumes that a G.729 codec will be used and is set to 16 Kb, no G.711 calls will be accepted, as they require 128 Kb.

Multiple Gatekeeper Configurations

Sometimes you might want to be able to route calls between zones that different gatekeepers control. An example of this might be in a large enterprise that has multiple business units. Each business unit might have a gatekeeper that is controlling its sites. This lets each business unit manage its own bandwidth and dial plans. The corporation as a whole needs to be able to route calls between all locations. A subset of the company location is shown in Figure 17-2. Each gatekeeper also controls additional locations that are not shown in the diagram. In addition, there is PSTN connectivity at every location.

A zone that a different gatekeeper controls is known as a *remote zone*. Setting up call routing to a remote zone is similar to the basic configuration discussed in the previous section. To begin, use the **zone remote** *zonename domainname ip-address* command. The *zonename* and *domainname* must match the names that are defined on the remote gatekeeper. The *ip-address* is the IP address of the remote gatekeeper.

The next things to configure are the zone prefixes for the zones in the remote gatekeeper. You do this in the same manner as the basic configuration. For remote zones, you must manually configure prefixes. Prefixes cannot be learned dynamically from the remote gatekeeper. You can still use dynamic prefix registration for local zones.

Optionally, you can code the **lrq reject-unknown-prefix** command. This command causes the gatekeeper to reject a Location Request (LRQ) message if no matching local zone prefix is coded.

Figure 17-2 *Multiple Gatekeeper Network*

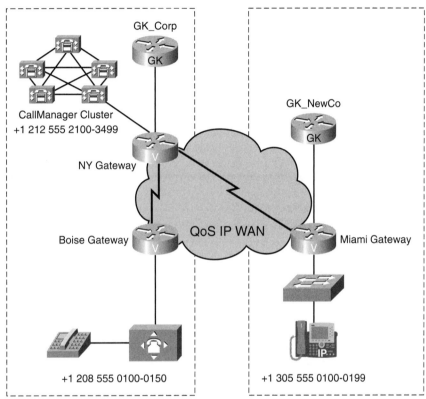

Overall, the process of configuring call routing with multiple gatekeepers is similar to configuring call routing with a single gatekeeper. The difference is the use of remote zone definitions. Example 17-7 shows the configuration of the two gatekeepers in the sample network.

Example 17-7 *Multiple Gatekeepers with Remote Zones*

```
CORPORATE GATEKEEPER

GK_Corp#show running-config
Building configuration...
!
!   Unnecessary output deleted
!
interface Loopback0
 description Gatekeeper interface
 ip address 10.100.101.1 255.255.255.255
 !
gatekeeper
```

continues

Example 17-7 *Multiple Gatekeepers with Remote Zones (Continued)*

```
 zone local ny cisco.com 10.100.101.1
 zone local boise cisco.com
 zone remote miami cisco.com 10.100.100.1 1719
 zone prefix miami 130555501..
 zone prefix boise 120855501..
 zone prefix ny 1212555....
 gw-type-prefix 1#* default-technology
 rrq dynamic-prefixes-accept
 arq reject-unknown-prefix
 lrq reject-unknown-prefix
 no shutdown
 !
 end

 NEW DIVISION GATEKEEPER

 GK_NewCo#show running-config
 Building configuration...
 !
 !  Unnecessary output deleted
 !
 interface Loopback0
  description Gatekeeper interface
  ip address 10.100.100.1 255.255.255.255
 !
 gatekeeper
  zone local miami cisco.com 10.100.100.1
  zone remote ny cisco.com 10.100.101.1 1719
  zone remote boise cisco.com 10.100.101.1 1719
  zone prefix miami 130555501..
  zone prefix boise 120855501..
  zone prefix ny 1212555....
  gw-type-prefix 1#* default-technology
  rrq dynamic-prefixes-accept
  arq reject-unknown-prefix
  lrq reject-unknown-prefix
  no shutdown
 !
 end
```

The signaling is quite different when an ARQ is received for a prefix in a remote zone from one that exists in a local zone. The local gatekeeper must issue an LRQ to the remote gatekeeper to attempt to resolve the IP address of the destination. For more information, see the "H.323 Call Flows Using Gatekeepers" section in Chapter 16.

Configuring Directory Gatekeepers

As the number of gatekeepers in a network grows, the administrative overhead that is associated with adding gateways or prefixes grows exponentially. You must replicate every change or addition in each gatekeeper. For large networks, a directory gatekeeper can reduce the administrative overhead that is associated with multiple gatekeepers. The following steps describe how to migrate from a full mesh gatekeeper environment to a directory gatekeeper:

Step 1 Configure a local zone in the directory gatekeeper. By convention, the hostname of the directory gatekeeper is used for the local zone name. No prefixes are configured for this local zone, because endpoints do not register with the directory gatekeeper.

Step 2 Configure each remote zone in the directory gatekeeper and the prefixes that are associated with each zone.

Step 3 Configure the directory gatekeeper to forward LRQ messages using the **lrq forward-queries** command. This command is what turns a standard gatekeeper into a directory gatekeeper.

Step 4 Add a remote zone in each gatekeeper for the directory gatekeeper.

Step 5 Add a prefix of * pointing to the directory gatekeeper. This causes the gateway to send an LRQ to the directory gatekeeper for all unknown prefixes. The directory gatekeeper forwards the LRQs to the appropriate gatekeeper based on the prefixes that are defined in Step 2.

Step 6 Remove all remote zones and prefixes from the gatekeepers except for the zone and prefix that point to the directory gatekeeper. Only the local zones and prefixes should remain.

Example 17-8 shows the configuration that is necessary to add a directory gatekeeper to the previous example.

Example 17-8 *Implementing a Directory Gatekeeper*

```
CORPORATE GATEKEEPER

GK_Corp#show running-config
Building configuration...
!
!  Unnecessary output deleted
!
interface Loopback0
 description Gatekeeper interface
 ip address 10.100.101.1 255.255.255.255
!
gatekeeper
 zone local ny cisco.com 10.100.101.1
 zone local boise cisco.com
 zone remote DGK cisco.com 10.1.10.15 1719
 zone prefix boise 120855501..
 zone prefix ny 1212555....
 zone prefix DGK *
 gw-type-prefix 1#* default-technology
```

continues

Example 17-8 *Implementing a Directory Gatekeeper (Continued)*

```
 rrq dynamic-prefixes-accept
 no shutdown
!
end
```
```
NEW DIVISION GATEKEEPER

GK_NewCo#show running-config
Building configuration...
!
!  Unnecessary output deleted
!
interface Loopback0
 description Gatekeeper interface
 ip address 10.100.100.1 255.255.255.255
!
gatekeeper
 zone local miami cisco.com 10.100.100.1
 zone remote DGK cisco.com 10.1.10.15 1719
 zone prefix miami 130555501..
 zone prefix DGK *
 gw-type-prefix 1#* default-technology
 rrq dynamic-prefixes-accept
 no shutdown
!
end
```
```
DIRECTORY GATEKEEPER

DGK#show running-config
Building configuration...
!
!  Unnecessary output deleted
!
interface Loopback0
 description Gatekeeper interface
 ip address 10.1.10.15 255.255.255.255
!
gatekeeper
 zone local DGK cisco.com 10.1.10.15
 zone remote miami cisco.com 10.100.100.1 1719
 zone remote ny cisco.com 10.100.101.1 1719
 zone remote boise cisco.com 10.100.100.1 1719
 zone prefix miami 130555501..
 zone prefix boise 120855501..
 zone prefix ny 1212555....
 lrq forward-queries
 gw-type-prefix 1#* default-technology
 rrq dynamic-prefixes-accept
 no shutdown
!
end
```

Troubleshooting Gatekeepers

If it looks like everything is configured properly and you are still having trouble placing calls, some tools are available to assist with troubleshooting. Some of the **show** commands already mentioned are quite useful. Several **debug** commands can also help you figure out the problem.

Of course, the first thing you need to do is make sure that the issue involves a gatekeeper call, rather than a more basic issue. Make sure all the trunks are operating cleanly, that dial peers are configured correctly, and that all the gateways and the gatekeeper are reachable on the IP network.

Registration Issues

If all the gatekeepers, trunks, dial peers, and gateways look okay, be sure the gateways are registered with the gatekeeper. You can do this by using the **show gatekeeper endpoints** command. If the gateway is not registered with the gatekeeper, you can find out more information using the **debug h225 asn1** command on the gateway. Example 17-9 shows the trace output for a successful gatekeeper discovery.

Example 17-9 *Gatekeeper Discovery Trace Using* **debug h225 asn1**

```
Miami#debug h225 asn1

value RasMessage ::= gatekeeperRequest :
    {
        requestSeqNum 7401
        protocolIdentifier { 0 0 8 2250 0 4 }
        rasAddress ipAddress :
        {
            ip '0A0C0102'H   ##  IP Address of gateway in hex (10.12.1.2)
            port 55895
        }
        endpointType
        {
          vendor
          {
            vendor
            {
              t35CountryCode 181
              t35Extension 0
              manufacturerCode 18
            }
          }
          gateway
          {
            protocol
            {
              voice :
              {
```

continues

Example 17-9 *Gatekeeper Discovery Trace Using* **debug h225 asn1** *(Continued)*

```
                    supportedPrefixes
                    {

                      {
                        prefix dialedDigits : "1#"    ## Technology Prefix
                      }
                    }
                  }
                },           h323 :
                {
                  supportedPrefixes
                  {
                  }
                }
              }
            }
            mc FALSE
            undefinedNode FALSE
          }
          gatekeeperIdentifier {"miami"}
          endpointAlias
          {
            h323-ID : {"miami@cisco.com"}    ##  H.323 ID of the gateway
          }
        }


value RasMessage ::= gatekeeperConfirm :
    {
      requestSeqNum 7401
      protocolIdentifier { 0 0 8 2250 0 4 }
      gatekeeperIdentifier {"miami"} ##  Local Zone Name the gateway will register
  to.
      rasAddress ipAddress :
      {
        ip '0A646401'H ##  IP Address of Discovered Gatekeeper (10.100.100.1)
        port 1719
      }
    }
```

If any of the parameters do not match what you expect, or if you receive no response, recheck the configuration on both sides to make sure a mismatch has not occurred. Example 17-10 shows a registration failure. Looking at the trace output, you can see that the gatekeeper zone name "boise" is misspelled. The gatekeeper reject reason "TerminalExcluded" in this case means that no zone name matched the registration request.

Example 17-10 *Gatekeeper Registration Failure*

```
! Unnecessary Output Deleted
value RasMessage ::= gatekeeperRequest :
    {
      requestSeqNum 6155
```

Example 17-10 *Gatekeeper Registration Failure (Continued)*

```
            protocolIdentifier { 0 0 8 2250 0 4 }
            rasAddress ipAddress :
            {
              ip '0A0105C8'H
              port 49785
            }
            endpointType
            {
              vendor
              }
              gateway
              {
                protocol
                {
                  voice :
                  {
                    supportedPrefixes
                    {

                      {
                        prefix dialedDigits : "1#"
                      }
                    }
                  }
            gatekeeperIdentifier {"boisy"}
            endpointAlias
            {
              dialedDigits : "0100",
              dialedDigits : "0101",
              h323-ID : {"boise@cisco.com"}
            }
          }

value RasMessage ::= gatekeeperReject :
    {
      requestSeqNum 6155
      protocolIdentifier { 0 0 8 2250 0 4 }
      rejectReason terminalExcluded : NULL
    }
```

Call Routing Issues

The **debug gatekeeper main 5** trace command is a useful, but undocumented, tool that can help identify call routing problems in the gatekeeper. The output of this command actually shows the decision tree steps that the gatekeeper takes as it processes the ARQ. Example 17-11 shows two examples of this trace output. The first shows a successfully completed call; the second shows one that failed to find a matching prefix.

Example 17-11 **debug gatekeeper main 5** *Trace Output*

```
CALL TO 911 SUCCESSFULLY HANDLED

*Aug  6 07:11:16.347: gk_rassrv_arq: arqp=0x840DD720, crv=0x7, answerCall=0
*Aug  6 07:11:16.347: gk_dns_query: No Name servers
*Aug  6 07:11:16.347: rassrv_get_addrinfo: (911) Tech-prefix match failed.
*Aug  6 07:11:16.347: rassrv_get_addrinfo: (911) Matched zone prefix 911 and
remainder
*Aug  6 07:11:16.347: rassrv_arq_select_viazone: about to check the source side,
rc_zonep=0x848CB0A8
*Aug  6 07:11:16.347: rassrv_arq_select_viazone: matched zone is boise, and
z_invianamelen=0
*Aug  6 07:11:16.347: rassrv_arq_select_viazone: about to check the destination
side,
dst_zonep=0x848CB300
*Aug  6 07:11:16.351: rassrv_arq_select_viazone: matched zone is miami, and
z_outvianamelen=0
*Aug  6 07:11:16.351: gk_zone_get_proxy_usage: local zone= miami, remote zone=
boise, call
direction= 0, eptype= 2050 be_entry= 0
*Aug  6 07:11:16.351: gk_zone_get_proxy_usage: returns proxied = 0
*Aug 6 07:11:16.351: gk_gw_select_px: Source and destination endpoints in different
local zones
*Aug  6 07:11:16.351: gk_zone_get_proxy_usage: local zone= boise, remote zone=
miami, call
direction= 1, eptype= 2050 be_entry= 0
*Aug  6 07:11:16.351: gk_zone_get_proxy_usage: returns proxied = 0
*Aug  6 07:11:16.511: gk_rassrv_arq: arqp=0x841FCA30, crv=0x6, answerCall=1
*Aug  6 07:11:16.591: gk_rassrv_irr: irrp=0x840DD720, from 10.12.1.2:50461
*Aug  6 07:11:17.099: gk_rassrv_irr: irrp=0x841FCF18, from 10.1.5.200:55005l

ARQ FAILED TO MATCH ZONE - CALL REJECTED
*Aug  6 07:17:19.731: gk_rassrv_arq: arqp=0x841FC1E0, crv=0xA, answerCall=0
*Aug  6 07:17:19.731: gk_dns_query: No Name servers
*Aug  6 07:17:19.731: rassrv_get_addrinfo: (91201555) Tech-prefix match failed.
*Aug  6 07:17:19.731: rassrv_get_addrinfo: (91201555) unresolved zone prefix
```

You can also use the **debug h225 asn1** command to see a great deal of detail about the RAS message. Although the output of this trace is verbose, it can provide invaluable information when you are trying to determine the reason that a call is not going through. The called and calling number, the bandwidth requested, and the gateway H.323 ID are all fields that you can easily see in the trace.

Example 17-12 shows the output of a call that failed because the called number was not registered. This indicates a misdialed number, an incorrectly coded dial peer, or an unregistered destination gateway.

Example 17-12   debug h225 asn1 *Trace Output*

```
ARQ TO GATEKEEPER

value RasMessage ::= admissionRequest :
    {
        requestSeqNum 81
        callType pointToPoint : NULL
        callModel direct : NULL
        endpointIdentifier {"83B7042800000001"}
        destinationInfo
        {
            dialedDigits : "91201555"
        }
        srcInfo
        {
            dialedDigits : "2085550100",
            h323-ID : {"boise@cisco.com"}
        }
        bandWidth 160
        callReferenceValue 11
        nonStandardData
        {
            nonStandardIdentifier h221NonStandard :
            {
                t35CountryCode 181
                t35Extension 0
                manufacturerCode 18
            }
            data '80000010290A1046585320302F322F3030002D49...'H
        }
        conferenceID 'D13AF02AAA2711DA802CC10D3BDE93AE'H
        activeMC FALSE
        answerCall FALSE
        canMapAlias TRUE
        callIdentifier
        {
            guid 'D13AF02AAA2711DA802EC10D3BDE93AE'H
        }
        willSupplyUUIEs FALSE
    }
ARJ FROM GATEKEEPER

value RasMessage ::= admissionReject :
    {
        requestSeqNum 81
        rejectReason calledPartyNotRegistered : NULL
        nonStandardData
        {
            nonStandardIdentifier h221NonStandard :
            {
                t35CountryCode 181
```

continues

Example 17-12 **debug h225 asn1** *Trace Output (Continued)*

```
            t35Extension 0
            manufacturerCode 18
        }
        data '80400160'H
    }
}
```

If the trace of the ARQ looks normal and the calls are still not being completed, the next step is to look at the call as it is processed in the destination gateway. Verify that the correct dial peers are being matched, the correct information is being sent to the PSTN or PBX on the outbound trunk, and so on. It is important to have an understanding of the end-to-end call flow, and to take a systematic approach to troubleshooting each step as the call progresses through the network components.

CallManager and Gatekeepers

Gatekeepers can provide the same call routing and CAC functionality for CallManager. You can use gatekeepers with CallManager between CallManager clusters in a pure IP Telephony network or in hybrid networks with CallManager clusters and voice gateways that are interfacing to PBX systems.

Configuring a CallManager Gatekeeper Trunk

You can set up CallManager to use a gatekeeper as follows:

Step 1 Define the gatekeeper to CallManager.

The only information that you need for this step is the IP address of the gatekeeper interface. Be sure that the **Enable Device** checkbox is also selected. An example is shown in Figure 17-3.

Figure 17-3 *Defining a Gatekeeper to CallManager*

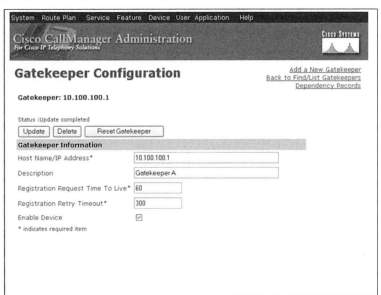

Step 2   Set up the actual trunk to the gatekeeper.

If your CallManager is running software version 3.2 or higher, Cisco recommends using H.225 gatekeeper-controlled trunks.

When you are configuring the trunk, you need to give it a unique name to be used to point traffic to the trunk in the next step. You also need to select the gatekeeper that you defined previously from a drop-down box. Add an appropriate technology prefix. You might want a different technology prefix for CallManager, because CallManager 4.0 and higher systems can handle both voice and video traffic. Always set the **Terminal Type** field to **gateway** for normal CAC.

Step 3   Enter the zone name.

It is almost always desirable to have a different zone name for each CallManager cluster that is defined on the gatekeeper. This helps when configuring bandwidth management.

Figure 17-4 shows an example of setting up a gatekeeper trunk. Some of the items on the configuration screen are not related to the gatekeeper and are not shown in this example.

Figure 17-4 *Defining a Gatekeeper Trunk on CallManager*

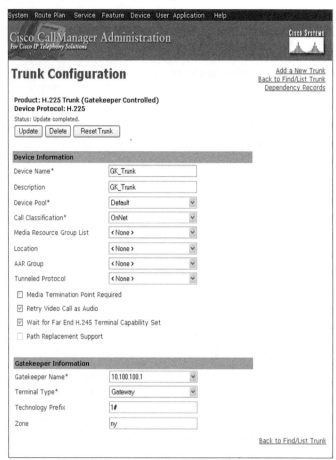

At this point, the trunk should be registered to the gatekeeper and ready for use. You can verify this by using the **show gatekeeper endpoints** command on the gatekeeper, as shown in Example 17-13.

Example 17-13   *Verifying CallManager Trunk Registration*

```
GK_A#show gatekeeper endpoints
                    GATEKEEPER ENDPOINT REGISTRATION
                    ==================================
CallSignalAddr  Port  RASSignalAddr   Port  Zone Name     Type      Flags
--------------- -----  --------------- ----- ---------     ----      -----
10.1.5.2        56105 10.1.5.2         60570 ny            VOIP-GW
    H323-ID: GK_Trunk_1
    Voice Capacity Max.=  Avail.=  Current.= 0
10.12.1.2       1720  10.12.1.2        56783 miami         VOIP-GW
    H323-ID: miami@cisco.com
    Voice Capacity Max.=  Avail.=  Current.= 0
10.1.5.200      1720  10.1.5.200       50240 boise         VOIP-GW
    E164-ID: 0100
    E164-ID: 0101
    H323-ID: boise@cisco.com
    Voice Capacity Max.=  Avail.=  Current.= 0
Total number of active registrations = 3
```

You can provide redundancy on the trunk by assigning up to three subscriber servers to the CallManager redundancy group that is associated with the device pool assigned to the trunk. This configuration causes all servers in the redundancy group to register with the gatekeeper. However, the H.323 trunk name that is used for the h323_id has a suffix of _*n*, where *n* is the node number of the CallManager server in the cluster. This ID is assigned automatically and cannot be changed.

This feature provides redundancy without adding administrative complexity. You configure a single trunk, but the gatekeeper registers multiple trunks, one from each subscriber in the CallManager redundancy group.

Step 4   After you have created the trunk, set up CallManager to use the gatekeeper trunk for specific dialed numbers.

You can include the trunk in CallManager route groups, route lists, and route patterns. Figure 17-5 shows a typical CallManager route pattern configuration using the gatekeeper trunk GK_Trunk. Dialed numbers that match this pattern cause CallManager to issue an ARQ to the gatekeeper to resolve the destination gateway IP address for this call.

Figure 17-5 *Associating a Route Pattern to the Gatekeeper Trunk*

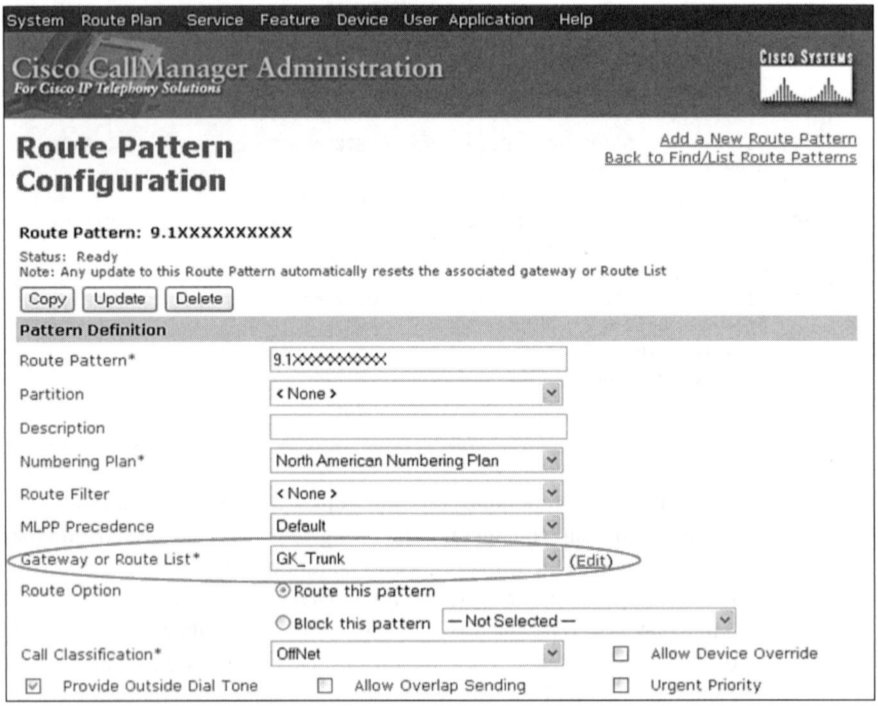

Cisco also recommends that you use the **arq reject-unknown-prefix** gatekeeper configuration command to prevent potential call routing loops that might occur across redundant CallManager trunks. If a called address does not match any of the known zone prefixes, the gatekeeper attempts to hairpin the call back through the originating gateway without **arq reject-unknown-prefix** configured. This action might cause loops in a CallManager environment with multiple trunks active to the gatekeeper.

CallManager does not support dynamic zone prefix registration. You must manually code zone prefixes on the gatekeeper for CallManager destinations.

You can verify proper operation and troubleshoot call routing problems in the same manner as with any registered H.323 gateway. CallManager uses the same RAS messaging format for call admission. For more information, see the "Troubleshooting Gatekeepers" section earlier in this chapter.

Gatekeeper Redundancy

A gatekeeper is a critical network component. It is responsible for most or all of the call routing, bandwidth management, and CAC. Because the gatekeeper centrally controls the dial plan, a failure can cause disruptions across the entire voice network under its control. Because of this criticality, it is advisable to implement gatekeeper redundancy to reduce the possibility of service interruptions.

Hot Standby Routing Protocol

One method of gatekeeper redundancy is the use of the Hot Standby Routing Protocol (HSRP). Following are the guidelines and caveats for implementing HSRP on a Cisco IOS gatekeeper:

- Only one gatekeeper is active at any given time.
    - The standby gatekeeper does not process calls unless the primary gatekeeper fails.
    - No load balancing is supported.
- All gatekeepers must reside on the same subnet.
- No state information is maintained between the gatekeepers, and current state information (calls in progress, bandwidth in use) is lost in the event of a failover. Oversubscription of bandwidth and call degradation is possible immediately after failover.
- Outage duration during a failover might be substantial because the endpoints have to reregister with the standby gatekeeper before calls can be placed. Active calls are not affected.
- Gatekeeper configurations must match exactly between the primary and standby gatekeepers. You must manually replicate any changes or updates to the standby. This adds administrative overhead and increases the chance of errors being introduced into the configuration.

Configuration of HSRP on a gatekeeper is straightforward. HSRP is not supported on a loopback interface, so it is necessary to use a physical interface as the gatekeeper interface. It is preferable to use a LAN interface for this, because LAN interfaces are more reliable than WAN interfaces.

Step 1   Configure IP addresses belonging to the same subnet on the LAN interfaces of both routers.

    For example, you could configure FastEthernet0/0 on gatekeeper GK_A as 10.100.100.2, and you could configure FastEthernet0/1 on gatekeeper GK_B as 10.100.100.3.

Step 2 Add a standby address to both interfaces using the **standby ip** *ip-address* command.

This address is active on only one of the two gateways at a time. This is the address you should use as the gatekeeper address. Endpoints use this address to register to the gatekeeper. The example uses 10.100.100.1 as the standby IP address.

Step 3 Copy the gatekeeper configuration from the primary to the standby gatekeeper.

After you set up HSRP redundancy, it is imperative that you keep the gatekeeper configuration on both gatekeepers the same. If you make a change on the active router, you should also make it on the standby. Put procedures in place to ensure that the configurations remain synchronized.

If the primary gatekeeper fails or becomes unreachable, the standby gatekeeper assumes the gatekeeper address, and the endpoints reregister to it. This can take up to a couple of minutes. You cannot place calls until the endpoints have reregistered.

HSRP provides an option to force a switch back to the primary after it returns to service. This option is typically not used for gatekeepers, because a switch back causes an unnecessary service interruption.

You can verify the status of each of the gatekeepers using the **show standby** and **show gatekeeper status** commands. Example 17-14 shows a dual gatekeeper HSRP redundancy configuration.

Example 17-14 *Gatekeeper Redundancy Using HSRP*

```
GATEKEEPER A

GK_A#show running-config
Building configuration...
!
!   Unnecessary output deleted
!
interface FastEthernet0/0
 ip address 10.100.100.2 255.255.255.240
 standby ip 10.100.100.1
!
gatekeeper
 zone local ny cisco.com 10.100.100.1
 zone local boise cisco.com
 zone local miami cisco.com
 zone prefix ny 2...
 gw-type-prefix 1#* default-technology
 rrq dynamic-prefixes-accept
 arq reject-unknown-prefix
 bandwidth interzone zone boise 16
```

Example 17-14 *Gatekeeper Redundancy Using HSRP (Continued)*

```
 no shutdown
 !
 end

GK_A#show gatekeeper status
    Gatekeeper State: UP
    Load Balancing:    DISABLED
    Flow Control:      DISABLED
    Zone Name:         ny
    Zone Name:         boise
    Zone Name:         miami
    Accounting:        DISABLED
    Endpoint Throttling:        DISABLED
    Security:          DISABLED
    Maximum Remote Bandwidth:              unlimited
    Current Remote Bandwidth:          0 kbps
    Current Remote Bandwidth (w/ Alt GKs): 0 kbps

GK_A#show standby
FastEthernet0/0 - Group 0
  State is Active
    5 state changes, last state change 00:03:08
  Virtual IP address is 10.100.100.1
  Active virtual MAC address is 0000.0c07.ac00
    Local virtual MAC address is 0000.0c07.ac00 (v1 default)
  Hello time 3 sec, hold time 10 sec
    Next hello sent in 0.816 secs
  Preemption disabled
  Active router is local
  Standby router is 10.100.100.3, priority 100 (expires in 8.924 sec)
  Priority 100 (Default 100)
    IP redundancy name is "hsrp-Fa0/0-0" (default)
GATEKEEPER B

GK_B#show running-config
Building configuration...
!
!  Unnecessary output deleted
!
interface FastEthernet0/0
 ip address 10.100.100.3 255.255.255.240
 standby ip 10.100.100.1
!
gatekeeper
 zone local ny cisco.com 10.100.100.1
 zone local boise cisco.com
 zone local miami cisco.com
 zone prefix ny 2...
 gw-type-prefix 1#* default-technology
 rrq dynamic-prefixes-accept
 arq reject-unknown-prefix
 bandwidth interzone zone boise 16
```

continues

Example 17-14 *Gatekeeper Redundancy Using HSRP (Continued)*

```
 no shutdown
 !
 end

GK_B#show gatekeeper status
     Gatekeeper State: HSRP STANDBY
     Load Balancing:   DISABLED
     Flow Control:     DISABLED
     Zone Name:        ny
     Zone Name:        boise
     Zone Name:        miami
     Accounting:       DISABLED
     Endpoint Throttling:        DISABLED
     Security:         DISABLED
     Maximum Remote Bandwidth:            unlimited
     Current Remote Bandwidth:            0 kbps
     Current Remote Bandwidth (w/ Alt GKs): 0 kbps

GK_B#show standby
FastEthernet0/0 - Group 0
  State is Standby
    4 state changes, last state change 00:06:04
  Virtual IP address is 10.100.100.1
  Active virtual MAC address is 0000.0c07.ac00
    Local virtual MAC address is 0000.0c07.ac00 (v1 default)
  Hello time 3 sec, hold time 10 sec
    Next hello sent in 1.880 secs
  Preemption disabled
  Active router is 10.100.100.2, priority 110 (expires in 8.020 sec)
  Standby router is local
  Priority 100 (default 100)
 IP redundancy name is "hsrp-Fa0/0-0" (default)
```

Gatekeeper Clustering

The gatekeeper cluster feature allows multiple gatekeepers to control one zone. When an endpoint, such as a voice gateway, registers with a gatekeeper, it is provided with a list of alternate gatekeepers for the zone in which it registers. These alternates were specified in the gatekeeper configuration. If the gatekeeper fails, the endpoint can use the alternate gatekeepers to continue operation.

NOTE Use of the alternate gatekeeper features requires Cisco IOS Software Release 12.2(1)T or later. CallManager Version 3.3 or later is required for redundancy on gatekeeper-controlled trunks.

Configuring gatekeeper clusters can be confusing. Each local zone is represented by a different name on each cluster member. It can help clarify if you think of a zone as having a "base name" and then an alias on the other cluster members. The gateways use the "base name" when they register to the gatekeeper zone.

For example, if a local zone base name is boise, and it is in a cluster with two alternate gatekeepers, you could use the names boise_gka and boise_gkb for the alternates. This could represent gatekeeper alternative A (gka) and gatekeeper alternative B (gkb) for the zone. In reality, the actual names used on the alternates can be anything as long as they are unique. Developing a naming scheme that has some meaning can help you to keep everything straight as you build the configuration.

Zone configuration is done in gatekeeper configuration mode. When you are configuring the gatekeeper, every local zone is listed with a **zone local** command and a **zone cluster** command. The **zone local** command defines the zone as it is known to the local gatekeeper. The **zone cluster** command identifies aliases for the zone and the IP addresses of the alternate gatekeepers that can process requests for that zone. The command format is **zone cluster local** *cluster-name zone-name*. The *zone-name* must match what is defined in the **zone local** statement. Aliases for the zones (names of the zones as they are known on alternate gatekeepers) are defined using the **element** *zone-alias ip-address* command. The IP address is that of the gatekeeper interface on the alternate gatekeeper where that zone alias is defined.

You might also find occasions where you want one gatekeeper to be primary for some zones and other gatekeepers as primary for other zones. This might be because of network topology, proximity, or other factors.

The following shows how a simple cluster can be built, based on the sample network. The sample network contains three local zones: ny, boise, and miami. GK_A is the primary gatekeeper for zone miami, and it is the alternate for ny and boise. GK_B is the primary for zones ny and boise, and it is the alternate for zone miami. Table 17-1 lists the names and aliases that are used to build the cluster.

Table 17-1 *Example Gatekeeper Cluster Zone Names*

	Gatekeeper GK_A	Gatekeeper GK_B
Zone Names	miami ny_GKA boise_GKA	miami_GKB ny boise
Cluster/Elements	miami_cluster miami_GKB	miami_cluster miami
Cluster/Elements	ny_cluster ny	ny_cluster ny_GKA
Cluster/Elements	boise_cluster boise	boise_cluster boise_GKA

After you have determined all the names, you can begin to configure the gatekeepers in the cluster. The configuration that you can apply for Gatekeeper GK_A and GK_B is shown in Example 17-15.

Example 17-15 *Simple Gatekeeper Cluster Configuration*

```
GATEKEEPER A

GK_A#show running-config
Building configuration...
!
! Unnecessary output deleted
!
interface Loopback0
 description Gatekeeper A
 ip address 10.100.100.1 255.255.255.255
!
gatekeeper
 zone local miami cisco.com 10.100.100.1
 zone local boise_GKA cisco.com
 zone local ny_GKA cisco.com
 zone cluster local miami_cluster miami
  element miami_GKB 10.100.101.1 1719
  !
 zone cluster local boise_cluster boise_GKA
  element boise 10.100.101.1 1719
  !
 zone cluster local ny_cluster ny_GKA
  element ny 10.100.101.1 1719
  !
 zone prefix ny_GKA 2...
 gw-type-prefix 1#* default-technology
 rrq dynamic-prefixes-accept
 arq reject-unknown-prefix
 bandwidth interzone zone boise_GKA 16
 no shutdown
!
end
GATEKEEPER B

GK_B#show running-config
Building configuration...
!
!  Unnecessary output deleted
!
interface Loopback0
 description Gatekeeper B
 ip address 10.100.101.1 255.255.255.255

 !
gatekeeper
 zone local ny cisco.com 10.100.101.1
 zone local boise cisco.com
 zone local miami_GKB cisco.com
```

Example 17-15 *Simple Gatekeeper Cluster Configuration (Continued)*

```
zone cluster local ny_cluster ny
 element ny_GKA 10.100.100.1 1719
!
zone cluster local boise_cluster boise
 element boise_GKA 10.100.100.1 1719
!
zone cluster local miami_cluster miami_GKA
 element miami 10.100.100.1 1719
!
zone prefix ny 2...
gw-type-prefix 1#* default-technology
rrq dynamic-prefixes-accept
arq reject-unknown-prefix
bandwidth interzone zone boise 16
no shutdown
!
end
```

Several tools are available to verify the setup and status of the cluster. These tools include the **show gatekeeper endpoint**, **show gatekeeper status cluster**, **show gatekeeper cluster**, and **show gatekeeper zone cluster** commands.

Example 17-16 demonstrates output from each of these commands.

Example 17-16 *Gatekeeper Cluster **show** Commands*

```
DEFINED CLUSTERS AND THEIR ELEMENTS
GK_B#show gatekeeper clusters

               CONFIGURED CLUSTERS
               ===================
Cluster Name    Type     Local Zone    Elements     IP
-----------     ----     ----------    --------     --
ny_cluster      Local    ny            ny_GKA       10.100.100.1 1719
boise_cluster   Local    boise         boise_GKA    10.100.100.1 1719
miami_cluster   Local    miami_GKB     miami        10.100.100.1 1719

CURRENT STATUS OF THE CLUSTER
GK_B#show gatekeeper status cluster

               CLUSTER INFORMATION
               ===================
                          Active    Endpoint    Last
Hostname       %Mem   %CPU  Calls    Count       Announce
--------       ----   ----  ------   --------    --------
GK_B           71     1     0        2           Local Host
GK_A           19     0     0        1           5s

CLUSTER INFORMATION BY ZONE
GK_B#show gatekeeper zone cluster
               LOCAL CLUSTER INFORMATION
```

continues

Example 17-16 *Gatekeeper Cluster* **show** *Commands (Continued)*

```
                          ===========================
                            TOT BW    INT BW   REM BW   LAST      ALT GK
LOCAL GK NAME ALT GK NAME  PRI (kbps)  (kbps)   (kbps)   ANNOUNCE  STATUS
------------- -----------  ---  ------  ------   ------   --------  ------
ny            ny_GKA        7   0       0        0        20s       CONNECTED
boise         boise_GKA     7   0       0        0        20s       CONNECTED
miami_GKB     miami         7   0       0        0        20s       CONNECTED


REGISTERED ENDPOINTS
GK_B#show gatekeeper endpoint
                    GATEKEEPER ENDPOINT REGISTRATION
                    ================================
CallSignalAddr  Port  RASSignalAddr   Port  Zone Name      Type     Flags
--------------  ----- ---------------  ----- ---------      ----     -----
10.1.5.2        61817 10.1.5.2         61819 ny             VOIP-GW
   H323-ID: GK_Trunk_1
   Voice Capacity Max.=  Avail.=  Current.= 0
10.12.1.2       1720  10.12.1.2        52237 miami_GKB      VOIP-GW A
   H323-ID: miami@cisco.com
10.1.5.200      1720  10.1.5.200       50240 boise          VOIP-GW
   E164-ID: 0100
   E164-ID: 0101
   H323-ID: boise@cisco.com
   Voice Capacity Max.=  Avail.=  Current.= 0
Total number of active registrations = 3
```

In the **show gatekeeper endpoint** output, the A flag listed after the *miami_GKB* zone indicates that this gatekeeper is currently alternate for that zone. Absence of the A flag means that this is the active gatekeeper for the zone.

Load Balancing

Load balancing allows the gatekeeper to move registered endpoints to an alternate gatekeeper or to reject new calls and registrations after a threshold is met. Load balancing requires that alternate gatekeepers be configured.

The syntax for the command to set up load balancing is **load-balance** [**endpoints** *max-endpoints*] [**calls** *max-calls*] [**cpu** *max-cpu*] [**memory** *max-memory-used*]. You apply this in gatekeeper configuration mode on each gatekeeper in the cluster where you want to load-balance. You can concatenate the parameters together to allow monitoring of multiple thresholds.

To verify that load balancing is enabled, use the **show gatekeeper status** command, as demonstrated in Example 17-17. The last four lines are displayed only when load balancing is enabled.

Example 17-17 *Gatekeeper Load Balancing*

```
GK_A#show gatekeeper status
    Gatekeeper State: UP
    Load Balancing:    ENABLED
    Flow Control:      DISABLED
    Zone Name:         miami
    Zone Name:         boise_GKA
    Zone Name:         ny_GKA
    Accounting:        DISABLED
    Endpoint Throttling:        DISABLED
    Security:          DISABLED
    Maximum Remote Bandwidth:            unlimited
    Current Remote Bandwidth:            0 kbps
    Current Remote Bandwidth (w/ Alt GKs): 0 kbps
    Call Capacity:         0 / 100
    Endpoint Capacity:     1 / 100
    Memory Utilization:    19% / 70%
    CPU Utilization:       0% / 80%
```

Troubleshooting Gatekeeper Clustering

Gatekeepers that are members of a cluster communicate with each other to update their status by using GUP. GUP messages are sent between cluster members periodically or when the status has changed. Each member gatekeeper in the cluster maintains the state information about activity on all the other gatekeepers. With that state information, failover to an alternate gatekeeper can be seamlessly completed. For more information on the GUP protocol, see the "Gatekeeper Update Protocol" section in Chapter 16.

You can use the **debug gatekeeper gup asn1** command to determine if the proper information is being passed in the GUP messages. The output of this trace allows you to easily determine if the updates are occurring and if they contain valid information. The number of calls by zone, the bandwidth used, and the load balancing information are included in the GUP announcement messages. You can use this information in addition to the troubleshooting tools previously discussed to help isolate problems with the gatekeepers.

Example 17-18 shows GUP messages that are sent to alternate gatekeepers within the cluster when a call is placed from Boise to Miami.

Example 17-18 **debug gatekeeper gup asn1** *Trace Output*

```
GK_A#debug gatekeeper gup asn1
*Aug  6 08:31:40.103: GUP INCOMING PDU ::=

value GUP_Information ::=
    {
      protocolIdentifier { 1 2 840 113548 10 0 0 4 }
      message announcementIndication :
      {
        announcementInterval 30
```

continues

Example 17-18 **debug gatekeeper gup asn1** *Trace Output (Continued)*

```
         endpointCapacity 24658
         callCapacity 24284
         hostName '474B5F42'H
         percentMemory 71
         percentCPU 1
         currentCalls 1      ## 1 call in progress
         currentEndpoints 1
         zoneInformation
         {

           {
             gatekeeperIdentifier {"ny"}
             altGKIdentifier {"ny_GKA"}
             totalBandwidth 0
    un          interzoneBandwidth 0
             remoteBandwidth 0
           },
           {
             gatekeeperIdentifier {"boise"}
             altGKIdentifier {"boise_GKA"}
             totalBandwidth 160
             interzoneBandwidth 160    ##  16Kb Bandwidth Currently in Use
             remoteBandwidth 0
           },
           {
             gatekeeperIdentifier {"miami_GKB"}
             altGKIdentifier {"miami"}
             totalBandwidth 0
             interzoneBandwidth 0
             remoteBandwidth 0
           }
         }
       }
     }
   }
 *Aug  6 08:31:40.123: Received GUP ANNOUNCEMENT INDICATION from 10.100.101.1
```

Configuring Resource Availability Indicator

The Resource Availability Indication (RAI) is a mechanism by which gateways can report the status of resources to the gatekeeper. If RAI is enabled, the gateway tracks the status of DS0 channels and DSP resources. This feature only tracks DS0s and DSP resources; analog trunk ports are not included.

RAI is useful in locations where more than one gateway is servicing a destination. An example of this might be a large location with multiple PSTN connections. You can have multiple trunks dispersed across several gateways for increased capacity and redundancy.

When RAI is enabled, resources are tracked against a defined threshold. When the high resource threshold is exceeded, an RAI message is sent to the gatekeeper indicating that the gateway is almost out of resources. When the resources have become available again and the low threshold is met, another RAI message is sent to the gatekeeper indicating that the gateway is no longer resource constrained.

The gatekeeper assigns a priority to gateways. If multiple gateways service the same destination, the gatekeeper routes the calls based on the gateway priority. If all the gateways have the same priority, the gatekeeper load-balances across them. The default gateway priority is 5. You can change the priority of a specific gateway using the **zone prefix** *gatekeeper-name e164-prefix* [**gw-priority** *priority gw-alias* [*gw-alias, ...*]] command. You can set the priority in a range from 0 to 10. The gw-alias is the H323-ID of the gateway that you want to change.

When the gatekeeper receives an RAI from a gateway indicating that it is almost out of resources, it lowers the priority of that gateway to 1. When that occurs, the gatekeeper sends calls to the other gateways that are servicing the destination with higher priorities. If no other gateway has a higher priority or if all gateways in that zone have priority 1, the gatekeeper still sends calls to the gateway that sent the RAI message.

When the low threshold is met and the gatekeeper receives the RAI message indicating that resources are again available, it restores the priority of the gateway to the original value.

No configuration is necessary on the gatekeeper to enable RAI.

RAI is enabled on the gateway using the **resource threshold** [**high** *percentage-value*] [**low** *percentage-value*] [**report-policy** {**idle-only** ׀ **addressable**}] command in gateway configuration mode. The optional report-policy parameter determines how to calculate resource utilization:

- **idle-only**—Utilization = (in-use)/(in-use plus free)
- **addressable**—Utilization = (in-use plus disabled)/addressable

The addressable channel calculation includes disabled channels; therefore, it provides a more accurate percentage of available channels.

You can also optionally code the **lrq reject-resource-low** command on the gatekeeper. Normally, all requests are processed even if the destination gateways are reporting that they are almost out of resources. If the **lrq reject-resource-low** command is included, the gatekeeper can reject (issue a Location Reject, or LRJ) requests from remote zones to a destination that is resource constrained.

Example 17-19 shows the configuration that is necessary to enable RAI on a gateway.

Example 17-19 *Enabling RAI*

```
Leeds#show running-config
Building configuration...
!
!   Unnecessary output deleted
!
controller E1 1/0
```

continues

Example 17-19 *Enabling RAI (Continued)*

```
 ds0-group 1 timeslots 1-4 type r2-digital r2-compelled ani
 !
 !
 interface Serial0/0.102 point-to-point
  ip address 10.13.1.2 255.255.255.0
  frame-relay interface-dlci 102
  h323-gateway voip interface
  h323-gateway voip id leeds multicast
  h323-gateway voip h323-id leeds@cisco.com
  h323-gateway voip tech-prefix 1#
  h323-gateway voip bind srcaddr 10.13.1.2
 !
 !
 voice-port 1/0:1
 !
 voice-port 2/0/0
 !
 voice-port 2/0/1
 !
 voice-port 2/0/2
 !
 voice-port 2/0/3
 !
 dial-peer voice 99 voip
  destination-pattern .T
  session target ras
  codec g711ulaw
 !
 dial-peer voice 1 pots
  destination-pattern 0113496....
  no digit-strip
  port 1/0:1
 !
 !
 gateway
   resource threshold high 75 low 50
 !
 end
```

In the example, only four timeslots are enabled on the E1 trunk. The high threshold is
75 percent, and the low threshold is 50 percent. Voice port 1/0:1 is referenced in a dial peer,
making the channels addressable. This is important—only DS0s that are associated with a
POTS dial peer are monitored. Usage of available DSP resources is also monitored and
compared to the thresholds for RAI reporting.

Even though the gateway has analog voice ports, only the DS0 ports are included in
calculating resource usage.

You can see which resources are being monitored and which thresholds are in use by using the **show gateway** command, as demonstrated in Example 17-20.

Example 17-20 *Displaying Resource Thresholds*

```
Leeds#show gateway
H.323 ITU-T Version: 4.0    H323 Stack Version: 0.1

 H.323 service is up
 Gateway  leeds@cisco.com  is registered to Gatekeeper leeds

Alias list (CLI configured)
 H323-ID leeds@cisco.com
Alias list (last RCF)
 H323-ID leeds@cisco.com

 H323 resource thresholding is Enabled and Active
 H323 resource threshold values:
  DSP: Low threshold 50, High threshold 75
  DS0: Low threshold 50, High threshold 75
```

To see the status of monitored DS0 and DSP resources, use the **show call resource voice stats** command. To see whether any of the configured thresholds have been exceeded, use the **show voice resource call threshold** command. Example 17-21 shows the results of both of these commands, in addition to the **show gatekeeper endpoint** command.

Example 17-21 *Displaying Resource Status*

```
CURRENT STATUS OF MONITORED RESOURCES
Leeds#show call resource voice stats
Resource Monitor -  Dial-up Resource Statistics Information:

DSP Statistics:

Utilization: 0.00 percent
Total channels: 76
Inuse channels: 0
Disabled channels: 0
Pending channels: 0
Free channels: 76

DS0 Statistics:

Utilization: 0.00 percent
Total channels: 31
Addressable channels: 4
Inuse channels: 0
Disabled channels: 4
Free channels: 0

THRESHOLD STATE INFORMATION
Leeds#show call resource voice threshold
```

continues

Example 17-21 *Displaying Resource Status (Continued)*

```
Resource Monitor -  Dial-up Resource Threshold Information:

DS0 Threshold:

Client Type: h323
High Water Mark: 75
Low Water Mark: 50
Threshold State: high_threshold_hit

DSP Threshold:

Client Type: h323
High Water Mark: 75
Low Water Mark: 50
Threshold State: low_threshold_hit

GATEWAY STATUS REPORTED BY GATEKEEPER
HQ#sho gatekeeper endpoints
                 GATEKEEPER ENDPOINT REGISTRATION
                 ================================
CallSignalAddr  Port  RASSignalAddr   Port  Zone Name      Type     Flags
--------------- ----- --------------- ----- ---------      ----     -----
10.12.1.2       1720  10.12.1.2       50196 miami          VOIP-GW
    H323-ID: miami@cisco.com
    Voice Capacity Max.=  Avail.=  Current.= 0
10.13.1.2       1720  10.13.1.2       51289 leeds          VOIP-GW O
    H323-ID: leeds@cisco.com
    Voice Capacity Max.=  Avail.=  Current.= 0
10.1.5.200      1720  10.1.5.200      51942 boise          H323-GW
    H323-ID: boise@cisco.com
    Voice Capacity Max.=  Avail.=  Current.= 0
Total number of active registrations = 3
```

In the example, you can see that 76 DSP resources exist, and all are free. Four DS0 resources are available, and all four are disabled, leaving zero free. This means that the gateway should be telling the gatekeeper that it is resource constrained via an RAI message. The **show gatekeeper endpoints** command in the example lists the *leeds* gateway with an O flag. This confirms that the gatekeeper has received the RAI message, and the gateway is flagged as out of resources.

You can also see the actual RAI message sent by the gateway and the gatekeeper response using the **debug h225 asn1** trace command. Example 17-22 shows the RAI that is sent to the gatekeeper.

Example 17-22 *RAI Message Captured with* **debug h225 asn1** *Trace*

```
Leeds#debug h225 asn1
*Jun 25 19:41:27.537: RAS OUTGOING PDU ::=

value RasMessage ::= resourcesAvailableIndicate :
```

Example 17-22 *RAI Message Captured with* **debug h225 asn1** *Trace (Continued)*

```
{
  requestSeqNum 1746
  protocolIdentifier { 0 0 8 2250 0 4 }
  endpointIdentifier {"8413BC2400000003"}
  protocols
  {
    voice :
    {
      supportedPrefixes
      {

        {
          prefix dialedDigits : "1#"
        }
      }
    },        h323 :
    {
      supportedPrefixes
      {
      }
    }
  }
}
    almostOutOfResources TRUE
}


*Jun 25 19:41:27.537: RAS OUTGOING ENCODE BUFFER::= 81380006D1060008914A00041E00
38003400310033004200430032003400300030003000300030003000300033023C05040100204020
05010080
*Jun 25 19:41:27.537:
*Jun 25 19:41:27.577: RAS INCOMING ENCODE BUFFER::= 820A0006D1060008914A0004
*Jun 25 19:41:27.577:
*Jun 25 19:41:27.577: RAS INCOMING PDU ::=

value RasMessage ::= resourcesAvailableConfirm :
    {
      requestSeqNum 1746
      protocolIdentifier { 0 0 8 2250 0 4 }
    }
```

In the trace, the almostOutOfResources flag is set to TRUE, informing the gatekeeper of a resource constraint. The gatekeeper acknowledges with a resourcesAvailableConfirm message, changes the priority of the gateway to 1, and sets the O status flag.

Configuring Gatekeeper Security

The options that are available for securing the gatekeeper-controlled H.323 network were discussed in Chapter 16. Proper planning and design up front of the desired security function simplifies the configuration.

To configure the gatekeeper to authenticate requests, it is first necessary to set up the authentication, authorization, and accounting feature (AAA) within Cisco IOS. AAA can use credentials that are configured in either a local database on the gatekeeper or an external RADIUS security server such as the Cisco Secure Access Control Server (ACS). AAA can also send accounting records to the RADIUS server to track events such as call duration, invalid login attempts, and so on.

The exact AAA configuration depends on several factors that are beyond the scope of this book. For guidance configuring AAA, please refer to Cisco.com.

When you are using authentication, it is important that you synchronize the time between the gatekeeper and all the gateways on the network. The Network Time Protocol (NTP) is the best way to accomplish this. To enable NTP, use the **ntp server** <*server_addr*> command in global configuration mode. The <*server_addr*> should be that of a known good NTP time source that is reachable on the network. More information on configuring NTP is available on Cisco.com.

The **security token required-for** {**all** | **registration**} command is used on the gatekeeper to authenticate gateways during registration or to do per-call authentication. If the **registration** option is selected, the gateway credentials are validated before the gateway can successfully register. If the **all** option is used, credentials are checked during registration and for each call that is presented to the gatekeeper.

On the gateway, the **security password** *word* **level** {**all** | **endpoint** | **per-call**} command is used in gateway configuration mode. If the **endpoint** option is selected, authentication occurs only during registration. The **per-call** option causes credentials to be sent on every call request. The **all** option enables both registration and per-call authentication. The *word* parameter sets the password to be used for the gateway.

You can use the tokenless call authentication feature for endpoints that do not support tokens, such as CallManager. To configure tokenless call authentication, you must create an access control list (ACL) on the gatekeeper. The ACL must include permit statements for the IP address of every device that is authorized to place call routing requests to the gatekeeper.

After you create the ACL, you enter the command **security acl answerarq** <*1-99*> in gatekeeper configuration mode. The <*1-99*> parameter refers to the ACL you just created. When this is complete, all ARQs that are received from gateways that have IP addresses permitted by the ACL are answered, whether or not they contain a security token.

It is important to note that tokenless call authentication applies to ARQs only and has no effect on gateway registration with the gatekeeper. Also, you can use token-based and tokenless call authentication at the same time. They are not mutually exclusive.

Example 17-23 shows the configuration that is necessary to enable gateway registration authentication. In this example, per-call authentication is not being done. The AAA feature is using locally configured user IDs and passwords rather than a RADIUS server.

Example 17-23 *Enabling Gateway Registration Security*

```
BOISE GATEWAY
boise#show running-config
Building configuration...
!
! Unnecessary output deleted
!
interface FastEthernet0/0
 ip address 10.1.5.200 255.255.255.0
 h323-gateway voip interface
 h323-gateway voip id boise multicast
 h323-gateway voip h323-id boise@cisco.com
 h323-gateway voip tech-prefix 1#
 h323-gateway voip bind srcaddr 10.1.5.200
 !
gateway
 security password goodguy level endpoint
 !
end

GATEKEEPER A
GKA#show running-config
Building configuration...
!
! Unnecessary output deleted
!
username leeds@cisco.com password 0 goodguy
username boise@cisco.com password 0 goodguy
username miami@cisco.com password 0 goodguy
!
aaa new-model
!
!
aaa authentication login default local
aaa authentication login h323 local
aaa authorization exec default local
aaa authorization exec h323 local
!
gatekeeper
 zone local boise cisco.com 10.1.5.1
 zone local miami cisco.com
 zone local leeds cisco.com
 zone prefix miami 21........
 security token required-for registration
```

continues

Example 17-23 *Enabling Gateway Registration Security (Continued)*

```
gw-type-prefix 1#* default-technology
rrq dynamic-prefixes-accept
arq reject-unknown-prefix
bandwidth interzone default 64
no shutdown
!
!
ntp server 10.1.5.200
!
end
```

If a RADIUS server such as Cisco Secure ACS had been used, the credentials would not have appeared in the Cisco IOS configuration. Also note that NTP has been configured and is being used to synchronize the gatekeeper clock.

CallManager does not support tokens for either registration or per-call security. If CallManager trunks are in use, you cannot enable registration security; otherwise, the CallManager trunk is unable to register. You can use per-call security with CallManager by using the tokenless call authentication feature.

Troubleshooting Gatekeeper Security

If registration or call routing problems occur due to security, you can use one of several tools to determine the problem. Some common causes of security issues include the following:

- **Clocks not synchronized**—If is the difference is too great between the time stamps on the request and the time in the gatekeeper, the request is rejected. Be sure that NTP is set up and working properly. You can use the **show ntp status** command to quickly verify NTP operation.

- **User ID mismatch**—The user ID that is used is the full H.323-ID. The user ID credentials must match.

- **No token being presented**—Some devices cannot use token authentication, as discussed previously.

Some of the tools that can assist in finding the cause of a problem include the **debug h225 asn1**, **debug gatekeeper main 5**, **debug aaa authentication,** and **debug aaa attr** trace commands. Example 17-24 shows how the **debug h225 asn1** trace can assist with a gateway registration problem.

Example 17-24 *Failed Gateway Registration* **debug h225 asn1** *Trace*

```
May 17 14:23:23.717: RAS OUTGOING PDU ::=

value RasMessage ::= registrationRequest :
    {
```

Example 17-24   *Failed Gateway Registration* **debug h225 asn1** *Trace (Continued)*

```
requestSeqNum 1150
protocolIdentifier { 0 0 8 2250 0 4 }
discoveryComplete TRUE
callSignalAddress
{
  ipAddress :
  {
    ip '0A0105C8'H
    port 1720
  }
}
rasAddress
{
  ipAddress :
  {
    ip '0A0105C8'H
    port 56775
  }
}
terminalType
{
  vendor
  {
    vendor
    {
      t35CountryCode 181
      t35Extension 0
      manufacturerCode 18
    }
    productId '436973636F47617465776179'H
    versionId '32'H
  }
  gateway
  {
    protocol
    {
      voice :
      {
        supportedPrefixes
        {

          {
            prefix dialedDigits : "1#"
          }
        }
      },              h323 :
      {
        supportedPrefixes
        {
        }
      }
    }
```

continues

Example 17-24 *Failed Gateway Registration* **debug h225 asn1** *Trace (Continued)*

```
          }
          mc FALSE
          undefinedNode FALSE
        }
        terminalAlias
        {
          h323-ID : {"boise@cisco.com"}
        }
        gatekeeperIdentifier {"boise"}
        endpointVendor
        {
          vendor
          {
            t35CountryCode 181
            t35Extension 0
            manufacturerCode 18
          }
          productId '436973636F47617465776179'H
          versionId '32'H
        }
        timeToLive 60
        keepAlive FALSE
        willSupplyUUIEs FALSE
        maintainConnection TRUE
        usageReportingCapability
        {
          nonStandardUsageTypes
          {

            {
              nonStandardIdentifier h221NonStandard :
              {
                t35CountryCode 181
                t35Extension 0
                manufacturerCode 18
              }
              data '40'H
            }
          }
          startTime NULL
          endTime NULL
          terminationCause NULL
        }
      }


May 17 14:23:23.865:
May 17 14:23:23.865: RAS INCOMING PDU ::=

value RasMessage ::= registrationReject :
      {
```

Example 17-24 *Failed Gateway Registration* **debug h225 asn1** *Trace (Continued)*

```
      requestSeqNum 1150
      protocolIdentifier { 0 0 8 2250 0 4 }
      rejectReason securityDenial : NULL
      gatekeeperIdentifier {"boise"}
   }
```

You can see that the registration request from the Boise gateway was rejected because of securityDenial. In this case, no security information was included in the RRQ. This most likely indicates a configuration error in the gateway. Example 17-25 shows the successful registration process after the configuration was corrected.

Example 17-25 *Successful Gateway Registration* **debug h225 asn1** *Trace*

```
value RasMessage ::= registrationRequest :
    {
      requestSeqNum 1170
      protocolIdentifier { 0 0 8 2250 0 4 }
      discoveryComplete TRUE
      callSignalAddress
      {
        ipAddress :
        {
          ip '0A0105C8'H
          port 1720
        }
      }
      rasAddress
      {
        ipAddress :
        {
          ip '0A0105C8'H
          port 52091
        }
      }
      terminalType
      {
        vendor
        {
          vendor
          {
            t35CountryCode 181
            t35Extension 0
            manufacturerCode 18
          }
          productId '436973636F47617465776179'H
          versionId '32'H
        }
        gateway
        {
          protocol
          {
```

continues

Example 17-25 *Successful Gateway Registration* **debug h225 asn1** *Trace (Continued)*

```
                  voice :
                  {
                    supportedPrefixes
                    {

                      {
                        prefix dialedDigits : "1#"
                      }
                    }
                  },              h323 :
                  {
                    supportedPrefixes
                    {
                    }
                  }
                }
              }
              mc FALSE
              undefinedNode FALSE
            }
            terminalAlias
            {
              h323-ID : {"boise@cisco.com"}
            }
            gatekeeperIdentifier {"boise"}
            endpointVendor
            {
              vendor
              {
                t35CountryCode 181
                t35Extension 0
                manufacturerCode 18
              }
              productId '436973636F47617465776179'H
              versionId '32'H
            }
            timeToLive 60
            tokens
            {

              {
                tokenOID { 1 2 840 113548 10 1 2 1 }
                timeStamp 1147876446
                challenge 'F64FAD4A17AFE3C1D0D51ADF38071BA8'H
                random 164
                generalID {"boise@cisco.com"}
              }
            }
            cryptoTokens
            {
              cryptoEPPwdHash :
              {
```

Example 17-25 *Successful Gateway Registration* **debug h225 asn1** *Trace (Continued)*

```
                    alias h323-ID : {"boise@cisco.com"}
                    timeStamp 1147876446
                    token
                    {
                      algorithmOID { 1 2 840 113549 2 5 }
                      paramS
                      {
                      }
                      hash "6D01394D6E13493CB7338E16EADDB9F"
                    }
                }
            }
            keepAlive FALSE
            willSupplyUUIEs FALSE
            maintainConnection TRUE
            usageReportingCapability
            {
              nonStandardUsageTypes
              {

                {
                  nonStandardIdentifier h221NonStandard :
                  {
                    t35CountryCode 181
                    t35Extension 0
                    manufacturerCode 18
                  }
                  data '40'H
                }
              }
              startTime NULL
              endTime NULL
              terminationCause NULL
            }
        }


May 17 14:34:07.073: RAS INCOMING PDU ::=

value RasMessage ::= registrationConfirm :
    {
        requestSeqNum 1170
        protocolIdentifier { 0 0 8 2250 0 4 }
        callSignalAddress
        {
        }
        terminalAlias
        {
          h323-ID : {"boise@cisco.com"}
        }
        gatekeeperIdentifier {"boise"}
        endpointIdentifier {"840F50B400000003"}
```

continues

Example 17-25 *Successful Gateway Registration* **debug h225 asn1** *Trace (Continued)*

```
                    alternateGatekeeper
                    {
                    }
                    timeToLive 60
                    willRespondToIRR FALSE
                    maintainConnection TRUE
                    supportsAdditiveRegistration NULL
                    usageSpec
                    {

                      {
                        when
                        {
                          end NULL
                          inIrr NULL
                        }
                        callStartingPoint
                        {
                          connect NULL
                        }
                        required
                        {
                          nonStandardUsageTypes
                          {
                          }
                          startTime NULL
                          endTime NULL
                          terminationCause NULL
                        }
                      }
                    }
                }
```

In this example, you can see that both the Cisco Access Token (CAT) and H.235 cryptoToken are included in the RRQ. The Cisco gatekeeper only processes the CAT; it ignores the cryptoToken. The cryptoToken is included for compatibility with third-party gatekeepers. You can also see the H.323 ID and timestamp in the trace output.

Case Study: Deploying Gatekeepers to Assist in Migration to VoIP

Your company migration to an IP Telephony infrastructure is well underway. Three out of six sites are completely converted. The design uses a centralized CallManager deployment at the New York headquarters location. CallManager location-based CAC is being used for CAC to the sites that have been converted. PBXs are still being used at the New York, Boise, and Shanghai locations.

Gatekeepers are being deployed as part of the migration. Two gatekeepers are located at the New York office and configured as a redundant cluster. You need to configure them to provide call routing between the IP Telephony sites and the PBX locations. The gatekeepers should also provide CAC to the locations that have a PBX. Figure 17-6 illustrates details of the network topology.

Figure 17-6 *Example Voice Network Topology*

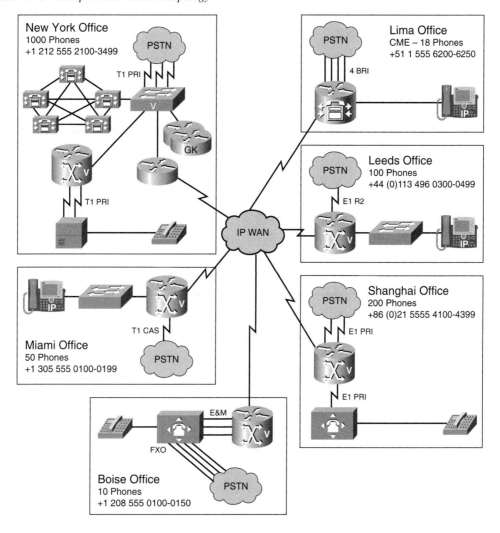

Planning the configuration prior to beginning deployment helps eliminate confusion and ensure a smooth rollout. As discussed previously, it is useful to lay out all the naming information in advance to simplify building of the gatekeeper cluster definitions. Zones have to be created for New York, Boise, Shanghai, and CallManager. The zone for CallManager will be used to route calls between sites with a PBX and sites that are CallManager controlled with IP Telephony endpoints.

The physical trunk count provides CAC for the Boise location, so the gatekeeper does not have to control it. Only three E&M trunks exist between the gateway and the PBX, so concurrent calls are limited to three.

The New York headquarters location has high bandwidth links, so you do not need to limit calls to that zone in the gatekeeper.

Shanghai has an E1 and a fairly high data requirement, so you should limit calls to that zone to a concurrent maximum of 20. A G.729 codec is used for all calls across the WAN. Because the gatekeeper uses a value of 16 Kb for each G.729 call, you need to set the limit to the Shanghai zone to 320 Kb (20 calls * 16 Kb).

CallManager is using location-based CAC to limit calls to remote IP Telephony sites, so you do not need to limit the bandwidth in the gatekeeper to that zone.

Zone prefixes are explicitly defined to the gatekeeper. Dynamic prefix registration is not used. This can provide more flexibility by allowing more generic prefixes to be defined to the gatekeeper to get the call to the right gateway. At that point, the dial peers in the gateway can selectively route the call to its destination.

Table 17-2 provides information on the gatekeeper planning for the case study.

Table 17-2 *Case Study Gatekeeper Planning*

	Gatekeeper GK1	Gatekeeper GK2
Zone Names	ny boise shanghai callmgr	ny_alt boise_alt shanghai_alt callmgr_alt
Cluster/Elements	ny_cluster ny_alt	ny_cluster ny
Cluster/Elements	boise_cluster boise_alt	boise_cluster boise
Cluster/Elements	shanghai_cluster shanghai_alt	shanghai_cluster shanghai
Cluster/Elements	callmgr_cluster callmgr_alt	callmgr_cluster callmgr

Table 17-2   *Case Study Gatekeeper Planning (Continued)*

	Gatekeeper GK1	Gatekeeper GK2
NY Zone	Prefixes: 912125552… 912125553… 0012125552… 0012125553…	Bandwidth: No limit
Boise Zone	Prefixes: 9120855501… 00120855501…	Bandwidth: No limit
Shanghai Zone	Prefixes: 901186 0086	Bandwidth: 320 Kb
CallMgr Zone	Prefixes: 901151 901144 9130555501… 0051 0044 00130555501…	Bandwidth: No limit

To begin implementation, set up two Cisco IOS routers as gatekeepers. To provide a high level of redundancy, locate these routers on separate power sources and Ethernet switches at the New York location. The gatekeeper interface on gatekeeper GK1 has an IP address of 10.100.100.1. Gatekeeper GK2 has an IP address of 10.200.200.1.

You can do all the gatekeeper configuration in advance. Subsequently, you can configure the gateways individually and verify them as dictated by the migration schedule.

Example 17-26 shows the full configuration of both gatekeepers that are necessary to support the design requirements. Be sure to add the **arq reject-unknown-prefix** command to prevent loops on the redundant CallManager trunks. The **bandwidth interzone zone shanghai 320** command limits the number of calls between any other location and Shanghai to 20 as planned.

Example 17-26   *Case Study Gatekeeper Configuration*

```
GATEKEEPER GK1

GK1#show running-config
Building configuration...
```

continues

Example 17-26 *Case Study Gatekeeper Configuration (Continued)*

```
!
! Unnecessary output deleted
!
interface Loopback0
 description Gatekeeper GK1
 ip address 10.100.100.1 255.255.255.255
!
gatekeeper
 zone local ny acme.com 10.100.100.1
 zone local boise acme.com
 zone local shanghai acme.com
 zone local callmgr acme.com
 zone cluster local ny_cluster ny
  element ny_alt 10.200.200.1 1719
 !
 zone cluster local boise_cluster boise
  element boise_alt 10.200.200.1 1719
 !
 zone cluster local shanghai_cluster shanghai
  element shanghai_alt 10.200.200.1 1719
 !
 zone cluster local callmgr_cluster callmgr
  element callmgr_alt 10.200.200.1 1719
 !
 zone prefix ny 912125552...
 zone prefix ny 912125553...
 zone prefix ny 0012125552...
 zone prefix ny 0012125553...
 zone prefix boise 9120855501..
 zone prefix boise 00120855501..
 zone prefix shanghai 901186*
 zone prefix shanghai 0086*
 zone prefix callmgr 901151*
 zone prefix callmgr 901144*
 zone prefix callmgr 9130555501..
 zone prefix callmgr 0051*
 zone prefix callmgr 0044*
 zone prefix callmgr 00130555501..
 zone prefix callmgr 9*
 zone prefix callmgr 001*
 gw-type-prefix 1#* default-technology
 arq reject-unknown-prefix
 bandwidth interzone zone shanghai 320
 no shutdown
 !
 end
GATEKEEPER GK2

GK2#show running-config
Building configuration...
 !
 !  Unnecessary output deleted
```

Example 17-26   *Case Study Gatekeeper Configuration (Continued)*

```
!
interface Loopback0
 description Gatekeeper GK2
 ip address 10.200.200.1 255.255.255.255
!
gatekeeper
 zone local ny_alt acme.com 10.200.200.1
 zone local boise_alt acme.com
 zone local shanghai_alt acme.com
 zone local callmgr_alt acme.com
 zone cluster local ny_cluster ny_alt
  element ny 10.100.100.1 1719
 !
 zone cluster local boise_cluster boise_alt
  element boise 10.100.100.1 1719
 !
 zone cluster local shanghai_cluster shanghai_alt
  element shanghai 10.100.100.1 1719
 !
 zone cluster local callmgr_cluster callmgr_alt
  element callmgr 10.100.100.1 1719
 !
 zone prefix ny_alt 912125552...
 zone prefix ny_alt 912125553...
 zone prefix ny_alt 0012125552...
 zone prefix ny_alt 0012125553...
 zone prefix boise_alt 9120855501..
 zone prefix boise_alt 00120855501..
 zone prefix shanghai_alt 901186*
 zone prefix shanghai_alt 0086*
 zone prefix callmgr_alt 901151*
 zone prefix callmgr_alt 901144*
 zone prefix callmgr_alt 9130555501..
 zone prefix callmgr_alt 0051*
 zone prefix callmgr_alt 0044*
 zone prefix callmgr_alt 00130555501..
 zone prefix callmgr_alt 9*
 zone prefix callmgr_alt 001*
 gw-type-prefix 1#* default-technology
 arq reject-unknown-prefix
 bandwidth interzone zone boise 16
 no shutdown
!
end
```

When the gatekeepers are active, you can configure the gateways to register with them. You do this by configuring an interface as a gateway interface, as just described. To control the registration process and ensure predictable behavior, use a specific IP address to point to gatekeeper GK1 instead of letting the gateway find it using multicast. This should complete the implementation of the gatekeeper for call routing and bandwidth management. It is also important to properly set up the dial peers in the gateways. Each of the PBX systems expects a four-digit extension across the connected trunks. Example 17-27 shows the gateway configuration for the Cisco IOS voice gateways in this case study.

Example 17-27 *Case Study Gateway Configuration*

```
NY GATEWAY

NewYork#show running-config
Building configuration...
!
!  Unnecessary output deleted
!
interface FastEthernet 1/0
 ip address 10.1.25.100 255.255.255.0
 h323-gateway voip interface
 h323-gateway voip id ny ipaddr 10.100.100.1 1719
 h323-gateway voip h323-id ny@acme.com
 h323-gateway voip tech-prefix 1#
!
voice-port 1/0:23
!
voice-port 2/0:23
!
dial-peer voice 999 voip
 destination-pattern 9T
 session target ras
!
dial-peer voice 11 pots
 destination-pattern 912125552[1-9]..
 port 1/0:23
 prefix 2
 preference 1
!
dial-peer voice 12 pots
 destination-pattern 912125552[1-9]..
 port 2/0:23
 prefix 2
 preference 2
!
dial-peer voice 21 pots
 destination-pattern 912125553[0-4]..
 port 1/0:23
 prefix 3
 preference 1
!
dial-peer voice 22 pots
 destination-pattern 912125553[0-4]..
 port 2/0:23
 prefix 3
 preference 2
!
gateway
 !
```

Example 17-27   *Case Study Gateway Configuration (Continued)*

```
end
BOISE GATEWAY

Boise#show running-config
Building configuration...
!
!  Unnecessary output deleted
!
interface FastEthernet 1/0
 ip address 10.20.25.100 255.255.255.0
 h323-gateway voip interface
 h323-gateway voip id boise ipaddr 10.100.100.1 1719
 h323-gateway voip h323-id boise@acme.com
 h323-gateway voip tech-prefix 1#
!
voice-port 0/2/0
signaling wink-start
type 1
operation 2-wire
!
voice-port 0/2/1
signaling wink-start
type 1
operation 2-wire
!
voice-port 0/3/0
signaling wink-start
type 1
operation 2-wire
!
voice-port 0/3/1
 shutdown
!
dial-peer voice 999 voip
 destination-pattern 9T
 session target ras
!
dial-peer voice 11 pots
 destination-pattern 9120855501[0-5].
 port 0/2/0
 prefix 01
 preference 1
!
dial-peer voice 12 pots
 destination-pattern 9120855501[0-5].
 port 0/2/1
 prefix 01
 preference 2
!
dial-peer voice 13 pots
 destination-pattern 9120855501[0-5].
 port 0/3/0
```

continues

Example 17-27 *Case Study Gateway Configuration (Continued)*

```
 prefix 01
 preference 3
!
dial-peer voice 21 pots
 destination-pattern 00120855501[0-5].
 port 0/2/0
 prefix 01
 preference 1
!
dial-peer voice 22 pots
 destination-pattern 00120855501[0-5].
 port 0/2/1
 prefix 01
 preference 2
!
dial-peer voice 23 pots
 destination-pattern 00120855501[0-5].
 port 0/3/0
 prefix 01
 preference 3
!
gateway
!
end
```

```
SHANGHAI GATEWAY

Shanghai#show running-config
Building configuration...
!
!  Unnecessary output deleted
!
interface FastEthernet 1/0
 ip address 10.30.25.100 255.255.255.0
 h323-gateway voip interface
 h323-gateway voip id shanghai ipaddr 10.100.100.1 1719
 h323-gateway voip h323-id shanghai@acme.com
 h323-gateway voip tech-prefix 1#
!
voice-port 1/0:15
 description PSTN
 trunk-group ToPSTN
!
voice-port 1/1:15
 description PSTN
 trunk-group ToPSTN
!
voice-port 2/0:15
 description PBX
!
dial-peer voice 990 voip
 destination-pattern 001T
```

Example 17-27 *Case Study Gateway Configuration (Continued)*

```
 session target ras
 !
dial-peer voice 991 voip
 destination-pattern 0044T
 session target ras
 !
dial-peer voice 11 pots
 destination-pattern 9011862155554[1-3]..
 port 2/0:15
 prefix 4
 !
dial-peer voice 2 pots
 destination-pattern 0T
 trunkgroup ToPSTN
 no digit-strip
 !
gateway
 !
end
```

The topology at each of the remote locations is slightly different, so you need to customize the approach used to address the individual requirements.

In the New York headquarters location, only a specific number range is routed to the PBX, so the dial peer needs to be specific to that range. PSTN access for all the PBX phones is via a CallManager-controlled gateway. For correct routing, all calls that are routed out of the PBX must go to the gatekeeper for resolution. If no match is available for one of the other gatekeeper-controlled remote sites (sites with a PBX), you must route the call to the CallManager in the *ny* zone. The CallManager then either routes the call to an IP Telephony site or to the PSTN.

In Boise, all the phones and the PSTN are connected to the PBX. Calls are only routed from the PBX to the voice gateway if they are destined for another on network location. This is controlled on the PBX, not the gateway. Therefore, the PBX should send all call setup requests to the gatekeeper.

The Shanghai gateway has connections between both the PSTN and the PBX. All the phones are on the PBX. PSTN access from the PBX is only available using the gateway. Inbound calls to the gateway from a different on-network location require passing the four-digit extension across the trunk to the PBX. Outbound calls from the PBX are more interesting. If they are to the PSTN, they must be routed out of one of the PSTN trunks. If they are to any of the other on-network locations, the call request must be forwarded to the gatekeeper. You can also take advantage of the topology to send calls with a U.S. country code to the gatekeeper so that they will be forwarded out of the New York gateway. This can reduce toll charges on calls between Shanghai and the United States.

Review Questions

1 What are two ways to verify that gateways have successfully registered with a gatekeeper?

2 Why is it necessary to configure technology prefixes when implementing gatekeepers on a voice network?

3 What do you need to do to the gatekeeper configuration to provide dynamic prefix registration support?

4 How much bandwidth does the gatekeeper count for each call using a G.729 codec? For a G.711 codec?

5 How can you provide redundancy on a CallManager H.225 gatekeeper-controlled trunk?

6 How is state information shared between gatekeepers in a gatekeeper cluster?

7 What three commands can provide detailed information about the status of a gatekeeper cluster?

8 Which undocumented trace command can you use to show the decision tree steps that the gatekeeper takes as it processes an ARQ message?

IP-to-IP Gateways

CHAPTER 18

Cisco Multiservice IP-to-IP Gateway

One of the latest buzzwords in voice-over IP (VoIP) infrastructure deployments is Session Border Controller (SBC). As VoIP deployments move from individual islands of voice networks to end-to-end voice solutions, SBCs become a crucial infrastructure device that sits on the border of two networks handling real-time voice and video sessions. Before SBCs, service providers implemented back-to-back time-division multiplexing (TDM) gateways when interconnecting with other service providers. They were able to create points of demarcations between the networks, but because of the involvement of the digital signal processors (DSP), not only was delay being introduced, but also degradation in the voice/fax quality because of the additional decoding and encoding of the voice/fax packets. Apart from creating points of demarcations, various other challenges arise when you interconnect two VoIP/video networks.

To benefit from low long-distance telephony charges, many enterprises have also started using IP interconnect services from service providers. SBCs are used between the two networks to handle their real-time communication needs. Cisco Multiservice IP-to-IP gateway (IPIPGW) is the Cisco Session Border Controller product that provides a toolkit of Cisco IOS features to resolve various interconnect problems.

This chapter helps you do the following:

- Understand the IPIPGW architecture
- Configure an IPIPGW
- Understand Voice Infrastructure and Application (VIA) zones
- Understand the features that are available on IPIPGWs
- Use **show** and **debug** commands

IP-to-IP Gateway Overview

VoIP has gained acceptance with enterprise, service provider, and commercial customers, and the migration of voice traffic from public switched telephone network (PSTN) to voice traffic over the IP network is underway. Increasing numbers of customers, looking for richer services than the PSTN can provide, are starting to interconnect their VoIP networks.

However, interconnecting disparate VoIP networks has a new set of challenges that need to be dealt with. These new network requirements include the following:

- Creating proper points of demarcation between enterprises and service providers, primarily for providing security and collection of call detail records (CDRs) for voice quality statistics and billing.

- Hiding internal network topology from the peering partner or the outside world for security purposes.

- Providing interworking between H.323 and Session Initiation Protocol (SIP)

- Addressing various other challenges, such as transcoding media, routing VoIP traffic to traverse firewalls and Network Address Translation (NAT), ensuring quality of service (QoS), and employing call admission control (CAC).

Cisco Multiservice IP-to-IP Gateway

The Cisco Multiservice IPIPGW facilitates simple and cost-effective connectivity between independent VoIP and video networks. Designed to meet enterprise and service provider SBC needs, the Cisco Multiservice IPIPGW is an integrated Cisco IOS application that runs on the following platforms:

- Cisco 2800 series integrated services routers

- Cisco 3800 series integrated services routers

- Cisco 2600XM series multiservice platforms

- Cisco 2691 routers

- Cisco 3700 series routers

- Cisco 7200VXR series routers

- Cisco 7301 routers

- Cisco AS5350XM and AS5400XM universal gateways

The IPIPGW images support not only IPIPGW functionality, but also a regular TDM gateway and gatekeeper functionality. The IPIPGW images are special images, which are integrated along with the routing, switching, and security features that are available in the regular Cisco IOS images.

Deploying IPIPGWs has three prerequisites:

- A supported Cisco router platform

- A Cisco Multiservice IPIPGW Cisco IOS image—INT VOICE/VIDEO, IPIP GW, or TDMIP GW

- Cisco integrated voice video license: gatekeeper IPIPGW feature license

Architecture

On a regular Cisco voice gateway, one call leg is a TDM connection on which the call is originated or terminated. The other call leg could be a VoIP call based on any VoIP protocol. With the IPIPGW, a single voice call has two VoIP call legs. The originating call leg is matched on the incoming VoIP dial peer and terminated at the IPIPGW. The second call leg is reoriginated based on the outgoing VoIP dial peer.

Figure 18-1 illustrates the IPIPGW architecture, which is based on the back-to-back user agent (B2BUA), which is SIP, or the back-to-back gateway (B2BGW), which is H.323.

Figure 18-1 *IPIPGW Architecture*

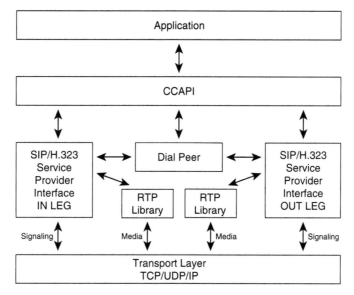

The IPIPGW implementation leverages Cisco voice gateway architecture. The main difference between the voice gateway and the IPIPGW is that no telephony service provider interface (SPI) or telephony signaling stack exists in case of IPIPGW. The IPIPGW has two IP legs for a given voice call, whereas the TDM-IP gateway has one telephony and one IP leg for a given TDM-IP call.

When a VoIP call arrives at the IPIPGW, it is matched at the configured inbound dial peer. The particular VoIP SPI (such as H.323 or SIP) processes the call and informs the application, which in turn routes the call using the configured outbound dial peer. The two SPIs talk using the application layer for the signaling messages. For capability, media address, and port exchanges, the SPI communicates directly or by using the Call Control API (CCAPI) layer.

Each IP leg has a corresponding Real-Time Transport Protocol (RTP) instance that is associated with it for media flow-through. The media stream that is originating from the IPIPGW carries the IP address and the port number of the IPIPGW.

NOTE   The only changes in the media stream are the IP address and port number. For media flow around calls, media flows directly between endpoints; therefore, you will not see RTP instances on the IPIPGW.

Media-Handling Modes

You can handle the passing of media in two ways:

- Media flow-through
- Media flow-around

Figure 18-2 illustrates the media-handling modes that are supported on the IPIPGW.

Figure 18-2 *Media Handling Modes*

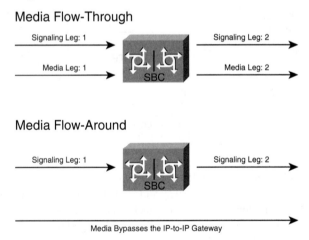

- **Media flow-through**—In media flow-through, the media stream passes through the IPIPGW, as shown in the top example of Figure 18-2. The IP address in the RTP packet is rewritten, with the IPIPGW inserting its own IP address. This provides complete privacy of the endpoints that are generating and terminating the call. None of the parties involved in the conversation would know the IP address of the other party. Both endpoints see only the IP address of the IPIPGW that is sending and receiving the RTP packets. Media flow-through is the default mode for media handling.

- **Media flow-around**—If media flow-around is configured, the media stream bypasses the IPIPGW and flows directly between the originating and terminating endpoints. This is shown in the bottom example of Figure 18-2. In this case, both the endpoints that are involved in the call would know the IP address of the other endpoint.

Protocol Support

The IPIPGW supports the following VoIP call combinations:

- SIP-to-SIP
- H.323-to-H.323
- H.323-to-SIP interworking

SIP Networks

For SIP networks, the Cisco IPIPGW functions as a B2BUA. It receives a SIP request, reformulates the request, and then sends it as a new request. The responses that the terminating endpoint sends to the request are also reformulated and sent back in the opposite direction. Therefore, the Cisco IPIPGW can sit between two SIP networks without either party knowing the uniform resource identifier (URI), IP address, or any other information of the other party.

To achieve this, the B2BUA reformulates a request with entirely new From, Via, Contact, Call ID, and Session Description Protocol (SDP) media information. The B2BUA also removes any other SIP header fields that might contain information about the calling party. When the B2BUA returns a response, it also changes the contact and SDP media information from the called party. The modified SDP points to the B2BUA, which then forwards RTP media packets from the called party to the calling party and vice versa. Thus, neither endpoint learns any identifying information about the other party during the session establishment.

H.323 Networks

In H.323 networks, the Cisco IPIPGW also functions as a B2BGW, or a terminator and reoriginator of voice, fax, or video calls. No DSPs are required for calls using the same codec, which provides better quality voice calls because hardly any delay is added for the RTP stream. DSPs are required only if you need to transcode between two codecs, such as G.711ulaw and G.729r8.

Protocol Interworking

Because the Cisco IPIPGW terminates and reoriginates VoIP calls, it can handle different VoIP protocols on each leg. This provides a valuable capability when protocol-disparate networks need to talk to one another. The Cisco Multiservice IPIPGW does protocol interworking between H.323 and SIP for voice and fax calls.

This provides flexibility to customers who are connecting their Cisco CallManager H.323 network to a VoIP service provider who offers SIP services. It also enables customers who want to migrate from H.323-based networks to SIP-based networks. With the media flowing through the gateway, complete network hiding for both signaling and media is achieved. Also, if the enterprise is using one codec, such as G.711ulaw, and the SIP VoIP service provider is using G.729r8, transcoding between these codecs is supported for the protocol interworking scenarios. Supplementary services between H.323 trunks of the Cisco CallManager and SIP service provider are supported. The H.323 trunk needs to configure a media termination point (MTP) so that services such as call hold/resume, call transfer, and so on can be used.

Basic Configuration

Cisco voice gateways, by default, support a TDM-to-VoIP or VoIP-to-TDM call. Enabling the VoIP-to-VoIP functionality is configured under the **voice service voip** configuration mode. The syntax for the **allow-connections** command is **allow-connections {h323 | sip} to {h323 | sip}**.

Example 18-1 illustrates the basic configuration to enable a VoIP-to-VoIP call. By configuring **allow-connections h323 to h323**, Cisco IOS can permit an incoming H.323 VoIP call to be accepted and sent out as an H.323 VoIP call on the second call leg. Also shown is the configuration for allowing SIP-to-SIP or H.323-SIP calls.

Example 18-1 *Enabling IPIPGW Functionality*

```
IPIPGateway#config t
IPIPGateway(config)# voice service voip
IPIPGateway(conf-voi-serv)#allow-connections h323 to h323
IPIPGateway(conf-voi-serv)#allow-connections h323 to sip
IPIPGateway(conf-voi-serv)#allow-connections sip to h323
IPIPGateway(conf-voi-serv)#allow-connections sip to sip
```

Media-handling mode is configured under the **voice service voip** configuration mode. The command syntax is **media {flow-through | flow-around}**. Example 18-2 illustrates the configuration commands for implementing media flow-through.

Example 18-2 *Configuring Media Flow-Through*

```
IP-to-IP_GW(config)#voice service voip
IP-to-IP_GW(conf-voi-serv)#media flow-through
```

Example 18-3 illustrates the configuration commands for implementing media flow-around.

Example 18-3   *Configuring Media Flow-Around*

```
IP-to-IP_GW(config)#voice service voip
IP-to-IP_GW(conf-voi-serv)#media flow-around
```

You can achieve the routing of the voice and video calls based on the configuration of the incoming and outgoing dial peers. You can apply the relevant protocol, dual tone multifrequency (DTMF) type, codec information, QoS parameters, and other parameters to each VoIP dial peer.

Example 18-4 illustrates a VoIP dial peer configuration. VoIP dial peer 1 is the incoming H.323 dial peer (default protocol, if **session protocol** command is not configured). The **session target** command designates the IP address for this VoIP dial peer, which in this example is the IP address of the originating endpoint. The **codec g711ulaw** command specifies that the codec to be used for this dial peer is G711u-law. The **dtmf h245-alphanumeric** command specifies that the dtmf type to use for this dial peer is H.245 alphanumeric. VoIP dial peer 2 is a SIP-based VoIP dial peer. This is explicitly configured in the **session protocol sipv2** command. The destination pattern is the called-party number that the originating endpoint dials. The **dtmf-relay rtp-nte** command specifies the RFC 2833 DTMF type to be used on the outgoing leg.

Example 18-4   *Configuring VoIP Dial Peers for IPIPGWs*

```
IPIPGateway#config t
!
! H.323 dial peer
IPIPGateway(config)#dial-peer voice 1 voip
IPIPGateway(config-dial-peer)#session target ipv4:9.13.8.150
IPIPGateway(config-dial-peer)#incoming called-number 8...
IPIPGateway(config-dial-peer)#dtmf-relay h245-alphanumeric
IPIPGateway(config-dial-peer)#codec g711ulaw
!
! SIP dial peer
IPIPGateway(config-dial-peer)#dial-peer voice 2 voip
IPIPGateway(config-dial-peer)#destination-pattern 8...
IPIPGateway(config-dial-peer)#session protocol sipv2
IPIPGateway(config-dial-peer)#session target ipv4:9.13.8.16
IPIPGateway(config-dial-peer)#dtmf-relay rtp-nte
IPIPGateway(config-dial-peer)#codec g711ulaw
```

Also, because the IPIPGW and gatekeeper functionality are supported in the same Cisco IOS image, you can run both these functionalities on the same router. You can run the IPIPGW in conjunction with the Cisco gatekeeper using a concept called *via-zones*.

Via-Zones

Chapter 16, "Deploying Gatekeepers," introduced the Cisco IOS gatekeeper and the concept of local and remote zones. The Cisco Multiservice IPIPGW feature introduces gatekeeper via-zones. A via-zone is a Cisco term for a zone that contains IPIPGWs. A via-zone-enabled gatekeeper is capable of recognizing via-zones and sending traffic to via-zone gateways.

You must configure IPIPGW to register to a local zone on the gatekeeper. You would use this zone as the via-zone. You could configure the **zone local** or **zone remote** command to take the incoming call through the IPIPGW. You can achieve this based on the invia and outvia configuration in the **zone** command. The **invia** command specifies the gatekeeper for the calls that are entering the particular zone, and the **outvia** command specifies the gatekeeper that is leaving that zone. When the **invia** and **outvia** commands are configured, the gatekeeper returns the IP address of the IPIPGW in the Admission Confirm (ACF)/Location Confirm (LCF) messages to the originating gateway. The originating gateway then sends an H.323 setup to the IPIPGW, which in turn terminates and reoriginates traffic to its final destination.

Figure 18-3 illustrates a gatekeeper via-zone call flow. A caller from area code 408 calls a party in area code 972, and the following actions occur.

Figure 18-3 *Gatekeeper Via-Zone—Sample Call Flow*

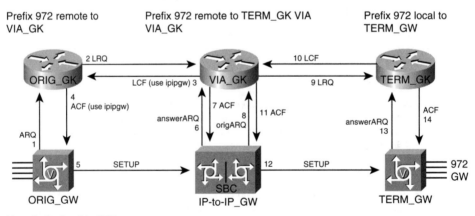

1 ORIG_GW sends an Admission Request (ARQ) with the 972-based number to ORIG_GK.

2 ORIG_GK sees prefix 972 as reachable through VIA_GK and sends a Location Request (LRQ) to VIA_GK.

3   The LRQ for 972 is received by VIA_GK. VIA_GK looks at the H.323 ID in the inbound LRQ to find the remote zone. Then it looks for a via-zone keyword associated with that remote zone. Because the via-zone gatekeeper ID is a local zone, it allocates the call to the IPIPGW in the via-zone and returns an LCF specifying IP-TO-IP_GW.

4   ORIG_GK returns the ACF, specifying the IP address of IP-TO-IP_GW.

5   ORIG_GW sends a SETUP message to IP-TO-IP_GW for the 972 call.

6   IP-TO-IP_GW sends an ARQ to VIA_GK to admit the incoming call (answerCall=true).

7   VIA_GK returns an ACF.

8   IP-TO-IP_GW has a dial peer specifying ras VIA_GK for the 972 prefix (or all prefixes) and sends an ARQ (with answerCall set to FALSE) to VIA_GK for prefix 972.

9   VIA_GK sees prefix 972 as TERM_GK, and there is no outvia zone, so VIA_GK sends an LRQ to TERM_GK.

10 TERM_GK sees prefix 972 as in its own zone and sends an LCF pointing to TERM_GW.

11 VIA_GK returns an ACF specifying IP-TO-IP_GW.

12 IP-TO-IP_GW sends a SETUP message to TERM_GW for the 972 call.

13 TERM_GW sends an ARQ answerCall to TERM_GK.

14 TERM_GK returns an ACF for answerCall.

Example 18-5 shows the configurations for the gatekeepers and IPIPGW to support the call flows shown in the preceding list.

Example 18-5 *Via-Zone Configuration*

```
ORIG_GK#config t
ORIG_GK(config)#gatekeeper
ORIG_GK(config-gk)#zone local ORIG_GK zone1 192.168.10.10
ORIG_GK(config-gk)#zone remote VIA_GK zone2 192.168.20.20 1719
ORIG_GK(config-gk)#zone prefix VIA_GK 972*
VIA_GK#config t
VIA_GK(config)#gatekeeper
VIA_GK(config-gk)#zone local VIA_GK zone2 192.168.20.20
VIA_GK(config-gk)#zone remote TERM_GK zone3 192.168.30.30 invia VIA_GK outvia VIA_GK
VIA_GK(config-gk)#zone remote ORIG_GK zone1 192.168.10.10 invia VIA_GK outvia VIA_GK
VIA_GK(config-gk)#zone prefix TERM_GK 972*
IP-to-IP_GW#config t
IP-to-IP_GW(config)#int f0/0
IP-to-IP_GW(config-if)#h323-gateway voip interface
IP-to-IP_GW(config-if)#h323-gateway voip h323-id IP-to-IP_GW
```

continues

Example 18-5 *Via-Zone Configuration (Continued)*

```
IP-to-IP_GW(config-if)#h323-gateway voip id VIA_GK ipaddr 192.168.20.20
IP-to-IP_GW(config)#gateway
IP-to-IP_GW(config)#dial-peer voice 1 voip
IP-to-IP_GW(config-dial-peer)#incoming called-number .T
IP-to-IP_GW(config-dial-peer)#codec g711ulaw
IP-to-IP_GW(config)#dial-peer voice 2 voip
IP-to-IP_GW(config-dial-peer)#destination-pattern 972*
IP-to-IP_GW(config-dial-peer)#session target ras
IP-to-IP_GW(config-dial-peer)#codec g711ulaw
TERM_GK#config t
TERM_GK(config)#gatekeeper
TERM_GK(config-gk)#zone local TERM_GK zone3 192.168.30.30
```

IP-to-IP Gateway Features

IPIPGW supports a rich set of features for providing the SBC functionality. As it supports both TDM and IP-to-IP calls, it also provides a smooth transition path for customers who currently have PSTN interconnects and are migrating to VoIP interconnects. Few of the features, which help in interconnecting voice and video networks, are described in more detail.

Video Support

Cisco Multiservice IPIPGW supports video calls for H.323 deployments. With the support for video, you can use the IPIPGW for extending the rich media experience between two enterprises by interconnecting their video networks while providing security, quality, reliability, and scalability. In addition to the benefits that the Cisco Multiservice IPIPGW feature offers in the voice network, it also provides the following features for video networks:

- H.261, H.263, and H.264 codec support.

- Far-end camera control (FECC) support, which enables an endpoint to control the remote camera on a video call that is connected through the IPIPGW.

- Support for T.120 data collaboration in flow-around mode.

- Resource Reservation Protocol (RSVP) synchronization and differentiated services code point (DSCP) marking for video streams. This feature provides enhanced QoS through RSVP synchronization with the H.323 signaling protocol and DSCP packet marking.

- New vendor-specific attribute (VSA) for improved accounting of bandwidth usage. You can configure Cisco gateways to use the max-bit-rate VSA to report bandwidth usage to accounting servers.

- Support for generic data capabilities for inline data content.

Codec transparent is a concept supported with the IPIPGW and is useful for video deployments. You can also use it in voice deployments. By configuring codec transparent on the incoming and the outgoing dial peers, IPIPGW transparently passes the codec from one leg to another. Only codecs that are supported by the IPIPGW are transparently passed. If an unsupported codec is requested, call setup will fail. The **codec transparent** command eases the configuration and leaves it up to the two endpoints to negotiate the codec for the call.

Address Hiding

The architecture of the IPIPGW has been built such that it inherently performs the function of hiding IP addresses, as shown in Figure 18-4. The call signaling is terminated at the gateway and then reoriginated using the IP address of the Cisco IPIPGW. The media can also be terminated and reoriginated, thus providing complete privacy of the endpoint or network that is generating the call. It also creates a point of demarcation between the two networks, which eases manageability and troubleshooting.

When configuring the interfaces on the IPIPGW, you can use various combinations:

- Two Ethernet interfaces, with different IP addresses associated with them.

- A single Ethernet interface or a single loopback interface, if it is properly routed between the two networks. Both sides of the networks would be communicating with this one IP address and receiving signaling and media information from this one IP address.

- One Ethernet interface and one loopback interface.

You can bind only one protocol, H.323 or SIP, to the single loopback interface.

Figure 18-4 *Address Hiding for SIP Call Flow*

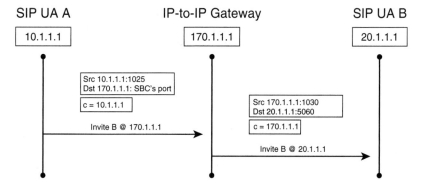

Security

With VoIP deployment on the rise, the need for providing security for voice calls is also increasing. IPIPGW supports a rich set of security mechanisms for both H.323 and SIP protocols.

H.323 Deployments

Security for VoIP calls is provided by using the following:

- IPsec tunnels for encrypting the H.323 signaling traffic
- Secure RTP (SRTP) for media encryption

One IPsec tunnel is created between the originating endpoint and the IPIPGW, and the second tunnel is created between the IPIPGW and the terminating endpoint. These static IPsec tunnels provide an end-to-end secure signaling channel for the H.323 messages. The keys, which are negotiated in the H.225 messages, are relayed by the IPIPGW from one leg to another. Media is also encrypted using SRTP, and it flows through the gateway without its payload being changed. Only the Layer 3 IP address of the SRTP packets is modified for providing the address-hiding feature.

SIP Deployments: Transport Layer Security

Another security feature that is supported on the IPIPGW is the Transport Layer Security (TLS) protocol. TLS is implemented over the TCP. TLS provides two security functionalities:

- **Mutual authentication**—This is based on mutually exchanging certificates signed by a trusted certificate authority (CA) server.
- **Signaling encryption**—During the handshake phase, the IPIPGW and the originating or terminating gateway negotiate a dynamically generated symmetric key and cipher algorithms through TLS. When the negotiation is successful, the SIP signaling is encrypted or decrypted using the exchanged symmetric key.

Digest Authentication

The Cisco IPIPGW supports HTTP digest authentication and provides a stateless challenge-response mechanism for authentication based on digest access. Figure 18-5 illustrates HTTP digest authentication. When the SIP proxy server receives a SIP request from the IPIPGW without credentials, it challenges the request with a 401 or 407 unauthorized. The IPIPGW then responds to the challenge and supplies the required credentials for the call to be successfully completed.

Figure 18-5 *Message Exchange for Digest Authentication*

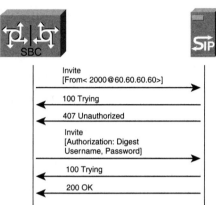

Digest authentication is configured under the **sip-ua** configuration mode. The command syntax is **authentication username** *username* **password** *password* [**realm** *realm*]. Example 18-6 illustrates the configuration commands for implementing digest authentication.

Example 18-6 *Configuring Digest Authentication*

```
IPIPGateway#config t
IPIPGateway(config)#sip-ua
IPIPGateway(config-sip-ua)#authentication username userone password jackson realm
cisco.com
```

DTMF Interworking

Because the IPIPGW terminates and reoriginates the signaling call leg, the DTMF relay tones need to be transmitted across the 2 call legs. Based on the configuration, you can send a similar DTMF type across the outbound VoIP type or, in certain cases, you can change the DTMF type from one type to another, as shown in Table 18-1.

For example, you can transmit H.245 alphanumeric as the same H.245 alphanumeric DTMF, or you can convert the H.245 alphanumeric on the H.323 call leg to SIP RFC 2833, or SIP NOTIFY on the SIP call leg, and vice versa. For DTMF types such as RFC 2833, the media must flow through the IPIPGW.

Table 18-1 *DTMF Types Supported on the IPIPGW*

DTMF Relay Type at Origination Side	DTMF Relay Type at Termination Side
H323 <-> H323	
H245 alphanumeric	H245 alphanumeric
H245 signal	H245 signal

continues

Table 18-1 *DTMF Types Supported on the IPIPGW (Continued)*

DTMF Relay Type at Origination Side	DTMF Relay Type at Termination Side
RFC 2833	RFC 2833
H245 alphanumeric	H245 signal
RFC 2833	H245 signal
RFC 2833	H245 alphanumeric
H323 <-> SIP	
H245 alphanumeric	NOTIFY
H245 alphanumeric	RFC 2833
H245 signal	NOTIFY
H245 signal	RFC 2833
RFC 2833	NOTIFY
RFC 2833	RFC 2833
SIP <-> SIP	
NOTIFY	NOTIFY
RFC 2833	RFC 2833

Admission Confirm (ACF)/Location Confirm (LCF) DTMF Relay is configured under the VoIP dial peer configuration mode. It needs to be configured under both the incoming as well as the outgoing VoIP dial peer. The command syntax is **dtmf-relay** *cisco-rtp|h245-alphanumeric|h245-signal|rtp-nte|sip-notify.* Example 18-7 illustrates the configuration commands for implementing RFC 2833 dtmf type.

Example 18-7 *Configuring RFC 2833 DTMF*

```
IP-to-IP_GW(config)#dial-peer voice 1 voip
IP-to-IP_GW(config-dial-peer)#dtmf-relay rtp-nte
```

Fax Support

A fax call is treated similarly to a voice call. Standards-based T.38 and other fax types such as Cisco fax relay and fax pass-through are supported. Interworking between H.323 and SIP fax calls is also supported. When you configure fax, you can use the regular fax commands either globally or under the specific inbound and outbound VoIP dial peers. Interworking between various fax types is not possible. For example, you cannot convert a T.38 fax call to a fax pass-through call.

Quality of Service

The Cisco Multiservice IPIPGW supports all the QoS features that are available in Cisco IOS. Features such as low-latency queuing (LLQ), IP precedence, and DSCP are supported on the gateway. You could remark the signaling, in addition to media packets, appropriately before sending the traffic into the network. By applying the right QoS policies, you can provide better service to selected traffic. You can use the regular Cisco IOS commands for QoS for configuration.

Call Admission Control

CAC is a deterministic and informed decision made before you establish a voice or video call. CAC is based on whether the required network resources are available to provide suitable QoS for the new call. Different CAC mechanisms are supported on the Cisco Multiservice IPIPGW and, based on the need and network design of the specific customers, you could apply one of the following mechanisms.

RSVP-Based CAC

Cisco IPIPGW uses RSVP to limit the accepted voice or video load on the IP network to guarantee the QoS levels of calls. The Cisco IPIPGW CAC that is using RSVP synchronizes RSVP signaling with the protocol (H.323 or SIP) signaling to ensure that the bandwidth reservation is established in both directions before a call moves to the alerting phase (ringing). This ensures that the called party phone rings only after you have reserved the resources for the call. With RSVP-based admission control, the IPIPGW can reserve network bandwidth and react appropriately if bandwidth reservation fails.

Max Connections-Based CAC

The maximum connections CAC mechanism involves using the **max-conn** VoIP dial-peer configuration command on a dial peer of the outgoing leg to restrict the number of concurrent connections (calls) that can be active on that dial peer at any one time.

IP Call Capacity-Based CAC

CAC can also be provided based on carrier ID. Carrier ID is an attribute that consists of up to 127 alphanumeric characters that identify the carrier that is handling H.323 calls. This CAC mechanism works in conjunction with a Cisco gatekeeper. You can match incoming calls that have a certain carrier ID configured. Only the configured maximum capacity of calls is allowed to traverse the IPIPGW.

You configure the IP circuit under the voice service voip and h323 configuration mode. The command syntax is **ip circuit carrier-id** *carrier name* **reserved-calls** *reserved*. The *carrier name* defines an IP circuit using the specified name as the circuit ID, and the *reserved* keyword defines the maximum number of calls for the circuit ID. Example 18-8 illustrates the configuration commands for **ip circuit**. **max-calls** sets the number of maximum aggregate H.323 IP circuit carrier call legs. The reserved-calls number has to be double the number of calls allowed to pass the IPIPGW. Therefore, in Example 18-8, 200 calls would be allowed through the gateway for carrier XYZ. Also, more than one carrier ID can be configured.

Example 18-8 *Configuring CAC Based on IP Circuits*

```
IPIPGateway#config t
IPIPGateway(config)# voice service voip
IP-to-IP_GW(conf-voi-serv)#h323
IP-to-IP_GW(conf-serv-h323)#ip circuit max-calls 800
IP-to-IP_GW(conf-serv-h323)#ip circuit carrier-id XYZ reserved-calls 400
```

Thresholds Based on CPU, Memory, and Total Calls

It is critical to configure the gateway so that it accepts calls based on certain resources. If the resources are being highly used or are falling below configured limits, you should reject the incoming calls with a configured type of treatment. You can configure call treatment to send a certain type of a cause code so that the originating gateway can reroute the call to the next available gateway. You can provision CAC based on monitoring certain resources of the IPIPGW, such as these:

- CPU
- Memory
- Total number of calls

You can configure the IPIPGW to handle VoIP based on the minimum and maximum limits that are configured. Based on the resource that is monitored, you could apply appropriate treatment when the resource reaches the configured low or high threshold window mark.

You configure CAC based on CPU, memory, and total calls in the global configuration mode.

The command syntax for configuring call threshold based on CPU utilization for the last 5 seconds is **call threshold global cpu-5sec low** *low-threshold* **high** *high-threshold*. Example 18-9 illustrates the configuration commands for setting a CPU low threshold of 5 percent and a high threshold of 90 percent measured in the last 5 seconds.

Example 18-9 *Configuring CAC Control Based on CPU*

```
IPIPGateway(config)#call threshold global cpu-5sec low 5 high 90
```

The command syntax for configuring call threshold based on average CPU utilization is **call threshold global cpu-avg low** *low-threshold* **high** *high-threshold*. Example 18-10 illustrates the configuration commands for configuring thresholds of the average CPU utilization for 5 percent (low) or 75 percent (high).

Example 18-10 *Configuring CAC Based on CPU*

```
IPIPGateway(config)#call threshold global cpu-avg low 5 high 75
```

The command syntax for configuring call threshold based on average CPU utilization is **call threshold global total-mem low** *low-threshold* **high** *high-threshold*. Example 18-11 illustrates the configuration commands for enabling CAC based on memory. The low threshold is set to 10 percent, and the high threshold is set to 75 percent of the gateway memory.

Example 18-11 *Configuring CAC Based on Memory*

```
IPIPGateway(config)#call threshold global total-mem low 10 high 75
```

The command syntax for configuring call threshold based on total number of calls that the IPIPGW would handle is **call threshold global total-calls low** *low-threshold* **high** *high-threshold*. Example 18-12 illustrates the configuration commands for enabling CAC based on the total number of calls to be handled. The low threshold is set to 1 call, and the high threshold is set to 800 calls.

Example 18-12 *Configuring CAC Based on Total Calls*

```
IPIPGateway(config)#call threshold global total-calls low 1 high 800
```

You need to turn on call treatment to take the appropriate action when the gateway resources hit the low or the high threshold mark. You can also configure call treatment so that a particular cause code is returned. The command syntax for enabling call treatment is **call threshold on**. Example 18-13 illustrates the configuration commands for enabling call treatment. Various options of what cause code could be sent are shown in the **call treatment cause-code** command.

Example 18-13 *Configuring Call Treatment*

```
IPIPGatewayconfig)#call treatment on
IPIPGateway(config)#call treatment cause-code ?
busy         Insert cause code indicating the GW is busy (17)
no-QoS       Insert cause code indicating the GW can't provide QOS (49)
no-resource  Insert cause code indicating the GW has no resource (47)
```

Transcoding

Transcoding functionality is supported on the IPIPGW routers. Using transcoding services reduces bandwidth on the WAN side, resulting in tangible cost savings. DSP farms provide the transcoding services using DSP resources that are installed either on the router motherboard or on high-density digital voice/fax network modules. The transcoding functionality is supported between G.711 and G.729 codecs. Table 18-2 lists the variants and packetizations.

Table 18-2 *Codec Support*

Codec	Packetization Periods for Transcoding (ms)
G.711 a-law, G.711 µ-law	10, 20, or 30
G.729, G.729A, G.729B, G.729AB	10, 20, 30, 40, 50, or 60

NOTE Only 2800s, 2600XMs, 2691, 3700s, and 3800s support transcoding.

You can use the DSP farm that is used for the transcoding on the same router platform as the IPIPGW or on an external router.

IPIPGW uses the Skinny server to talk to the DSP farm. When you enable transcoding on the IPIPGW, you use the same configuration commands that you used in the Cisco CallManager Express (CME).

VXML and Tcl Scripts

You can run voice XML and Toolkit Command Language (Tcl) scripts on the IPIPGW. DSPs are not required for use of this feature. You have to record prompts in the same codec type that you use for the call. For example, you should use prompts that are recorded in G711µlaw for G711µlaw calls. The scripts are applied to the VoIP dial peer. Because of the rich set of DTMF types that are supported (for example, H.245 alphanumeric, H.245 signal, SIP RFC 2833, and SIP NOTIFY), this is a useful feature for many customers who are deploying services, such as prepaid calling cards.

Billing

You can collect call detail records (CDRs) on the IPIPGW, similar to the way you collect them on a regular Cisco IOS TDM gateway. The CDRs are generated for both legs of the call, regardless of whether it is an H.323 or a SIP call. Conference ID is the common field, which you can use to corelate the two call legs for the voice call. Capability for gathering voice quality statistics based on packet loss, jitter, and round trip time is available.

show Commands

You can use many of the **show** commands that are employed on the Cisco voice gateways on the IPIPGW. Each voice call that passes through the IPIPGW has two VoIP media streams in the media flow-through. Example 18-14 illustrates the **show** command for checking the two VoIP media streams on the IPIPGW in the media flow-through mode. The command output displays the active RTP connections and the call identifiers for each leg of the VoIP. Connection 1, which is call identifier 31, signifies the connection between the IPIPGW and the originating endpoint. Connection 2 (Call ID 32) signifies the second call leg, which is the connection between the IPIPGW and the terminating endpoint. The User Datagram Protocol (UDP) ports are shown for the local (IPIPGW) and remote endpoints (originating and terminating endpoints). The LocalIP is the IP address of the IPIPGW, and the RemoteIP is the IP address of the originating and terminating endpoint.

Example 18-14 *Displaying Media Streams*

```
IP-to-IP_GW#show voip rtp connections
VoIP RTP active connections :
No. CallId  dstCallId  LocalRTP    RmtRTP      LocalIP       RemoteIP
1   31       32         17612       17978       200.1.1.3     60.60.60.75
2   32       31         18164       29128       200.1.1.3     200.1.1.75
Found 2 active RTP connections
```

debug Commands

The following **debug** commands are helpful for troubleshooting IPIPGW call flows. Based on the protocols that you are using, you can turn on the appropriate debugs to diagnose the problem.

- H.323–H.323 scenarios:
  - **debug h225 asn1**
  - **debug h225 events**
  - **debug h245 asn1**
  - **debug h245 events**
  - **debug h225 q931**
  - **debug cch323 all**
  - **debug gatekeeper main 10**
  - **debug voip ipipgw**
  - **debug voip ccapi inout**
- H.323–SIP scenarios:
  - **debug h225 asn1**
  - **debug h225 events**

  — **debug h245 asn1**

  — **debug h245 events**

  — **debug cch323 all**

  — **debug voip ipipgw**

  — **debug voip ccapi inout**

  — **debug ccsip all**

- SIP-SIP scenarios:

  — **debug ccsip all**

  — **debug voip ccapi inout**

- RSVP scenarios:

  — **debug call rsvp-sync events**

  — **debug call rsvp-sync func-trace**

Case Study: Providing Enterprise VoIP Trunking to VoIP Service of the Service Provider

The New York office needs to connect a CallManager H.225 trunk to a SIP service provider. The CallManager is version 4.1.3. To provide security and protocol interworking, you plan to implement an IPIPGW to connect with the service provider, as shown in Figure 18-6.

Figure 18-6 *New York IPIPGW Implementation*

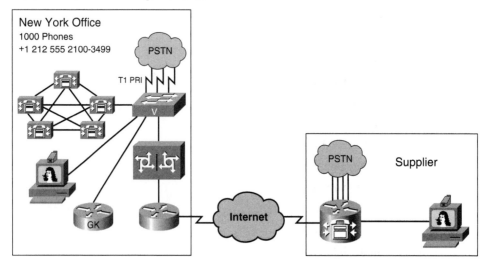

CallManager Configuration

Note the following points in CallManager trunk configuration:

- Configure the CallManager with an H.225 gatekeeper-controlled trunk
- Check Media Termination Point Required
- Uncheck Wait for Far End H.245 Terminal Capability Set
- Check Enable Inbound FastStart
- Gatekeeper Name should be IP Address Gatekeeper
- Gatekeeper Terminal Type should be Gateway
- Technology prefix should be 1#

Example 18-15 shows the configuration steps for implementing the IPIPGW. In this example, the Cisco IOS gatekeeper and the IPIPGW are running on the same router platform.

Example 18-15 *IPIPGW Implementation*

```
!
! Enabling IPIPGW functionality
!
IPIPGateway#config t
IPIPGateway(config)#voice service voip
IPIPGateway(conf-voi-serv)#allow-connections h323 to sip
IPIPGateway(conf-voi-serv)#allow-connections sip to h323
IPIPGateway(config-voi-serv)#exit
!
! Configuring the gatekeeper
!
IPIPGateway(config)#gatekeeper
IPIPGateway(config-gk)#zone local via_gk zone2
IPIPGateway(config-gk)#zone local CCM zone2 invia via_gk outvia via_gk
IPIPGateway(config-gk)#zone prefix CCM 2125553... gw-priority 6 IPIPGatewayTrunk_1
IPIPGateway(config-gk)#gw-type-prefix 1#* default-technology
IPIPGateway(config-gk)#no shutdown
IPIPGateway(config-gk)#exit
!
! Configuring the H.323 gateway to register with the gatekeeper
!
IPIPGateway(config)#interface GigabitEthernet0/0
IPIPGateway(config-if)#ip address 10.1.10.50 255.255.255.0
IPIPGateway(config-if)#h323-gateway voip interface
IPIPGateway(config-if)#h323-gateway voip id via_gk ipaddr 10.1.10.50 1719
IPIPGateway(config-if)#h323-gateway voip h323-id IP-to-IP_GW
IPIPGateway(config-if)#exit
!
! Configuring SIP user-agent section to point toward the service provider SIP proxy
!
IPIPGateway(config)#sip-ua
IPIPGateway(config-sip-ua)#authentication username ipip password 01100F175804 realm
CISCO
```

continues

Example 18-15 *IPIPGW Implementation (Continued)*

```
IPIPGateway(config-sip-ua)#sip-server dns:csps-release.gb.com
IPIPGateway(config-sip-ua)#exit
!
! Configuring the VoIP dial peers for routing calls from and to the Cisco CallManager
!
IPIPGateway(config)#dial-peer voice 1 voip
IPIPGateway(config-dial-peer)#destination-pattern 4088536...
IPIPGateway(config-dial-peer)#session protocol sipv2
IPIPGateway(config-dial-peer)#session target sip-server
IPIPGateway(config-dial-peer)#codec g711ulaw
IPIPGateway(config-dial-peer)#exit
!
IPIPGateway(config)#dial-peer voice 2 voip
IPIPGateway(config-dial-peer)#destination-pattern 2125553...
IPIPGateway(config-dial-peer)#session target ras
IPIPGateway(config-dial-peer)#incoming called-number .T
IPIPGateway(config-dial-peer)#codec g711ulaw
IPIPGateway(config-dial-peer)#end
```

Figures 18-7, 18-8, and 18-9 illustrate the CallManager H.225 trunk configuration.

Figure 18-7 *CallManager H.225 Trunk Configuration*

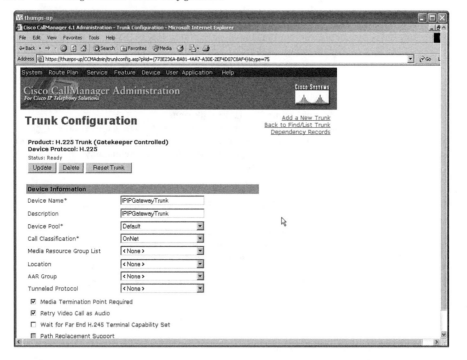

Figure 18-8 *CallManager H.225 Trunk Configuration (Continued)*

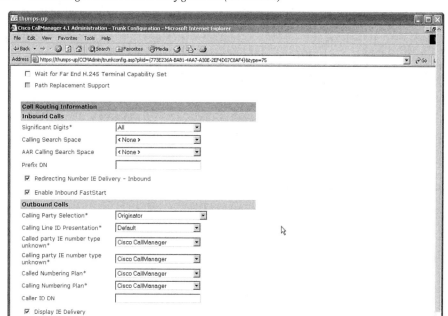

Figure 18-9 *CallManager H.225 Trunk Configuration (Continued)*

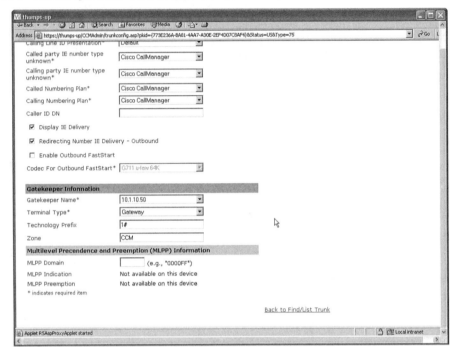

Review Questions

1 Why would you use media flow-around?

2 What is needed to implement an IPIPGW?

3 What is a via-zone?

4 Under what circumstances is a DSP needed in an IPIPGW call?

5 What platforms are supported for the Cisco Multiservice IPIPGW?

6 Can the Cisco Multiservice IPIPGW register to more than one gatekeeper?

7 Can you use the Cisco Multiservice IPIPGW without a gatekeeper?

8 Are translation rules and digit manipulation supported on the Cisco Multiservice IPIPGW?

Answers to Chapter-Ending Review Questions

Chapter 1

1 What are three tasks that a voice gateway performs?

Voice gateways perform some or all of the following tasks:

- Interfacing with the IP network and the PSTN or PBX
- Supporting IP call control protocols, in addition to TDM call control protocols
- Performing call setup and teardown for calls between the VoIP and PSTN networks by terminating and reoriginating the call media and signaling
- Providing supplementary services, such as call hold and transfer
- Relaying DTMF tones
- Supporting analog fax and modems over the IP network

2 What are two benefits of adding an IPIPGW between networks?

Placing an IPIPGW between networks gives added network privacy and additional security.

3 What are four tasks that an H.323 gatekeeper performs?

An H.323 gatekeeper can perform the following functions:

- Address resolution
- Call admission control
- Bandwidth control
- Zone management
- Security
- Call management
- Routing of call control signaling

4 Which call control protocol is an IETF standard that requires a call agent to function?

MGCP is a call control protocol that is an IETF standard and required a call agent to function.

5 Which call control protocol is an IETF standard, uses a distributed call-control model, and is able to control multiple types of media connections?

SIP is an IETF standard that uses a distributed call-control model and can control multiple types of media connections.

6 Which call control protocol is an ITU-T standard and uses a distributed call-control model?

H.323 is an ITU-T standard that uses a distributed call-control model.

7 What are three typical CallManager deployment scenarios?

Three typical CallManager deployment scenarios are as follows:

- Single site deployment
- Multisite deployment with centralized call control
- Multisite deployment with distributed call control

Chapter 2

1 What role does the call agent play when using an MGCP gateway?

A call agent is essential when you are using an MGCP gateway. It knows the dial plan, so it tells the gateway where to route calls. It controls the setup and teardown of connections to endpoints on the gateway, and thus the setup and teardown of calls.

2 List the control messages that MGCP uses.

NotificationRequest—RQNT

Notify—NTFY

CreateConnection—CRCX

ModifyConnection—MDCX

DeleteConnection—DLCX

AuditEndpoint—AUEP

AuditConnection—AUCX

EndpointConfiguration—EPCF

RestartInProgress—RSIP

3 How does MGCP Backhaul function?

The gateway terminates ISDN Q.921 messages but places the Q.931 messages in a TCP packet and sends them to the CallManager for processing.

4 What three commands do you need to enable MGCP on a router and identify Cisco CallManager as its call agent?

mgcp

5ccm-manager mgcp mgcp call-agent [*ip-address|hostname*] [*port*]

5 Why is there a need for DTMF relay in a VoIP network, regardless of the gateway protocol used?

When you are using codecs that compress voice, DTMF tones might become distorted or part of the signal might be lost. Then the receiver would not be able to respond correctly to the numbers that were sent.

Chapter 3

1 List at least four benefits of using H.323 as a gateway protocol.

- Caller ID from FXO and T1 CAS
- Use of a fractional PRI
- Interoperability with applications and devices from other vendors
- No version dependence between a gateway and CallManager
- Granular call control
- Tcl and VXML applications can be used
- Support for legacy systems
- Support for more types of TDM interfaces and signaling than MGCP
- Multimedia support
- NFAS support
- Use of a gatekeeper for call control and address resolution
- PRI call preservation

2 When you are configuring an H.323 gateway on a CallManager, what information do you enter for Device Name?

Enter the IP address of the gateway. If CallManager can reach the gateway with more than one IP address, use the **h323-gateway voip bind srcaddr** *ip-address* command to select which address to use.

3 Name four types of DTMF Relay that H.323 uses.

H.323 uses Cisco-RTP, RTP-NTE, H.245 Alphanumeric, and H.245 Signal.

4 What commands must you enter for a Cisco gateway to use H.323 Fast Start?

Cisco gateways assume that H.323 Fast Start is used. No commands are necessary to configure it.

5 Briefly describe toll bypass.

With toll bypass, calls between company locations are sent over the IP network as VoIP when bandwidth is available, and they are routed over the PSTN when no bandwidth is available.

6 If you configure conflicting commands globally under the **voice service voip** configuration mode, and under the dial peer using **voice class**, which commands will the router use?

The router will use the most explicitly applied commands, which in this case are the commands under the dial peer. It will use global commands only if more explicit ones are not configured.

7 How do you prevent active calls from being terminated when the CallManager becomes unreachable?

Turn off H.225 keepalives between the gateway and CallManager. The commands to do this are as follows:

GW1(config)#**voice service voip**

GW1(conf-voi-serv)#**h323**

GW1(conf-serv-h323)#**no h225 timeout keepalive**

Chapter 4

1 What do the acronyms UAC and UAS stand for? Define the difference between the two entities.

UAC stands for user agent client, and UAS stands for user agent server. The UAC originates the SIP session, and the UAS is the other endpoint of the session. It responds to INVITES and other messages sent from the UAC.

2 Name five types of SIP servers, and describe what they do.

The five types of SIP servers are proxy, registrar, location, redirect, and presence. Following is what each one does:

Proxy server—Receives SIP requests from a UAC and forwards them to the next-hop device, such as a SIP server or the UAS.

Registrar server—Registers UAs and provides location information upon request.

Location server—Maintains the location database for registered UAs.

Redirect server—Informs a UA about alternate locations for a called party that has moved.

Presence server—Gathers presence information and subscriptions, and sends notifications of events.

3 Name the five types of SIP methods that Cisco routers can both generate and respond to. What is the purpose of each one?

The five types of SIP methods that Cisco routers can generate and respond to are REGISTER, INVITE, ACK, CANCEL, and BYE. Following is what each one does:

REGISTER—Registers a UA address with a SIP server.

INVITE—Requests that a UA participate in a session.

ACK—Sent by the UAC when it has received the final response to an INVITE.

CANCEL—Ends a pending session, not one that has already been accepted.

BYE—Ends a call or session.

4 What command configures a dial peer to use SIP in its communication with its VoIP peer?

The **session protocol sipv2** command under dial-peer configuration mode configures a dial peer to use SIP in its communication with its VoIP peer.

5 How does CallManager 4.x interact with a SIP gateway?

CallManager 4.x can register a SIP trunk to the gateway. The trunk is referred to as a *signaling interface*. It can also trunk to a SIP server, a CME gateway, or another CallManager cluster.

6 What additional SIP capabilities does CallManager 5.x add?

CallManager 5.x can register SIP phones and can function as a B2BUA.

7 Which Layer 4 protocol does SIP use by default, and what is the default port?

SIP uses UDP by default, but you can configure it to use TCP. The default port number is 5060.

8 What is the function of the SDP in SIP call setup?

SDP is used to exchange information about endpoint capabilities and negotiate call features, such as in an INVITE message. The SDP part of a SIP message contains information, such as the SDP version, the calling party organization, the IP address, expected media, and media attributes.

Chapter 5

1 Which port type should you use to connect to a two-wire analog service connecting to the PSTN for both inbound and outbound calling?

A two-wire analog service from the PSTN is considered an FXS port. You should connect this to an FXO port in a gateway. You could connect an FXS-DID port to the PSTN, but this configuration would support outbound dialing only.

2 What types of signaling are required on a voice circuit?

Supervisory signaling, address signaling, and informational signaling are required on a voice circuit. Supervisory signaling is used to indicate on-hook and off-hook status. Address signaling is used to convey destination information. Finally, informational signaling is used to provide user feedback, such as dial tone and ringing.

3 What is the difference between CAS and CCS on an E1 circuit?

Although both CAS and CCS use timeslot 16 to carry signaling, CAS has specific bits within a multiframe that are dedicated, or associated to each channel. With CCS, messages are used to carry signaling information.

4 What is the difference between SF and ESF?

An SF consists of 12 T1 frames. The framing bit is used for synchronization. Robbed-bit signaling can provide two signaling bits per channel (A and B).

An ESF consists of 24 T1 frames. In addition to synchronization, the framing bits can be used to provide data link information and CRC error correction. Robbed-bit signaling can provide 4 signaling bits per channel (A, B, C, and D).

5 What two types of echo are possible on a voice circuit?

The two possible types of echo on a voice circuit are acoustic echo and hybrid echo.

Acoustic echo is caused by poor acoustic isolation between the speaker and microphone.

Hybrid echo is caused by an impedance mismatch in a 2-wire to 4-wire hybrid.

6 Which signaling types support ANI on T1 CAS circuits?

E&M-FGD supports reception of ANI. FGD-EANA supports transmission of ANI.

7 Which line signaling method should you use on an E1 R2 satellite link?

You should use R2-Pulse on an E1 R2 satellite link.

8 What component of an ISDN message is used to carry information about the call?

Call-specific information is carried in the Information Element of an ISDN message.

Chapter 6

1 What is a major drawback of using analog FXO trunks for inbound calls?

The drawback is that no DNIS information is provided, so calls cannot be directly routed to their destination.

2 Which command must you include when configuring a CAMA type 4 (KP-NPD-NXX-XXXX-ST) trunk?

You must use the **ani mapping** command to associate three-digit NPA numbers to a single-digit NPD.

3 You issue a **show controller** command on a digital trunk and see accumulated slip seconds in every interval. What could be the cause?

Incorrect clocking configuration on the physical port can cause slips. For a PSTN connection, line clocking is typically used.

4 When you are trying to set up Q.931 backhaul on an ISDN PRI using CallManager MGCP, the **isdn bind-l3 ccm-manager** command is not recognized. What could cause this?

The cause could be that you omitted the **service mgcp** keywords from the PRI group configuration on the controller for the physical interface.

5 What must you do prior to configuring a PRI group on an ISDN PRI circuit?

You must configure an ISDN switch type globally on the Cisco voice gateway prior to configuring a PRI group on an ISDN PRI circuit.

6 Which signaling type is necessary if you want to receive ANI information on a T1 CAS trunk?

E&M FGD is necessary if you want to receive ANI information on a T1 CAS trunk.

7 What are the two components of R2 signaling?

Line signaling (supervisory control signals) and interregister signaling (call setup control) are the two components of R2 signaling.

8 If it is necessary to use the **cas custom** command to modify the signaling on an E1 R2 trunk, what is the recommended first step?

Begin by configuring the **country** *country* **use-defaults** command under **cas custom**.

Chapter 7

1 How will caller ID work on an FXO to FXS connection between a PBX and a Cisco voice gateway?

Caller ID will work only in one direction, from FXS to FXO.

2 Which E&M trunk type is most commonly in use?

Type I is used most often in North America, and Type V is used most often throughout the rest of the world.

3 A four-wire E&M Type V trunk uses how many physical wires?

A four-wire E&M Type V trunk uses six wires.

4 Which command confirms the status of clocking for the TDM bus of a voice gateway?

The **show network-clocks** command lists available clock sources by priority.

5 How can you control the master/slave Layer 2 function of an ISDN PRI trunk?

You can control the master/slave Layer 2 function of an ISDN PRI trunk by using the **isdn protocol-emulate user | network** command.

6 What type of signaling is configured on DS0s that are used for T-CCS?

External signaling is configured using the **type ext-sig** parameter of the **ds0-group** command.

7 How do you configure the D-channel for an MGCP-controlled ISDN PRI trunk?

Configure Layer 3 backhaul to CallManager using the **isdn bind-l3 ccm-manager** command.

8 When you are using an MGCP-controlled PRI trunk, how can you verify the status of the ISDN Q.931 backhaul?

The **show ccm-manager** command shows the status of the backhaul channel.

Chapter 8

1 Voice is sensitive to delay, jitter, and packet drops. What are the recommended maximum values for each of these?

High-quality voice and interactive video have the following network requirements:

- A maximum of 150 ms of one-way delay
- A maximum of 30 ms jitter
- A maximum of 1 percent packet loss

2 When you use the Modular QoS CLI, or MQC, what steps are involved in setting a bandwidth limit for voice traffic that is sent out an interface?

Step 1	Classify the traffic using a class map.
Step 2	Create a policy map, and associate the class map with the policy map.
Step 3	Assign bandwidth to that class within the policy map.
Step 4	Assign the policy to an interface with the **service-policy outbound** *policy-map-name* command.

3 Data packets can be large compared to voice packets. Why is this a problem across a WAN link, and how can you remedy it?

Although voice might be placed in a priority queue, a voice packet can be delayed by a larger data packet if it arrives at the interface after the data packet has begun being serialized. To maintain the delay budget for voice, you should serialize all packets in 10 ms or less. This is not a problem on links of T1 speed or better, because you can serialize a 1500-byte packet within 10 ms. To remedy this, you can use LFI on slower-speed links.

4 What is the difference between fax/modem relay and passthrough?

In relay, the fax or modem analog data is demodulated by the sending gateway, packetized, and sent over the IP network. The receiving gateway remodulates it and forwards it as analog data to the fax or modem.

In passthrough, fax and modem calls are treated as any other analog voice call, with the data carried in-band in RTP packets to the remote fax or modem.

5 What are the two types of fax relay that Cisco routers use, and which is the default type?

Cisco routers use Cisco proprietary fax relay and the ITU-T standardized T.38 fax relay. Cisco fax relay is the default.

6 In which configuration mode are fax/modem commands given on MGCP gateways? How about H.323 and SIP gateways?

Fax/modem relay and passthrough commands are given at global configuration mode on MGCP gateways. On H.323 and SIP gateways, they can be given at either dial peer or voice service configuration mode.

7 How does SRTP protect voice media traffic?

SRTP encrypts the RTP voice media payload, but not the RTP header, using AES encryption. It authenticates the RTP header and payload contents by computing a one-way HMAC-SHA1 hash and placing the results in an authentication tag at the end of the packet. The receiver runs the same computation and compares its result to the contents of the authentication tag. If the contents do not match, the receiver drops the packet. SRTP also includes a replay protection process to avoid DoS attacks.

8 When using encrypted voice within a LAN, why is it a good idea to also encrypt traffic between the voice gateway and Cisco CallManager?

Voice media and signaling are not the only types of voice traffic that traverse the WAN. MGCP gateways communicate with Cisco CallManagers. IP phones download TFTP files and Dynamic Host Configuration Protocol (DHCP) information, if those servers are centrally located. DTMF tones and encryption keys might be exchanged. If you are encrypting the IP phone traffic, it makes sense to encrypt the other voice traffic also, unless your network is secure and trusted.

9 How is firewall function affected if an IPsec tunnel from a remote gateway terminates on the Cisco CallManager, rather than another device?

A firewall cannot thoroughly inspect IPsec traffic coming from the WAN and going through the firewall into the LAN. All the firewall sees is the IPsec header. It would have to be able to decrypt the packet to see the original headers and the payload information. Thus, terminating an IPSec connection on the CallManager prevents the firewall from inspecting that communication, but it also secures that traffic while it traverses the network to reach the CallManager.

Chapter 9

1 What determines whether a gateway does digit-by-digit matching?

A gateway uses digit-by-digit matching if the incoming dial peer is not configured for **direct-inward-dial**. If the incoming dial peer is configured for **direct-inward-dial**, the entire digit string is matched. The exception is an incoming ISDN call with overlapping receiving.

2 What is the default order of operation for matching outbound dial peers?

Most specific match is the first selection. If two equivalent matches exist, the peer with the highest configured preference is selected. If preferences are equal, the selection is random.

3 What is necessary for a dial peer to be considered operational?

You must configure the dial peer with an answer address or an incoming called number or both a destination pattern and a target.

4 Which factors must you balance when designing a dial plan?

You must balance ease of use for end users with administrative overhead and scalability.

5 What end-user issue can be caused by an overlapping dial plan?

An overlapping dial plan requires the interdigit timer to expire before the appropriate route pattern can be selected. This results in a long post dial delay. You can minimize this issue by reducing the interdigit timer or by training users to use the # to indicate they have entered all digits.

6 What is the default dial peer?

The default dial peer is a system dial peer that is used to match inbound calls if the call does not match a configured dial peer.

7 Which number is used to match the destination pattern on a dial peer?

For inbound dial peers, the calling number (ANI) is used to match the destination pattern. For outbound dial peers, the called number (DNIS) is used to match the destination pattern.

8 How are dial peers configured to accommodate an overlapping dial plan?

For the dial peers that have overlapping destination patterns, you need to add a T to the end of the digit string. This signifies that the digit matching should not occur until the interdigit timer expires.

Chapter 10

1 Define *digit manipulation.*

Digit manipulation encompasses adding, subtracting, and changing telephone numbers.

2 Of the digit manipulation techniques digit stripping, digit forwarding, digit prefixing, number expansion, and CLID, which are executed after the outbound dial peer is matched but before the numbers are transmitted?

All but number expansion are executed after the outbound dial peer is matched but before the numbers are transmitted.

3 By default, POTS dial peers strip any outbound digits that explicitly match their destination pattern. What are two simple ways to prevent the router from stripping all the digits?

Use either the **no digit-strip** command or the **forward-digit** *number* command under dial-peer configuration mode.

4 When is a number expansion executed, and how can you test its action?

A number expansion is a global policy that is executed before any outbound dial peer is matched. The command **show dialplan number** *number* can test its action.

5 Given the following voice translation rule, how would a dialed string of **913012345678** be translated?

```
/^\(91\)301\(.......\)/ /1\2/
```

It would translate to **12345678**. The **91** is translated to **1**, and then the contents of the second set (specified with the **\2**) are inserted. Because **301** is neither translated nor inserted, it is ignored.

6 Given the following voice translation rule, how would a dialed string of **913012345678** be translated?

```
/^\(91\)301\(.......\)/ /\1700\2/
```

It would translate to **917002345678**. The contents of the first set are inserted, the 301 is translated to 700, and then the contents of the second set are inserted.

Chapter 11

1 Name three types of CAC.

Three types of CAC include local CAC, measurement-based CAC, and resource-based CAC.

2 What CAC mechanism would you use to guarantee enough bandwidth for the duration of a call?

You could use RSVP, which reserves bandwidth on a call-by-call basis and rejects calls when any router in the path is unable to provide sufficient resources.

3 How are dial peers configured to be part of the same hunt group?

You can use a destination pattern that points the dial peers to the same phone numbers, and designate a preference value to control their order of use.

4 What is the difference between LVBO and AVBO?

LVBO monitors router interfaces and makes the busyout decision based on the state of the interface. AVBO sends a probe to measure network congestion and make its busyout decision based on the results of that probe.

5 Which CAC mechanism, other than AVBO, uses probes in making its call admission decision?

PSTN fallback also uses probes to make its call admission decision.

6 What is TEHO used for, and what are two issues with its use?

TEHO is used to minimize long-distance toll charges. Issues with its use include dial plan complexity and regulatory restrictions.

7 What are some differences between gateway-controlled RSVP and CallManager-controlled RSVP?

You can use gateway-controlled RSVP only with gateway protocols that have dial peers, because it requires some configuration under the dial peers. The gateway makes the CAC decisions based on its RSVP policy configuration.

You can use CallManager-controlled RSVP with all gateway protocols because it does not require dial peer configuration. RSVP policy configuration is done on CallManager, and CAC decisions are controlled by CallManager. CallManager-controlled RSVP uses SCCP to communicate with a media resource called an RSVP agent on the gateway.

8 Given the following dial peers, which would the gateway use first? Second? Third?

dial-peer voice 2200 voip

preference 1

destination-pattern 2200

session target ipv4:10.20.25.1

dial-peer voice 2201 voip

destination-pattern 2200

session target ipv4:10.20.26.2

dial-peer voice 2202 voip

preference 4

destination-pattern 2200

session target ipv4:10.20.27.3

Dial peer 2201 would be the most preferred. It has the default preference value of 0, which is the highest priority. (Lower preference values have higher priority.) Dial peer 2200 would be used second because its preference value is 1, and dial peer 2002 would be least preferred because it has the highest preference value.

Chapter 12

1 What conditions must exist for COR to restrict a call?

Both the inbound and outbound dial peers must have a COR list defined, and the outgoing COR list must be a subset of the incoming COR list.

2 An outgoing COR list is analogous to which Cisco CallManager Class of Control setting?

Partition

3 An incoming COR list is analogous to which Cisco CallManager Class of Control setting?

Calling Search Space

4 How many COR lists can you assign in SRST?

20

Chapter 13

1 Which two steps are required to enable MGCP Gateway Fallback?

Enable MGCP Gateway Fallback using the **ccm-manager fallback-mgcp** command, and set the alternate application to default.

2 Which device initiates SRST?

The SRST process is initiated by the IP phone sending a registration request to the SRST gateway.

3 Which gateway protocol can provide call preservation when using ISDN to the PSTN?

H.323 can provide call preservation when using ISDN to the PSTN.

4 Which command supports both extension addressing and E.164 addressing?

dialplan-pattern supports both extension addressing and E.164 addressing.

5 Which two SIP functions does a gateway perform to enable SIP SRST?

A gateways performs SIP Registrar Server and B2BUA to enable SIP SRST. Version 3.0 used Redirect Server instead of B2BUA.

6 Which certificate server can a Secure SRST router autoenroll with?

A Secure SRST router can autoenroll with Cisco IOS certificate server.

7 Which gateway protocol should you use for a remote site with an E1 PRI to provide the best call preservation?

You should use H.323 for a remote site with an E1 PRI to provide the best call preservation.

8 What is required to support integration to a centralized voice-mail system over a PRI?

The service provider must pass RDNIS. It might also be possible to support RDNIS using the **forward-digits extra inband** command on the dial peer if the router is running Cisco IOS 12.3(11)T or later.

Chapter 14

1 What is the purpose of a DSPFarm Profile?

The DSPFarm profile allows the DSPs of a gateway to be registered to multiple CallManager groups.

2 When is a DSP needed for an MTP?

You need a DSP when the packetization period for the voice streams is not the same. If the packetization period is the same, you can use a software-based MTP.

3 What is the default codec complexity for a C5510 DSP?

Flex complexity is the default codec complexity.

4 What is the major difference in the way C549 and C5510 DSPs handle voice termination?

When you are using a C549 DSP, voice termination is assigned statically. Each voice port is permanently assigned to a DSP when the voice port is created. When you are using a C5510 DSP, voice termination is dynamically assigned. Sequential calls on the same voice port might be handled by different DSPs.

5 You need to terminate 14 G.711 calls, provide transcoding for 6 G.729a to G.711 calls, and support 5 G.711 conference sessions with up to eight participants in each conference. What is the minimum number of DSPs required?

You need three C5510 DSPs. C549 DSPs support only six participants per conference. One DSP supports the voice termination for 14 calls. One DSP supports the six required medium-complexity transcoding sessions. One DSP supports up to eight G.711 conference calls.

6 You need to support one mixed-mode conference with up to eight participants. How should you configure the maximum sessions under the conference profile?

Because a DSP that is configured for conferencing cannot support another function, you should configure the maximum sessions to 2, which is the maximum number of conferences that a C5510 DSP can support. Setting the maximum sessions to 1 eliminates the possibility of using the DSP to its full capability.

7 Describe two benefits of DSP sharing.

- It reduces the possibility of oversubscribing DSP resources.
- It makes it easier to add DSP resources. DSPs can be added to an NM instead of having to dismantle the router to access the main board.

8 Your ISR 2811 has an NM-HDV with five PVDM-12s and two PVDM2-48s installed on the main board. The NM-HDV is configured for medium complexity and has one E1 voice port. There are also two E1 voice ports in HWIC slots. What is the maximum number of G.711 conferences that you can support with the extra DSPs?

The five PVDM-12s have three C549 DSPs each, which can terminate four medium-complexity calls requiring that 8 of the 15 DSPs are used for voice termination. You can configure the remaining seven DSPs to support one conference bridge each.

The two PVDM2-48s have a total of six C5510 DSPs. Four of these DSPs are required to terminate the 60 voice channels in the two E1s. The remaining two C5510 DSPs can each support eight G.711 conferences, for a total of 16.

Because using both Cisco IOS Media Resources (C549) and Enhanced IOS Media Resources (C5510) is not supported on a single router, you can register only the C5510s to CallManager. Therefore, the maximum number of G.711 conferences supported is 16.

Chapter 15

1 Why would you choose to implement an application in Tcl instead of VoiceXML?

A VoiceXML application requires an HTTP server, whereas a Tcl application does not require external servers.

2 Why would you choose to implement an application in VoiceXML instead of Tcl?

VoiceXML can interact with existing web applications requiring minimal development time to provide a voice interface to an existing web-based service. VoiceXML is also standards based, whereas Tcl IVR 2.0 uses Cisco proprietary APIs.

3 What is the precedence order for setting parameter values?

The precedence order is dial peer, service, and then package.

4 What is a package?

A package is a set of common functions that multiple applications use.

5 What is the purpose of a parameter namespace?

A parameter namespace allows multiple applications to use parameters that have the same name.

6 What application enhances the network management capabilities of Cisco routers?

Embedded Event Manager enhances the network management capabilities of Cisco routers.

7 What protocol can you use to increase the size and number of prompts available to an application?

You can use RTSP to increase the size and number of prompts available to an application.

8 What are the requirements for recording an application prompt?

You should record audio prompts in 8-bit, μ-law with 8-KHz encoding and save them in au format.

Chapter 16

1 List the two primary functions of a gatekeeper in an H.323 network.

Gatekeepers provide call routing with a centralized dial plan and CAC.

2 What is a gatekeeper zone?

A gatekeeper zone is used to logically group H.323 devices that an individual gatekeeper controls.

3 What is a technology prefix?

A technology prefix is an optional H.323 feature that the gatekeeper uses to group gateways by type or class or to define a pool of gateways.

4 Where is bandwidth management initially done?

Bandwidth management is initially done when processing an ARQ. You can modify it later during the call with a BRQ.

5 What is another name for a directory gatekeeper?

Another name for a directory gatekeeper is a hierarchical gatekeeper.

6 What is GUP, and what is it used for?

GUP is the Gatekeeper Update Protocol. It uses RAS messages to provide updates to alternate gatekeepers when using gatekeeper clustering.

Chapter 17

1 What are two ways to verify that gateways have successfully registered with a gatekeeper?

Use the **show gatekeeper endpoints** command on the gatekeeper or the **show gateway** command on the gateway.

2 Why is it necessary to configure technology prefixes when implementing gatekeepers on a voice network?

Typically, a called number matches a zone prefix, not a registered E.164 address. In this case, if a technology prefix is not also matched, the call is rejected.

3 What do you need to do to the gatekeeper configuration to provide dynamic prefix registration support?

Add the **rrq dynamic-prefixes-accept** command to the gatekeeper configuration.

4 How much bandwidth does the gatekeeper count for each call using a G.729 codec? For a G.711 codec?

The gatekeeper counts each G.729 as 16 Kb and each G.711 call as 128 Kb.

5 How can you provide redundancy on a CallManager H.225 gatekeeper-controlled trunk?

You can provide redundancy on the trunk by assigning up to three subscriber servers to the CallManager redundancy group that is associated with the device pool assigned to the trunk.

6 How is state information shared between gatekeepers in a gatekeeper cluster?

State information is updated to all members of a gatekeeper cluster using GUP messages.

7 What three commands can provide detailed information about the status of a gatekeeper cluster?

The **show gatekeeper status cluster**, **show gatekeeper cluster**, and **show gatekeeper zone cluster** commands are available to verify the setup and status of the cluster.

8 Which undocumented trace command can you use to show the decision tree steps that the gatekeeper takes as it processes an ARQ message?

You can use the **debug gatekeeper main 5** trace command to show the decision tree steps that the gatekeeper takes as it processes an ARQ message.

Chapter 18

1 Why would you use media flow-around?

You use media flow-around mode when you are not concerned with hiding your address. Because the IPIPGW is only involved in call setup and does not have to process media streams, more calls can be supported.

2 What is needed to implement an IPIPGW?

You need a supported router platform, an IPIPGW Cisco IOS image, and an integrated voice video feature license to implement an IPIPGW.

3 What is a via-zone?

A via-zone is a local zone that has been dedicated to only service IPIPGWs. Although it is not necessary to have a dedicated zone for the IPIPGW, it is often much simpler to troubleshoot networks in which we have an dedicated IPIPGW zone.

4 Under what circumstances is a DSP needed in an IPIPGW call?

A DSP is needed if the two call legs do not use the same codec or packet size. If the call legs use identical parameters, a DSP is not required.

5 What platforms are supported for the Cisco Multiservice IPIPGW?

The supported platforms are the Cisco ISRs (Cisco 2800, Cisco 3800), Cisco 2600XM Series (Cisco 2691, 2650XM, 2651XM, 2620XM, 2621XM, 2610XM, and 2611XM), Cisco 3700 Series (Cisco 3725, 3745), Cisco 7200 VXR, Cisco 7301, Cisco AS5350XM, and Cisco AS5400XM.

6 Can the Cisco Multiservice IPIPGW register to more than one gatekeeper?

No, it can register with only one gatekeeper. However, more than one gateway can register to one gatekeeper.

7 Can you use the Cisco Multiservice IPIPGW without a gatekeeper?

Yes, you can. You can run the Cisco Multiservice without a gatekeeper by configuring direct dial peers on the gateway.

8 Are translation rules and digit manipulation supported on the Cisco Multiservice IPIPGW?

Yes, they have the same support for translation rules and digit manipulation on VoIP dial peers as other Cisco H.323 gateways.

INDEX

C

N

POTS trunks, 147
CAMA connections, 154–157
FXO connection configuration, 147–154
trunk circuits, 145–147
public switched telephone network. *See* **PSTN**
PVDM versus PVDM2, 414
PVDM2 versus PVDM, 414

Q

Q Signaling. *See* **QSIG**
QoS (quality of service), 221
IP WAN design, 221
IP WANs, 221–222
AutoQoS, 248–249
classify traffic using class maps, 222–227
compression, 246–248
link fragmentation and interleave, 239–246
MPLS class mapping, 232–239
policy maps, 227–232
IPIPGW (Multiservice IP-to-IP gateway), 565
QSIG (Q Signaling), 141
ISDN digital circuits, 141
PRI trunks, 204–205
quality of service. *See* **QoS**

R

R2 signaling, 131
inter-register signaling, 132–133
line signaling, 131–132
R2-Compelled inter-register signaling, 133
R2-Noncompelled inter-register signaling, 133
R2-Semi-compelled inter-register signaling, 133
RAI (Resource Availability Indication), 348, 478
gatekeeper deployment models, 478–479
gatekeeper redundancy, 522–527
resource-based CAC, 348
random-detect command, 230
random-detect dscp-based command, 230
RAS signaling, gatekeeper signaling, 461–464
discovery, 464–465
H.323 call flow, 466–468

Real-Time Transport Control Protocol (RTCP), 14
Real-Time Transport Protocol (RTP), 6, 14
redirect contact order command, SIP voice service configuration, 101
redirect ip2ip command, 98, 101
redirect servers, SIP (session initiation protocol), 13, 81
redundancy
CallManager, MGCP (Media Gateway Control Protocol), 45–46
gatekeeper configuration
clustering, 516–520
HSRP (Hot Standby Routing Protocol), 513–516
load balancing, 520–521
RAI (Resource Availability Indication), 522–527
troubleshooting gatekeeper cluster, 521–522
gatekeeper deployment models, 476–478
H.323 protocol, 69–70
register servers, SIP (Session Initiation Protocol), 81
registrar command, SIP UA commands, 99
registrar server command, 101, 397
registrar servers, SIP (session initiation protocol), 13
registration, troubleshooting gatekeepers, 503–505
regular expressions, voice translation profiles, 309
changing call type or numbering plan, 313–314
deleting specific digits, 312
rerouting call over PSTN, 310–312
sets and replacement digits, 312–313
relay method, 249
remote sites
call preservation, 398–399
MGCP gateway fallback, 403–404
SRST (Survivable Remote Site Telephony). *See* SRST
residential gateways, 26
Resource Availability Indication. *See* **RAI**
resource-based CAC, call route selection, 346
gatekeeper zone bandwidth, 347

S

Safari
BOOKS ONLINE
ENABLED

THIS BOOK IS SAFARI ENABLED

INCLUDES FREE 45-DAY ACCESS TO THE ONLINE EDITION

The Safari® Enabled icon on the cover of your favorite technology book means the book is available through Safari Bookshelf. When you buy this book, you get free access to the online edition for 45 days.

Safari Bookshelf is an electronic reference library that lets you easily search thousands of technical books, find code samples, download chapters, and access technical information whenever and wherever you need it.

TO GAIN 45-DAY SAFARI ENABLED ACCESS TO THIS BOOK:

- Go to **http://www.ciscopress.com/safarienabled**

- Complete the brief registration form

- Enter the coupon code found in the front of this book before the "Contents at a Glance" page

If you have difficulty registering on Safari Bookshelf or accessing the online edition, please e-mail customer-service@safaribooksonline.com.